The Cultural Matrix

The Cultural Matrix

Understanding Black Youth

Edited by ORLANDO PATTERSON

With ETHAN FOSSE

 Harvard University Press

Cambridge, Massachusetts
London, England

Chapter 8 was originally published in "The Role of Religious and Social
Organizations in the Lives of Disadvantaged Youth" by Rajeev Dehejia,
Thomas DeLeire, Erzo F. P. Luttmer, and Josh Mitchell. *In The Problems
of Disadvantaged Youth: An Economic Perspective* edited by Jonathan
Gruber, pp. 237–274. Chicago: University of Chicago Press for the
National Bureau of Economic Research, Copyright © 2009 by the
National Bureau of Economic Research. Reprinted here in condensed
form by kind permission of University of Chicago Press.

Portions of Chapter 5 and Figure 5.1 were originally published in "Social
Altruism, Cynicism, and the 'Good Community'." In *Great American
City: Chicago and the Enduring Neighborhood Effect* by Robert J.
Sampson, pp. 210-236. Chicago: University of Chicago Press, Copyright ©
2012 by the University of Chicago.

First Harvard University Press paperback edition, 2016
Second Printing

Library of Congress Cataloging-in-Publication Data

The cultural matrix : understanding Black youth / edited by Orlando
Patterson ; with Ethan Fosse.
    pages cm
    Includes bibliographical references and index.
  ISBN 978-0-674-72875-2 (cloth: alk. paper)
  ISBN 978-0-674-65997-1 (pbk.)
    1. African American youth—Social conditions. 2. African American
    youth—Social life and customs. I. Patterson, Orlando, 1940–
    II. Fosse, Ethan.
  E185.86.C978 2015
305.235089'96—dc23   2014026484

Contents

PART IV: The CULTURAL STRUCTURING of CONFLICT and DIFFERENCES WITHIN and BETWEEN GENDERS

PART V: CULTURAL, SOCIAL, and MORAL TRIALS

The Cultural Matrix

Introduction

ORLANDO PATTERSON, *Harvard University*
ETHAN FOSSE, *Harvard University*

The past half century has witnessed remarkable changes in the condition of African Americans and, more generally, the state of race relations in America. These changes, however, have created a paradoxical situation. The civil rights movement and subsequent policies aimed at socioeconomic reform have resulted in the largest group of middle-class and elite blacks in the world, several of them leading some of the most powerful corporations in the nation and abroad; yet the bottom fifth of the black population is among the poorest in the nation and, as Hurricane Katrina exposed, often live in abysmal "Third World" conditions. Politically, blacks are a powerful presence and the most loyal members of one of the nation's two leading parties; yet, "race" remains a central lever of American politics and sustains its most fundamental regional and ideological alignments. Blacks have a disproportionate impact on the nation's culture—both popular and elite—yet continue to struggle in the educational system and are severely underrepresented in its boom of scientific and high-end technology. And although legalized segregation has long been abolished and anti-exclusionary laws strictly enforced, the great majority of blacks still live in highly segregated, impoverished communities. It is a record of remarkable successes, mixed achievements, and major failures.

Nowhere is this paradox more acutely exhibited than in the condition of black American youth, especially male youth. They are trapped in a seemingly intractable socioeconomic crisis, yet are among the most vibrant creators of popular culture in the nation and the world. President Barack Obama (2014) has lamented that:"Fifty years after Dr. [Martin Luther] King talked about his dream for America's children, the stubborn fact is that the life chances for the average black or brown child in this country lags behind by almost every measure and is worse for boys and young men." Only between 52 and 61 percent (depending on method of calculation) of

1

those entering high school graduate, compared with between 71 and 79 percent of white males. A third of all black men in their thirties now have a prison record, as do an astonishing two-thirds of all black men who have dropped out of high school. Violence has become endemic, with a murder rate of 34.4 per 100,000 among males aged fifteen to seventeen. Only 20 percent of black youth who are not in school are employed at any given time. Their lives are often impoverished, violent, and short, leading one group of social scientists to describe them as an "endangered species" (Gibbs 1988). A large number of social scientists have addressed the problem, but it is increasingly evident that the structural factors they emphasize, while certainly critical, can only explain the problem in partial, fragmentary ways. Further, these explanations confront the perplexing, stubborn fact that, for all their socioeconomic problems, black youth are the producers of a powerful popular culture that permeates, and in areas dominates, the nation's mainstream culture, including youth from other racial and ethnic groups.

What this paradox suggests is the need to explore the cultural life of black youth in order to deepen our understanding of their social plight as well as their extraordinary creativity. That is the primary objective of this volume. Doing so, however, requires some profound changes in the approaches of scholars who work on black youth, and poverty more generally. For several decades, there was hostility, approaching derision, to any cultural study of the poor, including black youth. While it has become legitimate again to probe the cultural life of the disadvantaged, social scientists continue to tread warily, and one kind of cultural analysis remains suspect: attempts to explain social problems in cultural terms.

Explaining the origin and full extent of scholarly discomfort with the culture concept in so far as it relates to the black poor, and especially its youth population, would require its own volume, taking us deep into the sociology of knowledge, and cannot be attempted here (see Patterson 2014). This introduction examines only in barest outline the main periods through which this fraught academic process has developed. There was, first, a classic period, beginning in the late nineteenth century with the sociocultural studies of W. E. B. Du Bois (1899) and ending with two of the greatest ethnographies ever written on urban black culture, Ulf Hannerz's (1969) study of Washington, D.C., and Lee Rainwater's (1970) detailed examination of a St. Louis housing project. Between them were classics such as Hortense Powdermaker's *After Freedom* (1939), Drake and Cayton's *Black Metropolis* (1945), E. Franklin Frazier's *The Negro*

Family in the United States (1948) and *Negro Youth at the Crossways* (1940), as well as Kenneth Clark's *Dark Ghetto* (1965). What we can gather from their analyses is that the authors of this classic era felt free to study black culture and its relation to social conditions as they saw fit, unburdened by any prevailing social science dogma concerning what was academically appropriate, either conceptually or terminologically.

The second period, which we might call a period of disjunctions, began in the mid-sixties, ironically the period that witnessed some of the best cultural studies on the urban poor, and it was sparked by reaction to the work of two authors, Daniel Patrick Moynihan's policy report *The Negro Family: The Case for National Action* (1965) and Oscar Lewis's badly theorized summary of his otherwise remarkable ethnographic works (1961, 1966). The reaction to the Moynihan analysis was by far the most virulent, inaccurate, and often grossly unfair. As the sociologist William Julius Wilson (1989) and others have pointed out (Rainwater and Yancey 1967), Moynihan's report simply summarized what was the consensus sociological position on the troubled black lower-class family at the time, including the views of leading African American sociologists. He identified the economic and social consequences of single female-headed households, *but further pointed out that this was the result of the racial and socioeconomic oppression of black Americans.* Critics, as William Julius Wilson (1989) has observed, egregiously neglected the corollary to his argument and pilloried him for "pathologizing" the black poor with language that was, in fact, common in sociological circles at the time. Kenneth Clark's work (1965), for example, published the same year as Moynihan's report, wrote at length on "The Negro Matriarchy and the Distorted Masculine Image" and "The Causes of Pathology." The greatest irony of all is that Moynihan was easily one of the most liberal councilors to advise a president and was deeply committed to the single most liberal policy agenda to aid black Americans in the history of the American government, Lyndon B. Johnson's "Great Society" program. History has been kind to Moynihan: a recent conference at Harvard by leading social scientists, all with impeccably liberal credentials, concluded that Moynihan was correct in his analysis and prediction. Looking backward, the criticisms of Moynihan were largely motivated by the racial pride of a newly resurgent black nationalism, (Draper 1971; Patterson 1977, ch. 6; 1997, 64–81), the fear of an emerging black middle class that undue attention to the sociocultural problems of the urban poor would redound unfavorably on them or diminish support for liberal social policies, and the mistaken belief that any reference to cultural practices was tantamount to blaming the victim, with the implication that the poor had to change their ways if there was to be any meaningful improvement in their condition.

History, however, has not been as kind to Lewis. A collection of papers published in the late 1960s (Valentine 1968) already fully laid out the major criticisms of the theory. The simple truth of the matter is that there is no such thing as *the* culture of poverty. Poor people all over America and the world adapt to their socioeconomic, physical, and political environments in a wide variety of ways. Indeed, even in a small island such as Jamaica, the poor of the shantytowns of Kingston have very different values, norms, and beliefs from the rural poor of the countryside; the latter are among the harshest critics of the former and are quite terrified of them. Apart from flaws in his theoretical statement, Lewis was also a victim of changing academic trends. His seminal works appeared at the height of the reaction against the Parsonian paradigm in sociology (Gouldner 1970; Habermas 1981), which portrayed culture as a highly integrated system of values and norms that regulated society and, by virtue of being internalized by deep processes of socialization, set the goals that were thought to guide human behavior. These justifiable criticisms of the Parsonian framework, combined with the ideological and policy criticisms launched at Moynihan, led many to adopt an exclusionary rule: all cultural studies, especially those on the poor, became suspect.

What followed was a third, revisionist period in the study of black America (Williams and Stockton 1973), which lasted from the end of the Lyndon Johnson era to the early 1980s. Not only did culture become a Typhoid Mary in academic social science but the very study of blacks was largely shunned by white scholars. Partially filling the void were studies, mainly by black scholars, which denied or downplayed problems in black families, and black lower-class life generally, claiming instead that the lives of black Americans were simply different and constituted a record of remarkable survival and resilience against white oppression, the best examples of this being Billingsley's (1968) *Black Families in White America* and Ladner's (1972) *Tomorrow's Tomorrow*. A collection of essays edited by Ladner (1973) entitled *The Death of White Sociology* laid out the revisionist position. White scholars took the title and contents seriously, and nearly all stayed away. The few who dared study the subject carefully toed the line. For instance, in her study *All Our Kin*, Carol Stack focused on "the adaptive strategies, resourcefulness and resilience of urban families under conditions of perpetual poverty" and "the stability of their kin networks"

(Stack 1974, 22). Scanzoni (1971) likewise took no chances: his study of black Americans focused squarely on stable, working- and middle-class households headed by couples married for at least five years. Predictably, given his self-censored sample, he found stable unions headed by nurturing, loving couples with childhood outcomes that varied strictly in terms of fathers' economic situations.

What is astonishing about the revisionist period is the discrepancy between the social science consensus and the reality of urban black life, for it was during the seventies and early eighties that major problems among the urban poor escalated greatly: family life disintegrated beyond anything Moynihan could have imagined (by the early 1980s, over a half of all births were to single mothers, compared with the 25 percent that had deeply troubled Moynihan), drug addiction soared with the catastrophic crack epidemic, and criminal victimization, including homicide, reached unprecedented levels in contemporary American history.

Inevitably, white and black social scientists were compelled to take the problems seriously, demarcating the fourth period in regard to the role of culture, which we call the structuralist turn. The response, both on the left and right, as well as those of neither political persuasion, was bad news for the study of culture. Leading the liberal resurgence were the pathbreaking works of William Julius Wilson, who laid out a strongly structuralist position, especially in a paper written with one of his students, Loïc Wacquant, who was later himself an important player in the study of black life. Wacquant and Wilson wrote: "Our central argument is that the interrelated set of phenomena captured by the term 'underclass' is primarily social-structural and that the inner city is experiencing a crisis because the dramatic growth in joblessness and economic exclusion associated with the ongoing spatial and industrial restructuring of American capitalism has triggered a process of hyperghettoization" (1989). To be fair, this overstated the structuralism of both authors, especially Wilson, who was always alert to the interactive role of culture in the understanding of lower-class black life, even if this was sometimes hidden in an overall structuralist tone.[1] For example, implicit in his 1978 book, *The Declining Significance of Race,* was the cultural argument that the withdrawal of middle-class roles and lifestyles from the ghetto had deleterious consequences for those left behind, an argument that elicited a good deal of carping from the hardline structuralists. With the publication of the *The Truly Disadvantaged* (1987), Wilson found himself in complex academic combat with both ends of the ideological spectrum, for by now the right had entered the fray with analyses and commentaries on the black poor and, sadly for the fortunes of the cultural approach to poverty, had embraced a cultural position that would certainly have appalled Oscar Lewis, even though it was often expressed in his name. Mercifully, poor Lewis was by now long dead, having prematurely passed away in 1970 at the age of fifty-six. Noting that the number of people in poverty stopped declining just as the expenditure on welfare was at its highest, Charles Murray (1984) blamed the welfare policies of the 1960s and 1970s for the growing social crisis among the urban poor. These policies, Murray argued, created a culture of dependency that incentivized the poor to remain idle and bear more children. Wilson responded by criticizing Murray's work as a rehash of the culture of poverty thesis, but at the same time faulted liberals for their failure to "address straightforwardly the rise of social pathologies in the ghetto" (Wilson 1987, 12). While insisting that social isolation and structural constraints were the major factors accounting for the problems facing poor black Americans, he nonetheless acknowledged that culture played some role though "as a response to social structural constraints and opportunities" (Wilson 1987, 61). Wilson's position, in which culture might be considered in the analysis as long as it is viewed as a dependent variable, remains the standard assumption when studying the lives of the poor. Interestingly, Wilson has recently given a more central place for culture in his most recent statement on the subject. In *More Than Just Race* (2009), he concedes that culture can operate as an intermediary variable in explaining the problems of black Americans. While agreeing with Orlando Patterson (2001, 2006) that "cultural explanations should be part of any attempt to fully account for such behavior and outcomes," he insists that in the final analysis "structure trumps culture" (Wilson 2009, 21). We respond to Wilson's newly nuanced position on this issue in Chapter 2.

We are now in the fifth, and current, phase of the treatment of culture in the study of African American problems and, more generally, the problem of poverty. It is what Mabel Berezin (1994) once called a "fissured terrain." First, it should be noted that culture has returned to center stage in the social sciences, including sociology, and was officially acknowledged in the founding of the Culture Section of the American Sociological Association in 1988. Enthusiasts have published thick volumes announcing "the cultural turn" in the discipline (Bonnell, Hunt, and White 1999). Accompanying this "turn" has been an even more vibrant development in "cultural studies" in the humanities, which bear a somewhat prickly relationship to cultural sociology. As far as the study of poverty, and black poverty in particular, is concerned, however, current developments in sociology are best described as a cultural half-turn. On the one hand, scholars such as Elijah Anderson (1979; 1992; 1999; 2008), Douglas Massey and Mary Denton (1993), Sandra Smith (2006), Martin Sanchez-Jankowski (2008), Alford Young (2004), Prudence Carter (2005), Annette Lareau (2003), Sudhir Venkatesh (2002; 2009), and others have forged ahead, probing complex, difficult issues on how culture can have an independent, semiautonomous effect on human behavior, including the lives of the poor. On the other hand, other scholars, most notably Lamont and Small (2008; see also Small 2004; Lamont, Small, and Harding 2010; Harding 2010), have sought to navigate between the Scylla of a crude culturalism and the Charybdis of a barren structuralism and have embodied what we call the cultural half-turn. Typically these analyses have replaced the language of norms, values, attitudes, and ideologies with those of scripts, toolkits, boundaries, narratives, repertoires, and frames. While the adoption of concepts from cognitive psychology and the humanities are potentially useful in expanding our approach to understanding how culture works, the cultural half-turn is limited in several respects.

First, the cultural half-turn focuses mainly, and often exclusively, on the pragmatics of culture, largely ignoring or downplaying the evaluative, normative, and informational components of culture. Even with symbolic boundaries, where an evaluative dimension could be incorporated, most research has been toward how an individual categorizes or differentiates others, or as they prefer to say, how people conduct boundary work, a concept borrowed largely from the Norwegian anthropologist Fredrik Barth, who developed it as an effective means of downplaying the role of culture in the conception and analysis of ethnic groups (Barth 1969). Second, scholars in the half-turn tradition have ignored how cultural constructs are persistent through time and across populations, both diachronically and synchronically (Patterson 2004, ch. 2). Persistence has been confused with coherence and simplicity, but norms, attitudes, values, and ideologies, as social psychologists have long demonstrated, are anything but coherent or simple. Unfortunately, as social scientists in the tradition of the half-turn have ignored cultural persistence, they have discarded related processes of diffusion and transmission. Third, as a corrective, the cultural half-turn has downplayed the shared aspect of culture. This neglect of the collective is also reflected in the disparagement of "subcultures," or of what we will call cultural configurations, the fact that cultural constructs cluster in meaningful, systematic ways (see Patterson, Chapter 1 in this volume), all such attempts being disparaged with the academic smear of being Parsonian or "culture of poverty." Fourth, and crucially, the half-turn culturalists have tended to view culture as something to be interpreted but not a force that explains behavior. This is particularly surprising since structural accounts increasingly include culture as a mediator between structure and behavior (except for orthodox Marxists and neoclassical economists, and even the latter has now begun to shift significantly). Even for the most die-hard structuralists, social class, for instance, impacts behavior through cultural mechanisms and thus has a role for explanation.

Finally, despite criticizing, and sometimes condemning, previous studies on the cultural lives of the poor for conflating culture with behavior, those embracing the cultural half-turn frequently do so, a common danger of extreme pragmatism. This conflation of culture and behavior is not a mere academic distinction: by combining culture with behavior, culture cannot logically explain behavior, since it *is* behavior. How culture works and influences becomes what people do or how they rationalize what they are doing (called "meaning-making"). The result can be frustrating for the progress of social science research as well as for determining policy implications of these analyses, since culture becomes an epistemological *ouroboros* of both explanandum and explanans.

By neglecting the persistent, collective, evaluative, explanatory, and ideational, culture is at worst treated as a hall of mirrors, a postmodern epistemological jungle in which no one (including, or rather especially, the social scientist) can conclude anything substantive from their non-privileged, inherently relational epistemological position. All that can be said is that "reality is complex" and "everybody is right." As an academic exercise, this may very well prove self-fulfilling. However, as a way for understanding and explaining the paradox of black youth, and for uncovering the solutions to the problems they face, it demands more. The social problems they face are too great and too important not to take culture seriously.[2]

Chapter Overviews

We now turn to an overview of the chapters in this volume. The work is organized into five parts. Part one, Overview, provides both a theoretical and substantive framework for the works that follow. In Chapter 1, "The

Nature and Dynamics of Cultural Processes," Orlando Patterson provides a more integrated and balanced approach to the understanding of culture than that generally available in contemporary cultural sociology. Patterson argues that there are two basic components of culture: that of cultural knowledge structures and of the pragmatics of culture. The distinction is directly analogous to Saussure's distinction between *langue* (language) and *parole* (speech), and the nearly exclusive emphasis of contemporary cultural sociologists on pragmatics is as untenable as a linguist who claims that speech is all there is to language. Patterson contends that cultural knowledge structures are shared schemata of three types—declarative, procedural, and evaluative—which are unevenly shared across a network of persons. He draws on knowledge-activation theory from social psychology to further explore cultural pragmatics and its relation to constituted knowledge structures. The chapter concludes with an introduction to the concept of sociocultural configurations, which provides a more useful way of understanding the constellation of values, norms, beliefs, and metaphors that motivate people in their daily lives.

In Chapter 2, "The Social and Cultural Matrix of Black Youth," Patterson further explores the diversity of lifestyles among black youth in inner-city neighborhoods of America. Drawing on the now rich resource of ethnographies and quantitative studies as well as his own work, he identifies four sociocultural configurations of black youth: the adapted mainstream of the inner-city middle- and lower-middle class, the proletarian configuration of the working class and working poor, the street configuration of the disconnected, and that of the hip-hop nation, the last of which most black youth embrace. Because the problem of violence is pervasive among the urban poor, a special section examines its extent and the factors accounting for it. Another section addresses the problem of unemployment and the question of the relation between cultural and structural factors in its explanation. Patterson concludes by addressing the paradox of black youth's extraordinary influence on the nation's popular culture, and attempts to show how it is related to the broader problem of what the late sociologist Daniel Bell called the cultural contradictions of American capitalism.

The chapters of part two examine the values, norms and beliefs of black youth as well as their remarkable aesthetic accomplishments in broad national terms. In Chapter 3, "The Values and Beliefs of Disconnected Black Youth," sociologist Ethan Fosse extends the analysis of culture to the values and beliefs of youth who are structurally disconnected—that is, those who are neither employed nor in school. He examines six main cultural domains: psychological well-being, sociocultural networks, career and educational attainment, risk and expectations, community and social problems, and finally government and society. Structural disconnection, Fosse finds, is not just a matter of socioeconomic position: black youth who are structurally disconnected are much more likely to express psychological distress, have less homogeneous social networks, express greater levels of distrust, maintain deeper pessimism of their own academic and occupational skills, and view both leaders and government policies with heightened skepticism. However, Fosse also shows that, despite their disadvantaged position in the labor market, disconnected black youth are in fact much more likely to evaluate a successful career and educational attainment as extremely important. The importance that disconnected black youth attach to their career and educational goals, while simultaneously doubting their educational skills and capabilities for upward mobility, highlights the key point of the chapter: that structural disconnection is not just a structural problem but a cultural one. He concludes with a call for recognizing that structural disconnection likely leads to a concomitant level of suffering and difficulty.

Chapter 4, "Hip-hop's Irrepressible Refashionability: Phases in the Cultural Production of Black Youth," by ethnomusicologist Wayne Marshall, provides a cultural-historical analysis of the rise and social implications of hip-hop. Several themes emerge from Marshall's chapter. First, his analysis is related to long-standing criticisms of hip-hop's content among the left, right, and artists themselves, as well as the perceived confrontational style of hip-hop. Yet Marshall suggests the problem with these debates on hip-hop is that there has been too much focus on the content and not enough on the form, which demonstrates immense creative inventiveness. Second, his chapter highlights a number of largely constructive aspects of hip-hop's form. Principally, hip-hop exhibits what Marshall calls extensive "refashionability" of form. For example, black youth have innovatively used media technologies to unique creative ends and reinvented cultural elements from mainstream popular culture, including other musical genres. Third, Marshall's analysis underscores how hip-hop's integrative form helps bridge disparate groups. For example, although born of, and reflecting, local culture in the Bronx, hip-hop has become part of what Marshall calls "global youth culture." Finally, due in part to the refashioning of technologies, hip-hop has been deeply participatory: for example, musical sampling obviates the need for an untalented "professional" musician, and new software has given hip-hop a democratic, widely accessible character. As such, hip-hop has been characterized by informal, independent, "do-it-yourself" modes of cultural production and distribution. Yet, Marshall cautions that there is a potentially dangerous mix of refashionability with bridging via commercial success: to wit, the gap between "the real" and reality is heightened, with the former widely disseminated and the latter removed from the cultural purview. Regardless of the perceived shortcomings of hip-hop, Marshall's analysis concludes that social and political groups can take advantage of hip-hop's refashionability, and its integrative and participatory form to help improve the lives of black youth.

The chapters of part three are fully engaged with one of the major themes of this work, discussed in Patterson's Overview: that cultural and structural forces cannot be viewed in isolation, but instead operate interactively in accounting for behavioral outcomes. Chapter 5, "Continuity and Change in Neighborhood Culture: Toward a Structurally Embedded Theory of Social Altruism and Moral Cynicism," by sociologist Robert J. Sampson, explores the ways in which neighborhoods reproduce cultural values and norms through conditions of structural disadvantage. In his analysis, he uses two unique data sets for measuring behavioral instances of altruism across Chicago neighborhoods: the likelihood of heart-attack victims receiving CPR and the proportion of lost letters that are mailed after being systematically dropped on the street. Based on these community-level data, Sampson uncovers five core findings relating culture and structure to instances of behavioral altruism. First, instances of cardiopulmonary resuscitation (CPR) and lost-letter returns are systematically related, varying in expected ways across neighborhoods. Second, these variations are influenced by long-term cultural characteristics of neighborhoods, such that altruistic events in the relatively distant past predict current levels of community-level altruism. Third, behavioral variations in returning lost letters are systematically related to people's cultural beliefs about morality, levels of neighborhood trust, and shared expectations for intervening to keep public order. Fourth, these cultural beliefs and norms are, in turn, systematically correlated with neighborhood-level conditions of structural disadvantage and deprivation, including crime and poverty rates. Finally, past conditions of structural disadvantage predict current variations in neighborhood level cultures, as measured by beliefs about morality, trust, and intervention to keep public order. Taken together, Sampson's findings highlight the fact that cultural beliefs and norms are inextricably connected not only with structural disadvantage but with observable behavioral instances of altruism across time and space.

In Chapter 6, "'I Do Me': Young Black Men and the Struggle to Resist the Street," sociologist Kathryn Edin and her colleagues examine poor black youth who have managed to avoid entirely, or interact minimally with, the common ways of life in their severely disadvantaged communities. Based on detailed ethnographic data and in-depth interviews of poor black youth living in Baltimore, they identify four broad sets of cultural strategies and supports that have helped these youth avoid some of the risks from their environment. First, all the youth they studied embraced an ideology of "I do me," in which one is entirely self-sufficient, with no expectation of support from others. This cultural set of beliefs and values helped the youth deal with the severe risks they faced growing up in their communities. Second, to avoid being the target of violence, youth reported the importance of knowing the people in their neighborhood, especially those youth most likely to be dangerous, in order to survive and accordingly escape a life of crime and poor socioeconomic circumstances. Third, youth also reported withdrawing from their neighborhood environments in various ways—with parents moving their children to schools outside the community, parents establishing curfews and restrictions, and older siblings warning about and providing a way of bonding outside the street life. Finally, youth developed hybrid or alternative cultural identities to avoid the risks of living in very poor neighborhoods, such as middle-class occupational goals, participating in sports, having children, and relating to adult role models with relatively stable occupations. The authors emphasize, however, that these strategies entail substantial costs. For example, withdrawal from the community can lead to social isolation, a feeling that one is not part of the "action" of the streets, and increased difficulty navigating both cultural realms. Similarly, cultivating alternative identities can result in potentially lower income over the short-term from conventional work, compared to drug-dealing, costs from raising a child, problems with finding secure employment, and lack of social support among those who succeed in going to college and attaining their career goals. Even the strategy of being known can have negative effects, since many also reported that to feel safe one must initially fight and develop a reputation that decreases the chances of being involved in fights over the long run.

In Chapter 7, "More Than Just Black: Cultural Perils and Opportunities in Inner-City Neighborhoods," sociologist Van C. Tran compares the experiences of second-generation West Indians with native-born black Americans. Using both in-depth interviews of poor black youth and quantitative survey data on second-generation immigrants, Tran shows that West Indians and native-born black Americans face broadly similar, although not identical, structural disadvantages, living in neighborhoods characterized by elevated levels of poverty, segregation, and violence. Tran further extends his analysis beyond neighborhood-level structural conditions to consider the role of cultural factors in affecting the different trajectories of native-born black Americans and West Indians. He finds three main cultural mechanisms that at least partially account for the attainment gap between West Indians and native-born black Americans: stricter parental strategies with closer supervision, lower levels of involvement in the local drug trade, and lower levels of involvement in peer networks.

Chapter 8, "The Role of Religious and Social Organizations in the Lives of Disadvantaged Youth," by economist Rajeev Dehejia and his colleagues examines how religious participation can buffer the negative impacts of severe disadvantage. Using quantitative panel data, the authors collect measures of disadvantage as well as parental involvement with religious and other social organizations when the sampled youth were ages three to nineteen and observe their outcomes thirteen to fifteen years later. They consider a range of definitions of disadvantage in childhood (including family income and poverty measures, family characteristics including parental education, and child characteristics including parental assessments of the child) and a range of outcome measures in adulthood (such as education, income, and measures of health and psychological well-being). In general, they find substantial evidence that youth with religiously active parents are less affected later in life by childhood disadvantage than youth whose parents did not frequently attend religious services. These buffering effects of religious organizations are most pronounced when outcomes are measured by high school graduation or nonsmoking and when disadvantage is measured by family resources or maternal education, but the authors also find buffering effects for a number of other outcomes and related measures of disadvantage.

Part four, The Cultural Structuring of Conflict and Differences Within and Between Genders, focuses on one of the major problems that black youth face in their disadvantaged neighborhoods, seemingly pervasive violence, and the cultural strategies they use to control and avoid it. A neglected issue, the gendered nature of violence, is also addressed. Chapter 9, "Keeping Up the Front: How Disadvantaged Black Youths Avoid

Street Violence in the Inner City," by sociologists Joseph Krupnick and Christopher Winship turns the question of violence on its head. Typically the question of violence in poor black neighborhoods is focused on why the crime rates are so high. However, Krupnick and Winship ask instead: Why are these neighborhoods not more violent than they are? They observe that, in fact, violent activity is typically not the initial impulse of poor black youth, and this is reflected in the fact that even the most violent areas have crime rates low in an absolute (though not comparative) sense. They contend that street violence is not usually intended, and that poor youth engage in posturing and posing that appear threatening, not to create violence but to avoid it. Based on extensive ethnographic research in the south side of Chicago, they uncover a variety of strategies that black youth employ to avoid or minimize violent encounters. For instance, they find that the most common way to avoid violence is by postponement. When poor youth walk past each other in the street, they put a great deal of effort into looking nonchalant and aloof, with little interest in the other person they pass. In the analysis by Krupnick and Winship, black youth are neither impulsive "superpredators" nor passive cultural dopes, but rather culturally embedded agents attempting to forge a sense of order by deferring violence with posturing, avoidance, and other microstrategies.

Chapter 10, "What about the Day After? Youth Culture in the Era of 'Law and Order,'" by ethnographer and sociologist Sudhir Venkatesh explores how cultural norms are related to patterns of criminal violence among the urban poor. As Venkatesh notes, the problem of violence in poor neighborhoods is typically posed as identifying individual-level structural and cultural causes of violent behavior. However, Venkatesh flips the analysis, examining instead how community-level responses to norm violations affect subsequent individual-level instances of criminal behavior. For example, in his years of first-person research with the urban poor, Venkatesh finds that residents frequently mediate potentially violent conflicts themselves instead of relying on the police. To understand why communities do this, Venkatesh emphasizes that when an individual violates a cultural norm by committing a violent act, the community-level response prevents an escalation of violence. Researchers thus would be well advised, contends Venkatesh, to consider community-level cultural factors as causes of criminal activity. This will entail, he argues, consulting community stakeholders who themselves mediate responses to criminal activity (instead of calling a third party such as the police), uncovering a longer temporal dimension in conditioning cultural norms, and using a variety of data sources, including qualitative data that can highlight the taken-for-granted assumptions of some quantitative research. Furthermore, Venkatesh calls on researchers to question simple categorizations of groups or communities as law abiding versus criminal, since traditions of community-based enforcement are prevalent in even the most violently dangerous neighborhoods.

Chapter 11, "Culture, Inequality, and Gender Relations among Urban Black Youth," by sociologist Jody Miller explores the intersections of gender inequality, culture, and poverty among black youth. Miller examines the sexual objectification of young black women, which she argues contributes to sexual violence against women. This violence can include sexual harassment, sexual assault, and group rape. Based on qualitative and survey-based research in St. Louis, Miller shows that black women experience shockingly high levels of sexual violence and contends that this sexual violence has deep cultural roots. Many violent acts are based on cultural ideologies that blame black women for their problems, on relationships with black men characterized by pervasive and mutual distrust, and on beliefs about male and female sexuality that encourage violent behaviors. Furthermore, she argues that particular forms of masculine identity, promoted within peer groups and popular culture, privilege and reinforce sexual harassment against women. To reduce sexual violence among the urban poor, Miller suggests encouraging young women to question and critically talk about the messages and images they consume regarding gender and sexuality. As well, young black men should adopt forms of masculinity that are not rooted in sexual dominance over women and should be encouraged to generalize the empathy they often already have for women in their lives. Miller further argues that the lives of young men and women are intertwined, so women should not be targeted separately from men, and vice versa. Ultimately it will take improving the social and cultural lives of both black men and women to prevent the sexual violence black women endure.

Part five, Cultural, Social and Moral Trials, shifts to a consideration of the sociocultural issues that bedevil policy interventions toward improving the lives of black youth through selected case studies and a broad social-philosophical analysis of all attempts at social and cultural change. Chapter 12, by sociologist Simone Ispa-Landa "Effects of Affluent Suburban Schooling: Learning Skilled Ways of Interacting with Educational Gatekeepers" examines how institutional standards within schools influence students' cultural beliefs and attitudes for dealing with educational gatekeepers. Her analysis is based on ethnographic observations and in-depth interviews with two groups of urban black adolescents (in grades 8–10) with similar familial backgrounds but in differing educational environments. Students in one group are enrolled in an urban-to-suburban racial integration program and are bused to schools in affluent suburbs where the majority of students are the children of upper-middle-class, white professionals. In contrast, members of the second group have been wait-listed for the racial integration program and attend low-performing, majority-minority public schools in the central city.

A central finding of her research is that teachers in suburban schools often perceived challenges by students to teacher practices or authority as legitimate. At the same time, the racialization of black students' gender performances led to efforts to "reform" them by bringing them into closer compliance with what guidance counselors and teachers believed to be middle-class or non-"ghetto" styles of feminine self-presentation. Teachers in urban charter and public schools were more likely to interpret students' voicing of complaints as "attitude" or "talking back" and to punish such behavior. As a result, wait-listed students had fewer opportunities than students in the busing program to cultivate skills and styles of self-assertion conducive to academic success. She concludes by emphasizing how both schools and families are important sites in which poor youth acquire much-needed cultural skills and strategies.

In Chapter 13, "'Try On the Outfit and Just See How It Works': The Psychocultural Responses of Disconnected Youth to Work," sociologists Orlando Patterson and Jacqueline Rivers analyze findings from a jobs training program that explicitly promoted cultural change in the participants. The target population were youth with very unstable job histories, and one aim of the program was to develop the "soft" skills to help with obtaining secure employment. The authors find that in general the participants in the program responded positively to the program's goals and reported no personal or identity problems as a result. Moreover, almost all participants did not think the program was trying to impose a "white" or middle-class cultural worldview. Indeed, these youth had a quite sophisticated ethnosociological model of society, which bore remarkable resemblance to Erving Goffman's dramaturgical theory and which led them to view the mainstream culture of work as simply another frame, another play in the game of life that they were free to enact or reject as they choose. This is a crucial finding for students of cultural analysis, for it reveals that explicit programs of cultural change need not be viewed as paternalistic or ideological by the participants involved. As the authors observe, this is likely a reflection of the fact that most respondents already embraced to some degree the cultural norms, values, and beliefs promoted by the program but had either disregarded them or had difficulty applying them to the circumstances they faced.

In Chapter 14, "Stepping Up or Stepping Back: Highly Disadvantaged Parents' Responses to the Building Strong Families Program," sociologist Andrew Clarkwest and colleagues examine the results of the Building Strong Families (BSF) project, which was sponsored by the U.S. Department of Health and Human Services' Administration for Children and Families (ACF). This project offered relationship skills education in small groups of unwed couples who had either just had a child or were expecting a child, with the goal of improving relationship quality so that couples would remain together. The authors, working with Mathematica Policy Research, conducted an experimental evaluation of the BSF program in eight sites across the country. Their findings are sobering for those interested in policy interventions to change the lives of the urban poor. Clarkwest and colleagues find that fifteen months after the intervention, the BSF program had no statistically or substantively significant effect on the relationship status or quality, nor on the level and kind of involvement of fathers with their children.

Indeed, the intervention revealed an extraordinarily counterintuitive finding: the authors found pronounced negative effects of the program at the Baltimore site. In particular, the unwed couples in Baltimore were much less likely to remain in a relationship after the program, and fathers were much less likely to provide meaningful financial support or see their children consistently. On top of this, after the program, the mothers were much more likely to report experiencing a severe physical assault. How could a program designed to improve relationship quality not only have no effects, but actually make relationships worse? To answer this question, Clarkwest and colleagues use the Baltimore site as a comparative case study with the other sites. The sample of unwed couples recruited from the Baltimore site were unique in several respects, most importantly in the large proportion of African American couples who were living in conditions of severe economic and social disadvantage. In other words, the couples who were recruited into the sample had unique characteristics that interacted with the intervention of the program to produce negative effects.

Based on these differences, the authors evaluate several competing explanations for the pronounced negative effects for the Baltimore site.

They outline three main explanations. First, although the program had no impact on their earnings or drug use, after the program fathers were more likely to fault themselves for the end of the relationship, citing their inability to contribute financially to the relationship and their abuse of alcohol and other drugs. Second, because of the fragility of the relationships before the intervention, the program likely had a triggering effect, causing couples to reevaluate their relationships and breaking apart a relationship that would have broken apart anyway but at a later point in time. Finally, the intervention may have had interference effects. Unlike several other sites, the couples in the Baltimore sample were all unwed and had not been in their relationships as long. Thus, the lack of role models in the sample may have exacerbated the relationship expectations, fostering a sense of hopelessness about the possibility of staying together.

In Chapter 15, "Beyond BA Blinders: Cultural Impediments to College Success," educational researcher James Rosenbaum and colleagues explore how access to higher education presents many barriers to upward mobility, especially for disadvantaged youth. These authors contend that there exists a pervasive set of cultural norms they call "BA blinders." This is the view that college must encourage all students, regardless of their career goals, to purse a BA degree that involves four years of full-time courses, with no interim credentials or partial payoffs, and an emphasis on a broad range of academic fields. These cultural beliefs, which are also embedded in norms and values promoting this model of higher education, present severe barriers to disadvantaged youth, according to the authors. For example, the course load can be daunting, there is little payoff with partial completion, the obligations are often uncertain and conflicting with nonschool obligations, and some degrees may be entirely unrelated to secure employment. Many of these problems are exacerbated by the fact that poor youth often grow up in cultural contexts in which the goals and structure of a BA-style system is unfamiliar and daunting, requiring the extra burden of "code switching" to even participate in higher education.

The authors conclude that there is a set of specific, clearly-obtainable procedures that colleges, in particular community colleges that overwhelmingly educate poor youth, can use to improve the institutional goals of higher education. Specifically, Rosenbaum and his coauthors argue that community colleges should front-load rewards by identifying desirable credentials and occupations that can be quickly attained, presenting quick payoffs, back-loading obstacles by delaying remedial and general education until they are absolutely necessary, creating incremental success sequences (or "degree ladders," as they call it), identifying pathways and time slots for courses that are the most optimal for each student, providing guardrails that monitor progress, and investing in extensive information and support in the job-search process. The chapter reinforces the theme that policy interventions are themselves embedded in cultural contexts that influence their efficacy. Moreover, policies can reflect norms and values of the general population (or economic elites), which may in fact not be optimal for some subset of the population. Although a college education may be a universally desired goal, it may be a barrier to success if it fails to take into account the needs of those who are actually obtaining the degree.

Finally, in Chapter 16,"Liberalism, Self-Respect, and Troubling Cultural Patterns in Ghettos," social philosopher Tommie Shelby discusses the moral and political aspects of policies based on cultural change. Shelby begins by emphasizing that the phrase "the culture of poverty" has long been abandoned by social scientists, given that it has come to represent a simplistic, pseudoscientific causal relationship between culture, structure, and people's life chances. Yet there is a growing awareness that there are indeed cultural aspects of poverty, with people's attitudes, values, and beliefs affecting or reflecting their structural conditions. For people who have been the victims of systemic racism and segregation, these cultural differences may become more pronounced (although not necessarily more important). He argues that there are two versions of what he calls the "cultural divergence thesis" relating culture to poverty. The "weak" version is that the norms, values, and beliefs of the poor reflect their current structural conditions, while the "strong" version is that these cultural aspects are derived from both diachronic and synchronic structural conditions. Shelby then contends that, regardless of the broad claims, either version of the cultural divergence thesis suggests cultural changes might be appropriate, since within a single generation switching across cultural contexts can be a barrier to educational and occupational advancement.

In the latter part of his essay, Shelby considers how what he calls "cultural reform," or positive cultural change, might be useful in improving the lives of the severely disadvantaged, in particular black youth. He distinguishes among three types of cultural reform: cultural augmentation, in which otherwise absent or latent beliefs, values, or norms are introduced to the poor; second, cultural removal, in which cultural aspects are eliminated or "neutralized"; and finally, some combination of cultural augmentation and removal, or what Shelby calls "cultural rehabilitation."

Shelby further emphasizes that cultural reform may range from the unobjectionable alteration of people's beliefs, which is a type of cultural reform so widespread in the educational system that it is taken for granted, to the controversial attempt to change the values or cultural identities of the poor. Yet Shelby suggests that the alterations of people's values or identities, because they orient what is worthwhile and desirable, are impossible to avoid, since they undergird all the most basic questions of what policies should be in place. When cultural reform entails explicitly changing people's values and identities, in which the aim is "to restructure the soul," cultural change is tantamount to "moral reform." This leads to Shelby's crucial question: Can liberals support moral reform as one part of a variety of strategies in improving the lives of the poor without sacrificing their own political values? Shelby argues that even if there is a cultural divergence between the poor and the rest of society that worsens their life chances, cultural reform based on changing the values and identities of the poor attacks the social bases of their self-esteem and violates their basic right to self-respect. Furthermore, such a campaign is incompatible with the value of personal autonomy consistent with modern liberalism.

Given the pitfalls of moral reform, Shelby sees a way forward that incorporates cultural reform with liberal-democratic principles and a market-based society. At a minimum, racial discrimination should be minimized, conditions of equality of opportunity should be maximized (by promoting regulations that secure market competition and minimize the intergenerational transfer of economic advantage), and there should be a guaranteed social minimum so that no one lives in "degrading forms of poverty." To realize these fundamental changes to American society, a broad coalition will be required, including among the black poor. To pave the way for cultural change, which will at some point entail changes in people's norms and values, Shelby calls for an appeal to the self-respect of poor blacks, with reform coming not from the state (which in his view currently lacks the moral authority to implement changing people's values and norms) but from grassroots community and political organizations.

We conclude with a section titled "What Have We Learned?" in which we provide an overview of the main themes of the volume, discussing the implications for cultural analyses of poverty as well as the role of culture in social policy. We also review and briefly evaluate, in light of our findings, several of the major policy interventions aimed at improving the lives of black youth.

Ultimately it is our hope that by bringing together a diverse set of scholars from a wide range of disciplines, from economics to ethnomusicology, grounded in both data as well as theoretical insights from the humanities and social sciences, the chapters in this volume contribute not just to academic research but also to public discourse on the facts and realities facing black youth every day. To date, far too much public discourse on the relation between culture and disadvantage has veered toward crude ad hoc speculations on the one hand and a taken-for-granted position that all cultural explanations are either irrelevant or anathema on the other. Neither approach is conducive to the advancement of empirical research or to public discourse. In the final analysis, it is only by listening to the voices of the poor and taking the interacting structural and cultural conditions they experience seriously as both a scientific and policy matter that we can tackle the problems they face without repeating the mistakes of the past or ignoring the enormity of the challenges ahead.

I

OVERVIEW

The Nature and Dynamics of Cultural Processes

ORLANDO PATTERSON, *Harvard University*

Introduction

This chapter provides an overview of the conception of culture that informs this work. We offer a preliminary definition in this introduction. Sections 1 and 2 explore the two basic components of culture. Section 3 introduces the concept of sociocultural configuration, which we deploy in our study of the social and cultural matrix of black youth in the following chapter.

Culture is the product of two interconnected sets of processes. One is a dynamically stable component of collectively constructed knowledge about our world that is unevenly shared and distributed among given networks of persons. We follow Sahlins (2000) in calling this the constituted component of culture. Such knowledge provides predictability and regularity, coordination, continuity, and meaning in human thought, actions, and interactions. Cultural knowledge is grounded in, and emerges from, pragmatic usage, which is its second component. This component refers to the ways in which cultural knowledge is used in ongoing individual and interpersonal actions. It is in the interactions of cultural users that cultural knowledge is transmitted, produced, reproduced, and changed (Patterson 2004; 2001; 2010).

One way of illustrating the distinction, and relation between, the two components is to think of a similar relation between the two components of language, first emphasized by Saussure (1977): the relation between language with its lexicon and rules of grammar, syntax, and deep structure on the one hand, and speech or utterance on the other, which are the pragmatics of speakers communicating with each other. While individuals have a great deal of leeway in how they use language, it remains the case that no communication is possible without a recognition and knowledge

25

of the rules of language. Furthermore, as social linguists and students of linguistic pragmatics have shown, there is a substratum of practical rules of usage in language, proper ways of communicating that take account of context, the social attributes of speakers and their intent, making it possible to overcome the ambiguities of talk. The analogy holds directly with the two components of culture, more broadly conceived. Interaction is not possible without a minimum set of shared cultural knowledge and meanings among persons, including the explicit and often implicit rules prescribed in social norms, values, shared metaphors, and models of reasoning. This would seem screamingly obvious, but in the face of current skepticism among cultural sociologists, microsociologists have found it necessary to document the fact that a fundamental "feature of interaction in groups is that members must share their interpretations of behaviors (i.e., shared meanings) in order for them to coordinate their activities and accomplish the task" (Burke and Stets 2009, 153). At the same time, shared knowledge and meaning structures and the rules and values relating to them provide sufficient flexibility to impart unique qualities to each interaction.[1]

Section 1. The Component of Constituted Cultural Knowledge

The basic processes of cultural knowledge are shared schemata (DiMaggio 1997). They are of three broad types: the domains of declarative, procedural, and evaluative knowledge. Schemata are mental shortcuts, "precompiled generic knowledge structures" in memory that organize and process incoming information and perceptions in the light of previously stored knowledge about given objects, concepts, events, and evaluations (Brewer 1987, 189). They are rooted in our capacity to categorize, which makes it possible for the perceived world to come "as structured information rather than as arbitrary or unpredictable attributes" (Rosch 1978, 28–30). Schemata also retrieve knowledge structures from memory to make judgments (Brewer and Nakamura 1984). Schemata may be purely individual and idiosyncratic, which is the form usually studied by psychologists. They only become cultural *when they are public or shared* by a given group of persons (D'Andrade and Strauss 1992; DiMaggio 1997; Cerulo 2010). Schemas are also often hierarchically combined: specific instances of schemata are united with more abstracts ones to generate schema assemblages, which dynamically allow for the removal from memory of inappropriate schemas and their replacement by others. These assemblages, in turn, can themselves be assembled into higher-order configurations, to which we return in the final section. Schemas, according to D'Andrade and Strauss (1992), also have motivational force, depicting "natural and appropriate responses" and guides to action.

Not all knowledge is cognitively processed as schemata. As Brewer notes, we often face novel situations that cannot be adequately represented or processed by them, in which case we turn to mental models and to our natural capacity to reason, based on our use of innate or "generic knowledge of space, time, causality, and human intentionality" (1987, 189). There are, however, three ways in which our reasoning can become cultural: when they are prefigured and internally represented in our shared beliefs, ideologies, narratives, metaphors, metonymies, and tropes (Lakoff and Johnson 2003; Denzau and North 1994); when externally represented in institutions, which, as Douglas aptly puts it, "think for us" (Douglas 1986); and when they are distributed knowledge embedded in social interactions (Hutchins 1995), discussed below.

Cultural knowledge is not only shared but can also be held in common. Knowledge is *common* when all persons in a group not only know a given fact but knowingly know that all persons know it, ad infinitum. It is possible for most persons in a given community to share knowledge of something, yet be unaware of the fact that it is widely known. In an inner-city neighborhood, for example, most persons may be aware of the fact that the greatly admired head of a locally based antipoverty foundation may be corrupt, yet be unaware of the fact that this is generally known. Once this fact is made public, however, say by a muckraking article in the local newspaper, and thereby becomes common knowledge, everyone may come forward with accusations of their own. The manipulation of common knowledge is important in indirect speech and in the face-saving and face-losing of everyday interactions (Pinker 2007, 418–25). It is also a critical element in interactions in inner-city and other communities where respect and face-saving are often essential for the avoidance of violence (see the chapter by Krupnick and Winship in this volume), and indirection has long been shown to be an essential element of African American signifying and other vernacular language and folkways (Gates 1988). Common knowledge is also important in explaining social movements and other forms of collective action: a person's decision to join a demonstration or a revolt, for example, may depend on her knowledge of other people's knowledge of the intention of others to join the protest (Chwe 1999).

Domains of Cultural Knowledge Structures: Declarative, Procedural, and Evaluative

We distinguish between three domains of shared schemas, henceforth referred to as cultural knowledge: declarative, procedural, and evaluative. Declarative knowledge is simply knowledge of facts and events, whereas procedural knowledge is "know-how," skills, or how to do things (Smith 1994, 100). Declarative knowledge is explicit, expressional, and often acquired in one-trial learning: once told what a slam-dunk is, we know it. We distinguish broadly between internal and external declarative cultural knowledge, the former referring to shared beliefs, ideologies, language, narratives, metaphor, and so on (Larson 1994, 20), the latter to artifacts, social rituals, conventions, and the more formal, structured conventions we call institutions. However, it is largely one of analytic convenience. Lakoff points out that narratives, which are complex schemata, "exist outside the body—in our culture—and inside the body—in the very building blocks of our brain" (Lakoff 2009, 21; see also Ignatow 2007, 119–24). Furthermore, physical objects, including our bodies, are means through which we think, by providing "the basis for an extraordinarily wide variety of ontological metaphors, that is, ways of viewing events, activities, emotions, ideas, etc., as entities and substances" (Lakoff and Johnson 2003, 25–32). To be sure, in purely cognitive terms, all thought and language are embodied since, ultimately, they are largely based on image-schemas or primary metaphors that originate in prelinguistic, neurologically wired structures of experience going back to childhood, which associatively shape the more complex conceptual metaphors by which we think. Thus, "in all aspects of life . . . we define our reality in terms of metaphors and then proceed to act on the basis of the metaphors. We draw inferences, set goals, make commitments, and execute plans, all on the basis of how we in part structure our experience, consciously and unconsciously, by means of metaphor" (Lakoff and Johnson 2003, 158).

Nonetheless, sociologists and other students of culture find it more analytically convenient to broadly distinguish knowledge structures and social objects that are phenomenologically more external from those that are more obviously embodied. This allows us to highlight those behaviors and modes of being in which knowledge is clearly invested in our bodies and is performed nonconsciously. It is what we call procedural knowledge, that which can only be acquired through demonstration and practice. The French phenomenologist Merleau-Ponty used the example of touch-typing to illustrate what he called "knowledge in the hands, which is forthcoming only when bodily effort is made, and cannot be formulated in detachment from that effort" (Merleau-Ponty [1945] 1962, 144). One may know what singing a rap song, boxing, or a bicycle are all about, but doing them can only be learned through performative training and, once acquired, become automatic and nonconscious, that is embodied (Hutchins 1995, 311). While some procedural knowledge requires initial training in formal settings, it is also the kind of knowledge not normally learned in class-rooms but at home, in one's community and personal network, and on the job—itself made possible by one's personal network. Bourdieu's widely acclaimed concepts of "habitus" and "cultural capital" are grounded on the principle of procedural knowledge acquisition, as he himself recog-nizes: "The essential part of the modus operandi which defines practical mastery is transmitted in practice, in its practical state, without attaining the level of discourse" (Bourdieu 1977, 87–95; see also Bourdieu 1986, 241–58; 1990, 66–67; Wacquant 2004b).

It should be pointed out that the relation between cultural knowledge and the body can move in either or both directions. Thus, Bourdieu's classic account of gender roles and values and their relation to public and private life among the Algerian Kabyle is an example of cultural declara-tive knowledge and values being inscribed in what he calls "bodily hexis": "The opposition which mythico-ritual logic makes between the male and the female and which organize the whole system of values, reappear, for example, in the gestures and movements of the body, in the form of the opposition between the straight and the bent, or between assurance and restraint" (Bourdieu 1977, 94). Mary Douglas describes this as the natu-ralization of social relations through the analogic use of the body: "The institutions lock into the structure of an analogy from the body. . . . In modern society the analogical relation of head to hand was frequently used to justify the class structure, the inequalities of the educational system, and the division of labor between manual and intellectual work" (Douglas 1986, 48–53).

Procedural cultural knowledge is of two broad types: routines or scripts, and distributed knowledge. Scripts are cultural algorithms—stored knowl-edge of "predetermined, stereotyped sequences of actions that defines a well-known situation" (Schank and Abelson 1977, 41). Even simple scripts are prone to misconceptions and can usually only be learned by doing (Chen 2004, 98). Routines can further be subdivided into types: individual and divisional. Individual routines are those performed by a single person, such as learning the recipe for food preparation. Divisional procedures, or drills, are those that require alignment with others, such as learning one's role in an army parade or navigation team or orchestra. Hutchins shows how the pelorus operators of the navigation team on a navy ship need only know what to do when certain operations occur in their environment, and need have no knowledge of the entire script. They simply "do X when Y" (Hutchins 1995, 199–200). Even so simple a procedure, however, has to be learned through repeated drills: one small error can ruin an entire parade, docking maneuver, or orchestral performance.

Distributed cultural knowledge is that in which the interaction of two or more agents' knowledge sets yields new knowledge that is not known to them separately. Monique has just noticed that JJ, the local hip-hop artist and hit-maker, has his dreadlocks tied in a neat ponytail; Kelly knows that the only time JJ ever wears his dreadlocks in a ponytail is when he goes to Manhattan to sign a contract for a new rap song he has just created. From the intersection of these two sets of knowledge, they arrive at the aggregate or distributed knowledge, unknown to each separately, that a new hip-hop hit is on the way. This new knowledge is embedded in their information states taken together. Such knowledge is often fundamental for the performance of ongoing, complex human action, as Hutchins (1995, 219–24) has demonstrated in his study of the navigation team on a U.S. navy ship. Note that the distinctive feature of distributed knowledge is not only that it is embodied in persons but also that it is embedded in interactions between them.

The importance of procedural knowledge for an understanding of ethnoracial inequality cannot be overstated. It is, in fact, the basic mechanism whereby the social iniquity of segregation is achieved. The systematic separation of blacks from the social life of whites, especially middle-class and more successful whites, amounted to a sustained, centuries-long deprivation of the acquisition of all the fundamental procedural knowledge required for successful functioning in mainstream American society. This denial was, and remains, especially acute for youth and young children. Cognitive scientists have shown that procedural knowledge is the first to be learned, is partly independent of declarative knowledge, and is located in a different part of the brain (Bloom and Lazerson 1988). One gets better at skill performance the earlier one starts to acquire it, and the longer one practices it (Ten Berge and Van Hezewijk 1999, 607–09, 615–18). Schools cannot compensate for this deficiency since teachers rely heavily on verbal expression, whereas procedural skills, especially the all-important social ones, are implicit and distributed and hence often not even consciously known; nonetheless, there are grounds to believe that they are more important for survival than declarative knowledge such as that acquired at school (Ten Berge and Van Hezewijk 1999, 607).

The evaluative domain of cognitive knowledge refers to the shared schemas we call values and norms. Cultural sociologists, in overreacting against previous generations of scholars who misinterpreted and misused these concepts, have gone to the other, absurd extreme of denying their significance in social life, a denial that is especially true of those who study racial inequality. This denigration has simply brought ridicule to the discipline, since other fields of study, most notably social psychology, economics, and law, consider them foundational. There is also a good deal of contradiction within sociology itself, since one of the most advanced areas of the discipline, organizational studies, regards values and norms as critical components of organizational structure and functioning. Happily, recent studies have now largely discredited this untenable dogma in the discipline (see Hechter and Opp 2001, pt. 1 and ch. 13; Bardi and Schwartz 2003; Lefkowitz 2003; Hitlin and Piliavin 2004; Inglehart and Baker 2000).

Values refer to the ways we evaluate objects—the degree to which we favor or disfavor them. They are similar to attitudes, except that they are shared or collective. They are of two kinds: what Weber (1949, 111) called "ultimate and final values, in which the meaning of existence is rooted," and particularized values which are domain specific, collectively shared likes and dislikes. Others refer to the same distinction with terms such as "terminal and instrumental," or general and domain relevant (Lefkowitz 2003, 145–47; Rokeach 1973). Ultimate values are prototypic evaluations of the desirable or undesirable: individualism, the work ethic, love of God, nation, and family on the one hand, and negative ultimate values such as anti-Semitism, racism, and homophobia, which may be as foundational as favored ultimate values. The view that values only refer to positive evaluations is incorrect (Hitlin and Piliavin 2004). Racism, for example, was a foundational value of the Old South, right down to the middle of the twentieth century. Particularized values are things like the preference for home ownership, spectator sports, hip-hop music, hypermasculinity, and so on.

Of course, persons are not slaves to their values, and it is easy to show that their behaviors often depart from them, but this in no way vitiates their significance in social life (see Barth 1993, 44). Every criticism that has been leveled at values—that several may serve the same ends, that different ends may be served by the same value, and that they are repetitive and redundant—can be said of genes, yet such observations have not led geneticists to abandon the study of genes. A large number of studies have now fully established the fact that values, especially ultimate ones, are extremely stable and have powerful effects on human life (Rokeach 1973; Feather 1995; Inglehart and Baker 2000; Bardi and Schwartz 2003; Hitlin and Piliavin 2004).

An important distinction, which clears up much of the confusion about values, is that between espoused and experiential values: those that persons consciously advocate and acknowledge and those they actually live by and that can be inferred from their behavior (Argyris and Schon 1978; Epstein 1989). Espoused values, however hypocritical, may still be consequential, since the constant public expression of a preference may eventually lead people to accept it, especially if there is also institutional support for it. This seems to have been the case with the change in white attitudes toward blacks since the middle of the twentieth century or the more dramatic shift in values toward homosexuality and gay marriage over recent decades.

Ultimate values are desired for their own sake, are deeply internalized, and are strongly reinforced by public myths, narratives, and popular culture (Hechter, Nadel, and Michod 1993, ch. 1; McBride and Toburen 1996). Indeed, as Lakoff and Johnson (2003, 22) point out, "The most fundamental values in a culture will be coherent with the metaphorical structure of the most fundamental concepts in the culture." They account for basic divisions in political life (Haidt 2012, chs. 4, 7, 11), and because they are the foundations of our stability, they have enormous consequences when they change or shift (see Inglehart 1990; Inglehart and Welzel 2005). Furthermore, people often are prepared to act against their own interests and even physical survival in the pursuit of ultimate values (Fiske and Tetlock 1997; McGraw and Tetlock 2005). After the tragedy of 9/11, no one, except perhaps a dogmatic cultural sociologist, can sensibly deny the power of religious and political values to motivate the behavior of people (Atran 2006, 164).

Value strength or salience is an important aspect of values, since two groups may have the same value object—say, work is desirable—but differ sharply in how strongly they feel about it: one group may work to live, another may live to work, considering work fundamental to their self-esteem (Lakoff and Johnson 2003, 23–24). However, values may simply be in conflict, leading to conflicts in the metaphor associated with them, and this may be resolved not simply by a shift in priorities, as Lakoff and Johnson argue, but by a deliberate inversion of the associated metaphor. A good example of this is the Jamaican Rastafarian rejection of the implicit metaphor of certain English words. Thus "oppression," with the first syllable "op" phonetically suggesting the favored orientation metaphor "up," is considered an imperialist linguistic trick to make black people comfortable with their condition, and is thus changed in Rasta dread talk (speech) to "downpression," and the word "understanding" with its belittling "under" (meant, they believe, to trick the poor into not gaining knowledge) is transformed to "overstanding" (Pollard 2000, 3–18, 86–93), both of which make perfect sense in light of the role of metaphor in cultural coherence (Lakoff and Johnson 2003, 14–34).

Norms are the shared rules we live by. They prescribe and proscribe what we ought to do in given situations, unlike values, which express what we like or profoundly desire to do. They presume a reference group that we expect to reward or punish us for our conformity or failure to conform, and whom we expect to behave accordingly. Norms are fundamental to social order, and there is some evidence that we may be cognitively hard wired toward normative behavior (Therborn 2004, 868, 870; see also Hechter and Opp 2001, xii and ch. 13; Coleman 1990; for interesting recent reviews of the evolutionary literature on norms, see O'Gorman 2008, 77; Dubreuil 2010, 19–50).

Norms may be injunctive—prescribing what we ought or ought not to do—or observational (also called "descriptive" by some psychologists), our conception of what is normal, based on the observed behavior of others. The former applies to all situations, the latter only to the contexts in which the behavior has become typical (Cialdini and Trost 1998, 161). Among inner-city male youth, respect for one's person is an injunctive norm, to be defended under all circumstances and even to kill for; however, flirting with or hassling every passing woman on the street is an observational norm best confined to the 'hood (Anderson 1999; Bourgois 1996). A more complicated situation is one in which persons may hold both behavioral and injunctive norms regarding a given social behavior but with different relative strengths. Thus, almost every survey on the attitudes and norms of inner-city youths reports a norm of strong disapproval of out-of-wedlock birth and misogynistic rap songs, yet these same youths are observed to practice or consume both to a considerable degree (Cohen 2012). One interpretation of the discrepancy is that they are reporting their weak injunctive norms to survey researchers while abiding by the observational norms of their neighborhoods. Another interpretation is consistent with one theory of norm emergence, namely, that a behavioral regularity will, over time, require justification and "a sense of oughtness," and thus become institutionalized as an injunctive norm (Horne 2001, 6; see also Fine 2001, 139–64). Thus, Ethan Fosse shows (this volume) that, among disconnected black youth, out-of-wedlock fathering and misogynistic attitudes are already injunctive. It is also possible that persons hold several injunctive norms in regard to particular behaviors, in which case the most salient, or the one with the strongest subjective salience, will be most effective. Researchers in social psychology have long reached a consensus that informal social norms are strongest in their influence when there is uncertainty about the situation, when the person we are interacting with is similar to us, or when it is very important that we initiate or maintain a relationship we are particularly concerned about (Cialdini and Trost 1998, 162).

Norms and values may or may not complement each other. Schwartz (1977) proposes the category of personal norms to which people conform because they are consistent with their most deeply held values, independent of external pressures to conform. However, it is very often the case that we do not necessarily like doing the things we are obliged to do, and societies may go through periods in which there is dissonance between what is collectively desired and what is still injunctively prescribed. This was the case with norms and values pertaining to marriage, divorce, and romantic love during the second half of the twentieth century in most Western societies (Balistrino and Ciardi 2008).

Finally, it should be noted that informal norms—those lacking legal sanction—are often as important as formal ones in understanding formal social institutions and economic change. Douglass North (1991), the institutional economist, considers informal norms to have been as important as formal ones in the emergence of capitalism. Organizational sociologists generally agree that they are critical for organizational culture, functioning, and isomorphism, as well as the adoption of innovative changes (DiMaggio and Powell 1983; Scott 2005; Russell 1992). The informal norm of reciprocity has also been shown to be vital for productive employer–employeee relationships (Akerlof 1982).

Section 2. The Component of Cultural Pragmatics

Rules of Practice

As noted earlier, this component refers to persons' use of culture in their interactions. However, and again in contrast to prevailing dogma, while people exercise agency in their practice of culture, they do so within limits set by rules of practice. There are routine ways of interactionally using the constituted cultural structures as well as an alternate body of practical rules of conduct that complement, though sometimes compete with, the knowledge structures of the constituted component. These are meta-cultural rules of interaction, similar to the meta-linguistic rules of conversation that social linguists have long identified (see, for example, Myers 1998; Van Leeuwen 2005, 248–67). What's more, as we saw earlier in our discussion of distributed procedural knowledge, we may not even consciously know what the implicit, rule-bound knowledge is that we are interactively following, though conscious of the desired outcome, since this only emerges from our interaction with each other.

However much their personal projects may motivate persons to deviate from the constituted culture, it is usually the case that they try hard to reconcile, or at least appear to coordinate, their interests with established norms and values, and the effort to appear to conform has important consequences. Bourdieu (1979) refers to this as "second order officiating strategies" (I prefer the term "performative strategies"), in which even the minority of strong-willed persons willing to bend the rules deliberately espouse, and show respect for, the constituted norms and values, precisely because the achievement of their private goals requires a smoothly functioning social order. Free-riding and disruptive deviance are prevented, or muted, by people's awareness of the dangers of overtly undermining the constituted order. The age-old principle of justice holds for the practice of all-important domains of constituted culture: that the appearance of performance (including performative beliefs) is as critical as the act of performance. Furthermore, as identity theorists have shown, for those asserting leadership, "the behavior in which person A engages to display the meanings of his or her leadership identity must be similarly interpreted by person B. If what A does to show leadership is not what B takes to be leadership (because they don't share meanings), then B will not respond in ways that verify A's leadership identity. For the system to work, B must perceive A's behavior in the same way that A perceives behavior—taking the role of the other" (Burke and Stets 2009, 153).

Affect-control theorists in social psychology provide powerful support for the view that what people do in their normal interactions is not obsessive-competitive boundary work or the manipulation of cultural toolkits so as to get the better of others (Swidler 1986; Lamont and Fournier 1993; on Swidler's view see Vaisey, 2008, 2009) but rather makes every effort to reinforce cultural expectations. Far from being compulsive "meaning-makers," as contemporary cultural sociology would have it, affect-control theory, expanding Goffman's microsociological theory of expressive order, has demonstrated compellingly that "humans are . . . *meaning-maintainers,* who continually reconstruct the world to fit intuitive knowledge generated from sentiments, with cognitive and logical constraints. In this perspective, rational analysis is rare rather than routine" (Heise 2002, 17; emphasis added). Further, these sentiments are deeply rooted in more fundamental "shared cultural sentiments." Individuals, in their interactions, seek to maintain not just the meaning of self or of situated identity, "but to maintain understandings generally" (Heise 2002, 35; for a review of affect control and other identity theories, see Owens, Robinson, and Smith-Lovin 2010, 486).

In addition to such performative strategies, however, it is often the case that a parallel structure of practical rules emerges which sometimes contradicts, sometimes substitutes for, but most often sustains the constituted order. Freilich and Schubert (1989, 219) argue that, at the level of social units such as work groups, clans, clubs, and cliques, a parallel system of pragmatic or "smart rules" exists which guide practical action, taking account of the contingencies of human interaction on the ground that no set of rules of "proper action" can fully anticipate. The point is illustrated with a study of police behavior on the street in which a set of practical or "smart" rules of discretionary behavior derived from experience facilitates police action. The resulting greater efficiency of the police in maintaining public order reinforces, rather than undermines, the rules of the constituted order. Like the Algerian group studied by Bourdieu, the American police "learn to use street wisdom *and learn, simultaneously, how to appear to be operating within the law*" (Freilich and Schubert 1989, 220). The tension between smart and proper or constituted culture is not always as productive as Freilich and Schubert found. Peter Moskos's (2009) more recent study of police pragmatic behavior in the inner cities of Baltimore shows that, while appearing to promote the constituted culture, police smart rules actually did little to reduce crime or promote constituted norms and values among the African American population they were meant to serve. Of course, they worked well in safeguarding the dominant bourgeois groups (white and black) as well as the "war on drugs" bureaucratic structure, which raises the Gramscian issue of hegemony, of what groups, and what ultimate end values, the constituted cultural order serves, questions that are best explored by social philosophers (see the chapter by Shelby in this volume).

Another, quite different example of a set of rules of pragmatic action that coexisted with the constituted cultural order is given by the historical sociologist Biernacki who shows how wool textile workers in Germany and England during the nineteenth century developed "different kinds of tacit pragmatic suppositions (that) center larger clusters of practices and beliefs" (2000, 292) with very different outcomes for the workers of both countries. These pragmatic rules of conduct constituted a "component of cultural structure in their own right" (306) and changed at different paces from the overarching constituted culture. A final, more recent example is taken, ironically, from Lamont's study of how panelists judging academic grant applications developed "customary rules" of "pragmatic fairness" in their meetings. These rules, however, ended up strongly reinforcing the constituted ultimate norms and values of impartiality and transparency that undergird the entire academic system (Lamont 2009, 111, 107–58).

What all these cases show is that people do not arbitrarily use the constituted culture like toolkits to serve their peculiar whims and interests. Instead, as with the pragmatics of language, there are well-defined rules of practice that regulate how they use the constituted domains of culture, and these practical rules of conduct are themselves not only an integral part of the cultural system but are dynamically interconnected with, and usually in support of, the ultimate values and norms of the constituted component of culture.

Cultural Change

Cultural processes are dynamic, and there is change in both components, although at difference rates. Cultural change comes about in two ways: formal and deliberately by the action of state legislatures and other leaders; and informally, and often unintentionally, through the pragmatics of cultural usage. Norms can be changed by edict, as happened dramatically in the dismantlement of America's culture of Jim Crow with the passage of the civil and voting rights laws. Another way in which cultural practices can be made to change is through changes in enabling institutions that sustain them, although this varies with domain. Thus, the use of legislation to change the segregation of schools and neighborhoods that severely handicap African American children and youth have been far less successful than in their use to change the political culture.

As with language, culture changes nonformally in the pragmatics of usage. At the pragmatic level, there is constant pressure to change due to errors in the transmission process, idiosyncratic interpretations of the constituted processes, deliberate innovations and inventions, and simple accidents. Cultural pragmatics is like an evolutionary hothouse from which, however, very few innovations survive to become either part of the rules of practice or, far less so, of the domains of the constituted component (see Sperber 1996, 73, chs. 4–5). Most attempts at innovation or invention die without moving from the heads of their inventors or their small circle of friends; others simply cancel each other out. In the final analysis, the norms and values of the evaluative domain act as a powerful filter against innovation moving beyond small cliques and circles.

Nonetheless, change does occur, and the recent path-breaking work of Padgett and Powell (2012) offers us one of the best models of how this happens, especially in cases of major innovations. They show that the most powerful source of cultural change may be generated by the intersection of multiple networks through which flow production rules and procedures as well as established interactions. Innovation emerges when routine skills and relational patterns are transposed from one network to another and given new functions and roles. Innovations become inventions when they "cascade out" to influence the procedures and relationships of other networks, tipping the entire system into radically new ways of thinking, doing, and interacting. Padgett has brilliantly applied his model of change to the rise of early capitalism in renaissance Florence and to other major Western cultural innovations (Padgett and Powell 2012, chs. 5 and 6), but the model works remarkably well in an innovation-cum-invention close to the subject of this volume: the invention of the hip-hop genre of music in the South Bronx during the seventies and eighties of the last century, resulting from the new wave of urban-working and shanty-town migrants from Jamaica into the heart of the South Bronx. The network folding of some of the young immigrants' relational patterns with those of native blacks and the transposition and refunctioning of certain musical forms they brought with them—distinctive DJ boasting styles, dub-shouts, record scratching, the outdoor sound system—into preexisting musical routines of native black youth, such as their own traditional form of rapping, toasting, DJing, and house partying, were culturally explosive, rapidly catalyzing into a set of new procedures such as break-beating, punch phrasing, scratching, crossfading, cutting, mixing, and socially conscious lyrics, that eventually tipped into the new genre. We do not have the space here to examine this striking instantiation of Padgett's theory. However, Wayne Marshall's splendid history of hip-hop in this volume, though not directly engaged with Padgett's theory, provides a rich account that is fully consistent with it.

Knowledge Activation in Sociocultural Pragmatics

We now shift toward a fuller consideration of the microlevels of cultural action. Here we ask: How much and what domains of their culture do individuals know? How do they utilize such knowledge? How do context and broader structural forces interact with constituted and pragmatic cultural knowledge to achieve the goals that individuals and groups set themselves? And what local group-level interactions are engaged in the activation of cultural processes? One important branch of social cognition studies offers a powerful tool in preparing to answer such questions: knowledge activation theory (Higgins 1996; Forster and Liberman 2007; Anderson et al. 2007).

Knowledge activation refers to the cognitive processes involved in the retrieval and use of cultural knowledge. First, there is the availability of cultural knowledge. Cultural knowledge must be stored in memory for it to be available for use in given situations. The acquisition of such knowledge, then, is of prime concern. Many studies of black youth, including several of the chapters in this volume, are concerned with this question. However, as we have seen, there are several domains of culture, both at the constituted and pragmatic levels. Black youth, we will see in Chapter 2, must rely on inadequate schools, segregated role models (themselves with limited knowledge of the constituted culture), and popular media to acquire much of what they know about the dominant mainstream middle-class knowledge domains. These provide varying degrees of knowledge of the declarative and evaluative domains but are completely inadequate for the acquisition of vital procedural knowledge. Of course, as we show in

Chapter 2, they have several other knowledge systems, generated mainly in the inner-city environment, on which to draw.

Second, assuming given sets of cultural knowledge in memory, there is the question of their accessibility. This refers to the degree to which knowledge in memory can be quickly or automatically activated. Even if the appropriate cultural knowledge is available, it cannot be assumed that this will happen on a regular basis, or at all. Automatic activation is subject to subtle shifts of cues in the environment, and hence the extent to which available knowledge becomes accessible varies from one context to the next. Accessibility further may be chronic or transient. When a knowledge structure is frequently used, it becomes chronic in the sense that it is the cultural schema that most readily comes to mind in response to social or other environmental stimuli. Transient accessibility occurs in response to some recent priming, which may temporarily override the more chronically accessible, default response. Knowledge activation, then, has to be seen as the product of the interaction between available knowledge, stimulus and social context (Anderson et al. 2007, 142–43). Thus an unemployed youth may have in memory the declarative knowledge of proper behavior in a job interview, which he learned from an employment prep agency, but upon confronting a white, unfriendly, and clearly skeptical employer, accesses the street culture response of a mean scowl and aggressive body language that is automatically accessible in the face of such perceived hostile cues (see the chapter by Patterson and Rivers in this volume).

The third process concerns the applicability of cultural knowledge. Even if available and accessible, a particular knowledge structure may not be appropriate for a given situation. Take the schema of making eye contact. Among most ethnicities, and in most contexts, this is considered appropriate behavior. However, on many streets of the inner cities, returning another person's glance too directly could be taken as an affront and sign of disrespect and invite a violent response, if the person making the eye contact is male, and will almost certainly lead to sexual harassment if the contact is made by a female (see the chapters by Krupnick and Winship; Miller; and Patterson and Rivers in this volume).

The fourth element of the knowledge-activation process is not always mentioned but is given special emphasis by Anderson et al. (2007, 139)— what they call self-regulation, which are psychological processes "such as inhibition, suppression, adjustment, or enhancement" that can "short-circuit activation at the outset, or re-direct it once it has occurred, and can also prevent application or introduce a post-application correction." People, in short, are not slaves to their automatic reflexes.

Section 3. Sociocultural Configurations

Knowledge activation theory informs our development of a key construct in the study of black youth and, I suggest, all meso- and microlevel studies of culture: the sociocultural configuration. I mean by this the availability and activation of any cluster of cultural knowledge and practices structured around a core set of values and norms, motivated by a common set of interests, goals, or needs. Configurations vary in duration, density, complexity, and availability. They are often durable, such as a lodge group, sports club, or entrenched street gang, but they may be instantaneous, such as flash mobs. They vary in levels of complexity, from those which meet the specialized needs of professional or informal communal groups, to those of gangs, clubs, lodges, organizations, and ethnic groups. Higher-order or macroconfigurations are simply configurations of lower-order ones orchestrated by ultimate values. With complex macroconfigurations, no single individual can know all the constituent microdomains, but it is essential that all persons know, have chronically accessible, and abide by the fundamental articulating values and norms—what Shore calls "foundational schemas" (1998, 312)—that orchestrate the entire configuration. The construct gets us away from the totalizing view of different groups of people each having a single, all-embracing culture or subculture. People, especially those in modern complex societies, know and have access to a variety of cultural configurations (although there tends to be a primary focal one) and, contrary to the mistaken view, are usually able to shift from one to the other, although there are special cases where this may become problematic.

Such shifts are possible because, as social identity theory makes clear, in modern, complex, highly differentiated societies, people are capable of "as many identities as distinct networks of relationships in which they occupy positions and play roles" (Stryker and Burke 2000, 286). Furthermore, identities are understood "as cognitive schemas—internally stored information and meanings serving as frameworks for interpreting experience," and are organized within the self "in a salience hierarchy" (286).

The concept of sociocultural configuration is partly congruent with the dynamic constructivist approach in cultural psychology developed by Hong and Mallorie (2004, 63) who conceptualize culture, "not as a general, monolithic entity, but as a loose network of domain-specific cognitive structures" and that individuals can have several such networks, even if they contain conflicting views (see also Benet-Martinez et al. 2002). The construct is also indebted to Fine's (1979) concept of "ideocultures," especially his recent foregrounding of the ways in which groups' cognition, identity, performance, and emotion are integrated in practice (Fine and Fields 2008) but differs in several important respects. Thus, while the pragmatics of such configurations are observed microsociologically, such configurations may be available in the broader "landscape" of an entire nation, or even globally. Thus the hip-hop configurion has long sprung from its South Bronx crucible to become nationally available to American youth of all ethnicities and classes, indeed, to global youth. It is now a vibrant ensemble of foundational cultural slots that are instantiated , on the ground—in Harlem, Chicago, LA, the *banlieues* of France and elsewhere—in ways that, however "recontextualized," creatively reproduce certain dynamically stable aesthetic modes and signifiers— rapping, DJing, MCing, graffiti art, breakdancing, distinctive fashions and embodied styles—as well as "black-inflected identities" and themes such as antiracism, equality, hypermasculinity, authenticity, and subaltern rage (Alim 2008, 1–24; Drissel 2009; Patterson, ch. 2 in this volume).

In modern societies, especially urban ones, people can often access many configurations relating to different roles or aspects of their lives (Fischer 1975, 1324–28). Stryker and Burke state the matter elegantly: "Society is seen as a mosaic of relatively durable patterned interactions and relationships, differentiated yet organized, embedded in an array of groups, organizations, communities, and institutions, and intersected by crosscutting boundaries of class, ethnicity, age, gender, religion and other variables" (2000, 285). As we show in Chapter 2, an inner-city youth may have available some aspects of the dominant mainstream culture, a good deal of the popular culture, the hip-hop variant of popular culture, the vernacular black culture of his proletarian parents, or the violent street culture of his neighborhood.

I use the term sociocultural focus to refer to the most chronically accessible or default configuration of a group, the one that is most crucial to identity salience, emotional security, normal functioning, and emergencies. People, however, are not permanently wedded to their focal or primary configuration. It is always possible to override chronically accessible knowledge structures, behavioral habits, and identity salience through transient accessibility or frame switching, documented, for example, in Hong and Mallorie's (2004) study of Korean frame switching in their relations with white Americans.

A final feature of cultural configurations concerns the role of trust and norms. Karen Cook and Russell Hardin (2001, 327–47) have argued that in large urban areas with many networks of ongoing relationships, there is "a shift from reliance on normative regulation of behavior to the use of ongoing trust relationships" because the sharing of common or generalized norms cannot be fully relied on. I think that norms remain important, but there is a shift from injunctive to within-group observational and personal norms. However, the basic insight is well taken and applies nicely to the behavior of inner-city street gangs. In the absence of formal sanctioning institutions or respect for authorities, gang members must rely on "modal trusting relationships [that] grow out of ongoing interactions that give each party an incentive to be cooperative" (Cook and Hardin 2001, 327–28). As one Milwaukee gang member explained, the only thing required of an initiate to the gang was "to prove your trust" (Hagedorn 1998, 91). Many acts of violence among such groups are the result of the betrayal of such trusting relationships (Venkatesh 2006, 371–73).

Conclusion

In this chapter, we have departed from the pragmatic extremism of contemporary cultural sociology with its excessive emphasis on meaning-making, symbolic manipulation, and status seeking; its dismissive treatment of norms and values; and its demonstrably false view that the component of constituted cultural knowledge is an incoherent gallimaufry of toolkits that people use as they please in their endless interpersonal power struggles and boundary wars. Instead, we have attempted to restore balance to the conception of culture by defining it as the dynamically stable product of a bicomponential set of shared processes that, on the one hand, provide predictability, coordination, coherence, direction, prefigured information, and meaning maintenance in people's lives, and, on the other hand, flexibility in individual and social action, pragmatic rules for their usage, as well as contextually bound alternate knowledge structures. From the interaction of the two also emerges institutional structures as well as change, sometimes rapidly, but usually over the long run, language development being the prototype of such changes. I have also proposed that we focus on the sociocultural configurations of those smaller networks of persons, embedded in larger social structures, that are more typical of the contexts in which people conduct their lives. An analysis of such configurations, informed by the view of culture discussed above, will be offered in the following chapter.

The Social and Cultural Matrix of Black Youth

ORLANDO PATTERSON, *Harvard University*

Introduction

It has long been established in sociological studies going back to the early 1940s (Drake and Cayton 1945, chs. 19–22) that black urban neighborhoods cultivate a variety of sociocultural configurations offering individuals a range of options for dealing with their own neighborhood and the wider dominant world. "The diversity of lifestyles," Hannerz wrote over forty years ago, "has a great impact on the ordering of ghetto social relations"; not only was there "drifting between lifestyles," but for those who remain committed to one such style, the necessary skill of "managing coexistence" (1969, 34, 61–69). In the previous chapter, we saw that people are quite capable of assimilating and shifting between different cultural constructs and configurations. Indeed, the acquisition of more than one system of cultural codes—most notably language—can be a cognitive and social asset rather than a problem for such persons (Oyserman et al. 2003). A major recent study of second-generation Americans concludes that there is a "second generation advantage" that springs precisely from their heterogeneous cultural environment (Kasinitz et al. 2008).

It is therefore somewhat puzzling to be told in a recent sociological study that a key, newly rediscovered feature of disadvantaged black neighborhoods is their "cultural heterogeneity" and that the basic problem of black youth is the "negative effects of cultural heterogeneity" due to the problem of having to shift between cultural models, the "dilution" resulting from the presence of other models, and the inevitably unsuccessful attempt to simultaneously mix "multiple competing models," all of which result in "ineffective strategies for accomplishing the desired ends" (Harding 2010, 5). If there is one group of Americans whose history has prepared them for adapting to and exploiting heterogeneity, it is

African Americans. Prudence Carter has sensibly pointed out that "racial and ethnic group members hold multiple intersecting identities shaped by varied forms of socialization and experience" and that this is a source of strength rather than weakness. Among the group of low-income minority youths she studied, it was precisely the bicultural "straddlers" who did best educationally and were college bound (Carter 2005, vii, 37–39). There are, indeed, differing cultural configurations in the inner cities of America, and one of these is a major source of the problems black youth face. But the problem arises not from the plurality of configurations or from low multicultural competence, but rather from the destructive reign of violence from one of them—the sociocultural configuration of a minority that has captured the streets of the inner cities and spread what has been called a "culture of terror" on their neighborhoods (Wacquant 2008, ch. 2; Ferguson 2001, 99, 105).

Poor people, Frank Furstenberg has reminded us, are not all alike, and their differences may be as great as what they have in common (1993; 2000). Anderson's distinction between decent and street cultures in inner-city neighborhoods (1999, ch. 1; see Venkatesh 2006, 37–38), while not inaccurate, underplays the complexity of the social and cultural situation in these neighborhoods. There are, in fact, at least three main social groups and four focal cultural configurations among the disadvantaged black neighborhoods of America. The three main groups are what may be called the ghetto middle class, the black working class, and the disconnected street people. The four focal cultural configurations will be labeled the adapted mainstream, the proletarian, the street, and the hip-hop. Hip-hop is now the common cultural configuration of nearly all black youth, as accessible as the focal configuration of the group in which they were brought up (Rose 2008, 8). Needless to say, these are not mutually exclusive categories. There is a striking degree of social and cultural mobility among black youth, a major reason for both their problems and creativity. Nonetheless, the rich research literature upon which I draw strongly suggests that these are robust types.

The majority of disadvantaged youth, and certainly the most impoverished and problematic, live in the neighborhoods of segregated and concentrated poverty, and we will therefore pay greatest attention to these. However, not all disadvantaged black youth live in disadvantaged neighborhoods. Many live in so-called middle-class ghettos such as those studied by Mary Pattillo. Others also live in integrated working- and lower-class neighborhoods and projects such as the "Brothers" of

Cambridge, Massachusetts, studied by Jay MacLeod. Our analysis will incorporate these experiences.

Two further preliminary points of note are, first, that our analysis will be on the sociocultural configurations of black youth, not exclusively on what has been called "black youth culture." Our aim is to understand all cultural processes that influence disadvantaged black youth. This means that we will be as concerned with their culture of orientation and the wider dominant culture as much as the youth cultures they create. Second, while there is a greater likelihood of those having a mainstream, proletarian, or street configuration to belong to middle-class, working-class, and disconnected segments of disadvantaged neighborhoods, the match is far from even. Thus while the majority of youth from the economically marginal population studied by Carter seem headed for the street culture, or were already there, 7 percent of them were what Carter calls mainstreamers, and over a third were solidly proletarian on an upwardly mobile track (2005, ix, 31–46). Conversely, both Pattillo (2000, 117–45) and Hassett-Walker (2010) document youth from solidly middle-class backgrounds partly or already fully ensnared in the street culture of crime and delinquency.

This chapter will examine the diversity of sociocultural configurations among disadvantaged black youth in ten sections. Section 1 briefly describes the main groups of disadvantaged youth and their neighborhood contexts. Because all cultural configurations among Americans relate in one way or another to the dominant mainstream, we begin our cultural analysis in section 2 with a brief description of its hegemonic and popular components. Section 3 examines the adapted mainstream configuration; section 4, the proletarian; section 5, the street; section 6, the hip-hop configuration; section 7 probes more deeply into the special problems of youth violence, crime, and the crisis of incarceration; section 8 uses a deeper analysis of the causes of unemployment to highlight the issue of the relation between structural and cultural forces in understanding the plight of black youth; section 9 summarizes and discusses the sociocultural matrix, showing its main interactions; section 10 concludes with a reflection on the broader significance of the culture of black youth for the culture of capitalism in America.

Section 1. Disadvantaged Contexts and Groups

Unlike their white counterparts, most poor black youth, as well as a significant proportion of middle-income ones, live in disadvantaged neighborhoods.

Although earlier studies based entirely on census data and questionable definitions of neighborhoods had tended to underplay the effects of neighborhoods on life outcomes (Mayer and Jencks 1989), later works based on rigorously collected field data, more sociologically meaningful conceptions of neighborhoods, and previously missing variables have documented the serious negative consequences of growing up in disadvantaged neighborhoods and the mechanisms whereby such influences are transmitted (Gephart 1997; Wilson 1997; Rankin and Quane 2002; Sampson, Morenoff, and Earls 1999; Sampson 2013). Furstenberg (2000, 902–04) has also drawn attention to another deficiency in the sociological literature on youth and neighborhoods: the fact that the focus of most studies is usually on a single context, whereas the reality is that youth are exposed to multiple contexts in the course of making their way through adolescence and early adulthood. These contexts may overlap but are often relatively independent of each other—school, work, church, youth center, shopping mall, clubs, hangout sites, neighborhood of upbringing, peer-group neighborhood—and while the influence of each context may be small, the cumulative effect can be quite powerful, but one that will not be captured by single neighborhood or monocontextual studies. One of the many virtues of Pattillo's (2000) excellent study of the black middle class was to show precisely how the adjacent ghetto neighborhoods powerfully influenced their youth in spite of the more advantaged contexts they had provided for them. Of special note is that we will take account of one set of neighborhood variables that has been conspicuously missing from sociological studies of the ghetto: the chemical toxicity of such neighborhoods and the ways in which negative socioeconomic neighborhood qualities are neurologically transmitted (National Scientific Council on the Developing Child 2006). One common academic practice has been to differentiate black social groups by income and to distinguish their neighborhoods in terms of the proportion of poor persons living in them. Using this conventional approach, we find that in 2011 over a half of the black population was either poor (27.6 percent) or low income (23.7 percent; i.e., earning below twice the poverty rate; DeNavas-Walt 2012, table 3). Children and youth bear the brunt of poverty: 63.3 percent under 18 were in low-income families (39 percent below the poverty level). The income method also indicates that a quarter of all African Americans (7.6 million persons) live in areas with over 30 percent poor people and nearly half in areas with more than 20 percent poor (Pendal et al. 2011, 4) This may seem bad enough, but the conventional emphasis on income actually underestimates the depth of the problem. A more sophisticated approach, which we adopt, is that proposed by Sharkey who uses a multidimensional definition of disadvantaged neighborhoods based not only on poverty rates but on levels of unemployment, welfare receipt, segregation, and female headed families. Sharkey found that 78 percent of *all* black children (under 18) were brought up in neighborhoods of "high disadvantage" during the period 1985–2000 (Sharkey 2012a; 2012b). It is safe to say that nearly all disadvantaged youth live and were brought up in neighborhoods that are highly disadvantaged.

While there is obviously a fair degree of variation, the typical disadvantaged neighborhood has the following rough distribution of the three main groups mentioned above. At least half of the population belongs to the proletarian group. This group includes working-class persons who earn stable incomes in the formal economic sector, low-income earners, and the working poor (a little under half of all blacks with income below the poverty line are working; Bureau of Labor Statistics 2012b; Newman 2000, chs. 1–3).

On the better-off side of the proletariat is the ghetto middle class, which constitutes roughly 25 percent of disadvantaged neighborhoods. It may seem odd to describe a middle-class group as disadvantaged, but one of the two most remarkable features of the black middle-class condition in America is that half of all black children born between 1955 and 1970 into families earning solidly middle-class incomes of $62,000 or higher grew up in highly disadvantaged neighborhoods (Sharkey 2013)! The comparable percentage for whites approaches zero. This means that they were exposed to all the social and environmental toxicity of these disadvantaged neighborhoods that we will discuss in detail later. The second remarkable feature of middle-class blacks is that those who did not grow up in disadvantaged neighborhoods continue to live in highly segregated communities that border on, and are partially exposed to, the cultural and social influences of these neighborhoods (Pattillo-McCoy 1999). The most recent census data fully confirms Pattillo-McCoy's important ethnographic demonstration that the black middle class did not fully withdraw from the working and lower classes. "A central new finding," writes the social demographer John Logan, "is that blacks' neighborhoods are separate and unequal not because blacks cannot afford homes in better neighborhoods, but because even when they achieve higher incomes they are unable to translate these into residential mobility" (2011).

At the other, more deprived side of the proletariat is the disconnected population, which, by our estimate, constitutes about 25 percent of these neighborhoods in their entirety (i.e., adults, youth, and children). I refer to the group that Wilson and others previously labeled the underclass. Their defining structural feature was that they were outside the mainstream of the American occupational system due to their lack of training and skills and were chronically unemployed or not in the labor force (Wilson 1987; 1996). The current term, *disconnected,* is usually used mainly to refer to the youth segment of this group. However, we should note in passing that while many disconnected youth eventually find jobs and settle down in the proletarian group, most do not. Instead, they simply join the older segment of the disconnected, chronically unemployed, street-corner and sidewalk people. What is more, their numbers are increased by youth and adults who are downwardly mobile from the proletarian and middle-class groups. Edelman and his coauthors define disconnected youth as persons ages sixteen to twenty-four, unenrolled in high school or college, who experience full-year idleness (Edelman, Holzer, and Offner 2006). By their measure, 10 percent of young black men in 1999 in the civilian population were disconnected or idle. However, when account was taken of the incarcerated population, this percentage rose to 17, with a lower rate of 10 percent for women (14). Sadly, the situation grew much worse during the first decade of this century. In late 2011, the idle or disconnected among the civilian youth population amounted to 20.3 percent (Bureau of Labor Statistics 2012b, tables 1 and 2). These figures include both males and females. Slightly over a half are males. If we assume the same ratio of incarcerated to idle among males as existed in 1999 (seven out of ten), the disconnected male youth population rises to 34 percent of all male youth ages sixteen to twenty-four. The closeness of this proportion to another, often cited, is striking: the fact that one in three of all black youth will experience time in a federal prison or jail. A recent study (Measure of America 2011), based on 2010 data, finds substantial variation between the metropolitan areas of the nation. With an average of 22.5 percent (not including the incarcerated) disconnected among African Americans, San Diego (12.1 percent), Boston (13.1 percent), and Denver (15.8 percent) were the least disconnected cities, while Chicago (24 percent), Detroit (25.3 percent), Seattle (26.9 percent), and Phoenix (28.2 percent) had the highest proportions of disconnected black youth.

Here, to sum up, are the important estimates to bear in mind in the discussion that follows. Taking account of all age groups, disadvantaged neighborhoods consist, respectively of 50, 25, and 25 percent working class, ghetto middle class, and disconnected persons. Considering the youth population only, defined as those between ages sixteen and twenty-four, these neighborhoods contain approximately 46 percent working class, 34 percent disconnected, and 20 percent ghetto middle-class youth.

Section 2. The American Mainstream: Hegemonic and Popular

Understanding the cultural configurations of any particular group of Americans must begin with recognition of the fact that all Americans engage in one way or another with the dominant, overarching macroconfiguration that we call the mainstream. This is true even of those groups who are held by many to define their configuration in antihegemonic terms; as we will see, such rejections pertain to only one domain of their values, and, paradoxically, a good deal of their deviance can be attributed to their very exposure to the more undesirable configurations of mainstream culture. Black Americans, like other ethnic Americans, are thoroughly engaged in this reciprocal process: their cultural productions involve varying degrees of appropriation from mainstream configurations in addition to evolving vernacular processes that are partly creolized ancestral models syncretized with borrowings from the mainstream to forge entirely new American constructions.

Far from the old conception of a static hegemon rooted in an Anglo-American core, American mainstream culture is best viewed as a dynamic process that is constantly shaped by, even as it shapes, old and new immigrant and minority sub-cultural processes. Alba and Nee write that

> . . . the mainstream culture, which is highly variegated in any event—
> by social class and region, among other factors—changes as elements
> of the cultures of the newer groups are incorporated into it. The
> composite culture that we identify with the mainstream is made up
> of multiple interpenetrating layers and allows individuals and sub-
> populations to forge identities out of its materials to distinguish
> themselves from others in the mainstream—as do, for instance,
> Baptists in Alabama and Jews in New York—in ways that are still
> recognizably American. (Alba and Nee 2005, 12)

Behind this dynamic heterogeneity, however, is "a core set of interrelated institutional structures and organizations regulated by rules and practices that weaken, even undermine the influence of ethnic groups per se" (Alba and Nee 2005, 12). This is the hegemonic mainstream: the capitalist economy, the political system, the educational system, and the vast set of national organizations that define and meet Americans' basic and ulti-mate desires and goals.

The ultimate or primary values of mainstream America are widely prop-agated and, as such, at least cognitively available to all Americans. We follow Rokeach (1973) and Gans (1988) in specifying what these are: popular individualism, which entails taking responsibility for one's self and life outcomes; a deep commitment to the free-enterprise system; acquisitiveness and materialism; the ability to make choices; personal freedom and especially freedom of expression; a highly qualified idealiza-tion of equality; the work ethic and attendant belief that everyone should have an even chance at making a success of life; and a more personal set of values, including the strong valorization of self-respect, self-actualization, love of family, romantic love, fairness and honesty, and love of God and nation. Gans also adds suspicion of organizations (what he calls "organi-zational avoidance"), but this seems to be more a distinctive value of con-servative, Euro-American Protestants. These values do not form a harmonious whole, by any means. The equality value ideal, for example, has been the source of endless debate and strife among elite and masses: "Ships have been launched, lives given, governments toppled, all in the name of this one ideal" (Verba and Orren 1985, 1). And even values that appear to be little contested, such as individualism, on scrutiny turn out to be highly paradoxical. As Fischer (2008, 370) recently pointed out, Americans are at once the most intensely individualistic and also the most familistic and moralistic of the advanced industrial nations, which leads him to conclude that we have mis-specified American distinctiveness in claiming individualism as its master value. Rather, the primary value is voluntarism: people voluntarily choose their associations and joint goals, but having chosen, they commit themselves to abide by the association's rules and ends and to act as its agents.

While available to all, with growing edcational and income inequality, the proportion of the population for whom the values and ideals of the dominant middle-class mainstream can be anything but a dream is increasing, and to a much greater extent among the Hispanic and black members of the society. However, it is also the case that the white poor, who constitute the numeric majority of poor people, also suffer many of the exclusions and discrimination experienced by nonwhite minorities. In her recent study of class and classism in America, Bernice Lott (2002) found that, contrary to the egalitarian ideal famously inscribed in the Declaration of Independence, the dominant response of the nonpoor to the Euro-American poor is that of "separation, exclusion, devaluation, discounting, and designation as 'other,' and that this response is identified in both institutional and interpersonal contexts" (100–01). "White trash" means "them" not "us," she notes, and some researchers have argued that the rural white poor are being increasingly racialized and "morally excluded" by the well-off (101–02). (The fact that these primary values and ideals of the mainstream are less attainable does not mean that they are unimportant, a recurring fallacy of contemporary sociology.)

This is definitely not the case in the popular component of mainstream culture, which may be defined as all cultural representations that are generally available, usually through the commercialized and commodifying mass media, are cognitively accessible and valued by the majority or large plurality of consumers, and require no formal authorizationn for their production (Willis 1990, 1–29; Freccero 1999, 13; Storey 2006, ch. 1; Parker 2011). Ray and Pat Brown have offered a lyrical definition of what this is:

> Popular culture is the way of life in which and by which most people in any society live. In a democracy like the United States, it is the voice of the people—their likes and dislikes—that form the lifeblood of daily existence, of a way of life. . . . It is the everyday world around us: the mass media, entertainments, and diversions. It is our heroes, icons, rituals, everyday actions, psychology, and religion—our total life picture. It is the way of living we inherit, practice and modify as we please, and how we do it. (2001, 1–2)

Like scales on a fish, they add, American popular culture incorporates, and in the process transforms into a distinctly American way, the "overlapping and interworking" tributary cultures of the many ethnicities and regional groups that constitute the society (2001, 1–2). Later we will discuss how this process works in the case of black American youth.

Section 3. The Adapted Mainstream

The adapted mainstream refers to the focal configuration of the black middle class living in disadvantaged neighborhoods as well as neighborhoods that adjoin and are influenced by them. Mainstreamers are those African Americans for whom the essential configurations of the declarative and procedural knowledge of mainstream America, as well as its norms and values, are largely accessible and are usually applicable to their daily lives, except where their living environment requires some adaptation. Like most urban Americans, they also have access to the distinctive cultural knowledge, styles, values, and norms of their ethnic group, which they activate in their private lives, using the frame-switching mechanisms discussed in the last chapter. In this regard, they are no different from Jewish, Italian, Chinese, or the various subgroups of urban, middle-class Latino Americans.

They do differ, however, in the two important ways mentioned above: their segregation in, and the greater exposure of their children to, the other cultural configurations that thrive in poor, black, urban neighborhoods. They do so for a variety of reasons: some because they love the rhythm and style of the inner city, its dangers notwithstanding; some because of its familiarity, being the neighborhoods where they grew up and are sentimentally attached to; some because they have inherited property, which they choose to keep in spite of declining values; some because they are downwardly mobile from more exclusive middle-class jobs and neighborhoods; and a few who belong to the increasing waves of the gentry, anticipating the reclamation of the inner city by the wealthy and powerful, bored with the suburbs (Mary-Pattillo 1999, chs. 2–3; Sharkey 2012b).

Procedural knowledge is acquired primarily through interaction, observation, and practice, and a major consequence for the African American middle class is that they are excluded from the acquisition of such knowledge while growing up and must acquire it as young adults at college, work, or in adult friendships with successful whites or the truly advantaged blacks (Lacey 2007; Pattillo 1999, 186–200). Pattillo found that most middle-class black parents have the financial, social, and human capital, including parenting skills, that are typical of mainstream middle-class families. Their cultural priorities are similar to those described by scholars of middle-class parenting (Lareau 2003), and they try hard to prepare their children for participation in the dominant culture: private schools, sports, ballet, money for movies and other mainstream events (Pattillo 1999, 102–03). Sadly, these strategies do not seem to be enough. By their mid-teens many are ensnared, "consumed," and "thrilled" by what she calls the "ghetto trance" of the street and hip-hop configurations, especially boys (Pattillo 1999, ch. 6).[1] Many youth do follow the middle-class track of their parents, but a puzzle that emerges from Pattillo's ethnography is that success and failure seem to be largely random, especially in regard to boys, as the detailed, firsthand accounts of three of her young informants indicate (Patillo 1999, chs. 7–9).

The puzzle may be *partly* explained by differences in the socialization strategies of black middle-class parents. A recent study found that parental monitoring by black inner-city residents had mixed results (Quyen, Huizinga, and Byrnes 2010, 271–72). Among nondiscordant two-parent families (the minority), monitoring predicted better adjustment, consistent with what others have reported. However, such monitoring was found, *on the whole,* to predict greater levels of antisocial behavior, especially in single-parent households, which the authors of this study attributed to black youths' perception of such parenting as mistrust and intrusiveness, leading them to get even more involved with peers, including delinquent ones. Another recent work on parenting and socialization among black Americans found that the values of parents and children are weakly associated and that the two differ greatly in their perceptions of what is going on in the childrearing process, especially in relation to racial socialization. In striking contrast with whites, black mothers who emphasized the value of self-direction had no impact on their adolescents' academic performance and school activities (Ford 2009).

Gender, however, strongly mediates the processes of childrearing among middle-class African Americans (as it does in other classes; Turnage 2004). There is much greater congruence in the perceptions of socialization messages between mothers and daughters, which is hardly surprising in light of the fact that not only is the only parent present often the same gender as the daughter but also that even when fathers are present there is considerable mismatch between perceptions of the interaction in the father-daughter (as well as father-son) dyad (Ford 2009). Added to this is the finding that mothers transmitted different socialization messages to their daughters, especially in regard to racial stereotypes and mainstream values. With their girls, they emphasized pride, self-respect, spirituality, deportment, and control, all aimed at building self-esteem and countering stereotypes about black women, a childrearing strategy called "armoring" by two researchers (Bell and Nkomo 1998). Considerable socialization energy is also devoted to protection against the risks of sexual predation and infectious diseases, especially AIDS, with African American girls accounting for 57 percent of cases in the age group thirteen to nineteen (Townsend 2008, 432, 435). A side effect of promoting these values is a greater feeling of closeness to the mainstream, extending even to traditional gender roles, on the part of girls.

With their boys, there is far greater emphasis on preparation for racial prejudice from majority persons and, more generally, racial barriers against black men, an important consequence of which is boys' greater sense of solidarity with other blacks and more alienation from the mainstream (Ford 2009). Interestingly, mothers deny or fail to perceive such differences in their parental signals. Furthermore, even when boys and girls received the same content and number of messages, mothers' style in communicating with girls led to greater congruence, especially in behavioral socialization (Ford 2009, 142–43). Other studies suggest that African American parents were somewhat more likely to be involved with the education of their daughters than with their sons (Jeynes 2005). To use the childrearing typology of Furstenberg et al. (1999), girls are socialized with *promotive* parental strategies as well as protective ones, whereas with boys the emphasis is largely on protective strategies designed to prepare them for the intra-black violence and out-group hostility against young black males they are likely to face. However, the "armoring" of girls is not always without its problems. In their emphasis on survival, mothers often prioritize protection and deportment over affection, resulting in intense and sometimes antagonistic relationships. This can lead girls to do precisely what the "armoring" was meant to prevent: seeking refuge in the arms of an "understanding" sexual rogue, the female counterpart to boys seeking love and direction from gang leaders. Unlike boys, though, girls do seem to have an alternative resource to the overmothering of their "blood mothers": sympathetic "other mothers," who are not as invested emotionally in the survival and middle-class reproduction of the adolescent and can offer the unconditional affection, understanding, and nonjudgmental communication their overanxious, middle-class oriented mothers find hard to give (Townsend 2008, 437).

We know, however, that the black middle class, even those not confined to the ghetto, is not reproducing itself (Acs 2011, 13–19). What this indicates is that the hard cultural work of middle-class childrearing and socialization is not enough. The environment, as we will see in our consideration of the other configurations, is as important as how parents bring up their children. We will probe the nature of this environment in our consideration of the other configurations, but before getting to them, we should note several other factors that work against class reproduction among the ghetto middle class.

Peter Kaufman, writing of Americans as a whole, has argued persuasively that middle-class social reproduction results from the activation and negotiation of structural advantages by middle-class youth (Kaufman 2005). The reproduction of middle-class status is not simply the product of the cultural capital they inherit but is rather "the ongoing action of individuals who are responsible for the production and reproduction of their own social-class position as well as *the production and reproduction of the rules and resources that constitute the social structure that affects their lives*" (Kaufman 2005, 248; emphasis added). Although he does not frame it in these terms, what he calls the reproduction of rules and resources is, of course, the unconscious learning of the procedural knowledge of middle-class life. Three themes are evoked in this process: (positive) resistance and contestation, the importance of the peer group, and the structural location of the family. It is precisely in this interplay of social structure and human agency that middle-class black youth appear to lose their way.

When advantaged middle-class youth resist their parents' choices for them, they engage in a positive process of self-actualization that usually results in career choices that perpetuate and even enhance their status, though not in the exact trajectories their parents planned for them (becoming high-powered nonprofit executives, art dealers, and even sociology professors instead of doctors and corporate lawyers). They can do so because they know the rules and procedures, the tacit knowledge of the mainstream success game, which is often precisely what is lacking in the segregated upbringing of the ghetto middle class. They learn these procedures, of course, not only from observing (instead of just learning the instructions of their successful parents' behavior) but also from their peer group, the second major theme in the cultural play of advantaged middle-class young people. Not only does interaction with peer groups provide training in the structural resources that allow them to reject the particular trajectories of their parents in the full, though thoroughly implicit, knowledge that they can find another path to suburban bliss, but it provides "a strong sense of belonging in which the group largely shapes individual behavior, values, and attitudes through social comparisons and reflected appraisals" (Kaufman 2005, 257). White ethnoclass segregation means that the peer group reflects the social class of their parents, and their social interactions both mirror middle-class values and provide friends whose own successes strongly discourage working-class job choices and out-group friendships. In regard to the influence of families, we have seen that disadvantaged middle-class parents try hard to impart the socialization messages of the mainstream middle class. However, their kids do not benefit as much as they might because of the structural and residential location of the parents, and possibly also because their parents' own jobs and behavior, while they may place them squarely in the middle-class income bracket, might not be effective models for success in the fast-moving, deindustrializing, knowledge-intensive economic sector of the dominant mainstream (a disproportionate number of middle-class blacks, for example, work in the declining public sector). It is interesting that working-class parents seem to succeed more with their parenting strategies, as we discuss later, possibly because they are more alert to the counteracting influence of the peer group.

Where this is most pronounced is in middle-class black youth views and practices of masculinity. A good deal has been written on the cultural configuration of black masculinity. We will be examining this subject at greater length in our discussion of disconnected youth, but at this point two generalizations are worth mentioning. First, it is in this domain that older blacks most differ from their youth, especially among the middle class and stable working classes. Second, there has emerged a remarkable degree of uniformity in the culture of masculinity among all classes and regions of black youth in America. Differences exist, to be sure, but only in degrees of emphasis on certain practices; however, the knowledge structures, norms, and values of the configurations are strikingly similar, the reason almost certainly being the massive diffusion and celebration (sometimes to the point of caricature) of black youth views and performance of masculinity in the popular culture, abetted and increasingly defined by corporate entertainment interests.

To illustrate this point, I will consider a limiting case: not that of ghetto resident middle-class black youth, but of a group of black youth studied in the best possible environment—that of an integrated, northeastern suburban school district where black youth go to a well-resourced, "good" school with dedicated teachers (A Study of Gender Differences).[2] The middle-class parents of these youth exhibit all the standard parenting skills of middle- and upper-middle-class parents; indeed, they were more engaged with the school than the white parents, assertively interacting with teachers to ensure that their children got the best possible schooling. Parents were also very attentive to the educational performance of their children, grounding them (in one case for an entire summer) if they failed to perform up to their standards. The black girls in this school all responded as expected to their advantaged situation; nearly all did well academically and all went on to college. The boys performed poorly academically. There was no disdain for education among male or female youth, and the author found no support for Ogbu's (1993) "acting white" thesis or an oppositional culture toward education (consistent with findings elsewhere, e.g., Harris 2011). Black girls, like Euro-American females and males, were admired and popular for doing well academically; black boys all recognized the necessity of education for getting ahead and did not disdain the few among them who did well in their schoolwork. However, no black boy (whatever his academic achievement) became popular for academic excellence. Black boys took an entirely instrumental view of education; they saw the need for it in order to get ahead, but they cared little for the intrinsic worth of learning and aimed for the minimum possible academic achievement in order to graduate. Instead, they were rewarded with popularity and respect only by excelling at black male identity, the focus of which was a particular constellation of cultural practices and values that emphasized their masculinity. Attesting to the wide distribution of the masculine configuration among black youth, the author found exactly similar traits as those observed by Majors and Bilson (1992) as well as Staples (1982) and Carter (2005) in their studies of black youth masculinity: a "cool pose" demeanor consisting of a distinct style of speech, posture, and walk that signaled strength, control, lack of emotion verging on indifference, fearlessness and toughness, a preoccupation with sports and black music, a demonstration of prowess in terms of sexual conquest, athleticism, and success at fighting when necessary. A distinctively black activity was chillin', spending hours each day with no planned activity, talking, flirting with passing girls, or taking turns rapping, generally showing how "cool" one could be. Walking home while chillin' could take as long as three hours. Another was preoccupation with clothes, and the necessity to be seen wearing the right, usually expensive brands. Among these students, "if you don't wear the right gear, you ain't nobody." It was not enough simply to wear baggy jeans and certain kinds of sneakers, shirts, and boots; wearing the right brand was of equal importance, the brand in fashion usually determined by the clothes of favored rap stars: Pepe, Nike, Jordans, Girbaud, Sean John, Enyce, Iceberg, and Rocawear being the desired brands at the time of the study. The worst faux pas a youth could commit was to wear knock-off brands or "fakes"; boys whose financially sensible or strapped parents had gotten department store brands like Karl Kani, Fruit of the Loom, or South Pole were mercilessly mocked, their waistbands pulled over to reveal the true label. Playing and watching sports were also an essential part of black youth male identity, although only basketball and football mattered; baseball was considered "gay" by the youth in this high school, partly because of the "really, really tight pants" of baseball players. The author agrees with Majors and Bilson that the strong emphasis on black masculinity was for many a compensation for failure to do well academically; the lowest achievers were those that most strongly exhibited the style, postures, and behaviors associated with the tough, cool, athletic, sexually aggressive displays of black masculinity, but it was also found that even those few black male students who did well academically felt pressured to conform to this configuration. They were never mocked for doing well academically, but they certainly "straight up [got] laughed at" if they appeared weak, wore the wrong clothes or brands, didn't chill enough, or were not into sports, rap music, or girls. The author found that academically inclined black males, by going out of their way to conform, all tended to underperform. The enactment of black youth masculinity, in its all-consuming time demands; materialism; nonintellectualism and wholly instrumental attitude toward education; intense orality; sheer, physical pleasure of its performance; and tremendous rewards in terms of popularity among all groups, undermined academic performance.

What we have just described may be called black youth masculinity lite. It is the bourgeois extreme of a distinct cultural configuration, the other end of which we find among the disconnected youth of the ghetto's streets. Nonetheless, its benefits and costs are already clear. There is no gainsaying its gratification for these young people: their life is exciting, thrilling even, physically engaged, sartorially stylish, verbally rapturous; they are expertly knowledgeable about the world's greatest popular culture; their days as leisurely as aristocrats (and let's not forget that European aristocratic youth similarly "chilled" their time away for centuries—just read Jane Austen); they are admired, envied, and popular, especially with the girls. We may be scholars, but we cannot be such fogies as to forget what joy it was as teens to have been popular or perhaps, more to the point, what misery it was to have been one of the nerds. However, we already see the costs for this style and performance of masculinity.

Section 4. The Proletarian Configuration

Mitchell Duneier has rightly upbraided researchers and journalists for their neglect or misunderstanding of the cultural life of the ghetto working class (Duneier 1992, 137–57). It is best to view their socioeconomic status on a continuum. At one extreme is the minority of moderately secure wage earners. At the other is the economically marginal who must settle for poverty-level jobs, which they supplement either by doing several such jobs or by hustling in the informal and/or underground economy. "The shady world," Venkatesh observes, "plays a critical role in their work to create a stable household," and this forces them to live in a valuational and normative "space between 'ought' and 'is,' between what exists and what is possible" (Venkatesh 2006, 40–41; see also Anderson 1999, 42–45, 53–65). Between these two extremes is the majority, "struggling at the threshold of stable socioeconomic integration" (Wacquant 2004, 43). They are, in addition to those with regular jobs paying barely livable wages in the formal sector, the home-based seamstresses, handymen, food vendors, gypsy cab drivers, unlicensed electricians, carpenters, and others whose incomes evade the tax system (Newman 2000, 201), and it is on the cultural practices of this segment that we concentrate.

Middle-class declarative knowledge structures are partly available to proletarian youth—acquired from school, especially grade school and early high school (Ferguson 2002, 97–113) and the media, especially TV and radio—a cultural fact as true of Chicago of the early 1940s as it is of Chicago and other cities of the Black Belt today (Drake and Cayton 1945; Nightingale 1993, 74). Such cultural knowledge is also acquired from middle-class role models in their neighborhood and also from parents, especially mothers who learn these models from their own upbringing as well as from work (Hannerz 1969, ch. 2; McCord et al. 1969; Rainwater 1970; Dill 1980; MacLeod 1995, 53–60, 74–81, 98–110; Holloway et al. 1997, 73, ch. 7; Anderson 1999, 180–215; Venkatesh 2000, 160–63; Sanchez-Jankowski 2008, 74, ch. 10; Carter 2005, ch. 1).

What is open to question is the amount and depth of this knowledge. This is most evident in the knowledge of, and fluency in, mainstream standard English in both its spoken and written form. In their classic study of differences in knowledge exposure between mainstream middle-class, working-class white, and welfare families, Risley and Hart (1995, 236) found that "parents in professional families characteristically devoted over half again more time and said three times as much to their children as did parents in welfare families." The cumulative effect is that by age three the child of middle-class mainstream parents has heard thirty million words; the child of working-class parents, twenty million; and the child of unemployed black parents, ten million. Furthermore, there are marked differences in the "quality features" of language used—the richness of vocabulary and the exposure to the nuances of standard English—and these have important broader cultural consequences since vocabulary quality familiarizes children with the distinctions made in the culture and to causal, temporal, and qualitative relations that are critical for thought (Hart and Risley 1995, 100).[3]

This language difference has major consequences for later academic and social development for working-class black kids, many of whom "enter kindergarten with oral language skills and early literacy-based skills that differ significantly from those needed to support early classroom success (and) . . . complicate the transition from the home culture into the classroom culture" (Washington 2001, 214; see also Phillips et al. 1998; Bradley et al. 2001a, 2002). Acquiring full competence in the knowledge and use of standard English is further complicated not only by dialectal variation in the speech of African Americans, especially disadvantaged children who are far more likely to use African American vernacular English by as early as age four in their everyday speech, boys more so than girls (Washington 2001, 216–17). We hasten to add that, viewed purely in linguistic terms, there is absolutely nothing that is inferior about black proletarian speech or Ebonics, which is simply another fully developed variant of English. However, because it is the standard language of education, commerce, government, and all important communication, competence in the standard dialect is essential for success in the broader society.

What is true of language holds equally for other domains of mainstream middle-class cultural knowledge: it's not that there's a total absence of such knowledge, but there is far less frequency and depth of exposure—to its social rules, roles, and patterns of relationships; the basic facts of its history; knowledge of things considered important; ready availability of essential objects such as computers, books, magazines, and newspapers; museum and other out-of-home activities, and so on. These all add up to the totality of what Hirsch calls "crucial background knowledge" that persons literate in the mainstream culture know, or must know if they are to acquire competence in negotiating their way through it (1987, 26; 2006). Hirsch and his associates have attempted the daunting task of identifying the minimum set of cultural knowledge that competence in mainstream American culture requires. Any such list will always invite legitimate controversy (see, for examples, Squire 1987, 76–77; Schwartz 1987, 77), but the criticism that the effort amounts to a form of cultural superiority is baseless and completely misses the point. Like standard English, regardless of whether it is superior or inferior to other areas of American culture, the fact remains that the availability of a minimum set of mainstream cultural knowledge is vital for negotiating one's way through it.

The African American working class is fully aware of this. The declarative knowledge of the mainstream world is not something resented but rather one they find gratifying to engage with because it gives them a sense of participation in the wider American world. MacLeod (1995, 44–45) found that the group of black Cambridge high school students he calls "the Brothers" was remarkable for its degree of acceptance of mainstream values and behavior. Unlike the delinquent lower-class white kids in the project, the Brothers "accept the dominant culture's definitions of success and judge themselves by these criteria," and the academically successful one among them was actually admired for his motivation and achievement. MacLeod, however, goes too far in claiming that there is nothing distinctive about their cultural values and practices.

A distinctive element of working-class black cultural configuration is the strong emphasis on immediate kin relations and close friendships. In this regard, black individualism, while espoused, departs crucially from mainstream individualism. The latter encourages a self-regarding success ethic that places personal ambition and occupational achievement over particularistic and affective ties. Middle-class parents encourage their young adult children to leave home, even if there are several empty-nest rooms, and indeed become alarmed if their children, especially boys, show any reluctance to strike out on their own; young adults are also expected to be as geographically mobile as their occupations require, paying no regard to how far removed they are from their family of orientation and friends with whom them grew up. Black working-class Americans, somewhat like their white counterparts but even more so, strongly value such affective attachments, and this influences their career choices. A striking example of this was Derek, the only academically successful youth among the Brothers, who twice turned down the opportunity for certain economic security: once by giving up the offer to become a policeman in an upper-middle-class suburb after acing the police examination, a job he had long yearned for; and, again, by refusing the offer of a promotion to a supervisory position at Logan airport where he worked. On both occasions the prospect of diminished ties to family and close friends at work was the reason. His wife "and a million other people" talked him out of the first; the supervisory job was turned down because he feared losing his friendships with coworkers whom he would then have to supervise, his "niche," as he called it: "The pay really doesn't matter," he said. "It's not the most important thing, it's just being with the people, y'know, people who care, that's what it is" (MacLeod 1995, 200–03). This is very touching, but it certainly does not seem to reflect mainstream American individualism. We did note earlier that friendship is a mainstream value, so perhaps a better way of putting this is to say that working-class black Americans are distinctive in selectively emphasizing the mainstream value of friendship, one that is far more frequently trumped by self-regarding individualism and career mobility in the dominant configuration of middle-class mainstream values.

This emphasis on friendship is lifelong and seems to grow with age. We find it in full bloom among the older men who gather daily at Slim's table in a café in Chicago located outside, but not too far from, the ghetto. The men are attracted to the order and power embodied in the wider world, one that exudes American mainstream power, diversity, and values (Duneier 1992, 100–01). Nonetheless, they refuse to see themselves as mere mimic-men. Those aspects of the broader mainstream they admire they consider to be very much a part of their own heritage, one that they see sadly slipping away under the onslaught of the street culture they abhor (127). As such, the mainstream world "rather than simply being a civilizing influence . . . is a vehicle for them to express their own civility" (159).

The situation is far more problematic in regard to procedural knowledge of mainstream middle-class American culture. Works on the childrearing practices of Americans all really amount to studies on the acquisition of procedural knowledge, and they all point to extraordinary differences in knowing how to do all that is critical for competence in mainstream culture (Risley and Hart 1995; Lareau 2003; Bradley et al.

2001a; 2001b; Phillips et al. 1998; Holloway et al. 1997, chs. 5–6; Mayer 1997; Brooks-Gunn, Klebanov, and Liaw 1995). These differences pertained to every category of childrearing: "from parental responsiveness to parental teaching, from the quality of the physical environment to the level of stimulation for learning present, and from the likelihood of being spanked to the likelihood of having significant contact with one's father" (Bradley et al. 2001a, 3). Income is the main factor explaining these differences, but for African American children, this was compounded by the isolation and disadvantaged features of their neighborhood environments.

Annette Lareau's (2003) distinction between what she calls the "concerted" childrearing practices of middle-class, mainstream Americans and the "natural" childrearing of the lower and working classes (Risley and Hart 1995, 55, 119–34) describes "two sets of competences" which, however, "are not equally valued in the institutional worlds" of mainstream America (67). Middle class children are "trained in the rules of the (mainstream) game" (6). Along with their greater verbal facility, knowledge of abstract concepts, and tightly scheduled exposure to a wide range of activities, they develop "skill differences in interacting with authority figures in institutions and at home" (6). On the other hand, the natural, "open-ended," largely unattended upbringing of working-class children (of all ethnicities) results in "no training in the enactment of organizational rules" (81). In stark contrast with middle-class children, African American proletarian children have far less interactive time with adults and even when in the presence of adults they are urged to be passive and obedient. There is also a paucity of involvement with organized activities by means of which the implicit procedural skills, the "how-to" of mainstream culture are learned through doing (141).

Lareau's distinction, while it captures the important factor of the transmission, or lack thereof, of procedural knowledge, is nonetheless too limited in that it fails to identify important variations within working-class parenting strategies, a point already thoroughly documented by Furstenberg et al. (2000, 1999). It also does not take into account the way these strategies are mediated by neighborhood variables and individual characteristics of parents and children. These parenting strategies can make all the difference, not so much in whether their children make it to the middle class (very few do) but in whether they avoid the pitfalls of the ghetto and end up with good, well-paying jobs. Drawing on earlier work by Baumrind (1991), Steinberg et al. (1992), and Furstenberg (1999), Rankin and Quane

(2002, 87–91) distinguish between three dimensions of parenting strategies: that of *parental monitoring,* which measures the degree to which parents monitor the whereabouts of their children when not directly under their control, *parental involvement,* which measures the level of involvement of the mother in coactivities with the child as well as the latter's school activities, and *family rules,* which assesses the degree to which parents clearly and consistently enforce rules regarding household chores, TV watching, and homework. Striking variation was found within class and neighborhood, and these parenting strategies largely had the expected effects: better-monitored youth were more competent socially and educationally, had friends who held mainstream values, and were less likely to be delinquent. Youth whose parents held them to consistent rules were also more competent and had more positive peer-group relations, although they were not necessarily better behaved. Parental involvement was associated with greater competence but also with less desirable friendships. This seemingly odd result was possibly due to the fact that it may have been precisely because their kids were falling into bad company that parents became so much more involved with them.

One striking result of this study was that, controlling for family management, economically more advantaged African American youth did only marginally better than more disadvantaged ones. They were somewhat more socially competent, but children of welfare families actually had more prosocial friends, further quantitative support for Pattillo-McCoy's finding that middle-class children are often just as exposed to negative peer group influences as poorer ones. One of the strongest results of the study was that youth who associated with a positive peer group espousing mainstream values were most likely to be socially and educationally competent and to have the least behavioral problems (Rankin and Quane 2002, 91). This work also lends strong support to the position that parental norms and values matter a great deal, especially among the working class. Regardless of economic background, youth whose parents transmitted more mainstream values and took a nontolerant view toward deviance ended up being more competent. Parents who espoused mainstream norms and values were also those most likely to employ all three family strategies (88). Indeed, parenting strategy and the enactment of mainstream norms even trumps the negative effects of family structure. While single parenting did have negative consequences, due mainly to the fact that the sole parents had less time to monitor and otherwise parent their children, it was surprising how little *direct* effect these had on youth outcomes, once allowance is made for such time constraint.

The remarkable takeaway result of this study, then, is that "parenting and family normative orientations matter more than socioeconomic resources or family structure. For the most part, the advantages of socioeconomic status for urban African-American youth *are transmitted through more effective parenting and, to a lesser extent, family norms and values. Youth of parents who hold conventional (i.e., mainstream) values are more intolerant of youth deviancy and report higher levels of social competency*" (94; emphasis added). More recent work supports this finding with an additional factor: among the working class where there is coparenting, the quality of the relationship between the parents strongly predicts delinquency outcomes (Hassett-Walker 2010, 278–79).

Although, as we noted earlier, schools make available some of the basic declarative knowledge of the dominant mainstream (for those students interested in learning it), they largely fail to complement such knowledge with the procedural skills essential for success in the mainstream economy. According to Sanchez-Jankowski (2008), while "some education takes place in these schools," the number of students who acquire the procedural knowledge necessary for college is extremely small. Instead, the vast majority are simply "schooled," in the course of which, of course, they acquire basic declarative knowledge of mainstream culture. However, many students typically "viewed their high school years as their last chance for leisure and fun," rather than the place to acquire critical educational and related procedural skills: "the value orientations that permeated the neighborhoods were brought into the school, and the more these values could influence the thoughts and behaviors of the students, faculty and administration, the more the school reinforced the neighborhoods' social structure" (307–08; see also Carter 2005). While this may be true of the majority, Sanchez-Jankowski paints too bleak a picture of the working-class youth educational experience. We suspect that Carter's portrait tells it more like it is: even though she studied an extremely poor population at the least secure end of the working-class spectrum, 43 percent of her subjects were performing either adequately or quite well; not good enough, but hardly the funhouse disaster implicit in Sanchez-Jankowski's account.

While their segregation largely explains the lack of procedural knowledge, one tendency among the black working class, including the most stable wage earners, may well reinforce this problem: what has been called the "attitude-achievement paradox" (Mickelson 1990): a sharp discrepancy between educational aspiration and the belief in the value of education on the one hand and actual educational performance on the other. To be sure, this paradox is not peculiar to the working class since "A Study of Gender Differences" found it among the male middle-class males studied (39–44). Carter's explanation of the "paradox" is that it is a reflection of cultural disengagement from school and a sense of not fitting in among a subgroup of students (2005, 11–12, 39–46). However, this was clearly not the case among the middle-class students studied in "A Study of Gender Differences," which explained it in terms of a strongly instrumental view of education rather than an intrinsic liking of knowledge for its own sake, or even as something that was considered important for one's personal development (44–57). Duneier (1992), while not directly addressing this issue, reported something else that might be relevant: a suspicion of book learning and overemphasis on "common-sense understanding" among the working-class men he studied (81). To be sure, while a characteristic emphasis, this is far from being peculiar to the black working class, and here again, we find that distinctiveness lies, not in a different belief or domain of declarative knowledge, but in a different weight—value in the literal sense—placed on certain mainstream knowledge structures. The suspicion of intellect has long been known to be a feature of mainstream American values (Hofstadter, 1966). However, this thread of anti-intellectualism is more than balanced by other preferences in the middle-class mainstream, if only by ensuring that children go to good schools strongly biased toward progressive educational values. It is the selective overemphasis on their own practical knowledge (itself severely confined by segregation) that distinguishes this as a black proletarian value. And this brings us to the prescriptive domain of black proletarian culture. More recently Harris (2011) has vigorously argued that the paradox might best be explained in terms of "a lack of academic skill sets necessary for academic success," which result from early and preadolescent socioeconomic, health, and other disadvantages (126), a position consistent with what we argue later.

The values and norms of mainstream American culture are widely available to black working-class Americans and their youth, acquired partly by the same means, mentioned earlier, as mainstream declarative knowledge (Anderson 1999, 37–45; Venkatesh 2000, 164; Harding 2010, 5–6, 132–34). However, more importantly, mainstream values and injunctive norms are widely, indeed relentlessly, transmitted through its powerful mass media, to which black Americans are on average more exposed than other Americans since they listen, watch, and participate so much more. No one has emphasized this more than the cultural historian Carl Nightingale, who on the basis of six years of ethnographic research in the Philadelphia inner city, concluded that the dominant view of the lives of black youth as a group isolated and alienated from American mainstream culture is mistaken. Black youth, he found, are thoroughly American in all their tastes, values, and norms, and although some of them "prefer to be known as citizens of something called the 'hip-hop nation,' most tend to sound like so-called red-blooded, patriotic Americans," who love the military, support the troops at war, and are completely saturated by America's "ethic of conspicuous consumption" material values and dreams (Nightingale 1993, 2).

Survey and ethnographic data also indicate that most proletarian black youth know and espouse mainstream *injunctive* norms. This is especially pronounced in norms relating to sex, childbirth, marriage, and divorce, as researchers going all the way back to the sixties attest (Rodman 1963; Hannerz 1969, ch. 4; Rainwater 1970; Anderson 1999; Patterson 1998; Edin and Kefalas 2005). All demonstrate that proletarian African Americans, especially women, espouse strong belief in both the ultimate values and norms of premarital chastity; marriage as the rightful state for couples who live together; marital fidelity; and strong negative norms against divorce. How, then, do we explain the striking disjuncture with behavior, one that researchers in the sixties were already reporting? The distinction between injunctive and observational norms is critical for understanding this and other anomalies in black working-class life. In a St. Louis project during the sixties, one teenager, after insisting that having a baby after marriage was the right thing to do, nonetheless responded when asked if she would be ashamed to have a baby out of wedlock: "It's really no reason to feel shame because there are a lot of people walking around here unmarried and you'll just be one more in the crowd. You shouldn't feel inferior or anything because there are a lot of people in your class" (Rainwater 1969, 310, 390) As Rainwater commented, "It is possible to live a life that departs significantly from the way one thinks life ought to be lived without ceasing to exist, without feeling totally degraded, without giving up all self-esteem." It was also found, in these early studies, that the very mainstream idealization of stable, faithful marriage—as ultimate value and injunctive norm—itself became a major factor in promoting the observational norm of single parenting. "No ghetto-specific model for a male-female union has anything close to the normative validity which the mainstream model enjoys in the ghetto as well as outside it," wrote Hannerz, "and this makes it hard for couples to find a state of the union which is as morally satisfying to them" (1969, 102). The result is that women, by their late twenties, came to view men as untrustworthy and marriage not worth the risks, preferring the independence of single mothering. For women also, having children was an emotional imperative invested with great personal value but uncoupled from marriage. Similarly, male incapacity to live up to the cognitively available mainstream male ideal of the sole breadwinner coupled with their marginality in their households alienated men "even further from the mainstream model" (89).

Fast-forward nearly forty years, and we find an identical disjuncture reported by Anderson (1999, 142–78) as well as Edin and Kefalas (2005, chs. 2, 4, and 5) and Harding (2010, 162–88). The mainstream "culture of decency," Anderson shows, is present and readily available in the inner city today, transmitted in the neighborhood by role models such as ministers, teachers, parents, and upwardly mobile peers who all "serve as a powerful inspiration to those who may be otherwise disadvantaged" (1999, 143). There is, however, one important difference from the sixties: today, the great majority of working-class and nearly all poor black children are born to single mothers or to cohabiting or married parents who soon break up. The forces accounting for this development, emerging in the seventies, while their impact has been much greater on the black working class and poor, were not ghetto specific, since they applied also to the white poor and increasing numbers of their working class. Edin and Kefalas (2005) attribute this to "profound cultural changes America has undergone over the last thirty years." Their findings—that "while the practical significance of marriage has diminished, its symbolic significance has grown;" that "adherence to the marriage norm, albeit, on their own terms, is more than merely lip service to a middle-class ideal;" that most "are strongly opposed to divorce;" that most women are deeply suspicious of male motives, promises, and behavior, and that "you can't get a decent man you can really, really trust;" and that, regardless of their union status or circumstances, having children is strongly valued, and that childlessness is "one of the greatest tragedies in life,"—read like the ethnographic reports on poor black women in the sixties, except for their much wider application today (187–212). The suspicion of marriage on the part of poor, working-class, and even a growing number of middle-class black women is well founded: a recent study of the lifetime probability of marital dissolution finds that 70 percent of *all* first marriages among black women will end in divorce, compared with only 47 percent among whites. The figure is higher for the working class, since this rate varies with education (Raley and Bumpass 2003, 250). For men also, especially those at the working-poor end of the proletarian spectrum, there is the persistence of the alienation from the role of father brought on, in part, by their inability to live up to the norm of provider (Wilkinson 2003, 96–97, 116–18). The best explanation for this cultural change is offered by the economist George Akerlof (1998)—what he calls technology-reproduction—to which we return in section 8.

It should come as no surprise that this pattern of marital and familial fragility is reproduced among black youth and is reflected in their romantic relationships from their adolescent years. A recent study found that growing up with troubled parental relationships and marital disruption, combined with the harsh parenting found more frequently among African Americans, as well as exposure to violence, discrimination, and economic insecurity leads to "negative relational schemas" among African American adolescents that, in turn, create "conflict and hostility with romantic partners" (Simons et al. 2013). Adolescent relationships, these authors point out, act as rehearsals for adult ones, and consequently, these stormy relationships "give rise to unfavourable views about marriage." What these authors claim to have shown, correctly, are the mechanisms by which historically fraught gender relations and marital fragility, accelerated by developments in the seventies, are reproduced in each generation, beginning in the adolescent years (93). Although marriage is not working, most working-class African Americans, like nearly all white Americans, are still normatively committed to it and feel compelled to give it a shot at some time during their lives. Thus, a majority of working-class blacks will have been married, or previously married, by the waning years of their youth—some 55 percent by age thirty, slightly more men than women—and by their mid-forties over 80 percent will have been in the category of ever married persons (Ruggles and Fitch, n.d., slides 73–76). In this respect, they are different from disconnected youth and adults, among whom marriage has largely disappeared except for the somewhat strange increase since 1990 in the marriage rate among incarcerated young men, for which there is, as yet, no reasonable explanation (Ruggles and Fitch, n.d., slides 73–76).

Turning to values of work, there is a strong commitment to the work ethic among all working-class black Americans, including those at the poorest end of the spectrum. Although the "McJobs" of the working poor in this group are denigrated, especially by the disconnected street people in their own neighborhoods who "proudly" prefer unemployment to such seemingly lowly work, the ghetto working poor maintain their dignity in what Newman calls a "rebuttal culture" that draws on the mainstream value of the work ethic, which allows them to see themselves as strongly connected with conservative mainstream contempt for the welfare-dependent and jobless (Newman 2000, 98). Smith shows that there is a pattern of distrust and deep unwillingness to refer others to job openings unless the recommenders are themselves secure in their own status and employment and are assured of the reputation of the job-seekers, especially that their behavior is not "ghetto," meaning of the street culture (Smith 2005, 23–26, 47). Sadly, even where working-class inner-city residents are willing to shield their distrust and take a chance on recommending another person from the neighborhood, the result is often a disappointing job. In their multi-city study of job searches, Green, Tiggs, and Diaz (1999) concluded that blacks who use multiplex relationships—relatives, friends, neighbors, coworkers—to find jobs, end up earning substantially less than those who did not, in striking contrast with Euro-Americans, whose multiplex searches yield higher wage returns than those who did not. What this shows, as the authors remark, is that living in the ghetto compounds the weakness of one's social capital, while for white workers, living in advantaged communities multiplies their human capital accumulation (269–76). To them that hath, the advantaged neighborhoods give; to them that hath not, the ghettos take away.

Because of the pervasive violence of their environment, all working-class black Americans, but especially those at the more marginal end of the spectrum, must know and have readily accessible the cultural configuration of the street, what one called "street intelligence," enabling them to cognitively switch configurations rapidly as circumstances, indeed physical survival, dictate. Researchers have observed this for over a half a century, and one of the best accounts of the cognitive processes involved comes from Rainwater's (1969) neglected classic. He found that two meaning systems defined important relationships among the proletariat, especially the working poor. "For any one individual at any one time, both systems are possibly alive for him at once; much of his thinking will be devoted to determining which way things are going for him—toward the good life or toward an ordinary ghetto life—and which way they are likely to go in the future. Both conceptions are present for him as he grows up" (48). This account is nearly identical to what observers of the black working class report today (see Anderson 1999, 36; Venkatesh 2006, 40; Harding 2010, 5–6, 106–07).

One area of life where this tension is most pronounced is the working-class boy's development of his masculinity. On the one hand, working class youth have a valuable model of masculinity from their culture of orientation provided by the hardworking men of their parents' generation in stable employment. They may not interact with them as often as they would like to, given the number of hours these older men must work, many holding down two low-paying jobs, the fragility of working-class marriages, and the tendency of working-class adult men to bond with each other after work, but they see them constantly in the male relatives and friends of their mothers as well as in their own fathers, whether or not they co-reside with their mothers.

In his study of working-class black men, Duneier (1992) has given us a finely etched portrait of this model of masculinity:

> They are consistently inner-directed and firm, and they act with resolve; their images of self-worth are not derived from material possessions or the approval of others; they are disciplined ascetics with respect for wisdom and experience; usually humble, they can be quiet, sincere, and discreet, and they look for those qualities in their friends. They are sensitive, but not "soft" in any sense that the (Euro-American) men's movement sees as the basis of its gender crisis. They know how to put their foot down, and how to "show their swords." (163)

All well and good. But the problem that all black working-class boys face growing up is the pervasive menace of the street culture. Like their parents, survival is the name of the game, except that, in their case, it is the constant need to either avoid or defend themselves from the inevitable encounters with street youth. In doing so, they are required to assume some of the toughness, the bravado, and the mean-mug qualities of the street. It's a constant balancing act—one that no doubt takes its toll on their studies and their other attempts to become the men of their parents' generation. The marvel is that this works for most of them most of the time; the majority of working-class boys in the ghetto end up becoming working-class men, and a few of the most fortunate even realize the American dream of upward mobility into the middle class. Unfortunately, a far too large minority become ensnared by the street, joining rather than fighting or evading it. In some cases, tragically, they get into trouble simply by trying to protect themselves and their relatives. A sad example was David, an academically promising working-class boy from the Philadelphia ghetto attending an academically elite public school who, in an attempt to protect his thirteen-year-old sister from the sexual advances of much older street boys, and himself from their threats after he defended her, started carrying a concealed pen knife to school, only to have it discovered, causing him to be expelled from the school in police handcuffs (Gunn 2008, 28–37). Gunn adds that working-class boys can use "any number of strategies, but the most common is to simply toughen up, to perform masculinity in ways that are recognized by other residents of that community" (33).

All young women in the ghettos, but especially working-class girls, face the equivalent of a social and cultural nightmare every day, both outside on the neighborhood streets and inside in relationship violence. Young black women in the ghettos not only experience the highest victimization rates of all females in the nation, but their risks for nonfatal violence are almost as great as those for boys and, astonishingly, their risk of non-stranger violence is actually higher than those faced by boys in the ghettos (Lauristen 2003 quoted in Miller 2008, 8). This highly gendered violence is "a systematic and overlapping feature of their neighborhoods, communities, and schools" and is played out in the context of virulent sexist ideologies (Miller 2008, 192). Their main strategies for dealing with this pervasive violence—avoiding public spaces and relying on the company of others—themselves create further problems, since they become virtual prisoners in their own homes and are robbed of the opportunity to participate in public life. Furthermore these strategies are often ineffective, in that the greatest risk of abuse comes from intimate partner violence and there is very little support for them either from the community, or the police. Even in schools, where they face the gravest risks of sexual harassment, they get little or no institutional support (Miller 2008, chs. 3 and 5). Fully half of inner-city African American girls sampled in a recent study had been abused psychologically or physically by their partners (Alleyene-Green, Coleman-Bower, and Henry 2012). Indeed, young women are often blamed for acts of violence against them. Adolescent girls face two related kinds of contradictions that greatly add to the stressfulness of their condition. First, there is the tension between their mothers' insistence that they should "act like a lady" and never get into fights and the view of their peer group that not fighting back when provoked indicates being soft and weak or a "punk" (Carter 2005, 94–104). Second, among their peers, they gain status for being attractive to boys, but they are also taunted for being sexually precocious and risk getting into fights if they are too attractive or engage in sexual relationships (Miller 2008, 7, chs. 3–4). The heavy toll on mental and physical health that living in the ghetto takes has now been well documented (Turney, Kissane, and Edin 2012; Gennetian et al. 2012, 156).

There is, however, one powerful institutional buffer to this terrible neighborhood hazard that young girls face daily, and that is the black church. Before discussing its special significance for black women, including youth, let us look briefly at the role of religion in black working-class life. On every measure—church attendance, frequency of praying, absolute certainty in the existence of God, belief in the devil, miracles, angels, demons, life after death, and the literal interpretation of the Bible—African Americans are the most religious group of Americans. Even among those who rarely go to church, belief in the certainty of God's existence and the value of prayer is stronger than the national norm (Pew Forum 2010a). MC Hammer raps that "we got to pray just to make it today," and even Jay-Z, the bad-boy tycoon, admits that "I'm not an angel, I'm sure / but every night before I lay / I drop my knees to the floor and pray."

However, there is a sharp division between the very poor and disconnected on the one hand and the better off on the other. The working class is the backbone of black American religious life, with higher church attendance than the more secular middle class above them or the less-believing disconnected street people and impoverished. Almost all working-class blacks have a religious affiliation and at least 80 percent claim that religion is very important in their lives. Although more true of older blacks, much the same pattern holds for black youth between eighteen and twenty-nine who attend church weekly at a higher rate (55 percent) than the national average (33 percent) and are even more absolutely certain in their belief in God (88 percent) than conservative (mostly white) Evangelicals (86 percent; Pew Forum 2010b). At the individual level, it has been shown that church attendance does have positive consequences for African American youth, even after they have stopped going to church (see Chapter 8 in this volume).

At the same time, contrary to conventional wisdom, black religiosity does not always enhance neighborhood welfare or efficacy; class decisively mediates its influence. In the middle- and solidly working-class neighborhood of Groveland studied by Mary Pattillo-McCoy (1998) "the black church culturally and religiously binds together the black middle class and the black poor," an "anchoring institution" and center of activity providing "a common language that motivates social action" in both religious and secular life (768–71, passim). However, this is less true of churches in many of the low-income inner-city neighborhoods because congregations often do not live in the areas where their churches are located (due to cheaper rents or the fact that they have moved away as the neighborhood deteriorated), and they feel little sense of commitment to them, which is not to say that they do not have broader, transneighborhood ethnic interests (McRoberts 2005). Furthermore, the disconnected are as unconnected to church as they are to work. Although they claim to believe in God and consider religion "a positive thing" (Young 2004, 141), Smith found that religion was not a significant factor in the lives of the majority of residents in the housing projects of Indianapolis he studied (Smith 2001, 317). This is not a new development. In the late 1930s, fewer than a third of lower-class adults in Chicago were regular, dues-paying church members (Drake and Cayton 1945, 612). Thus the black church's support for black women does not necessarily come from its effect on their neighborhoods, although in less deprived areas it certainly does.

The religiosity of the black proletariat might more properly be viewed as a subconfiguration, because church life and beliefs anchor a set of generally conservative spiritual and social values and norms that are orthogonal to the beliefs and practices of their political and everyday secular lives. Thus black proletarians closely resemble conservative white evangelicals—the backbone of the far right of the Republican party—in their strong disapproval of abortion, their homophobia and disapproval of gay marriage, and their support for a greater role of religion in public and political life (Pew Forum 2010a). They also favor more patriarchal gender relations and, as already noted, strongly disapprove of premarital sex and nonmarital cohabitation. This contrasts sharply with their very strong support for the Democratic party and for a greater role of government in national life.

A major puzzle quickly emerges after any consideration of black American religiosity. Why is it that the most religious group in the nation, proclaiming the most conservative Christian values, have the highest rates of crime, the lowest rates of marriage, the highest rates of out of wedlock birth, the highest rates of marital disruption, and the most hedonistic cultural creations. We suggest that these separate configurations are justified by a dualistic, two-kingdoms view of the world. God's spiritual kingdom is a separate realm in which He reigns supreme and is joyously given praise in weekly church worship, where sermons loudly warn of the wages of sin and proclaim God's divine laws and his *injunctive* norms for people. Outside church, God is certainly there, though in the highly personified presence of the crucified, penitent Christ. However, Satan is also alive and well—as every middle-aged black critic of rap music will attest (Cohen 2010, 73), even as they once did of the "devil music" called the blues—and life is a constant struggle to withstand his temptations. Only by virtue of being sanctified and saved (as are 59 percent of all blacks, compared with 46 percent of Americans nationally) are the trials and seductions of sin held at bay. Inevitably, there are lapses and, not infrequently, hard falls. The compromise that emerges is the temporal world of *behavioral* norms. To the black proletariat then, life in the inner cities of America is a quasi-Augustinian world of two cities: an inner city of righteousness, of a demanding God, in cathartic worship of whom, one is cleansed, sanctified, and redeemed and made able to bear all the misfortunes of "Man," especially *the* man; and an outer, earthly city of a surely tried but ever-forgiving Christ, the Son of Man and sacrificial Savior, whose grace and mercy comes only through praying longer and harder and more frequently, in and out of church, than any other group of Americans.

And this is especially the case for working-class African American women who, unlike the men of the group, remain profoundly spiritual between church services on Sundays. In her probing ethnography of the spiritual lives of black women, Marla Frederick (2003) shows how spirituality is central to their daily lives, giving meaning and direction to a degree experienced by few black men. This spiritual configuration is anchored in a constellation of three "predominant" expressive values: gratitude, empathy, and righteous discontent (65). First, they live in gratitude to God's benevolence for "making it through" the daily trials of their world.[4] Second, there is empathy for the gift of being able to feel the pain of others, especially neighbors and kin—their losses, bereavements, and hardships which—but for the grace of God—they too could so easily have suffered. And thirdly, there is righteous discontent, expressed mainly in public spaces and interactions, especially church, which "challenges the conditions that give rise to poor education, poor quality health services and poor living conditions" and "translates into active community building as well as open confrontation with systems of oppression" (94).

Among the things African American working-class women pray hardest for is to be spared what haunts them (especially mothers) daily: the prospect of their children falling prey to the cultural configuration of the street.

Section 5. The Street Configuration

The third sociocultural configuration in the inner cities is the one that has received the most attention: the street culture of the economically disconnected, socially alienated, and disproportionately delinquent group (Anderson 1992; 1999; 2008; Wilson 1987; 2009; Wacquant 2008; Venkatesh 2002; 2009; Miller 2008). The emphasis is justified because, although they constitute, on average, no more than a quarter of the population of the inner cities, their cultural configuration and behavior create a virtual state of siege for all others who live in the ghetto. This configuration is not new in black American life. Du Bois (1899) gave a vivid portrait of what seemed like an incipient street culture in his sociological study of Philadelphia, and Roger Lane's more recent study traces the origins of the city's violence as far back as 1860 (Lane 1989).

Seven cultural processes, or subconfigurations, form the interactive core of the focal street configuration: (1) the centrality of bounded physical space, the 'hood, as the source of identity and meaning; (2) surviving and living with pervasive violence, expressed primarily in the invasion and defense of bounded spaces or turfs; (3) "hegemonic masculinity"; (4) the salience of respect; (5) a counterhegemonic, and near nihilistic, rejection of mainstream educational values, especially among those still at school; (6) a seemingly paradoxical embrace of several other core mainstream values, especially individualism; and (7) identification with a threatening vision of blackness acknowledged as "thug life," or that of the "real nigga."

The ghetto neighborhood—grim, hypersegregated, impoverished, with dilapidated buildings, poor or nonexistent infrastructural services such as police protection, bereft of formal institutions such as banks and super-markets—is the crucible of street culture. Harrison White (1992), in his fertile (if consciously denied) theory of culture, notes the importance of locality in the definition and enactment of identity. "Different sets of identities may generate and perceive different spaces," and further, "locality as a construct implies some approximation to a partition of phys-ical space in order to gain self-consistency in the social accounting of localities" (129). White's observations resonate with an older school of scholarship that focuses on territoriality as a fundamental human attri-bute. As Lyman and Scott (1967) noted many years ago, "peculiar identi-ties are sometimes impossible to realize in the absence of an appropriate setting" (236). They recognize four kinds of territories: public territories, those areas where most citizens have free access by virtue of their rights as citizens; home territories, those where a group of persons are not only free to roam but have a sense of intimacy, control, and possession on the space so bounded; interactional territories, spaces where people gather and that are shielded by an invisible boundary during the course of the interaction, such as the street corner where youth hang out; and embodied territory which are the spaces enclosed by the human body and its anatomical spaces, usually protected by strong norms regarding personal space and the right to repel the attempts of others to touch or even stare too hard.

There is a complex relationship between these four kinds of spaces, which directly applies to the territorial behavior of disconnected black youth. In the first place, the defense of territory seems to be the last stance in the preservation of human dignity, identity, and worth for those who feel despised, excluded, persecuted, and powerless; to the degree that there is nothing left to lose or defend, this defense is exaggerated in its salience. Secondly, where persons are denied their citizenship rights by being hounded out of public spaces—legally or illegally—as are black youth from middle-class neighborhoods, malls, or the "nice" public spaces of their cities, there is a compensatory emphasis on protecting what little one has, one's own home space or 'hood. Protecting this space is not just a psychological but a physical and economic necessity. It is the main arena for the informal, underground economy so well documented by Venkatesh and others—drug selling, pimping and prostitution, bootlegging, hus-tling, informal trading—all "unpredictable, dangerous and poorly paying" but the only means of survival in places where formal work has disap-peared (Wilson 1996, 2–24, 142–43; Venkatesh 2009, 34; see also Young

2004, 67). Thus, every area of the inner city has been marked out as turf to be defended. However, thirdly, if the home space is an extremely over-crowded ghetto and subject to environmental toxins that themselves induce violent behavior (to be discussed below), there will be a strong tendency toward encroachment of other, especially neighboring territories through invasion, violation, and contamination: gang-banging, drive-by shootings and killings, the insult or rape of women from the other area, stealing, and burning (Lyman and Scott 1967, 243–45). Such encroach-ments are, of course, met by turf defenses based on a "retaliatory ethic" that, in turn, elicit reactions in a vicious downward spiral of violence (Jacobs and Wright 2006).

Embodied territoriality, personal space, relates in interesting ways to home territoriality. This kind of "claim," to use Goffman's (1972) termi-nology, is ego centered and moves around with the claimant. One impor-tant element in the extreme emphasis on respect is, in fact, simply an expression of the need to defend one's bodily space. Defending respect for bodily space, however, is itself often identified with defending respect for home territory: "body territory is also convertible into home territory" (Lyman and Scott 1967, 241). Body markings, tattoos, indicate gang membership and home territory. The sexual conquest of a woman's body from a rival turf is symbolically identified with territorial invasion and pol-lution of that territory, and it is no accident that a large number of turf wars in the ghetto result from such sexual penetrations. The main things these youth talk about are girls, money, and revenge (Young 2004, 57). Staring at a person the wrong way may also be taken as an invasion of body and turf space and result in violent responses. Learning how to avoid and defend oneself from, and with, violence is essential cultural knowl-edge for all boys growing up in the presence of street culture: "There is no protection, no haven for childhood in this context of social terror" (Ferguson 2001, 120; see also Anderson 2008, 42; Wilkinson 2003, 226; Harding 2010, xi). While violent acts do not happen every day, the "enduring sentiment" is that it can happen any time: "The possibility of violence looms large because it is random and unpredictable. It can occur in the form of organized gang activity, the wrong thing being said to somebody during a street corner discussion, the misreading of someone else's intentions, or simply being in the wrong place at the wrong time" (Young 2004, 44–45). The reason why this fraught situation does not collapse into total anarchy is that well-established codes of conduct exist for both the expression and avoidance of violence, as Krupnick and

Winship as well as Venkatesh show in this volume (Chapters 9 and 10; see also Venkatesh 2009, 186–87).

A hypermasculinity lies at the core of self-identified "bad boys." In her penetrating study of the subject, Ferguson (2001) found that male pride and respect is gained and exhibited by the use of three strategies of masculinity: gender power, the disruption of mainstream normalcy, and fighting. A predatory sexuality with regard to women—quite apart from the use of sex as a form of territorialism—beginning from early teens, is central to being male. As noted earlier, the highly gendered nature of violence in inner-city neighborhoods is widely attested (see Miller, this volume, Chapter 11). Initiation into sex begins early: 21 percent of black youth have had their first sexual experience by the age of thirteen (compared with 9 percent of white youth and 12 percent of Latinos) and over 40 percent between ages fifteen and seventeen. Nearly a third of all black male youth report that they have gotten one or more women pregnant, which is mirrored by the statistic that between the ages of twenty and twenty-five some 65 percent of all black women have been pregnant (Cohen 2012, 55–56). Cohen's figures are for black youth in general; it is a reasonable assumption that the percentages would be much higher for disconnected youth. In the culture of the street, being able to "pull the girls" and then "cutting" and "hitting" them are essential attributes of masculinity (May 2008, 101–28). Women are commodified; objects to be played; "hoes" to be fucked, pimped, and (if they have the goods) trafficked; "bitches" to be impregnated, violently put in their place and discarded, along with the children they produce who simply become notches on their phallocentric poles to brag about with other predators on the corner and to enhance feelings of control. Thus 86 percent of black male youth reported that when they have sex they "feel in control" or "feel good about themselves," compared with 65 percent of white males, although it should be noted that 78 percent of young black women reported feeling the same way (Cohen 2010, 60).

Hegemonic masculinity (or hypermasculinity as some call it) is also expressed through violent competition with other male youth in an endless "campaigning for respect," which "may be viewed as forms of social capital that [are] very valuable, especially when various other forms of capital have been denied or are unavailable" (Anderson 1999, ch. 2) although, as Young (2004) notes, it is the kind of cultural capital that guarantees the impossibility of gaining any other kind (70). Attracting attention as a badass nigga, "a 'beast' with a 'fearsome reputation'" is an essential first step in gaining respect, which at school may involve no more than being disruptive in class, but, as Ferguson (2001) notes, from very early the "danger is that in the desire for recognition, the subject of one's identification becomes the fantasmatic threatening figure of black masculinity. The act becomes the reality" (125; see also Young 2004, 68). Indeed, being seen as just outright crazy in the degree of one's recklessness is an esteemed value. Nathan McCall wrote in his 1994 memoir of growing up in Portsmouth, Virginia, that "It was a big thing then to be considered a crazy nigger. We regarded craziness as an esteemed quality, something we admired, like white people admire courage . . . craziness and courage were one and the same" (56). Not much had changed in the forty years between McCall's teenage years and 2012, when a young gang member told a team of *Boston Globe* researchers on violence in the Boston inner city how he proved his loyalty: "When everyone was like, 'Yo, let's go do this,' I'm like, 'Fuck that! I'm going.'" He added: "That's why they call me Livewire, because I used to do a lot of stupid shit" (Cramer et al. 2012). Studying violence in the same city a few years earlier, Harding (2010) found that picking fights, or "beefs" between individuals, in retaliation for perceived harm or insults as well as defending oneself when challenged are "the essence of manly behavior," and individual beefs have their direct collective counterparts in beefs between neighborhoods, which are "to some extent about a neighborhood's reputation and the relative safety that comes from being known as a rough neighborhood" (32–33). Violence is also the means by which disapproved acts are punished—snitching, especially to the police, being among the most brutally sanctioned.

Anderson (2008) has recently pointed out that this image has major implications that go beyond the ghetto and the street people themselves. In the broader society, young black men are "too often feared and considered guilty until proven innocent," and this stereotype is often attached to even elite and upper-middle-class black youth: "All males of color are then referenced by the stereotype of the 'bad boy'" (6).

One less-overtly violent expression of manly behavior is athletic prowess. "To be 'the man among men,'" writes May, "through athletic competition is one of the greatest accolades that a man can receive. Such endorsements can solidify a man's sense of masculinity" (2008). Clearly, this applies to only the small minority who are talented enough to survive the tryouts and cuts of high school coaches, although all black youth are deeply involved with athletics, whether as average players or spectators (May 2008, 30–49). Nonetheless, it is interesting that there is a gendered element even in this domain, itself related to the value of being tough. Among the basketball-playing youth studied by May, "descriptors like 'crying like a girl,' 'being soft,' 'weak as water,' 'sweet,' or 'bitch-like' and their accompanying gestures are meant sometimes as lighthearted jokes and sometimes as serious insults. To convey signs of femininity—most notably through emotions or feelings—links the players to women rather than to masculine signifiers of toughness or stoicism linked to men" (104).

By the time they have dropped out of school, sometimes long before, the street gang has replaced home—or that fragment of it left in the impoverished, overworked, stressed-out maternal figure too exhausted or incapable of exercising any parental control—as the new haven for the kid being swallowed by the street. The typical gang has been defined as "three or more youths between the ages of 11 and 21 that identify themselves by a common name, set of symbols and rules, as well as locations, and who engage in regular delinquent and criminal activity" (East Harlem Juvenile Gang Task Force 2011, 5). Almost every study of street culture finds that the gang, in addition to its dangerous demands of working in the underground economy, also offers desperately needed attention, direction, affection, and the authority figure of the gang leader. This sometimes happens even where a father is present, but the necessity of eking out a living at poverty-level wages, or hustling, leaves both parents little time for childrearing. As one such youth told Wilkinson's (2003) interviewer, himself an ex-offender from the New York neighborhood she studied:

> So, that's why I grew up in the streets. I grew up as looking for somebody to love me in the streets. You know, my mother was always working, my father used to be doing his thing. So I was by myself. I'm here looking for some love. I ain't got nobody to give me love, so I went to the streets to find love. (70)

We hear the same refrain from a gang leader in Chicago: "These guys [the Black Kings] are my family" (Venkatesh 2006, 279). Indeed, gang leaders sometimes directly challenge parental authority. Alex Kotlowitz (1992) reported one case in which a distraught mother, having found her long-missing son, was told pointblank that her son was no longer hers and now belonged to the gang leader. The leaders of gangs are the top of the hier-archy of older youth who constitute the alternate role models for younger male kids growing up in the ghetto. These older youth, long out of school and work, who are either gang members or denizens of the less-structured street-corner groups, may be seen as the main agents of reproduction of the street culture, whose enforced or chosen idleness gives them lots of time to cultivate and express in endless chatter the fine points of the code of the street and to transmit it in their active socialization of younger men and unattended schoolboys, a point emphasized by Harding (2010, 106).

However, it should be noted that in a nontrivial number of cases, youth were socialized into the street culture by their own parents or relatives, as we discovered in our study of Boston youth (Patterson and Rivers, this volume, Chapter 13). In the inner-city neighborhood of New York Wilkinson studied, one in five of the single mothers of her sample were either addicted to drugs or engaged in other criminal activity. Among two-parent families 54 percent of fathers and 28 percent of mothers were addicted to drugs, and 43 percent of fathers were involved in illegal activ-ities while bringing up their children. As one respondent painfully recalled:

> . . . I was growing up my parents were involved in drugs and shit. I seen all that, man. Well that's the way they were. A lotta shit happen to me because of that. Yeah man, too much shit. Just too much drama. Everybody in my family been locked up before. So I'm used to it already, man. It's all I heard, you know. (Wilkinson 2003, 71)

Another youth, commenting on the fact that he was on his own from a very early age, described himself as "an old man in a kid's body" (Kornblum and Williams 1998, 19; and on Chicago, see Young 2004, 76).

One often-noted element of the street culture is the fact that it actively promotes opposition to mainstream values; indeed, this is often taken as the central component of the culture with the name "oppositional cul-ture." There is undoubtedly a strong strand of deviation from mainstream injunctive norms and values in the culture of the street, but the idea needs to be qualified in several respects. Active resistance to mainstream norms, as a consciously pursued goal, is true more of younger street people still in school and is focused on the rejection of mainstream educational declarative knowledge, values, and norms. It is now well established that an oppositional culture is not typical of the great majority of black

American youth (Harris 2011). Nonetheless, more fine-grained research indicates that some elements of it certainly characterize the attitudes and behavior of a minority. The hard core of this minority are students being socialized into the street culture, but, sadly, as Karolyn Tyson (2011) persuasively demonstrates through the voices of the students she studied, some 65 percent of her informants claim to be influenced in some way by the oppositional group, their best efforts to avoid it notwithstanding (80, ch. 3 passim). Tyson attributes the persistence of this oppositional disruption to the "racialized tracking" of schools, especially those that are ethnically mixed, since this results in the institutional association of giftedness with whiteness, the great majority of high-performing tracks being Caucasian (2011, 3–16, 127–62). Hence, educationally successful blacks find themselves isolated from fellow blacks and from socially unaccepting whites, and it is this that leads to them being targeted with the "acting white" slur. To be sure, the "acting white" slur has long been a feature of black life—hurled at blacks who spoke and behaved in too imitatively "white" ways—but, Tyson points out, it only became associated, in a "cultural shift," with high educational achievement after the integration of schools and their subsequent internal resegregation through ability and performance tracking (12, 34–78). This is a very suggestive account, although it raises the issue of regional sample bias (the work was done in North Carolina) and leaves unexplained the reasons why so few black students end up, in the first place, isolated in the high performing tracks (cf. Harris 2011, 144–62).

Taking a different tack, Carla O'Connor (1997) argues that such opposition is more a conarrative rather than a simple counternarrative, a view endorsed by Young (2004, 142), and this seems consistent with what survey data and his own findings suggest. Finally, Ann Ferguson (2001) offers a rather nuanced account of what this all really means. Troublemakers at the school she studied, already stereotyped as prison material by their teachers, respond to the realization that success in the mainstream educational system has been foreclosed by disidentifying in what has been called a process of "active nonlearning." This happens when those designated as "bad boys," who may be no less intelligent than the "good kids" who follow the rules, reject the education being offered by teachers who are viewed as strangers from outside the neighborhood and who seem to disrespect the culture of the 'hood. The "local knowledge" of the street culture observed among the unenrolled and unemployed older youth become "the generative matrix for an oppositional discourse about the

contrasting treatment they observe and experience" (98). This oppositional disidentification hardens into a central component of their emerging
masculinity about the time those destined for the street enter fourth
grade, the so-called "fourth-grade syndrome" in black ghetto schools
(204). Ferguson also proposes an institutional interpretation of the
"acting white" claim, but with a novel, more cultural twist, when compared with Tyson's: to the degree that it exists, she argues, it is more a
response to the institution giving up on them than of peer pressure: "the
claim that 'acting white' is a prerequisite for success becomes an insight *on
the part of youth* into the normalizing techniques of the institution" (204).
The bad boys, she is saying, have instinctively grasped the Bourdieuan
logic of schooling as a disciplinary imposition of the dominant mainstream culture, which requires conformity as the price of success, a success which, in any case, is reserved for the few and the lucky (cf. Carter
2005, 64–72).

Whatever the truth—and it will be some time before we settle this
matter—what seems certain is that being bad and nonconforming are
simultaneously identified with real, "authentic" blackness. Being black, a
real "nigga," "becomes the source of a subversive reverse discourse to
recoup personal esteem" (Ferguson 2001). But it also involves an exaggerated performance of everything that distinguishes them from the mainstream: black talk; black dress; loud black music; disruptive classroom
performance; fighting; heterosexual power and misogynistic attitudes
toward women; identification with the pimp, drug pusher, gangster, the
incarcerated, and the ex-con.

In paradoxical contrast to their attitudes toward middle-class mainstream educational values (at least while in school), disconnected youth
and adults are avid consumers of the popular culture and have strongly
assimilated many of its values, including the major primary national ones.
To his surprise, Young (2004) found that even the most hardened disconnected youth insisted on attributing their failures to their own shortcomings and refused to blame racism. "Like many Americans, all of the men
professed a belief in individual initiative as essential for successful upward
mobility . . . all of the men appeared to subscribe to the traditional American creed—the notion inherent in the 'Protestant Ethic'—that hard work
begets positive results for getting ahead. In this respect the men under-
scored the centrality of hard work, education, and social ties to explain
how people move up the American hierarchy" (139). Later he adds: "In

the end, we find that all of the men shared the common ground of an adherence to the traditional individualism and moralism of the standard notion of the American Dream" (141). These findings are strongly supported by survey data. Cohen (2012), for example, found that the poorest black youth were those most inclined to say that they were responsible for their condition due to their own limitations and bad decisions (25; see also Ethan Fosse in this volume, Chapter 3). Young is here clearly bothered and uncomfortable with his own findings. As a first-rate ethnographer, he is professionally reluctant to treat his subjects as what Garfinkel (1967, 68) calls "cultural dopes," (the rejection, as epiphenomenal, of subjects' commonsense knowledge of social structures and their own interpretations of their lived situations) which, in any event, would cast doubt on the subjective authenticity of all his other findings. At the same time, their unreconstructed mainstream individualism and insistence on blaming themselves for their own failings goes against the liberal grain of contemporary sociological doctrine (on which, see Lynch 2012). Sociologists love subjects who tell truth to mainstream power; they grow uncomfortable when these subjects tell mainstream truths to sociologists. Young attempts to resolve the dilemma by arguing that the extreme segregation and isolation of the young men he studied makes it difficult for them to "articulate a more complex understanding of how personal mobility unfolds" and the role of racism in explaining their condition (Young 2004, 144). Interestingly, the more isolated they were, the greater their espousal of mainstream individualism.

The clue to understanding this seeming paradox is that social isolation does not amount to cultural isolation. Black Americans are, in fact, more exposed to the mass media than any other group, from which they absorb a good deal of their expressed values and injunctive norms. Cathy Cohen (2012) is on the right track in arguing that black youth are "taught a certain set of norms and values, which they internalize and reiterate when asked to judge behaviour" (53). This may be so, but the situation is far more complex. The truth of the matter is that a good deal of the negative values, and possibly some of the behavior of disconnected youth, can be attributed directly to what they have learned from their exposure to mainstream culture, not only from school and adults, but from the mass media.

African Americans spend an average of seven hours and twelve minutes each day watching TV, substantially above the national average of five hours and eleven minutes (Nielsen 2011). And while younger African Americans, ages eighteen to thirty-four (so-called Generation Y), now watch fewer hours than black baby boomers (ages forty-five to sixty-four)—six hours and three minutes per day compared with eight and a half hours—this is still nearly an hour more than the average watching time for the nation (Nielsen 2012, 20). Nielsen also finds that the black digital consumer is very socially connected to others, with 72 percent of adults online having more than one social networking profile, Twitter being the most popular. African Americans, and black youth in particular, are also avid users of new media such as gaming consoles. Nielsen adds that they "can be reached through the online features of these devices for advertising, marketing and information collection" (2012, 23). They also downloaded video and music at 30 percent and 10 percent higher rates respectively than the population at large. Finally, African Americans attend movies at a rate 10 percent greater than the national average.

With such massive exposure, it's no wonder that African Americans are so connected to mainstream injunctive norms as well as its popular values and beliefs, in spite of their social isolation. There are, however, several major negative consequences of being so besotted with the media. The epidemic of obesity among blacks and other Americans has been attributed in good part to extreme TV watching (Dietz and Gortmaker 1985; Harvard School of Public Health 2013), and there is an association with lowered levels of academic achievement, although the causal direction has yet to be determined (Thomson and Austin 2003). Based on his seven-year ethnographic work, Nightingale (1993) speculatively attributes not only the strong espousal of celebrated mainstream values and norms but nearly all the problematic values and behaviors of inner city youth—violence, hypermasculinity and misogyny, drug addiction, educational failure, unemployment—to their near total immersion in the mainstream mass media, which he claims infuses them with all the evils of a materialistic culture that glorifies violence, greed, and success at any cost while failing to provide them with meaningful jobs or the procedural skills necessary for the jobs they would like. This immersion, he further argues, has isolated them from their own traditional culture, which was a far more effective shield against the ravages of their impoverished condition. Instead, "American culture in general, and mainstream mass media have infused the socialization of inner-city kids with racial caricatures and an extremely compelling set of sanitized, glorified images of violence" (75). While Nightingale overstates his case, especially in his too-romantic view of the protective armor of the vernacular black urban culture and in his neglect of its persistence, there is truth to his argument that the norms, values, and much of the declarative knowledge, beliefs, and goals that motivate disconnected black youth (and a good many of the connected) behavior are derived from either the underside of the popular mainstream or exaggerated versions of it. The outlaw and gangster, the celebration of violence, the reverence for the gun, the legitimation of greed, and the idealization of material possession are all fundamental elements of America's mainstream culture, reinforced by the foundational myth of the Wild West and gun-toting cowboy and bad man or antihero, and by their relentless celebration by Hollywood (Martinez 1997; Kubrin 2005, 376). So, too, is the commodification and marketing of teenage sexuality (Giroux 1998, 39; Sharpley-Whiting 2007, 5) and, as Tricia Rose (2008, 109) recently pointed out, the "aggressive, sexist, and confrontational style of masculinity" often associated with gangsta rappers is perfectly exhibited in the iconic mainstream figure of Governor Schwarzenegger with his belittling of opponents as "girlie men" and impregnation of his housemaid.

What Nightingale and Rose were not able to do was to offer evidence that supported a causal link between exposure to the violent and more negative images, stories, values, and norms of the mainstream media and subsequent violent behavior. Earlier work by experimental psychologists had established a strong, short-term increase in aggressiveness following exposure to violent video clips (Anderson et al. 2003) as well as higher levels of self-reported violence after viewing media with violent content (Johnson et al. 2002), but they did not demonstrate long-term effects or causal direction. However, recent psychological and econometric research have done just that. In a major longitudinal study of the same subjects as children (ages six through ten) and as adults fourteen years later, it was found that early exposure to TV violence by children strongly predicted serious physical aggression and criminality among them when they became adults, as well as a greater likelihood of women engaging in indirect aggression. In the case of men, the effects were heightened by "their identification with same sex characters and perceptions of realism in TV violence." These effects held even after controlling for class, parental variables, intelligence and early childhood aggression (Huesmann et al. 2003). More recently, the causal link between TV watching and actual behavior has been even more compellingly demonstrated by Kearney and Levine (2014) who, using an IV methodology designed to avoid the endogeneity problems that beset such studies, showed that teenaged girls who watched the reality TV show, *16 and Pregnant* gave birth at a significantly lower rate than expected, accounting for a third of the decline in such births between June 2009 and and the end of 2010. Importantly, the impact was greatest for black, non-Hispanic teens, who were 30 percent more likely to watch the shows (Kearney and Levine 2014, 32). It may seem reasonable to assume that if the media can have positive causal consequences it is equally likely to have negative ones, but another recent econometric study, based on a natural experiment, complicates the story, providing causal evidence that "on days with a high audience for violent movies, violent crime is lower, even after controlling flexibly for seasonality" (Dahl and Della Vigna 2009, 280). However, as the authors themselves go on to note, their findings do not necessarily contradict the experimental results of the psychologists, since the decline in violent crime after viewing violent movies is a substitution effect: time spent watching movies is time not available to commit robberies and other crimes. The study makes no claims regarding the reinforcing or long-term causal impact of violent media on violent behavior.

Whether listening to music with violent lyrics has the same effect as watching violent videos is still to be determined, although both genres are now thoroughly conflated. It is important to keep in mind that rap, and hip-hop generally, however much they may reinforce these defining features of the popular mainstream, were hardly their originators, and gangsta rappers themselves, as Robin Kelley reminds us, "are consistent about tracing criminal behavior and vicious individualism to mainstream American culture" (Kelley 1994, 201).

What happens to disconnected youth and the cultural configuration of the street when they get older? Some of them do manage to straighten their lives out, get and keep a low-paying job, and return to the working-poor end of the working class in which they may well have been brought up, before turning to the street culture as teenagers; and there are the odd successes either via a rap hit, athletic success, or getting out after a big drug haul before being caught by the police. But these are the exceptional few; if there is alarming downward mobility from even the black middle class, it is not surprising that upward mobility from the bottom hardly exists. The great majority remain disconnected from the mainstream economy and simply drift into a tired, slightly less violent version of the street configuration. Mitchell Duneier, having given us a warm portrait of older working-class black men and the maturation of their proletarian cultural configuration in *Slim's Table,* proceeded to do the same for the disconnected in *Sidewalk,* his ethnography of a group of scavengers, panhandlers, and street vendors on the streets of Greenwich Village, New York. Although he tries hard to present these men in the best light possible, documenting at length the few "redeeming aspects" of their economic hustling and the effort of the less downtrodden to encourage them to lead "better" lives (Duneier 1999, 314–15), his data leave us in no doubt about the sad, sordidly banal state of their existence. With the exception of Hakim Hasan, an intelligent, well-read, college dropout who "went into exile in the street" and is hardly typical, these men are in a prolonged state of human aestivation, a debased condition of lowered mental, cultural, and socioeconomic torpor and underemployment in bemused and uncomprehending response to the postindustrial energy of the great American city in which they drift. At some point in their thirties, the heat of the city's criminal justice system and the mental and physical risks of the youthful street culture and underground economy became too much for them, and they developed a "fuck it mentality (which) is a kind of retreatism with pervasive effects on a person's life, and [at] its most 'severe level' reflects an indifference to basic standards that will be destructive to others" (Duneier 1999, 60–62). At this point, they simply turned to scavenging, panhandling, street-living ("unhoused" in Duneier's sympathetic terminology), or bumming off of older relatives. Elements of the youthful street configuration persist, such as the misogynistic contempt for, and harassment of, women; the fighting over territory (in their case a desirable place on the street to "lay their shit out," rather than neighborhood turf); drug addiction; confrontations with the police (who now see them as a nuisance rather than a threat to public order); and a chronic incapacity to sustain meaningful relationships, especially with women. But there were changes: the sartorial glamour of youth was gone, replaced by vile-smelling clothes, befouled by their own excrement as they ease themselves in street corners, as was the intermittent high-rolling times of the underground economy. Physical violence was replaced by verbal aggression, and the puffed-up pride and bravura of youth had given way to resignation, sloth, and bitterness. Even Hasan, for all his unusual learning and intelligence, found himself abandoned by his lover in favor of another "vendor" on the sidewalk, and as he prepared to depart from his life as a self-styled, Jane Jacobs "public character" and return to the trials of ordinary life, he was wracked by the fear that he might never make it, aware that "this conflict between my aspirations and my bitterness is the essence of my story," which may never be resolved (Duneier 1999, 328).

Section 6. The Hip-Hop Cultural Configuration

Black youth engagement with popular mainstream culture presents a radically different picture from their experience with the hegemonic middle-class processes. In stark contrast to their isolation from middle-class procedural practices and skills, African American youth today constitute an integral part of modern American popular culture, in the production of which they are virtual overachievers. They are both active consumers of this culture as well as major, and in expressive areas, often dominant players in the formation and functioning of this component of modern America. This holds for both the social as well as the expressive dimensions of American popular culture. And in knowledge-activation terms, mainstream popular culture is known and chronically accessible and applicable to the daily lives of black youth in all its forms: the declarative, procedural, and the regulatory domain of values and norms.

Here we come upon one of the central paradoxes of American civilization: the near complete socioeconomic isolation of disadvantaged black youth from middle-class American mainstream culture and from its most critical procedural knowledge base, in conjunction with the complete integration and constitutive role of black youth in its popular culture, to the degree that the very identity of this culture, in America and in the world, is in good part recognized as black. This asymmetric "outside/inside dynamic," as Iton (2008, 4) aptly calls it, is not new. Indeed, the history of popular culture in America, from its birth with minstrelsy in the early nineteenth century, is a story of the wholesale plundering and appropriation of black popular cultural productions performed by white performers in blackface right down to the 1940s. The minstrel show, as recent scholarship has made clear, was the TV, cinema, and Broadway of the nineteenth century, the main entertainment of the masses (Ogbar 2007, 9–36). From its emergence in Jacksonian America, white entertainers had no doubt about the value of black cultural creations and the love of the white masses for them, and many such as Thomas D. Rice, who invented the term Jim Crow, went on what amounted to field trips down South in search of new African American materials. At the same time, their own, and their audiences', chronic racism required that they not only exclude the creators of the cultural artifacts they had appropriated, but that they ridicule them in blackface and other public indignities (see Lott 1993, ch. 1; Toll 1974; Lhamon 1988, ch. 1; Brungage 2011). This began to change only with the rock-and-roll movement in music and dance and the desegregation of sports in the late 1950s and early 1960s. That decade was mainly transitional: whites continued to plunder and appropriate black expressive cultural productions—only now without the mocking prop of blackface—and black performers began to directly reach a white audience, if to a far lesser degree, and their economic returns were considerably less than what was being earned by white performers such as Elvis Presley and the Rolling Stones performing black music (Neal 1999, 25–54; Floyd 1995, 177–80).

The hip-hop configuration constituted a radical new departure in black youth's involvement with the expressive component of mainstream popular culture. In the first place, it marked a decisive shift of black youth cultural creators form the margin to the mainstream in all its components—rap, dancing, fashion art, and argot. Cornel West's (1982) view that it is a rebellion from the margin, which sees "little use in assimilating into the American mainstream," is no longer an accurate description of this movement, if it ever was (80, quoted in Perry 2004, 103). Perry (2004, 194) more accurately describes the movement as "a subculture of American music, of American culture, and of black America. And as much as it resists the philosophical and aesthetic pressures of mainstream America, it finds itself in constant conversation with, response to, and a part of Americana." It is important not to be misguided by the ideological camouflage of hip-hop leaders who, in denying the contradiction of a movement loudly proclaiming its street cred and ghetto authenticity even while being obsessed with mainstream success, broadcast the trope that it was the mainstream that crossed over to hip-hop rather than hip-hop to the mainstream. But as S. Craig Watkins (2005) compellingly argues, it was a two-way movement, and the camouflage actually underplays "the complex genius of the movement's creative class." He adds:

Just as the cultural mainstream actively pursued hip-hop, many of the movers and shakers within hip-hop sought out the mainstream. In the end, hip-hop did not simply join the mainstream; in effect, it redefined the very meaning and experience of the mainstream. (126)

The contradiction of successful hip-hop leaders is, however, the complementary counterpart to an equally pronounced contradiction among the corporate entrepreneurs of America's thriving popular cultural economy. Not only have they vigorously promoted hip-hop's cultural influence among middle-class mainstream white and black youth, including, presumably, their own children, but have selectively reinforced the most lewd, grotesquely masculinist and misogynistic, violent, and "gangsta" version of the movement. As David Samuels (1991) notes: "The more rappers were packaged as violent black criminals, the bigger their white audiences became" (quoted in Forman and Neal 2004, 147; see also Kelley 1994, 186–227, 224; Lena 2006, 489). Many cultural critics have complained that this has resulted in the commercialization and commodification of the movement, with negative artistic consequences, to which we return below (Rose 1994, 40–41; 2008; Watkins 2005, 52–53, 238–39; Perry 2004, 196–203). It is interesting to note that this was not the first time that white commercialization encouraged a shift toward the bawdy and illegal: during the first period of recording of black music in the twenties, singers were urged to depict men "stealing, cheating, and dying for a piece of their women's jelly roll, angel food cake, or shortening bread" (Levine 1977, 242–43).

Be that as it may, hip-hop's enormous influence on popular culture, both domestically and globally, has now been thoroughly documented (Neal 1999; Forman 2003, chs. 4, 7, and 9; Forman and Neal 2004; Watkins 2005, chs. 1–3; George 1998, chs. 5–10; Kitwana 2002; Perkins 1996, ch. 1). "From the pimped out rides we drive, technology we adopt and brands we wear to the beverages we drink, music we listen to and language we speak," writes the marketing entrepreneur and analyst Erin Patton, "the Hip-Hop generation has had an intoxicating effect on popular culture and the global economy" (2009, 29). Not only is this the case, but it is so perceived by the great majority of Americans—73 percent of Euro-Americans and 67 percent of Hispanics believe that blacks are a "driving force for popular culture" (Nielsen 2012, 5). This influence has had major feedback consequences for black youth, not always to their best interests.

The black proletariat—especially the working poor—were historically the primary sources and transmitters of black aesthetic cultural production and of the broader black vernacular culture. Black music (sacred and secular), dance, language, oral traditions, humor, folk and visual arts, religion, style, and athleticism are derived predominantly from the working poor and, from the early twentieth century, primarily the urban working poor (Levine 1977; Floyd 1995, 76–86). Cultural work, as often as not, was, and remains, substitute and compensation for, expression of, relief from, and improvement on exploitative and demeaning manual work (Kelley 1994, 40–53, 109–20). In ways both obvious and subtle, black cultural work has long been a critical medium of political expression, what made the denial of dignity bearable and what motivated the young to work at low-paying deadend jobs (Watkins 2005, chs. 6–7; Alvarez 2008, ch. 3; Imani 2004, ch. 2). During the war economy of the 1940s, for example, the only thing that motivated young blacks to work at the discriminatory poverty-level wages offered them, in spite of the booming war economy, was the powerful cultural desire to support and express their cool zoot style. "If non-white youth were denied their dignity through discrimination, violence, and negative discourse," writes Alvarez in his excellent study of zoot culture, "zoot suiters reclaimed it by asserting control over their own bodies and performing unique race and gender identities," and in doing so, they came to identify themselves "as a group based on members' *insubordination* to domination" (Alvarez 2008, 78, 80; emphasis in original). The insubordination, however, was motivated not from a desire to separate themselves but from their insistence on sharing in the mainstream culture of consumption. Seventy years later, we find a similar cultural dynamic of resistance through participation in the underground economy aimed squarely at their desire to share, by any means necessary, in America's mainstream culture of conspicuous consumption. "In an act of defiance," Cathy Cohen wrote in her recent study, "these young people create alternative spaces for income production— the 'underground economy'—but they do so not with the intent of challenging or resisting dominant norms of work but for the normative goal of consumption. They want to participate in, not restructure, the consumer culture that in many ways defines their status and worth" (2012, 90).

As with the street and proletarian configuration, place and locality play a central role in hip-hop culture. While sociologists have focused on the negative social consequences of living in the confines of the 'hood, hip-hop scholars have emphasized the aesthetic dimension of the cultural geography of culture (Rose 1994, 21–34; Forman 2003). As Forman emphasizes: "Space and place figure prominently as organizing concepts delineating a vast range of imaginary or actual social practices," some represented in the violent rituals of daily life, others expressively (Forman

2003, 3; see also Rose 1994, 21–34). Chief among these, of course, is the unending war with the despised justice system and its prison-industrial complex. Kanye West echoes the central thesis of Alexander's new Jim Crow in his song *New Slaves*: "They tryna lock niggas up / They tryna make new slaves / See that's that private owned prison / Get your piece today / They probably all in the Hamptons / Bragging 'bout their maid / Fuck you and your Hampton house / I'll fuck your Hampton spouse."

The cultural configuration of the hip-hop nation is simply the latest manifestation of this long tradition of cultural creativity and resistance emerging from the syncretic interaction of the inherited vernacular cultural processes with creolized African survivals and fragments reinterpreted and reconstructed in light of the American experience—with the mainstream popular culture and the challenges of concentrated, segregated poverty on the one hand, and the violence of the street culture on the other. Bakari Kitwana (2002, 8), writing as both an analyst and a member of the hip-hop generation, cautions us not to completely identify the worldview of the hip-hop generation with that of hip-hop culture, as is so often done. Many of the values of the preceding civil rights generation, he notes, are still present (in what I referred to earlier as their culture of orientation) but are often superseded by new values that tend toward a new configuration. For example, while black pride is still valued, personal financial success "by any means necessary" and "obsession with materialistic and consumer trappings" are far more important than the older generation's emphasis on communal integrity (6). There is also a new kind of social activism that is often at odds with the civil rights generation political activists such as Jesse Jackson and Al Sharpton (Cohen 2012, 186–89). However, by far the most important factor distinguishing the hip-hop generation is their complete engagement with the national popular culture, largely mediated through the constitutive influence of hip-hop, which has become for black youth "the fundamental matrix of self-expression for this whole generation" (Davis 1991, quoted in Rose 1994, 20). There is a good deal of irony, ambiguity, and outright hostility involved in this engagement, reflected in the best of the rappers' lyrics, which we will return to in our final reflection.

We noted above that the black vernacular was largely the construction of the black proletariat. While this remains true, there has been a shift away from the poorer end of the proletarian spectrum. This is true even of gangsta rap, notwithstanding its celebration of violence, misogyny, hypermasculinity, and hatred of the police, all attitudes and postures that run counter to the values of their culture of orientation. This is so not simply because proletarians, together with middle-class youth, constitute the great mjority of youth in the inner cities, but because they have more resources, intellectually and materially, on which to draw. The same goes for athletic prowess: Wacquant (2004) observes that youth from the most disadvantaged families in the inner city are quickly eliminated from boxing because "they lack the habits and inclinations demanded by pugilistic practice" (43–44). Rap music and its apotheosis, the rap performance, contrary to many ill-informed and biased reports, is, *at its best* quite challenging lyrically, musically, mentally, and physically (Dyson 2004, 67–68). That high-wire integration of "flow, layering and ruptures in line" and "ability to move easily and powerfully through complex lyrics," analyzed by Tricia Rose (1994, 34–41) is simply beyond the capabilities of the majority of semiliterate dropouts whose lives focus on the street culture. One cannot use a past or a radical tradition one knows little or nothing about or write complex rhymes if one is illiterate, or go through the amazing orchestration of body, mind, rhythm, timing, voicing, and charismatic engagement with an enraptured audience—the essential attributes of a rap performance—if one's executive neurological functions have been impaired. Nor can one engage for any sustained period in the inventive repurposing of "consumer-end technologies, from turntable to Twitter," to sampled previous hits, found tropes, immigrant "riddims," dubs, and other vocal musical styles, that Wayne Marshall (this volume, Chapter 4) argues is the defining genius of the movement. My analysis of the thirty-two singers who produced the fifty bestselling rap songs in the history of the genre shows that less than a third (ten) were of genuinely street culture background (among them, 50 Cent, Puff Daddy, and DMX); fourteen were either from the working-class or lower-middle-class segment of the proletariat (e.g., Outkast, MC Hammer, Dr. Dre) or from the working poor (Jay-Z, Lil Wayne, Ja Rule). The remaining quarter were of comfortable middle-class background (e.g., Lauryn Hill, Will Smith, Ludacris, and Kanye West, whose late mother was formerly Professor and Chair of the English Department at Chicago State University). Rap music is not sociology, in spite of its performers' frequent assertion that they are "keeping it real," an effort that all too often goes wrong, as Sharpley-Whiting acerbically notes (2007, 2).

This does not mean that rappers are lying when they make these claims. Rather, what they rap about—at least up to the point of the complete

"hyper-gangsterization" of the music, is their experience of the terrify-
ingly violent culture to which they were exposed, against which they
struggled, and which they eventually survived, in good part by knowing
its brutal declarative codes and procedures, when to make them cognitively accessible, and when to perform the rituals of avoidance that ensured
their survival (on which, see Krupnick and Winship, this volume, Chapter
9). There is a kind of Stockholm or survival identification syndrome in the
lyrics of every rapper who was not *of* the street but who, growing up daily,
lived *in* it, and the over-the-top exaggerations of many gangsta raps
coming from performers who were more likely terrified victims of real
gangsters rather than street gangstas themselves lends support to such an
interpretation. Danny Brown's experience being brought up on the east
side of the Detroit ghetto by better-off, very protective parents, was typical: "I used to get beat up all the time . . . And I'm kind of not really
gangster like that" (Ahmed 2012). And there is wicked irony in Outkast's
famous hook: "Do you really wanna know about some gangsta shit?" But
rap, before its corporate appropriation and artistic descent, was also more
than the aesthetic sublimation of post-traumatic psychology. For both
performers and their ardent listeners, rap lyrics were, as Kubrin notes, "an
interpretive schema" and resource "for seeing and describing violent identity and behavior" (2005, 375). However, unlike Kubrin, I see the best of
these lyrics, in their precorporate heyday, not as Austinian "reality-
producing activities," but as raw, compulsively musical reliving of, relief
from, and cathartic transcendence of its exploited, exploiting, and
degrading local contexts, a powerful American counterpart to the primal
reggae dub-screams of the Kingston slums that had partly inspired them
(Marshall 2007; this volume, Chapter 4; Martinez 1997, 272).

Like reggae, too, rap represents a primal, default culture of honor that
emerges, especially among youth, where formal institutions break down
or have lost all legitimacy. It is unlikely that any rap artists (with the possible exception of Kanye West) has ever read or cared much for Nietzsche,
but in their lyrics and behavior, they represent a primeval culture of honor
that comes closest to the realization of Nietzsche's (2008) Dionysian exis-
tentialism in today's world (see Patterson 1998b). Drawing on the street
culture's hegemonic masculinity, they are hard men, who, like Nietzsche,
philosophize in their raps with a hammer: "Yes this is a mission that I'm
on / Taking out the weak on the microphone / I'm hype so talk about the
hard hitting Hammer" (MC Hammer 1990). There is also the glorification of self-esteem and near-manic claim and defense of respect for its

own sake. In Nietzschean terms, this is the engine of creativity, as he proclaims in *Thus Spoke Zarathustra*: "To esteem is to create. Hear this you creators! Esteeming itself is of all esteemed things the most estimable. Through esteeming alone is there value . . ." (1954, 171). For esteem alone, the hip-hop artist is sometimes prepared to kill or be killed, as the intertwined tragedies of Tupac Shakur and Biggie Smalls amply illustrate. "As I walk through the valley of the shadow of death," intoned Nas, "New York to Cali for the money, power, and respect." Closely related to this is the obsession with what Nietzsche, in *Twilight of the Idols*, called the "spiritualization of hostility . . . a profound appreciation of the value of having enemies. Acting and thinking in the opposite way from that which has been the rule" (1954, 488). For Jay-Z, there is godlike power in having enemies: "The takeover, the break's over nigga / God MC, me, Jay-hova / Hey lil' soldier you ain't ready for war / R.O.C. too strong for y'all." There is a Nietzschean intoxication, too, with the rebellious vitality of youth, the idea that "one remains young only as long as the soul does not stretch itself and desire peace." Thus spoke Jay-Z: "Forever young. I wanna be forever young / Do you really want to live forever, forever and forever? / Forever young. I wanna be forever young."

Hip-hop does not exhaust the influence of black youth on the expressive areas of popular culture; and, furthermore, black youth involvement goes well beyond the mainly expressive. That broader influence, going back to the late nineteenth century, and well documented in Boyd's (2008a) useful recent compendiums of studies and commentaries extends to film and TV, radio, theatre, comedy, fashion, photography, video arts, pornography, and, most notably, sports. To be sure, the style, aesthetic, and values of hip-hop have become so pervasive in American popular culture that its influence can now often be found well beyond the original core components of the movement—rap music, breakdancing, graffiti, and street language (Rose 1994, 34–61; Alim 2006, chs. 1 and 4; Chang 2006). Todd Boyd's study of the growing merger of basketball and hip-hop culture makes the point tellingly: "Far from being simply music played on one's headphone that is unconsciously imitated by those who listen, hip-hop is the soundtrack to a lifestyle; and basketball tends to be the most visible stage where this lifestyle is played out" (2008b, 14–15). The megastar Jay-Z is the apotheosis of this development; his recently formed Roc Nation Sports expands a corporate enterprise that includes, in addition to his own musical company, nightclubs, a fashion line, video games, and part ownership in the Brooklyn Nets.

Viewed in terms of the cultural matrix, then, black youth are virtual overperformers in their command of the declarative knowledge, procedural processes, and important domains of the norms and values of American mainstream popular culture. Their superior knowledge of the popular culture springs not only from the avidity with which they consume its artifacts, representation, metaphors, metonyms, and values but by virtue of their audacious replication, reinvention, and symbolic appropriation of the urban dimension of these processes (Rose 1994, 22). However, there is a deep downside to all this. In the first place, the so-called golden generative period of hip-hop, when almost every new album challenged the boundaries of creativity and there was a high level of socio-cultural consciousness and political progressivism, is almost over—although we should be careful not to idealize this period too much since many of the problematic issues that emerged later were already evident in the eighties, as Sharpley-Whiting points out (2007, xvii, 120). Nor should we wholly dismiss the present period; for while the irredeemably vulgar Lil Wayne is all too typical, not only are there several excellent socially conscious rappers performing in the shadows, but arguably the best lyricist and performer ever produced by the movement, Kayne West, is presently at the height of his powers and getting better and better. Nonetheless, Cathy Cohen's view that recent condemnations of hip-hop are more moral panic than informed argument may be too defensive (Cohen 2012, 27–49). Very sympathetic observers lament the fact that instead of artistically representing and transcending the realities of ghetto life, under the pressure of corporate packaging, elements of the street and prison cultures have now been morphed into hip-hop, so much so that it is often difficult to differentiate the two (Kitwana 2005, 3). It has been argued that this extreme focus on the ghetto neighborhood and its street culture, abetted by corporate interests, is what undermined the previous progressivism of the movement since this was associated with an antipathy to anything outside the 'hood, making broad-based alliances impossible and East Coast-West Coast and other internal feuding more likely (Nielsen 2012, 357–58). Even very sympathetic analysts more inclined to blame the corporate world and white racism for hip-hop's problems concede that the genre is in crisis (Rebollo-Gil and Moras 2012). Tricia Rose (2008) is even more pessimistic. She has pronounced the movement "gravely ill" if not yet quite dead as a creative and critical force in popular culture and for black American youth.

Where's the fun in actually living in the kind of environment in which street-level drug dealers, street prostitutes, and pimps ply their trade? Instead of this grim reality, hip-hop gives far-flung fans—many of whom populate relatively comfortable and nonblack environments—the black pimp, criminal, ho, trick, drug dealer, bitch, hustler, gangsta, and parolee without the actual suffering, without any reference to the larger social policies that have disproportionately produced these figures and the conditions in which they flourish. (225; see, however, Marshall, this volume, Chapter 4, who rejects the declension view of the movement)

Among the most troubling developments since the late nineties is the deep involvement of hip-hop with the multibillion-dollar pornographic industry. The strip club has long been an integral part of both the music video and business end of hip-hop, but since the start of the new century, there has been a complete crossover into pornography, with well-known hip-hop stars such as Snoop Dogg, Mystikal, Lil Jon, and Eastside Boyz participating in hardcore porn. Scenes from these productions, with hip-hop the necessary musical background, involve the most degrading and abusive depictions of women imaginable. No wonder then that this view of women has become pervasive in the purely musical component of the movement, many lyrics being little more than aural pornography in which violent sexual fantasies such as gang rape, snuff rape, and brutal, forced abortions ("One hit to the stomach she's leaking it") are celebrated (Sharpley-Whiting 2007, 53–84). As Sharpley-Whiting makes clear, not only has hip-hop lent its power in popular culture to the mainstreaming of pornography, along with the degrading view of all women as hos and porn sluts, but it has been especially poisonous in exacerbating and normalizing the worst aspects of gender relations among black youth. The denial of female, especially black female agency, has become a central preoccupation of the genre: "Much of black male rappers' energy is spent trying to keep women quiet or getting them to shut up. The rest is spent trying to get them into bed or in some cases even condoning or bragging about sexual assault/rape which ultimately has the same silencing effect" (Rebollo-Gil and Moras 2012, 125–26). Sexual abuse has become so common and viewed as so normal that women who complain are virulently attacked: "Critiques of sexual abuse in hip-hop by black women seem to invite more pugilism—physical and lyrical. It is not so much that we don't count. We do . . . but we also in truth do not add up to too much—certainly not more than the profits to be had at our expense" (Sharpley-Whiting 2007, 67). In addition, priming experiments indicate that exposure to gangsta rap music by whites leads to a significant devaluation of black women (Gan, Zillmann, and Mitrook 1997).

There is, to be sure, a long tradition of such musical celebration and sublimation of pimping and outright criminality among the urban black poor, a classic case in point being the mythologizing of Stacker Lee, the St. Louis pimp who murdered his acquaintance, William Lyons, in cold blood in 1890, but went on to be celebrated in the folk-blues as "Stagolee" and in the later R&B hit "Stagger Lee." "Like rap music a century later," wrote Cecil Brown in his excellent excavation of the ballad, "Stagolee became a trope for the resentment felt by people marginalized by the dominant white society. For almost seven decades, Stagolee remained a symbol of rebellion, oppositional, subversive, 'underground,' and largely invisible as part of the unofficial subculture of prostitutes, gamblers, criminals, and other 'undesirables'" (Brown 2003, 120). Indeed, Brown thinks Stagolee had a direct influence on hip-hop culture (Brown 2003, 220–28).

There are two big differences, however, between the mythologizing of Stagolee in the first half of the twentieth century and the celebration of violence and misogyny in gangsta hip-hop today: when Stagolee thrived, there were firm checks and balances coming from countervailing moral forces within the black community who knew and fearlessly chastised "devil music" when they heard it; and, unlike today, they did not have to struggle against the mighty weight of the mainstream corporate system, cynically drenching all youth with unqualified celebration of rape, prostitution, drug use, and murder in the pursuit of profits (Levine 1977, 177–78).

To what degree this celebration, normalizing, and even mainstreaming of violence and misogyny has any direct effect on actual violence remains controversial. At the macro level, the evidence points against such a direct causal link. Thus the golden era of hip-hop, between the early eighties and mid-nineties, when the music and other elements of the movement were more socially conscious and politically motivated (George 2004; Dyson 2004) coincided with the escalation of criminal violence among black youth, while the plunge in rates of violence from the mid-nineties until the present (with the exception of the recent rise in the rate among teens, discussed below) coincides with the domination of the genre by gangsta rap. It is best to say that gangsta hip-hop reflects the violence of the ghetto and may indirectly influence crime through its celebration of street culture youth and its reinforcement of the hostility toward snitching, thereby worsening the problem of law enforcement and neighborhood collective efficacy. However, as we pointed out in the last section, a well-designed longitudinal study (Huesmann et al. 2003) on the micro or individual level has pointed to a direct causal link between aggressive and sexually risky behavior on the one hand and exposure to violent TV shows, sex videos, and lyrics, although even on this level the evidence is far from decisive (Zillmann et al. 1995; Johnson, Jackson, and Gatto 1995; Hansen 1995; Ballard, Dodson, and Bazzini 1999). Interestingly, the hip-hop star Ice Cube, while admitting the influence of the popular culture, blames the media rather than hip-hop for pervasive violence, telling a *New York Times* reporter:

> The TV taught the kids more than the parents because the TV was 24 hours a day. And you sit up here 24 hours a day looking at foolishness, and so you're addicted. You want to see the cartoons—very violent. That's the first thing. There are more weapons in Toys "R" Us than there are at the gun shop. Now the people from the older generation, they remember life without television. We don't know that. (Rule 1994, 42; quoted in Hansen 1995)

Regardless of the causal link, however, any cultural genre that routinely celebrates retaliatory murder and rape and dismisses women as hos, "hot pussy for sale," "hood rats," "dirty bitches," and "punannys" for the taking, trashing, and discarding is morally bankrupt, and it is academically trite and morally questionable to insist on sociological or psychological proof of harm before condemning it. These lyrics are self-evidently evil speech acts. That the men who sing them also act them out in their own lives and have become role models for an entire generation of youth simply makes matters worse.

Contrary to what is often claimed, there is little evidence that hip-hop, for all its popular success, contributes much to the employment of disadvantaged youth. Successful hip-hop artists and cultural critics who celebrate the movement's influence on American and global popular culture remind me of the Latin poet Horace, who boasted in the early first century of his conquered Greek slave ancestors' subaltern cultural conquest of Rome. What Horace failed to mention was that for every successful Greek poet and entertainer in Rome there were thousands of unsuccessful

Greek slaves and ex-slaves toiling in the vast underground economy, or at lowly and unrewarding tasks in the households, mines, and slave lati- fundia of the hegemonic Romans (Patterson 1991). What was true of Horace's Rome is no less true of Obama's America. The sad truth is that it takes only a small minority of creative minds to forge or influence a culture, especially its popular component. Hip-hop's consumption by black youth is pervasive (Cohen 2012, 74), and, its artistic degeneration notwithstanding, it may well continue to enhance racial pride (however questionably) and provide a means for the displacement of black youths' own frustrations and darker impulses (Dixon, Zhang, and Conrad 2009). But in spite of the vast sums made by the relatively few successful pro- ducers of the genre, hip-hop offers little in the way of meaningful employ- ment for the average black youth.

And the same holds for other areas of success in the popular culture, such as sports. One of the cruelest sociological hoaxes played upon black youth from the beginning of their integration into popular culture at the middle of the twentieth century is the myth that replaced the old "credit to your race" indignity, namely, that participation in sports and the pop- ular arts offer significant employment opportunities and mobility out of the ghetto (May 2008, 151–74; see also Hoberman 1997). In fact, these are among the most competitive areas of American life, characterized by the taunting penalty of winner-take-all economics (Frank and Cook 1995, chs. 1 and 10). It is not enough to be good at the practices of popular culture, as most black youth undoubtedly are; one has to be either a prodigy in sports or extraordinarily lucky in other areas, or both, to suc- cessfully make a living. Take basketball, for example, the national sport that blacks now dominate. A recent study by the NCAA (NCAA Research Report 2012) quantified the hopelessness of the hoop dreams of inner- city black youth. It found that pro basketball was the most difficult of all national sports to enter—seventeen times more so than pro baseball and two-and-a-half times greater than pro football. A high school basketball athlete in 2012 had only a 3 in 10,000 chance of making it to a profes- sional team. Note, however, that even this estimate paints too rosy a pic- ture, since the base population for calculating the odds includes only students who were already good enough to have made their high school's team. If we include all the dreamers who can play ball well enough and are so obsessed with the sport that it influences their aspirations, motivation, and behavior, especially their academic performance, with vain hopes of somehow making it into professional basketball, we are talking about at least a half of the 1,608,000 black male high school students who are currently between the ages of fifteen and nineteen (U.S. Census Bureau 2011), or 804,000 teenage black dreamers, only fifty-one of whom were drafted in 2012. This amounts to odds of .0063 percent or 1 in 15,764; a black high school youth is fifteen times more likely to be killed in a car accident in his lifetime than to become a professional basketball player, or 5,238 times more likely at some time in his life of going to a state or federal prison. The idea of professional sports as an avenue out of the inner city is what May aptly calls "the dirty trick" of modern sports (May 2008, 151–74).

But so too is the equally pervasive dream of making it out of the ghettos by means of a rap hit or by becoming an entertainment star in some other arena of hip-hop or the broader popular culture. Writing about his own hip-hop generation Bakari Kitwana (2002, 46) tells us that, in spite of their poverty, "it's nearly impossible to find a kid on the block who doesn't think he can be the next Puff Daddy or Master P, Chris Webber or Tiger Woods." This leads to "unprecedented dissatisfaction" and a "sense of entitlement," because "the American Dream means not just living comfortably but becoming an overnight millionaire while still young. . . . That a handful of widely celebrated hip-hop generationers have achieved the dream makes the possibility real, despite the odds." Indeed. Precisely because the qualifications and talent necessary for entry are less demanding than in professional sports—anyone can cut a disc or post a YouTube performance—the competition is even more brutal. What's more, a growing body of research on the criteria for the production of a successful hit song or video by a novice indicates that, whatever the performer's talents, the process appears to be purely stochastic (Salganik and Watts 2009). The rap dream of becoming another Jay-Z or Dr. Dre is even more improbable than becoming another Michael Jordan.

Section 7. Toward a Deeper Understanding of Youth Crime and Violence: Culture, Incarceration, and Environmental Toxicity

The roles of external mainstream cultural, as well as internal ones such as those we have discussed above, are undeniable in partly explaining inner-city violence, but they are hardly sufficient. The level of violence in the inner cities is too pervasive, too utterly self-destructive, too chronically accessible to be explained solely in terms of the cultural configuration of disconnected black youth. Any understanding of the reign of terror on the streets of America's black ghettos must consider all possible structural, environmental, and biological factors that generate, continuously interact with, and are sustained by the cultural processes we have examined above. Before doing so, let us briefly review the evidence on both past and current levels of crime and violence among disadvantaged blacks.

Although between 2002 and 2010 serious violent crime against youth (usually committed by other youth) declined quite sharply among whites (26 percent) and Hispanics (65 percent), the previous similar pattern of decline between 1994 and 2002 among black youth halted in 2002 and has not declined since them. In 2010, there were 24.5 acts of serious crime per 1,000 committed against black youth, more than twice the rate among Euro-Americans and Hispanics (Bureau of Justice Statistics 2012a, 4). Homicide rates give a more accurate picture of the level of violence in a group because it is not influenced by official definitions or popular views of what constitutes a crime. In 2008, the homicide victimization rate (the number of persons killed) for blacks (19.6 per 100,000) was six times that for whites. Having peaked at 39.4 in 1991, it fell to a low of 20 in 1999, where it has stabilized. The offending rates (number who killed per 100,000) followed a similar pattern, peaking at 51 in 1991 and falling to 24.7 in 2008. After declining substantially during the nineties, the racial gap has remained constant: in 2008 it was seven times that of whites.

An even grimmer picture emerges when we focus on youth. The homicide victimization rate for black teenagers ages fourteen to seventeen peaked at 79 per 100,000 in 1993, over eight times the white rate, and had more than halved to 31.4 in 2008, which was seven times the white rate. It is among young adults ages eighteen to twenty-four that one finds the highest rates among both whites and blacks. Among blacks of this group, there was a near carnage in the early nineties when the rate peaked at 195.9 in 1993, nearly ten times the rate for whites of that age group. By 2008, the rate had, mercifully, more than halved to 91.9 homicides per 100,000, nearly eight times the white rate for that age category. However, a disturbing new trend has emerged in the first decade of this century: the homicide offending rate (the number of killers per 100,000) for black male teens (ages fourteen to seventeen) has begun to rise again from its low of 54.3 in 2002 to 64.8 in 2008, which is eight times the white teen rate of murderers (Bureau of Justice Statistics 2011).

The good news, then, is that the rates have more than halved since the catastrophic drug-related homicide rates of the late eighties and early nineties and have fallen back to roughly where they were in the early eighties (LaFree, Bauner, and O'Brien 2010, 87); the not-so-good news, however, is that the rate of the early eighties was still, by national standards, extremely high, as they remain today. By focusing too much on the sharp oscillation period between the eighties and late nineties, social scientists working on crime run the risk of neglecting the historic pattern of high crime rates among blacks. The work of W. E. B. Du Bois and of the modern social historian Roger Lane thoroughly documents the long history of a high racial gap in crime rates. In the 1890s, the black homicide rate in Philadelphia was more than five times that of its white population. More tellingly, the trend in the black rate from the middle of the nineteenth century up to the 1960s moved in the opposite direction of whites: the latter witnessed a steady decline in its rate while the black rate increased. By the 1960s, the black homicide rate was 11.46 times that of the white rate (Lane 1986, 95–143; LaFree, Bauner, and O'Brien 2010, 87). Lane documents a "criminal subculture" in the nineteenth century that bore remarkable resemblance to the street cultural configuration today: then, as now, there was a thriving underground economy with a high rate of prostitution (one in eight of all black women fifteen to forty-five years of age engaged in prostitution, many under the control of pimps, some of whom grew prosperous; 122–33, 158–59); then, as now, there was deep cynicism and disrespect for the (often racist) police (160); then, as now, the conditions of urban life and culture were "deeply subversive of black family life" (156), with modern researchers finding much the same (Sampson, Morenoff, and Raudenbush 2005); then, as now, the black middle class found itself with a problem almost identical to that described by Mary Pattillo a hundred years later in the 1990s: its struggle for respectability was undermined by the proximity of the criminal underground and the devastating exposure of its children to delinquent temptations of a flashy criminal culture and ostentatious criminal entrepreneurs as well as pervasive violence (Lane 1989, 153–55, 159–61). Comparing the late nineteenth century with the early eighties, before the disastrous escalation of the drug induced rates, Lane wrote:

> Among Afro-Americans, then, current rates of criminality are relatively simple projections out of the past, products of a sub-culture of violence long nurtured by exclusion and denial. The roots of black crime are threefold: a different social psychology resulting from blacks' exclusion from the dominant experience with factory, bureaucracy, and schooling; a heritage of economic and other insecurities;

and a long and complex experience with criminal activity. Political subordination and dependence historically helped make the urban "vice district" largely congruent with its "black district." Residential segregation trapped large numbers into living in or near an underworld in which force was the predominant means of settling disputes. This condition aggravated the felt need to carry weapons, which was originally a kind of defence against white aggression and hostility. The effect of these three conditions over time has been an atmosphere in which violent behavior is not only accepted but often expected and even celebrated. (173)

The pervasiveness of violence in the nation's ghettos today was recently given vivid expression in an op-ed by the reporter, Jonathan Schuppe writing in the *New York Times* of a visit to Newark in the spring of 2013. He notes that the homicide rate gives only a partial picture of the consequences of gun violence, since for every one killed there are many who survived their injuries only to spend the rest of their lives living with the pain and trauma of their experience, like the teenage girl he met with a bullet near her heart, the seven-year-old boy who was shot in the leg while playing near his porch, the hot dog vendor, shot in the stomach by robbers, or the grandmother hit by a stray bullet as she left her church. Just as traumatic, though, were the effects of violence on those who constantly witnessed it, even if they themselves were not shot:

> I've talked to kids who have seen someone get shot; many of them are afraid to go outside, while others act as if it doesn't bother them at all. I've met their neighbors, who live in a constant state of fear and mistrust. I've spent many hours with their suffering parents . . . who desperately want their children to ride bikes on a warm spring Saturday evening without having to think about ducking and running. ("Gunshots on Warm Spring Evenings," *New York Times*, May 17, 2013)

Three broad sets of factors in the upbringing of the inner-city child are critical for a more complete, and interactive, understanding of ghetto violence: childhood maltreatment and neglect by caregivers; a preexisting socially and culturally toxic environment; and a chemically toxic environment, especially extreme exposure to lead. These factors operate conjuncturally to produce what neuroscientists studying the developing child have come to designate as toxic stress.

In a groundbreaking series of recent studies, the Harvard Center on the Developing Child (HCDC 2010) has established that "early exposure to circumstances that produce persistent fear and chronic anxiety can have lifelong consequences by disrupting the developing architecture of the brain" (National Scientific Council on the Developing Child [NSCDC] 2010a). Exposure to extreme stress during fetal and early child development generate enduring epigenetic changes in the cells of the brain that alter gene expression and influence the brain's development (NSCDC 2010b). Threatening factors in the child's environment that constantly generate fear and anxiety, culminating in the condition of "toxic stress" (NSCDC 2008/2012), include neglect and maltreatment of the child (physical, emotional, and sexual abuse) as well as abuse of one parent by another and the pervasive threat of violence in the neighborhood. The fear and anxiety so experienced in turn "trigger extreme, prolonged activation of the body's stress response system," which alters the neurological circuitry of the developing brain. These early experiences "literally become embedded in the architecture of their brains" (NSCDC 2004b). This has major cognitive and emotional consequences such as reduced learning capacity and ability to engage in typical social relationships later in life (NSCDC 2004a). Stress overload also adversely alters the region of the brain (the prefrontal cortex) crucial for the development of executive functions: ". . . abilities such as making, following, and altering plans; controlling and focusing attention; inhibiting impulsive behaviors; and developing the ability to hold and incorporate new information in decision-making." This body of research has also found that:

- Children come to associate fear-triggering events with the context in which they occurred and over time this is generalized to people and places that are only vaguely similar to the original stimulus that generated their trauma. Thus, a particular look may trigger the fear response and lead the individual to react violently. (NSCDC 2010a)
- Constant fear in the child's upbringing eventually distorts how the child perceives and responds to threat. There is also an increased tendency to assume anger on the part of others when their expression and behavior are ambiguous, leading the individual to react with defensive aggressiveness. (NSCDC 2010a)
- One counterintuitive finding is that neglect by caregivers, defined as "the absence of sufficient attention, responsiveness, and protection

that are appropriate to the age and needs of a child" (HCDC 2012), can be even more damaging than abuse and other forms of maltreatment. Psychological tests showed that neglected children, when compared with those who had suffered verbal or physical abuse, had the greatest difficulties handling frustrating situations and also showed least creativity, confidence, and assertiveness when faced with such challenges (HCDC 2012). We have already found hints of this in our earlier discussion of natural childrearing. There is a thin but deadly line between "occasional inattention" and "chronic understimulation" in which "caregivers exhibit an ongoing, diminished level of child-focused attention that fails to support a young child's need for cognitive, language, social, and emotional engagement" (HCDC 2012, 3).

Research on child maltreatment indicates that, while the overall rate has been declining, African American children experience the worst rates: 14.3 of every 1,000 black children in 2011 suffered from maltreatment, compared with 7.9 percent whites, 8.6 percent Hispanics, and 1.7 percent Asians (Child Trends Data Bank 2013, 5). Poverty, while partly important in absolute terms, cannot explain these ethnic differences since the official Hispanic poverty rate in 2010 was nearly similar to that of black Americans (26.6 percent versus 27.4 percent) and was actually higher using the more accurate alternate SMP rate (28.2 percent versus 25.4 percent; Lopez and Cohn, 2011).

This is especially true of the emphasis on spanking. Just such an argument has been made by Nightingale who, rejecting the view that spanking has less adverse consequences for black kids than for whites, concluded that the frustrations of living with poverty, combined with the traditional mainstream fundamentalist culture of forceful, at times abusive, childrearing—don't spare the rod and spoil the child—and reinforced by the law-and-order rhetoric of political leaders and the criminal justice system "legitimate parental behavior that leaves children with hurtful and even traumatic memories" (Nightingale 1993, 81; cf. Holloway et al. 1997, 36, 64–65, ch. 6; Ferguson 2001, 135–36).

This is consistent with the sociological finding that family type is "the strongest and most consistent predictor of differences" in the black-white homicide rate (LaFree, Bauner, and O'Brien 2010, 91). It is not so much the type of family structure as the fact that the probability of such abusive treatment is much greater in such financially and emotionally stressed household patterns. Many poor parents in the ghettos, to be sure, avoid this tragic outcome. As Furstenberg (1999, 4–5) and his coauthors point out, parents of adolescents must walk a "fine line between just the right amount of control and too little or too much control." A good deal depends on the nature of the relationship forged between parent and child in the latter's preadolescent years and the kinds of parenting strategies used by the parent (chs. 4–5).

By a socially and culturally toxic environment we mean three things: the pervasive culture of violence and threat of physical danger already existing in the community of upbringing; weak neighborhood efficacy; and institutional neglect and incarceration. We have already discussed the atmosphere of pervasive violence that exists in the typical inner-city poor neighborhoods. Most works on adolescent violence have focused on the causes of youthful generation of violence, but more recent works have examined the consequences of exposure to preexisting neighborhood violence as well as intimate partner violence, showing that they themselves are major factors in the further perpetuation of violence as well as psychological and other health risks (Hagan and Foster 2001). What the studies on the developing child clearly demonstrate is the neurological mechanism whereby this culture of violence is reproduced. Growing up in the presence of pervasive violence tends to make one violent.

The ethnographic data is uniform in reporting that all black children in the inner cities perceive their world as a violent, threatening place and, hence, like all children constantly exposed to such environmental trauma, they "learn to be fearful through a process called 'fear conditioning' which is strongly connected to the development of later anxiety disorders" (NSCDC 2010a). The emotional memories of growing up in the violent environment are powerful and persist throughout childhood and adulthood and "are re-lived by individuals who experience traumatic event when cues in the environment activate those memories" as happens nearly every time they step out into the streets. In quantitative terms, it has been shown that prior levels of homicide are highly associated with all measures of current homicide (Sampson, Raudenbush, and Earls 1997, 922). Thus living in the segregated ghetto becomes a self-generating production and reproduction of violence.

Collective efficacy has been defined by Robert Sampson and his associates as "social cohesion among neighbors combined with their willingness to intervene on behalf of the common good," and in this way they "maintain effective social controls" (918). This they distinguish from the more formal mechanisms of social control such as the police and courts and include actions such as "monitoring of spontaneous play groups among children, a willingness to intervene to prevent acts such as truancy and street corner hanging by teenage peer groups, and the confrontation of persons who are exploiting or disturbing public space" (Sampson, Raudenbush, and Earls 1997, 918). The willingness to intervene on behalf of the common good depends heavily on the existence of mutual trust and solidarity among neighborhood residents. The authors' (Sampson et al. 1997) measure to assess the level of such efficacy shows a high correlation between the composition of neighborhoods and degree of collective efficacy: black neighborhoods with concentrated disadvantage showed the lowest levels of collective efficacy, although "concentrated disadvantage more than race, per se, is the driving structural force at play" (923); and there is a strong negative relationship between the homicide rate and level of collective efficacy, even after controlling for prior violence (922). Sampson et al. see a clear analogy between individual and neighborhood efficacy, and in this regard, the absence of collective efficacy may well be termed *collective neglect,* with similar devastating consequences. When an adult sees a young girl being led into an abandoned building by an older man or a young boy being made to carry a gun or satchel of drugs for the local drug pusher, not intervening or taking some action to protect the child amounts to the same kind of neglect discussed earlier in regard to the relationship between caregiver and child.

Sampson, Raudenbush, and Earls's most important finding is one that strongly complements those of the neurological researchers' emphasis on the lasting effects of early toxic environments: the fact that concentrated poverty, combined with communal inefficacy, has lasting consequences for the cognitive capacity of ghetto children that persist for many years, even after being removed from the ghetto. Living in the ghetto during their early years accounted for a six IQ-point deficit compared with black children reared outside the ghetto, and these effects were delayed, being strongest after the children had left the ghetto (Sampson, Sharkey, and Raudenbush 2008; see also Sampson 2013). The mechanism by which this happened are those identified by the brain researchers discussed above.

There is, however, a second kind of neglect: the erosion of institutional facilities and support in the disadvantaged inner-city neighborhood. This is what Wacquant vividly describes as the "wider processes of organizational desertification" that have reduced the number and effectiveness of formal institutions in many of the worst ghettos of the nation (Wacquant 2008, 5–6, 11–12, 218–23). It includes police forces that have an extremely limited view of their role, concentrating on the failed war on drugs while turning a blind eye to clear evidence of maltreatment and abuse, such as domestic violence and the sexual harassment of young girls (Moskos 2008, 83–88). In the suburbs of California, any reported crime is responded to immediately by screaming police cars and thorough investigations. However, in the Oakland ghetto, it was recently reported that a single part time investigator was assigned to 10,000 complaints (NYTimes 5/10/2013, A14). The sociologist and former police officer Peter Moskos (2009), notes that the reliance on police cars, telephones, 911 calls, and other techniques of "scientific" police management, which replaced the "watchman" approach of the foot patrol officer, meant that police were considered to be working when they were simply cruising around, waiting to respond to 911 calls after crime had happened rather than being on the scene, interacting with residents, and in this way preventing crime from happening (94–97). "Citizens, rather than being encouraged to maintain community standards, were urged to stay behind locked doors and call 911" (93), in this way worsening the problem of low neighborhood efficacy.

Institutional erosion also includes dysfunctional schools in which too many teachers (though by no means all) write off large numbers of their students as "prison material" and make little attempt to teach them. Or schools get shuttered on narrow educational test-score grounds, neglecting the fact that the school is often the only significant governmental institutional presence in the neighborhood and often seen by residents as "an institution that promotes local values supporting the neighborhood's subculture" (Sanchez-Jankowski 2008, 300). The recent closing of purportedly underperforming schools in Philadelphia to ease a budget deficit illustrates the point. Critics told the *New York Times* that even failing schools can "serve as refuges in communities that have little else." One resident commmented that "the school is one of the foundations of the community. It's like a village. The schools know our kids and they look out for our kids" (Rich and Hurdle 2013). The *New York Times* added that there was little evidence that students were actually moved to better schools, and many were exposed to greater violence as they adjusted to the new, unfamiliar school environments.

Desertification is also evident in the abandonment and "planned shrinkage" of public facilities in inner-city neighborhoods, and the resulting disinvestment and spatial redistribution of private businesses out of the inner-city communities, along with the retrenchment of the welfare state and vital services, especially for the youngest children, who must be left unattended and neglected by single mothers forced to work, a process well documented by Wilson and Wacquant (Wilson 1987, 1996; Wacquant 2008, ch. 2).

In one case, however, it is not institutional erosion, but over-institutionalization that has had corrosive consequences: the mass incarceration of black male youth. The incarceration rate of the United States has grown astronomically in recent decades. At the end of 2011, there were 2,239,751 incarcerated persons in the country, or 1 in every 107 persons, a slight decline from the previous year (Bureau of Justice Statistics 2011). This is, by far, the highest total and percentage rate in the global history of imprisonment. Even more staggering is the number of adult persons under the supervision of the correctional system of the country: persons incarcerated plus those on probation or who are parolees. At the end of 2011, this number was 6,977,700 or one in thirty-four Americans (Bureau of Justice Statistics 2012b).

Black Americans make up a disproportionate fraction of the incarcerated and supervised. Although there was a welcome 9.8 percent decline in the incarceration of black men during the first decade of the present century, they still make up 38 percent of all prisoners, and 39 percent of all male prisoners (Bureau of Justice Statistics 2012b; Mauer 2013, 6–9). One in thirty-three of all black persons are in prison, a rate six times greater than whites. As remarkable as these national racial differences are, however, they pale in comparison with the more qualified data on youth. Thus, focusing on the working-age male population, Western and Pettit (2010) found that 11.4 percent of black males ages twenty to thirty-four (one in nine) are behind bars, and of those in this age group without a high school certificate or GED diploma, a staggering 37 percent are in prison or jail, a higher percent than the 26 percent who are employed; alternately, in 2009, almost 70 percent of this group of blacks is likely to have served time in prison by their early thirties (Western and Muller 2013, 129).

This increase is partly explained by the escalation in crimes—especially drug-related and violent crimes—by black youth, but there is general agreement that the major reason was the drastic shift in criminal justice policy, which required mandatory sentences and long-term imprisonment for repeat offenders, reinforced by the enormous profits to be made by the rapidly expanding private prison industry (Drucker 2013). There was also blatant racial bias in the application of these laws, especially those related to the different kinds of cocaine offenses. Research interests have shifted recently toward an understanding of the effects of such unprecedented mass incarceration. There is quite persuasive evidence that the increase in incarceration did account for the marked decrease in the crime rate over recent years, and it is acknowledged that this did substantially enhance the security and quality of life of ghetto residents, which explains why inner-city blacks were among the strongest supporters of the draconian penalties, including young unemployed urban blacks who were most likely to be penalized by the laws (Western and Muller 2013, 171). At the same time, there is evidence that mass incarceration is criminologic or crime-causing, "perhaps by promoting criminal behaviors, by integrating prison inmates into the networks of criminal offenders, or by conferring a stigma that limits legitimate opportunities" (170). Western and Muller might have added another: increased reputation within the street and hip-hop communities of the ghetto, imprisonment having become a sort of rite of passage that validates street cred, normalizes the prison experience, and diminishes the deterrent value of the threat of imprisonment, so much so that hip-hop artists with clean backgrounds either invent criminal records or deliberately invite arrest and imprisonment (Arnold 2008; XXL Staff 2010).

One group of scholars regards mass imprisonment as a new form of political control of blacks, virtually a new Jim Crow in which "a tightly networked system of laws, policies, customs and institutions that operate collectively to ensure the subordinate status of" black Americans, one based less on old-style direct racism and more on callous indifference to blacks (Alexander 2010, 20); or a new penal state with a mushrooming prison-industrial complex that hyperincarcerates blacks in order to contain the fallout from institutional desertification and the "retrenchment of the miserly welfare state"; thus poverty is criminalized "via the punitive containment of the poor in the increasingly isolated and stigmatized neighborhoods in which they are confined, on the one hand, and in jails and prisons which operate as their spillway, on the other" (Wacquant 2008, 276–79; cf. Useem and Piehl 2008, ch. 2).

Western and his associates have addressed another set of issues, the social and labor market consequences of mass incarceration, at both the individual and macrosociological levels. Western and Pettit (2010) claim that incarceration now critically influences inequality in America: it worsens the labor market prospects and mobility of ex-convicts, depressing their total potential earnings by 9 percent and incurring severe collateral damage to their children and spouses. There are serious selection problems with this work: we have no reason to believe that black men who end up in prison would have been the caring fathers and spouses Western assumes; indeed, a good body of evidence suggests the contrary. In fact, their children may well have been better off without them, given the evidence on child abuse and neglect among lower-class black children. Western seems to have backed away from the earlier strong claims of the Pew study in his most recent paper (Western and Muller 2013). At the individual level, the claim of collateral damage to the families of the convicted is, at best, mixed and "may be near zero," and at the aggregate level, there is no consistent relationship; in the nation as a whole, crime and incarceration is unrelated except for the period between 1985 and 1994 when incarceration did significantly reduce crime. Thus the evidence is mixed, at best, "for the idea that high rates of incarceration are deeply implicated in a new social logic of urban poverty" (Western and Muller 2013, 181; cf. Useem and Piehl 2008, ch. 6). Whatever the eventual conclusion of this line of scholarship, it is reasonable to say that incarceration has become counterproductive for two cultural reasons: its frequency among youth has made it observationally normative and has nearly obliterated its deterrent value on crime; worse, as we have already seen, going to prison has become a rite of passage for many youth in the street culture and is even celebrated by the now-dominant gangsta rap genre of hip-hop, which regards it as an important way of establishing their street cred. In other words, imprisonment has become injunctively normative for many youth.

Yet another kind of institutional damage that adds to the toxicity of the environment for black youth is institutional and lingering personal racism. We have seen that black youth themselves, while aware of racism, are inclined not to attribute their particular failings to racial discrimination but to their own bad decisions and immediate circumstances. While it is admirable of them to do so, and strongly indicates that they have not fallen into the kind of crippling despair that undermines all attempt at change, there can be no doubt that their hypersegregation constitutes the single greatest legacy of the earlier era of direct, dominative racism and, as such, perpetuates its influence in what may properly be called institutional racism. It is deplorable, and tragically ironic, that for the vast majority of black Americans, the America of Obama is as segregated as it was at the start of the civil rights movement. Inner-city youth live in an all-black world, a world that is completely marginalized economically and socially, and, as such, being black is inevitably perceived as being in some critical way the source of their marginality and failure. The stigma of being a black young person is made immediately obvious to them the moment they walk out of the inner city and try to enter mainstream spaces, either by being rejected for unskilled jobs through what economists call statistical discrimination or by being closely watched in shopping malls or shops or simply by seeing the look of mild apprehension on the face of non-ghetto middle-class persons (white and black) as they approach them. Indeed, they do not even have to leave the ghetto to experience discrimination. The employment practices of Burger Barn restaurants studied by Katherine Newman (2000) were located in the midst of a completely segregated part of Harlem, yet young blacks found even there that employers were more inclined to hire lighter-complexioned Puerto Rican and Dominican laborers commuting into the ghetto (2000 234–45). The segregation of neighborhoods and schools, Nightingale (1993) found in his in-depth ethnography of children in inner-city Philadelphia, and the outside world's identification of race with inner-city criminality are "humiliating lessons" that dominate the emotional memories of kids growing up in the inner cities, leading to "fundamental notions of racial difference in kids' worldviews" as well as "negative assessment of their own racial identity" (112–13, 119). Wacquant (2008) arrives at much the same conclusion from his study of inner-city Chicago and in a penetrating passage this acute French observer of the black ghetto writes:

> Race is inscribed everywhere in the ghetto: in the objectivity of space and of the separate and inferior institutions that confine its population in the manner of a snare, but also the subjectivity of categories of perception and judgment that its residents engage in their most routine conduct, thoughts, and feelings. Indeed, color consciousness in the Black Belt is so suffusive as to go without saying—so much so that it can go unnoticed even by careful observers because, precisely, it is embedded deep in what Alfred Schutz calls the "natural attitude" of everyday life. (74, 186)

As if all the above were not enough, we come to the third environmental factor accounting for the street culture of violence: literally, the chemical toxicity of homes and neighborhoods. Although a small group of researchers has long warned of the role of chemical toxins in explaining the mental and behavioral problems of inner-city youths, it is only in recent years that a growing body of evidence has persuaded many that neurotoxicity (the quality or state of having a poisonous effect on neurons or neural circuits) is another major factor explaining delinquency, violence, and the learning problems of black and other disadvantaged youth. These are of three kinds: (1) environmental chemicals, such as lead, mercury, and organophosphates, (2) recreational drugs, such as alcohol, nicotine, and cocaine; and (3) prescription medications, such as anticonvulsants (NSCDC 2006). These drugs alter the epigenome of the brain that determines which genes are turned on or off, with several adverse later consequences (NSCDC 2010b). Humans are most vulnerable to these drugs during the period of greatest brain growth, as fetuses and into early childhood. The role of recreational drugs, especially alcohol, and the growing abuse of prescription drugs and their consequences for the fetus and young child have been well documented, so we will focus here on the first set of chemicals, one of which, lead, is emerging as the major culprit in explaining teenage and later violence.

Heavy metals such as lead, mercury, and manganese are found in many places, like paint, dust, soil, chemical waste accumulated in water and plants, leaded gasoline, and, in the case of manganese, unleaded gasoline. The complex chemical structures in which they are found break down over time and release specific toxins that contaminate the bodies of children and placenta. They damage the brain by interfering with neural cell migration and synapse formation and with neurotransmitters, which are "responsible for all brain functions, including learning, control of emotions, social interactions, and such fundamental processes as movement, vision, hearing and touch" (NSCDC 2006). Lead is especially corrosive in its effects on the functioning of critical neurotransmitters such as dopamine, glutamate, and acetylcholine. One disturbing finding is that the absence of problems during early childhood does not indicate absence of brain damage, since there is often a delayed impact of these toxins; they may make their appearance during the teenage and adult years. Lowered IQ, impulsiveness, attention deficit, interpersonal difficulties, and aggressive behavior have all been shown to result from this exposure (Banks, Ferretti, and Schucar 1997; NSCDC 2006).

The studies of the National Scientific Council on the Developing Child have established the psychological mechanism whereby these toxins adversely affect the brain, leading to behavioral and cognitive problems.

Concurrent work by social scientists has demonstrated a remarkable link between lead exposure and both the rise and decline of the homicide rate in America, to a degree far greater, and more persuasive, than anything offered by criminologists (Denno 1990; Nevin 2000; Needleman et al. 1990; Reyes 2007; Wright, Boisvert, and Vaske 2009; Marcus, Fulton, and Clarke 2010). Using state-level observations, Reyes (2007) argues that the remarkable and wholly unanticipated 34 percent decline in violent crime between 1992 and 2002 is directly predicted by the removal of lead from gasoline in the late 1970s, mandated by the Clean Air Act, which accounts for 56 percent of the decline in violent crime, compared with 29 percent attributable to the increased effective abortion rate[5] and 23 percent to other factors such as police activity, decline in crack use, and incarceration (32). It has also been shown that a half of all African Americans are exposed to potentially harmful toxins (Wernette and Nieves 1992; Perera et al. 2003) and that those living in the inner cities have the greatest exposure of all (Chung et al. 1999). Thus inner city black youths' higher rate of violence can to a significant degree be attributed to such exposure (Dietrich et al. 1991; Dietrich et al. 2001; Mielke and Zahran 2012). In New Orleans, for example, soil lead levels, low-income, overwhelmingly black areas, and crime rates nearly completely overlay each other (Mielke and Zahran 2012). More directly, Perera et al. (2003) found that among African Americans, high prenatal exposure to PAHs (polycyclic aromatic hydrocarbons) was associated with lower birth rates and smaller head size.

Thus, to conclude, culture, as well as the socioeconomic, physical, and chemical environments all interact with each other in a causally conjunctural manner to create a wholly toxic context for those growing up and living in the inner cities. What is more, these effects are by themselves self-generating in that their epigenetic effects can in some cases last for several generations (NSCDC 2011). However, the sustained, intergenerational effects of the constantly toxic socioeconomic and chemical environment inevitably become normative—at the very least in an observational way—and for the minority who fall victim to the street culture, injunctively. In this way, cultural and the environmental toxicity mutually generate and recreate each other.

However, toxicity is not destiny. Notwithstanding all the dangers to the architecture of the developing brain that those growing up in poor, inner-city neighborhoods face, scientists working on child development take care to note that "there is no credible scientific evidence that supports the conclusion that young children who have been exposed to significant early stresses *will always* develop stress-related disorders. In both animal and human studies, interventions that provide more appropriate and supportive care help to stimulate positive growth and prevent poor outcomes" (NSCDC). Furstenberg and his associates (2000) have emphasized variation in life outcomes in the inner city and have shown how successful parenting can make a difference in even the most disadvantaged of conditions. A recent study found that strong bonding with family and teachers, involvement with extracurricular activities, lower degrees of parental discord, less involvement with delinquent peers, and fewer experiences of negative events growing up were moderately associated with resilience, and further, that there was a positive feedback loop wherein earlier resilience promoted later resilience (Quyen, Huizinga, and Byrnes 2010, 360–78).

Religion is another major buffer, as one of the chapters in this volume indicates. Besides caring parents and family members, there is the sheltering offered by a few teachers and selfless community leaders—coaches, choirmasters, scout leaders, and informal mentors—and similarly motivated peers (Cohen 2010, 79; Kornblum and Williams 1998, 10–11). Only this explains the fact that, in spite of the toxic nature of their environment, black youth in the ghettos of America have created an aesthetic cultural configuration that now occupies a major role in America's popular culture and has had an extraordinary impact on popular cultures globally, although, sadly, the aesthetic debasement of the genre may now have added to the cultural degradation and toxicity of the environment.

Section 8. Understanding Youth Unemployment: The Interaction of Cultural and Structural Forces

Unemployment and idleness, the defining structural features of the disconnected, are both interrelated with cultural factors in complex ways, which we examine in this section through an interrogation of the works of three scholars who have directly addressed the problem of causality and causal direction. More than anyone else, William Julius Wilson has argued for the devastating social costs associated with the disappearance of work from neighborhoods in which young persons are segregated (1996, chs. 2–3; 2009, ch. 3). Even the centrist *Economist* (2013, April 27: 12) agrees that "there are few worse things that society can do to its young than to leave them in limbo" and that throughout the world there is an association between violent crime and "startlingly high youth unemployment." However, the relation between the joblessness and cultural configurations of inner-city black youth is complex. Wilson has recently argued that the two processes are complementary while insisting that "structure trumps culture" (Wilson 2009, 21). One major feature of the high-tech, post-industrial economy that America has become is that the main available employment for the semiliterate and unskilled will be the most undesirable dirty jobs that do not provide a living wage, and even these might be hard to get where there is an unrelenting influx of legal and undocumented laborers from poor countries with much lower reservation wages eager to take them.[6]

The sociologist Roger Waldinger (1999), using New York of the mid-nineties for his case study, has strongly contested both the empirical and theoretical claims of Wilson and those arguing that post-industrialism has led to a complete loss of good blue-collar jobs in the cities of America. During the Clinton boom years of the nineties, there was an abundance of low-skill jobs in New York, as well as fairly well-paying blue-collar jobs, which, while declining in absolute terms, became available because whites were fleeing the city at a greater rate than such jobs were being lost to the forces of deindustrialization (Waldinger 1996, ch. 2; for similar patterns in Atlanta, Boston, Detroit, and Los Angeles, see Holzer 1996, 20–44). However, male youth were reluctant to take these jobs because they did not meet their aspirations or were below their reservation wage, holding out for higher-paid government jobs, which had become the black lower-middle and middle-class employment niche, but for which, however, they were not qualified. Prudence Carter has more recently given another reason why these jobs were not taken. Unlike the British working-class "lads" studied by Willis (1977) who identified manliness with manual labor, American working-class black youth disdained manual labor because it clashed with their notions of masculinity, not only because such work is dirty, but because it involved taking rather than giving orders. What's more, the soft skills required of many low-paying jobs as well as white-collar jobs were considered feminine and hence inconsistent with the hardness required of "real" men (Carter 2005, 90–94). Instead, the jobs were snapped up by immigrants. While many of these jobs were so-called dirty jobs, they were nonetheless entryways into the job queues, which opened the door to better, still-available blue-collar jobs later. However, once they established themselves in these niches, the various ethnic immigrant groups maintained them for later coethnic arrivals, in effect creating a monopolistic ethnic division of labor that excluded those not of their ethnic group, including those black youths who were willing to take such jobs (Waldinger 1996, chs. 3–4, 264–67, 286–95; on other cities, see Holzer 1996, 51–54). Added to this were persisting personal racial discrimination on the part of white employers, which led them to prefer non-black American males and black women, as well as so-called statistical racial discrimination, which was true even of some black employers: the use of black youths' appearance, manner (especially their street culture and hip-hop mode of being and style), and prison records as reasons not to hire high-risk employees with poor work ethic (Waldinger 1996, 30–31, 115–16, 158–60, 219–22, 280–82; see also Holzer 1996, 93–95; Carter 2005, 92). All this, of course, was self-fulfilling because prolonged unemployment eventually led to unemployability and deep resentment which intensified or led black youth into the street cultural configuration and its negative attitude toward work (Holzer 1996, 58–62; see also ch. 13 by Patterson and Rivers, this volume). Although he does not spell it out, there is clearly a strong cultural component to Waldinger's fine work. What he calls the unrealistic work expectations of poorly educated blacks is really nothing more than the result of the constellation of values defining male youth masculinity—the emphasis on respect and pride, the cool pose and "mean mug" manner and style of dress that turned off already prejudiced employers, the materialism (especially dress styles) that made even blue-collar wages seem ridiculously inadequate, the difficulty with taking orders from supervisors and with being punctual, and the quickness to take ambiguous comments as threats that had to be met with aggression, and, of course, the absence of basic work skills, including the "soft" social skills valued by employers (see Holzer 1996, 47–66). Thoroughly cultural, too, are the responses of white employers: racist distaste for blacks is simply a set of highly traditional cultural beliefs, values, and norms of interaction and exclusion. Statistical discrimination is a near-perfect example of a cultural schema (see also Holzer 1996, 59–62; Pager 2008). So, too, are the monopolistic collective job queues formed by immigrants who use insider ethnic connections and a common language and constellation of home-country cultural attributes to exclude blacks and other nonethnics. Culture, in fact, is everywhere in Waldinger's richly documented work, although, as a good card-carrying sociologist, he is extremely reluctant to use the C-word, which appears nowhere in his work.

Not so the Nobel laureate economist George Akerlof who, in two major papers, has directly challenged Wilson's earlier work as well as all hyper-structural sociologists on just this issue, making a strong case for the causal priority of cultural processes acting both directly and as the mediating mechanisms of legal and technical shocks (Akerlof, Yellen, and Katz 1996). Taking issue with Wilson's attribution of the soaring rate of out-of-wedlock birth since the mid-sixties and accompanying high-poverty, single-female households to the weak marriageability of black men due to job shortages (Wilson 1987, ch. 3; 1996, ch. 4), Akerlof and his coauthors show compellingly that this change had less to do with job scarcity and far more to do with the precipitous decline of an old cultural practice—the shotgun-marriage institution whereby men, under strong normative pressure, were obliged to marry women they impregnated—a decline they attributed to the "reproductive technology shock" of liberalized abortion laws and the ready availability of contraception, both occurring in the early seventies. They found that fully 60 percent of the increase in black out-of-wedlock births since the sixties can be explained by the decline in the cultural practice of the shotgun wedding, itself directly resulting from the mediating changing cultural norms of men regarding their responsibility for unplanned pregnancies and reasons for getting married, as well as of women regarding their freedom to engage in sex before marriage and to keep children born out of wedlock. However, the unanticipated massive increase in single-female households resulting from these cultural changes, by greatly increasing the extent of poverty, especially among the black poor, also explains the poor unemployment experience of black men, since growing up in a single-female household has been shown to directly predict chronic unemployment of persons reared in such households (McLanahan 1997). Thus a profound cultural change explains the decline in marriage, nonpoverty, and employability of poor black men, and not the other way around.

In yet another study, Akerlof more directly challenges Wilson's claim of causal direction in the relationship between marriage and jobs. Both agree that low marriage rates are associated with major social problems such as crime and drug addiction and that the data are clear that married men are more likely to earn higher wages and to be in the labor force as full-time workers, and are less likely to be unemployed, quit their jobs, or be part-year workers (Wilson 1996, chs. 3–4; Akerlof 1998, 291, 295–98). Changes in the degree of these differences are sufficiently large to have been explained, potentially, by major changes in the age of marriage over the same period since the mid-sixties. But there are two obstacles to the claim that the cultural change (in age at, and rate of, marriage) accounted for changes in the observed differences in the labor market attributes of married and unmarried men: selection bias and the fact that men do change their behavior at some predetermined age, which just happens to coincide with the time during which marriage typically occurs. An instrumental variable test indicated that selection bias is, in fact, very much at play in explaining the differences. Men who marry are quite different from those who don't, and these differences can be shown to exist before they get married. However, other studies have shown that, whatever the greater cultural capital men who marry bring to their marital state, these are compounded by marriage, leading to a faster rate of human capital accumulation and hence higher rate of *growth* of earnings. Thus there is (or was until recently) a marriage premium. The job performance of married men, adjusted for grade level, is better than that of the unmarried, and they have substantially higher chances of promotion. However, this premium has greatly declined in recent years, and by now, has perhaps disappeared (Akerlof 1998, 299–304). It would seem that as the marriage rate declines employers tend to distinguish less on the basis of marital status. These complexities lead Akerlof to recommend caution in interpreting the data, which "only weakly support the hypothesis that marital status matters for *aggregate* activity" (307). On the individual level, however, there is no doubt about the striking differences between the behavior of married and single men "and some of these (econometric) findings may even suggest that the differences are causal" (307).

Although Akerlof leaves the matter here, there is one major implication of his findings that he did not pursue, perhaps for disciplinary reasons. It has been shown definitively that men who marry are different, married men bringing substantially greater human capital to their marriage. The question left dangling, and which we may now legitimately ask is, what is the nature of this greater prior human capital that persists and is compounded by marriage? Isn't it what sociologists call culture, or more precisely, cultural capital, including disposition? Thus, while the selection bias instrumentally demonstrated by Akerlof partly undermines his own effort to demonstrate that the marital rite initiates a change in the behavior of the husband, it actually hands us one of the best possible supports for our position that culture matters, and may well be as important as, and even more important than, structural factors in certain circumstances and in certain domains: men socialized into a certain constellation of cultural qualities—possessing certain declarative and procedural knowledge as well as beliefs, values, and norms—called "human capital" by the economists who may be forgiven for not knowing that they are speaking cultural prose—greatly outperform men without these cultural attributes, and coincidentally, quite possibly for this very reason, are more likely to make the sensible decision to get married and settle down, which, in turn, is likely to accelerate the rate of accumulation of these prior cultural properties, with economic consequences that were once quite powerful but now seem to be waning with the socially troublesome decline in the rate of marriage, a decline that is fastest and most disastrous among young black Americans, especially the poor and disadvantaged. Akerlof's work, while showing clearly the importance of culture in both initiating and mediating major social change, cannot be said to prove that culture trumps structure. Instead, what he shows is the necessary interaction of cultural and structural forces.

Section 9. Summary and Discussion

The interactions of cultural and structural forces, as well as the arguments of the chapter as a whole, are diagrammed in the matrix of explanatory factors in Figure 2.1. A combination of major cultural, legal, technological, economic, and policy changes, most of which originated in the sixties and early seventies, were mainly responsible for a cascading series of other changes that culminated in the vicious circle of sociocultural forces directly accounting for the crisis of high unemployment, delinquency, and violence that continues to beset black youth in spite of the overall decline in violence since its peak in 1990. Some of these well-known early exogenous factors were not discussed in the chapter, and we mention them now for the sake of completeness: the rise of second-wave feminism, which motivated and largely facilitated the reproductive technology shock and also directly influenced dominant mainstream values and norms; the civil rights movement that led to the rise of the black middle class, which, however, remained ghettoized even after moving out of the old largely impoverished ghettos; and the 1965 immigration act that had the largely unintended consequence of initiating the new wave of mass migration from non-European nations, most arriving in gateway cities where they competed with blacks for jobs and housing in the new post-industrial order.

The diagram indicates that toxic stress, mass incarceration, educational failure, the street cultural configuration, and discriminatory practices of urban employers (dubbed employer statistical racism) are the direct, proximate causes of the plight of disadvantaged black youth. The double-headed arrows indicate that these proximate causes interact in negative

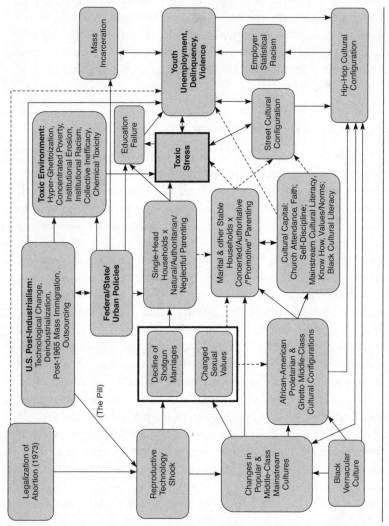

Figure 2.1. Matrix of interacting cultural and structural factors explaining the condition of black youth. Broken arrow lines indicate negative influence.

feedback loops. Of these, the most important is toxic stress, which mediates many of the major structural as well as cultural forces leading up to and sustaining the crisis. Of the structural forces in the matrix, the dark side of post-industrialism interacting with state, federal, and urban policies is shown to be one of the major contributing factors. Blue-collar jobs paying a living wage did not disappear from the economy, but they did disappear largely from the cities with the departing white working class; and those good blue-collar jobs that remained as well as entry-level "dirty jobs" were rapidly monopolized by immigrants who proceeded to shut black males (poor black women fared better partly because they were less feared by employers) out of the networks of job recruitment in the ethnic niches they formed. More important were its indirect effects through the creation of the devastating toxic environment of the inner cities, a development facilitated by state policies at the federal, state, and local levels. There was the racist herding of poor blacks into vast, segregated projects and dilapidated housing reeking with lead paint in the full blast of vehicular exhaust fumes and the erosion of institutional structures, including law enforcement (except to wage the losing war on drugs, which increased the price of illicit drugs and facilitated the rise of the murderous underground economy that, in turn, crippled collective efficacy as law-abiding residents huddled in silent terror behind their bullet riddled walls). Racially biased and completely counterproductive federal and state policies, combined with the increased criminality of black youth in the drug trade also account for the rise of the prison-industrial complex that has led to the globally unprecedented rise in incarceration and its disproportionate impact on black youth. A similar combination of poorly resourced and administered segregated schools, further crippled by the street culture configuration mediated through the cognitive impairment and violent behavior induced by toxic stress, led to chronic educational failure. A major legislative decision, the 1965 immigration act, leading (unexpectedly) to the mass immigration of low-skilled immigrants to the inner cities, also had some negative effects on the wages, employment prospects, and available housing stock of black youth and their families, although a recent review of the economic studies on the labor market impact of immigration concedes that this literature raises more questions than it answers (Bodvarsson and Van den Berg 2009, 133–55; see also Jaynes 2008, 87–101).

Turning now to the mainly cultural factors, the legal-cultural change culminating in the landmark *Roe v. Wade* Supreme Court decision (itself largely prompted by the politico-cultural movement of second-wave feminism) intersected with new birth-control medical technology to produce the reproductive technology shock, which had the unintended consequence of rapidly increasing the number of single-headed (mainly female) households (via its direct reduction of the cultural norm of shotgun marriages) and the liberation of female and male sexual values and norms of behavior. These changes influenced all ethnoracial groups and classes but was especially devastating for black women and their children, due to the long preexisting fragility of black male-female relationships and marriages. Elsewhere I have argued that this fragility goes all the way back to slavery and its two-and-a-half centuries of prohibition of formal marriage among blacks (Patterson 1998a, 44–70). The fact that the majority of black men and women were married prior to the 1960s does not invalidate my position. The tension between men and women persisted and may even have been made worse by the fact that women were forced by economic necessity to marry in spite of patriarchal treatment by their spouses because only black men held sharecropping titles during the Jim Crow era (white landowners extending their patriarchal biases to their sharecroppers). Furthermore, as Clarkwest (2005) demonstrates in his brilliant historical sociology of black marital disruption, premarital motherhood was always accepted among blacks, even during the period of higher marriage rates, and unlike whites, the image of the isolated and lonely "spinster" was far less prevalent. Hence, as the decision "whether or not to marry became increasingly elective rather than assumed, African American women were less constrained to marry when the options appeared poor," even though they continued to hope for better options (309). Both black men and black women seized the apparent liberation offered by the reproductive technology shock, although it would not be long before poor black women discovered that the cost of their liberation was the massive retreat of men from paternal responsibility and an upsurge of the inconsequential sexuality and biological fathering that had only been thinly veiled during the Jim Crow era, especially among the lower classes who, in any event, always had a much higher rate of out-of-wedlock births and single-mother households than working- and middle-class blacks and the rest of the American population. (White and black feminist women, too, would eventually begin to question whether "free sex" was really in their interests.)

The sexual revolution also had major wider consequences for both popular and middle-class mainstream culture. It intersected in important ways with the rise of youth culture, including the rapid emergence of rock-and-roll, which, as we noted earlier, marked a decisive shift in the role of vernacular black culture and its performers, rock-and-roll being simply the mainstreaming of one form of black vernacular music. These changes were to greatly influence both the black proletarian and middle-class cultural configurations and later stimulate the rise of the "golden age" of the hip-hop movement (early eighties to late nineties), which, it should be noted, was partly initiated by Jamaican and other West Indian migrants in the South Bronx (Hebdige 1990; Marshall, Chapter 4 this volume).

The positive influence of the proletarian and ghetto middle-class cultural configurations are mediated mainly through the stable households (marital and nonmarital) and cultural capital that they nurture, a major source of the latter being the intense religious faith and church attendance discussed above as well as in Chapter 8 of this volume. However, it is important to emphasize again that it is less the household structure and more their intersection (symbolized by x) with the kind of childrearing values and practices in both the stable and single-parent households that truly matter. Concerted and authoritative parenting are more likely to occur in stable two-parent households because of the greater resources and time that such households have to devote to their children as well as the greater likelihood of church attendance; however, where such households practice natural or authoritarian parenting, they are as likely to have deleterious consequences for children. Similarly, while authoritarian and natural parenting are more likely to occur in single-parent households resulting in child neglect and abuse, this is due less to being headed by a single woman (who with adequate resources and time is quite able to deploy the "promotive" and "preventive" parenting strategies, as Furstenberg calls them, that result in healthy children) and more to the amount of time she has to work, her lack of resources, and the stress of bringing up children in the ghetto without any individual or communal help (collective efficacy). Stable households and the cultural capital they generate act as buffers to the toxic stress of ghetto living, both directly and indirectly, through their protection from the dangers of the street culture and the now-dominant gangsta genre of the hip-hop configuration, especially during the high-risk period of late adolescence (Furstenberg et al. 1999, 171–213; Wingood et al. 2003).

Section 10. Concluding Reflections

While we have concentrated on the modern period, the awful plight of black youth is not new. We share Wacquant's (2001) view that their present condition must be placed within the historical context of racial oppression in America (see Patterson 1972; 2008). As we have seen, historians have found a similar constellation of problems going all the way back to the mid-nineteenth century. This tragedy has therefore been long in the making and is the cumulative outcome of two-and-a-half centuries of slavery, followed by another century of Jim Crow legalized terrorism. However, while it is true that America's prisons have acquired more and more the attributes of racial ghettos, we cannot quite support Wacquant's claim that the ghettos have at the same time become more like a prison. Mass imprisonment has certainly produced a "carceral mesh" that has had profound consequences for all black Americans living in the Black Belt, but there are two paradoxical elements of black-white relations in America that belie the claim that African Americans are prisoners in the ghettos.

The first is the fact that the great majority of black Americans are now fully integrated in the public and economic life of the country, even as they remain socially segregated. Black Americans are now an integral and powerful part of the civic life of the nation: in the last presidential election, they voted at a higher rate than whites; they are a major component of the Democratic party; and they hold offices at all levels of national life, including the presidency, the culmination of the political revolution initiated by the civil rights movement. The paradox here is that this quite remarkable level of civic integration (unparalleled among the heterogeneous, majority white nations of the world) has been accompanied by the stubborn persistence of high levels of social and residential segregation, a problem we have addressed elsewhere (Patterson 1997, 2008). Nor should we let the startling statistics on unemployment and incarceration among black youth blind us to the fact that these figures are far from true of the black population as a whole. In May 2013, the participation rate of blacks in the economy was 61.5 percent, only 2 percentage points behind that of whites, and their unemployment rate of 13.2 percent while deplorably high when compared with the white rate of 6.7 percent, nonetheless means that 87 percent of black Americans, including those in the middle- and working-class ghettos, are fully employed and connected to the mainstream economy, a rate that, in absolute comparative terms, is lower than the average of all the other advanced industrial nations (Bureau of Labor Statistics 2013). The reasons for the persistence of high levels of segregation, even among the middle classes, are complex and contentious; whatever they may be, the view that the black population in the ghettos are imprisoned there is unsustainable, even though it might in some real senses be true of the 20 percent who constitute the disconnected involved with the street culture.

Second, there is the paradox of mainstream popular culture, suffused with the creations of black youth from the ghetto: the age-old American pattern of cultural "love and theft" (Lott 1993) from the very group that is demonized and confined to the worst and most toxic regions of the ghetto. Understanding this paradox of cultural integration and social exclusion takes us to the heart of one of the abiding problems in the culture of American capitalism.

In his classic work *The Cultural Contradictions of Capitalism,* Daniel Bell (1976) argued that post-industrial American capitalism faced a cultural crisis in that its traditional legitimacy was built on a "moral system of reward, rooted in a Protestant sanctification of work" and an economizing system of rationality, efficiency, and discipline. At the same time, it thrives on, indeed requires, mass consumption and the glorification of plenty, which, along with long-simmering modernist and postmodernist antinomian cultural trends emphasize a "materialistic hedonism" as well as "anticognitive and anti-intellectual currents which are rooted in a return to instinctual modes" (54–61, 65–72, 84). The result of this contradiction "is that a corporation finds its people being straight by day and swingers by night" (xxv). Bell cites the "counterculture" of the 1960s and 1970s—extreme psychedelic experiences, sexual liberation, porno-pop, apocalyptic moods, the rise of a "hip-drug-rock culture on a popular level, and the 'new sensibility' of a black-mass ritual and violence in the arena of culture—as cultural actions that undermine the social structure itself" (54). However, within the realm of the counterculture, Bell finds another contradiction. It was no more than a "children's crusade" that was acting out what had long been the "closet behavior of its liberal parents" and grandparents: "it claimed to be new and daring when it was only repeating in more raucous form . . . the youthful japes of a Greenwich Village bohemia of a half century before. It was less a counter-culture than a counterfeit culture" (xxvii). To be sure, there were two major new features in what emerged with the sixties: first, the fact that unlike the avant-garde eudaemonism of their parents, the new counterculture made no distinction between art and reality—"what was previously played out in fantasy and imagination must be acted in life as well" (54). And secondly, what was previously practiced by a small bohemian elite is now practiced by many and is "acted out on the giant screen of the mass media" (54).

These important new features notwithstanding, the heart of the tension Bell described has long troubled the West. As he himself recognized, there was a long tradition in Western consciousness of a tension between the rational and irrational or instinctive, discipline and spontaneity, emotional restraint and hedonism, order and chaos. Nietzsche, whom he cites, had used the Greek metaphor of the Apollonian and the Dionysian to explore this tension in nineteenth-century Europe, especially his native Germany, one that earlier nineteenth-century writers such as Goethe had grappled with in terms of the opposition of the classical and the romantic (on which, see Del Caro 1989). What Bell did was to delineate the modern, American, capitalist version of this ancient antinomy. If there was a crisis, as Bell claimed, it would seem to have been well contained. But if so, how? And if a crisis existed and had been contained, who exactly paid the price for its resolution?

The answer lies in the cultural uses of black youth in America: the appropriation, near complete corporate control, and reconstruction of hip-hop as a "gangsta-pimp-ho" configuration within the broader fold of the mainstream serves the function of providing a perfect Dionysian antiphony to the disciplined, Apollonian call of the dominant culture. White youth, especially males of the baby-bust generation, find in gangsta rap's focus on violence, revenge, and thuggish claims of authenticity a sonic representation of their own darkest adolescent and early adult impulses, and a safe way to displace their repressed anger and dread at the hegemonic mainstream's tightening grip of middle-class normalcy and straightness on them, much as thrash metal and hardcore punk had done earlier. Or, in the words of Alexander Riley (2005), drawing on a tradition of neo-Durkheimian scholarship on popular culture, gangsta rap provides "a symbolic framework of orgiastic transgression and 'ex-stasis', which . . . is the literal stepping outside of the quotidian and mundane" (303).

A remarkable illustration of what is going on is given by Kitwana (2005) in his account of a group of middle class, white women in their late twenties and early thirties, who left their suburban Cleveland community on a girls-night-out visit to a sold-out hip-hop concert in Detroit. A thirty-three year old homemaker told him:

We spent our entire days trying to fit into a perfect little bubble. The perfect $500,000 houses. The perfect overscheduled kids. The perfect husbands. We love life, but we hate our lives. And so I think we identify more with hip-hop's passion, anger and frustration than we do this dream world. (5)

Hip-hop, Kitwana argues, is embraced by middle- and working-class white youth because it gives full expression to their own growing sense of alienation from the mainstream and their insecurities and "provides a public space that they can communicate within, unrestricted by the old obstacles" (78). No doubt; but this is too oversocialized an interpretation. More to the point is what his young, white female respondents told him. They come for the passion and to vent their anger and frustration, but more than anything else, we suspect, to be intoxicated by the sheer delirium and hedonistic abandonment of the hip-hop beat and wild, hypnotic energy. In the case of hip-hop groupies, white and black, they do so in order to have their fifteen minutes of fame at having "fucked a famous person," which in many cases, according to Sharpley-Whiting, is their exercise of agency as "self-assured women who have desires and who are firmly in control of their sexuality. They are not 'girls gone wild,' but women who have game . . . game enough to 'conquer and destroy' a hip-hop star for a night, several months or years" (2007, 109). Placing this in the broader context of America's current culture of capitalism, she adds:

> These freewheeling sexual practices are indeed individual choices that are at once coupled with the hedonism that hip-hop has come to signify and also our larger American cultural reflexes that celebrate capitalism, consumerism, and the individual over the collective. "Famously fucked" women dispense sexual favors in order to procure the capital and currency represented by the fame, power, and riches of the hip-hop star; and that currency in its turn is consumed, collected, and cosseted between thighs and lips. (110)

For a few, the intoxication can take them over the edge, the perennial danger of Dionysian excess, as was certainly the case with the young woman who, at a sold-out rap performance in Minneapolis by Danny Brown, ripped open his fly while he sang front stage, and like a character straight out of *The Bacchae* savagely consumed him (Pryde 2013).

For most, however, the hip-hop experience is not only cathartic but the expression of a desire for creative destruction, change, and becoming—what Nietzsche called Dionysian strength (Del Caro 1989, 601–02)—

providing just the right balance to the Apollonian order, structure, and control of their shrinking, hypercompetitive, bourgeois world.

Hip-hop performers are well aware of the fact that they are serving this psychocultural function and sometimes contemptuously mock their audience by letting them know they know. Jay-Z does it crudely: "I'm only tryin' to give you what you want / Nigga fuck shit, ass bitch, you like it, don't front." But just in case they take offense, he concludes, a bit lamely, "It's only entertainment." Kanye West, the ultimate Dionysian figure of rap, does it with devilish grace. He pumps his audience to hand-waving frenzy with mocking self-demonization: "Everybody know I'm a mutha-fucking monster / I'ma need to see your fucking hands at the concert . . . Less talk, more head right now, huh? / And my eyes more red than the devil is . . ." And in another, he doesn't even try to disguise his contempt: "Champagne wishes, 30 white bitches / I mean this shit is fucking ridiculous . . . By the way, what a way to act with me / We the black dynasty / These the days of our lives / Hating from the sidelines / Giving you the guidelines." It is hard to miss the cutting Dionysian punchline of the last word, for what better summarizes the Apollonian discipline of these corporate mainstreamers screaming at his feet: "straight by day, and swingers by night."

This use of the cultural constructions of black youth as a Dionysian counterbalance to the Apollonian demands of American capitalist culture is not entirely new. Of the white musicians and others attracted to jazz during the twenties, Levine (1977) has written: "It was not just the musical but the cultural freedom—the ability to be and express themselves, the sense of being natural—which they associated with jazz" (295). Much the same held for later white consumers of black culture: the hipsters and zoot suiters of the forties, the beatnicks and "white negroes" of the fifties celebrated by Norman Mailer, the swingers and rock-and-rollers of the sixties.

However there are two things that are startlingly new about the present white use of hip-hop and black street culture. First is the sheer scale of the white involvement—some 80 percent of hip-hop audience is white youth and young adults. Second, although blacks continue to dominate the performance of hip-hop, and hence remain a powerful and pervasive force among black youth, as we have seen, the content of the music itself, as well as its production, has been nearly completely taken over by the corporate entertainment system. In doing so, these coroporations not only receive most of the profit from what has become a $10 billion per year cultural industry, but they dictate the reconstruction and distortion of the musical genre into a form that, while it works perfectly as a Dionysian counterpoise for those already disciplined by their hyperscheduled suburban upbringing and schooling and the rigors of the corporate office, achieves just the opposite for the disconnected and deprived youth of the toxic ghettos— reinforcing their anger, misogyny, addiction, criminality, and violence— the destructive side of the Dionysian impulse that leads to chaos, the urge to disfigure and destroy all that is structured and enduring.

The only victims of their chaos, of course, are themselves and fellow blacks of the ghettos. To contain the chaos, to protect the orderly majority of working- and middle-class blacks who live in the inner cities, and to prevent any chance of their violence spilling out from the confines of the ghettos, there exists the vast network of profitmaking gulags that is America's prison-industrial complex. Thus the creative rage of the dispossessed resolves the cultural contradictions of post-industrial America and its bourgeois youth, even as it traps and eviscerates its creators in a matrix of internal self-destruction and external imprisonment.

II

BLACK YOUTH CULTURES ACROSS *the* NATION

3

The Values and Beliefs of Disconnected Black Youth

ETHAN FOSSE, *Harvard University*

There is growing concern among both policymakers and the general public that America's youth are becoming structurally disconnected from the dominant institutions of American society. These youth are neither in school nor at work, and their ranks have only grown in an era of systemically high unemployment and inequality (Bridgeland and Milano 2012). Black youth in particular have been affected, with some studies estimating that their disconnection level is upwards of 30 percent, even though many are in prison (Belfield et al. 2012; Burd-Sharps and Lewis 2013; Eckholm 2006; Smith et al. 2012). The economic consequences of the structural disconnection of America's youth, especially black youth who have historically been disadvantaged from a legacy of discrimination and slavery, have been widely discussed and debated (Belfield and Levin 2007; Mincy 2006). However, there has been much less attention on the likely cultural effects from such pervasive structural segregation and marginalization from the institutions of school and work (cf. Strayhorn 2009). In short, an outstanding question remains: are the structurally disconnected also culturally disconnected, and if so, in what ways?

In this chapter, I move beyond previous work on the structural disconnectedness of black youth by comparing four groups on their cultural values and beliefs: disconnected white youth, disconnected black youth, connected white youth, and connected black youth. Based on quantitative data from a wide variety of sources, the empirical analysis of the cultural views of disconnected black youth reveals a set of new findings. I examine six domains of values and beliefs: psychological health, sociocultural networks, work and school, risk and expectations, and American government and policy. The results are clear: on a wide range of values and beliefs, disconnected youth are more culturally divergent than their connected

139

counterparts. Substantively speaking, this means that disconnected black youth are less accepting of many of the values and beliefs of prototypical "mainstream" society, tending to view helping others as unimportant and reporting a lower tendency to engage in altruistic behaviors such as letting others in line, donating blood, or lending a valuable item to another person. Accordingly, disconnected black youth are much more pessimistic and cynical of the world around them, and compared to connected black youth, they have lower levels of psychological well-being. For example, disconnected black youth have markedly lower trust in governmental institutions and express much less overall satisfaction about the direction of their own lives. Additionally, they are considerably less likely to expect they will be employed full-time, graduate from college, or even survive young adulthood.

The empirical findings in this chapter show strong support for the argument that the structural disconnection of America's youth is not just an economic or demographic issue but a cultural one. Furthermore, the findings reinforce the view that structural disconnection interacts with race to impact profoundly the cultural lives of black youth in ways that are deeply worrying. In almost all cases, the evidence supports a *triplici discrimine* against black youth: not only are they suffering from structural disconnection and the continued barriers of racial segregation and discrimination, both historical and contemporary, but their situation is compounded further by the cultural effects of their disconnection from the institutions of work and school. By expressing often justified feelings of pessimism, cynicism, and distrust, inter alia, disconnected black youth are in danger of abandoning what has hitherto been a main source of hope and progress for black Americans: cultural resilience in the face of steep structural disadvantages.

The analysis in this chapter builds on previous work on disconnected youth by policymakers and social scientists (Besharov 1999; Bridgeland and Mason-Elder 2012; Edelman, Holzer, and Offner 2006; MaCurdy, Keating, and Nagavarapu 2006; Pfeiffer and Seiberlich 2010). However, most of this prior literature largely sidelines the cultural aspects of black youth, focusing instead on demographic and structural outcomes such as income, education, and employment. The work that does in fact examine structural disconnection and culture is limited (Jordan and Cooper 2003; MacDonald and Marsh 2001), with few in-depth analyses other than policy reports that provide a general overview without more complex analyses. The best work has been by qualitative researchers, who have documented in detail the emotional and psychological impact of structural disconnection (for example, see MacDonald 2008). This literature is often at odds with the relatively slim quantitative literature, which tends to show that disconnected youth are not strikingly different from their connected counterparts in nationally representative surveys of attitudes and values (cf. Bridgeland and Milano 2012).

The rest of this chapter is structured as follows. Part I describes the variety of data used in the analysis, the process of identifying disconnected youth, and the cultural dimensions of structural disconnection. Part II provides the empirical evidence in greater detail on the various values and attitudes of disconnected black youth compared to other youth. Finally, Part III concludes with the implications of the findings in this chapter as well as possibilities for further research on the cultural aspects of disconnected black youth.

Part I: Defining the Disconnected

The lack of systematic empirical research on how disconnected black youth fare relative to connected white and black youth on cultural outcomes is due in large part to data limitations. Few data sets have specified cultural values and beliefs while also having a sample size large enough to identify disconnected black youth. Furthermore, studies that have rigorous data on structural factors, such as employment and demographic characteristics, typically have no more than one or two variables that can be called cultural in any sense of the term. Thus, most studies on disconnected youth have focused on examining relations among structural factors.

To overcome these data limitations, I took a three-pronged approach. First, I gathered a large number of quantitative studies that have not only the minimum amount of information required to identify disconnected black youth, but also data related to their values and beliefs. Second, I focused on using data with black or youth oversamples to ensure that as many disconnected youth could be identified as possible. Finally, I sought to include data sets that allow for a relatively detailed set of control variables to ensure that estimates of the cultural values and beliefs of disconnected youth would not be ostensibly spurious. The final set of twenty-four data sources used in this chapter are shown in Table 3.1. Combined, these data sets sample over 50,000 individuals and cover a wide range of cultural variables, from mental health to perceived risks and expectations. All are nationally representative and have oversamples for youth or black

Americans. All cross-sectional studies were conducted by either landlines or cell phones with a random sampling technique, with the exception of the General Social Survey, which is based largely on face-to-face interviews. All three of the longitudinal studies in Table 3.1 are drawn from personal interviews supplemented with on-site questionnaires and computer-aided personal interviews to reduce response bias and ensure confidentiality. For all analyses in this chapter, I used sampling weights to ensure that the estimated findings are representative.

Who Are the Disconnected?

While most researchers and analysts agree that *disconnected* refers to those neither working nor in school, in practice there are varying approaches to measuring and classifying the level of disconnection.[1] There is greater agreement among researchers on the age of disconnected youth, with the majority of studies focusing on categorizing youth between the ages of sixteen to twenty-four who are neither in school nor working as disconnected. For the purposes of this chapter, I relied on self-report by the respondents on their labor force and educational participation to determine whether or not they were disconnected. Each data source included in this analysis has questions asking the respondent to indicate whether or not they are working full or part time, enrolled in school, unemployed, laid off, on disability, retired, or working as a homemaker. For all analyses, I classified full- or part-time respondents or those who were enrolled in school as connected, while those who were unemployed or laid off as disconnected. For all analyses, I also included those on disability, but neither at work nor in school, as structurally disconnected.[2] Those retired or working as homemakers were coded as missing for the purposes of this analysis. As shown in Table 3.1, all three studies examine youth as they transition through the eighteen to twenty-four age range of interest to researchers and policymakers. Finally, for race I relied on self-identification from the surveys, which, although differing, tended to produce similar estimates. Further analyses based on perceived race of the respondent by the interviewer yielded nearly identical results.

Although researchers differ somewhat regarding who is to be considered a disconnected youth (MaCurdy et al. 2006), the conceptualization used here is broadly consistent with previous measures of disconnection. Several categories of youth are excluded from being classified as disconnected. Across most studies, part-time students are not considered disconnected, but this suggests that some estimates of disconnection may

Table 3.1. Structural Disconnection of White and Black Youth by Survey Type, 2000–2012

Survey Type	Year	White Disconnected	Black Disconnected	Youth Subset
Longitudinal				
Add Health (Wave 3)	2001–2002	11.8%	26.5%	18–28*
Add Health (Wave 4)	2007–2009	13.9%	21.0%	25–34*
General Social Survey Panel (Wave 1)	2006	7.8%	12.6%	18–34
General Social Survey Panel (Wave 2)	2008	9.1%	21.8%	20–36
General Social Survey Panel (Wave 3)	2010	8.5%	16.5%	22–38
National Longitudinal Study of Youth 1997 (Round 4)	2000	5.5%	13.6%	16–21*
National Longitudinal Study of Youth 1997 (Round 10)	2006	7.9%	16.5%	22–27*
National Longitudinal Study of Youth 1997 (Round 12)	2008	7.9%	15.5%	24–29*
National Longitudinal Study of Youth 1997 (Round 15)	2011	12.6%	23.3%	27–32*
Cross-Sectional				
General Social Survey	2000	4.0%	7.1%	18–34
National Survey of American Life	2001	7.1%	19.9%	18–24*
General Social Survey	2002	7.2%	10.6%	18–34
American Mosaic Project Survey	2003	9.5%	14.7%	18–34
Emerging Adulthood Survey	2004	13.9%	21.8%	18–24*
General Social Survey	2004	5.7%	8.8%	18–34
Youth Culture Survey	2005	8.1%	13.8%	15–25*
African-American Men Survey	2006	7.9%	12.9%	18–34
General Social Survey	2006	7.1%	11.0%	18–34
Generation Next Survey	2006	15.0%	25.8%	18–25*
Racial Attitudes in America Survey	2007	18.1%	21.1%	18–34
Race Relations Survey	2008	12.6%	23.7%	18–34

Table 3.1. *(continued)*

Survey Type	Year	White Disconnected	Black Disconnected	Youth Subset
General Social Survey	2008	8.2%	15.1%	18–34
Capitalism Survey	2010	19.4%	35.0%	18–34
General Social Survey	2010	9.6%	11.1%	18–34
Millennial Survey	2010	20.4%	23.4%	18–29*
Black Women in America	2011	13.0%	19.9%	18–34
Youth and Economy Survey	2011	16.7%	28.0%	18–34
Teens and Digital Citizenship Survey	2011	15.0%	23.0%	14–17
General Social Survey	2012	7.5%	15.0%	18–34
Millennial Values Survey	2012	19.7%	23.0%	18–24*
	Average	12.6%	19.7%	

Notes: Table shows percentage of disconnected youth by racial group. All estimates are adjusted using sampling weights. *Indicates the survey is based on an oversample of youth.

be on the low side, since many youth now take online classes and thus qualify, in a formal sense, as part-time students. Similarly, part-time workers are also not classified as disconnected youth. Given the increase in temporary jobs, as well as online ad hoc employment, this, too, likely leads to an underestimate of the level of disconnection among youth. As well, even if youth are looking for a job, they are classified as disconnected if they are nonetheless neither working nor in school. Some studies exclude from the disconnected category those who are actively looking for work, but this determination is not possible for all data sources used in this chapter. As well, again consistent with most other studies, youth in the military are not considered disconnected.[3] Lastly, when the data were available, I coded respondents living in institutions (such as the military or medical establishments) as connected, even if they were unemployed and not in school.

Table 3.1 above shows the percent of youth who are structurally disconnected in the twenty-four studies used in this chapter. The longitudinal surveys track the same individuals over time as they transition to adulthood, while the cross-sectional surveys are based on a different randomly-selected sample of the population. Analyses based on the American Community Survey, a 1 percent subsample of the U.S. Census,

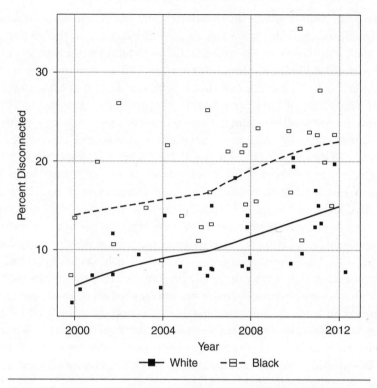

Figure 3.1. Percent disconnected youth by race, 2000–2012

estimate that about 23.5 percent of black youth aged eighteen to twenty-four were structurally disconnected in 2010, in contrast to 11.5 percent of white youth (Wight et al. 2010). These national-level estimates, based on demographic data as well as survey results, correspond well with the overall estimates from the longitudinal and cross-sectional surveys shown in Table 3.1. Based on the longitudinal data sets, on average I estimate that since 2000 approximately 18.6 percent of black youth are structurally disconnected compared to 11.4 percent of white youth. I find a similar but narrower gap for the cross-sectional surveys, although the gap is somewhat smaller. These findings are consistent with previous research, which shows that across various measures the disconnection rate of black youth is roughly double that of white youth (Burd-Sharps and Lewis 2013; Wight et al. 2010).

In Figure 3.1, the estimated level of structural disconnection for white and black youth is plotted over time for all of the data sets analyzed overlaid with a fitted curve giving the overall trend by race. Consistent with prior research, the estimates here show an alarming increase in the percentage of black youth who are structurally disconnected over the past decade,[4] reflecting conditions of rising inequality and joblessness not only in the wake of the 2008 financial crisis but well before. The fitted curve suggests that nearly 25% of black youth were structurally disconnected in 2012, consistent with 2010 findings from the American Community Survey (Wight et al. 2010). In contrast, although they, too, have experienced an increase in disconnection, white youth have remained below 15 percent.

The structural disadvantages facing black youth are indeed severe, as shown in the estimates above. The high measures expressed here are worth comparing to another, related measure of structural disconnection: the employment-to-population ratio. For black youth aged sixteen to twenty-four, as of 2010 the percentage employed was 34.4 percent, compared with the national average for all youth, which was 48.9 percent. As a robustness check, I calculated the same measures for all samples used in this analysis and obtained similar percentages for black youth versus all youth. This lends credence that the disconnection measures used for the analyses in this chapter reflect those used by demographic researchers and policy analysts. In total, the findings here suggest that upwards of seven million youth are structurally disconnected, with black youth representing a sizable and growing share of this population.

The consequences of structural disconnection are striking: higher rates of poverty, delayed or absent transitions to adulthood, and lower levels of educational attainment. Indeed, according to nationally-representative survey data from 2011, I find that structural disconnection among black youth is related systematically to a number of related experiences of disadvantage and poverty. Compared to connected black youth, those who are structurally disconnected are more likely to say they or another family member living in their household have, in the past year, been laid off or lost a job (39.2 percent versus 18.3 percent), lost health insurance coverage (32.8 percent versus 18.7 percent), had problems paying medical bills (44.0 percent versus 39.6 percent), had problems paying their rent or mortgage (33.1 percent versus 27.0 percent), had difficulty getting a loan from a bank or any other type of personal credit (45.8 percent versus 29.6 percent), and had increased their credit card debt (43.6 percent versus 20.7 percent).[5]

These patterns accord with those for young adults more generally: those who are disconnected for three or more years are about fourteen times more likely to be poor and earn about two-and-one-half times less in earnings and are about two to three times less likely to be employed full time than young adults who had never been disconnected (Wight et al. 2010). The demographic consequences are also striking, with traditional markers of adulthood delayed or absent altogether. For example, survey and demographic research shows that young adults, especially black youth, are more frequently delaying or avoiding marriage and childbearing. Previous research has documented extensively that children are living at home longer than they were thirty years ago (Besharov 1999). For instance, in 1970 about 47 percent of young adults aged eighteen to twenty-four were living at home. However, by 2009 young adults living at home had increased to nearly 53 percent. As well, youth are staying in school longer. Simlarly, nearly 30 percent of young adults were enrolled in school in 1970 but by 2008, the percentage of young adults enrolled had reached over 45 percent.

Part II: The Cultural Aspects of Disconnected Youth

In this section, I describe the main facts about the cultural values and beliefs of disconnected black youth on the six main cultural domains discussed in the previous section: psychological well-being (e.g., life satisfaction, measures of self-esteem and anxiety, concerns related to physical safety), sociocultural networks (e.g., beliefs on the diversity of one's social network as well as measures of trust in others), risk and expectations (e.g., positive evaluations of risky behaviors and self-assessment regarding future expectations), orientations toward work and school (e.g., values toward having a socially meaningful and high-paying occupation, respondent's views on the importance of school), community and social problems (e.g., importance of what is causing declining marriage rate among blacks, importance of causes of black men becoming incarcerated, quality of life for black men in America, opinions of rap and hip-hop music, portrayal of black men in the media), and American government and policy (e.g., trust in institutions and interest in political affairs). In total, the full number of estimated outcomes is 250. Given the number of estimates, results are described by focusing on a snapshot summary of the estimates pooled across all surveys as well as a smaller set of differences for discussion and interpretation. I first turn to the snapshot summary of the results for each of the cultural domains.

Figure 3.2 presents the main results from the regression analyses for all 250 outcomes pooled by the cultural domain. From each of these domains, an adjusted mean was calculated for each group defined by the cross tabulation of race and structural disconnection. In this analysis, the reference category is connected white youth, with disconnected black youth, connected black youth, and disconnected white youth as the comparison groups. For this overall snapshot, scores for all outcome variables have been normalized so that a relative ranking can be visualized.[6] For each cultural domain, higher values can be interpreted as "better," and lower values are "worse." For example, referring to the first set of coefficients in Figure 3.2, a higher value for psychological well-being implies higher levels of self-esteem, lower levels of anxiety, and lower incidence of depression, among other items.

The overall findings are striking: although there is some variation in the outcomes, disconnected black youth are consistently the most divergent on a range of outcomes as compared to white disconnected, black connected, and white connected youth. Moreover, they are the most consistently "worse" on each of these cultural domains. I turn to each of these cultural domains referred to in Figure 3.2. Regarding psychological well-being, the summary indicates that white youth have the highest level of reported psychological well-being, followed by connected black youth and disconnected white youth, with disconnected black youth lowest. Despite relatively high scores on some self-esteem measures, the findings here indicate that disconnected black youth are still at an elevated risk of worse psychological outcomes. In terms of sociocultural networks, the findings here show that black youth report the most disconnection across all groups, with the least diverse social networks and the lowest levels of trust in others. Turning to values and beliefs toward work and school, the findings further suggest that disconnected black youth are the most pessimistic, with the most negative evaluations toward occupations and work. Regarding risk and expectations, the findings show that disconnected black youth are the most likely to positively evaluate risky behaviors and have negative views about their future success in life. The next cultural domain concerns community and social problems. In general, disconnected black youth express highly critical and negative views toward the social problems facing their communities, but in this respect they are not substantially different from disconnected white youth overall. Particular attention to rap and hip-hop music is warranted: disconnected black youth are by far the most critical of these forms of media. These findings are

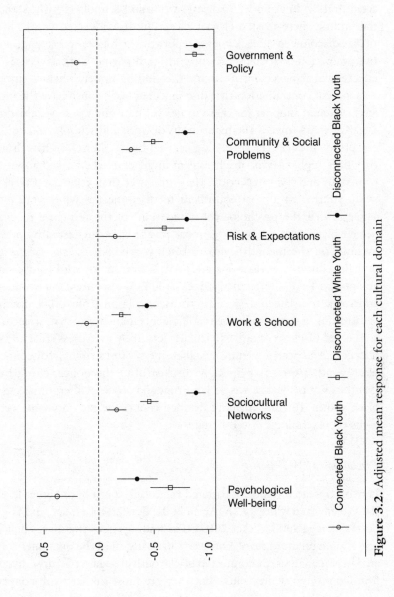

Figure 3.2. Adjusted mean response for each cultural domain

consistent with the general negative attitudes and values expressed by those who are disconnected structurally.

The snapshot findings here are consistent with those expected from youth who are structurally disconnected from the twin institutions of acculturation in American society: work and school. Notwithstanding, the findings here mask a crucial exception: disconnected youth, in particular disconnected black youth, report by the highest percentage a positive evaluation of socially meaningful, high-paying work as well as high educational achievement. I discuss this finding in detail below, since it is an apparent contradiction that disconnected black youth have the highest level of stated support for these values yet have the most pessimistic and negative views toward the institutions of work and school. An additional exception concerns the psychological well-being of black youth: although they have higher levels of self-esteem in general, when asked about their own skills and life satisfaction, they are lower than connected black and white youth and almost equivalent to disconnected white youth. This suggests that the psychological foundations of the resilience of disconnected black youth may be far more fragile than suggested by previous findings on the mental health of black youth. Finally, the last cultural domain concerns evaluations and beliefs toward American government and policy. To put it succinctly, does structural disconnection from school and work translate into a cultural disconnection from other dominant institutions of American society? The general answer is that, indeed, disconnected black youth are particularly less likely to express trust and confidence in American government and business. Most strikingly, disconnected black youth are overwhelmingly distrustful of the police, citing beliefs that the criminal justice system is corrupt and prone to discriminate against black youth. Turning to more detailed results for each domain, we first focus on psychological well-being.[7]

Psychological Well-Being

Previous research has demonstrated that black youth have higher levels of self-esteem than white youth (Ajzen 2001; Forster, Liberman, and Higgins 2005; Twenge and Crocker 2002). The findings from the survey data portray a more nuanced story, however. On nearly all of the outcomes considered in this analysis, disconnected black youth are again the most divergent from connected white youth, but they are most similar to disconnected white youth. This implies that, as expected, structural disconnection may have profoundly negative cultural consequences, leading to higher levels of anxiety, depression, and stress overall. In the aggregate, the results on psychological well-being are consistent with the interpretation that structural disconnection is emotionally and ideationally harmful.

Beginning with general measures of psychological well-being, compared to their connected counterparts, disconnected black youth are much less likely to say that they are very satisfied with their life as a whole these days (40.3 percent versus 52.6 percent) and are less likely to agree strongly that they have a high self-esteem (69.0 percent versus 53.7 percent).[8] Similarly, black youth who are disconnected are much more likely to say they are not too happy with their lives (32.2 percent versus 7.1 percent). The findings also show that in the past year, disconnected black youth are much more likely to say they have rarely laughed (16.0 percent) or cried (29.1 percent), consistent with the claim that emotional expression is restricted among many black youth.

Additionally, structural disconnection is related to elevated levels of perceived stress. For example, disconnected black youth are more likely to say they frequently experience stress in their daily lives (38.1 percent versus 33.3 percent). Accordingly, disconnected black youth also express higher levels of worry on various aspects of their daily life, such as not getting adequate health care (62.0 percent versus 37.5 percent), getting HIV/AIDS (51.3 percent versus 25.8 percent), being a target of a violent crime (34.7 percent versus 23.6 percent), experiencing discrimination of any kind (51.4 percent versus 27.0 percent), providing for an aging family member (46.9 percent versus 1.1 percent), and experiencing or having a family member suffering a chronic illness (37.2 percent versus 33.6 percent).[9] They are also much less likely to be satisfied with their housing situation (53.8 percent versus 44.3 percent). Perhaps more striking, black youth are more likely than those who are connected to say that in the past month things have not been going their way (50.1 percent versus 21.3 percent), that they've been losing hope either very often or somewhat often (66.3 percent versus 20.3 percent), and that they have been unable to control the important things in their life (59.7 percent versus 44.2 percent).

As another aspect of psychological well-being, I also examine questions related to their future and life goals. Disconnected black youth are also less likely to believe they will have a better life compared to their parents.

I find that 77.9 percent of disconnected black youth think they will have a better life than their parents, while 88.4 percent of connected black youth think this will be the case. Similarly, a smaller percentage say they are mostly optimistic about their future: 73.4 percent in contrast to 82.3 percent. Additionally, when asked to consider the standard of living for their children, disconnected black youth are less likely to say the condition will be much better (45.2 percent versus 53.7 percent). More generally, findings show that 65.6 percent of disconnected black youth are more optimistic than pessimistic, while 69.7 percent of connected black youth view their future this way.

Sociocultural Networks

Regarding sociocultural networks, previous research on structurally disconnected youth has focused on their economic and educational outcomes (Edelman et al. 2006), but far less research has examined the sociocultural networks of structurally disconnected youth. Findings reveal that, across a wide range of analyses related to sociocultural networks, disconnected youth in fact fare much worse than their connected counterparts, with black youth particularly affected.

I first turn to the diversity of the social networks of disconnected versus connected black youth. While 14.4 percent of disconnected black youth say all or most of their close friends are of a different race, over 28.0 percent of connected black youth say this is the case for them. I find similar lower levels of cross-race interactions for disconnected youth when they describe not only their day-to-day interactions but also their neighborhoods and communities.[10] Likewise, analyses show that there's a 44 percent chance that disconnected black youth rarely see whites in their daily social interactions, while this number is 12 percent for connected black youth. Reflecting their relative structural segregation, the findings further show lower levels of trust among disconnected black youth. For instance, while there's a 78 percent chance connected white youth trust others in their community, there's only a 24 percent chance of disconnected black youth saying they trust others.

Consistent with these results, disconnected black youth are more likely to say that other people do not treat them with respect, with 29 percent saying disrespect occurs very often in their daily life in contrast to 14.6 percent of connected youth. Furthermore, black youth say that people often act as though they're not smart (15.5 percent versus 8.7 percent), and people ignore or overlook them (30.1 percent versus 24 percent).[11] Additionally, black youth who are disconnected say that other people act as if they are afraid of them (20.0 percent versus 14.0 percent) or that they are dishonest (20.1 percent versus 14.2 percent). The evidence also suggests that disconnected black youth have resigned to such apparent mistreatment, with a smaller percentage of those who are disconnected likely to say that being respected by others is very important (63.4 percent versus 71.7 percent).

As another aspect of sociocultural networks, I examine the effect of structural disconnection on measures of perceived societal conflict. For example, the data indicate that disconnected black youth are also more likely to say that racism is a big problem in society (61.1 percent versus 44.9 percent) as well as sexism (63.6 percent versus 36.8 percent). Yet black youth who are disconnected are less likely to believe there are strong conflicts between young people and older people (28.3 percent versus 44.0 percent), poor people and rich people (61.0 percent versus 84.2 percent), and immigrants and people born in the United States (43.4 percent versus 76.2 percent). They are, however, more likely than connected black youth to think there are conflicts between black and white Americans (58.2 percent versus 48.5 percent). This finding is consistent with the greater structural segregation of disconnected black youth, who report having fewer interactions with white Americans than their connected counterparts.

Risk, Expectations, and Decision Making

Previous research has shown that disconnected youth are more likely to engage in risky behaviors, such as drug abuse, criminal activity, and unprotected casual sex (Turner et al. 2011). However, much less is known about the values and beliefs of disconnected youth in regards to risky activities. As shown in Figure 3.2, based on an index of all the surveys, I find some evidence (albeit mixed) that disconnected youth are more likely to express favorable views toward behaviors that are risky. For example, I find that on an index of views about whether or not they prefer risky behaviors such as unprotected sex, out-of-wedlock births, and drug abuse, disconnected black youth are more likely than their connected counterparts to express a higher preference. Furthermore, findings indicate that disconnected black youth have a 52 percent chance of agreeing with the statement that "I'm a person who likes to take risks" as opposed to 27 percent of connected black youth. I examined for interaction effects with gender, and as expected, I found statistically significant differences, with men more likely than women to prefer taking risks. I also examined the expectations youth had about their own futures. The results are sobering: disconnected black youth are much less likely than connected black youth to believe they will live to age 30 (94 percent versus 75 percent), eventually become married (85 percent versus 72 percent), and earn a middle-class income by age 35 (74 percent versus 38 percent).[12] In sum, I find some evidence that structural disconnection is systematically related not just to the enactment of risky behaviors but to preferences for risk taking as well as negative expectations about one's own future.

Work and School

I now turn to values and beliefs related to work and school. Previous survey research on disconnected youth has shown that 85 percent of disconnected youth say that it is "extremely important" to have a good job or career in order to live the life they want (Bridgeland and Milano 2012). Additionally, most disconnected youth say they are personally responsible for their futures, with 77 percent agreeing that getting a good education and job is their own responsibility (ibid.). Our findings are broadly consistent with these unadjusted estimates. In fact, disconnected black youth are, if anything, more likely than their connected counterparts to report that a career is "very important" in their lives (94.2 percent versus 87.3 percent). Moreover, this evaluation does not vary meaningfully by gender, with young black men and women saying at equally high levels that they value a career in their lives. Similarly, I find few differences between connected and disconnected black youth in the importance they attach to being wealthy: in fact, if anything, disconnected black youth value being wealthy even more than those who are connected (25.1 percent versus 37.0 percent). Additionally, the findings show that black youth are willing to sacrifice job security and a socially meaningful career for a higher income. While 90.1 percent of connected black youth think having a career that benefits society is highly important, 64.1 percent of disconnected black youth feel this way. However, nearly 94.0 percent of disconnected black youth say being successful in a high-paying career or profession is highly important, compared to 70.1 percent of connected black youth. In fact, when asked to choose between job security versus a higher-paying career, disconnected black youth are more likely to prefer a high-paying career (50.2 percent versus 36.5 percent) over job security (48.2 percent versus 60.0 percent).

Although highly valuing a successful career, disconnected black youth express an elevated level of pessimism and awareness of the barriers they face. For example, disconnected black youth are much more likely than connected black youth to worry about not having enough money to pay for their bills (64.6 percent versus 45.0 percent) and providing a good education for their children (69.3 percent versus 50.0 percent). Disconnected black youth also see greater barriers to college, with 53.4 percent saying that it's harder to get into college today than for their parents' generation (compared to 41.9 percent for connected black youth). Additionally, 40.5 percent of disconnected black youth say they are very dissatisfied with their current financial situation, compared to just 20.0 percent of connected black youth.

Disconnected black youth are also surprisingly self-critical of their educational and occupational skills. For example, when asked to assess their own financial literacy on a grading scale from A to F, disconnected black youth generally report a lower report card, with 37.0 percent giving themselves a grade of C or lower compared to connected black youth, of which 26.9 percent give themselves such a grade. Disconnected black youth are also aware of the barriers they face, with 63.8 percent saying they do not have the skills or education to compete in the workforce (compared to 51.0 percent of connected black youth). Additionally, disconnected black youth are more likely to say that acquiring such skills is somewhat or very difficult (51.2 percent versus 38.4 percent).

Consistent with their self-assessment of the barriers they face, the findings show that disconnected black youth express high levels of discontentment with their occupational history.[13] For instance, among those youth who are structurally connected, there is a stark contrast in how they perceive their current job. Just 10.8 percent of black youth view their current job as a career, while 37.7 percent of connected white youth view their current job as a career. Moreover, just over 50.0 percent of black youth say that their current job is "just another job" and a little less than 40.0 percent say it's a "stepping stone to a career." Similarly, black youth who are disconnected are less likely to say they are very or somewhat satisfied with their educational attainment (61.0 percent versus 72.4 percent). Accordingly, 71.6 percent of disconnected black youth say they do not have the education and training necessary to obtain the kind of job they want.

As an additional measure of values and beliefs toward work and school, I examine how disconnected and connected black youth responded to the worsening economic conditions since the 2008 financial crisis. When asked how they have adjusted their life due to economic conditions in 2011, disconnected black youth report making more adjustments than connected black youth. In particular, a higher percentage say that in the past few years they have had to move back with their parents after living on their own (15.8 percent versus 13.4 percent), postponed having a baby (26.5 percent versus 21.8 percent), gone back to school at some point (26.5 percent versus 21.8 percent), and taken an unpaid job just to gain work experience (33.4 percent versus 21.2 percent). Most strikingly, 77.3 percent of disconnected black youth say they have taken a job they did not really want "just to pay the bills," compared with 52.8 percent of connected black youth. However, disconnected black youth are less likely to say they have postponed getting married (16.2 percent versus 24.9 percent) or going back to school (36.3 percent versus 53.0 percent).

Community and Social Issues

The analyses summarized in Figure 3.2 also included a cultural domain related to community and social problems. For these analyses, I focused in particular on problems facing majority-black communities such as out-of-wedlock births and an elevated rate of violence by young black men as well as values and beliefs toward rap and hip-hop music. The findings show that in general disconnected black youth hold more negative evaluations of their communities and social problems.[14] I find few aggregate differences in terms of structural disconnection regarding the declining marriage rate of black youth and possible reasons why black men are more likely to be incarcerated. However, there are large, statistically significant differences on the problems facing black families and communities, with disconnected youth consistently more likely to say that issues such as out-of-wedlock births and joblessness are "very big" problems. Furthermore, I find that disconnected black youth are particularly critical of black men as well as rap and hip-hop music. For example, disconnected black youth have a 74 percent chance of saying that black men "don't take their education seriously enough" as opposed to 62 percent of connected black youth.

I also examined the values and beliefs of black youth toward rap and hip-hop music, with the findings similarly showing that disconnected youth are especially critical of these musical forms. For example, compared to their connected counterparts, disconnected black youth are more likely to say rap and hip-hop music "places too much emphasis on sex" (64 percent to 52 percent), is "demeaning toward black women" (51 percent to 43 percent), does "not focus enough on political issues" (30 percent to 5 percent), and "has too much bad language" (20 percent to 15 percent). In short, across a range of issues facing their communities including the role of rap and hip-hop music in their lives, disconnected black youth are among the most critical, consistently reporting more negative evaluations and beliefs.

I focus here in particular on the values and beliefs black youth have toward marriage, given the importance of the topic and the degree to which it is widely discussed. The findings from the surveys show that disconnected black youth are less likely than those who are connected to say that being married is a very important value in their lives (35.2 percent in contrast to 47.9 percent).[15] I additionally find that connected young black men are more likely than connected young black women to say that this is very important (49.1 percent versus 32.8 percent); among disconnected black youth, this gender difference is smaller but still apparent (36.8 percent versus 29.0 percent). However, disconnected black youth are more likely to say that they value being in a good romantic relationship, with 58.6 percent saying this is very important in contrast to 48.2 percent of connected black youth. Furthermore, a higher percentage of young black men than women say this very important (56.8 percent versus 48.8 percent). Additionally, black youth are more likely to value being a good parent, with 57.0 percent of young black women and 53.7 percent of young black men saying this is "one of the most important things" in their life.

Consistent with prior research, there is strong evidence of intergenerational differences in values toward marriage and having children, with younger cohorts of black Americans much less likely to say either being married or having children is a very important value in their lives. However, the one exception concerns connected black youth who, compared to older cohorts, are slightly more likely to say being married is very important to them (47.5 percent for those below thirty-five years of age in contrast to 39.1 percent for those above age thirty-five).[16] Likewise, there is evidence of a generational difference in values toward having children.

While 57.1 percent of black youth aged eighteen to thirty-four say having children is "very important," this percentage is 62.6 percent for black Americans aged thirty-five to forty-nine and 66.0 percent for those sixty-five years or older.[17]

Regarding values toward children, I find evidence that disconnected black women are much more likely to value having children (75.7 percent) compared to connected black women (57.9 percent). However, for young black men, the pattern is reversed, with connected black men more likely to value having children (61.6 percent) compared to disconnected young black men (45.6 percent). Likewise, when asked about whether nor not they think abortion or having a child while not being married is morally wrong, black youth who are connected are more likely to strongly agree that abortion and having children out of wedlock are morally wrong. Specifically, 11.0 percent of disconnected black youth say they strongly agree that abortion is morally wrong (compared to 27.8 percent of connected black youth), while 1.4 percent say the same about having a child out of wedlock (compared to 10.9 percent of connected black youth).

Government and Society

The final cultural domain concerns views on government and society more generally, including aspects of social policy. As expected, I find that disconnected black youth report the lowest levels of trust in American government and business. For example, there is a 55 percent chance that disconnected black youth will say big business "should not be trusted" compared to 48 percent for connected black youth. I similarly find that disconnected black youth have negative evaluations of law enforcement, with 72 percent saying the police "should never be trusted" compared to 51 percent for connected black youth. Additionally, findings show that disconnected black youth are considerably more likely to say they are very or somewhat worried that they will be unfairly treated by the police (44.2 percent versus 26.0 percent).

Another aspect of government and policy concerns the views that black youth have toward government and policy making more generally. The results show that disconnected black youth in contrast to connected black youth are less likely to say they believe voting is important (73 percent to 84 percent) and that government is responsive to the needs of "people like them" (45 percent to 71 percent). As well, I find that, compared to their connected counterparts, disconnected black youth are much more likely to say "a conspiracy is behind things in the world" (32 percent to 20 percent). There is some limited evidence that disconnected black youth are also more likely than connected youth to view the economic system as inherently unfair and "stacked against" black Americans, although these do not reach conventional levels of statistical significance.

Lastly, as another aspect of government and social policy, I examined the beliefs of disconnected youth on the legitimacy of the economic system. The data show that there are few differences between disconnected and connected black youth in their views on whether the American economic system is "stacked against blacks." While 35 percent of connected black youth think the system is stacked against them, 31.6 percent of disconnected black youth report this belief. Additionally, when asked about what matters in getting ahead in life today, overwhelming majorities of connected and disconnected black youth say that getting a good education and working hard are more important than coming from money and knowing the right people (79.5 percent compared to 73.8 percent, respectively).[18] In sum, across a range of outcomes, I find that disconnected youth, especially black youth, express values and beliefs that are negative and distrustful of the American political and economic system.

Part III: Discussion and Conclusion

Since at least the 1970s, there has been a steady increase in the number of youth who are neither in the workforce nor in school, especially among black youth. While a great deal of research has described the structural aspects of disconnected black youth, very little has examined the cultural aspects. In this chapter, I used quantitative data tracking the same youth over time to examine the effects of structural disconnection on the values and beliefs of black and white youth. Of note is that these findings are among the first to show that structurally disconnected black youth are in turn culturally divergent on a wide set of cultural beliefs and values (see also Carter 2003; O'Donnell et al. 2003; Woods and Jagers 2003).

Broadly summarizing, the results show striking evidence of a growing cultural disjuncture between disconnected youth and their connected counterparts, with black youth in general holding more negative evaluations and beliefs.[19] Specifically, in comparison to connected black youth, disconnected black youth have much lower levels of psychological well-being, lower levels of trust in others and less diverse sociocultural networks, more negative views toward the institutions of work and school, a higher preference for risk taking along with lowered expectations about their own futures, more critical views toward the problems in their communities and the role of rap and hip-hop music in society, and less trust in the fairness of American government and the economic system. In this respect, disconnected black youth are culturally divergent from connected youth, who overall have more positive evaluations and beliefs on each of these dimensions.

One exception worth pointing out is that black youth who are structurally disconnected are the most likely to say they strongly value a socially meaningful, high-paying career as well as educational advancement, even while expressing negative evaluations of the institutions of work and school. One explanation for this apparent discrepancy between strongly valuing work and school while reporting negative evaluations of the institutions of school and work is related to the distinction between descriptive and injunctive norms (see Orlando Patterson, Chapter 1). Descriptive norms are based on what other people do. For example, black youth may be more likely to commit robberies because it is more common among their peers. In contrast, an injunctive norm is based on what other people approve of. For instance, a youth with many peers who commit robberies may nonetheless say that robbery is "wrong," since this is the injunctive norm. In this sense, black youth may in fact be reporting on the basis of injunctive norms regarding whether or not they value work and school but on the basis of descriptive norms when asked to evaluate particular aspects of work and school.

Another issue worth attention concerns the relationship between structural disconnection and cultural disjuncture. As discussed in the section on the model of interactivity between structure and culture, it is not a determinant conclusion that disconnected black youth would diverge culturally. Why does this kind of structural disconnection lead to a corresponding albeit less salient cultural disconnection? Structural disconnection is in fact a de facto removal from the two main institutions of cultural transmission in contemporary American society: the workplace and school. The mainstream values and norms transmitted in these cultural sites are not transmitted if no one is present. Consistent with social learning, it is widely known that behaviors that are acquired or modified by individual learning can subsequently be transmitted and social learning can be biased so that some variants are more likely to be transmitted than others. These processes are modeled as deviations from accurate, unbiased transmission. To the extent that black youth are disconnected even partially, these deviations will be much greater, leading to a stunted or even non-existent cultural transmission through the institutions of school and work. Furthermore, the overall finding that disconnected black youth are not just structurally disconnected but the most culturally divergent from the main categories of race and disconnection is not necessarily to be interpreted in a wholly negative light.

First, cultural divergence also implies cultural cohesion. For example, as shown in the findings on religious beliefs and values, the turning away of black youth from their religious beliefs may in fact make them more similar to white youth. Similarly, on several measures, white youth who are disconnected are in fact more similar to black youth who are disconnected than their connected pairs. Second, cultural divergence may lead to a political or social movement to change the existing power structure, as has been advocated by the sociologist William Julius Wilson (Wilson 1987, 2010). Although unlikely given the current political motivations and engagement of black youth today, this may nonetheless be the basis for greater social change. Third, cultural divergence as it is related to structural disconnection is in one sense a symptom of how people are thinking and feeling in ways that "make sense." For example, it is not bad itself to distrust the government when the government is guilty of corruption or other forms of malfeasance or when leaders express contempt for the poor and disconnected. Fourth, cultural divergence, even when unrelated to any particular scientific or artistic cultural domain, can nonetheless lead to cultural innovations through boundary spanning and transmission (for a related point, see Chapter 4 by Wayne Marshall on hip-hop music).[20] Similar innovations have occurred among black youth in the area of hip-hop and rap. Finally, it should be emphasized that cultural divergence is not unique to the youth studied in this chapter. As long as people have been on this planet, there has been cultural change through structural disruptions (Kaufman and Patterson 2005).[21]

Notwithstanding, there is also a dark side to the results presented in this chapter (for a similar point, see Cherry 1995). Structural disconnection and cultural divergence, in unison, has the potential to cause enormous suffering beyond what is already occurring. When American youth lose hope, and there are few structural or political changes to improve their situation, the danger is that they will further separate structurally and culturally. This may in fact be a problem if normative views rejecting occupational mobility and educational attainment become more widespread, views that are counterproductive at best and self-destructive at worst. Ultimately, the disconnected structural position of black youth is nothing new, although it has become more decisive in recent years (Jordan and Cooper 2003; Lomax 2000; Sullivan 2003). Indeed, in the history of racial and class relations in the United States, it is surprising that severely disadvantaged groups have not risen en masse, as is often hoped by social reformers. The policy implication is to ignore the structural realities or listen to what the culture of black youth are telling us. Many scholars often bemoan the decline of various forms of cultural cohesion (Bell 1965; Coward, Feagin, and Williams 1974; Eisenstadt 1986), but this is in some respects a potentially facile understanding to the problems at hand. Distrust, or any other "undesirable" cultural outcome is not ipso facto to be bemoaned when it is in fact warranted by the structural conditions in which people live every day. It is both a rationally bounded way of dealing with life's realities as well as a signal of the deeply engrained problems of joblessness, inequality, and segregation. The structurally connected members of American society would do well to look closely and listen to what black youth have to say.

Appendix: Theoretical and Methodological Notes

This appendix provides an overview of the cultural outcomes used in the analysis, how the estimates were obtained, and the expected hypotheses. The outcome variables analyzed in this chapter are related to the cultural values and beliefs of black youth. I examine six domains of values and beliefs: psychological well-being, sociocultural networks, work and school, risk and expectations, community and social problems (including views on rap and hip-hop music), and American government and policy. I focus exclusively on outcomes related to the values and beliefs of the respondent to the extent possible rather than on self-reported behavior and actions, with the exception of sociocultural networks, which includes outcomes based on self-reported altruistic actions.[22]

The outcomes related to *psychological well-being* include clinical measures of anxiety, depression, and aggression. These also include items measuring self-esteem, whether or not one is pessimistic or optimistic, and overall concerns related to physical safety. The questions on *sociocultural networks* include measures of perceived beliefs on the diversity of the respondent's social networks as well as measures of trust in others. Cultural values and beliefs related to one's *career and educational attainment* include the perceived importance of being successful in a career, views on what matters for "getting ahead" in the workplace, and how much one values wealth. We also include questions on financial self-literacy, such as an item asking the respondent to rate themselves a letter grade from A to F in terms of understanding personal finance, managing money, budgeting, and saving for retirement. The questions on *risk and expectations* focus on the respondent's self-assessment of their risk taking and their expectations about their future. Regarding risk taking, these include the respondent's views on activities such as drug abuse, criminal activity, and unprotected sex. For example, one set of questions taps the respondent's views on premarital sex as well as the perceived normative consequences of becoming pregnant as a teenager. The outcomes related to *community and social problems* capture values and beliefs of their neighborhood and ethnic group. We also include questions related to rap and hip-hop music, asking questions such as the perceived possible negative effects of rap and hip-hop music on the cultural lives of black youth (e.g., giving a distorted portrayal of black men or exposing youth to "bad or offensive" language).[23] Finally, we include a set of questions on *American government and policy*. These include questions on whether or not respondents view the world as riven with conflict across racial, class, and ethnic groups. Included, also, are measures of trust and confidence in the dominant institutions of American society, such big business and elected officials.[24]

The wording of many of the questions raised technical issues. Specifically, many of the questions in the surveys have a general form, such as "I'm going to read you a list of some things that different people value in their lives . . . How about being respected? Is that very important, somewhat important, not too important, or not important at all?" For questions such as these, answers are ordinal, but the cardinality is not always clear. Accordingly, to estimate the outcomes in this chapter, I use the stereotype logistic model.[25] While the multinomial logistic and ordinal logistic regressions are most commonly used in quantitative analyses of categorical variables, for surveys measuring the cultural values and beliefs of respondents, the stereotype logistic regression is usually most suitable since when respondents are asked to assess or judge an outcome they may do so without a ranking or they may use a different ranking altogether. The stereotype logistic regression model can be understood as a more flexible model that, unlike the multinomial logistic regression, allows for unranked categories and, unlike the ordered logistic regression model, does not impose the proportional-odds assumption (see Anderson 1984). For those outcomes with only two categories, in all cases we use the logistic regression model over the stereotype logistic regression model, since they had fewer parameters to estimate.

The stereotype logistic regression model can be viewed as restriction on the multinomial logistic regression. To see this, note that in a multinomial logistic regression model there are $m-1$ parameter vectors $\tilde{\beta}_k$ to be estimated, where m equals the number of levels in the outcome and k is an index from 1 to $m-1$. In the stereotype model, there are d parameter vectors, where d is between 1 and $\min(m-1, p)$ and p is the number of predictors on the right-hand side of the equation. Accordingly, the coefficients for the stereotype logistic regression model are given as β_j for $j = 1, \ldots, d$. These two models are related in that the coefficients for the multinomial model can be expressed as a scaled sum of the coefficients of a stereotype model, such that $\tilde{\beta}_k = -\sum_{j=1}^{d} \phi_{jk}\beta_j$, where ϕ_{jk} is an estimated scale parameter for each coefficient β_j. Thus, for a vector of covariates x we let $\tilde{\beta}_k = -\sum_{j=1}^{d} \phi_{jk}\beta_j$, where ϕ_{jk} is a parameter for outcome k that allows for an unrestricted constant term for each equation. We can then state that the probability of observing outcome k as the following:

$$\Pr(\Upsilon_i = k) = \begin{cases} \dfrac{\exp(\eta_k)}{1+\sum_{l=1}^{m-1}\exp(\eta_l)}, & k > m \\ \dfrac{1}{1+\sum_{l=1}^{m-1}\exp(\eta_l)}, & k - m \end{cases}$$

Note that if $d = m - 1$, then the stereotype logistic regression model is just the multinomial logistic model except with a reparameterization. When estimating the models in this chapter, we use the so-called corner restraints of $\phi_{jj} = 1$ and $\phi_{jk} = 0$ to identify the scale parameters ϕ_{jk} and coefficients β_j (see Anderson 1984).

Besides using the stereotype logistic regression model, the estimates in this chapter are predicted probabilities derived from regression models with parameters for a three-way interaction among indicators for youth status (typically defined as eighteen to twenty-four versus twenty-five and up), race (either black or white), and disconnection level (either disconnected or connected).[26] This three-way interaction is simply a way of modeling the difference in the youth indicator within the four categories defined by race and disconnection. Accordingly, we estimated a stereotype logistic regression model of the following form:

$$\eta_k = \theta_k - \phi_k[\beta_1(black)+\beta_2(disconnected)+\beta_3(black*disconnected)+\beta_4(youth)$$
$$+\beta_5(black*disconnected)+\beta_6(disconnected*youth)$$
$$+\beta_5(black*female*disconnected)+\beta_8 X]$$

where k is less than the total number of levels of the outcome, η_k equals zero for the highest value of k, and $\mathbf{X}$ is a set of controls, and the parameters θ_k as well as θ_k are as described previously. After fitting this model, we set the youth indicator and then calculate the predicted probabilities for the outcome for each of the other groups defined by the cross tabulation of disconnection status and racial category. Finally, because most data were from complex surveys, we adjusted using sampling weights when appropriate.

Based on prior research, we expect the coefficient β_1 for whether the respondent identifies as black to be generally negative, with the exception of psychological well-being inasmuch as some research has shown that black youth may have higher levels of self-esteem (Twenge and Crocker 2002). We similarly expect the coefficient β_2 to have generally "worse" outcomes (cf. Besharov 1999; MaCurdy et al. 2006; Wight et al. 2010), with differences greater for disconnected youth such that the coefficient β_3 is statistically significant. Note that for each of the cultural domains analyzed there is a solid theoretical rationale with structural disconnection. Briefly, disconnection from the twin dominant institutions of acculturation in American society, work and school, is expected to provide negative psychological states of well-being, altered views on education and work, a greater willingness to take risks, lowered expectations, more pessimistic views on community and social problems, as well as greater distrust and cultural distance from the American government and public policy. Although not shown systematically in previous research, these expected findings are consistent with the literature on the centrality of work and school in American society (Carr 2001; Smeeding, Garfinkel, and Mincy 2009).

The advantage of using a three-way interaction to examine the relationship between structural disconnection and cultural difference is twofold. First, rather than subsetting the data to youth, it allows one to model the full variation in the data rather than discarding it unnecessarily. Second, from this interactive model, we can then calculate the predicted probabilities for youth alone, without displaying the full interaction or its coefficients since that is not the focus of the issue at hand (that is, the structural disconnection of black youth and its relation to cultural differences). In short, the approach we use here allows an examination of a subset of the data while avoiding throwing away information used to analyze that subset.

Besides the terms for a three-way interaction between race, age, and disconnection level, note that in all models we adjust for a set of background characteristics X that may otherwise confound the relationship among age, race, and disconnection. In particular, we adjust for the respondent's gender, place of birth, marital status, geographic region, metro status, household income, and a time variable (when appropriate, as in cross-sectional studies). In preliminary models, we also adjusted for household income, which was available in most (but not all) of the studies used in this analysis. This adjustment had no substantive effect on the estimates or the conclusions of the analysis, and was often statistically insignificant, so in the final models, we did not include this as an input on the right-hand side of the equation.

The interactive model here, in which age, race, and disconnection are defined by their cross products, has a theoretical relation to the structure and culture. The idea that structural disconnection is ipso facto related to cultural divergence is not a foregone conclusion, especially for the case of black youth (for example, see Bridgeland and Milano 2012). There are four main combinatorial considerations. First, structurally disconnected youth may culturally differ only or primarily by race. In this scenario, any level of structural disconnection is unlikely to have a significant impact on the enduring cultural fault lines between whites and blacks, either due to continued racial discrimination, particular religious and cultural traditions of black Americans, or the persisting legacy of segregation and slavery. Second, cultural differences are most stark across structural disconnection rather than race or age, inasmuch as the workplace and school are important sites of cultural transmission. Third, cultural differences may exist primarily by age. According to this logic, the information-saturated, technologically connected world today alters the consumption and diffusion of culture. A related reason refers to the fact that cultural views can change over one's life as part of the process of maturation. Fourth, it is possible that there are no cultural differences by race, age, or disconnection. This effectively implies that structural differences are not divisive enough to lead to cultural disconnection or that the spells out of the workplace or school are not long enough to have important cultural effects. To put it another way, structural disconnection may have negative impacts, but culturally there may be few negative effects given the cultural resilience of black youth. The framework here implies a fifth approach: race, gender, and structural disconnection interact with culture to create divergent outcomes. Indeed, from theories on the relationship between culture and demographics, we expect there to be cultural differences across racial and age groups (Borofsky et al. 2001). This expectation is in fact consistent with theories of cultural diffusion and persistence (Kaufman and Patterson 2005; Patterson 2004), cultural memory theories, and frameworks for understanding generational and demographic cultural differences (D'Andrade 1981; Eisenstadt 1986; Schudson 1989). In short, we expect that structural differences will create fault lines that redound culturally, effectively splitting disconnected black youth from their connected counterparts.

4

Hip-Hop's Irrepressible Refashionability

Phases in the Cultural Production of Black Youth

WAYNE MARSHALL, *Harvard University*

Since its first mass media appearances in the early 1980s, hip-hop has served as an increasingly prominent site for discussions about African American cultural production and its relationship to troubling socioeconomic indicators for black youth. According to both defenders and detractors, hip-hop reflects its circumstances, giving voice, form, and meaning to the challenging conditions from which it issues, including urban impoverishment and unemployment, a failing education system, institutional racism and police brutality, and the scourge of drugs and violent crime. As such, hip-hop has both been championed and condemned as a powerfully informing force, shaping the very culture that it would seem to represent by offering powerful scripts, myths, and all manner of cultural resources to be taken up and reworked by youthful practitioners (Rose 2008; McWhorter 2008). While dramatizing a set of tragic social problems and bringing them to center stage in American and global popular culture, hip-hop stands as neither an easy scapegoat nor a simple solution for policymakers, eluding gross generalization with its wide variety of shapes and forms. Hip-hop's projection of black male authenticity may appear at times utterly dominant, but such notions have also been shown to be both unstable and remarkably malleable. Moreover, whether at the level of noncommercial production or modest entrepreneurial efforts—which continue in myriad ways, enabled by creative uses of new media technologies—or in full integration with the entertainment industry (Charnas 2010), one can behold in hip-hop's aesthetics a great dynamism, an undeniable degree of self-determination, and a prizing of innovation which together might give both skeptics and devotees new ways to engage and understand hip-hop and black youth alike.

Public debates about the genre are far too often bogged down by objections to the specific contents of hip-hop productions. Here I argue that hip-hop's discontents, if you will, would do better to put questions of content aside, at least momentarily, in order to appreciate the importance of craft, innovation, media literacy, and other practices that have made hip-hop such an enduring and inspiring force in the lives of young people, especially black youth. To refocus questions about the relationship between black youth cultural production and socioeconomic outcomes, this chapter offers an historical overview foregrounding hip-hop's power and potential as a set of forms and procedures—in particular, how its sonic and social priorities have remained remarkably consistent even as they have shifted in step with changes in technology, economic opportunity, and sociocultural circumstances. Specifically, I contend that hip-hop's roots in and continued use of repurposed consumer-end technologies, from turntables to Twitter, deeply informs its aesthetic principles and possibilities as a constructive force in American social life.

Brass Knuckles and Wheels of Steel (1973–1979)

In the 1970s, the Bronx was like a place besieged, isolated and impoverished by urban planning that favored other parts of the city and other citizens, gutted by a rash of insurance arson, terrorized by gang warfare and police brutality, and neglected by local government. But its residents persevered, listened to music and danced at parties, went to school and tried to look fresh for their peers, all of which demanded a creative and flexible approach to self-fashioning, especially for the growing numbers of migrants from the Caribbean and their children. Amidst such poverty and malaise that a 1977 visit from President Carter focused international attention on the Bronx's seemingly shell-shocked streets, a remarkable, resilient, and eventually global phenomenon took root as local culture. Hip-hop's tale of origins has become well worn by now, but particular details—namely, the refashioning of consumer electronics and musical recordings, youth culture, and public space—merit special emphasis. Attending to these details of hip-hop's origins, we can better appreciate how hip-hop emerges as a distinctive set of practices, ideas, and institutions that have been widely transmitted and significantly transformed in the decades since.

As the story goes, hip-hop was born on a summer night in 1973 in a modest recreation room on the ground floor of 1520 Sedgwick Avenue, an apartment building in the West Bronx (Chang 2005). It was there that Clive Campbell, better known as Kool Herc, hosted a party with his older sister Cindy, looking to raise some cash for back-to-school clothes. Born and raised in Kingston, Jamaica, Campbell moved to the Bronx in 1967 to join his mother. Although not yet a teenager when he left Jamaica, Campbell was well familiar with the key local institutions known as soundsystems: mobile disco units operating in local dance halls, with a branded reputation based on the power and clarity of their speakers, the cachet of the records they played, and the talents of their personnel. Most crucial to any soundsystem, after the system itself, are the selector, tasked with playing and manipulating the music, and the DJ (or disc jockey), who, in the Jamaican context, rarely touches any records but rather presides over the event, commenting on or singing along with the music, exhorting attendees to dance, and generally turning the experience of listening to recordings into something closer to a locally customized, live performance. Knowing the importance of these elements, Herc borrowed a powerful Shure P.A. system from his father, an occasional soundman for local R&B acts, and played the role of selector (or DJ in American parlance), handpicking and cueing up the records, as well as master of ceremonies, or MC, using a microphone to greet and praise party-goers with short rhyming routines, hype the musical selections, make announcements, and encourage dancing.

Like any good DJ, Herc sought to respond to the demands of his audience. Given his context, this entailed embracing and extending certain soundsystem techniques—namely, the license to manipulate a record rather than honoring the integrity of a particular performance—even while departing somewhat starkly from what one might have heard at a dance in Jamaica. Despite borrowing liberally from soundsystem culture, Herc did not play reggae at the party. At least among his peers, Jamaican music and style had yet to undergo the cool recuperation that eventually followed Bob Marley's success and, perhaps more important in New York, the violent dominance of the drug trade by Jamaican gangs, or posses, in the 1980s (Gunst 1995; Marshall 2005). Rather, just as Campbell made an effort to swap his Jamaican accent for a more local one, he played soul, funk, and driving disco tracks—especially records featuring stripped-down, percussion-led break-downs, or "breakbeats"—in place of reggae anthems (Chang 2005; Marshall 2007). Having noticed that specific passages on the records seemed to get the otherwise nonchalant crowd moving, Herc took the liberties so common to Jamaican soundsystem practice and began making his own live edits of the songs. Later dubbed the "merry-go-round" technique, Herc would attempt to extend these breakbeats by picking up the needle toward the end of the break and dropping it back down again at the beginning. This innovative isolation and extension of popular breaks lit a fire under the feet of Bronx denizens looking for a little uplift, especially the so-called b-boys (or break boys) who symbiotically developed acrobatic routines in step with the explosive soundtrack. Herc and his sister Cindy began to throw parties regularly, and the audience steadily grew—as did Herc's crew, now including dedicated MCs, such as Coke La Rock, and a coterie of flashy dancers. Eventually, running out of room at 1520 Sedgwick, Herc relocated to nearby Cedar Park where, repurposing what little civic infrastructure remained in a place haunted by the politics of neglect, electricity from a utility pole powered his soundsystem. In contrast to clubs, where cover charges and age restrictions kept teenagers out, these "park jams" were active incubators, stylistically and socially, of a new kind of public youth culture. In this way, Herc's burgeoning audience, some driven west by gang violence in the South Bronx, helped essentially to coproduce a remarkable phenomenon: a vibrant party scene where local culture thrived as DJs, MCs, and dancers wrested new forms out of the resources at hand.

Often the story of hip-hop's beginnings focuses on a lack of access to such things as music education, musical instruments, and so forth, positioning the use of turntables and records as a remarkable example of resourcefulness (e.g., Rose 1994, 34–35; Sublette 2008, 186; West 2009, 116). But this perspective, as if hip-hop would not have happened if Bronx youth could have taken trumpet lessons, can also obscure the deliberate, vanguard embrace of electronics and recordings by enterprising DJs working to create their own musical and social worlds. It is worth pausing for a moment to appreciate the cultural revolution entailed by turning forms of consumption (i.e., buying records) into modes of production, transforming asynchronous consumer culture (we all listen to these records in private contexts) into real-time participatory culture (not only do we listen together in the same space, we are all party to the fundamental re-creation of these tracks). The rise of the DJ in hip-hop's formative years thus offers an excellent example of how cultural production is shaped by the interplay between structural conditions on the one hand and acts of improvisation and innovation on the other. Approaching polished audio commodities as incomplete performances to be activated in a live setting had precedent in reggae culture, but hip-hop artists refashioned this practice in distinctive and influential ways. Just as Herc had localized and transformed Jamaican soundsystem style, his rivals and acolytes extended these innovations according to the demands of local tastes. Hence, Joseph Saddler, a.k.a. Grandmaster Flash, improved upon Herc's "merry-go-round" technique with a more precise and smooth stitching together of breakbeats and other recorded fragments—innovations predicated upon Saddler's technical expertise (rigging up cues and crossfaders to facilitate the process), his admiration of the extended mixes of local disco mavens such as Pete DJ Jones, and finally, a fierce devotion to practice and improvement. Likewise, Grand Wizzard Theodore, an apprentice of Flash, developed the technique of scratching records rhythmically—perhaps the most obvious hallmark of hip-hop musicianship. Today such reuse of previously recorded performances—most often in the form of digital sampling—stands as absolutely ubiquitous musical practice, regardless of genre.

The radical refashioning of Bronx sociality instigated by hip-hop extends beyond the cultural alchemy of turning consumer-end commodities into raw materials for collective creativity or public spaces into community havens; it applies also to the stunning transformation of Bronx gang culture in the wake of this musical phenomenon. Credit typically goes to the South Bronx's Afrika Bambaataa, an imposing, fearless ex-gang member with ecumenical tastes and a vision for harnessing hip-hop's energy into a genuine social movement among Bronx youth. Under the banner of the Universal Zulu Nation, Bambaataa invited local gang members to leave their colors and disputes at home and come jam together at his parties. In an artful sublimation of actual violence into symbolic clashes between performers, b-boy crews engaged in vigorous physical but generally noncontact battles, DJs competed with their selections and skills, MCs jockeyed for crowd approval, and graffiti writers took territorialism into greater and greater realms of abstraction and mutual regard. One obvious legacy of this shift in Bronx youth culture is the macho posturing and spectacular rivalries (or "beefs") that remain so central to hip-hop. Because its modes of performance and presentation emerge from a rather tough context, a fundamentally competitive and confrontational stance continues to undergird a great deal of hip-hop style. In other words, the genre's innovations with regard to questions of form are not always so neatly separated from content. Of course, staging battles between the Bronx's best DJs, MCs, and dancers also served to attract large audiences, a boon for the occasional party charging a cover, revealing an entrepreneurial logic at work as well. But economically speaking, the early days of hip-hop made for modest returns on the blood, sweat, and tears of the genre's pioneers.

By the late 1970s, hip-hop could be considered a modest commercial success on one hand and an incredible aesthetic triumph on the other, but history would soon show the former to be a mere product of shortsightedness. Hip-hop was so tied to real-time social gatherings in its early years, and so predicated on other musicians' recordings, that the idea of committing such performances to tape and selling them as musical commodities in their own right required a leap of logic. Recordings of parties were made, of course, and tapes circulated informally and noncommercially, but it was not until a seasoned and savvy record executive, Silvia Robinson of Sugar Hill Records, saw the potential in the form that the recorded rap song emerged as such, some six years after Herc's back-to-school jam on Sedgwick Avenue. Most of hip-hop's biggest names at that time were not easily convinced or drawn away from the relatively lucrative party circuit, so Robinson's first attempt to record hip-hop was more of a studio simulation than a faithful rendering of contemporary party practice. Assembling a ragtag crew of aspiring rappers under the name of the Sugar Hill Gang, Robinson released a fifteen-minute single called "Rapper's Delight" that stitched together original lyrics as well as a number of popular routines drawn from such prominent MCs as Grandmaster Caz over a replayed loop from Chic's "Good Times," then a current favorite among hip-hop DJs. Despite its unusual length for a pop single, a genuine artifact of hip-hop's sprawling, party-suited style, "Rapper's Delight" became a massive hit on urban radio, selling millions of copies and ultimately offering the first exposure to hip-hop for much of the world beyond the Bronx (Charnas 2010, 43).

The great success of the Sugar Hill Gang initiated a profound turn for hip-hop aesthetics. If it had begun as a DJ- and dancer-oriented phenomenon, by the end of the 1970s a rising focus on MCs and the stunning popularity of "Rapper's Delight" would serve to cement a new hierarchy among the genre's practitioners, not to mention a shift in the sites of hip-hop production from parks and clubs to studios and mass media. Hip-hop would change irrevocably after the advent of rap records, especially as a next generation of kids striving to be fresh and cool embraced the new possibilities for hip-hop performance afforded by studios, live musicians and drum machines, and, eventually, digital samples of the very break-beats that so reliably excited dancers at the seminal parties thrown by the likes of Herc, Bambaataa, and Flash. Perhaps more radically, commercial hip-hop recordings, circulating far and wide, would enable the genre to transcend its local context, making these new and exhilarating forms available to a diverse range of new devotees, not all of whom shared the orientation produced by such a high-pressure cultural crucible as the Bronx. The compelling aesthetic innovations of hip-hop's founding fig-ures would inspire countless variations in the ensuing decades, addressing and inviting new participants into an increasingly translocal and mass-mediated youth culture. A great deal of this subsequent activity remained grassroots, amateur, local, and independent, but new industrial partners from corporate record labels to Hollywood studios would follow. A dynamic, if occasionally tense, feedback loop between small-scale and corporate enterprise has animated hip-hop aesthetics ever since.

The Golden Age: Commercial Inroads and the Rise of Gangsta (1980–1989)

On the heels of "Rapper's Delight," Sugar Hill Records and other small New York-based labels, such as Tommy Boy, Profile, and Wild Pitch, sought to capitalize on the growing interest in rap. These efforts would bring hip-hop to far wider attention, disseminating while reshaping its distinctive aesthetics. In the first half of the 1980s, hip-hop enjoyed an increasing presence in mass media, appearing in documentary reportage on such novel forms as "breakdance" (an outsider term for b-boying) and graffiti as well as in such stylized films as *Breakin'* (1984) and *Beat Street* (1984). These mainstreaming trends would continue through the latter half of the decade as hip-hop developed into a commercial force, epito-mized by the "crossover" success of Run DMC and other acts on Def Jam Records. Regional variations on the genre, especially those issuing from Los Angeles, reconfigured hip-hop's geography and, in the rise of gangsta rap, its very ethos. All the while, hip-hop persisted and spread as grass-roots participatory culture, taking root in cities across the United States— and with slightly more lag, the world—where the genre's insurgent energy produced an efflorescence of do-it-yourself (DIY) recording artists, labels, and party promoters.

Almost immediately, the shift to a recorded medium produced stark changes for hip-hop form and content. Born in the parks and community centers of the Bronx, hip-hop fashion had long mixed streetwise style with an aspirational and occasionally exotic touch. New commercial vistas ushered in a sartorial regime that took even stronger cues from showbiz. On record sleeves, at higher profile concerts, and, before long, in music videos, hip-hop's most prominent performers—e.g., Flash and Bambaataa and their extended crews, the Furious Five and Soul Sonic Force—styled themselves in garish garb that seemed at once post-apocalyptic, Afro-futuristic, and downright campy. This line of experimentation also informed new studio productions. To refigure their acts from live stage to studio, Bambaataa, Flash, and other early hip-hop recording artists took care to produce their tracks according to hip-hop's aesthetic priorities even as they embraced new possibilities afforded by state-of-the-art studio equipment and knowledgeable engineers and producers from other sectors of the dance music world, such as Arthur Baker, who collaborated with Afrika Bambaataa on his breakthrough single "Planet Rock" (1982). Together with Grandmaster Flash's "The Message," also released in 1982, "Planet Rock" pointed at once to hip-hop's past and its future. A brief consideration of these two early hip-hop hits reveals how the sound and purview of the genre were shifting, even as certain crucial elements remained firmly in place.

On both "Planet Rock" and "The Message," hip-hop's central sonic signposts—funk-derived rhythms, foregrounded drums, palpable bass, and musical allusions to contemporary and perennial favorites—sit alongside bracingly new sounds like the orchestral bursts of a digital sampling keyboard, the sustained bass decay of a synthesized kick drum, or vocal effects that make rappers sound like robots. In place of cherished break-beats coaxed from well-worn vinyl or a studio band replaying loops inspired by DJs' live edits of popular tracks (as heard on "Rapper's Delight"), "Planet Rock" and "The Message" feature funky rhythms pro-grammed using the drum machines of the day. An up-tempo track (close to 130 beats per minute) and thus well suited for dancing, "Planet Rock" brims with the electronic sounds of the latest in synthesizer technology, a quintessential example of what some have called electro-funk—a niche that Tommy Boy Records was eager to exploit. High-tech sheen aside, it also bears the hallmarks of old school hip-hop. Ensemble party raps, including call-and-response chants, alternate with a haunting melody bor-rowed from a seemingly unlikely source: "Trans-Europe Express," a 1977 dance hit by Kraftwerk, a German electronic music outfit who, despite their robotic rhythms and cold synthesizers, enjoyed a remarkable following in African American club scenes and had long held a special place in Bambaataa's eclectic record collection. For all its futuristic departures, then, "Planet Rock" was firmly anchored in the specific aesthetics developed by Bronx DJs in the 1970s.

For its part, "The Message," another rather contrived but ironically seminal production from Sugar Hill Records, also presented continuities with earlier practices even as it engendered a bold new trend for hip-hop. Though it shared a funky rhythmic framework with hip-hop's favorite breakbeats, at 100 beats per minute, the track was far slower than the driving soul and disco beats that had long been hip-hop's bread and butter. Indeed, Grandmaster Flash and his group were so dismayed by the plodding tempo that they rejected the project and declined to participate, intent on making a party track. Only one of Flash's MCs, Melvin "Melle Mel" Glover, agreed to work on the song, contributing his vocals and a final verse. The rest of the production, including the eerie synthesizer lines, features the work of Clifton "Jiggs" Chase, Sugar Hill's in-house producer and arranger, and Edward Fletcher, a.k.a. Duke Bootee, another musician and songwriter at the label. Fletcher composed and performed the chorus and opening verses, which offer vivid ruminations on the psychological tolls of urban blight. (Grandmaster Flash and the Furious Five would remain the artists named on the record, though publishing credits went to Fletcher, Glover, Chase, and Silvia Robinson.) The song's strong narrative structure offered a clear contrast to hip-hop's more typically party-centric lyrics. Its immediate resonance—climbing to number four on the R&B charts—made an indelible impression on the fledgling hip-hop industry, and on public perceptions of the genre itself. Injecting a certain gravitas into hip-hop's festivities, "The Message" refashioned the genre as specially positioned to offer timely commentary on black urban life. While up-tempo party raps have never receded from hip-hop, gritty tales about the ills of urban poverty, delivered over a brooding soundtrack, have come to occupy a dominant place in the genre. In one stroke, the song sowed the seeds of activist "conscious rap" as well as gangsta rap's vivid depictions of street violence.

Hip-hop's biggest commercial breakthrough to that point, the crossover triumph of Run DMC and Def Jam Records, follows clearly and closely on these developments. A trio hailing from Queens comprising two MCs and a DJ, Run DMC's mix of big synthetic drums, hard rock guitars, commanding voices, and spartan but striking street fashion (black leather, gold chains, fedoras, and crisp Adidas sneakers) grabbed the attention of hip-hop's core New York audience and then, in an unprecedented manner, the national mainstream. Making party music with a realist edge, Run DMC deftly mixed social commentary, catchy refrains, and bravado. But what propelled the trio into uncharted territory for hip-hop—into the top five of the Billboard Hot 100, regular rotation on MTV, and multiplatinum album sales—was the savvy choice on the part of their producer, Rick Rubin, to fuse their brash vocals and booming beats with the squealing electric guitars still dominating the pop-rock landscape. The formula proved popular on the trio's tellingly titled second album, *King of Rock* (1985), and then enormously successful with the group's remake of Aerosmith's "Walk This Way" for their third album, *Raising Hell* (1986). An admirer of hard rock and hip-hop alike, Rubin was poised to broker this marriage, though it is telling that hip-hop DJs had long reserved a special place in their crates for "Walk This Way" (originally released in 1975), thanks to its stark opening drum break. Hence, Def Jam's lucrative merger of rap and rock was itself presaged by the ecumenical selections of early hip-hop DJs, cued into the magic of such moments, it bears repeating, by discerning dancers.

Hip-hop acts and labels made sustained commercial inroads during the latter half of the 1980s. Joining Def Jam, Sugar Hill, Tommy Boy, and other established labels were a rash of independent ventures increasingly based outside New York, such as LA's Priority Records or Delicious Vinyl, often operating as subsidiaries of the majors or with national distribution deals. The relentless and competitive release of rap records made hip-hop aesthetics more widely available while at the same time reshaping the sound of hip-hop through inevitable regional variation. Thanks to the reach of rap records and increasing dissemination via radio and television, scenes were springing up across the country, from Boston to Houston, where aspiring artists and enterprising promoters formed groups, recorded demos and organized shows, distributed small-batch releases via local shops and directly out of their cars, courted local radio play, built a home-town fan base, and so on. Hip-hop's privileging of immediacy and participation over polish, together with the advent of more affordable and sophisticated music production equipment, fostered a cottage industry of home recordings, small-label ventures, and thriving local media ecologies. This DIY spirit and local orientation also gave rise in the mid-1980s to the mixtape, a cassette featuring a local DJ's mix of the latest rap songs, often mixing regional and national acts and typically for sale in informal commercial settings like sidewalk stands and swap meets. In contrast to the tapes that circulated in the seventies, capturing a DJ's live set in low-fidelity, mixtapes were more often assembled carefully at home or in a studio, sometimes using a multitrack recorder, and they were conceived as commercial products in their own right. As rap records were treated as malleable materials, not unlike breakbeats before them, mixtapes served to extend the practice of editing and activating recordings for particular listening contexts.

Another mid-eighties extension of seventies DJ practice, and a crucial development for hip-hop (and modern music production writ large), is the embrace of sampling as primary compositional technique. As noted, the first rap recordings departed radically from hip-hop tradition by replacing the DJ's real-time manipulation of breakbeats with studio reproductions performed by in-house musicians or programmed into synthesizers and drum machines. The result was a certain loss of aura and meaning as a central feature of hip-hop's affective charge—namely, the use of particular timbres from beloved performances to jog the musical memory—receded from the sound of the genre. With the advent of relatively affordable digital samplers such as the SP–1200 or the MPC, however, sampling offered a way to bring breakbeats and all manner of resonant audio fragments back into the mix. The aesthetic parameters forged in the feedback loops of Bronx dance parties thus returned resurgent, powerfully informing sampling practice in terms of form and content alike: source material remained ecumenical but grounded in funky percussion; drums and bass routinely pushed to thrilling, palpable effect. Although hip-hop producers were not the first to employ the procedure, they quickly became sampling's foremost practitioners and innovators—with regard both to subtle details (such as the ways drum breaks were chopped up, processed, and reassembled) and to densely layered, unprecedented, album-length masterpieces (e.g., the work of Public Enemy's Bomb Squad). Prior to Marley Marl's famous epiphany upon discovering he could isolate and manipulate a single snare drum from a classic James Brown record (Rose 1994, 79), no one had attempted such a brazen and integral appropriation of commercial recordings. Looping and chopping up hip-hop's beloved breakbeats soon became not only commonplace, but for many artists and devotees, absolutely paramount to the genre's sound, feel, and philosophy—a position redoubled in the wake of prominent copyright infringement litigation (Schloss 2004; Marshall 2006).

As with the mixtape, the art of sampling revived and reinvigorated hip-hop's radical approach to musical commodities as the phenomenon transitioned from live, local practice to a more mediated experience. Treating the audio recording not merely as a consumer end product but as a creative resource served to decommodify it (even if to be recommodified later), an approach consonant both with timeless cultural traditions of reuse and allusion and with the utterly modern (and largely academic and avant-garde) techniques of *musique concrète*.[1] Moreover, obviating the need for a band or "professional" musicians, sampling represented yet another way that hip-hop aesthetics fostered a democratization of popular culture. Suddenly, anyone with access to the equipment and an ear for arrangement could be a composer. This legacy remains important and immense. Today's popular plug-and-play music software (e.g., GarageBand or FruityLoops), which has itself initiated another phase of popular music's democratization and disintermediation, takes for granted the centrality of hip-hop's once pioneering approach to contemporary musical play and production. If once the product of a leap in logic and a lot of labor, sample-based loops have today become the default option for music production. But not only did sampling extend hip-hop's powerful and democratic aesthetic, as an approach grounded in the specific affective resonances and amplified frequencies of particular recordings, it also enabled a suggestive and referential sonic language that added a vivid dimension to hip-hop's cultural politics. Directly figurative samples—conjuring everything from familiar funk to modern jazz, dangerous dancehall to childhood schmaltz—could colorfully support a growing range of expressive styles, rhetorical positions, and archetypes employed by rap vocalists (some of whom still styled themselves as MCs).

Some pivotal examples stand out among the new figurations brought into being in the late eighties by savvy acts of sampling. One is *Criminal Minded* (1987) by Boogie Down Productions (BDP), released on B-Boy Records, the group's own modest imprint (supported by a small, South Bronx label called Rock Candy). At the same time that Run DMC were enjoying platinum record sales with their fusion of hard rock and reverberant drum machines, BDP refashioned the sound of hip-hop by delivering Jamaican patois-laced lyrics about the ravages of the crack age over choppy, distorted, and stark backing tracks that beckoned from the bleeding edge of audio culture. Jarringly truncated samples—drums from James Brown breaks, a guitar riff from a reggae instrumental—explode over a timeline held in place by hi-hats so quantized they possess a sort of anti-swing. As familiar as it sounded in some ways, it still sounded like nothing else. And if KRS-One's street-level realism takes inevitable cues from "The Message," the narrator of "P Is Free" and "9mm Goes Bang" is a very different character, less a wary observer or victim and more an eager participant, a ready reaper of dubious Reagan-era spoils. *Criminal Minded* signaled a strong tonal shift in hip-hop's representation of urban malaise and its effects on community relationships, and the album's first-person badman perspective—informed and inflected by dancehall reggae's mirror images of black, modern gangsters—helped to kick-start the "gangsta" rap movement. Notably, it also recentered the Bronx in the hip-hop imagination, at least temporarily, even as it reaccented the birthplace of hip-hop so strongly that it was difficult to imagine Kool Herc hiding his Jamaican accent a decade earlier.

A more infamous touchstone of gangsta rap, *Straight Outta Compton* (1988) by Los Angeles-based NWA, refashioned the emergent subgenre by drawing on the spectacular sheen of Hollywood. Taking their sartorial cue from Run DMC, NWA adopted a striking but muted look to suit their theatrical menace: black jeans, LA sports gear, and dark sunglasses. The group's producer, Andre "Dr. Dre" Young, propelled their gangsta imagery using a battery of samples: loping funk bass lines, explosive breakbeats (sometimes layered for effect, and usually looped rather than reassembled from fragments), dialogue from vintage cop-and-robber films, wailing sirens and other effects, including, in a true nod to Hollywood, the Foley-style sounds of running, fighting, and, of course, gunshots. Styling themselves as cool but crazed, NWA marshaled as they modernized the exaggerated, profanity-laced boasts of African American oral, literary, and audio traditions, and they courted controversy and publicity with songs such as "Fuck the Police" (which led the FBI to send a letter of concern to Priority Records, the distributor for NWA's label, Ruthless Records). At a moment when gang violence was becoming a national preoccupation, NWA gave voice to a popular dissatisfaction with the circumstances of inner-city life, in particular police brutality and other forms of pervasive racism, cannily foreshadowing the 1992 LA uprising, despite notes of nihilism. ("When something happens in South Central Los Angeles," intones Ice Cube during the first seconds of the album's eponymous song, "nothing happens; it's just another nigger dead.") Gangsta theater emerges here as complex and compelling racial politics, taking cues from badman archetypes and mobster flicks alike. The mix of cartoonish violence and self-proclaimed realism made for an intoxicating but toxic cocktail, a feedback loop through which hip-hop's sense of "the real" would be reconfigured by gangsta rap's surreal and salacious media spectacle.

Even as it became an increasingly big tent, full of funhouse mirrors, hip-hop remained a small enough world in the late eighties that an act like NWA could go on national tour with Long Island's De La Soul without too much cognitive dissonance. In contrast to NWA's black garb and noir sensibilities, De La Soul proposed more playful racial politics through day-glo colors, Africa-shaped medallions and peace signs, and sample-based backings that whimsically recycled pop detritus. Along with such affiliates as the Jungle Brothers and A Tribe Called Quest, De La Soul opened up space in hip-hop for positive, practically bohemian depictions of black middle-class life that aligned with Afrocentrism while resisting the strictures of archetype and stereotype. (It is telling that NWA and De La Soul could tour together on the strength of rather different hit singles centered on self-expression, "Express Yourself" and "Me, Myself, and I.") Together with other sample-laden acts from greater New York—many, notably, hailing from Long Island's middle-class black enclaves—these groups helped to rearticulate, against the rise of gangsta, hip-hop's conception of black community. Perhaps none would do so as forcefully, and with so avant-garde a sonic backdrop, as Public Enemy. On formative albums such as *It Takes a Nation of Millions to Hold Us Back* (1988) and *Fear of a Black Planet* (1990), Public Enemy put forward a bracing critique of racial injustice over a barrage of densely layered samples. For many listeners, the group's noisy militancy seemed less a contrast than a complement to NWA's strident, street-level drama, and all of this activity amounted to a sea change for the genre's wider representation and resonance (not least because of both groups' ability to captivate mainstream media). On several occasions in the late eighties, Public Enemy's frontman, Chuck D, compared rap music to CNN, or to TV news more broadly, for hip-hop's commercial success and growing diversity allowed an unprecedented set of depictions of the everyday concerns, struggles, and fantasies of African Americans to circulate publicly.

Ironically, even as sampling advanced the art of hip-hop production and offered vivid backdrop for new acts, the effect of these successful "sampladelic" records (to invoke an awkward term used seriously by music critics[2]) was to accelerate a longstanding trend: the ascension of the rapper—formerly a master-of-ceremonies assisting a DJ and interacting with a live audience of dancers—to primary and sometimes sole focus. This shift (which had long transpired in Jamaica) was already underway by the late seventies as Herc, Flash, and Bambaataa—who yet retained top billing—increasingly integrated MCs and vocal groups into their live acts. The ascent of rap recordings served to cement this hierarchy, minimizing the DJ's role, if not effacing it altogether. Popular nomenclature provides a guide here, for *hip-hop*—a broad term encompassing styles of dance, dress, visual art, and other practices—was overshadowed at this time by *rap*. The popularity of music videos no doubt played a paramount role in this shift as well, framing rappers as actors; the two biggest shows were tellingly named *Rap City* and *Yo! MTV Raps*. As hip-hop further integrated with the mainstream music business, the most successful rappers functioned as rock stars, transcending their vocations as performers to serve in the wider culture as celebrities. This represented another phase of refashioning for hip-hop, from recorded form to full-fledged media phenomenon, allowing its commercial possibilities—as well as its shapes and sites—to multiply.

Between the growing investment by artists in fashioning their personas (as much as, say, their lyrics) and by labels, magazines, television, radio, and other media in promoting rap as pop spectacle, hip-hop's power to inform young people's own processes of self-fashioning had never been more freighted with possibility and danger. Although early DJs and MCs took on honorific titles, donned outlandish costumes, and no doubt seemed larger than life to some, hip-hop as a local, live practice constrained one's ability to invent a character too out of step with one's rep. To put it another way, cultural norms restricted the distance between one's character and one's personality. The move to studios, however, invited all manner of experimentation, and the mediation of audio and video offered safe distance to play with *dramatis personae*. This shift was profound but subtle enough that rappers continued to collapse their recording selves and their actual selves—all the better for imbuing performances with authenticity, that slippery coin of the realm. As an artist who began in the late 1980s by styling himself as a spry-tongued, mildly Afrocentric Brooklynite (which he was), found success in the late 1990s posing as a former drug hustler among the best rappers "in the game" (which he was), and spent the last decade as a part-time executive, part-time pop star, and part-time art collector (all of which he is)—or in his own words, "not a businessman" but "a business, man"—Jay-Z knows this open secret as well as anyone. In his recent book, *Decoded*, bearing the apt cover image of one of Warhol's Rorschach paintings (which he owns), Jay-Z minces no words: "The rapper's character is essentially a conceit, a first-person literary creation" (2010, 292). But he notes that artists themselves can forget this:

> You can be anyone in the [recording] booth. It's like wearing a mask. It's an amazing freedom but also a temptation. The temptation is to go too far, to pretend the mask is real and try to convince people that you're something that you're not. (292)

Despite this widely recognized practice, then, the sly elision of the rap persona and the person doing the rapping has made hip-hop in the age of its technological reproducibility a powerful but problematic resource for young people of all stripes and, given the ascendance of glossy gangsta theater, for young black men in particular.

The Platinum Age: Pop Integration and Cooptation (1990–2005)

Over the course of the 1990s and into the twenty-first century, hip-hop maintained an impressive trajectory into nearly every corner of popular culture and all manner of commerce. Beyond placing hits on the pop charts and in television, film, and advertising, hip-hop aesthetics more generally influenced nearly every other popular genre, including rock and country but especially R&B, which has increasingly blurred into hip-hop. As such, the transmitted if transfigured sonic priorities of 1970s Bronx DJs now suffused popular culture as thoroughly as jazz and rock had in earlier decades. During this period, hip-hop was refashioned by a host of entrepreneurial efforts into a broad sort of brand, a cultural and economic force that could bring to market more than musical commodities: from clothing lines and other lifestyle products, to magazines and straight-to-DVD videos, to the public relations revolution embodied by the "street teams" that began by promoting new recordings and quickly branched out into any conceivable urban product pitch. Although such commercial success sometimes entailed embarrassing collusion with corporate visions, in more independent sectors, such as the burgeoning regional industries in southern cities like Atlanta and New Orleans, hip-hop's rising tide enabled a fair amount of artistic and economic autonomy. As the tools of professional-grade production and global distribution became ever more affordable, a staggering amount of hip-hop production ensued. From major labels to independents of varying scale to self-released or noncommercial efforts, hip-hop remained a remarkable culture engine. In turn, this rash of activity propelled a continued expansion of settings and styles (not to mention a perennial revival of old school and golden age practices), which extended not only across the United States but, especially with the Bob Marley-like resonance of Tupac Shakur, to every corner of the globe.[3]

And yet, while it would be wrong to downplay this dazzling diversity, despite subtle shifts in the genre's textures and timbres, the formal innovations of the 1980s as pertaining to musical form, thematic content, and media strategy remained pretty much in place: recycled funk rhythms were enhanced with the latest in digital studio trickery; audio recordings supported by videos remained the primary product; and an array of self-styled macks, hustlers, gangstas, and players refused to relinquish their dominant grip on the genre. With greater access to resources than ever, hip-hop became blinged-out (as the soundtrack for conspicuous consumption) and pimped-out (knowingly, in a "pimp the system," "pimp myself," "pimp my ride" manner). From a certain perspective, hip-hop's imperatives during this phase might be reduced to two key positions: (1) an individualist aspiration for the good life; and (2) the work ethic, or grind, to make it a reality. But against a certain decadence, hip-hop's popularity and aggressive transmedia practices served to spread other core ideas of hip-hop as well, among them some that would not have seemed too out of place in the Bronx decades before: resourceful repurposing (of ideas, styles, technologies), community commitments, technical mastery, and carefully crafted performances that come across as effortlessly cool.

Marking the genre's turn toward full-scale pop integration, two of hip-hop's biggest commercial breakthroughs arrived in 1990, inevitable if perhaps regrettable outcomes of the genre's mainstreaming trend. Vanilla Ice's "Ice Ice Baby" and MC Hammer's "U Can't Touch This" were massive hits, propelling both artists' albums to multiplatinum status (i.e., millions of units sold) and occupying pop radio playlists for months. Notably, both employed long samples from previous pop hits (and both were sued for unauthorized use), and each in its own way seemed to illustrate an inherent tension between hip-hop's assumed street authenticity and the commercial circulation that made it available to all. Whereas MC Hammer actually hailed from rough-and-tumble Oakland despite embracing ridiculous parachute pants and shimmying across stages like a showbiz veteran, Vanilla Ice masqueraded as an urban tough from Miami despite hailing from Texas. Mainstream audiences swallowed these confections whole, but vocal quarters of the hip-hop industry—including artists and burgeoning media outlets (especially magazines)—expressed strong dissatisfaction with both acts, increasingly ambivalent about the aesthetic and political costs of cross-over success. This anticommercial resentment was further stoked by the ways commercial success had begun to reshape hip-hop aesthetics as a matter of economic course, at times impinging on beloved traditions. Following a series of high-profile copyright lawsuits and settlements in the early nineties, for instance, sample-based hip-hop producers adopted a marked hesitancy on the one hand and a certain militancy on the other. Some, such as DJ Premier of Gang Starr, craftily upheld sampling as central to his and to "real" hip-hop aesthetics, obscuring his sources while flaunting their sampled-ness; others simply embraced synthesizers, live instruments, and, when affordable, legally licensed samples. The result was a two-tier system for the genre: the mainstream or "commercial" sphere, flush with cash and in-house access to sample-rich back catalogs, and the so-called underground, a term expressing at once an aesthetic stance and economic marginality.

It is hardly surprising that two of the genre's most successful labels in the 1990s bridged the gap, at least aesthetically, between the underground and mainstream. If hip-hop had been trending toward full-blown media spectacle since the late 1980s, the famous and fatal feud between Bad Boy and Death Row Records made good on this promise. Had the two labels not so effectively threaded the needle between hardcore and commercial aesthetics, it seems unlikely that magazines such as *The Source* or *Vibe* would have cared enough to throw fuel on the fiery exchange that developed mid-decade between the two labels' biggest stars, Tupac Shakur (a.k.a. 2Pac) and the Notorious B.I.G. (or Biggie Smalls). Run by the thuggish Marion "Suge" Knight, who brokered Dr. Dre's departure from Ruthless Records, Death Row established a national profile first with the massive success of Dr. Dre's *The Chronic* (1992), which served to introduce Snoop Dogg (Calvin Broadus Jr.), soon to be a star in his own right, as well as the "G-Funk" sound, a new take on the gangsta aesthetic Dre developed with NWA. Suturing the slinky funk of seventies groups like Parliament-Funkadelic (or P-Funk) to steroidal drums, Dre provided enthralling backing for menacing raps about gun violence, drug use, misogyny, and revenge fantasies. With Snoop's *Doggystyle* arriving months later (1993) and outselling *The Chronic*, it was clear that they were on to something (namely, that the suburbs could not get enough gangsta story-telling). By this point, the aesthetic and geographic center of hip-hop had decisively shifted to Los Angeles. But around the same time, almost in response—at least it would be heard and dramatized that way—Sean

"Puffy" Combs challenged this realigned cartography. Launching Bad Boy Records in 1993, Combs began producing a string of hardcore New York rappers and R&B groups, imbuing his acts with a signature sound that harkened back to New York's golden past—in part, by employing the sort of dusty breakbeats that still resonated as intimately part of hip-hop—without sacrificing a contemporary sheen. Combs introduced Biggie Smalls on a series of remixes, including a popular version of Craig Mack's "Flava in Ya Ear" (1993), Bad Boy's first release. When Smalls's debut album, *Ready to Die* (1994), followed a year later to multiplatinum sales, Puffy and Biggy found themselves presiding over a New York rap renaissance alongside such kindred acts as Nas, Jay-Z, and the Wu-Tang Clan.

Although initially friendly, Biggie and Tupac grew increasingly estranged and antagonistic after public disputes between Suge Knight and Sean Combs, and their recorded and press-released taunts escalated a war of words to a heightened pitch. By 1996, Tupac had become Death Row's flagship act, enjoying idol-like popularity effaced perhaps only by his posthumous legend. His story uncannily embodies hip-hop's narrative arc: the product of Black Panther parents and art school, Tupac starts his career as a roadie and dancer for the Bay Area's quirky party-rap group Digital Underground; he makes his solo debut rapping about incarceration, police brutality, and teenage pregnancy (*2Pacalypse Now,* 1991), and spends the next few years recording increasingly paranoid and nihilistic material along with occasional anthems of compassionate uplift (e.g., "Keep Ya Head Up" [1993] and "Dear Mama" [1995]); after several brushes with the law, bailed out by Suge Knight, Tupac signs to Death Row and embraces the unabashed "thug life" to stunning commercial success (*All Eyez on Me,* 1996). Jailed repeatedly and nearly killed in a November 1994 shooting in New York, Tupac's vivid gangsta theater had long blurred into his real life. Biggie, similarly, appeared eager to prophesy his end with albums titled *Ready to Die* and *Life After Death* (released two weeks after his murder in March 1997). As if to prove wrong the critics who claimed gangsta was just "theater," life would soon imitate art. Both artists were killed in drive-by shootings, a mere six months apart. Judged as media spectacle, this was as good as show business gets—better even, given the tragic conflation of the real and "the real." As such, Tupac's and Biggie's duel-to-the-death offered a sort of apex, or rather nadir, in the trend toward highly profitable, media-stoked animus, or "beef," between rival rap stars. (On the other hand, the posthumous cottage industries grown up around both figures can reach lows of their own.)

Against the backdrop of nearly unchecked commercial ascent and tragic thematic theater, a groundswell of independent production and distribution continued from Brooklyn to Oakland and Atlanta to Houston. A number of enterprising producer-rapper-entrepreneurs, perhaps none as singularly successful as New Orleans's Master P, sold millions of CDs "out of their cars" (literally and figuratively). Their small business practices, already grounded in two decades of DIY hustle, would lay a foundation for the coming age of Internet-abetted disintermediation. Moreover, advancing both "anticommercial" and fully aspirational stances, these diverse efforts offered a variety of alternative scripts to the gangsta ethos, as well as no little variation on that well-worn theme. In the wake of the sad, sizeable losses of Tupac and Biggie, Brooklyn-based duo Black Star reanimated the sound and spirit of Boogie Down Productions for their song "Definition" (1998). The group deployed samples and melodic allusions to two seminal BDP songs—one a proto-gangsta celebration of violence ("Remix for P Is Free"), the other diametrically opposed ("Stop the Violence")—in order to propel an urgent critique of rhetorical and actual violence in hip-hop. Black Star, dead prez, Common, the Roots, and other "socially conscious" groups would thus emerge from hip-hop's aesthetic underground (with commercial recording contracts) to inspire a generation of backpack-toting, politically engaged formalists. But assailing "hater-players" from the economic underground ultimately proved less popular than styling oneself as a modern-day, media-savvy meta-pimp beset by phantom "player-haters." Despite being bankrolled by James Murdoch, son of Rupert, Black Star's label, Rawkus Records, could hardly compete with the commercial juggernaut that was Bad Boy. An underground hit, commonly played in clubs and on hip-hop radio, "Definition" topped out at number sixty on the Billboard Top 100. In contrast, in the months following Biggie Smalls's murder, Bad Boy commenced a chart-topping run, including Combs's treacly tribute to B.I.G., "I'll Be Missing You," which spent eleven weeks at number one in the summer of 1997. Hip-hop's (partially willing) cooptation by the larger culture industry would continue apace, even alongside steady expansion at all levels, with no end of new avatars willing to step into the void left by the sudden departure of two of the genre's most outsize characters.

In the first years of the new millennium, with hip-hop singles dominating the charts, the genre essentially became coterminous with global youth culture. Thanks to steady commercial gains by hip-hop artists and labels, the Top 40 changed radically in character as teenyboppers—

teenagers, especially girls, still comprising the major market for pop recordings—abandoned boy bands for airbrushed thug balladeers. This was hardly a superficial shift; thanks to hip-hop, there were more black faces and voices in the mainstream than ever before. Not only did hip-hop acts consistently generate hits, as they had since the early nineties, now they downright dominated Billboard's pop charts. A widely reported milestone, during one week in October 2003 the Top 10 was entirely filled by black artists for the first time in history: nine of the ten were bonafide rap acts and the number one spot, "Baby Boy" by Beyoncé and Sean Paul, may as well have been (Lewis 2003). But despite this immense cultural footprint and sea change in the relationship between American popular culture and race, the main difference for hip-hop was a matter of scale. With regard to formal aesthetic features, little had changed since the mid–1980s. For instance, one of the genre's biggest stars of the last decade, Eminem, may merit special mention for the ways he refashioned whiteness through hip-hop (and refashioned hip-hop in the process), but his central schtick, a schizophrenic train wreck of person and persona, was simply an intensification of an approach developed in the early days of gangsta rap. Likewise, while 50 Cent deserves attention for his hefty record sales, incredibly profitable venture with Vitamin Water, and remarkable transmedia strategy—he even appears as the action hero of a video game, *Blood on the Sand* (2009), allowing players to indulge urban-guerilla fantasies of killing Middle Eastern terrorists with a gangsta flair—none of this is terribly new.

Given hip-hop's rise to the top, criticism of the genre remains rife from both sides of the political spectrum. On one hand, conservative African American commentators, such as John McWhorter and Thomas Chatterton Williams, follow in the footsteps of would-be censor C. Delores Tucker, arguing that hip-hop's lyrics and imagery demean women and African Americans and contribute to a deeply counterproductive culture enthralling black youth. An October 2010 op-ed by Williams in the *Wall Street Journal* levels this critique at hip-hop's biggest star in recent years, Lil Wayne, starting from the dismaying news that President Obama has some of the rapper's songs on his iPod:

Lil Wayne is emblematic of a hip-hop culture that is ignorant, misogynistic, casually criminal and often violent. A self-described gangster, a modern-day minstrel who embodies the most virulent racist stereotypes that generations of blacks have fought to overcome. His music is a vigorous endorsement of the pathologies that still haunt and cripple far too many in the black underclass.

On the other hand, if not entirely in disagreement, critics from the left contend that if gangsta rap ever had any sort of political valence, even that seems to have evaporated in the face of unfettered commercial success. "Back in the days, gangsta rappers faced off against label executives in corporate boardrooms over freedom of speech," notes Eric Arnold in *Colorlines*. "Now they entertain marketing meetings over energy drink endorsements" (2010). Still others, not surprisingly including many rap stars and so-called hip-hop moguls, view hip-hop's accumulation of capital and power as a revolutionary political project in line with Booker T. Washington's ideas about African American self-determination (Simmons 2002; Neal 2004).

As hip-hop, continually refashioned by practitioners and investors, has in turn reconfigured not only the music business but popular culture and commerce more broadly, one might legitimately wonder who has co-opted whom. Hip-hop artists and entrepreneurs may make compromises on the road to riches, but a certain insistence about the shapes and forms the genre takes—partly a product of stubborn artistic prerogatives, partly derived from a savvy grasp on which visions of blackness sell—has also radically changed the face and tone of American popular culture. Whether this change is for better or worse is up for debate, but to focus solely on the top sellers and stars is to overlook hip-hop's profound reorganization of how popular culture is made and is made meaningful. Hip-hop's platinum-plated reshaping of public culture has not only lined the pockets of a few lucky individuals, it has also initiated and sustained an explosion in local, amateur production, fostering a participatory turn in popular culture that, with the rise of the World Wide Web and social media, now appears as the norm. For community organizers, activists, educators, policymakers, and stakeholders of all sorts seeking to engage and support black youth, this more humble, if still impressive, sphere of activity is a far better target than the personal shortcomings of celebrities.

The Silicon Age: MP3s, Social Media, and New Plasticity (2005–present)

If hip-hop's fortunes rose from gold to platinum between 1985 and 2005, such upward mobility seemed to plateau with the advent of MP3s and socially networked media-sharing sites. While it should not be too surprising that hip-hop's profits would parallel those of the larger recording industry, it should not be too lamented either. The changing media landscape, especially the shift from top-down to peer-to-peer topographies, may threaten business as usual for the major record labels, but such informal, independent modes of production and distribution are hardly alien to hip-hop with its history of DIY practices, premium on innovation, and early adoption of new technologies. Of course, during its ascent to the pinnacle of music consumer culture, certain quarters of the hip-hop world—which is to say, record-label executives and the rare artists with fair contracts—benefitted from the same exploitative practices and artificial scarcities that propped up the recording industry at large. But more importantly, as a participatory culture that uses consumer goods as part of its set of tools and repertories, another large swath of the hip-hop world—e.g., independent artists and the audiences that engage and sustain them—has been well poised to weather the radical disintermediation presented by what some have called the social web (or "Web 2.0," reflecting the shift toward so-called user-generated content). The last decade offers a series of rather remarkable success stories in this regard, all of which point to new possibilities for understanding hip-hop's power as a positive, productive force in the lives of young people.

Hip-hop's irrepressible ability to be refashioned by the next generation comes into fine focus with the shift—or, one might argue, return—from hip-hop as primarily gathered around musical commodities to hip-hop as a set of forms and practices circulating more or less freely (on the Internet but offline, too, of course) in order to be activated in real time and real space. As a genre that long encouraged amateur practice communities and robust participation, grounded in the feedback loops of live interaction, hip-hop not only continues apace during a turbulent moment for popular media of all kinds, it has continued to expand its remit, drawing in more participants and greater variety than ever before. The driving factor behind this change is, of course, the digital turn—namely, the unprecedented availability of professional-grade audio and video production software together with the advent of Internet sites and services that provide free global publishing capacity. These developments allow hip-hop's already thriving "underground" to proceed with little need for record labels or other intermediaries. Accordingly, hip-hop aesthetics have shifted again under this new regime, permitting a less polished aesthetic to sit comfortably alongside utterly pristine pop (which hip-hop still is too, at the top). While other genres struggle to find footing in this brave new world, hip-hop's longstanding appreciation for relatively unvarnished expression has placed the genre at the cutting edge of contemporary popular culture. In contrast to the garish products that glisten from billboards and corporate mass media, a certain "fruityloopy" minimalism is the order of the day.[4] Moreover, it is increasingly difficult to locate hip-hop's "products," for a popular song or dance today might reside across dozens of YouTube videos rather than in some reified object available at a store (even if the iTunes store). This riles certain purists and Golden Age devotees of virtuosic formalism, but it also represents a return to hip-hop's "old school" roots—namely, the emphasis on local performance and interaction (as embodied by the recent resurgence of dance crazes), and the resourceful refashioning of commodities, technologies, media, fashion, and so on. Further, by allowing a greater diversity of voices to circulate publicly, the genre shows promising signs of loosening its well-worn strictures of keep-it-realism. Thousands of everyday producers and participants, who make hip-hop a crucial part of their media-suffused lives, have already strongly refashioned hip-hop in their image, including rather direct challenges to longstanding mores around black masculinity. How could they do any less?

Although no hard line exists, one might as well pick 2005 as marking an epochal shift, for that is the year YouTube launched. The popular video-sharing website exemplifies a deep change in our mode of popular culture production. In some cases, YouTube has become the primary, if not sole, platform not just for musical artifacts but for social lives. Essentially the world's second most popular search engine and an absolutely immense site (serving, at last count, some three billion videos per day, with forty-eight hours of material uploaded each minute), YouTube has become a crucial platform for major acts and bedroom loners alike.[5] A great deal of hip-hop on YouTube embodies the phenomenon set in motion in the Bronx some forty years ago: that is, hip-hop remains as vibrant a grassroots phenomenon as ever. A profusion of self-produced songs and videos reside on YouTube, many with no commercial aspirations but, rather, simply uploaded for local peers (if circulating publicly, by default, and hence available globally). A staggering variety of other forms of hip-hop practice also thrive on the site: countless dance-alongs, rap-alongs, freestyle battles, remixes and mashups, and all manner of tutorials and demonstrations. On the other hand, hip-hop's outsize presence on YouTube also shows it to be as industrial as ever: half of the top twenty most viewed videos all time, at the time of writing, are either hip-hop songs or clearly bear the marks of hip-hop's broader cultural influence. *Industry* is a key term when discussing YouTube as a central hip-hop site, for while the recording industry does its best to "monetize" its wares there, a broader sort of industry—a decentralized industriousness on the part of media-savvy young people—is also on full display, with significant consequences.

It is worth noting that as a distribution platform, YouTube emerges somewhat seamlessly from the genealogy of the so-called mixtape—long divorced, despite the name, from cassette technology as well as DJ-style mixing. Over the last decade, the mixtape has emerged as one of hip-hop's primary forms, a largely noncommercial method for projecting one's voice into a crowded public sphere. Major label artists and fully independent acts alike release mixtapes for a variety of reasons: to stoke anticipation and actual sales of official releases, to gain or maintain presence in a world of rapid turnover and fleeting attention spans, or simply to share via an imperative to produce and represent oneself as close to real time as possible. Initially a way for DJs to establish their brand and for audiences to keep up on the latest productions, mixtapes originated as semicommercial products, sold on the street, in the subway, or at barbershops and other nonconventional, informal retail sites—then subsequently duplicated and passed along hand to hand.[6] The rise of the MP3 mixtape, however, has exploded as it extends this practice, sidestepping commerce almost entirely as mixtapes circulate freely on websites like datpiff.com or via blogs, digital lockers (such as Mediafire and Hulkshare), and other peer-to-peer methods of exchange. This shift has also extended to the content of mixtapes, which have mutated from DJ vehicles to showcases for rappers to present original material with little or no assistance from traditional intermediaries. The impressive ascent of hip-hop stars like 50 Cent or, more recently, Lil Wayne and Drake stems directly from the aggressive and successful circulation of their mixtapes. But if this shift seems to parallel hip-hop's trajectory from DJ practice in the seventies to the rap recordings of the eighties, in other ways the shapes and forms of hip-hop in the age of MP3s and YouTube suggest an altogether different sort of configuration. Whereas one could argue that hip-hop resided in the parks of the Bronx in the seventies and in the personal media players—home and car stereos, boomboxes, and walkmen—of consumers in the eighties and nineties, hip-hop today might be said to reside on the distributed network of the World Wide Web and the devices through which people access and contribute to it. This is an important development with regard to notions of industry and community. "Make no mistake," argued hip-hop scribe Andrew Noz in spring 2010, "the future of the genre lies not in the hands of the industry, but at your corner bootlegger or favorite blog."

Some of the most remarkable hip-hop success stories in this brave new world reveal at once how new modes of production and circulation are extending decades-old hip-hop traditions even as they present direct challenges to longstanding orthodoxies of the genre. Black youth have consistently proven to be early adopters of new information and communication technologies, and several savvy avatars of the so-called millennial generation have marshaled their familiarity with the digital domain into substantial followings and, in some cases, considerable commercial success.[7] Perhaps the most notorious example is "Crank That (Soulja Boy)" (2007) by DeAndre "Soulja Boy" Way, who self-produced and self-published the song as a seventeen-year-old. Building the track out of stock sounds from the popular and user-friendly music software FL Studio (formerly FruityLoops), Soulja Boy deployed chintzy steel drum samples and stark percussive accompaniment (synthesized snaps and hi-hats) to propel a catchy refrain, which, as a clever branding strategy, prominently includes his name. Sharing the MP3 with online peers on sites such as Soundclick and MySpace, Soulja Boy found that it enjoyed remarkable resonance as peers and supporters uploaded videos of themselves dancing to the song using a set of simple steps choreographed by his friends. In turn, Soulja Boy celebrated and encouraged such activity by embedding the videos on his increasingly trafficked MySpace blog. The song and dance became a "viral" hit on YouTube, inspiring hundreds to try out the steps and share them with the world (and to remix the song in myriad ways), eventually bringing Soulja Boy to the attention of Atlanta-based producer Mr. Collipark, who signed him to a deal with Universal. This resulted in a higher fidelity version of the song as well as an official video, which helped to propel "Crank That" to the top of the charts, where it stayed for seven weeks in late 2007. "Crank That" went on to set new records for digital song sales as well as ringtones. Today Soulja Boy leverages substantial followings on Twitter, Facebook, and YouTube to promote a constant flurry of free mixtapes and commercial releases, including collaborations with such established acts as 50 Cent. At the same time, Soulja Boy's popularity has also made him the target of hip-hop stakeholders who bemoan this "participatory turn" for the genre. Veteran rapper Ice T (today better known as a television actor), for instance, famously accused Soulja Boy of "single-handedly kill[ing] hip-hop," a sentiment shared widely—just see the dissenting comments on "Crank That" videos—but also one that underlines a generational shift with regard to what hip-hop should look and sound like.

Writing about Soulja Boy for the *New York Times,* Jon Caramanica (2010) registers this change: "His brand of low-barrier-to-entry rap has become the template for a new generation of teenage artists using the Internet as their primary promotion tool, creating rabid fan bases outside of usual industry structures." There may be no artist who better exemplifies this shift than the Bay Area's Lil B (a.k.a. Brandon McCartney), who seems to approach hip-hop in the age of social media more as a conceptual artist than a recording artist. For one, nearly everything he releases is available for free. A prolific producer of his own songs, Lil B has released somewhere in the range of 3,000 tracks over the last three years, some 700 of them via 150 separate MySpace accounts (Noz 2011). His quirky videos on YouTube garner millions of views and, perhaps more impressively, recruit thousands of willing participants to help spread his odd gospel. Lil B's dances and catch phrases are gleefully embraced and amplified by everyday fans, established rappers (Soulja Boy among them), and professional athletes, all of whom appear less as unwitting replicants of so-called viral memes than as active participants in the phenomenon— "friends" (in the MySpace/Facebook sense) and "followers" (in Twitter's terminology) who are in on the jokes. While the actual content of his songs can range from dada-esque absurdity to bald misogyny, this seems less important to Lil B's acolytes—and for understanding hip-hop's latest incarnation—than his impressive abilities to navigate the new media landscape and manage his public relations to such popular support and critical acclaim.

An important complement to Soulja Boy's and Lil B's individual stories of Web 2.0 triumph is the more faceless Los Angeles hip-hop phenomenon known as jerkin. Although the scene did launch one local act, the New Boyz, into the national mainstream, jerkin is better appreciated in the story of hip-hop precisely because of its lack of stars. Centered around home-produced rap songs and dance videos—generally intended for high school friends but, because of the open default settings of YouTube, broadcast far and wide—the jerkin scene seemed to encourage participation as a matter of principle, keeping the barriers to entry relatively low. Video tutorials abound on YouTube for making jerkin-style beats or mastering the small, relatively simple repertory of jerkin dances, and while many of the

DIY dance videos or songs could stand up to contemporary commercial standards of quality (especially in the age of Soulja Boy), others bear the unmistakable "watermarks" of unlicensed or demo software, showing a clear preference for immediacy and immersion over polish or posterity. Consistent with earlier moments in hip-hop fashion, jerkin style called for a creative combination of relatively accessible consumer goods (at least for middle-class kids): brightly colored, close-fitting pants or "skinny jeans"; T-shirts, hats, and other accessories nodding nostalgically to cartoons and other childhood icons; and the latest in personal digital gadgetry. As such, jerkin's participatory ethos embodies many of hip-hop's earliest priorities: interacting in real time and real space, with an emphasis on fun; harnessing competitive energy to express personal style; and repurposing public space and consumer-end media technologies. Moreover, jerkin represents one of dozens of regional scenes gathered around distinctive, local takes on hip-hop (which, in turn, travel translocally). From Compton to Harlem and Dallas to Memphis, black youth have gathered around specific dances such as the "Stanky Legg" or the "Dougie"—or turfing or krumping or bucking—all of them essentially sharing the same spirit and set of core competencies. As with "Crank That" or the New Boyz' "You're a Jerk," the signature songs animating so much of this activity are often approached as communal resources—distributed assemblages scattered across dozens of dance videos, remixes, and all manner of personalized instantiations, revisions, and extensions, which, taken together, appear to take hip-hop's originary repurposing of vinyl and subsequent adoption of sampling into yet another phase of the genre's challenge to notions of authorship and ownership in popular culture.

As the very ontology of musical commodities has been joyfully dismantled on YouTube and the like, so have many other things, including hip-hop itself. For all of hip-hop's outsize presence on YouTube, one could also argue that YouTube—standing in synecdochically for the larger Internet—has itself radically refigured hip-hop by placing it alongside an unprecedented collection of other forms, genres, and styles. The vast cultural cornucopia at YouTube can even make something so dominant as hip-hop seem but another thing to sample from the culture at large, especially for curious young people with broadband connections and plenty of time. Like so many other things, faced with the irreducibility of its own diversity, hip-hop's formerly hegemonic self-image—forged in the tough crucibles of gang-ridden cities and made hyperreal by gangsta theater— has cracked in the digital mirror that is YouTube. Clearly, a previously stringent regime of representing black masculinity has yielded to a marked openness to idiosyncrasy, if not outright taboo crossing. The current generation reshaping hip-hop are data flâneurs, empowered by the generally safe distance provided by digital mediation and engaged in the sort of playful theatrics that the web seems to engender (Watkins 2009). These are young people so confident in—or at least bold about—their own understanding of what's important and what's cool that they are comfortable challenging longstanding sartorial and behavioral mores. "I'm doing me" has become the mantra of this generation, a sentiment echoed and affirmed in the complex feedback loop between grassroots hip-hop scenes like jerkin and such mainstream avatars as Lil Wayne, Kanye West, and Drake, all of whom wear their sensitivities on their sleeves (if in alternation with an unmistakable machismo). Hence, jerkin could be said to embody and revive classical hip-hop forms and values even as its specific content sometimes serves to propel a profound turn for hip-hop. So comfortable are some of these kids in their own skin that a mixed-gender jerkin group like AirBorn Allstarz can boast, tongues only partly in cheek, that they look so fresh and clean in their "White Girl Clothes" and "White Boy Clothes" (2008). More explicitly courting controversy, Lil B recently released a mixtape with the provocative (if misleading) title, *I'm Gay* (2011). But such button pushing is hardly a settled matter. For some, especially stakeholders of the old order, all of the acts mentioned in this final section have crossed the line into a sort of buffoonery. For other observers, however, hip-hop's reinvigorated plasticity might offer a hopeful sign.

Conclusion: The Choice Is Yours

Some forty years after hip-hop took root as local youth culture in the Bronx, the genre shows few signs of abating as a cultural force. Hip-hop's reign over popular culture is remarkable at this point, especially if we compare to the heydays of jazz, rock, or soul. Like these earlier genres, hip-hop stands both as a marker of the resilience of African American culture and as an expression of national integrity. Although produced and consumed by people spanning all racial categories and social classes, hip-hop's persistent, putative blackness means that it stands as a special, and freighted, resource for black youth. Even as that may give concerned parties pause, an appreciation of hip-hop aesthetics that goes beneath glossy gangsta surfaces to emphasize the genre's irrepressible refashionability offers great ground for engagement. Indeed, it is difficult to imagine a more compelling explanation for hip-hop's longevity as popular (and grassroots) culture than its essential flexibility, its imperative to "flip the script"—a restless orientation toward remaking the world of popular culture, and all the models and myths it offers up, developed out of an originary and sustained play with technologies of media reproduction. This orientation entails a number of central values and practices—technical competency and media savvy, competitive creativity and inventive reuse, communal engagement around shared texts—that should be of interest to anyone anxious about the ironic disparity between hip-hop's remarkable cultural production and socioeconomic outcomes for black youth.

The refashioning of popular culture—an increasingly commonplace activity in today's world of socially networked, embeddable media—necessarily involves an articulation of one's own relationship to it, and hence, if sometimes subtly, a remodeling of the self. So it makes sense that across hip-hop's varied expressions since the 1970s one of the more salient threads to emerge is how powerfully the genre fosters a commitment to self-fashioning—as a DJ or a producer, an MC or a rapper, an artist or a hustler (or both). The brave new attempts at public self-fashioning so central to youth culture—and to hip-hop—in an age of social media could thus prove galvanizing and useful, even if the content of a particular Soulja Boy or jerkin song is absurd, vulgar, or needlessly demeaning. Rather than dwelling on such content, better to attend to the aesthetic principles and procedures that have made hip-hop such an enduring and inspiring force in the lives of young people. Targeted toward education and policymaking, recent research on the intersections between new media and youth cultural production have taken special note of how hip-hop offers, in the words of Patricia Lange and Mizuko Ito, "a particularly important case" for understanding how young people deal with the profusion of media in their everyday lives (2009, 269). The lead authors of an ambitious effort to document how contemporary youth practices "change the dynamics of youth-adult negotiations over literacy, learning, and authoritative knowledge" (2), Lange and Ito argue for hip-hop's special significance as "a genre of music that was ahead of the curve in terms of developing styles of sampling and remix, as well as being grounded within very active amateur production communities where youth develop creative identities and competencies" (269).

As outlined in the preceding section, hip-hop provided a solid cultural foundation for today's moment of media turbulence, interactivity, and coproduction, especially for black youth; in turn, hip-hop is undergoing yet another phase of reconfiguration by a generation for whom the entire procedure is second nature. This is certainly an opening—first and foremost for hip-hop's devoted practitioners, but also for the broader constituency of stakeholders concerned with the feedback loop between culture and society, from activists and educators, to parents, politicians, and producers. Hence, to ignore or suppress rather than support hip-hop's uncontainable dynamism, its openness to shape shifting and syncretism, its imperatives for "flipping the script" and independently producing oneself (and one's sense of self), represents more than a missed opportunity. Overlooking hip-hop's irrepressible refashionability is tantamount to giving up on connecting with young people at all.

III

THE INTERACTION *of* CULTURAL *and* SOCIAL PROCESSES *in* INNER-CITY NEIGHBORHOODS

5

Continuity and Change in Neighborhood Culture

Toward a Structurally Embedded Theory of Social Altruism and Moral Cynicism

ROBERT J. SAMPSON, *Harvard University*

A puzzling feature of contemporary social life is the strong continuity in multiple forms of neighborhood disadvantage that characterize the "inner city" and, increasingly, the outer edges of cities and the suburbs. Perhaps in an earlier era of *de jure* racial segregation, it was simply expected to find the severe concentration by place of "disease and death" or "poverty and social disorganization," as Drake and Cayton ([1945] 1993, 203, 205) described things in *Black Metropolis* during the mid-twentieth century. Later observers used more contentious language to describe similar phenomena, the most well-known being Daniel Patrick Moynihan's (1965) assertion of a "tangle of pathology" in the black community during the Johnson administration. Setting aside his troubling analogy to disease and the ensuing controversy, Moynihan's description of racialized stratification and neighborhood marginalization in the American city was difficult to ignore. Whether unemployment, poverty, crime, or single-parent families with children, the data showed that urban black communities experienced a disproportionate burden of social stress.

Despite landmark civil rights legislation, the Fair Housing Act, and a sharp liberal turn in American culture in the mid-1960s, what came next surprised many observers of the urban scene. Instead of the hoped-for equality and harmony, cities experienced riots, outmigration of the middle class to the suburbs, industrial decline, unprecedented increases in violence, and a crisis in public education. Taken together, these phenomena fueled an even greater concentration by neighborhood of social disadvantage. The

201

best-known effort to make sense of these setbacks to expectations of social progress in the latter decades of the twentieth century was William Julius Wilson's ([1987] 2012) *The Truly Disadvantaged*. He argued that the social transformation of inner-city neighborhoods in the 1970s and '80s led to an increased concentration of the most disadvantaged segments of the urban black population, especially poor, female-headed families with children. Wilson argued that the racialized concentration of poverty and joblessness resulted from macrostructural economic changes in central cities where low-income minorities were disproportionately located, including a shift from goods-producing to service-producing industries, the increasing polarization of the labor market into low-wage and high-wage sectors, and the decline of manufacturing jobs. According to Wilson, the exodus of middle- and upper-income black families from the inner city also removed an important "social buffer" that could potentially deflect the effects of prolonged joblessness and deindustrialization.

In *American Apartheid* (1993), the sociologists Douglas Massey and Nancy Denton pick up the thread of Wilson's work but focus on racial segregation as the primary causal variable. They describe how economic dislocation interacts with the spatial concentration of a minority group to create a set of structural circumstances that reinforce the effects of social and economic deprivation. In a racially segregated environment, economic forces that cause a downward shift in the distribution of minority income not only bring about an increase in the poverty rate for the group as a whole, but also cause an increase in the geographic concentration of poverty. This geographic intensification of poverty occurs because the additional poverty created by macroeconomic conditions is necessarily spread unevenly over the metropolitan area. Segregation by race and poverty, then, rather than out-migration, is their key concern. Along with *The Truly Disadvantaged*, *American Apartheid* stands out as one of the dominant pieces of scholarship on urban poverty at the closing of the twentieth century. Although these books posited different causal mechanisms, both were powerful statements on neighborhood effects.[1]

Neighborhood Inequality Today

One might have thought that the twenty-first century would finally usher in the irrelevance of neighborhood stratification. In fact, that was the explicit prediction of many scholars and public intellectuals. Globalization is increasingly triumphant according to a dominant narrative, rendering the world "flat" and "placeless" (Friedman 2005; Giddens 1991). It is not only profound technological change and globalization that have reshaped cities. The new millennium has seen the greatest economic crisis since the 1930s, and the war on terrorism has led to charges of coercive policing and the hyper-surveillance of public spaces (Beckett and Herbert 2010; Wacquant 2014). Counter to the narrative of decline, however, other changes bespeak vitality and are similarly large in scope, including unprecedented declines in violence; unexpected population return and gentrification in formerly dying cities; the economic revitalization of poverty neighborhoods through foreign immigration; and the large-scale transformation of public housing, including the tearing down of dilapidated high-rise projects and the dispersal of thousands of poor families through housing voucher programs. In particular, the federally designed "Moving to Opportunity" housing demonstration (Briggs et al. 2010) was explicitly designed to overcome the kinds of concentrated poverty featured in Wilson's ([1987] 2012) theory.

Yet neither upheaval nor renewal has altered the enduring footprint of neighborhood inequality—disadvantage and affluence alike. For the poor, "moving to opportunity" turns out to look more like "moving to inequality" (Sampson 2008), and the legacies of disadvantage from decades prior can still be seen across the neighborhood landscape. For example, despite the rapid population turnover of individual residents and much social change, the poverty rate in Chicago's neighborhoods correlated highly and significantly (0.78, p < .01) from 1960 to 2000, a period of vast social change (Sampson 2012, 105). The correlation in Chicago is nearly identical to that for all neighborhoods in the United States, so Chicago is not simply an outlier. This "stickiness" of inequality by place can also be shown at the high end of affluence.

A similar pattern exists for other characteristics that underwent large changes in absolute level, as occurred with the unexpected decline in violence in the United States starting during the mid-1990s. Similar to the rest of the country, for example, robbery and homicide rates declined approximately 50 percent in Chicago from 1995 to 2006. Remarkably, however, neighborhoods overall did not switch places in their relative violence rankings during this period. The prediction line over time is nearly perfect: high-violence areas tend to persist and low-violence areas remain so (Sampson 2012, 110). There was almost no relative change in position, in other words, even as violence plummeted and nearly all neighborhoods benefitted from the secular change. In the other direction, as incarceration increased in the United States from the 1970s onward, the concentration in a small number of communities of very high rates of incarceration was stubbornly persistent.

In *Great American City: Chicago and the Enduring Neighborhood Effect* (2012), I present a systematic theory and detailed empirical examination of this broad phenomenon. Logic demands that if neighborhoods do not matter, identities and inequalities by place should be rapidly interchangeable, the durable inequality of a community rare, and neighborhood effects on both individuals and higher-level social processes weak or nonexistent. The effects of spatial proximity should likewise be weak. By contrast, I demonstrate with a wide variety of data sources that differentiation by neighborhood is not only widespread, but that it has durable properties—with cultural and social mechanisms of reproduction—and with effects that span a wide variety of social phenomena. Whether crime, poverty, child health, protest, leadership networks, civic engagement, home foreclosures, teen births, altruism, social disorder, residential mobility flows, collective efficacy, or immigration, to name a few subjects I investigate, the city is socially ordered by a spatial logic ("placed") and yields differences as much today as a century ago. I therefore argue that spatially inscribed social differences constitute a family of "neighborhood effects" that are pervasive, strong, cross-cutting, and paradoxically stable even as they are changing in manifest form.

A Role for Cultural Continuity?

In this chapter, I draw on *Great American City* to focus more intently on cultural mechanisms of continuity in neighborhood social differentiation. As Patterson (2004) has argued, the emphasis on change in the social sciences has obscured the systematic theoretical probing of large-scale historical and cultural continuities. Although he focuses primarily on societies, Patterson's observation parallels the literature in community studies and neighborhood effects. From the early studies of the Chicago School of urban sociology to Wilson ([1987] 2012) to the present day, the dominant focus has been on urban structural change, including in my own work. This structural orientation makes considerable sense for the reasons noted at the outset: cities underwent dramatic socioeconomic changes, and key indicators such as poverty and unemployment are highly concentrated spatially. Furthermore, socioeconomic characteristics can be measured with high degrees of reliability and accuracy, both across places and time. By its very design, for example, the U.S. decennial census provides a straightforward way to document long-term patterns of neighborhood economic inequality.

Culture has proven much harder to confront, both conceptually and empirically. Scholars have debated for decades over the proper theoretical definition of culture, and whatever side one might take in this different kind of "culture war," most would likely agree that there are few, if any, direct indicators of culture that are measured in consistent ways over time, such that stability and change can be assessed. A further problem attaches to the poverty literature in the form of the long shadow cast by Oscar Lewis's (1969) notion of a "culture of poverty." Its association with blaming the victim, and the ensuing acrimony over the Moynihan report's focus on black poverty, lingers to this day (Gans 2011; Massey and Sampson 2009). As recently as 2011, a reviewer invoked the language of "blaming the victim" to excoriate Wilson's (2009) *More than Just Race: Being Black and Poor in the Inner City* for its attempts to integrate structure and culture in the study of racial inequality. As Darity (2011, 469, 474) would have it, the effort equates to "cultural determinism" and "scholars need to dispense with cultural factors altogether." Clearly, the culture war among scholars is alive and well.

There would thus seem to be little gain to exploring aspects of culture where neighborhood inequality is concerned. But there are several reasons to rethink the study of culture when it comes to neighborhood effects. For one, to study the relationship of culture to structural poverty is by no means logically equivalent to asserting the culture *of* poverty. Transcending or replacing the framework set by Lewis is increasingly the aim of urban cultural analysis (Patterson 2000; Small et al. 2010). Second, to jettison culture from the study of poverty means ignoring the role of cultural mechanisms that operate among the *non-poor* and that serve to perpetuate poverty (such as racial stereotypes or schemas that trigger neighborhood disinvestment by elites). Third, *pace* Darity, to study mechanisms of culture does not imply that one is attributing racial differences in inequality to inherent cultural differences.

Fourth, and perhaps most important, there is increasing recognition across a wide swath of the social sciences that the continued separation of structural and cultural accounts of social behavior is analytically misleading. Even demographers and economists are studying culture (Akerlof and Kranton 2010; Bachrach 2014; Nunn and Wantchekon 2011), underscoring the vibrancy of interdisciplinary attempts to reconcile explanatory accounts that integrate the apparent subjectivity of culture with the objectivity and structure of the material world. Theoretically nuanced definitions of culture, moreover, see it as embedded in structure or, as the political scientist Alan Patten (2011, 741) recently put it, as a "precipitate." Patten argues that what makes the beliefs, attitudes, and ideas of a culture shared is that the people or group who hold them share a common *social lineage* rooted in exposure to a *distinctive environment*. By this view, culture is embedded in historical environments, thus leading to an intertwined causal process and making a strict dichotomization misguided.

The intellectual move I make in this chapter is to pursue the neighborhood context of two understudied but potentially powerful cultural mechanisms: (1) shared beliefs regarding moral and legal cynicism, and (2) other-regarding norms with respect to altruistic public behaviors. Although the concept of norms (like culture itself) has been widely debated and definitional clarity is rare, I focus on norms of an informal rather than legal or official nature, which Horne (2001, 4) refers to as the social "expectations" that arise in the context of everyday repeated interactions. As Goffman (1971, 97) argues, informal social norms rooted in expectations and perceived codes of conduct are "little explicated"; they are tacit and couched in general, rather than specific, terms. Such norms are also governed informally rather than centrally coordinated (Ellickson 1991). The concept of "collective efficacy" that I describe below, for example, is rooted in the idea of shared expectations for public action that encompass a variety of behaviors, from monitoring neighborhood children to helping keep open a fire station targeted by the city for closure. The other-regarding behaviors I examine are similarly disparate in manifest form, but I argue they nonetheless signify a general underlying norm.[2]

Within this scheme, the evidence of durable neighborhood disadvantage motivates me to take a longitudinal approach to cultural continuities and deep structures in the contemporary city. I highlight the structural and temporal *conditions of culture* and hence treat culture as *variable* rather than constant (Kornhauser 1978). From this view, social norms and coordinated beliefs are rooted in cognitive processes (Bachrach 2014), but in a structurally patterned and temporal way. Unlike the image conjured up by the metaphor of "tool kit" (Swidler 1986), whereby individuals can access and then discard from a variety of options seemingly at will, my framework places emphasis on the idea that shared beliefs and norms have staying (and motivating) power across a wide spectrum of life.

I thus consider cultural and structural mechanisms of continuity as part of an interlocking dynamic rather than as rigidly competing.

My goal, then, is to not to address culture writ large or to wade into the hoary debate over race and culture.[3] Nor do I proclaim or assess the independent "effect" of culture on some human behavior. My aim is more modest but perhaps more productive in the long run: to establish whether there is evidence of cultural continuities at the neighborhood level and their relation to both past and present structural features of the environment—*cultural structures,* in other words. Before turning to my hypotheses and analytical strategy, I highlight the theoretical underpinnings of two types of cultural mechanisms that I link to legacies of disadvantage.

Other-Regarding Norms and Moral Cynicism

I consider first the concept of other-regarding behavior, which in turn necessitates theoretical reflection on the public good.[4] Achieving common goals has proven especially problematic in an age of individual rights and increasing population diversity. But procedural justice and community are not the contradiction that common wisdom suggests. At the end of his magnum opus *A Theory of Justice,* John Rawls emphasized "the idea of social union" and argued that justice is grounded in interdependency and social cooperation as opposed to the rational actor notion of "private society" ([1971] 1999, 456–458). Writing as a sociological philosopher might, Rawls argues that "it follows that the collective activity of justice is the preeminent form of human flourishing. . . . Thus the public realization of justice is a value of community" (463).

Rawls invokes the intellectual tool of the "original position" to derive social conditions that we can defend as constituting the just society, and, in turn, what I have called the "good community" (Sampson 2012, Chapter 9). The original position is only a thought experiment, but, like counterfactual thinking generally, it is productive for explicating hypotheses and empirical expectations. The essential idea is that individuals do not know in advance their economic or social position, and so must decide future principles in conditions of initial equality and under a "veil of ignorance" (Rawls 1993, 23–28). Under such hypothetical conditions, Rawls derives principles of "justice as fairness" and spells out institutional implications for equality and the inclusion of individual rights, the details of which I set aside for present purposes. I wish to focus instead on the argument that the counterfactual of the original condition, combined with a conception of justice as rooted in social interdependence, leads to basic principles of socially altruistic behavior, or what we might think of as "urban ethics."[5] I argue that under a "veil of ignorance," individuals will choose neighbors that respond to others in need rather than those who ignore them, and neighbors that contribute everyday acts of kindness rather than free riders; helping behavior and human cooperation are widely desired goods.[6] But once exposed to the material and social exigencies of everyday life, human tendencies for cooperation and other-regarding behavior are tested. I thus argue that the capacity for altruism is socially conditioned, especially by persistent concentrated disadvantages.

There is evidence to back my linkage of normative with contextual considerations. Under experimental conditions where all else is equalized, research shows that humans act in other-regarding fashion far more than theories of selfish or rational man would have it. All of us have had the experience of a store clerk or cab driver returning money when we have inadvertently overpaid. This is no fluke behavior. In recent years, social scientists have carried out hundreds of experiments under names like the social dilemma game, ultimatum game, and dictator game. Generally speaking, these experiments force subjects to make a choice between maximizing their own payoffs or helping others. In game after game, cooperation is higher and defection rarer than expected under assumptions of perfect rationality, demonstrating that other-regarding preferences are commonplace.[7] Equally common are "cheater-detection" mechanisms and the tendency of humans to punish those who violate social norms of fairness, even if it means self-sacrifice. There is evidence that subjects in experiments fear that others will in turn punish them if they violate norms of fairness, such as making a "lowball" offer. As the legal scholar Lynn Stout (2006, 14) puts it, this finding means not only that other-regarding preferences exist, but also that we know that other people have other-regarding preferences, ultimately supporting the existence of a social sanction or social norm.

The social context of the environment (here, the experiment) matters greatly in the shaping of other-regarding behaviors. When players are allowed to speak to one another, when group identity is promoted, when the benefits of cooperation are made better known, and when subjects believe that their fellow players will behave fairly, altruistic behavior is increased. One way to recast these findings is to say that under conditions of cohesion and perceived legitimacy of the experimental context, other-regarding preferences are enhanced—hence, the evaluation of the game matters. It follows that under conditions where the experimental context is stigmatized or publicly devalued, we would expect other-regarding preferences to be attenuated. This reasoning is at odds with accounts that reject evaluative elements of culture, but is consistent with the literature on procedural justice in psychology and on social identity in economics.[8] Simply stated, when people believe that the rules are fair and followed properly, voluntary self-sacrifice and support of other-regarding behavior is more common.

We can extend this line of thinking to naturalistic environments such as neighborhoods. Although sparse, extant research suggests that members of low-income and minority-group populations are most likely to perceive injustice in the application of legal norms, and to express cynicism about the legitimacy and the ability of institutions, such as the police force, to do their jobs in an effective and non-discriminatory manner (Bobo 2001; Sampson and Bartusch 1998). The differential ecological distributions of social resources by race intensify this pattern: at all levels of socioeconomic status and after accounting for residential moves, even to the suburbs, blacks do not get nearly the same return as whites when it comes to the income level of their neighborhood destination. For the reasons originally emphasized by Wilson and Massey, neighborhoods that combine racial segregation with concentrated resource disadvantage are the places where the inability to influence the structures of power that constrain lives, along with exposure to violence and other social harms, is greatest. Such neighborhood disadvantage is also linked to public stereotyping and external denigration (Waquant 2010), reflected for example in common references to poor neighborhoods (especially black) as "ghetto," "slum," or "disordered." The concentration of multiple forms of disadvantage and devaluation in turn breeds cynicism and undermines norms of public other-regarding behavior.[9] Cynicism, after all, is socially corrosive and works to render its holders indifferent to the concerns of others; it is in effect a kind of anti-altruism embodied in a deep sense of alienation from what is perceived as a hostile, unjust world.

To be clear, my conceptualization does not imply wholesale rejection of conventional norms; it is more about the process of attenuation in the face of prolonged experiences and situational exigencies rooted in structural disadvantage. Conventionality clashes with a public environment where exposure to violence, physical disorder, state disinvestment, and external stigmatization are commonplace, serving as a constant reminder of the precariousness of everyday life (Anderson 1999; Hannerz 1969; Liebow 1967; Wacquant 2014). This interpretation helps to explain the inconsistent or weak support shown for subcultural values in surveys (Sampson and Bartusch 1998). Ultimate values are similar across the spectrum, but the existential considerations of life in severely concentrated disadvantage foster a cynicism about the utility of other-regarding norms. As Kornhauser has cogently argued (1978, 225), "What is inevitable cannot be deplored with as much conviction as what is avoidable." According to this view, judgments that seem to justify predatory or nonaltruistic behavior need not be viewed as cultural approval. The experience of widespread disorder, crime, and disadvantage instead leads to beliefs and attitudes that are adaptations to contextual realities rather than the embodiment of deep cultural values: what Liebow (1967) famously called a "shadow culture."

Importantly, though, when structural exigencies are deeply rooted and persistent over long periods of time, associated beliefs and other-regarding norms likewise become hardier, inducing a cultural lag or persistence (Hannerz 1969; Nunn and Wantchekon 2011). Indeed, it would run against human nature to expect instantaneous cultural change in response to structural change. In the cognitive realm, for example, my colleagues and I have shown that there is a long-term negative effect of concentrated disadvantage on the verbal performance of children even if their families moved out of poverty (Sampson et al. 2008). I suggest that the severe disadvantages in American "hyper-ghettos" are equally tenacious in their temporal grip on symbolic denigration and what Wacquant (2010, 2) terms "collective demoralization," in turn shaping the perceptions and actions of external observers who have the power to shape the fate of neighborhoods. In particular, if a neighborhood gains a reputation as a "no man's land" where residents do not care about others, this devaluation is likely to be reinforced by institutional representatives of real estate, finance, and politics, and also outsiders in the form of potential residents, further undermining that neighborhood's economic future and contributing to its "territorial stigmatization" (Wacquant 2014). In this sense, while culture and structure are separate concepts, they are simultaneously manifested in social action and are thus empirically entangled.

Strategy and Hypotheses

A major challenge to my perspective is to find empirical indicators of other-regarding behavior and moral or legal cynicism that can be applied to neighborhoods and that satisfy social-scientific standards of measurement. I propose two indicators of social altruism that are free from subjective reinterpretations by participants: intervention in a personal health crisis, and a more mundane matter, the mailing of a lost letter. Providing aid to someone suffering a cardiac arrest is an almost classically altruistic behavior: CPR is not without risks, including both mild (disruption or delay in one's daily rounds; anxiety at performing in public) and serious (guilt or public blame if not performed properly; potential death of the victim). These risks might prompt people to avoid providing help, but they do not diminish the desirability of providing aid for those in critical need. The provision of CPR also greatly enhances one's probability of surviving a heart attack, so its contribution to the collective good is not in dispute. If someone mistakenly drops a stamped letter on the street in an urban area, the act of mailing it by a stranger likewise constitutes a reasonable proxy for other-regarding or cooperative behavior, albeit with less cost and fewer stakes. It takes little time and few downsides to the intervener, but the benefit to the "victim" is still potentially great (e.g., a letter to an employer or an insurance company). One can imagine other altruistic acts, such as helping a car-accident victim, organ donation, dousing a small fire about to spread to a house, giving directions, and calling a lost child's parents. Manipulating or controlling opportunities for their enactment is crucial, however, making it difficult to measure between-community variations based on observational data.[10]

Using theoretically appropriate sources of data that I shall describe shortly, I therefore investigate community-level variations in (a) giving CPR to heart attack victims conditional on a cardiac arrest, and (b) mailing lost letters systematically dropped in the street by trained researchers. I merge these data with systematic assessments of moral cynicism and shared expectations for public behavior gathered from a representative community survey and a set of structural and organizational measures of neighborhood context spanning four decades. I exploit these integrated longitudinal data to examine five hypotheses derived from the theoretical framework that I have outlined:

- *Hypothesis 1:* CPR and lost letter returns vary substantially across neighborhoods and are spatially concentrated to a degree beyond that expected by chance.
- *Hypothesis 2:* These variations are influenced by long-term cultural dynamics, such that other-regarding behavior at one time should predict its future level. Social altruism is part of the enduring social

character of a community, in other words. To assess this hypothesis, I examine whether the rate of neighborhood CPR predicts lost-letter return rates many years in the future, net of material conditions, and racial composition.

- *Hypothesis 3:* Behavioral variations in other-regarding behavior are predicted by moral and legal cynicism, neighborhood trust, and shared expectations for maintaining public order (what I term "collective efficacy"). Where cynicism about others is high and trust and shared norms about public intervention are dampened, the behavioral manifestation of other-regarding behavior (returning lost letters) will be lower.
- *Hypothesis 4:* These relationships, however, are embedded in neighborhood contexts of everyday experience. Concentrated disadvantage entails deprivation across multiple domains of life, including physical deterioration in the environment, public denigration and conflict over resources. I therefore expect that exposure to disadvantage and social marginalization will foster cynicism, lower shared expectations for public control, and reduce other-regarding behavior.
- *Hypothesis 5:* Legacies of disadvantage simultaneously matter. I hypothesize that concentrated disadvantage has both enduring and concurrent effects on other-regarding behavior as well as on moral and legal cynicism. I test this prediction by examining the influence of initial conditions in concentrated disadvantage in addition to the effects of subsequent structural changes in disadvantage on current neighborhood-level cultures.

In short, I argue that the idea of urban ethics in general and social altruism and moral cynicism in particular can be studied empirically and not just philosophically, as well as contextually in naturalistic neighborhood settings and not just in laboratory experiments. In doing so, I explore the challenge to the Rawlsian hypothetical community that is presented by actually-existing positions in real neighborhoods governed by structural processes of inequality.

Methods

The Lost Letter Experiment

The letter-drop technique derives from the pioneering work of Stanley Milgram, the social psychologist commonly associated with the finding that any two people are separated by "six degrees of separation." In the original lost letter experiment, Milgram and colleagues were interested not in degrees of separation, but rather in uncovering unobtrusive measures of political attitudes. In their initial study, Milgram and his co-authors varied the addressee list of some four hundred letters that were distributed in New Haven, Connecticut. Two addresses were benign (a generic name for an individual and "Medical Research Associates") while the other two were "Friends of the Communist Party" and "Friends of the Nazi Party." Rates of return were selective, with only a quarter of the latter group mailed back compared to 70 percent of the first two (Milgram et al. 1965, 438).

To date, there have been few attempts to implement Milgram's original lost letter experiment systematically using probability sampling. In 2002, the Project on Human Development in Chicago Neighborhoods (PHDCN) set out to incorporate the strengths of the lost letter technique and adapt it to a sociological context. The idea was to randomly scatter letters across neighborhoods of Chicago and measure the situational aspects of each letter drop and whether the letter was later returned. This idea was implemented during the interview phase of a community survey carried out by the Institute of Social Research in collaboration with PHDCN.[11] Project staff unobtrusively dropped two preaddressed stamped envelopes on opposite random corners of each home block of study participants who themselves had been randomly selected. Conditions at the time of each drop were recorded. One letter was addressed to a fictional person and the other to a fictional company. The delivery address on both letters corresponded to post office boxes at the Institute for Social Research in Michigan, and the return address was a fictional street in Chicago. Some 3,300 letters were dropped, and just over a third were returned to the mail and delivered to the addressee. I calculated the lost letter return rate for Chicago's census tracts, neighborhood clusters, and larger "community areas" that average just under 40,000 in population (N = 77), after adjusting for the influence of letter-drop conditions (including weather, time of day, day of week, month, and local and ecological conditions such as housing type and local disorder). Because the average number of letters dropped in census tracts was quite small (< 5), I focus primarily on the city's community areas, which averaged about forty letter drops each and thus yielded highly reliable measures. Community areas are also well-recognized by Chicago residents and institutions (Sampson 2012, 78–79).

The Cardiopulmonary Resuscitation (CPR) Study

For my second set of data, I draw on a study originally conducted in the late 1980s by medical sociologists at the University of Chicago. During 1987 and 1988, the Emergency Medical Service (EMS) unit recorded data on all cardiac arrests that occurred in Chicago, including detailed information on the characteristics of the cardiac arrest, the victim, and its location. Iwashyna et al. (1999) geocoded these data and reported that the rate of giving CPR varied substantially across census tracts. I obtained these data and linked them to the PHDCN family of studies. The incident-level unit of analysis comprised the population of all cardiac events serviced by EMS (N = 4,379 events). Like the original authors, I begin by examining two sets of characteristics central to CPR by a bystander. The first describes the cardiac arrest itself, including where it occurred (at or near home versus outside one's block of residence), the time of the 911 call, and whether or not it was witnessed. The second set includes characteristics of victims (age, race, and sex). Consistent with the original study, I found that CPR was more likely if it was witnessed, if it did not occur at home, and if the victim was older or white. There were no gender differences, and the race differential disappeared once other factors were controlled.

I then examined both raw and adjusted CPR rates that took these individual and situational factors into account at the census tract, neighborhood cluster, and community area levels. Although the patterns are similar across these ecological units, the reliability of measurement increases with the sample size, so I again focus primarily on community areas, where over fifty cardiac arrests occurred on average. The adjusted mean probability of CPR across communities is 0.22, meaning that in just under a quarter of the cases of pulmonary crisis in Chicago a victim received CPR from a bystander circa 1988.

PHDCN Community Survey

The Community Survey (CS) of the PHDCN is a multidimensional assessment by residents of the structural and cultural properties of their neighborhoods that was carried out at two points in time. To gain a complete picture of the city's neighborhoods, researchers personally interviewed 8,782 Chicago residents representing all of the city's neighborhoods in 1995. In 2002, a separate sample of 3,105 residents was interviewed.

The basic design for the CS had three stages: at stage one, city blocks were sampled within each neighborhood cluster; at stage two, dwelling units were sampled within blocks; at stage three, one adult resident (18 or older) was sampled within each selected dwelling unit. The final response rate was over 75 percent in both waves. The design yielded a representative sample of Chicago residents that was large enough to create reliable between-neighborhood measures.[12]

The concept of *moral and legal cynicism* was assessed by asking five questions about beliefs toward conventional legal and social norms. Respondents reported their level of agreement with five statements: "Laws were made to be broken"; "It's okay to do anything you want as long as you don't hurt anyone"; "To make money, there are no right and wrong ways anymore, only easy ways and hard ways"; "Fighting between friends or within families is nobody else's business"; and "Nowadays a person has to live pretty much for today and let tomorrow take care of itself" (1 = strongly disagree, 2 = disagree, 3 = neither agree nor disagree, 4 = agree, and 5 = strongly agree). Taken together, these questions measure whether laws or rules are considered binding in the present lives of respondents. Put differently, the items capture variation in respondents' attitudes about of "how the world works" with respect to acting in ways that are "outside" conventional legal and social norms. A five-item scale based on these items has been validated in prior research using the Chicago data (Sampson and Bartusch 1998).[13]

Although not my main theoretical focus, in the analysis below I also examine two other culturally related constructs: collective efficacy and norms about substance use and fighting among adolescents. The concept of collective efficacy combines *social cohesion* (the "collectivity" part of the concept) and *shared expectations for control* (the "efficacy" part of the concept). To capture shared expectations about social control, we designed vignettes. Residents were asked about the likelihood that their neighbors could be counted on to take action if: (1) children were skipping school and hanging out on a street corner, (2) children were spray-painting graffiti on a local building, (3) children were showing disrespect to an adult, (4) a fight broke out in front of their house, and (5) the fire station closest to home was threatened with budget cuts. Social cohesion was measured by coding whether residents agreed with the following propositions: "People around here are willing to help their neighbors"; "People in this neighborhood can be trusted"; "This is a close-knit neighborhood"; "People in this neighborhood generally get along with each other"; and

"People in this neighborhood share the same values." Social cohesion and social control were strongly related across neighborhoods and were combined into a summary measure of collective efficacy.

Finally, I examine variations across neighborhoods in the condemnation of minor deviance among teenagers. Rather than being questioned about crimes such as robbery or rape that are nearly universally condemned, respondents were asked, "How wrong is it for teenagers around thirteen years of age to (a) smoke cigarettes, (b) use marijuana, (c) drink alcohol, and (d) get into fist fights?" These items were measured on a five-point scale: "not wrong at all" (1), "a little wrong" (2), "wrong" (3), "very wrong" (4), and "extremely wrong" (5). Four corresponding questions asked how wrong the same acts were for "teenagers around nineteen years of age." These measures thus tap the tolerance that residents express for acts of substance use and fighting among teenagers. I combined the items to construct an overall tolerance of deviance scale.

Findings

Hypothesis 1: The Spatial Variability of Altruistic Behaviors

My first empirical question concerns spatial variability: Does where a heart attack takes place matter for receiving critical help? It does: the rate of giving CPR varies significantly from a low of 13 percent to over a third (37 percent) across Chicago's community areas. I found substantial variation across census tracts and neighborhood clusters as well. If we define CPR as a form of social altruism, there is clear empirical evidence of neighborhood differentiation.

The same pattern emerges for the behavior of returning a lost letter. Considerable variation emerges across all geographic units, with return rates ranging from a low of zero to a high of over 75 percent. Interestingly, the neighborhood with the highest level of returned letters, at 82 percent, is the heterogeneous community of Lakeview on Chicago's dense and very urban North Side. Apparently, this form of anonymous yet other-regarding behavior is not inhibited in the big-city environment.

Hypothesis 2: Temporal Persistence in Community Altruistic Character

A second and perhaps more intriguing theoretical question is the temporal "reach" or connection in forms of social altruism: do communities exhibit similar altruistic patterns over time? Translated to the present empirical case, does the CPR rate predict future acts of returning a lost letter? To be sure, performing CPR in 1988 does not cause someone to mail back a lost letter a decade or more hence. But if my theoretical approach is correct, then communities should exhibit detectable levels of durability and generality in their other-regarding character. Norms of altruism have general self-reinforcing properties, I suggest, whether through social learning, institutional support, or mechanisms of reward such as public acknowledgement of unselfish acts. These are the sorts of mediating mechanisms that undergird cultural reproduction.

Although more than a dozen years elapsed between giving CPR and the lost letter experiment, the correlation of the two rates of behavior is nonetheless positive and statistically significant (0.34, p < 0.01). This phenomenon is depicted visually in Figure 5.1. There is a clustering of high-intervention communities in the north and along the lake (e.g., Near North, Edgewater, Uptown) and in the northwest-side communities of Portage Park and Norwood Park. By contrast, there is a large cluster of low-intervention areas in the south-central areas of the city, although there are a number of socially altruistic communities nearby as well (e.g., West Elsdon, Beverly, and Morgan Park [just below Beverly]). Although the magnitude of the relationships is not large, the fact that community clusters of altruism from 1988 reappear many years later provides intriguing hints of a durable structure to norms of other-regarding behavior.

The reader might object, however, because we know that communities differ widely in demographic composition, as do cardiac-arrest victims. Race and age, for example, predict who gets medical help (blacks a bit less, the elderly a bit more), as does who is at home at the time of crisis, which is correlated with lifestyle. Perhaps more importantly, poor or uneducated residents may be less familiar with CPR techniques and so afraid to intervene even if motivated. Or people may be less likely to intervene where there are many other public bystanders. A poor, high-density neighborhood with a concentration of blacks, for example, might then bias the correlation, leading to an over- or underestimate of the factors that predict neighborhood variations in altruism. To address these concerns I controlled not only event-level factors, but also neighborhood poverty, age and racial composition, and population size from the 1990 census, which is most proximate in time to the cardiac arrests. Yet I still found a long-term connection despite these multiple adjustments—the partial (or

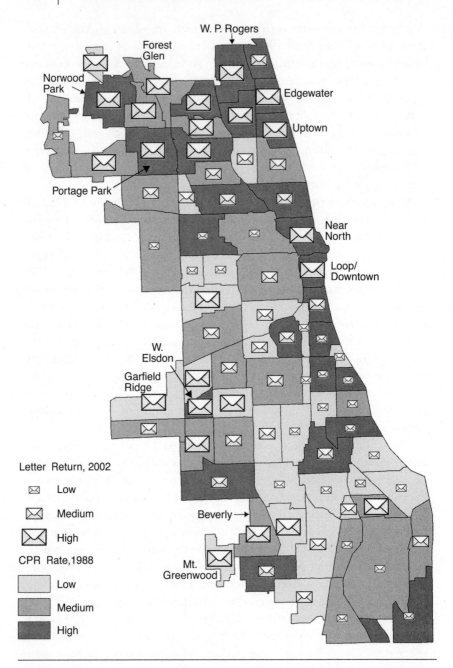

Figure 5.1. Community variability in CPR after a cardiac arrest and returning lost letters. Source: Reprinted from Sampson (2012: 222, © The University of Chicago Press).

adjusted) correlation was not substantively different and remained statistically significant (0.32, p < 0.01).

Overall, then, despite the relatively small number of cases and possible measurement error, the data reveal a reasonably persistent type of social altruism across communities: it consistently matters where you have a heart attack or lose something.

Hypothesis 3: Altruistic Behaviors Vary Systematically with Cultural Structures

I hypothesized earlier that socially altruistic intervention is more likely in environments where shared expectations for public intervention are high, where people trust their neighbors, and where moral cynicism is lower. I tested this prediction using the community surveys carried out in Chicago in 1995 and 2002. Because collective efficacy is persistent over time (R > 0.70) and to reduce measurement error, I employ the mean collective scale from 1995 to 2002 to predict later lost-letter return rates in 2002. The correlation is statistically significant (0.41, p < 0.01) at the community-area level. Shared expectations for control and trust in neighbors in 2002, which are constituent elements of the collective efficacy scale, also correlate with letter drops at 0.32 and 0.60, respectively (p < 0.01). Trust therefore appears to be the most directly related to altruistic behavior in the form of letter returns, a pattern that also holds once neighborhood compositional factors are controlled.

Recall that moral cynicism captures beliefs about the sense in which laws or collective moral rules are not considered binding in the lives of Chicago residents. Lost-letter return rates are much lower (−0.46, p < 0.01) in communities with high levels of cynicism and a perceived lack of legitimacy of conventional norms and legal rules. These findings thus confirm that behavioral variations in altruistic behavior are not only linked over time—the persistence dimension—but they are also significantly linked to concurrent survey-based indicators of shared expectations and collective beliefs about other-regarding norms.

Hypothesis 4: Altruistic Behaviors Are Linked to Community-Level Structural Conditions

The spatial concentration, temporal continuity, and connection of other-regarding behaviors with shared cognitive appraisals do not imply the irrelevance of structural factors, such as neighborhood-level poverty rates. Nor does it question the importance of dynamic structural changes within communities. Quite the opposite: my theoretical framework explicitly predicts that cultural mechanisms are shaped by long-term legacies of disadvantage and systematic changes in neighborhood structure.

I first tested this basic claim by considering the concurrent relationship of community-level structural factors with other-regarding behavior (see also Sampson 2012, 220–24). Controlling for population density, population size, and the age composition of the neighborhood in addition to the characteristics of the cardiac event itself (e.g., age, race, sex of victim), I found that concentrated poverty in 1990 was linked with a lower rate of bystander CPR across neighborhoods. I also considered the role of community-based organizations as an institutional factor that helps sustain both norms and opportunities for altruism.[14] To assess this notion, I examined the density of nonprofit organizations per capita for the year closest to the CPR study, 1989. Controlling for population density, population size, and the age, race, *and* economic composition of the neighborhood in addition to the characteristics of the cardiac event, the density of nonprofit organizations in the community had a positive significant association with bystander CPR. These findings thus support the argument that there are simultaneous organizational and poverty effects on social altruism (see also Sampson 2012, Chapter 8).

I next conducted an analysis of the letter-drop experiment analogous to that conducted for CPR. The approximately 3,300 lost letters were first analyzed as a simultaneous function of situational predictors (such as time of day, month, housing conditions, and weather) and a set of neighborhood-level predictors, including a multi-item scale of concentrated disadvantage, ethnic and immigrant diversity, residential stability, and population density.[15] Consistent with the findings discussed earlier, there was statistically significant ($p < 0.01$) variation in the letter-drop return rate across neighborhoods both before and after adjusting for situational factors, from census tracts to community areas. The reliability of the letter-drop return rate is higher at the community-area rather than census-tract level, at 0.75, so I highlight the structural- and organizational-level predictors of community-level variations in the rate of returning lost letters, taking into account both letter drop (e.g., time of day, type of addressee) and local ecological conditions. In multiply-disadvantaged ·communities (namely, poor *and* racially segregated), the rate of returning letters was significantly lower (t-ratio = −6.60). The magnitude of association was substantial and perhaps surprising, in that there is nothing immediately apparent in a materially deprived community that would prevent someone from returning a lost letter.[16] The second largest factor was nonprofit organizations. Like the bystander CPR findings, the density of nonprofits had a direct association with the rate of lost-letter returns.[17]

The structural predictors of these two distinct but correlated other-regarding behaviors are thus similar in nature, suggesting a latent construct of altruism that persists over time. The data further suggest that concentrated disadvantage undermines, and the density of organizations supports, altruistic communities. Institutional practices apparently bear on the explanation of some forms of altruistic behaviors. Going against widely popularized assumptions, ethnic heterogeneity and population density made little or no difference.

Furthermore, I found that concentrated disadvantage had by far the largest direct association with moral and legal cynicism. Lost-letter return rates are also much lower in communities with high levels of cynicism and a perceived lack of legitimacy of conventional norms and legal rules (-0.46, $p < 0.01$), but this association is largely explained by concentrated poverty and its link to racial isolation ("disadvantage"). Specifically, once concentrated disadvantage is controlled, along with residential stability and race/ethnic diversity, the link between community moral cynicism and letter-drop returns weakens.

Although residents in severely disadvantaged neighborhoods may be cynical or bear signs of hopelessness, this stance does not signify rejection of mainstream norms (Hannerz 1969; Kornhauser 1978). In fact, while the data reveal that blacks and Hispanics are significantly more likely than whites to perceive legal norms as less than binding, they are more *intolerant* of substance abuse by children. This pattern occurs in both the 1995 and 2002 surveys. Moreover, once neighborhood disadvantage is taken into account, blacks hold views about legal norms and police behavior similar to those of whites (Sampson and Bartusch 1998). My interpretation is that African Americans are more cynical because they are more likely to live in environments of concentrated disadvantage. Yet at the same time, minority groups are more intolerant of deviance and fighting than whites, even taking into account neighborhood-level factors. It thus appears that poor minority residents juggle complex cultural norms that are closely tied to the ecological and neighborhood structural environments in which they live.

*Hypothesis 5: Community-Level Cultures Are Shaped by Initial
Conditions and Dynamic Changes*

For the purposes of this chapter, I estimate a new set of models that build
on the findings above and in Sampson (2012). I do so by assessing stability *and* change in concentrated disadvantage, and then examine corresponding links to an underlying construct measured by behavioral
variations in neighborhood altruism and evaluative variations in moral/
legal cynicism as assessed by residents. Theoretically, I am most interested
in contrasting low-cynicism and high-altruism communities with high-
cynicism and low-altruism communities. To accomplish this goal, I took
the first principal component of letter-drop returns and moral cynicism,
each measured in the same year (2002). We know that there is measurement error in each indicator, but these indicators are based on such different methods—shared beliefs from a survey and observed behavior from
a field experiment—that there is unlikely to be a common source of measurement bias. I thus examine only the common variance; in this case, the
first principal component captured 66 percent shared variance. The result
is a unified scale with a positive loading for cynicism and a negative loading
for social altruism in the form of letter-drop returns.

I then created a summary index of concentrated racial disadvantage.
Consistent with the segregation argument of Massey and Denton (1993),
the correlation between racial isolation and concentrated poverty is quite
high in Chicago neighborhoods—on the order of 0.70 or higher, depending on the decade in question. Rather than trying to tease out independent effects of these highly intertwined factors, I therefore followed
previous work; however, for conceptual clarity, I focus here on a simple
indicator of "concentrated racial disadvantage" based on the first principal
component of percent black and percent in poverty. I did so going back to
1960, a period before the widespread riots and other large-scale social
changes that upended the landscape of American inner cities, Chicago
included. I defined the same construct for 2000, exactly forty years later,
and then measured the unadjusted change that each community experienced over that time period. In 1960, percent black and concentrated
poverty shared over 90 percent common variance; forty years later, in
2000, the shared variance was less but still substantial, at 83 percent.

The persistence over time in the basic pattern is telling when considered
against the backdrop of national and local social change. Chicago had
undergone not only riots, but also rapid racial transitions, outmigration,

deindustrialization, and increases in violence; and, by the new millennium, widespread immigration, gentrification, and unexpected decreases in violence—all of the social forces noted at the outset of this chapter. It is remarkable, then, that across these forty years the temporal correlation of concentrated racial disadvantage at the community level is a substantial 0.74 (p < .01). The question at hand is the extent to which the initial conditions in racially structured poverty in 1960 shaped later adaptations, cultural or otherwise. According to my theoretical framework, we should see evidence of both path dependence *and* change: culture is dependent on initial conditions, but not invariant, and thus responds to structural change.

Figure 5.2 presents the basic picture of stability and change from 1960 to 2000. The reader will note first the powerful connection of concentrated racial disadvantage across this period of vast social upheaval. The communities of Riverdale and Oakland, for example, experienced extremely high disadvantage at both ends of the observation period, while the Loop/Downtown area and a cluster of white well-off communities on the northwest side (e.g., Forest Glen, Norwood Park) remained oblivious to such disadvantage. Structural persistence is indeed strong. Second, however, one sees a set of communities that sit noticeably above the regression line; these are places that grew more disadvantaged relative to their position in 1960. Areas below the line improved: while persistence is dominant, it is not absolute. Indeed, communities such as the Near North Side and Near South Side witnessed considerable change due to public investments, gentrification, and the redevelopment of public housing. Third, and most important, community profiles of cynicism and altruism align with both of these structural realities. Every single community in the upper half of concentrated racial disadvantage in 1960 and that grew more disadvantaged over time is in the top tercile of high cynicism and low altruism (e.g., Washington Park, North Lawndale, Englewood, Riverdale). Hence both increases *and* initial conditions in concentrated racial disadvantage are systematically related to neighborhood cultural continuity.

Is it possible that this pattern is the outcome of other processes? To address competing explanations, I estimated a series of multivariate panel models that included potentially confounding factors such as population size, changes in population, ethnic heterogeneity, and residential stability. After controlling for these variables, the results show that baseline racialized poverty in 1960 and later increases in disadvantage over the course of 1960 to 2000 were directly associated with higher levels of cynicism and

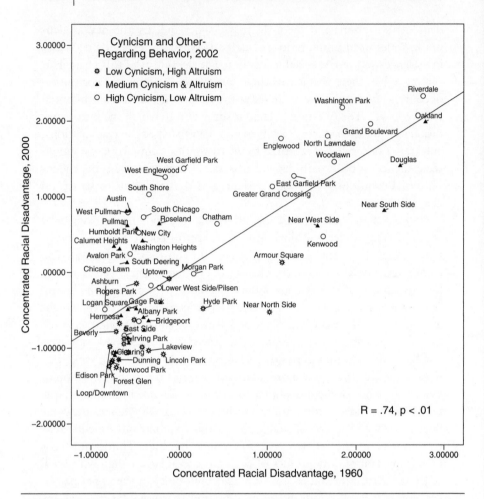

Figure 5.2. Initial conditions and change in concentrated racial disadvantage, 1960–2000: Community implications for moral cynicism and other-regarding behavior

lower levels of other-regarding behaviors in the form of letter returns in the year 2002. In fact, the largest coefficient of all is concentrated racial disadvantage in 1960 at the beginning of the study period (standardized coefficient = 0.96; t-ratio = 6.96, p < 0.01). The second largest predictor was changes in racial disadvantage (standardized coefficient = 0.71; t-ratio = 6.94, p < 0.01). The pattern in Figure 5.2 thus holds up and is not accounted for by correlated characteristics: both stability and change in structural disadvantage explain variation in the other-regarding character of neighborhoods.[18]

Summary

This chapter has shown that altruistic or other-regarding behaviors follow a spatial and temporal logic, consistent with a neighborhood-level path dependence that unfolds over the long-term. This idea was confirmed through the prediction of lost-letter return rates and CPR administration rates from more than a dozen years prior, controlling for the composition of the neighborhood. I posited that bystanders giving CPR to heart attack victims and mailing lost letters provide direct indicators of the "good community" that pass the classic Rawlsian test of what we might think of as "urban ethics." Lost-letter methods are also unobtrusive and subject to systematic manipulation, allowing me to adjust for opportunity conditions. CPR conditions were not manipulated, but the random nature of heart attacks provides a type of quasi-natural experiment.

It is thus telling that other-regarding behavior is shaped by levels of concentrated poverty and racial segregation laid down as far back as 1960. Despite macro political changes, urban social transformation, and pronounced gentrification toward the end of the twentieth century, neighborhoods remained remarkably stable in their relative standing of racialized disadvantage, despite the inflow and outflow of individual residents. Recent evidence also suggests that the degree of gentrification is shaped by racialized disadvantage, with poor black areas gentrifying less rapidly than poor white areas (Hwang and Sampson 2014). Poverty and its correlates are thus stubbornly persistent in terms of neighborhood concentration, especially in black and minority group areas. Yet when concentrated poverty does decline, as for example when induced by the dispersal of public housing or during times of intense foreign immigration, other-regarding behaviors and related cultural beliefs correspondingly increase.

I took a very different approach to neighborhood-level culture in my analysis of community survey data. I demonstrated distinct variations across neighborhoods in moral and legal cynicism and shared expectations for control. The key to this method was assessing intersubjective or shared assessments among residents, what might be thought of as "neighborhood narrative frames" (Small 2002) of cynicism about human nature and public order. Yet like other-regarding behavior, moral cynicism was structured—it was sharply amplified in communities of severe disadvantage. Similarly, shared expectations for social control were attenuated in contexts of resource deprivation. Moreover, levels of cynicism were also related to community differences in disadvantage dating back to 1960, and increases in disadvantage were associated with additional increases in cynicism.

There are, of course, a number of limitations to this study that need to be emphasized. Norms were not directly manipulated, and in the case of other-regarding behavior, the chief empirical indicators were behavioral in nature. My data are also limited to a single city, causality was not demonstrated in any definitive way, and mediating mechanisms that might explain continuity over long periods of time—what Nunn and Wantchekon (2011) call "channels of causality"—were not explored. I necessarily worked at a level of abstraction and theoretical speculation when discussing the link between structural disadvantage and cultural processes many years later. Furthermore, the decade from 2000 to 2010 witnessed changes that I was unable to study, such as Ehrenhalt's (2012) "Great Inversion"—the intensified gentrification (Hwang and Sampson 2014), shift of poverty to the suburbs, and population return to the central city. Of course, the Great Recession was another major event that I did not study. But the letter drop, CPR, and survey data were collected in 2002 or earlier, before these changes had fully unfolded. I suspect that patterns of neighborhood social character may well have changed more in this most recent decade than in earlier decades, and I hope that future research is able to assess stability and change in the early decades of the twenty-first century. I consider my findings as characterizing an important slice of history in American cities, but the long-term reality remains to be seen.

Although caution is clearly warranted, taken as a whole the findings are nonetheless reasonably consistent with the claim that there was an enduring cultural component to Chicago neighborhoods circa the close of the twentieth century that was not simply a result of individual, demographic, or purely economic explanations. Put simply, there appear to be cultural mechanisms embedded in reinforcing cycles of structural disadvantage. In communities with high levels of inter-subjectively shared cynicism and the perceived irrelevance of societal rules, lost-letter return rates are significantly lower. It is important to note that this association is largely explained by disadvantage, suggesting a feedback loop whereby concentrated disadvantage is corrosive with respect to other-regarding norms.

This process feeds cynicism, which reinforces behavior that is outside of the law (e.g., using violence to settle disputes), in turn further undermining trust and notions of the just community. Legal cynicism also helps explain the persistence of violence in certain communities and racial disparities in violence, with African Americans more likely to condemn crime and violence even as they are disproportionately exposed to greater disadvantage as well as moral and legal cynicism (Kirk and Papachristos 2011; Sampson and Bartusch 1998).

Conclusion

The historical reality of the American city is that neighborhoods with high concentrations of African Americans and economically impoverished residents have been stigmatized by highly visible problems of crime, disorder, and public disrepute. These persistent and psychologically salient correlations are experienced subjectively, but they are not a mirage: they have deep roots in the concrete reality of American stratification and segregation and are not likely to lapse in the face of short-term interventions. Importantly, they are also not easily lost on residents, leading to collective forms of demoralization that have diffused into popular culture.

Consider the imagery and cultural framing of hip-hop music as a manifestation of this process. Although generating worldwide impact and appeal, the origins of hip-hop can be traced to the same sort of neighborhood environments investigated in this chapter (Marshall 2014). In the Grammy Award-winning "The Message," Grandmaster Flash and the Furious Five are unrelenting in their portrayal of everyday life in the American ghetto:

> It's like a jungle sometimes it makes me wonder
> How I keep from going under
> Broken glass everywhere
> People pissing on the stairs, you know they just don't care

References to danger, violence, crack cocaine, unjust police, physical disorder, and, most relevant to this chapter, the perception that people "just don't care" dominate the lyrics of hip-hop, and not by accident. As the sociolinguist Marcyliena Morgan (2009, 4) puts it, "there is little question that gangsta' rap expressed hopelessness." The lyrics of this song and many more like it were born in deprived neighborhoods from the South Bronx of Grandmaster Flash to the South Central neighborhoods of Los

Angeles studied by Morgan. Shaped by the physical and structural environment, the public recognition that cynicism is high in poor urban neighborhoods and that norms of other-regarding behavior are precarious is something that is cognitively powerful and that is itself a shaper of future change.

I thus conclude that there is a community structure to normative orientations and cultural beliefs: "cognitive landscapes" where simmering disadvantage corrodes expectations of public other-regarding behavior and institutions of social control are mistrusted. Such perceptions and cognitive frames take on new life and cohere into a cumulative texture that is refracted through social interactions, practices, and collective reputations (Small 2002; Suttles 1984). But because race and neighborhood disadvantage have been bound together for long periods of American history, scholars must be careful not to attribute to African Americans a unique subculture of beliefs and attitudes that operate independently of the environment. Indeed, one of the most salient features of American history is persistent neighborhood inequality by race that has been sanctioned by the state, whether explicitly or implicitly.[19] Consider also that a durable pattern of social alienation has emerged among whites in impoverished rural settings (Duncan 2009). Perhaps we should not be surprised that those most exposed to the numbing reality of pervasive economic inequality and racial segregation become cynical about human cooperation and legal systems of justice—which can in turn lead to feedback loops that reinforce those very disadvantages—even as they personally condemn acts of crime and violence that make life more precarious. In this case, the interplay of culture and structure is given potent but tragic meaning.

6

"I Do Me"

Young Black Men and the Struggle to Resist the Street

PETER ROSENBLATT, *Loyola University Chicago*

KATHRYN EDIN, *Johns Hopkins University*

QUEENIE ZHU, *Harvard University*

Children who grow up in high-poverty urban neighborhoods disproportionately experience more crime and violence, attend resource-poor schools, and face constrained labor market opportunities relative to those raised in middle-income or affluent neighborhoods. Over and above their individual and family characteristics, neighborhoods of extreme disadvantage place children and young adults at risk. As they reach their teen years, young people living in these environments are more prone to school dropout, criminal and delinquent behavior, early sexual debut, and adolescent childbearing (see reviews by Ellen and Turner 1997; Leventhal and Brooks-Gunn 2000; Sampson, Morenoff, and Gannon-Rowley 2002). While both boys and girls are impacted by neighborhood violence, sociological research suggests that young men in disadvantaged neighborhoods spend far more time in public spaces in the neighborhood than do young women (Clampet-Lundquist et al. 2011). For these reasons and others, their interactions with peers often revolve around strategies to negotiate neighborhood violence and may disproportionately expose them to criminal activity (Harding 2009).

Indeed, popular accounts of these neighborhoods, such as HBO's *The Wire,* might lead one to guess that the probability of young men becoming involved in delinquent activity is quite high or even a veritable certainty. Yet our in-depth interviews with young men from disadvantaged neighborhoods in Baltimore reveal a tremendous range in the degree to which they were "caught up" in crime and violence, with a sizable number resisting delinquent activity despite their deleterious neighborhood origins.[1]

By late adolescence and early adulthood, more than half of those we interviewed (thirty out of fifty-eight) had no current or prior involvement with neighborhood violence (save as witnesses or occasional victims of crime), and roughly another 20 percent (eleven) had only dabbled in delinquent activity, perhaps getting in an occasional fight or hanging out with drug dealers. And while just under a third (seventeen) have been seriously involved in crime and violence at some point in the past, only a handful say that they are involved at present.

In now-classic studies of the inner city, sociologists have explained high levels of delinquency and violence in the lives of youth as a cultural response to the social isolation and limited opportunities for upward mobility in the communities in which they live (Wilson 1987; Massey and Denton 1993). These studies posited a lack of mainstream norms operating in these neighborhoods. Ethnographic research, however, often rejects the notion of a monolithic "ghetto" subculture and highlights the ways in which youth and adults in disadvantaged neighborhoods often attempt to take more traditional paths toward school or work in the formal economy (Furstenberg et al. 1999; MacLeod 1995; Newman 1999; Duneier 1992; Anderson 1999). Our findings extend this line of research. We find that despite variation in circumstances and outlook, nearly every young man we interviewed attested to the dominance of "the street"—a shorthand for neighborhood crime and violence—in their daily lives. The norms of street life are known to all of these young men (see also Anderson 1999). As they explain, "the streets" are a powerful force to be reckoned with: one that must be actively and forcefully resisted if one is to avoid getting "caught up." Meanwhile, those seeking alternative paths seldom have the tools or opportunities to do so easily and must navigate these alternative paths with little guidance and ample false starts.

This chapter considers the *strategies* youth in disadvantaged neighborhoods employ to resist the pull of the street and carve out an alternative identity. These strategies, while varied, reflect a common emphasis on autonomy—or, as several described it, "I do me." We also examine the external *supports* that aid them on their way. As we will show, coming of age in the crime-ridden projects of West Baltimore (such as the neighborhood nicknamed "Murder Mall") or even in the somewhat better-off working-class sections of the city does not make resisting street culture easy or costless, nor does it guarantee a successful path into the middle class. While outlining how youth avoid getting caught up in the neighborhood's violence and crime, we take into account the possible social and psychological costs of these strategies. We conclude by considering what these strategies really buy these young men in the end, given the tremendous and unyielding structural barriers and notable lack of social support they find when, after managing to craft an identity that is in opposition to the street, they seek to transition to a more conventional pathway to adulthood.

In 2010, we interviewed a sample of 150 youth (seventy-four females and seventy-six males) in Baltimore, Maryland, between the ages of fifteen and twenty-four. These young men and women shared similar origins; all were African American and grew up in highly distressed high-rise Baltimore public housing. Nearly all were raised apart from their biological fathers, and almost all were currently living in neighborhoods that were at least 20 percent poor.[2] In this chapter, we focus on males and limit our sample to the fifty-eight young men in our study who were between the ages of eighteen and twenty-four (omitting the younger males in the sample). We focus on men because of their greater vulnerability to neighborhood violence and crime, and on those over eighteen because we wanted to understand how strategies for resisting street culture were related to the process of pursuing postsecondary schooling, finding employment, and locating independent housing—key tasks that young adults face.[3] Out of those fifty-eight, we profile six in detail, in order to better illustrate the variety of strategies, coping mechanisms, and consequences that come with turning one's back on the path of illicit activity in the neighborhood. We include profiles of these men in Table 6.1.[4]

Results

"They Know Me; They Know What I Stand For":
Strategies for Engaging with the Street

Marcus, at nineteen, has one year of high school left, plans to go into the navy (inspired by the naval career of an uncle), and lives with his mother and two sisters in a turn-of-the-century brick row house in Northwest Baltimore. This bone-thin young man has lived in both the city and the suburbs—which our youth call "the county"—and explains, "Baltimore is a good place to live, but you have to pick the right area. If you pick the wrong area, your children or your husband or yourself is gonna be killed." Upbeat and quick with a joke, Marcus has nevertheless had people close to him die in the streets. When he was fourteen, his best "homeboy" (who

Table 6.1. Respondents in Study

Name	Age	Snapshot	Example of Strategy to Resist the Street	Future Plans
Marcus	19	• Close "homeboy" shot in front of him when he was fourteen, and his cousin was shot by the police • Used to sell drugs but stopped because got tired of "going to jail over and over again"	• Avoids drug dealers in the neighborhood by leaving entirely: "to stay out of trouble, you can't stay in one spot, you gotta move all over the place"	• Inspired by the naval career of an uncle, he plans to join up
Gary	23	• Owns a vintage silver Cadillac, which he detailed himself. It attracts attention from the police and respect from neighborhood youth • Graduated from a county high school but also spends time with friends in a rough part of West Baltimore. He refers to himself as "living between two worlds"	• Refuses to hold drug packages, and pats people down before they get into his car to make sure they are not carrying anything that could get him arrested	• Currently working as a Certified Nursing Assistant. Plans to use connections at work to gain a career in physical therapy
Tony	21	• Lives in a crowded row house in West Baltimore • Has two older brothers "in the streets" and an older sister who is a college grad and a mentor	• Draws a bright line between himself and drug activity in neighborhood, refusing even to buy cigarettes for young men on the corner	• Attending a local community college. Plans to go to pharmacy school and keeps a list of prerequisite classes on the fridge, crossing them off as he takes them

Terrell	21	• Describes himself as a "tough dude, nice, real great to get along with." Also explains, "I don't like people messing with me" • Used to hang out with neighborhood boys who sold drugs until their father stabbed him in a fight	• As a young man, taught himself to fight in order to keep from being picked on. Now he keeps to himself: "I'm a grown man, so I don't need no friends"	• School wasn't for him, and he stresses about job interviews; plans to make a career out of a warehouse distribution job
Doug	22	• Used to sell drugs, has had trouble finding a job with a felony conviction • Engaged and living with his fiancée and son in a quiet Northeast Baltimore neighborhood	• Differentiates between friends and associates— knowing the difference between the two keeps him out of trouble	• Priorities changed when his son Dwight was born—he left hustling behind and is looking for a job
Bob	23	• Transferred out of a magnet school and finished at a local high school, where he finished tenth- and eleventh-grade classes in one year • Into Pokémon and anime, Goth and heavy metal	• Growing up, spent a lot of time in the house by himself. He enjoys dressing in Goth attire to distinguish himself in the neighborhood	• Once worked his way up to shift manager at a fast-food restaurant, now working for minimum wage and hoping to do work his way up again

was in the process of switching neighborhood gang affiliations) was shot as the two were walking to a 7-Eleven convenience store. Marcus's first instinct was to flee the scene, not only because he wanted to avoid getting shot, but because he did not want the police to know he had witnessed the crime, in case he would be called upon to testify. He ran home, took off a shirt stained with blood and brain matter, threw it into the garbage, and showered away the remaining evidence, telling no one about what he witnessed.

This incident occurred while Marcus was living in Brooklyn Homes in South Baltimore, one of the city's most notorious housing projects. Youth who lived in non-project neighborhoods told stories of witnessing violence as well; in fact, nearly every youth had witnessed at least one incident of serious violence. Moving between the neighborhoods where they sleep at night, those where they visit family members, and those in which they have lived in the past and sometimes revisit, these young men confront innumerable challenges to their safety and must make choices on a daily basis about whom to trust and whom to avoid.

Male teens in Baltimore tend to spend their free time out and about in the neighborhood, hanging out on the corner or playing sports in vacant lots and public parks (Clampet-Lundquist et al. 2011). This pattern of leisure behavior regularly exposes them to environments rife with drug activity and violence. Even those who have no involvement with illicit activity but who merely wish to socialize with friends or play basketball or other sports must learn to navigate the street and to adopt defensive strategies if they wish to avoid getting caught up in violence or drug dealing. In creating these strategies, young men must still adapt to the norms of street life even while they do not embrace them. This involves adjusting their behavior to create physical and social distance between themselves and other youth in the neighborhood who are caught up in the streets. Sometimes, though, they must selectively embrace behaviors that are normative within street culture to survive. Avoiding getting caught up requires an intimate knowledge of the norms of street life.

A number of young men described the early teenage years as a time when other youth in the neighborhood start to test them to see how tough they are or "where your mind is at." At more than six feet tall with thick shoulders and neck, Terrell, age twenty-one, is built like a lineman. He describes himself as a "tough dude," but his contagious smile and easygoing manner speak to the gentler side of his personality. Growing up in a rough neighborhood, he described feeling powerless as his bike was stolen out from under him when he was riding home from school and as he watched older kids rip a video game out of his younger brother's hands. He became tougher in order to defend himself, explaining, "I [finally] got my fighting skills up," and feels that people avoid picking on him now because he has the skills to protect himself and is constantly on guard.[5] Other young men have similar memories of strategically choosing to fight—even over the slightest insult—when they first moved to a neighborhood or changed schools, in order to establish their reputation.

Fighting in the short term can ultimately mean less trouble in the long run.

Another way youth adapt to street life is through "being known." Marcus lives in Pimlico now—a step up from the Brooklyn projects—but the neighborhood is so crime infested that the landlord has bricked over all but one window in his apartment. His past experience selling drugs full time (he took a hiatus from school at the end of ninth grade) has taught Marcus a lot—whom to hang out with, and how to tell who is on a path that leads to jail. He says, "All I do is look at 'em, you see how they is." He is recognized by many in the neighborhood because of his mother, a recovered crack addict and Supplemental Security Income (SSI) recipient, but also a self-proclaimed "missionary" who helps the neighborhood's elderly and routinely chastises the neighborhood's drug dealers. Like Marcus, many young men talk about the critical importance of "being known" in the neighborhood, but being known doesn't indicate friendship or intimacy; Marcus is one of the most isolated young men in our study, so for him, nothing could be further from the truth. "Being known" involves making himself familiar enough to those who are involved in dangerous and illicit activity that he is not perceived as a threat or a target. As many young men in our study explained, it is fine to walk around after dark in a place where people are familiar with you, because they are less likely to jump you or assume that you are there to cause trouble.

Gary, age twenty-three, also talks about how "being known" matters. He grew up in the Lexington Terrace housing projects and now lives with his father in a quiet working-class neighborhood at the outer edge of Northeast Baltimore. He spends a lot of time in his meticulously detailed vintage silver Cadillac, traveling back and forth to a close high school friend's home in West Baltimore, in a neighborhood that is under de facto martial law because of the amount of drug trafficking there. Although the neighborhood is outwardly dangerous, Gary explains that he knows a lot of people there, and this provides a measure of safety. He explains, "If people don't know your face they're going to go after you, especially if you come around to talk to one of their girls. They don't like that at all." But because they know him and acknowledge that he is not an outsider, he feels safe.

In addition to developing ways to stay safe, youth also develop strategies for negotiating the advances of the drug dealers who often dominate public spaces in the neighborhood. The teenage years are the prime age when boys can be recruited to sell drugs. Juvenile and adult offenders face very different penalties, so dealers strategically recruit the young through the lure of large sums of money with low risk of jail time. This contact can begin with an older dealer asking a youth simply to hold onto a drug package for a period of time.

One strategy used by youth to negotiate this aspect of street life is to draw bright boundaries between themselves and drug activity. Twenty-one-year-old Tony, who developed his plans to go to pharmacy school during a high school internship, moved out of the projects when he was eight, eventually coming to stay in a house on a tree-lined street in a struggling working-class neighborhood in the western part of the city. While his present neighborhood is much quieter than the projects, there is still drug activity at all hours of the day. He describes how the dealers on the corner know him but also know that he is not "out there" or trying to become involved. He does this by drawing a bright line between himself and the illicit activity he sees every day. Juxtaposing himself against other young men in his neighborhood, he describes those who hang around the liquor store on the corner selling drugs as "misled youth." He will say hello but is wary about the ways that he might be tested. Young kids will ask him to buy cigarillos for them, even though they are under age. He refuses, because "certain stuff like that leads to other things, 'cause if you do it once he'll ask you to go buy alcohol." He explains, "That's how it works—if you do one thing, they gonna ask you to do another, and another, and another . . . until eventually it's like, 'Can you hold that package?'"

Gary ties his shoulder-length dreadlocks back with a hair band, revealing the diamond stud in his left ear. He is thoughtful and engaging and is an avid observer of street life. He has been asked directly to hold packages and carry drugs in his car, but he refuses, explaining, "It's too much of a risk. I don't want to get locked up for carrying a whole pound of weed." Gary's car is his signifier to others in the neighborhoods he visits—a pristine early-nineties silver Cadillac that he bought on Craigslist and detailed with tinted windows and chrome rims. He pats people down before they get in his car to make sure they are not carrying anything that could get him arrested. This is a necessary step, because although the car's tinted windows grant him protection and respect while driving around rough neighborhoods in West Baltimore where he visits a childhood friend, they also draw significant attention from the police, especially as he travels outside the city limits to his job in a hospital. He is especially serious about not letting drugs into the car. He says he has "too much going on to get locked up for someone else's stuff." Because he's drawn a bright line as to what he is "about," Gary has never had a problem when refusing to carry a package. He says of the dealers, "They know me, they know what I stand for."

Being "known" in the neighborhood, as mentioned earlier, does not imply intimate friendships. Lack of trust is a common feature in the lives of many young men growing up in disadvantaged neighborhoods in Baltimore. Young men are quick to differentiate between friends and "associates," the latter being people they know in the streets or conduct illicit activities with but don't get too close to. Doug, a twenty-two-year-old father, has a felony record and has been incarcerated more times than he can remember. He is clear on the differences between friends and associates. As his fiancée, Mayra, works and his son Dwight is in daycare, Doug "chills" with other unemployed men around his age. Importantly, the men are not his friends. "I don't have no friends, for real," he explains. "I got a lot of associates." While associates, who make up the majority of one's social circle, are people who are connected to each other through ulterior motives, friends—called brothers—are those "who've got your best interest at heart." Distinguishing between the two is vital in Doug's world: "Just call people associates, and you don't get disappointed" when they let you down, he says. His security in knowing the difference between an associate and a friend keeps Doug grounded and out of trouble. When approached by a recruiting Crips gang member in prison who tried to coax him to "come home" and join the gang, Doug laughed and replied, "I'm trying to *make it home*, man." He reflects, "I don't need any protection. . . . I've been doin' this too long, by myself. I can't rely on other niggas to help me."

Doug's comments reflect the self-reliance—the "I do me"—that is central to many of these neighborhood engagement strategies. While the teenage years can be a time of shifting friendships, growing up in the neighborhoods they do means that the consequences of ending a friendship are heightened for many of these young men. A number of youth have stories of friendships gone wrong, which reinforces their belief that friends are no substitute for being able to rely on oneself. Terrell, the broad-shouldered "tough dude," was close friends with two brothers who lived next door to him in his East Baltimore row home. For seven years, he hung out with these boys and their father at clubs and houses of acquaintances across the city. One night when they were all hanging out, their father became paranoid that Terrell was going to tell his girlfriend that he was cheating on her and came after Terrell with a knife. Shocked at this betrayal by a man whom he considered a father figure, Terrell did not fight back and was stabbed in the stomach. The experience has soured him on the concept of friendship—he says, "I'm finished with friends. I'm a grown man, so I don't need no friends."

In places where friendships can turn violent and the trust of associates is often in question, many youth adopt the motto "Family over Everything." Some sport tattoos with the abbreviation FOE, often emblazoned on a heart. This does not always connote a close, trusting family (though intense allegiance to family is sometimes evident). More commonly, the FOE ethos functions as a shield against forming risky loyalties to those who are not blood relations.[6] For this reason, a number of youth, both those caught up and those who resisted street life, described cousins, siblings, and other family members as their closest—and only—friends. Marcus, for example, was very close to his cousin, whom he looked up to like an older brother. But when Marcus was twelve, he says this nineteen-year-old young man, who was waiting for the bus at the time, was shot in the back five times by the police after being asked to kneel and place his hands over his head. Seven years later, Marcus still thinks about his cousin every day. And while he has had other friends killed in the streets, including his closest "homie," his cousin's death is an immeasurable loss. When asked to compare his reaction to the death of his cousin to the murder of his best friend, he shrugs, and states simply, "You can always get another friend, but you can't get another cousin."

In short, these youth must adapt to the norms of street life in their neighborhoods in numerous ways, even while seeking to reject becoming caught up in street culture. Choices about where to spend time and whom and what to avoid begin at an early age, as youth are forced to negotiate the drug dealers, gang members, and danger in their neighborhoods. For the large majority of the young men in our study, establishing oneself as a familiar, known face was critical to successfully negotiating the streets. Even Tony or Gary, who refrained from any contact with illicit activity, still emphasized how being known kept them safe. For many, fighting was a component of this strategy, especially when moving to a new neighborhood or school.

The strategy of drawing bright boundaries, exemplified by Gary's vigilance over who and what comes into his car, is meant to create a clear distance in their interactions with caught up youth. In deploying the strategy of being known, Gary is aided by his iconic car and the meticulous care that it shows. He explains that the bright line he draws with regard to the car has earned him the respect of the dealers in the neighborhood, whom he believes admire his resolve. By garnering this respect, Gary has taken the strategy of being known to another level; he is not only a familiar face, but people know the boundary he has drawn. Tony, too, explains that the boys on the corner know him but also respect the fact that he is pursuing college and a career rather than being "out there" with them on the streets.

Turning away from the street often leads these young men to adopt a strong code of self-reliance, which several describe with the expression "I do me." I do me is about controlling what you are able to control and not worrying about the rest. It emphasizes handling your own business and letting other people deal with theirs. It is about establishing an autonomous lifestyle, where intimacy, trust, and self-revelation are eschewed. This phrase captures the shifting relationships and general distrust of peers and reveals the strong current of social isolation that accompanies the rejection of street culture.

"You Gotta Move": Rejecting the Street through Selective Withdrawal

As young men in these environments age, many begin to withdraw from the neighborhood. The strategy of drawing bright boundaries, mentioned above, reflects a partial withdrawal. Although they still rely on complex schemes to navigate the neighborhood safely, many of the young men we interviewed in their early twenties came into less frequent contact with those involved in street life than they had when they were younger. Some changed their leisure routines, treating the outdoor environs of their neighborhoods as a route leading directly to or from school or work. Others were able to cultivate different outlets in which to socialize; becoming more involved with school, at church, or by intensive engagement in hobbies. Sometimes, this withdrawal, and the concomitant engagement in alternative activities, allows young adults to develop strong alternative identities. At times, youth may deploy these alternative identities to actively confront, and signal disdain for, the street, as we discuss toward the end of this chapter.

A self-described loner and outcast, Bob carries himself like an actor on a stage—confident and purposeful in each movement of his hands and flicker of his eyes. When Bob was eleven, his mother and stepfather divorced, and his mother, depressed, began using cocaine. She soon lost her Section 8 voucher, and the family moved multiple times, eventually landing at Bob's grandmother's house. Since his uncle and aunt also lived there, Bob had to sleep on the living room couch. Despite not having much space in the house, he spent very little time in the neighborhood, going from school directly home where he would play video games, indulge his interest in Japanese anime, or hang out playing card games like *Magic: The Gathering* with high-achieving friends from school whom he met in eleventh and twelfth grade. Bob, like a number of other youth who avoided illicit activities, did not make close friends until late in high school. By withdrawing from the neighborhood, he did not make even the weak connections that some youth made with "associates" who were caught up.

Marcus, the young man who witnessed the murder of his friend in the Brooklyn Homes projects and who sold drugs for a while, had to withdraw almost entirely once he stopped dealing because he was tired of "going to jail over and over and over again." Now he and two trusted "homeboys"—his only friends—either retreat into his bedroom and play video games or leave the neighborhood entirely to avoid contact with those who still sell drugs. He explains that the secret to "staying out of trouble is don't hang around with people out there selling drugs or nothing." "I know a lot of people out here sell drugs," he continues, "[so] I won't be around here. I'll be [leaving the neighborhood altogether]. Or I'll be in the house, that's about it." This takes some work on his part— when he and his homeboys want to escape the confines of his stifling hot bedroom, they take the bus to the inner harbor and other public venues across the city that are not dominated by street activity. "To stay out of trouble you can't stay in one spot, you gotta move all over the place," he states.

Deciding to withdraw from the neighborhood is often aided by having a social support system. Tony's two older brothers spent a lot of time in the streets—one is still selling drugs, and the other is recently out of jail and struggling to find a job with a felony record. They stress to him that he should not follow in their footsteps.[7] His older sister, in contrast, is a college graduate who works as a teacher in the city school system. Ever since he can remember, Tony's parents have told him to emulate his sister, and he has followed in her footsteps by becoming a full-time community college student with plans to go to a local university, where he has already been accepted, and then on to pharmacy school. Older siblings who have resisted involvement with drug activity and street violence can play a significant mentoring role, offering youth an example of a path to follow, while the experience of older siblings who were involved with the streets is often raised as a cautionary tale, notably by these siblings themselves.

In other cases, parents have pushed youth to limit their contact with the neighborhood. Some youth point to parents' strict curfews and attitudes toward work or school as influential forces that have kept them away from the streets. One young man who graduated from a county high school credits his mom with "always being on top of me and always keeping me positive and keep me going forward versus pulling me back, or having them to go to for a problem instead of reaching for the streets. I guess you can say I had, like, a family I could go to." Gary's father, who drove a delivery truck before he retired and owns his own home, played a strong role in steering Gary away from the streets when he was in middle school. When he was twelve, Gary's father was awarded custody of him, and he used his sister's address to send Gary to an inner suburb for high school. The suburban school was more economically and racially mixed, with white and Korean students as well as African Americans. It was also "quieter," a phrase youth used to denote lack of overt violence or criminal activity. Over time, Gary learned to straddle the two worlds of his school and his neighborhood and now utilizes that ability each day as he drives in his Cadillac between his job as a Certified Nursing Assistant in the eastern suburbs down to the West Baltimore corner where he spends time with two childhood friends.

Yet in our interviews, almost the same number of young men felt they had little support from immediate family members. Fathers, in particular, were rarely involved. Of the boys profiled here, only Gary lives with his dad. The others described fathers who were painfully absent from important moments in their lives—a promised childhood trip to the zoo, a high school graduation—or missing altogether (Marcus explains, "My mother was my father"). Mothers, too, could be more of a burden than a source of support at times. Bob, Marcus, Terrell, and Gary all had mothers who struggled with drug addiction. Doug esteems his mother—to the point of tears—for being "a queen" by cleaning up her heroin and cocaine habit and dealing with his father's failure to do the same, but her addiction had led to considerable suffering. Marcus's mother now volunteers full time through her church serving the neighborhood's elderly, but while Marcus was dealing drugs in ninth and tenth grades, she was willing to accept a large portion of his profits. "For once, all the bills were paid," he recalls with a guilty pride.

Doug, the young father, now dresses in a clean-cut maroon and gray American Eagle T-shirt that perfectly matches his sneakers—attire that seems contrary to his strong self-identification as someone from the "ghetto" who grew up in the streets—and exhibits an air of maturity and eloquence. As he articulates his struggles in coming to terms with his responsibilities as a father, it becomes apparent that of all the sacrifices he has made to be a good parent, rejecting the street is one of the most difficult. While cognizant of the high crime and disorder of the streets of West Baltimore where he came of age, Doug reflects back on "the 'hood" with nostalgia. "It's real tough," he warns. "If you're not hustling, and you ain't tryin' to get to jail or get shot, you stay away from the ghetto, stay in your house." Nonetheless, he misses the parties, the girls, and all the "action" available in the hustle and bustle of the 'hood. Doug laments that this stimulation is lacking in "boring" Lakeside, in Northeast Baltimore, the working-class neighborhood where he now lives with his fiancée and youngest son. Wrinkling his nose, Doug says of this place, "I don't even call this my 'hood. It's just where I live. It's somebody else's 'hood, not mine. I hate it." He chuckles as he says, "The only thing I like is that my son can go out and play, and I don't gotta worry about bullets hittin' his little head."

For youth like Doug and Marcus, who engaged in illicit activity for a time, selective withdrawal means accepting a tradeoff between greater safety and maintaining relationships. Several young men who had sold drugs in the past took to staying inside the house and avoiding completely their friends who were still engaged in street life, because they worried that any association could make them targets for street violence or the police. But there are also social costs for young men who never engage with or withdraw from the street early on. They do not generally develop the connections to "homeboys" as readily as those who were immersed in the street for a time. One young man's story is telling. Picked on constantly when he moved to his West Baltimore neighborhood from a white neighborhood in the inner suburbs, where his mother had lived for a time after leaving public housing, he was so committed to avoiding the street that he petitioned the local school for permission to come in early in order to escape having to take the same bus as kids from his neighborhood. Isolated and depressed for much of his teenage years, he did not make any friends until late in high school, and these friends did not live in the neighborhood.

Often, youth who disengage from the neighborhood end up growing up between worlds, never fully detaching themselves from the streets of their neighborhoods but also not completely embracing an alternative world. Gary, who went to high school in the county and now works in the suburbs, reflects, "Living in two different worlds, yeah . . . people look at me a certain way, city people look at me in a certain way, county people look at me in a certain way. Like, city people can't believe I work in a hospital; they look at me like, 'Can't believe you work there!' Like, 'It doesn't seem like it's you,' probably 'cuz they don't see that other side of me. They don't see that caring side. The friends from the county don't say anything about it. They say, 'Oh you work there? That's a nice place to work.'" He laughs and shakes his head. "It's kind of crazy."[8] As Gary bridged these worlds, he says he was left feeling that few people really understood where he was coming from.

As we described in the previous section, friends are commonly seen as less trustworthy sources of support than family members. When support from friends or family diminishes or is nonexistent, the "I do me" ethos again emerges as a guide for how to accomplish selective withdrawal from the streets. More than a few young men, like Bob, describe themselves as loners and say they have few close friends. As one young man who ran away from an abusive mother at age eight and spent his childhood in foster care describes it, "[What] I'm doin' now, like training myself to not be codependent, I guess you would call it, you know . . . having like this complex where you've been through so much that you feel like you *need* people, when I really *don't*, you know?"

Being "About Something" (Else): Developing Alternative Identities

By drawing bright boundaries that limit their engagement in the neighborhood or by withdrawing altogether, youth in our sample avoid becoming entangled with the risky behaviors associated with the street. But rejecting street culture, with its familiar courses of action, seldom means that these youth can easily select among alternative cultural pathways, largely because they seldom know the courses of action these alternatives involve. Nonetheless, some youth did adopt strong alternative identities and did so in ways that demonstrated their sharp opposition to the street. Sometimes, these were school- or career-focused. More often, however, they centered around hobbies or avid engagement in some institutional setting, such as a church. Most of the young men who described themselves with the phrase "I'm *about* something" described an alternative something else that was clearly distinct from the street, such as the commitment to raise a child, being part of an active alternative subculture (such as anime), or even the love of Shakespeare sonnets. These alternative identities functioned both as a shield from pressure to become caught up—a symbol that youth felt projected a message of social distance to drug dealers and gang members—and as a psychological coping mechanism that validated their decision to resist street life.

Gary is an old soul at twenty-three. He values what he refers to as the "old school upbringing," which preaches respect and hard work, and laments what he sees as the decline of these values among youth of his generation—many of whom he believes have little patience or loyalty to each other. Though Gary grew up in the projects, he vows to never live in that kind of neighborhood environment again. He asserts, "When I go to West Baltimore, East Baltimore, it reminds me where I come from. . . . I don't want to go back here. . . . I don't want to go back at all." He is focused on the future and on work, although he has faced a series of challenges due to the poor economy. After graduating from high school and working steadily for two years at a Coca-Cola distribution warehouse six days a week, he was unemployed for two years and spent many days going to the library to fill out job applications. His vintage Cadillac again played an important role in his life, as he used it to make ends meet by working as a "hack," an unlicensed cab driver.[9] He spent mornings waiting at supermarkets for "old ladies" and evenings trolling for passengers downtown, but he cautions that "you better be careful because you don't know who you're picking up." Sometimes hacks are targets for armed robbery, while other times people will use them and not pay, but Gary developed a regular clientele by relying on his ability to read people and the streets. "You can tell who to pick up and who not to pick up, just by looking," he explains. Eventually, he won a scholarship to a training program and was one of only eight people in his class of twenty to get a job in the field for which they had trained. As a Certified Nursing Assistant (CNA), Gary finally feels like he is on the right track and is leaning toward a career in physical therapy.

Tony is focused on becoming a pharmacist. He keeps a list of college classes that he needs to take, from prerequisites like algebra to core courses in chemistry, and reviews it every morning, crossing classes off as he completes them. At this point, the list is faded and marked up, pinned with a magnet to the refrigerator in his mother's brick row house in Franklintown in West Baltimore.[10] Tony did not develop these plans until twelfth grade. During an internship at the Maryland Red Cross, Tony made deliveries to the University of Maryland School of Pharmacy and began talking to people there about what it took to become a pharmacist. This experience established the goal of pharmacy school in his mind and solidified his commitment to staying away from the "drama" of the streets that had already claimed his two older brothers. While he knows it will take most of the next decade to achieve his plan, he is patient, explaining, "I took my time, chose to do what I have to do to make an honest living. . . . I'm not the type to waste time with foolishness."

The variety of "something else" that the young men in our study latched on to reflects the limited exposure that many have to viable alternatives to street life. For example, a couple of weeks spent making deliveries to the pharmacy school set Tony on a course for the next decade of his life. For many, becoming "about" a career is made easier through the intervention of a mentor—sometimes a teacher, coach, or pastor who takes an interest, other times an older sibling who is working, or a father figure who provides guidance. These mentors connect these young men to something outside of the neighborhood and validate the career plans they develop. Tony's older sister has inspired him. He chuckles as he recalls, "Everything I did, my moms would bring Tamika up; 'Tamika's doing this, Tamika got her degree, Tamika just moved out,' and I was like, 'OK, Tamika's doing something right.'" On his path to pharmacy school, Tony plans to complete his bachelor of science degree at the same university his sister graduated from. He was accepted the spring prior to our interview, but plans to defer in order to get more prerequisites out of the way at the local community college, where classes are cheaper.

Gary's mentor is his father. Gary recounts that "he always told me the right things to do, stay in school, what to do, what not to do." During his extended unemployment, Gary's dad was an important source of support: "I used to think something was wrong [with me]," Gary explains, "but my father would say, 'No it's not you, it's the economy.'" He looks to his father for advice: "I'm open for any conversation, but when it comes down to advice I listen to my father, because I can't take advice from somebody that's my age, because they've never been through anything." Having someone who has been there before, who has been through the struggles of finding and maintaining a career path, is vital for sustaining life goals. Mentors like Tony's sister and Gary's father validate their search for something else to be "about."

Bob, the self-described outcast and anime fan, has also had a series of mentors in his life: an elementary school teacher who invited him and his classmates over to his house to watch football, the middle school teacher who taught him chess, his stepfather who taught him to "be a gentleman" and introduced him to the church Bob still attends every week, and a pastor who noticed his actor's comportment and got him involved in community theater. Bob describes these mentors as each contributing in their own way to his becoming a man. While none of them connected him to a career in the way that Tony's and Gary's mentors did, by taking an interest in his pursuits they helped validate his sense of himself as someone who "stood out from the crowd."

Bright-eyed and smiling, Bob talks eagerly about his interest in Shakespeare, Poe, and the poet Paul Lawrence Dunbar and says, "I always knew I was going to be different; I always knew I was going to be an outcast." He first realized this in middle school, when he was flipping through channels and saw a cartoon that was "so fast paced, and high octane, and colorful, and awesome!" The cartoon was Pokémon, and this rapidly spawned a lifelong interest in Japanese anime, a "whole different world" from the East Baltimore housing project where he spent much of his childhood. For a long time, however, Bob was the only one in this world. It was not until eleventh grade that he met a small group of peers who were into anime. Through this group, he got into the Goth subculture, heavy-metal music, and the rock/hip-hop group Insane Clown Posse and learned that "you can be black, but you don't have to be like these guys out on the street." Bob uses Goth and the role of the outcast as part of his repertoire as he seeks to connect to an alternative pathway and to avoid becoming, as he puts it, "a statistic: [one of] the percentile of young men ages eighteen to twenty-five to be a father, or in and out of jail, or to be unemployed, or uneducated." He explains, "I was going to be in the percentile of young men who actually grow up to *be* something, young men who [have legitimate jobs], are competent fathers, who are things that I never had." The Goth attire and the interest in anime and rock are still an important part of his identity even in his mid-twenties. They continue to mark and validate his separation from the streets and reinforce his belief that he can take a different path. Bob's black clothing, black makeup, and pants with chains serve as a visible symbol to the caught up youth in the neighborhood that he is not participating in street culture. He becomes animated when describing how adopting Goth attire allows him to "stand out because I *am* different. . . . When somebody sees you [dressed] like that, people in my neighborhood, it was definitely protection—like this is *me*, I am not *that*."

Bob does not have any children yet, and he is proud of this, but his desire to be a better father to his future offspring than his father was to him is a sentiment shared by a number of young men in our sample who *are* fathers. For them, having children was often what sparked the drive to leave the streets; fatherhood became the alternative identity they were "about" and what gave them the motivation to reject street involvement in favor of a "legitimate" path. Doug was incarcerated for the entirety of Mayra's pregnancy with his youngest son. When Mayra finally brought the baby to the prison to meet Doug, the prison guard allowed him to hold Dwight briefly, relaxing the rule against physical contact with visitors. Doug was moved when the baby clung to him and refused to let go when pulled away by his mother. Taken aback, he said to his son, "Man, you've never even met me before, I didn't ever rub your mother's belly when you were inside, yet you hold onto me like that?" That experience transformed Doug's priorities and outlook on life, as he realized, "Yo, I gotta do something for this little dude."

From then on, Doug sought ways to separate himself from the streets, and determined to settle down and look for a legitimate job—"something real nice to get me out of this"—because a father "has to build some type of foundation for the kid." This decision, however, entails substantial costs. Doug now finds himself fighting for jobs he would not have even considered before, like stocking shelves at PetSmart for $10 an hour, when he boasts he could easily earn $1,000 in one night by hustling drugs in the city. He no longer views this as a real alternative, though, since "the money is good, but the consequences are horrible" if he gets caught. Doug feels he needs to "be there" for his son—"if I'm gone, there's gonna be other people telling my son what to do? That's crazy. What if he gettin' bullied in school by kids and I can't go there and bully their parents? I gotta teach [Dwight] to be a man and stand on your own two [feet], and ain't nobody gonna show him but me. I'm gonna raise him right."

Being about something is an important way for these young men to maintain their determination to resist the streets. Having an alternative identity both bolsters and validates their decision to turn away from the street, but the decision to "go straight" can be hard. Tony bears the weight of being the only one of his three brothers "trying to do right" on his shoulders, noting, "If you trying to do the right thing, man, keep doing it, don't let anyone tell you otherwise, 'cause it's rough as it is, man." Mentors play a key role in supporting these young men, but there are limitations—the further they get into territory that no one in their family or social circle knows, the more they end up being on their own, without guidance. Community college can become frustrating, as many youth who come from Baltimore City Public Schools are unprepared academically and must spend a year or more completing remedial nondegree courses. In Baltimore, where the majority of our youth went to school, fewer than one-quarter of high school graduates who enroll in college end up earning degrees (Durham and Westlund 2011). These astonishingly low numbers, even among those who do enroll, reveal how difficult it is for youth who are committed to the college path to actually succeed in realizing their goal. Our interviews uncovered stories of students who had to take multiyear hiatuses from college in order to work fast-food jobs to make enough to pay for another semester. One young man, discouraged by the lack of "seriousness" on the part of students and the poor quality of the instruction at the local community college, ruefully noted that it had the reputation of being the cheapest school in the United States, but "you get what you pay for."[11]

Others, like Doug, the young father, can get discouraged by barriers that impede efforts to start anew. A competent job applicant, Doug actively ensures that he makes eye contact, sits up straight, has a firm handshake, and knows "how to talk" during interviews, yet he always gets "shot down," causing him to conclude that "the [felony] record just speaks more" than his actual qualifications.

Even for those without a criminal record, employment opportunities are bleak. The 11 percent unemployment rate in Baltimore is higher than the national average, but for black men it is an even more dismal 17 percent.[12] Even finishing a degree or a job-training program is not a guarantee of employment—a couple of young men in our sample ended up taking minimum-wage fast-food jobs despite completing certificate programs in information technology or video game design. These experiences can be demoralizing and leave some adrift, depressed, and even more isolated. Another young man returned to Baltimore after his plan to move in with his grandparents in Florida and go to community college fell through. Depressed and demoralized, he blames himself for making "stupid" choices and at the age of twenty-one has difficulty envisioning any future for himself other than sitting around getting high with his cousins.

Conclusion

Despite the struggles and obstacles that characterize their personal histories, the majority of these young men have turned their back on the highly visible path of engaging in the crime or violence of the streets, at least for now. However, rejecting the street leaves young men with few concrete alternatives. Although many would agree with the youth who said of drug dealing, "You can't win in that lifestyle," few have the tools and opportunities to easily, or effectively, pursue another, more conventional path to adulthood. This does not mean that they become caught up, however. Instead, many who resist the street espouse an ideology of "I do me," which involves focusing on one's own goals without reference to the reactions of others and, most importantly, espouses the idea that a young man should not have to rely on anyone else.

Our story concurs with other accounts that show that while childhoods spent in disadvantaged neighborhood environments are associated with significant risk, many youth do make conscious efforts to avoid involvement in violence and delinquency (Harding 2009, 2011; Hannerz [1969] 2004), while others desist over time (Laub and Sampson 2003). Consistent with these studies, our interviews challenge the conventional wisdom that youth raised in high-poverty neighborhoods are entirely isolated from "mainstream" norms of conduct. Clearly, this is not so. Yet we argue that it would be a mistake to conclude, as David Harding (2011, 336) has claimed, that "it is inaccurate to conceptualize the cultural context of the poorest neighborhoods as fundamentally different from that of other neighborhoods." Despite evidence of exposure to mainstream or middle-class orientations and goals among our youth, the norms of the street clearly exert an influence on these young men's lives, whether they embrace them or not (see also Anderson 1999).

In the face of pressures to become (or remain) caught up in the streets, youth employ a range of strategies. Some strategies are rooted in adaptation to street norms such as the importance of "being known," or fighting to establish one's street reputation in order to prevent further threat of violence. Other strategies are more oppositional to these norms but strike a middle ground. Youth may draw bright boundaries around certain illicit behaviors, making clear they don't engage in them, while still making an effort to be "known" in the neighborhood. Still other strategies call for more overt rejection of street life. This can involve withdrawing from the neighborhood altogether, or "being about something"—a goal or activity that is clearly different from street culture. As Bob puts it, the "something" is a set of involvements that indicate to those caught up in the streets that "this is *me,* I am not *that,*" while also validating the decision to turn away from street life. There is some evidence that over the early life course, at least some youth move from the former set of strategies to the latter. This leads some to experience quite striking levels of isolation, while others manage to embrace an alternative identity. Our data suggest, though do not prove, that those who manage to construct a strong alternative identity, whether through anime, a vintage car, a child, or a clear career goal, might be more likely to be successful over time than those who do not. Yet the sheer variety of what constitutes that "something else" indicates that, contrary to Harding's claims, there are few clear, ready-made, cultural alternatives to the street available to these youth. Instead, they must, and do, innovate. Even the slightest contact with an alternative cultural model (through happenstance deliveries to a pharmacy or flipping the television channel to a Pokémon cartoon) can spark the start of what will constitute their "something else." Mentors can play a role in helping young men find that alternative, but often youth end up in situations where mentors lack the required expertise, especially when it comes to navigating the array of postsecondary school options available. And even a determined youth with a dedicated mentor may be no match for the structural barriers these young people face as they move through life. Thus even for those who deploy strategies of resistance and hold to some form of an alternative identity, it is difficult to forecast what the future holds.

Resisting the risk behaviors associated with the streets is not a guarantee of success, something that these young men realize as they talk about struggling, and "trying to do right." There are also social costs that come with this individualism in the form of isolation from peers and even family members. In place of these bonds, many young men deploy the "I do me" ethos as they navigate a different path. Despite the sharp structural obstacles they face, these youth believe that this ethos, and their determination to abide by its dictates, sets them apart from more delinquent peers.

Some of the young men in our sample believe they have exhausted all that the city has to offer. Doug plans to take his young family and start anew somewhere else, like Virginia: "I basically already laid my path in Baltimore, so the only thing to do now is get up and leave," he reasons. He does not, however, regret his choices and lifestyle thus far. Speaking about his experiences in the street and his run-ins with the law in West Baltimore, where he sold drugs, he asserts, "It let me know who I am. I'm bigger than this. It's nothing. And I can get out of this. It can't hold me down."

7

More Than Just Black

Cultural Perils and Opportunities in Inner-City Neighborhoods

VAN C. TRAN, *Columbia University*

Introduction

My first introduction to sociology was through William Julius Wilson's work on urban poverty among native blacks in Chicago and Mary Waters's work on West Indian immigrants in New York. I quickly realized that these scholars were talking about two very different ethnoracial groups, even though I found it difficult to distinguish between them with my then relatively untrained eyes. Later, I also learned that these groups often lived in very similar, if not adjacent, neighborhoods and were often portrayed by the media as simply "black." Yet for the most part, urban poverty scholars were happy to delegate the study of West Indians and other immigrant groups to the sociologists of immigration, despite the increasingly foreign sounds, sights, and smells permeating many inner-city neighborhoods. Immigration scholars, meanwhile, were too preoccupied by the focus on coethnic community to pay adequate attention to how neighborhood context, independent of the coethnic setting, shapes the ways in which ethnic groups function and conduct their daily lives.[1]

And yet, everywhere I looked in New York City, I saw how these immigrants and their children were reshaping and remaking neighborhoods, often with vivid imagination and tenacity (Kasinitz 1992; Waldinger 1996; Smith 2006; Iceland 2009). Though neighborhoods were often mentioned in the major studies of the post–1965 second generation, with the theory of spatial assimilation being a key component of both classical and contemporary accounts of immigrant incorporation (Portes and Rumbaut 2001; Portes and Zhou 1993; Kasinitz et al. 2008), neighborhood as an object of study is often secondary in this research to the more immediate concerns of identity choices, socioeconomic mobility, and educational achievement (but see Brown 2007). At the same time, urban scholars have focused on the problems of the inner city, most notably the disadvantages facing native blacks, which significantly worsened in the 1970s and 1980s, coinciding with the rise of immigration in these same cities and neighborhoods.

Over the last decades, a large literature on urban poverty has explored the challenging experiences of growing up black and poor in inner-city neighborhoods (Anderson 1999, 2008; Edin and Kefalas 2005; Patterson 2006; Sampson 2012; Venkatesh 2000, 2006; Wilson 1987, 2009). And yet, there has been a dearth of research examining the neighborhood experiences of second-generation West Indians who grew up in similar neighborhoods and often live in close proximity to native blacks. This chapter seeks to bring both "neighborhood" and "culture" back into the immigration research agenda by exploring how different ethnic groups navigate disadvantaged, inner-city context. More specifically, I will compare and contrast the experience of second-generation West Indians to that of native blacks. Drawing on geocoded survey and qualitative data from the Immigrant Second Generation in Metropolitan New York study, I will examine how neighborhood context and ethnic-specific cultural strategies interact in shaping divergent socioeconomic outcomes for both groups.

By examining two different ethnic groups in a similar structural context, this chapter contributes to the ongoing debate on the relative importance of ethnic culture and social structure in shaping one's life chances (Lee and Zhou 2014; Patterson 2000, 2004; Wilson 2009; Waters 1999; Kasinitz et al. 2008; Lamont and Small 2008; Tran 2011). On the one hand, the reality of enduring racial segregation and discrimination means that both groups continue to live in highly segregated neighborhoods, with similar structural constraints and physical environments. On the other hand, many studies documented a clear advantage for West Indians over native blacks in the labor market, even after adjusting for relevant background factors, with immigrant selectivity among West Indians playing a central role in this debate (Model 2008; Waters 1999). As the sociologist Suzanne Model (2008) has pointed out, attempts to compare foreign-born (i.e., first-generation) West Indians and native blacks cannot fully rule out the immigrant selectivity factor.

By comparing native West Indians (i.e., second-generation) to native blacks, this analysis explicitly deals with the selectivity issue in several ways. First, because second-generation West Indians were born and raised in the American context, they did not make the decision to migrate to the U.S. and are not selective in the same ways that their first-generation parents might be. Second, many speak English without an accent and are virtually indistinguishable from African Americans, suggesting that native whites' preference for West Indians over native blacks (i.e., white favoritism) is unlikely to be an explanation for their relative advantage. Third, because second-generation West Indians were raised in mostly immigrant households, their experiences are often shaped by the cultural understandings and expectations from their immigrant parents. As a result, this provides a unique opportunity to observe how ethnic-specific cultural elements might contribute to their relative advantage in socioeconomic outcomes. Taking both immigrant selectivity and cultural differences seriously, I then ask how selectivity in the West Indian first generation shapes the social mobility of the second generation. More importantly, I explore the specific cultural mechanisms that contribute to differences in socioeconomic attainment between second-generation West Indians and native blacks.

My results generally confirm the advantage in both educational and labor market outcomes among second-generation West Indians over native blacks, though I found no difference between the two groups on arrest and incarceration rates.[2] On the one hand, I find that both native blacks and West Indians grew up in neighborhoods that are segregated from native whites, though West Indians lived in areas that are relatively more advantaged compared to native blacks. These findings confirm the importance of race as the "master status" in shaping residential patterns (Foner 2001), suggesting that West Indians have not fully achieved spatial assimilation across immigrant generations by moving into areas in closer proximity with native whites. On the other hand, I also document the different ways in which second-generation West Indians and native blacks navigate their neighborhood environments, with the former reporting stricter parenting, lower levels of unsupervised playtime in the streets, different reactions to drug use and dealing, and fewer neighborhood-based social ties. As a result, West Indians are less connected to their local peer network compared to native blacks. In turn, this has the unintended consequence of sheltering them from neighborhood gangs, drugs, and crime as well as facilitating their social mobility.

West Indians and African Americans in New York City

This chapter draws on data from the Immigrant Second Generation in Metropolitan New York (ISGMNY) study which was conducted by Philip Kasinitz, John Mollenkopf, and Mary Waters (Mollenkopf et al. 1999). The ISGMNY study includes a multi-staged stratified random survey of 3,415 respondents living in New York City and the inner suburbs of New Jersey, Westchester, and Long Island.[3] The study focuses on the experiences of young adults (aged eighteen to thirty-two) from both native and second-generation background. In this chapter, my analysis focuses on the comparison between second-generation West Indians and native blacks, with data from native whites also being used as a reference point.

The ISGMNY study is one of only three major studies in the U.S. that focus on the post–1965 second generation and the only major study that includes a substantial number of second-generation West Indians. In addition to information on family background and educational and occupational trajectories, ISGMNY gathered detailed information about the neighborhoods where the respondents grew up. For this chapter, I use questions about the neighborhoods where respondents were born, where they lived the longest between the ages of six and eighteen and where they resided at the time of the survey. Specifically, the survey asked for the name, location, cross streets, and other pertinent details of the respondents' birth, childhood, and current neighborhood at the time of the survey. This information made it possible to geocode respondents' addresses to identify the census tracts and block groups in which they lived. The qualitative data provides detailed information on the respondents' experiences growing up in the neighborhood and the decisions that shape their mobility process. Overall, the data set contains 408 native whites, 421 native blacks, and 407 West Indian respondents.[4]

Comparing the experiences of native blacks and West Indians is important for four reasons. First, both groups are racially "black" (Waters 1999; Foner 2001; Reid 1939) and tend to live in very similar, and often adjacent, neighborhoods from each other (Crowder and Tedrow 2001). Second, this comparison takes into account the increase in intraracial heterogeneity among blacks as well as the emergence of the black middle class (Pattillo 2013; Lacy 2007). Third, by comparing two culturally distinct groups living in similar types of neighborhoods, this analysis reveals the relative importance of ethnic culture and social structure in shaping life chances (Patterson 2000, 2004; Wilson 2009; Waters 1999; Kasinitz et al. 2008; Lee and Zhou 2014). Fourth, this comparison contributes directly to the ongoing debate on the underlying causes of the West Indian advantage over native blacks (Waters 1999; Model 2008).

New York City provides a unique context for this comparison. Whereas the West Indian population in other states such as Florida and Maryland is relatively small and more selective, New York City has long been the favored destination for West Indian immigrants in the United States (Kasinitz 1992; Patterson 1995; Foner 2001). Furthermore, the West Indian population is as large as the native black population, comprising a substantial portion of the city's black working class (Kasinitz 1992). In their daily life, they are also as likely as blacks to experience discrimination and prejudice from native whites and others, because internal ethnic distinctions among blacks often elude many native whites (Vickerman 1999). The sociologist Mary Waters (1999, 3) referred to this as "the invisibility of the Caribbean immigrants as immigrants and their visibility as blacks."

As many incidents that involved violence against black immigrants in New York City made clear, West Indians' invisibility continues to persist, despite significant research over the last two decades on this ethnic group (Kasinitz 2001). As the anthropologist Nancy Foner (2001, 10) observed, "For West Indian New Yorkers of African descent, being black is the 'master status' that pervades and penetrates their lives." From the Crown Heights riots and the Church Avenue boycott of greengrocers to the killing of Michael Griffith by a white mob and police brutality against Abner Louima, the fact that all of these cases involved black immigrants was rarely highlighted in the national media, except in the occasional local coverage where reporters are more sensitive to the ethnic differences among the black population (Foner 2001; Waters 1999; Kasinitz 1992). These incidents confirm what second-generation West Indians reported experiencing in their life, where they are just as likely as native blacks to report being discriminated against by the police, at work, at school, at local shops, and at other establishments (Waters and Kasinitz 2010).

Immigrant Selectivity and the West Indian Advantage

A long literature has documented the so-called West Indian advantage over native blacks in obtaining secure employment (Model 2008). Indeed, conservatives have used these differences as evidence that continuing marginalization of African Americans is partially due to their lack of the right "cultural" values (for example, see Sowell 1978). Though immigrant selectivity clearly plays a role in this debate, other aspects of West Indian culture and native whites' preference for West Indians over native blacks might potentially matter (Model 2008; Waters 1999; Patterson 1995). For example, the sociologist Suzanne Model (2008, 57) has pointed out that "selectivity theorists believe that only a subset of Caribbean-raised individuals have these desirable traits: those who chose to migrate. Those who choose to stay home are not exceptional. Culturalists, on the other hand, believe that all Caribbean-raised individuals, both movers and stayers, have these desirable traits." Adjudicating among these competing perspectives, Model concludes that positive selectivity is the key factor that underlies this advantage. Specifically, she finds that "immigrant adults are more positively selected on education, and immigrant workers are more positively selected on occupation than their non-migrant compatriots" in her analysis of a sample of movers and stayers from the West Indies to the United States (30).

This chapter builds on this debate by comparing the experience of second-generation West Indians with native blacks, essentially avoiding immigrant selectivity among the first generation as a likely explanation for differences in socioeconomic outcomes. That said, second-generation West Indians are still selective in the sense that they might have parents who have brought with them certain outlooks or motivations, which shape the way in which the second generation makes sense of the opportunities in the United States. And yet, what selectivity indicates is not that ethnic-specific cultural strategies do not matter, but that the cultural elements operating are those of the selected group of immigrants who migrated from their home country and who have established themselves in the U.S. setting, not those of their parents' culture from their home country (Patterson 2000). Put differently, this chapter starts with the premise that any cultural influence on an ethnic group can only be understood interactively with the structural conditions and the physical environment in which ethnic groups live in the United States—a point that is also made in the agenda-setting chapter of this volume (Patterson and Fosse).

Instead of focusing exclusively on individual-level variables, the chapter also broadens the scope of this long-standing discussion on the West Indian advantage over native blacks by taking seriously the neighborhood context in which members of both groups grew up. This kind of geocoded data on the second generation has not been available until recently, and this analysis is the first attempt to document this intraracial difference in residential environment between the two groups. This is because the U.S. census stopped asking the parental birthplace question after 1970, making it impossible to separate second-generation West Indians from those in the later generations using census data. Whereas the quantitative analyses establish the differences in socioeconomic outcomes and neighborhood environments for the two groups, the qualitative evidence provides details on the social dynamics occurring within these neighborhoods and the cultural strategies that members of both groups adopt to navigate their life in this context. In particular, this chapter highlights how cultural understandings shape the ways these groups "live" in their neighborhoods, which also carry implications for their socioeconomic outcomes.

The West Indian Second-Generation Attainment Gap

Whereas studies on the West Indian advantage mostly focused on labor market outcomes,[5] this chapter extends this discussion by including educational outcomes as well as delinquency rates. Overall, data from the ISGMNY study confirm the second-generation advantage among West Indians across eight measures: high school dropout, unemployment rate, NEET[6] rate, college graduate, professional attainment, arrest rate, incarceration rate, and teenage pregnancy. These eight measures are standard outcomes in urban poverty research, providing a comprehensive snapshot of socioeconomic attainment. Native blacks reported the most disadvantaged outcomes, while West Indians reported outcomes similar to those of native whites. For example, 11.4 percent of the native black sample did not have a high school education, compared to only 6.9 percent of West Indians and 4.2 percent of native whites. Native blacks were twice as likely to be unemployed compared to West Indians (11.8 percent) and native whites (9.1 percent). Similarly, their NEET rate (25.7 percent) was twice higher than West Indians' (13 percent) and four times the rate of native whites (6.3 percent). On attainment measures, native blacks were less likely than West Indians and native whites to have completed a bachelor's degree or to be in a professional occupation by the age of twenty-five. Among native black females, the teen pregnancy rate (24.7 percent) was also double West Indians' (12.7 percent) and six times higher than native whites' (3.5 percent). Among native black males, the arrest rate was 31.9 percent and the incarceration rate was 15.7 percent, higher than those for West Indians and native whites.

Moving beyond descriptive statistics, Figure 7.1 presents selected predicted probabilities for eight outcomes for all three ethnic groups based on multivariate logistic regression analyses that include controls for key demographics and family background. Controlling for observed background conditions, West Indians are much less likely than native blacks to drop out of high school, be unemployed, be idle, or have a child by the age of eighteen. They are also much more likely than native blacks to have graduated from college and to be in a professional occupation by the age of twenty-five. However, there are no significant differences between native blacks and West Indians (or native whites) in arrest and incarceration rates.[7] These results indicate a clear West Indian advantage in educational and labor market outcomes, even after controlling for parental background characteristics (i.e., measurable characteristics in immigrant selectivity).

What factors might account for this persistent gap in socioeconomic attainment, even after adjusting for basic background conditions? In what follows, I argue that community-level structural conditions matter, but so do cultural understandings that are specific to these groups. I first attempt to show that West Indians tend to live in slightly better neighborhoods compared to native blacks, both in childhood and young adulthood. Though this neighborhood advantage partially accounts for the gaps in attainment, there are important differences in how both groups choose to "live" within their neighborhood. Specifically, I point to particular cultural strategies relevant to the navigation of the disadvantaged context: parenting strategies, involvement with the drug trade, and the engagement with the local peer network. I contend that these cultural factors interact with structural environment in shaping the divergence in mobility across groups.[8]

How Structure Matters: Concentrated Poverty, Violence, and Racial Segregation

In this section, I begin by using the geocoded ISGMNY data to describe the neighborhood structural context for both groups from birth to young adulthood. I then turn to the qualitative data to describe their

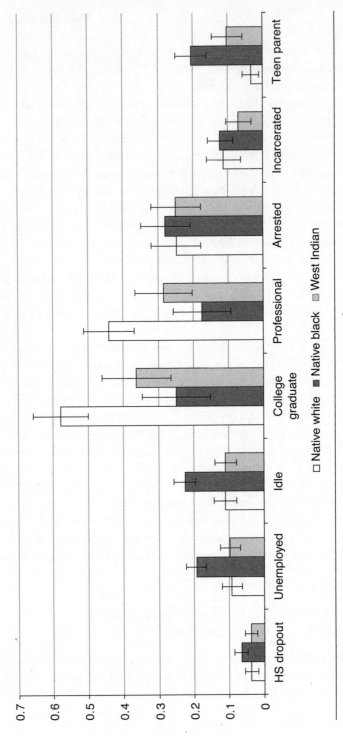

Figure 7.1. Predicted probabilities on selected outcomes by ethnic groups[9]

Legend: □ Native white ■ Native black ▨ West Indian

subjective experiences of these structural conditions. Together, this provides a comprehensive overview of the lived experiences on the ground for both groups.

Neighborhood Context from Birth to Young Adulthood

To begin, Figure 7.2 provides bivariate results on neighborhood trajectories over time using share of non-Hispanic whites and mean household income at the census tract level for West Indians, native blacks, and native whites. Mean household income was adjusted using the Consumer Price Index and benchmarked in the year 2000. As expected, the average native white respondent was born in a predominantly white neighborhood and continued to live in such neighborhoods well into young adulthood. In contrast, native blacks and West Indians live in areas with much lower levels of non-Hispanic whites. In young adulthood, native blacks live in neighborhoods where non-Hispanic whites comprised only 9 percent of the tract population, whereas West Indians are almost equally segregated from non-Hispanic whites. On mean household income, there are important differences between native blacks and West Indians. Native blacks live in the neighborhoods with the lowest mean household income across the three time points, whereas West Indians live in areas of much better quality. Overall, these results demonstrate that second-generation West Indians have not become spatially assimilated into the white mainstream, with many still living in black neighborhoods, though they are more likely to be in neighborhoods characterized by less concentrated disadvantage.

To further explore intraracial differences in neighborhood structural context, Figure 7.3 presents results from multivariate analyses restricted to only native black and West Indian respondents. The top panel indicates that West Indians on average live in neighborhoods with mean income that is $8,180 higher than native blacks, a large, statistically significant gap that remains even after controlling for all observed, relevant background conditions. Similarly, the lower panel presents the coefficients for ethnic dummies for both the adjusted and unadjusted models for percent non-Hispanic white, concentrated disadvantage,[10] and affluence.[11] The first variable captures the extent of segregation from whites, while the latter two variables capture the extreme ends of the distribution of neighborhood structural conditions. On the one hand, there is no statistically significant difference between West Indians and native blacks in both models

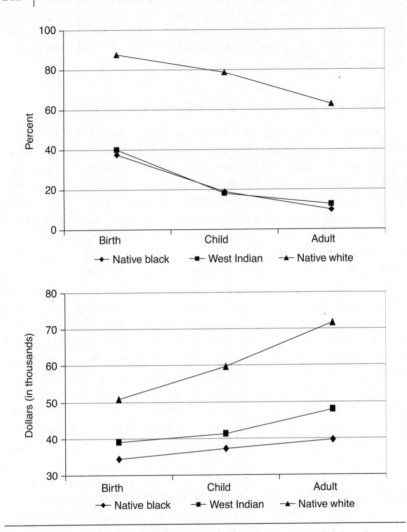

Figure 7.2. Neighborhood trajectory from birth to young adulthood: percent non-Hispanic white and mean household income[12]

regarding the proportion of non-Hispanic whites. On the other hand, West Indians live in neighborhoods that are much less disadvantaged and more affluent than those of native blacks, even after adjusting for all relevant observed background conditions.

These findings point to the distinction between racial and socioeconomic composition in the two groups' residential contexts, which is crucial to our understanding of their experiences. Though native blacks and

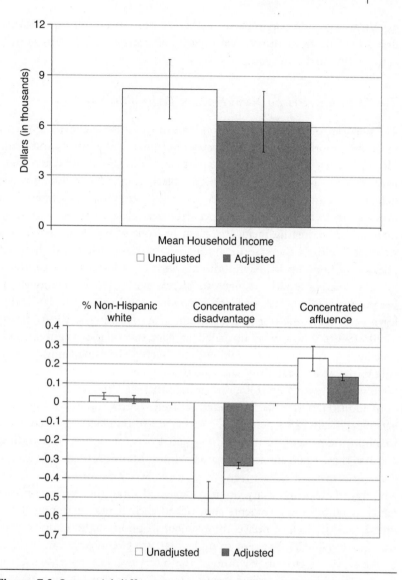

Figure 7.3. Intraracial differences in neighborhood attainment in young adulthood[13]

West Indians live in neighborhoods with similar proportions of native whites and are equally segregated from whites, West Indians also live in neighborhoods that have less concentrated disadvantage and have access to more resources than those of native blacks. In the following section, I turn to the qualitative evidence to explore respondents' subjective experiences growing up in these neighborhoods. Specifically, this analysis draws on data from thirty native black and thirty West Indian respondents in the qualitative sample.

The African American Narrative: The Perils of the Street

The majority of native black respondents in the survey reported growing up in neighborhoods with high rates of crime (72.9 percent) and drugs (66.3 percent). Among those who participated in the qualitative component, twenty-two of the thirty native black respondents also provided detailed accounts of drugs and crimes in the neighborhoods where they grew up. In fact, many incidents occurred very close to home, with some interviewees reporting incidents "right in front of my door" or "in the staircase." This is the case for both working-class blacks and the black poor, who grew up in neighborhoods with high levels of concentrated poverty. Navigating the dangerous streets within their neighborhood became both a daily task for black respondents and a skill that they had to learn early on in life (for similar findings, see Harding 2010; Anderson 1990, 1999). Those who managed to "get out of the neighborhood" quickly learned that they would end up "seeing the same things," referring to the widespread drug sales and dealing networks that they encountered when growing up (for a similar account, see Venkatesh 2006).

In addition, native blacks were more likely to grow up in housing projects. Specifically, 15.4 percent of native black respondents reported living in a housing project, compared to only 5.4 percent among West Indians and less than 1 percent among native whites. Many recalled early experiences in Brownsville, East New York, or the South Bronx—the most disadvantaged areas in the city. Some complained about the resignation with which neighborhood residents approached their living environment and noted that the lack of police enforcement in poor neighborhoods made the situation much worse. For example, Juan was twenty-seven and worked in the service sector at the time of the interview. Having grown up in Crown Heights, he described "project living" as "normal living," though he was aware of how different his neighborhood, which he referred to as "the ghetto," really was from the suburbs:

Q: What was it like to grow up in that neighborhood, in East New York?
A: See, it's hard to describe because as me being black, I mean, it was normal living. See it's different if you have any person from the

suburbs living out there and it be different for them living out in the ghetto like out here. It was hard growing up. I mean, street drugs, bodies, murders, I mean to me all of this was the typical life-style out there. That's how it was. They settle down short; that was the lifestyle out there; that was when I was growing up. (twenty-seven-year-old African American male)

Middle-class blacks were not fully immune to drugs and violence because middle-class black neighborhoods were often positioned in close proximity to other disadvantaged black areas (for a similar point, see Pattillo 2013). Put differently, middle-class blacks often live in "pockets of affluence" amidst wider swaths of concentrated disadvantage. For example, Molly described her family background as "middle class." Her father worked as a health inspector for the City of New York, and her mother was a supervisor at a local company. She attended a private university as an undergraduate but did not complete her four-year degree. At the time of the interview, she was working as a receptionist and lived in Jamaica (Queens), which she then compared to her childhood experience in Flatbush (Brooklyn):

Q: How would you compare where you live now [Jamaica] to Flatbush?
A: The community is great. They have a lot to offer for the children. . . . It's better. I mean I cannot be afraid to let them run outside ahead of me, whereas in Flatbush in Brooklyn, you don't know where a bullet is coming from. So it's a big step up.
Q: What are the bad things about this neighborhood?
A: What I would say is bad is the Boulevard. It's got a lot of drug traf-ficking. And that's the only downfall of the neighborhood, which they are trying to stop, but that's about it really. You don't see much rape going on or robbing or stealing or any of that source but they are very well protected around here. Security is good. Twenty-four hours. It's just the Boulevard mainly trafficking with drugs. That's the downfall. (thirty-two-year-old African American female)

To sum up, many native black respondents reported growing up in some of New York's most disadvantaged neighborhoods with higher levels of crime along with significant gang- and drug-related activities. They also lived in some of the most segregated neighborhoods with the lowest presence of non-Hispanic whites and often in close proximity of West Indians. Navigating and surviving in this disadvantaged context is one of the most salient themes in the interviews. This includes reflections on how to stay safe, how to avoid fights, how to resist the pressure to join a youth gang, as well as involvement with the drug trade, which often opened the door to more serious criminal involvements. These topics will be further explored in the second half of this chapter, which focuses on how group-specific cultural strategies matter for social mobility.

The West Indian Narrative: Islands in the City

One-third of the West Indian respondents in the survey reported growing up in Flatbush, Crown Heights, Bedford-Stuyvesant, and Jamaica. In contrast to native blacks, West Indians were more likely to live in mixed neighborhoods or in close proximity of other mixed areas, with a presence of whites or other non-white ethnic groups. Their neighborhoods also differed from those of native blacks in one important dimension: they are often surrounded by other coethnics from the West Indies. For example, Jarrell, a recent graduate of a public university and a case manager at a social service agency, described his experience in Flatbush as living in "an island in the city":

> Q: What was it like to grow up in Flatbush?
> A: Flatbush is like living on an island, (laughter) in the middle of a big city.
> Q: Why do you say that?
> A: Because 99 percent of the residents of Flatbush are from the Islands, and it's kind of like [a] melting pot of Caribbean culture mixed with American. The way things are done, the way people speak is still kind of representative of where they come from but always with the capitalist kind of twist to it because we are American. (twenty-three-year-old West Indian male)

Many West Indian respondents in the survey also reported growing up in neighborhoods with high rates of crime (68.1 percent) and drugs (57 percent), though there was a reduction in scale and nature of these incidents compared to native blacks. For example, whereas shooting was a regular occurrence in the neighborhoods described by black respondents, it was infrequently mentioned among West Indian respondents. Middle-class West Indians described growing up in relatively decent neighborhoods in Queens where children got along with their peers, though they were still likely to be in close proximity with native blacks.

Among respondents in the qualitative component of the study who did grow up in the most disadvantaged neighborhoods such as East New York or Brownsville, neighborhoods that were notorious for their high concentrations of social problems, almost all lived in the areas with less crime and violence, while native blacks tended to concentrate within public housing projects in these neighborhoods. In terms of crime, stories of "car stolen in front of one's house" or "three or four cars went missing on the same street overnight" were prevalent in these neighborhoods and were seen as matter-of-fact parts of life. These crimes, though widespread, do not compare to drive-by shootings, which are more common in inner-city native black neighborhoods.

As expected, residential segregation also affects a large proportion of West Indians (for similar findings, see Crowder 1999; Crowder and Tedrow 2001). Several reported watching their neighborhood turn from mostly white to predominantly black over a short period of time. This ethnic transition also mapped onto the increase of violence, which featured prominently in the lives of the second generation. For example, Jackie, a recent college graduate and a teacher in the New York City public schools, describes her experience growing up in Flatbush:

> Q: Can you tell me what it was like to grow up in [Flatbush]?
> A: It was a good experience. I think at the time when we first moved here, I guess it was one of those big influxes of people coming in from the West Indies, so we had mostly African Americans and West Indians in that neighborhood, and that's when the West Indians really started to come in and so it was always a good experience. I think the area that we lived in, I lived in what I consider to be projects. They weren't public housing, but they just kind of ended up like projects because all the white people left and all the black people came [laughter]. I guess by the time I got to junior high school and high school there was a lot of violence and the drugs, the influx of crack and things like that. So that had its effect. But I think it was a good experience, and I think that it toughened me up. (twenty-five-year-old West Indian female)

Half of the respondents in the qualitative sample also noted Flatbush's familiar feel to the "islands," including the availability of ethnic food right around the corner and the diverse mix of people from the West Indies, which added a specific flavor to neighborhood life. This sense of familiarity is an aspect of city living that they appreciated, especially in the larger context of a global city like New York. All nostalgic longing for home aside, respondents often remarked how violent Flatbush actually was. To place this into context, our respondents in the ISGMNY study grew up in the late 1980s and early 1990s at the peak of the crack epidemics. The large coethnic presence in their neighborhood does help ameliorate some of the prejudice, violence and fear of trouble. However, even in the most "ethnic" West Indian neighborhoods, the presence of African Americans is still quite significant. (For example, the proportion of West Indians in East Flatbush in 2010 was 51% and this was the neighborhood with the highest concentration of West Indians.) When asked to identify the worst things about Flatbush and Crown Heights, drugs and crime were often the most likely responses. Though respondents observed the positive aspects of the mixture of different cultures, many also remembered Flatbush as a place where there were "guys selling drugs" and "guys getting girls pregnant" along with "kids getting beaten up." And yet, some respondents managed to "pull thorough all of that" and ended up doing well, providing a vivid contrast between the West Indians and native blacks. For example, Tony, a twenty-nine-year-old West Indian respondent from a working-class background, reflected on his experience in Flatbush as "tough." Despite his proximity to the drug trade, he was determined to "never [get] sucked in and involved in all of that," went to college, and eventually found work in the financial sector.

The West Indian case also illustrates the spatially embedded nature of structural (dis)advantages. In this sense, the residential experience of West Indians is similar to middle-class native blacks who often share the same vulnerability (see Pattillo 2013). For example, Mark's parents were both middle-class professionals: his mother worked as a registered nurse, and his father was a bank clerk. A graduate of the City University of New York, Mark worked as a system administrator for a foreign bank at the time of the interview. Though Mark grew up in East New York, he did not realize that his family lived in close proximity of public housing projects in the neighborhood because the area in which he grew up was more family friendly and sheltered—a "pocket of affluence" amidst a highly disadvantaged area.

Q: What was it like to grow up in East New York?

A: East New York has been kind of a bit of a rough neighborhood at least for the last thirty years, but at the time that I was growing up there, a lot of what has really torn it up over the last ten years had not really happened yet. So from the way I saw it, it was not really all that bad, from the perspective of a child growing up there. I lived on a block and in a part of East New York where there are a lot of houses, one- or two-family houses where a lot of the people on the street knew each other, so your neighbors knew you. So the part of East New York where I lived in was a place where I think there was a pretty strong sense of community. Now, five blocks away were the projects, and I did know that there was a very different thing happening in the projects. I didn't really spend much time there . . . So at least for the very first early part of my growing up there, I didn't really think much about the fact that I lived in East New York. As I got a little bit older and actually probably explored the neighborhood more, I got to understand that kind of little corner of it that I was in was not all of it and came to kind of appreciate everything that was going on in the neighborhood. (twenty-eight-year-old West Indian male)

To sum up, West Indians reported growing up in relatively segregated neighborhoods in close proximity with native blacks, but with lower levels of crime and violence. They are also more likely than native blacks to report the presence of other coethnics as well as non-black populations in their neighborhoods. Even though respondents from both groups faced similar structural disadvantages in poverty, segregation, and violence in their neighborhoods, they draw on different group-specific strategies to navigate this disadvantaged context. The following section turns attention to three sets of cultural mechanisms and describes them in more details.

How Culture Matters: Parenting Strategies, Delinquency, and Local Peer Networks

The previous section documented that native blacks and West Indians grew up in structurally similar, yet not identical, neighborhoods. Though both perceived similar levels of drugs, crime, and violence in their neighborhoods, West Indians reported a greater presence of other racial groups. I now turn to the specific strategies that each group adopts to navigate this disadvantaged context and the cultural understandings that both groups exhibit, showing how these differences shape their experiences in their neighborhoods. Specifically, I point to three cultural mechanisms that partially explain the attainment gap between West Indians and native blacks: parenting strategies, involvement with the local drug trade, and the neighborhood peer networks. I argue that these strategies have the unintended consequences of facilitating social mobility among second-generation West Indians while potentially hindering the prospects of native blacks.

Parenting Strategies and Supervision

Growing up in Brownsville in close proximity to public housing projects, twenty-four-year-old Rachel was aware of the dangers of the streets. She shared that "there was a lot of violence" and that "there was nothing good" about her experience there. In fact, Rachel recounted being shot by a stray bullet in her own home. Her father lived in Barbados, but he did provide financial support and visited occasionally throughout her adolescence. Though there was no expectation that she had to finish college, her mother encouraged her "to go as far as she [could] go" in her education. Having attended a private university, she was working with the mentally challenged as a social worker at the time of the interview. She emphasized the importance of upbringing and expressed concern that young children today do not show as much respect to their parents:

> My friends and I, we would hang outside. When the streetlight came on, I had to be in the house. And my friends used to laugh at me, "Oh, the warden is calling you." But as an adult now I see children not being called in for lunch or supper. You are really free to roam the streets all day, and my mother's upbringing—she raised me how she was raised. Like my mother said, back home, these children out here doing these things, I would be able to beat them, send them home to their mother, and they would get beat too, again. But here, everyone minds their own business, because you complain to the parent and the parent gets upset that you complained. Or the child themselves gets very disrespectful. And you've got to worry about whether you're going to get a bullet in you. So you kind of are conditioned to just sit and watch and not really do anything. (twenty-four-year-old West Indian female)

In general, West Indians tend to be stricter with their children compared to native blacks. The use of corporal punishment in disciplining children is a case in point. Waters and Sykes (2009, 72) describe this key difference as "one between 'strict' Caribbean parenting and 'lax' American parenting." At the same time, parenting strategy is crucial in a disadvantaged context. As immigrants, West Indian parents had fewer ties to their immediate neighborhood, were more apprehensive of their surrounding and tended to be more protective of their children. This often led to stricter parenting strategies because they believed that "physical punishment was the way to deal with a child who had misbehaved" (Waters and Sykes 2009, 73). Many second-generation respondents recalled closely supervised visits to the neighborhood playground during childhood, hours spent at the local museum or library, and stricter curfew times during adolescence. When they went outside to play, they "could just be in front of the house" and "couldn't go to too many places" because their parents were afraid to let them out of sight. For example, Sheena, a thirty-one-year-old West Indian female, described her mother's decision not to allow her to play outside as a "typical kind of West Indian immigrant thing" because her mother did not want her to "mix with the Americans and all that foolishness."

Another key difference was family structure. West Indians also grew up with more adult figures in the household because they were more likely to grow up in two-parent households and their household tended to include both kin and non-kin adults (see also Bashi 2007; Kasinitz et al. 2008). In contrast, native blacks were more likely to grow up in single-parent households where the father was absent and the mother bore the burden of parenting, disciplining, and supervision. Specifically, 34 percent of native black respondents reported growing up with a single mother, compared to 25.6 percent of West Indians. This closer supervision has several implications for delinquency among the second generation, from drug use to skipping school. For example, the following respondent's attitude toward drugs use is illustrative:

Q: Were you around people dealing drugs?
A: Maybe, but I wasn't aware. I was around people that used to smoke reefer.
Q: How did you feel about that?
A: I just knew don't do it, or you're gonna get your butt whipped.
(thirty-one-year-old West Indian male)

In contrast, many native blacks reported a more lax attitude when it came to drug use. The following example might be an extreme case, but it highlights the range of parenting approaches.

A: I didn't know what I was smoking. I thought it was a cigarette, to tell you the truth. And I was walking around saying things to people I shouldn't have said to them. And there was a time when I come in from a bout of smoking and just pass out on the couch and my stuff would drop out of my pocket and my mother would find it.

Q: What did she say?

A: She'd take it and hide it just to see what I would do.

Q: What would you do?

A: Take it back and smoke it. It was mine. I bought it. (twenty-five-year-old African American female)

To be fair, there are examples and counterfactuals of "stricter" parents among native blacks. Twenty-five-year-old Camille grew up in a South Bronx housing project with a single mother. She described her neighborhood as a place where "very few people worked." She reported being afraid to go outside because of the gunshots and murders that occurred in the neighborhood. This was in spite of the fact that the neighborhood was generally family oriented in the sense that "everyone knew everyone." And yet, she was able to stay out of trouble, and she attributed this to her "strong" mother who kept her on track:

Q: What was it like to grow up there, in your childhood neighborhood?

A: Basically it was pretty rough. You walk outside the building, and there were drug dealers and everything else. Thank God most of my family lived in that building so that somewhat protected me and my sister from everything that was going [on] around us. Basically it kept them away from us, and my mother was very strong as far as us going to school and not listening to the gang. She made sure me and my sister were going to school, [and] she would make sure we was going someplace far away. It's just me and my sister, so we went to Aviation High School so she made sure we wasn't around the vicinity as far as the Bronx was concerned. (twenty-five-year-old African American female)

What these examples demonstrate is the importance of parenting strategies and how they shape the neighborhood *spaces* where youths spend time growing up as well as how much *time* they spend both inside and outside the home. More generally, these findings point to how space and time matter for theories of neighborhood effect and how parents often serve as an important mediating mechanism in disadvantaged context. Strict parenting has a more immediate impact on whether youths become involved in the local drug trade, which leads to downward mobility. The next section explores this theme in more detail.

Delinquency and the Local Drug Trade

One direct consequence of less parental supervision is native blacks' higher propensity to be involved in the local drug trade. Because drugs permeated many of the neighborhoods where West Indians and native blacks grew up in the 1980s and early 1990s, they also reported coming into contact with drugs early on in life and began engaging in drug selling as an informal income-generating strategy. For many, the "allure of the streets" often came a little too early, which was difficult to resist in the face of poverty and disadvantage. For example, Justin was born in Harlem and spent his earlier years with his mother, who worked as a nurse. Even though he reported being close to his father, his father had passed away when Justin was only eight. At the time of the interview, Justin had just completed a GED program and was working in the food services industry. He recounted his experience growing up in Harlem and how his involvement with the drug trade eventually led him to drop out of high school and into other criminal activities. Unfortunately, his experience is not atypical:

Q: Have you ever sold drugs?
A: Yeah. Crack, weed. It ain't something I do every day. I ain't like none of these other bums; they'd be on the corner all day every day. I'm the type of person, if I need some money real bad. Like if I really want something, like if I wanted a pair of sneakers, and I've got like 50 and the sneakers cost like 125, I'll go out there, sell a little bit of drugs just so I can get some sneakers, and that's it; I won't do it for like a year. It's just for when I really really want something. Like if I want to go to a party or something, I'll go do it for like twenty minutes, half an hour, get enough money for the party, and I'm done. I ain't no full-time, real into it, heavy, it's just when I need some money. (eighteen-year-old African American male)

Whereas native blacks often stated that "you have to hustle to make money" to justify their involvement in the drug trade, West Indians' reaction was quite a different one. Many protested that drugs were "killing" their neighborhood and "destroying" their community:

Q: Have you ever been around people dealing drugs?
A: (laughter) Yes. [And] I think it is destroying our community.
Q: What makes you say that?
A: Because when there's a need for something and you're not working, you got to find somehow to get it, so obviously you're going to have to steal and thief to get it. Drugs is the root of that. (twenty-four-year-old West Indian male)

Though they were not immune from their neighborhood environment, female respondents made an effort to avoid the drug trade. Among female respondents with children, some noted the lack of recreational facilities and institutional resources in their neighborhood that could provide children with safe, supervised play spaces in controlled environments. Others have observed that there was "not enough oriented towards the children" and that there was "nothing to do" when they were growing up. As a result, they found themselves spending time on the streets, which many white respondents also reported doing. However, in contrast to the clean, safe streets in predominantly white neighborhoods, street life in black neighborhoods often presents its own perils and challenges, potentially leading to negative consequences for adolescents and young adults. For example, twenty-five-year-old Rhonda described how her neighborhood changed from a pretty peaceful neighborhood into one with gangs and other forms of violence.

Q: So what do you think caused the change?
A: Anybody who wants to make the quick dollar. The quickest way to do it is drugs, and I guess that's what everybody's into. Everybody, I guess for the youth, I guess it's, you know, you see the videos, Jay-Z and everybody, and everything is diamonds and gold and money money this and money money that. You know, most of them don't have an education; they don't want to go to school; they just want to make quick money. The quickest way is drugs, for them.
Q: So you think that's what happened?
A: I mean, I can't blame it on rap. [But] a lot of rappers in their rap, say how they got their money hustlin', and that's how kids see—oh, I got to hustle now to get money, and that's what they look up to. So they don't want to [go] the long route of going to school and

workin'; they want to do it quick. So they don't understand. You can't get a pension selling drugs. What's gonna happen when you're too old to sell drugs? They don't see that far. (twenty-five-year-old African American female)

These experiences show that native blacks and West Indians also differ in their involvement with the local drug trade. While both reported that the "using and dealing of illegal drugs" was a major problem in their neighborhood while growing up, West Indians are more likely to distance themselves from the drug trade. One reason for this "distancing" strategy among West Indians is their lower connections to the neighborhood peer network. The next section highlights this theme and shows how it protects against downward mobility among second-generation West Indians.

Neighborhood Peer Networks and Social Mobility

As immigrants, West Indians had not spent as much time as native blacks in their neighborhoods, and as a result, had fewer local ties. Their neighborhoods were more transient, with a constant influx of new immigrants. Furthermore, West Indians were more likely to attend schools outside of their neighborhood and less likely to spend time in their own neighborhood of residence.[14] As a result, West Indian youths were less connected to their neighborhood peer networks which has the unintended benefit of protecting them from their neighborhood. In contrast, 70 percent of the native blacks in the ISGMNY survey reported that they grew up in neighborhoods where "most neighbors knew each other." For example, Erin grew up in a working-class family where both of her parents worked in the service sector. After graduating from a two-year community college, she found work at a local bank and was thirty-one at the time of the interview. Erin's experience growing up was generally pleasant, and she appreciated the fact that everyone on the block knew and spent time with each other:

Q: What were the best things about Bedford Stuyvesant at that time?
A: The best things? I mean, the best thing—having friends on that block to have fun with, and everybody knowing everybody so if you needed something and your mother or father wasn't home, you knew you could go to that next person, and they was gonna take care of you, 'cause they knew your mother and whatever you got from them, your mother or father would pay it back or give it back

or whatever. It was just more of a family-oriented type of situation. (thirty-one-year-old African American female)

In contrast, West Indians found themselves more withdrawn from the neighborhood, even when they lived in areas that were heavily coethnic, either because of prejudice against them or because they wanted to "stay out of trouble" and not "[get] into other people's business."

Q: What kinds of people lived in that neighborhood?
A: Mostly my block happened to be the block of the West Indians. We kind of all lived on the same block. We stayed friendly with each other, and we all pretty much knew each other that were from the West Indies. We knew where each other were from and things like that. That was on one side of the street, and on the other side of the street is all Americans. So it was like a long time ago, before everybody learned about West Indian culture, it used to be more like, "Oh you're West Indian; you're banana boat." As a child, in elementary school, it's kind of frustrating, but it's still kind of frustrating now because everyone thinks West Indian, they're Jamaican, and that is still frustrating because we're not all from one place . . . But like I said, I got shot by a stray bullet, and that kind of altered my thinking about a lot of people that were around me. I knew what they did, but it was none of my business per se, so I kept out of it. And they did what they had to do. As long as we were respectful of each other, I found a lot of people around that were pretty much struggling, and my family included. (twenty-four-year-old West Indian female)

In turn, being embedded in the local peer network increases the likelihood of delinquency involvement. For example, eighteen among the thirty native black respondents in the qualitative sample described how involvement in the local drug trade shaped the experience of youths in their neighborhood, with junior high marking a key turning point that separated drug dealers from those who chose not to deal. Moreover, nine of these eighteen native black respondents reported initially adopting drug dealing purely as an informal income-generating strategy, which enabled them to afford the luxury items that their parents might not be able to provide, such as a pair of Nike sneakers, a gold chain, or a new car. However, some of these young people found themselves increasingly unable to resist the pull of the streets and the allure of fast money.

Q: How did you get into [drugs]?

A: The streets. Just like I said, I was living with my older sister. My oldest sister, she could never buy me the things I wanted, and first of all, I was selling drugs actually and that was the type of thing where that money, in fact, there's a picture of me right there when I used to be back in my bad days. That's a $12,000 chain over there. That's straight gold link, and it's $12,000, and I used to be into that. And then I was, "You know what? This is slow money." Then I started doing robberies, and that was it.

Q: About what time did you drop out?

A: In my junior year. The money just got too good to me, and I just didn't want to go to school no more, so I just was chasing the dollar. So that was it. (thirty-year-old African American male)

These stories show that embeddedness in the local peer networks in a disadvantaged context can carry negative consequences. To be sure, close neighborhood ties can bring certain benefits, such as a stronger sense of neighborhood social cohesion and ongoing social support. However, the majority of West Indian second generation reported being detached and removed from their neighborhood. In other words, West Indians grew up in some of these poor neighborhoods, but were never fully integrated with their local peers. Their experiences highlight the divergent paths to mobility that could result even when ethnic groups grew up in similarly disadvantaged setting. On the one hand, West Indians are less affected by their neighborhoods given the stricter parents and the cultural frames that distance themselves from the local drug trade. On the other hand, these findings highlight how poverty shapes the cultural strategies that these youths adopt and the choices they make in light of structural constraints. This also points to the important role of *both* cultural and structural conditions in shaping individuals' life chances.

Discussion and Conclusion

This comparison seeks to highlight the interaction between structural conditions and cultural strategies in shaping second-generation social mobility. Though both ethnic groups are equally segregated from native whites, I find that West Indians lived in neighborhoods with lower levels of concentrated poverty. In cases where second-generation West Indians share the same high-poverty neighborhood with native blacks, West Indians are more likely to live in the smaller "pockets of affluence" within the neighborhood—blocks that are slightly more advantaged and have lower levels of violence. In addition, these two groups adopt different cultural strategies in their navigation of this context, with parenting strategies being an important tool that shapes both how much time youths spend and where they spend their time within their neighborhood.

The West Indian experience also illustrates the spatially embedded nature of advantaged and disadvantaged neighborhoods. West Indians were in closer proximity to integrated or mixed neighborhoods, whereas native blacks were in the midst of the most disadvantaged areas. West Indians were more likely to be surrounded by their coethnics, even when they lived in segregated neighborhoods. As immigrants, West Indians' social mobility over time also facilitated spatial mobility into residence in better, though segregated, neighborhoods. This spatial proximity to other native blacks had some negative consequences, but by and large, West Indians reported being shielded from the nearby violence, mostly by their parents who would "keep them inside." The role of family support in sheltering and protecting their children is repeatedly emphasized by West Indians. In sum, there is a combination of cultural strategies that promote social mobility: strict and protective parenting; a supportive home environment; and spending time inside doing homework and distancing from the street life in poor neighborhoods. These cultural strategies are neither specific to a particular ethnic group nor to a particular social class, though the qualitative data presented here suggest they were more prevalent among West Indians than native blacks.

What does this analysis reveal about the assimilation of the West Indian second generation? On the one hand, the theory of segmented assimilation predicts that West Indians will adopt the oppositional cultural outlook among native blacks and will be at risk of downward assimilation (Portes and Zhou 1993). In many ways, West Indians provide the most direct test of this theory, not only because they are phenotypically black, but they also live in neighborhoods adjacent to native blacks and often experience similar levels of discrimination in the casual setting by the police and others. On the other hand, other scholars emphasize the importance of a "minority culture of mobility" which refers to key cultural elements that provide "strategies for economic mobility in the context of discrimination and group disadvantage, and respond to distinctive problems that usually accompany minority middle-class status" (Neckerman et al. 1999, 946). Put differently, minority status can confer certain advantages. They can provide connections to ethnic resources that might promote social mobility, such as ethnic schools (Lee and Zhou 2014) or minority professional associations (Agius-Vallejo 2012). This minority culture of mobility is further supported by affirmative action and institutional policies that aim to reduce barriers to social mobility among blacks and Latinos in the post-civil-rights era, which disproportionately benefits the West Indian second generation (Kasinitz et al. 2008). And yet, as a racially black group, West Indians have yet to achieve parity with native whites, although they are certainly outperforming native blacks. These results show no evidence in support of downward mobility, while also provide partial support for the role of "selective acculturation" which emphasizes the importance of parental supervision and support in facilitating the process of assimilation (Portes and Rumbaut 2001). More importantly, these findings suggest that the very mechanisms that lead to downward assimilation (i.e., proximity to native blacks, inner-city youth culture, and local peer networks) based on the theory of segmented assimilation are operating in the opposite directions. While many West Indians grew up in poor black neighborhoods, they are not embedded in their local peer networks and are more likely to adopt a distancing stance when it comes to the local drug trade and other delinquent activities. Instead of assimilating into the black underclass, as theorists of segmented assimilation might have warned, West Indian parents adopt elements of the minority culture of mobility in their navigation of a disadvantaged context. In other words, the cultural practices that they have recreated in their host society as a result of their structural position and neighborhood context seem to be a form of selective acculturation that also ensures the strongest mobility outcomes possible among the West Indian second generation.

More broadly, these findings suggest that race is "more than just black" (Wilson 2009) and the complex link between ethnicity and culture deserves further research (Lee and Zhou 2014; Smith 2014). In other words, the very meaning of blackness has changed in the last decade with the country's first black president, the solidification of the black middle-class, the emergence of the black elites and the diversification of the black population. There is more than one way to be "black" and this heterogeneity invites a reexamination of the assumptions underlying our theories of assimilation, including the theory of segmented assimilation, which has adopted a certain historical specificity to the meaning of "blackness," along with heightened concerns about the permanent black underclass in the 1990s. Finally, this analysis is specific to New York City and to the historical period during which this sample of respondents came of age. The linkage between neighborhoods and social mobility might be more tenuous in other cities with lower levels of residential and school segregation. And yet, West Indians and native blacks would likely confront the perils and opportunities that this analysis reveals, but they can also be creative about the cultural strategies that they employ.

8

The Role of Religious and Social Organizations in the Lives of Disadvantaged Youth

RAJEEV DEHEJIA, *New York University*

THOMAS DELEIRE, *Georgetown University*

ERZO F. P. LUTTMER, *Dartmouth College*

JOSH MITCHELL, *Urban Institute*

1. Introduction

This chapter examines whether religious and social organizations benefit youth by offsetting the long-term consequences of growing up in a disadvantaged environment.[1] Disadvantages suffered during childhood not only impose an immediate cost on children and families but have also been shown to impose harm that lasts well into adulthood. Research in economics and other social sciences has documented that children who grow up in poverty have worse physical health, lower levels of cognitive ability, lower levels of school achievement, more emotional and behavioral problems, and higher teenage childbearing rates. Other sources of disadvantage include growing up with a single or less educated parent; parental job loss, divorce, or death; and growing up in a poor neighborhood. Moreover, the consequences of a disadvantaged upbringing may be compounded by weak ties to the community and the family.

Not all children who grow up disadvantaged suffer negative outcomes to the same extent. Families and children can adopt strategies to try to minimize the negative impacts of their surroundings. In this chapter, we examine one such strategy: engagement with religious and other social organizations. The link between poverty and poor outcomes has been hypothesized to be partially due to deficiencies in parenting, home environments, and neighborhoods. Religious and social organizations could

281

therefore make up for some of this lost social capital by providing counseling, social services, income support, or a network of social contacts. Our previous research (Dehejia, DeLeire, and Luttmer 2007) has found that religious organizations enable adults to partially protect their consumption patterns and mental well-being against drops in their income levels. This chapter builds on those results by examining whether involvement with religious or social organizations mitigates the long-run negative effects on youth of growing up in a disadvantaged environment.

In particular, we examine whether, by adulthood (thirteen to fifteen years later), children whose parents were involved with religious and social organizations suffered less harm from growing up in a disadvantaged environment than children whose parents were less involved. We consider fourteen measures of disadvantage in childhood: family income and poverty (measured by household income relative to the poverty line, the poverty rate in the census tract where the child resides, and by whether the child's household received public assistance); family characteristics (measured by the mother's level of education, by whether the child's parent was unmarried, by whether the parents' marriage broke up, and by an indicator for nonwhite households[2]); and child characteristics (parental assessments of the child, whether the child has repeated a grade, and an index of disciplinary problems). We consider twelve outcome measures in adulthood to capture whether these disadvantages had lasting detrimental consequences: the child's level of education, household income relative to the poverty line, whether the child receives public assistance, and measures of risky behavior (measured by smoking, age of first sex, and health insurance coverage) and psychological well-being (measured by subjective happiness and locus of control). Thus, in total, we test for buffering of religious participation in 168 (= 14 × 12) possible combinations of a measure of youth disadvantage and a measure of adult outcome.

We find that religious organizations provide buffering effects that are statistically significant at the 5 percent level for 38 out of a total of 168 disadvantage-outcome combinations examined. We can formally reject at the 1 percent level that this number of significant effects could arise by pure chance, and we conclude that religious organizations play an important buffering role against disadvantage experienced during youth. Of course, it is quite plausible that religious organizations also provide buffering effects for many of the disadvantage-outcome combinations that were not significant in our analysis. In those cases, we simply do not have the statistical power to prove or disprove buffering effects.[3] The buffering effects of religious organizations are most often statistically significant when outcomes are measured by high school graduation or nonsmoking and when disadvantage is measured by family resources or maternal education, but we also find statistically significant buffering effects for a number of other outcome-disadvantage pairs. Our data do not allow us to determine to what extent the buffering effects are driven by religious organizations actively intervening in the lives of disadvantaged youth (through tutoring, mentoring, or financial assistance) as opposed to providing the youth with motivation, values, or attitudes that lead to better outcomes.

Because participation in religion is often a choice that a child's parents actively make, we must be cautious in interpreting the buffering effect of religion as a causal effect of religious participation. For example, the effect of participation could be confounded with other coping strategies that families adopt in response to disadvantage, leading our estimated buffering effect to capture the combined effect of all of these strategies. Reverse causality is less of a concern since outcomes for disadvantaged youth are observed thirteen to fifteen years after we measure involvement with religious and social organizations and whether the child had a disadvantaged upbringing.

We believe our results show that religious organizations play an important role in shaping the lives of disadvantaged youth by mitigating at least some of the long-term consequences of disadvantage. We view our research as a first step in the important task of understanding whether—and through what mechanisms—disadvantaged youth benefit from participating in religious organizations.

2. Literature Review

The consequences of growing up in disadvantaged circumstances have been extensively documented in the academic research literature. In this section, we provide a brief overview of three aspects of this literature: the sources of disadvantage, the consequences of growing up in disadvantaged circumstances, and adaptive behaviors that families may adopt to protect themselves, in part, from these disadvantages. Finally, we review the less extensive economic literature on the role of religion in the lives of youth.

Sources of Disadvantage for Youth

Children can be disadvantaged if they grow up in poverty or if they experience any one of a large number of other circumstances. Collectively, researchers have considered a large number of potential disadvantages when examining consequences for youth. These include low family income and poverty (e.g., Duncan and Brooks-Gunn 1997), growing up in a single-parent family (McLanahan and Sandefur 1994), having a less educated mother (Currie and Moretti 2003; Black, Devereux, and Salvanes 2005; Oreopoulos, Page, and Stevens 2006), having a parent on public assistance (Antel 1992; Page 2004), having obese parents (Anderson, Butcher, and Schanzenbach 2007), and poor parenting behaviors (Currie and Hyson 1999; Bitler and Currie 2004).

Consequences of Growing up Disadvantaged

Many studies have documented the correlation between poverty and youth outcomes (inter alia Brooks-Gunn and Duncan 1997; Duncan and Brooks-Gunn 1997). Growing up in poverty is related to having worse physical health (Korenman and Miller 1997), lower levels of cognitive ability, lower levels of school achievement, and a greater number of emotional or behavioral problems (Smith, Brooks-Gunn, and Klebanov 1997). Low income is unlikely to be causally responsible for all of these outcomes. Longitudinal analysis has suggested that omitted parental characteristics that are correlated with income are likely responsible for many of these negative outcomes (Mayer 1997). However, there is also evidence from social experiments (Currie 1997) and sibling fixed effects models (Duncan et al. 1998) suggesting that income does at least partially matter. Shea (2000), Dahl and Lochner (2005), Oreopoulos, Page, and Stevens (2005), and Page, Stevens, and Lindo (2007) use plausibly exogenous income variation due to industry shocks, changes in EITC rules, and worker layoffs. These studies generally find effects of parental income on subsequent educational and labor market outcomes for the youths, and in many cases the effects are strongest for disadvantaged youths.

Having an unmarried parent has also been found to be associated with a range of negative outcomes for youth. McLanahan and Sandefur (1994, 3) argue that "growing up with only one biological parent frequently deprives children of important economic, parental, and community resources, and . . . these deprivations ultimately undermine their chances of future success." Their analysis suggests that roughly one-half of the deficit associated with having a single parent is due to low income and one-half is due to inadequate parental guidance and a lack of ties to community resources. Other research has also suggested that parenting behavior is an important determinant of child outcomes (Hanson, McLanahan, and Thomson 1997).

Parental education also matters. In addition to being associated with higher levels of family income, research has shown that parents' level of education has a strong, causal effect on children's health (Currie and Moretti 2003) and children's educational attainment (Black, Devereux, and Salvanes 2005). Other parental behaviors can influence children's outcomes as well. Even otherwise positive behaviors can have negative consequences. For example, Anderson, Butcher, and Levine (2003) find a causal relationship between maternal employment and the likelihood that a child is overweight.

Growing up in a poor neighborhood may also have a negative effect on outcomes later in life. Identifying these effects is complicated by the likely correlation of neighborhood conditions with unobserved parental characteristics and behaviors. Moreover, it is difficult to determine the sign of the bias stemming from this correlation, as parents who live in poor neighborhoods may have unobservable characteristics that lead to worse outcomes for their children or, alternatively, parents in poor neighborhoods may invest more in compensating activities to partially alleviate those effects. A number of studies have sought to overcome these biases to identify the effects of growing up in a poor neighborhood on children's outcomes using sibling fixed effects models (e.g., Aaronson 1997) or instrumental variables (Case and Katz 1991; Evans, Oates, and Schwab 1992).

Strategies to Minimize the Consequences of Disadvantage

Families and children can adopt strategies to mitigate the negative impacts of their surroundings. For example, single mothers can improve the educational outcomes and reduce the delinquency of their children by living with their own parents in multigenerational households (DeLeire and Kalil 2002). Guralnick (2004) describes how parents of children with developmental challenges adopt strategies—including expanding their networks of social support—in order to best meet the needs of their children. These strategies to mitigate the negative impact of disadvantage may or may not have value in and of themselves. While some adaptive strategies may be intrinsically valuable, others, such as not venturing outdoors in response to living in a dangerous neighborhood, may not.

Economic Consequences of Religion

In an overview of the growing literature on the economics of religion, Iannaccone (1998) discusses a range of studies on the economic consequences of religious participation, for example Freeman's (1986) finding that black youth who attend church are less likely to smoke, drink, or engage in drug use. More recent studies have also focused on the consequences of religious participation, but it has been difficult to determine whether the consequences are causal or driven by omitted variables. Gruber (2005) succeeds in credibly establishing causality by instrumenting own religious attendance by the religious market density of other ethnic groups sharing the same denomination. He finds that increased religious participation leads to higher educational attainment and income, less dependence on social insurance programs, and greater levels of marriage. Gruber and Hungerman (2006) use variation in "blue laws" to find causal evidence that religious attendance reduces drug use and heavy drinking. Lillard and Price (2007) show a strong association between religious participation among youth and reduced criminal and delinquent behavior, smoking, drug use, and drinking. Moreover, they use a variety of methods including propensity score matching, instrumental variables (using the "blue laws" instrument described above), and Altonji, Elder, and Taber's (2005) method of using selection on observables to infer the degrees of selection on unobservables to suggest that at least some of their observed associations between religious participation and outcomes are indeed causal relationships.

There is also a large literature showing that religiosity correlates with health outcomes and subjective well-being. Studies show a relationship between religion (variously measured by self-reported "religious coping" or religious activity including prayer) and a range of health outcomes (including depression, mortality, and immune system responses). These are exclusively correlation studies (see, for example, McCullough et al. 2000). Similarly, there is widespread evidence that religiosity is correlated with measures of subjective well-being (see inter alia Diener, Kahneman, and Schwarz 1999 and the meta-analyses by Parmagent 2002 and Smith, McCullough, and Poll 2003).

A number of studies also examine the buffering effects of religion on subjective well-being in the context of traumatic life events. Using cross-sectional data from the General Social Survey, Ellison (1991) finds that people with stronger religious beliefs have higher well-being and are less affected by traumatic events. Strawbridge et al. (1998) find nonuniform buffering effects using cross-sectional data from California. They find that religiosity buffers the effects of nonfamily stressors (e.g., unemployment) on depression but exacerbates the effects of family stressors (e.g., marital problems). This finding dovetails with Clark and Lelkes (2005) who find that religiosity may dampen or exacerbate the happiness effect of a major life shock depending on the denomination and the type of shock. Dehejia, DeLeire, and Luttmer (2007) find that religion buffers subjective well-being against income shocks. Moreover, in that paper we document that religious involvement also insures consumption against income shocks, i.e., religion provides more than spiritual support alone.

3. Data Description

The National Survey of Families and Households

We use three waves of the National Survey of Families and Households (NSFH), a panel data set collected by demographers (Sweet, Bumpass, and Call 1988; Sweet and Bumpass 1996, 2002). The NSFH contains detailed information on participants' family structure, living arrangements, educational attainment, religiosity, and economic and psychological well-being.

The first wave of interviews took place in 1987–1988 and was conducted in a face-to-face setting with respondents taking self-administered questionnaires for more sensitive topics. The sample consists of 13,007 individuals and is nationally representative of individuals age nineteen or older, living in households, and able to speak English or Spanish. If these "main respondents" lived in a household with children age nineteen or younger, one of these children was chosen at random to be the "focal child." The respondent answered a series of questions about this focal child, including questions about the child's behavior and school performance. Wave one contains information on 5,684 focal children. A second wave of interviews with the main respondents took place in 1992–1994. This allows our analysis to consider changes in variables of interest over the first two waves, such as whether the household experienced a marital breakup.

The third wave of interviews took place in 2001–2003. This wave included interviews with both the main respondents and with people who were focal children in wave one (for convenience we continue to refer to them as "focal children," though by wave three they are adults). We use the information from these grown-up focal children to construct our outcome measures. The NSFH conducted telephone interviews with eligible focal children, namely those aged eighteen to thirty-four in wave three (and who were age three to nineteen in wave one). The NSFH originally identified 4,128 focal children as eligible but were only able to locate and successfully interview 1,952 of them. (This raises issue of sample attrition, which we discuss in Dehejia et al. 2009.) These interviews asked about the focal child's educational attainment, income, risky behaviors, and subjective measures of well-being.

The NSFH granted us permission to use a limited-access version of the data set that contains characteristics of the respondent's neighborhood from the 1990 census at the tract level. A census tract is a local area that is fairly homogenous and typically contains between 2,500 and 8,000 people. We use log median household income and the poverty rate as tract-level measures of disadvantage.

Data Description and Choice of Variables

The full sample of wave-three interviewees who were focal children in wave one includes 1,952 observations. In some specifications, we restrict the sample to individuals older than twenty-five in wave three. This sample consists of 1,125 observations. The age restriction is useful for outcomes that are best measured in adulthood (for example, education or income). Figure 8.1 provides a snapshot of the samples. Households are mostly white (with 8 percent black, 5 percent Hispanic, and 1 percent other nonwhite). Of the wave-one adult respondents, 91 percent are biological parents (for convenience we refer to both biological parents and guardians as "parents"). Parents' ages range from nineteen to seventy-one in wave one, with an average age of thirty-nine.

We use a range of variables to measure household disadvantage in wave one of the data. Summary statistics for household disadvantage are presented in Figures 8.2 and 8.3. Our first set of measures, summarized in Figure 8.2, is based on family resources or poverty: log household income relative to the poverty line, an indicator for household income less than 200 percent of the poverty line (21 percent of the full sample), log median

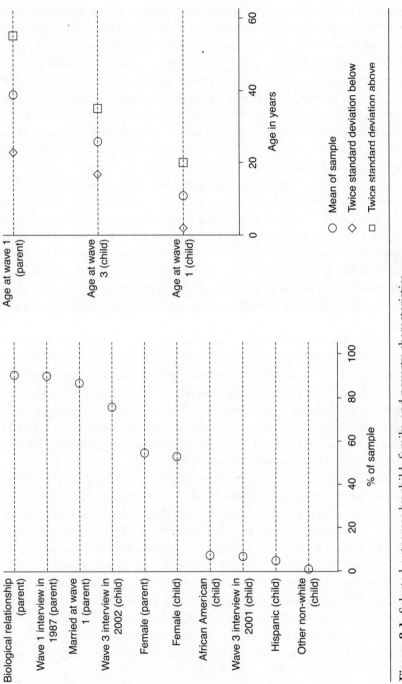

Figure 8.1. Selected outcomes by child, family, and poverty characteristics

household income in the census tract, the poverty rate at the census-tract level (11 percent of the full sample), and an indicator for the households receiving public assistance in wave one (5 percent of the full sample). The second set of disadvantage measures, summarized in Figure 8.3, is based on family characteristics, namely indicators for: nonwhite parents (14 percent of the full sample), an unmarried parent (13 percent of the full sample), a breakup of the parents' marriage (divorce or separation) occurring between wave one and wave two (10 percent of the sample, conditional on having married parents at wave one), a mother with less than a high school education (11 percent of the full sample), and a mother with high school education or less (52 percent of the full sample).

The third set of disadvantage measures, also summarized in Figure 8.3, is based on child characteristics: indicators for whether the parent thinks the focal child is unlikely to graduate from college or is difficult to raise; an indicator for the focal child having repeated a grade; and a composite measure of discipline difficulties. Some child characteristics reflect the parent's perception of the child, and as such must be interpreted with great care. For example, if religious parents systematically assess their children differently than nonreligious parents, then our estimates of buffering could be spurious.[4]

Figure 8.4 summarizes the measure of religious participation that we use in this chapter: the parent's percentile rank in the wave-one distribution of attendance at religious services.[5] We see that the distribution is substantially skewed to the right: the parent at the tenth percentile never attends, the median parent attends twice per month (24 times per year), and the parent at the ninetieth percentile attends twice per week (104 times per year). We also examine the robustness of our results to alternative specifications of parental religious attendance.

Finally, our wave-three outcome measures for the adult focal child are as follows. We examine measures of educational attainment (indicators for having a high school education or more, some college or more, and being a college graduate) and income (the age-specific percentile rank of a household's income to poverty-line ratio, an indicator for a household's being above the twenty-fifth percentile in the age-specific distribution of the income-to-poverty-line ratio, and an indicator for receiving public assistance). We also include measures of behavior and psychological well-being: an indicator for being a nonsmoker, an indicator for whether the child's age at first having sex was sixteen or older, an indicator for a normal body mass index,[6] an indicator for being covered by health insurance, a measure

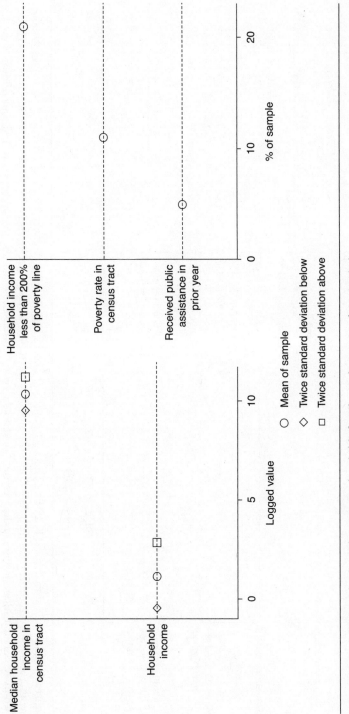

Figure 8.2. Additional selected outcomes by child, family, and poverty characteristics

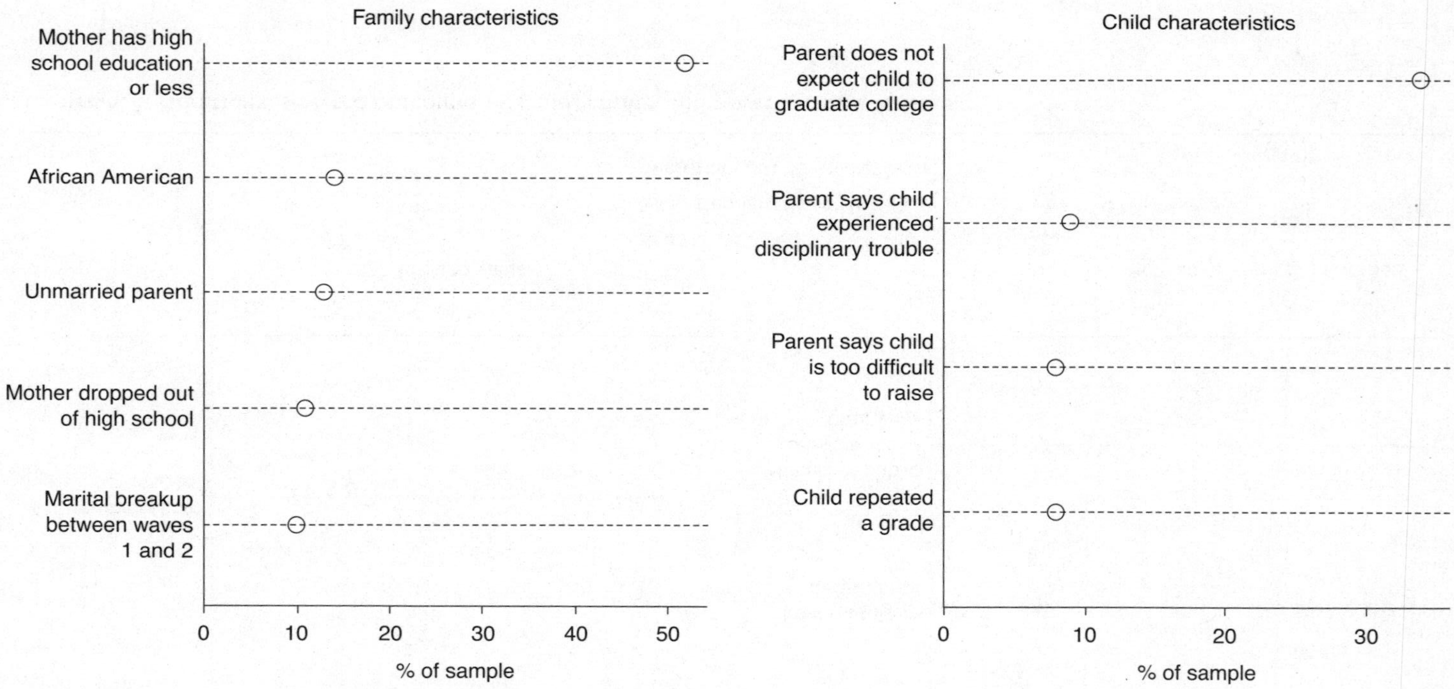

Figure 8.3. Sensitivity analysis of buffering effects. Robustness checks include a direct effect (predicted attendance, neighborhood income, and religious belief) and its interaction with disadvantage to the baseline specification. Standard focal child controls along with maternal education, parent gender, region, household size log of household income to poverty ratio, and four dummies for degree of agreement (on a scale from 1 to 5) for each response to four values statements are used to predict religious attendance, with R-squared of 0.17. Dotted lines indicate baseline buffering effect of religious participation.

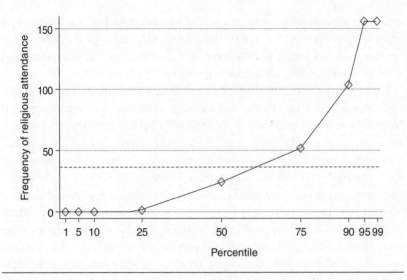

Figure 8.4. Distribution of parental religious attendance

of overall happiness, and a composite measure of locus of control (i.e., the extent to which someone perceives himself or herself to be in control of his or her environment).

4. Empirical Strategy

In this section, we present our empirical strategy and discuss related identification and econometric issues.

Specification

To examine whether religious and other organizations help to attenuate the effect of a disadvantaged upbringing, we estimate models of the form:

$$(1)\ Outcome_{it} = Disadvantaged_{i,t-1}\ \beta_1 + Religious_{i,t-1}\ \beta_2 + Disadvantaged_{i,t-1} \times Religious_{i,t-1}\ \beta3 + X_{i,t-1}\ \beta4 + \alpha it + \delta t + \varepsilon it$$

where $Outcome_{it}$ is a particular youth outcome in wave three, $Disadvantaged_{i,t-1}$ is an indicator of a disadvantaged household in wave one of the survey, and $Religious_{i,t-1}$ is a measure of parents' religiosity in wave one (or a measure of the parents' participation in other social organizations). $X_{i,t-1}$ is a set of controls for the characteristics of the household in which the youth grew up as well as the race/ethnicity and gender of the youth; α_{it} is a set of dummies for the age of the youth at the time of the wave-three interview; δ_t is a set of year-of-interview dummies for the wave-one and wave-three interview; and ε_{it} are error terms.

Based on the literature, we expect to find a negative β_1 (disadvantage leads to worse outcomes in adulthood) and a positive β_2 (growing up with religious parents is generally associated with better outcomes). However, since any measure of disadvantage is likely correlated with several omitted measures of disadvantage, β_1 merely measures an association. Similarly, since parental religious participation is a choice and is likely to be correlated with many other omitted characteristics that have a beneficial effect on later outcomes, the effect of parental religious participation is unlikely to be causal. Our main coefficient of interest is β_3, which measures the extent to which children of religious parents are less affected by growing up under disadvantaged conditions. Thus, we take a positive β_3 as suggestive evidence of the buffering effect of religion.

Despite omitted variables problems that bias β_1 and β_2, it is possible, under strong assumptions, to give a causal interpretation to β_3. The key condition for identification is that omitted characteristics are correlated with religious attendance to the same degree for disadvantaged and non-disadvantaged households. However, we prefer to interpret the estimates of β_3 as associations rather than as causal evidence of buffering because we are concerned that this identification condition does not hold in practice. In particular, it is possible that parental religious involvement is more strongly associated with omitted characteristics that affect later outcomes for disadvantaged children than it is for nondisadvantaged children. For example, it is possible that parents who participate in religious activities out of concern for their children growing up in a disadvantaged environment might also decide to enroll their children in after-school activities that could mitigate the effects of disadvantage. We could fully address this issue if we had an instrument for parental participation in religion, but unfortunately no such variable is available in our data.[7] We also acknowledge that the disadvantaged religious families form a selected sample for which religious participation did not succeed in overcoming their disadvantage in the first wave of our data. Thus, our estimated buffering effect should be interpreted as the average buffering given the selected nature of the sample in wave one. We are less worried about reverse causation, because we measure disadvantage in wave one of the survey and outcomes in wave three, thirteen to fifteen years later.

Joint Significance of the Buffering Effects

Given the large number of effects we investigate (fourteen measures of disadvantage and twelve outcomes), we would expect to find some statistically significant buffering effects of religion simply as a matter of chance. It would be problematic, indeed data mining, only to present the significant effects. Furthermore, there is a danger of ex-post theorizing to justify the particular pattern of effects we find. We deal with this issue in two ways. First, we present our results—both significant and insignificant—for a range of disadvantage and outcome measures that we believe reasonably spans the data available to us. Second, we show the whole distribution of t-statistics on the buffering effects of all disadvantage-outcome pairs and compare this with a simulated distribution of t-statistics under the null hypothesis of no true buffering effect, that is, we test whether we observe more statistically significant effects than would be expected by chance if religious organizations did not buffer at all against disadvantage.

5. Results

Direct Effects of Wave-One Disadvantage on Wave-Three Outcomes

It has been widely documented in the literature that there is a substantively significant ongoing association between childhood disadvantage and outcomes in adulthood. In prior work (Dehejia, DeLeire, Luttmer, and Mitchell 2009), we showed that, although it is appealing to interpret these results causally, they are fundamentally correlations. From other studies (especially Currie 1997; Duncan et al. 1998; Currie and Moretti 2003; and Black et al. 2005), we know that at least part of the effect of the family resource and poverty measures is causal. For child characteristics—particularly parental assessments of whether the child is expected to graduate from college or is difficult to raise—the scope for omitted variable bias is higher because both these assessments and the future outcome may depend on factors that are known to the parents but not to the researcher.

Religion and Buffering

Before examining the full set of religion-disadvantage interactions, we begin by discussing in detail the results for a single specification: the effect of having a mother with a high school degree or less (measured in wave one) on the child's educational attainment as an adult in wave three.

Since all wave three outcomes are scaled so that movements in the positive direction are beneficial to the individual, positive buffering effects reflect the advantage conferred by the religious attendance of the adult on the child in wave three, when he or she is now an adult.

The direct effect of having a mother with no more than a high school education on the child's level of education as an adult in wave three is negative: it reduces the probability that the child as an adult has at least some college in wave three by 23 percentage points relative to a mean of 65 percent (an effect that is statistically significant at the 1 percent level). The effect of religious participation is positive: moving from the twenty-fifth to the seventy-fifth percentile of parental religious participation is associated with an 8 percentage point increase in the child's probability of having some college or more education as an adult in wave three (which is statistically significant at the 1 percent level). Our main interest in this chapter is whether, as adults, children of religious parents are less affected by childhood disadvantages than children of less religious parents. This is captured by interacting the direct effect of the childhood disadvantage (in the example above, having a mother with no more than a high school education, although we consider many other measures of disadvantage below) with our measure of parental religious participation. We find that the interaction of religious participation and mother's education is positive (and statistically significant at the 1 percent level for OLS and at the 5 percent level for the probit specification), indicating that parental religious participation buffers children from some of the effects of childhood disadvantage. Having a mother with no more than a high school degree reduces the probability that the child has at least some college by 31 percentage points if the parent was at the twenty-fifth percentile of religious participation, i.e., a typical nonparticipant. This effect is reduced to 16 percentage points if the parent was at the seventy-fifth percentile of religious attendance, i.e., a religiously active parent. The difference between the two, 15 percentage points, is the estimated beneficial effect of religious participation. Expressed as a fraction of the disadvantage experienced by children of nonreligious parents, we find that religious involvement buffers 48 percent of the negative effect of having a mother with no more than a high school degree on the child's probability of having some college or more education as an adult in wave three.

In Figures 8.5 to 8.10, we present the buffering effect of religion computed in this way for the full set of measures of disadvantage and the full set of outcome variables. For simplicity, we present the results for the OLS specifications, but the results are similar for probit specifications (Dehejia et al. 2009).

Figures 8.5, 8.6, and 8.7 show whether measures of youth disadvantage have less of a detrimental impact on the high school graduation rates of youths with religious parents than on youth whose parents do not frequently attend religious services. In Figures 8.5 and 8.6, for all measures of family resources and poverty and for most measures of family characteristics, we find statistically significant buffering effects (i.e., the interval of plus-minus two standard errors from the estimated coefficient does not include zero). However, in Figure 8.7, we find no significant buffering effects with respect to any of the child characteristics. The magnitude of the buffering effect ranges between 42 and 113 percent for the significant effects.[8]

In Figures 8.5, 8.6, and 8.7, it is notable that we do not find many significant effects when education is measured using an indicator for having some college or more or using an indicator for being a college graduate in columns (2) and (3). This suggests that the buffering effects of religion are concentrated on the high school dropout margin. It is also notable that we do not find a uniformly statistically significant buffering effect for any of our income measures, including those that might be expected to pick up the effect of high school or more versus less than high school education (such as the indicators for being above the twenty-fifth percentile of the ratio of household income to the poverty line and for being on public assistance). One potential explanation for this puzzling result is that annual income is a noisy measure of permanent income in the age range at which we observe respondents in wave three.

The most uniformly significant buffering effect of religion against disadvantage as measured by child characteristics is for the public assistance indicator (Figure 8.7), with statistically significant buffering effects for "not expected to go to college," "difficult to raise," and repeated a grade; among disadvantages associated with child characteristics, the statistically significant buffering effects range from 35 to 130 percent.

Figures 8.8 and 8.9 present the buffering effects for behavioral outcomes and psychological well-being. We find the most uniform buffering effects for the indicator for being a nonsmoker. We find buffering effects

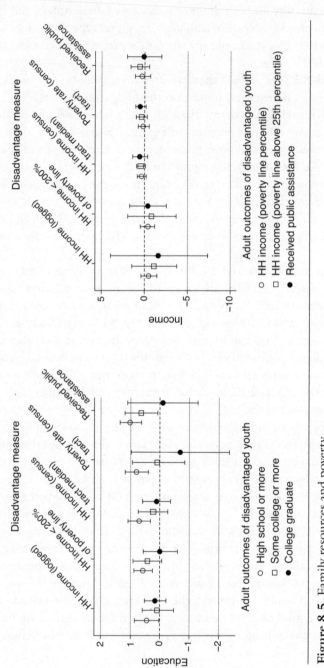

Figure 8.5. Family resources and poverty

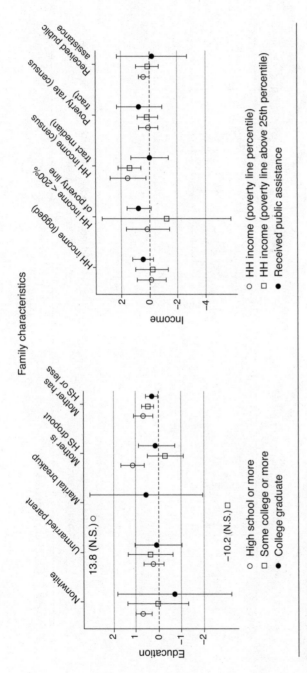

Figure 8.6. Family characteristics

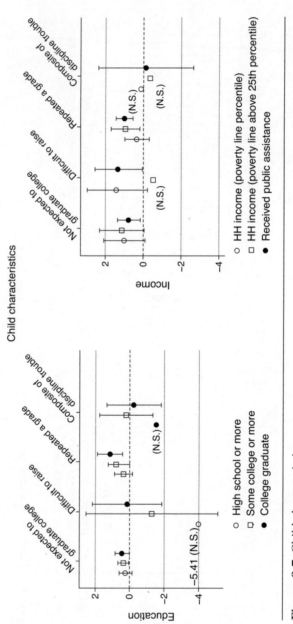

Figure 8.7. Child characteristics

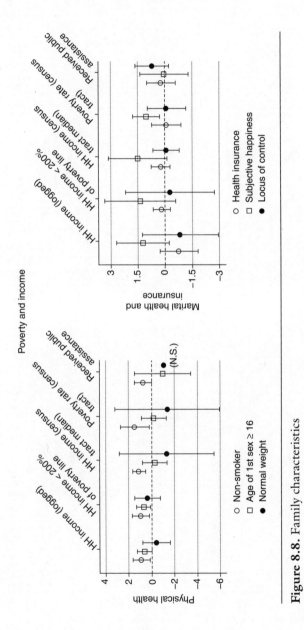

Figure 8.8. Family characteristics

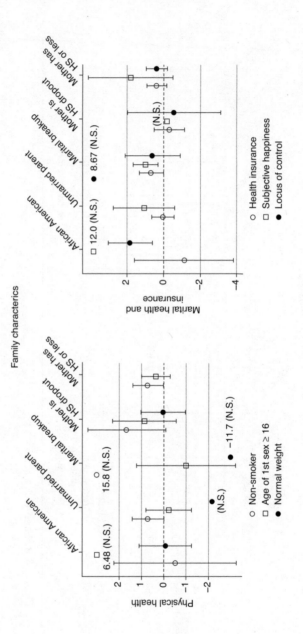

Family characterics

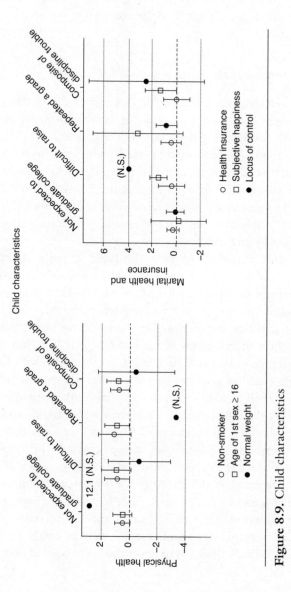

Figure 8.9. Child characteristics

of religiosity for all family resource measures of disadvantage, some family characteristic measures of disadvantage, and one of the child characteristics. For the statistically significant effects, the degree of buffering ranges between 71 and 181 percent. For other behavioral and psychological well-being outcomes, we do not find any uniformly statistically significant buffering effects.

Joint Significance of the Buffering Hypothesis

Although our discussion thus far has examined the buffering effect of religion for each disadvantage-outcome combination, we have not yet addressed the overarching hypothesis of the chapter, that participation in religious activities buffers disadvantaged youth later in life. Overall, we find that just over 20 percent of the buffering effects from all disadvantage-outcome combinations are significant at the 5 percent level, and we find no cases of a significantly negative buffering effect. Given the number of coefficients in question, is this statistically significantly more than we would expect by chance?

We test this formally. We order the 168 t-statistics of the buffering effects presented in Figures 8.5 to 8.9 from smallest to largest. We compare the actual distribution of t-statistics of our estimated coefficients with the expected value (and the 99 percent confidence interval) of each percentile of ranked t-statistics that we would expect under the null hypothesis of no buffering effect in any disadvantage-outcome pair (the thin lines).[9] This analysis is shown in Figure 8.10. Comparing the actual with the expected distribution confirms that we observe significantly more significant buffering effects than would be expected by chance. In particular, at the critical values for the 5 percent and 1 percent levels of significance (1.96 and 2.57), the observed distribution of t-statistics lies not only above the expected distribution of t-statistics, it also lies above the 99 percent confidence interval for the expected distribution of t-statistics. Moreover, all t-statistics greater than 0.5 lie above the 99 percent confidence interval for ordered t-statistics. Thus, we are able to reject the joint null hypothesis of no buffering effect of religion across all outcomes. Overall, we observe significantly more significant effects than would be expected by chance alone, which allows us to reject the hypothesis of no overall buffering effect.

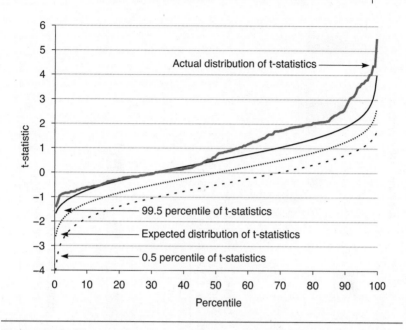

Figure 8.10. The actual and predicted percentiles of the distribution of t-statistics

Sensitivity Analysis

In Figure 8.11, we examine the sensitivity of the buffering effects of religion that we found in section 5.1 to the inclusion of a second buffering mechanism in the specification, in addition to religious attendance. In particular, we consider: religious attendance as predicted by covariates in our model; neighborhood income as a proxy for peers, schools, or other neighborhood institutions that provide buffering effects; and religious beliefs (as measured by belief in religious doctrine and in the literal truth of the Bible). The figure presents the estimated coefficient on the disadvantage-religious attendance interaction, the estimated coefficient on the interaction of the additional buffering variable and disadvantage, and the estimated buffering effect of religious attendance (as scaled in Figures 8.5 to 8.9).

The point estimates of buffering remain similar to those in the baseline specification, but only one estimate remains statistically significant at the 5 percent level, while the other four are now merely significant at the 10 percent level. Despite this decline in statistical significance, the robustness

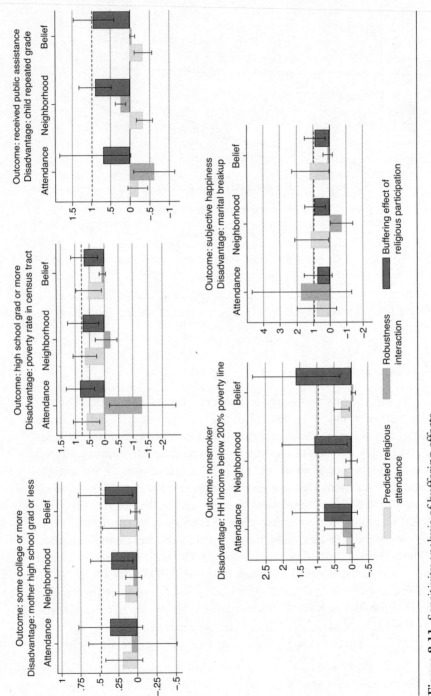

Figure 8.11. Sensitivity analysis of buffering effects

of the point estimates suggests that our estimates of buffering in our main specifications are due to actual religious attendance rather than the underlying covariates associated with religious attendance.

When including neighborhood income, we find that religious attendance continues to have significant buffering effects, suggesting that our findings are not driven by selection of religiously active parents into higher income neighborhoods.

Finally, when we include religious beliefs in addition to attendance, we continue to find a significant buffering effect of religious attendance, suggesting that attendance over and above belief buffers children against a disadvantaged upbringing. Taken together, the results from Figure 8.11 suggest that it is religious participation itself, rather than a likely correlate of religious participation, that provides the buffering effect against growing up in a disadvantaged environment.

6. Conclusions and Discussion

We draw two conclusions from our results. First, there are significant long-term effects of childhood disadvantages on subsequent outcomes in adulthood. This is not surprising given the large and expanding literature on intergenerational correlations in income, health, and education. Second, we find a substantial buffering effect of religion for a significant subset of outcomes. In particular, we find that religion buffers against a broad range of measures of disadvantage along the high school or more dimension. The buffering effect of religion on education, however, does not seem to translate into a buffering effect for income. In looking at behavior outcomes, we find some significant buffering effects for the likelihood of smoking. Finally, for health, health insurance, and psychological outcomes, we find few systematic buffering effects of religion.

Overall, we believe that our results support the notion that religion plays an important role in how households respond to the disadvantages they face. Our results are especially strong when disadvantage is measured by maternal education and outcomes are measured by the youth's educational attainment. Given that education has been shown to have far-reaching consequences for a range of outcomes, including mortality, voting, and crime, we believe our results shed light on a potentially important mechanism that can mitigate the intergenerational transmission of disadvantage.

IV

THE CULTURAL STRUCTURING *of* CONFLICT *and* DIFFERENCES WITHIN *and* BETWEEN GENDERS

9

Keeping Up the Front

How Disadvantaged Black Youths Avoid Street Violence in the Inner City

JOSEPH C. KRUPNICK, *Harvard University*
CHRISTOPHER WINSHIP, *Harvard University*

1. Introduction

Much of the literature on inner-city black youth culture has focused on the high levels of street violence, particularly involving gangs. Generally ignored is the fact that the overwhelming majority of interactions among young black gang members are neither conflictive nor violent.[1] Among the many encounters in which gang members participate, very few involve fights—much less shootings or homicides. Given the seemingly pervasive potential for violence in these relations, we ask: How is it possible that "peace" and "order" are preserved in the large majority of encounters on the inner-city street? Rather than thinking about why there is so *much* violence in this young African American world, we examine here why (and how) there is not more.[2]

We base our analysis on eighteen months of ethnographic and social observation and in-depth interviews with members of the Woodlawn community of Chicago. We study peacekeeping and violence in the inner city with a microlevel focus on understandings, performances, and action-oriented rituals of twenty Woodlawn young men who call themselves "Hustlas"—each is either a current or former member of a gang. Based on our ethnographic analysis, we adduce three main arguments. First, we find that social understandings on the street are fundamentally rooted in fear of physical conflict. Owing to socioeconomic marginality, a structural shift in the social relations of Woodlawn gangs, and the constant threat of a predatory social type Hustlas call "Crazy Killers," even the most innocuous face-to-face encounters are fateful events where social standing is on the line and where there is always potential for violence. However, in a street culture where status is so crucially tied to displays of masculine invulnerability and to being seen as a "badass" or "hardman," this creates a double-bind: Hustlas must find ways of warding off physical threat while simultaneously asserting themselves as street elites worthy of fear and respect.

Our second—and central—argument is that Hustlas negotiate these demands and limit violence through a series of interactional techniques we call "symbolic substitutions." Symbolic substitutions involve the use of aggressive front-staged posture, display, and verbal brinkmanship as strategic substitutes for face-to-face physical violence. While Hustlas talk a great deal about violent crime and organize their street styles around its danger, they stop short of actual physical conflict with threatening bluffs and blusters that substitute for situational closure. What makes these ritualized performances so effective, we find, is the cunning double-sidedness of a repeated street phrase like "Don't fuck with me" or "I'll get you . . . next time"—that both asserts situational dominance and obviates the risk of actual hand-to-hand conflict. Low-pitched phrases like these and menacing gestures like a cold stare or a closed fist earn Hustlas respect and status while limiting violence to artful display and mere front-staged sound and fury.

We organize Hustlas' performances around five types of ritual interaction—each carrying a risk of violence that Hustlas attempt to avoid. Following sociologist Erving Goffman, we decompose these violence-limiting interactions into five corresponding categories of symbolic substitution: postponement, accomplishment, keying, fabrication, and reframing. As interactions become more threatening, Hustlas deploy increasingly elaborate substitutes for violence. Less threatening situations like ordinary passages on the street require spontaneous signals that keep up the front by *postponing* violence to a vague and unspecified "next time." More threatening confrontations involve for-an-audience storytelling and cut-throat contests of "shit talking," which symbolically *accomplish* and *key* violence by replacing it with the aggressive suggestibility of dramatic language. Most dangerous are situations that call for acts of retaliation and others, including stickups and armed robberies, which are already framed by criminal intent. Hustlas operate in these fateful worlds by *fabricating* and *reframing* violence via psychological mind games that preserve the face of dominance and leave their victims "beaten"—psychologically, far more than they are physically.

Our third claim is that when violence occurs, it may well be neither necessary nor intended. Notwithstanding strategically planned and premeditated events like drive-by shootings and execution-style gang murders—which are publicized but account for only a small fraction of overall rates of inner-city violence—many instances of street violence are unintended and avoidable. Much of the time, violence is a consequence of misunderstandings, fear-driven breaks of frame, and impulsive accidents that are notable primarily as inconsistencies in a generally successful cultural project of peacekeeping. To put it in the Hustlas' own language, violence often erupts when people are caught "slipping"—a term that at once suggests the precariousness and the avoidability of most physical acts of violence. And, as we will discuss, even when Hustlas do "slip," there are often social designs in place that keep violence from escalating to all-out urban warfare, which, in this case, we will tentatively discuss via the role of handguns.

This chapter operates in the phenomenal foreground of social interactions, drawing on the interactionist and phenomenological methods made famous by Erving Goffman and with roots in Durkheim ([1912] 1964) and Simmel. In theory and method, this means we depart from the dominant positivist tradition that seeks explanations in the structural background of fixed causal categories (like poverty or residential segregation) (Skogan 1990; Sampson and Wilson 1995; Thornberry et al. 2003). One problem with the standard positivist approach is that most people who engage in acts of violence do not fit these causal categories. Second, most people who do fit into these categories are not violent. And, third, even those who are violent are not violent most of the time (Katz 1988; Collins 2004, 2008). We study violent *experiences,* then, not violent individuals, which means ethnographically investigating the sensual tug and pull of (often conflicting) emotional impulses and how they are tethered to particular situations that may end in bloodshed but must also start somewhere concrete.

But even the more descriptive ethnographic tradition tends to treat violence as an epiphenomenal symptom rather than on its own terms. For one thing, ethnographic sociology—like most quantitative work—generally remains wedded to structuralist assumptions that violence is straightforwardly shaped by "ghetto-specific" behavior and macrolevel antecedents like racism, residential segregation, and socioeconomic disadvantage (Wilson 1996; Venkatesh 2000, 2006). Second, urban ethnographers usually find it necessary to package violence together with culturally similar dynamics like gang membership, guns, drug dealing, and other phenomena that are presumed to lead to violence—often only by implication or untested association (Sanchez-Jankowski 1991; Majors and Billson 1993; Bourgois 1995; Jackall 2005; Harcourt 2006; Wacquant 2003, 2008; Klein and Maxson 2010). While this may in part reflect the technical challenge of gaining access to a criminal "underworld" (Becker [1963] 1997, 168–71), the upshot is that urban ethnographers rarely get close enough to violence to see how threatening situations actually unfold in everyday social interactions on the street.

The most notable exception is Elijah Anderson's *Code of the Street* (1999). In Anderson's analysis, persistent, racialized urban poverty combines with distrust of police and mainstream political institutions to create a cultural "code" that governs the use of violence as street justice. While residents divide themselves into fluid, folk ethnographic social categories of "street" and "decent," the code of the street takes a particular toll on "decent" residents who are often forced to switch codes and demonstrate "street credibility." Violence, however, is path dependent and situational, because one's degree of street credibility will in some circumstances invite and in others preclude physical challenges. For Anderson, this means violence is primarily a defensive move and that interactions are negotiated by methods of linguistic and paralinguistic signaling that either catalyze physical conflict or keep it at the level of posture and display.

Empirically, we build on Anderson's conception of violence in *Code of the Street*. We are particularly attuned to the role of defensive moves and front-staged postures involving what Anderson calls "showing heart." As we will discuss, the street requires an inversion of the Goffmanian code of presentation—in which we are generally presumed to be putting our best selves forward. Here, we find an antinomian world where respect is staked on front-staged threats, aggressive one-ups, and fierce displays of personal antagonism. In this connection, the inner-city "campaign for respect" creates a catch-22 for its participants: young black men must at once find ways to protect themselves physically (which means avoiding violence) and they must assert themselves socially (which means projecting the potential for violence). In Anderson's *Code of the Street*, there is no reliably safe way out. When it comes down to it, according to Anderson, "street credibility becomes a highly valuable commodity in the community, something for which some people will fight and die; ironically, often in response to a challenge or threat" (Anderson, pers. comm.).

Our argument is less pessimistic than Anderson's. In Woodlawn the rituals of interaction make it seldom necessary to "fight and die." Also, while Anderson does not problematize the link between what he calls the "capacity" and the "use" of violence, we argue that front staging a capacity for violence not only forestalls but also causally leads to its reduction. It is by affecting violent postures and displays that Hustlas in Woodlawn find ways to successfully protect themselves physically while still convincing their peers they are badass street elites not to be "fucked with."

In exploring how violence is strategically avoided, this chapter also has affinities with recent scholarship outside the context of inner-city life. Outside sociology, researchers in military history and warfare have become interested in the implication that, contrary to dominant depictions in mainstream political discussions, violence on the battlefield is fundamentally difficult, inefficient, and even incompetent (Marshall 1947; Keegan 1976, 1993; Holmes 1985; Grossman 1995). In sociology, Randall Collins (2008) in his path-breaking book *Violence: A Microsociological Theory* frames a vision of interactional life that is also quite similar to what we propose for the inner-city context. Collins cuts across a much broader swath of social life than we do, but he makes the critical distinction between performative brinkmanship and actual violent expression. Still, Collins stops short of arguing that bluster and bluff are pragmatically motivated to limit violent behavior. Violent presentation and practice do have the character of separateness in Collins, but we systematize the distinction by introducing the concept of symbolic substitution for the types of threatening interactions on which these performances work.

In the next section, we discuss our research methods. In the subsequent section, we describe the Woodlawn neighborhood, discuss the structural bases for our microlevel results, and explore the signs and significance of membership in the Hustla community. We then examine in detail five increasingly threatening street interactions and how Hustlas organize their involvement around displays of symbolic substitution that limit violence. Following this, we analyze circumstances under which peacekeeping fails and violence does occur. Finally, we offer a tentative note, incorporating into the discussion the complex and perhaps paradoxical role of Hustlas' handguns.

2. Research and Methods

This chapter is based on eighteen months of ethnographic fieldwork conducted by Krupnick in the Woodlawn community in Chicago's historic Black Belt. We chose Woodlawn for three reasons: first, like many South

Side neighborhoods in Chicago, Woodlawn has over the past twenty-five years suffered severe job losses, significant working- and middle-class depopulation, and escalating rates of concentrated disadvantage. Second, Woodlawn has been targeted for large-scale urban revival and gentrification, making it an opportunity to study a community in transition. Third, Woodlawn figures saliently in many ethnographic old and new classics like Park and Burgess's *The City* (1925), Thrasher's *The Gang* (1927), Drake and Cayton's *Black Metropolis* ([1945] 1993), Venkatesh's *American Project* (2000), and Wacquant's *Body and Soul* (2003).

We participated in detailed social observation and over 100 formal and informal interviews with twenty African American young men aged sixteen to thirty (all names used are pseudonyms). Our ethnographic work was conducted in the summer of 2008, the summer of 2009, and September 2010–September 2011. Each of our informants is a member (or former member, when noted) of a Chicago gang, including the Blackstone Rangers, the Black Disciples, the Gangster Disciples, and the Woodlawn branch of the Vice-Lords. We used a "snowball" sampling method to reach our informants, starting with extensive conversations with former Vice-Lord officer, Leroy, who lives in Woodlawn and has maintained close ties to young members of the community who run with the Vice-Lords and other prominent gangs in the neighborhood.

We first met Leroy in June 2008 on Chicago's north side, where he works as a doorman, and spent that summer becoming acquainted with Woodlawn in one-hour-per-day conversations on the corner of 63rd and Dorchester in Woodlawn. In the summer of 2009, Leroy introduced us to other Woodlawn Hustlas—Percy (twenty-four), Mike (twenty-one), Michael (twenty-five), and L. L. (twenty-five)—who, in turn, helped link us with the other informants in this study. Each of our interviews lasted between thirty minutes and two hours, some were conducted in groups, and many of our informants we followed up several times for purposes of clarification and elaboration. While most of our interviews were conducted on-site in Woodlawn (usually in a car, local restaurant, or on the street), a few were in a neighboring community or (in a handful of follow-up interviews) over the phone. In addition to our conversations with the young men, we also draw on conversations with Woodlawn community leaders, business owners, and local police officers who must go unnamed but were nevertheless essential for purposes of orientation.

In the course of our fieldwork, we made use of observational experiments in the microinteraction tradition of sociologists like Erving Goffman and ethnomethodologists like Harold Garfinkel (1967). We learned, for example, about the concepts of "slipping" and "staying on point" largely in the course of experiments in which we walked down the street with Hustlas and compared notes. We studied "everyday passages" by comparing different kinds of momentary interactions—including encounters with individuals versus those with larger groups, and encounters that we ourselves participated in versus those among Hustlas that we observed at a distance. In querying Hustlas in different social, chronological, and spatial contexts, we wanted to get a sense of the role of situational influences on their attitudes and styles of impression management. We sometimes asked Hustlas a series of questions one-on-one and then followed up with the same questions in a larger group discussion, and we also took note of how their interactions with us changed over time and in the different geographic settings where we conducted interviews. A final strategy involved cross-checking narratives and testimonies with as many Hustlas as possible. When one Hustla described an event whose consequences implicated others, we found it necessary to query as many Hustlas about it as possible. For corroborative evidence, we also asked Hustlas about other Hustla stories that did not involve them personally but which they might be in a position to discuss or elaborate on. In doing these things, our goal was to understand as precisely as possible how interactions actually unfold among Hustlas and to minimize the potential for narrative bias and fabrication.

Still, like all ethnographically driven research, this one is vulnerable to certain methodological limitations. In the course of our eighteen months in Woodlawn, we did not observe a single physical confrontation that might be called "overtly violent." We witnessed a number of verbal arguments and threats, some bluster-driven scuffles, and a few instances of clandestine crime, but not one fistfight, stick-up, or targeted weapon display or discharge. This means we must depend largely on accounts and stories—rather than direct observation—of encounters with violence and physical conflict. This is a notable limitation, especially if there is a wish among Hustlas to underplay violent deeds for reasons of concealment or, alternatively, to overstate involvement due to the cultural premium placed on ornate imagery and "badass" expressions of honor.

A second source of potential bias owes to the particular brand of intimacy that developed between Krupnick, a Euro-American male, and his all-black, male respondents. Interactions with Hustlas were often organized around male-bonding tropes (e.g., fist-bumping, joking, running commentary on women as they passed on the street, etc.). Krupnick also created trust based on his own physical stature (six feet two inches, 190 pounds, and "swoll as hell, not like a dorky professor," according to Leroy)—the latter being an important marker of social status among Hustlas in Woodlawn. These things are, of course, a double-edged sword. On the one hand, such intimacy may guard against a common ethnographic pitfall that Howard Becker calls informant "dummying-up"—in which respondents either refuse to participate in the study or simply feign ignorance or interest in what is being discussed (Becker [1963] 1997). On the other hand, there is also the risk of *too much* intimacy, that we have become too sympathetic to the plight of our respondents and have unwittingly elicited exaggerated or embellished testimonies. While we have tried our best to shield ourselves from naive moralism, we can only guard against respondent fabrication—as we have already suggested—by cross-checking reports with as many Hustlas as possible for tone and veracity.

A third methodological caveat involves ethnographic generalizability. The claims we make about Hustlas in Woodlawn are, we must remember, a product of time, place, and circumstance. It is unclear if one would observe similar social interactions in other inner-city centers like New York, Los Angeles, or Philadelphia. Nor is it clear that a study of Woodlawn in the 1970s (or even 1990s) would have yielded the same observations. There is also the matter of sample selection. While we are primarily interested in making claims about Hustlas who are actively engaged in gang life, it is worth noting that some of our respondents are not presently members of a Woodlawn gang. Two of our lead informants, Leroy and Percy, dropped out of the Vice-Lords, and although they retain close connections with their former "running buddies," their testimonies may reflect the idiosyncratic perspectives of former gang members who have (self) selected out of the process. Leroy's "former" status is particularly salient here given that Leroy provided us with an entrée to four of our other respondents—his good friends, who might be expected to share some of his idiosyncratic perspectives despite being still active in the gang system. While we cannot make the claim that our respondents constitute a perfectly representative cross-section of gang members in Woodlawn, we do argue that they belong to a self-defined and delimited community of young black men who strongly identify with the gang world and the members-only world they have self-consciously organized around the culture of what Leroy calls "street hustling." (See our section entitled "Street Membership.")

3. The Streets of Woodlawn

A. *The Neighborhood and Its Social Structure*

Before exploring the ethnographic results and implications of our study, the distinctive ecology and economics of the Woodlawn neighborhood merit a brief discussion. Woodlawn is located at the heart of Chicago's historically black South Side and covers a two-square-mile strip of land bordered by Lake Michigan on the east and Hyde Park and the University of Chicago on the north. Like so many U.S. urban communities, Woodlawn is rooted in a history of mid-century white flight and the twin evils of economic disinvestment and state abandonment. In the 1960s, it was a bustling 90,000-person African American neighborhood lined with specialty shops, grocery stores, and famous jazz clubs. It was an era where vital and progressive politics held sway, Saul Alinsky worked with one of the nation's first community organizations (the Woodlawn Organization), and a gang known as the Blackstone Rangers exerted national leadership as a forerunner of African American self-empowerment (Brazier 1960).

If one were to walk down the streets of present-day Woodlawn, how-ever, one would not see much of its progressive history. Despite recent commitments from city, community, and university-partnered urban revival, the area continues (as of 2011) to show signs of benign neglect. Sixty-third Street and Cottage Grove, once the hub of South Side com-merce and culture, looks bombed out—abandoned—a "community of last resort." It is the usual scene with construction and cigarette butts and shards of glass littering the streets. Young men pass each other with a glance, hustling past gang lines, and keeping their heads up en route to somewhere else. Older men loiter on street corners, drinking out of bags and forty-ounce bottles, sometimes retreating into a local store or com-munity organization to chat or to bum a smoke. There is the occasional gunshot, a little bit of running, drug dealers who are on the sly, and fields with dug-up grass and no children playing. There are closed storefronts, torn-down basketball rims, boarded up churches, and not many thriving centers of commerce. What remains are historic haunts, like Daley's Restaurant on 63rd—where they still serve chicken gumbo and breakfast all day; the once-influential community organizations like TWO and WECAN; and a 20,000-member megachurch, the Apostolic Church of God, that nobody in the community seems to attend (McRoberts 2003). Political and community leaders promise that this will all change in a few years—that Woodlawn will once again become a mixed-income "community of choice" (Quality of Life Plan 2005). But for now, Woodlawn's street life is largely defined by its young men who hang out in the daytime; mix it up on contested street corners; drive by with blares of threats and loud hip-hop; and spend their time looking for business or girls to holler at or just a physically safe way to get through the day.

Against the broad backdrop of post-1960s socioeconomic continuity, the Woodlawn neighborhood has witnessed a massive change in the social relations of the gang. In the 1980s and 1990s—as Venkatesh describes in his ethnographic research on the Robert Taylor Homes—Chicago gangs were large, solidary, and highly structured organizations governed by pyramid-shaped corporate hierarchies and divisions of labor (2000, 2006). Since 2007, large-scale, city-sponsored demolition of many of the city's largest public housing projects (most notably the Taylor Homes) has contributed to a splintering in the gang's traditional structure. Driven out of public housing where they previously consolidated territory, South Side gangs have attempted to establish new areas already occupied by other Chicago gangs. The immediate result, according to the Chicago Crime Commission's 2012 *Gang Book,* was an explosion of turf-related violence—2008 corresponding to a marked spike in Chicago gang homicides. In the longer term, it has meant that the traditionally hierarchical gang has been dislodged into warring factions, many being led by young men under twenty and controlling only a single city block. In Woodlawn, this has produced a fracturing of gang-level loyalty. There is now just as much risk of conflict with members of your own gang as there is with your historic rivals. Social relations, divested of much of their group status, must be settled among individuals who often don't know, in Hustla Leroy's terms, "who's a friend [and] who's an enemy."

B. Street Membership

In this changing gang group context, each of our twenty informants belongs to a class of Woodlawn citizenry whose members call themselves "Hustlas." Hustlas are young, black, males, ages sixteen to thirty, and residents who are active (or formerly active) in a subgroup of a local gang—the Rangers, the Black Disciples, the Gangster Disciples, or the Vice-Lords. They also share a common "street" orientation, which means that they organize self-presentations around displays of masculine toughness and a capacity to use violence. All twenty claim to own guns, thirteen say they carry guns with them "all the time," fourteen have spent time in jail or prison, eight grew up in Chicago's infamous Robert Taylor Homes, a slight majority are high school dropouts, and only two are employed in the mainstream labor market.

Perhaps most important is that our twenty informants share a strong sense of cultural membership. They explicitly define themselves as a group, often using expressions like "us players" or "g's like me" to locate themselves in a community of Hustlas who self-identify with the culture of honor on the Woodlawn streets. This means that they know each other by name, they know about each other, and some of them are siblings, cousins, or gang "running buddies." But, as our informants told us, the clearest dividing line between Hustlas and non-Hustlas involves gun ownership. It is worth exploring this on the logic of one of our informants—Xman:

> *Xman:* I gotta gun. A Glock. We all got 'em and the only difference is what kind of gun you have. But, yeah, part of what it means to live here is to be strapped, 'cause you never know what's gonna happen 'round here, man. So you gotta know who's carrying, who's not, and who's not even in the game. We hustlas, but I mean some of these shorties are just in another world. They never seen a gun. Like they live somewhere else, that's how they act, all uppity, trying to get smart you know. But, we respect them smarties, man, I mean we're all trying to figure out our way outta here, so they didn't bother us, we didn't bother them. Well, sometimes a joke or two if you a real scrawny little chump and you get caught slippin' or whatever. Or if you're a little rat and you talking to the police, then it's different. But, mostly they did their own shit, and we did ours. Different worlds, bro.

In saying "they didn't bother us, so we didn't bother them," Xman suggests that part of what distinguishes a Woodlawn "Hustla" from a Woodlawn "Smartie" is that the latter are not beholden to the same rules of honor and masculine toughness. As other Hustlas emphasized, Smarties are given a pass and tend to go unpunished even if they act like "pussies."

They do, however, play a crucial role on the street, typically filling in the background as onlookers or observers to the rhythms of the streets. Smarties are also treated with some measure of social respect—something Xman frames in the racialized language of collective struggle. This means that in a larger sense Hustlas share a common culture—or, in the terms of sociologist Orlando Patterson, a shared understanding about "what one must know to act effectively in one's environment" (Patterson 2000). They identify and understand themselves as part of a larger American inner-city street culture with idioms and dialects that are rooted in the black community of Woodlawn.

In spite of their strong association with street life, Hustlas also take pains to distance themselves from another social type they call "Crazy Killers." Crazy Killers represent the ultraviolent few in Woodlawn— young men on the fringes with reputations for heinous acts of murder, manslaughter, and even torture. Crazy Killers represent the ten to twenty hardest "hardmen" in all of Woodlawn and, according to our respondents, commit more than half of all the neighborhood's homicides in a given year. Some are hired by gangs for their capacity to instill fear, others are independent contractors, and a few are essentially contract killers who might be hired by a non-Crazy Killer to do somebody in. Crazy Killers are considered crazy because their behavior is so unpredictable; sometimes they'll let a grievance go, other times they will walk into a restaurant and, for no apparent reason (as Xman puts it) "spray bullets all over the fuckin' place and kill six innocent people." Although many of Woodlawn's craziest Killers are behind bars serving long sentences, in any given moment, at least a handful are at large on the streets of Woodlawn— either because they are awaiting criminal trials or because they have somehow, despite their histories of murder, managed to evade the justice system. Complicating matters further, many Crazy Killers have achieved almost mythological or urban-legend status: many Hustlas know them by name and by stories, but could not identify them if they passed on the street, and some Crazy Killers come into Woodlawn from other South Side neighborhoods like Englewood and Washington Park. The result is these violent few arouse in our respondents a distinct blend of awe and awfulness that colors everyday life on the streets in Woodlawn. Percy summarizes the Hustla experience of life among Crazy Killers:

You know, us guys, we're just trying to get through the day. Yeah, we sometimes do some stupid shit, but something has to happen—I mean, usually there's some reason or whatever. But, there a few guys, like fucking crazy killers, who just go around and kill people for no reason at all. They just wake up and are like "I feel like killing somebody," and they fucking do it! We all know about these guys, like this one Anthony James who's got like ten bodies under him minimum. James once walked into a Church's Chicken, he was chasing some mothafucka Johnny or whatever and shootin' down the street, so the guy Johnny runs into the chicken shack, and Anthony follows him and just starts blowing people away. Killed a woman, a kid, an old man, and I don't even know he even hit Johnny. Don't even take the money from the register or anything. Just walks out like it's no big deal and shit. Them guys out there. You get caught slippin', and you get your head blown off by one of these crazy mothafuckas. Can't be too careful.

If "can't be too careful" turns out to be a refrain for our Hustlas, it is in part due to the constant threat of Crazy Killers like Anthony James. That they comprise such a small fraction of Woodlawn's young black male population is not enough to quell the dread of a chance run-in. No matter how unlikely, a single bullet is enough to end things *in medias* and for all time.

4. Street Interactions

In a world where gang affiliations are increasingly tenuous and where Crazy Killers may always be lurking around the corner, Hustlas are faced with a double bind—how to create a reputation as a badass, while preserving a modicum of safety and social order. To resolve the double bind, Hustlas have adopted street presentations that display masculine toughness, strength, and conspicuous invulnerability to potential danger. To be seen as weak or "soft" is to make yourself a mark, an easy target for violence. Hence the importance of cultivating and keeping up the self-image that you are a badass. Particular emphasis is paid to physical semiotics, such as the building up of one's muscles (or, "getting swoll"); wearing garments that look like they belong on the battlefield (camouflage pants, fatigues, and boots); ostentatiously displaying tattoos (as a symbolic boundary from the world); growing, and carefully maintaining, facial hair (especially for "shorties" to look older); and brandishing a concealed weapon (sometimes with a conspicuous pants bulge). Use is also made of a distinctive language invoking familiar inversions (to be "sick" is a virtue),

Table 9.1 Interactional Profiles

Interaction Type	Threat of Violence	Symbolic Substitution	Respect Accrued
Ritual Passings	Low	Postponement	Minimal to Moderate
Boasting and Storytelling	Low	Accomplishment	Very High
Shit-Talking	Moderate	Keying	High
Revenge and Retaliation	Moderate to High	Fabrication	High
Armed Robbery	High	Reframing	Minimal

a paralinguistic style that is often highly gestured, and performative styles that favor bluffs, blusters, and an ornate choreography of verbal brinkmanship.

In the present section, we show how Hustlas limit physical danger in five increasingly dangerous types of street interactions: (1) simple passages on the street; (2) ritualized sessions of elaborate storytelling; (3) shit-talking and other language games; (4) interactional occasions for vengeance and revenge; and (5) the commissioning of armed robberies and criminal stickups. What emerges is a corresponding set of symbolic substitutions that we categorize as *postponement, accomplishment, keying, fabrication,* and *reframing*.[3] With each, there are cunning feints, sleights-of-hand, and rhetorical magic tricks that protect street hustlers from the real dread of physical violence. Table 9.1 renders a schematization of the findings in consolidated form. Here for each type of interaction we have indicated the potential threat of violence, the symbolic substitution used for limiting violence, and the degree of respect at stake. We then discuss each form of interaction in detail.

A. Ritual Passages as Violent Postponements

The most common interactions on the street occur in seemingly prosaic encounters where Hustlas simply walk (or drive) past each other on the street. Unlike most U.S. neighborhoods where these momentary exchanges tend to be quite casual and unmemorable, on the Woodlawn streets they often become rituals of fateful significance. We find that the most threatening street passages—usually involving members of rival gangs—undergo a series of contingent stages in which interactants limit violence by agreeing to postpone it. Here, we rely on our own observations of rival-gang Hustlas as they pass each other on the street in Woodlawn. When two Hustlas pass each other and are "staying on point," they become entrained in a nonverbal confrontation that generally unfolds roughly in the following sequence of embodied cues.

1. Fifty to twenty-five feet away, you do not make eye contact with your interactant and instead seem to be absorbed in something else—typically iPod/walkman, often beat boxing to the sounds of the music. Look around you—right and left—rather than directly in front or behind, but the appearance should be nonchalant or casual.
2. Keep your hands out of your pockets and in plain and visible view. When we questioned K. J. about this, he replied, "It's to show each other they're not planning on using a gun. No harm here, gotta have your hands out."
3. Make less than one second of eye contact when passing your interactant. Nod at each other affirmatively, fist-pound, high-five, and/or say something casual like, "What's up cuz" or "You straight," engage in light banter if situation compels it.
4. After passing, go back to the beat boxing or casual display of attentiveness. Don't look back. Looking back, after an encounter, would be a form of "slipping," unless you are looking for conflict, and might lead to an unwanted altercation—inadvertently or not.

In these simple passages, staying on point involves the ordered signaling of three kinds of cues. (1) Recognition—you have to demonstrate that you are cognitively aware that you are co-present with another person. This is straightforwardly achieved through Goffmanian civil inattention and, subsequently, by momentary eye contact and a head nod or verbal greeting. (2) Invulnerability—you are expected to affect casualness (listening to music, beat boxing, etc.) and "badness" (the effect of the guttural "wassup, cuz"). (3) Nonthreateningness—you are not holding a gun, you deploy the affirmative "nod," and you do not look back after the passage (Anderson 1990).

We might expect some slippage in the requirement to affect both invulnerability and nonthreateningness, but this would miss the crucially situational dimension of the latter. Just as the exchange itself is momentary, so is the display of nonthreateningness, which strategically says, "I'll let you go, *for now.*" To keep your hands in full view is not intended to show that you are unarmed or incapable of discharging your weapon; rather, that you are carrying a weapon but choosing in this instance not to point it at your interactant. Robert helps clarify this point:

> *Robert:* Dude, it's not like we out there looking to get fucked up. I don't want to die, you know, just like you. So if I'm running up on a guy, I gotta show him he's straight and no point in fronting like I'm going to smoke him or you know. . . . So, the other day, I'm on 65th just minding my own self, drinking, you know, and that shorty Zo *[from the Rangers, a historically rival gang]* steps up on me like he wants to hit a lick. So I gotta think fast and shit. I take my hands out, put 'em up totally innocent *[changes his voice],* "Zo, I'll let you pass here. You can go this time." Cause I don't need this shit now, you know. But, Zo's got points to prove you know, like he's just a kid and needs some action like all kids do. He needs to prove himself. So, the only thing I can do is squash it and like be cool and shit. So I'm like, "What's up, Zo, you straight?" Said it like we friends, and I'm like watching his back and want to make sure he doesn't think I'm switching up on him.

In saying "I'll let you pass here," Robert suggests that although he's a threatening person in general, on this particular occasion his intent is to "squash it." Robert achieves the double purpose of preserving the content of his badass image while crucially postponing anything potentially bad until a vague and unspecified next time (see also Suttles 1968, 125). Robert's nonviolent passage is also a striking example of associative reasoning in action. There is no time for Robert to ponder which cultural toolkit to use, just the fast-thinking heuristic much like what Kahneman (2003, 2011) calls the cognitive "System 1."

B. Boasting and Storytelling as Violent Accomplishments

On the street, where public knowledge depends on word-of-mouth circulation, encounters entrain Hustlas in boasts, brags, and "awe"-ful stories that are necessary for the staging of reputation and respect. Hence, the texture and detail with which Hustlas describe—and embellish—stories of themselves as outlaw sovereigns of dread (Katz 1988). In our observations in Woodlawn, we frequently overheard Jalen relating these kinds of anecdotes to fellow Black Disciple, Xman—anecdotes that invariably cast

Jalen playing comic book-type roles of vigilante superhero. In one story, Jalen describes himself as a kind of street soldier and superman. Jalen's story features his running buddy K. J.:

> *Jalen:* It went down in that building right there. Second floor. Cops like banging down the door, and I mean . . . we're up there, smoking, getting high, and I'm doing my thing *[i.e., selling drugs]*. Two floors up, and we jump out the window, me and K. J. and A-bomb, and I start runnin. So like a block later, I look around, can't see K. J., look back and he's being like jacked by the Po-lice. I'm like fuck this shit. Then, I say, no, can't let 5–0 think they run this place. So I just come up on the officer, creep up, and knock him down with my fist. Then, I put my fist into the other cop's head. Just pounded the fuck out of both. They're both down. And when we get back, wouldn't you know, K's talking shit, saying I shoulda kept running, that he was straight you know, didn't need help. So I reach for my Nine *[millimeter gun]* and that just shut him right the fuck up. Squashed that shit right away an' then some. So, you know, I'm the motherfucking man, nobody fucks with me down here.

The story contains the performative elements that keep up Jalen's badass reputation. First, there is the imputation of heroic courage in running back to confront the cops. Second, there is the matter of righteous honor in establishing himself, Jalen, as avenger against an unjust criminal system. Third, there is the demonstration of physical strength in punching out both cops. Finally, there is Jalen's display of invulnerability and capacity to use violence both in brandishing a weapon and in his story's coda: "I'm the motherfucking man, nobody fucks with me down here."

More subtle, however, are things that Jalen's story does not say. Jalen makes a point of conveying his capacity for violence (by brandishing the weapon), but it is just as important that he decides not to use it. Despite the fact that he says he has already fought with the cops, and despite K. J.'s apparent decision to goad Jalen into a second fight, Jalen responds by showing (but not firing) his gun. On the one hand, the gun is essential to Jalen's story because it demonstrates his invulnerability and status as someone "nobody fucks with." On the other hand, the gun also functions to deescalate tension, establish situational closure, and defuse the threat of violent repercussions. "Shutting him right the fuck up" both establishes situational dominance and restores peaceful equilibrium by deterring the expression of actual violence.

But, in being so taken by Jalen's story, we must be careful not to be taken in by it. Jalen's story, in other words, is both a description of a staged performance and an example of a staged presentation, which means that the telling of the story itself must be similarly scrutinized. We told it to other Hustlas—Michael, Xman, Leroy, Mike, and K. J. himself. We found that Michael had heard the story from Jalen, framed in almost identical terms (and believed it); Leory, Xman, and Mike had heard it in various guises from other people in Woodlawn (and believed it); and K. J.—who of course was part of the story—remembered the event unfolding very differently. Leroy called the story "awesome"; Mike said it was "straight badass"; and Michael expressed respect/fear for Jalen both because of the terrifying deed Jalen described and because of Jalen's story's capacity to narratively slander the image of fellow Hustla K. J.

> *Michael:* You gotta remember man these things *[stories]* get around and they can just fuck you up. K. J.'s a straight chump in that story, and you know what, I mean yeah it prolly fucking went down like that, but Jalen went around tellin' everybody just to show he's the man. That's what fucking bugs me, bro. It's not just that it happened; I mean what's the big deal that it happened—who's going to know, you know? But, Jalen has this mouth on him and that's the fucking important thing. That's the thing that ruins a man, because how else is it gonna get around, you know? It's like an advertisement or a commercial on television *[Jalen's story]* and that's what gets me about that punk J. I mean what if it didn't even happen like J says? What's the fucking difference, right, because all that matters is that J got in his story before anyone could even talk to K. J. So it doesn't even matter. All that matters now is the rep K. J.'s got because of Jalen's gossip. If enough people find out, it's not just gossip; it's fucking true, man.

In this sense, Jalen's story—even if purely fabricated—accomplishes violence purely by dint of the narrative power to make people believe it. That seems to be what Michael means when he says, "That's what fucking bugs me." What scares Michael is not Jalen's violent actions against K. J., but Jalen's even more threatening capacity to circulate a story that, because everyone hears and is contained by it, can ruin K. J.'s image (Suttles 1968, 201–02).

Quite significantly, K. J. himself remembered the event quite differently. According to K. J., Jalen did not land—or even attempt—a punch on the officer, but instead both of them defused the situation with the cops by talking their way out of it. Furthermore, K. J. had no memory of Jalen drawing a gun on him and found it surprising that Jalen would present it that way since, according to K. J., the whole situation involved them working together. In K. J.'s words:

> *K. J.:* Naw, man, that motherfucker's making up shit. You tripping if you believe that shit; he's just trying to front like he's a G. Just wanted to impress you, man, that's all. Dude's like my best friend, and that fucker wouldn't pop a cop if he *[the cop]* had a pussy. Dude fights like a bitch. You seen 'em? *[laughing]*

Whose version of the story, Jalen's or K. J.'s, is closer to reality is not what is at stake here. As we infer from Michael, Xman, Leroy, and Mike, fateful stories circulate in the Hustlas' close-knit network, and the better they are constructed, the more likely others will be taken in by them. Mike's response helps to generalize the point that reputations can be earned on the rising shoulders of the street-styled raconteur:

> *Mike:* Yo, Jalen's my boy, he's a straight Hustla. I heard 'bout that from Chris back in the day. Heard it a bunch of dudes man. I 'member I'm locked up and my boy Rob was talking about that shit. Busting on 5–0 like that man, my boy J's fucking Robocop. Crazy, yo, with nunchucks. Heard that cop he bombed on was sent to the ER and after that like was too 'fraid to even bust on *[arrest]* Jalen cause of what happened to him and shit. Nobody fucks with J 'cause of that shit. Not even the police *[laughing]*.

Legends make men in Woodlawn, and since people are often not around to see the events as they unfold, awe-inducing stories produce respect, even if they come straight out of the creative imagination and do not involve violence or even as much as a closed fist.

C. "Shit-Talking" as Violent Keying

As street games, stories have a peculiar power of consensual imposition. The storyteller, if charismatic or clever enough, wills his image of himself into the hearts and minds of an enchanted listener/audience. His symbolic power to shape their impression is expressed in a voice so magnetic that it not only transfixes but compels them to remember and repeat it to others—ideally, with a similar sense of awe. But, there are other language games that Hustlas play that limit the bloodshed of hand-to-hand conflict. In particular, the phenomenon of "shit-talking." Unlike storytelling, shit-talking involves interactionally bilateral exchanges, and the threat of conflict is more direct because of their turn-taking escalation and capacity to explode into violent catharsis. That they do not ordinarily lead to anything physical is what we must explore here.

To "talk shit" (or trash) is now a familiar mainstream expression that connotes aggressive verbal brinkmanship bordering on—though not quite ever reaching—overt hostility. Talking shit points to a theatrical, for-an-audience exchange, particularly during athletic events where the word "shit" seems short for "bullshit" and suggests a kind of talk so situationally narrow that after the game it will be thrown away (like shit or trash) and forgotten. On the street, there is considerably more at stake. Shit-talking rituals invoke a different set of metaphors for our Hustlas, the object being to reduce opponents to existential "shit" (Katz 1988, 85–86). Nineteen-year-old Robert gives us a vivid sense of what makes shit-talking so distinctive in a story about a game with twenty-three-year-old Marcus:

> *Robert:* Okay, you didn't hear this shit from me, yo. But, it goes like this. When you're talking shit, it's like playing basketball. One-on-one, or whatever, cause sometimes there are more guys. And there's almost always someone around payin' attention. So okay: You and I are hanging out chilling, just whatever, bunch of other guys around, and you get into it with me over some bullshit. So if you say something cold, I have to respond. I mean, I can't just walk away or, you know, like act like a pussy and ask you to say sorry. I can't even hit a lick *[get into a fistfight]*, see, cause that'd be unfair, and you'd have me then. So I gotta say something to you, and it's got to be even colder. And then it's your turn, and you gotta say something even motherfucking badder than what I said. And on and on . . .
>
> But, see, here's the fucking thing, bro. During this whole time, we are, you know, fronting like it don't mean nothing, but your game is on the line, bro. I mean, people are watching, and you know they remember if you got game or you don't . . .
>
> So, I got into it with my boy Marcus the other day, and we were straight working each other down, I was talking about what a pussy

he is, how I macked on his sister, and he didn't do anything, you know, and then he came back and said something to me. I won't even tell you what it is, but it was bad . . .

I just bombed on him, started punching him like crazy. I mean I wasn't even thinking, yo, but it was the end right there. His homies stepped in, held me back, and they all left laughing and chuckling, with me just standing there holding my dick. Next time, I gotta stay on point, not let that happen, not acting like a chump, throwing up in the air, you know?

Shit-talking exhibits what Goffman calls *keying*, the real threat of violence being transformed into something mutually understood as merely playful (Goffman 1974, 41; Radcliffe-Brown [1952] 1965, 90–116; Bateson 1971). Because it is all just fun and games, the give-and-take of shit-talking demands that you play by the rules and act like there's nothing particularly important at stake.[4] Shit-talking therefore requires a double evasion: You must feign casualness about both the content of an emotionally threatening exchange and the serious social price if you do not remain casual.

In the shit-talking game with Marcus, Robert broke frame by impulsively punching Marcus—an act both against the rules and grounds for declaring Marcus the conversational victor. Like many staged battles, this one ends with onlookers rallying around the exultant winner and the loser standing there alone "holding his dick." Not only does Robert lose the game, he has played so unfairly that the onlookers come on stage to rescue him from "looking like a chump." He has been caught fighting *and* fighting badly—the audience here being both judge/jury of foul play and limit-setting agent of informal social control. But it is also the awkwardness of "throwing up in the air" that is a source of Robert's regretful, "Next time I gotta stay on point, not let that happen." A repeat performance risks further loss of respect, illustrating further the contrast between the smooth élan of verbal sparring and the flailing gracelessness of hands-on conflict. Leroy helps us generalize the point, by way of personal confession:

Leroy: I used to run with Vice [Lords], but now I got a job working as a doorman. And you know what? I made as much money in a day back then as I do in a week here. But I wouldn't trade this job for anything. Why? Because it's fucking easy compared to being out there on the street slinging drugs and shit. But, so, what happened? I got fat and old *[laughing]*, and I can't compete out there anymore, bro. Bottom line is it just don't look pretty when I hit a lick. I used to be like Ali, yo, I could smoke 'em all and look like fucking Rambo or Predator. But, dude, that was then. This is now, and look at me, man! You think I can fight like this? *[Leroy points to the paunch in his belly]*. So I don't front like that any more, bro. When you grown, you realize you gotta learn to use your brain, not animal brawn . . . most of us guys look foolish, get laughed at, out there fighting. That's why boyz got my back on the street, because I know everything that's happening here . . . and I can talk 'em down with this *[pointing to his head]* not with this *[putting his palm on his fist]*.

Here, not fighting turns out to be a face-saving technique to prevent Leroy from looking incompetent via actual violence. In an environment that so highly values "looking pretty" in Leroy's somewhat ironic linguistic inversion, it is not easy to be like Muhammad Ali—especially when you are bare knuckled, standing on the street, and with so much at stake. It is the grace and restraint of ritualized shit-talking that heightens the primitiveness of physical fighting, gradually transforming the latter into a childish act of desperation that, in comparison, looks something like a temper tantrum (Collins 2008).

D. Shame as Vengeance and Violent Fabrication

It may not always be enough just to talk the talk. If backed by nothing more than shit-talking or memorably violent stories, there is no guarantee that you will earn lasting respect. This is why street respect requires Hustlas to "always stay on point." In practice, this means that each Hustla is trying to live up to the reputation that he is fundamentally the kind of person nobody should ever mess with. Reputation assumes particularly important transsituational implications in the social logic of revenge. Unlike the spontaneous and in-the-moment dominance Jalen established in his storied altercation with K. J., revenge takes us outside the immediacy of the interaction and into a new situation that depends on strategic calculation and the right timing. It is especially this unpredictability that makes revenge the "coldest" and most effective way to show one's capacity for violence. According to Xman:

Xman: It's about being the guy you can't fuck with. Jalen said it. But, being that guy, you need to be on that shit all the time. And, sometimes you gotta wait a little while, like show him who's boss. Say he fucked with your bro. He knows you're coming for him, because he hasn't seen you, so he knows. It's like horror movies— you just sit there waiting for the bad guy. You can't rest until you see him. The longer you wait, the worse that shit is.

With so much significance ascribed to the "when" of revenge, what is omitted is Xman's take on whether taking such violent action is in fact always necessary. Many of our Hustlas talk in florid language about the abstract importance of revenge, and many describe ornately embroidered plans for future acts of promised payback; however, very few Hustlas gave depictions involving actual experiences of it. A discussion with Leroy helps us think this through:

Leroy: No it ain't that simple. It's not like you get caught slippin' and you always come back at the guy. Sometimes you do, sometimes you don't. With gangs it's the same way. Mostly it's about what happens, and it's about respect, man. I mean, let's say someone runs up on you, maybe catches you slippin,' takes your wallet. Are you going to come back on him? Well, maybe not. I mean, it depends if it's worth it and what difference it makes to you. If lotsa people watching, then yo, you wanna make it look like you comin' back for him, 'cause that's how the game works.

But, whether you do come back like down the road, that's on you. Maybe it's a shorty who got you, like took your wallet. I mean, is it really worth it? I mean, what do you get out of hitting a lick on some kid like that . . . but, if shorty's like flaunting it, you know, running his mouth on the street how he took you, then it's another story. Same thing with gang shit. Sometimes it's enough, you just gotta make it look like you can't fuck with me. . . . But, whether you do or you don't, you gotta rep like you not gonna be fucked with.

When pressed for clarification about what it means to "rep like you not gonna be fucked with," Leroy pointed out that even when other people are watching it's often enough just to use certain kinds of suggestive language and tactics of humiliation to keep everyone scared of you.[5] He used an example involving his eighteen-year-old brother (Mike) who was pressured to avenge their younger sister's (Jasmine) honor after being slapped in the face by a sexually jilted seventeen-year-old male acquaintance (Nelson) from the neighborhood. What follows is an excerpt of our conversation:

> *Leroy:* Yeah, so we all expected Mike to come back at him like stone cold. He [Mike] was up in the house and didn't see the shit go down there. Comes in, sees Jas screaming, and goes like fucking crazy. So, a few days later he comes back down at Nelson up on 60th, down on Stony, bunch a people around in the daytime, you know how it is. He creeps up real slow, Nelson's fronting like he isn't scared. So Mike walks up and stands like this *[very, very close]* and just stares him down. I mean stares him all the way down to like his toenails! Then he takes his fist and points it at N's skull *[pulls JK toward him and simulates this by making a pistol out of his finger]*. Then, N's starting to like piss in his pants, Mike makes him put his hands up, gesturing like he's going to kill him. And, you're gonna love this, he waves his hands away like it's not worth it, and then out of nowhere suddenly pulls N's pants down! Everyone's like cracking up. He got 'em, and you think anyone's gonna fuck with Mike now?
>
> *JK:* But, why didn't Mike beat him up? It was enough just to pull his pants down?
>
> *Leroy:* Yeah, it was fucking perfect man. It was even better than that. You think N didn't learn his lesson—everybody laughing and shit like that? Damn straight he did. Just walked away. You ever seen a black person blush? *[laughing]* It got the job done, and Mike's on probation. That little pussy's not worth going to prison over. Not by a mile, man.
>
> *JK:* What did people think of the "pantsing"? I mean did people talk about it later?
>
> *Leroy:* Yeah, everyone's on that shit man. It got him respect and, shit man, probably fear. Mike's a crazy motherfucker, doing shit like that. I mean uncontrollable. If a guy's capable of "pantsing" you in front of like all his fucking boyz, I mean that's one unpredictable mofo, you know?

An important feature of Leroy's story about Mike is, "That little pussy's not worth going to prison over," which conveys symbolic dominance without recourse to physical violence. "You're not worth it" is a clever inversion of the traditional way to construct honor; in Mike's case, it turns out to be *dishonorable* to fight, because it would bring him down to the level of someone who's simply "not worth it."

But, most important Mike has severely limited Nelson's range of options for future retaliation. He got right up in Nelson's face, made him think he was going to beat him up, and then—as if to make fun of Nelson for flinching—simply pulled his pants down. Whatever sense of relief Nelson might have felt is immediately transformed into humiliation—both from what Mike chose to do instead and from his own embarrassment at having felt a sense of relief. The embarrassment, in this case, is somewhat similar to Robert's shit-talking misadventure, but the situation unfolds in reverse. In the shit-talking ritual, the frame was broken when a game was taken seriously; here, what first appears to be quite serious turns out to be a deviously fabricated practical joke. "Pantsing" someone is a classic prank, a practical joke right out of the elementary school playbook, and one that seems ironically suited for someone who has already been sexually jilted and turns out to be literally the butt of the joke. Therefore, as familiar as pantsing may be in the social realm of play, it is most emphatically *not* playful—the disjunction being precisely what makes the prank such a threatening display of situational dominance. Nelson cannot retaliate with violence because that would treat the joke seriously and make him look pitiful (or boorish). Nor can he act like he is in on the joke by playing along, because this would make him look foolish (or dense)—as though he fails to understand the joke's on him. The only thing to do is to acknowledge his own shame by pulling his pants up, walking away, and recognizing Mike as the situational victor.

Mike has also severely limited Nelson's range of options for future retaliation. Because the present interaction has already been socially framed as a joke, Nelson will only lose further respect if he comes back later and attempts to exact serious revenge. This testifies to the onlookers' third-party importance; everyone knows that Nelson has been "chumped"—just as everyone knows the joke was not entirely a joke—but they are likely not quite aware of the retaliatory seriousness of Mike's gesture. The laughter fabricates the event in a way that splits the onlookers off from Nelson and defines the encounter as too unserious for Nelson to be justi-fied in a violent response. When we finally flagged Nelson down to discuss the episode (now six months after the fact), Nelson could only say, "Fuck that, man. Don't ask me about that shit." In his terseness, Nelson implicitly acknowledges his final defeat.

As a retributive act, the humiliation tactic is perhaps more effective than violence because of its sly opportunism and constructive capacity to pass itself off as nonserious. It uses the practical joke as a strategic manipulation that proxies for raw, uncontrolled physicality and with onlookers present, it is perhaps more emotionally damaging for its victim.[6] Given the choice, Nelson would have likely preferred it if Mike had thrown a punch, because at least that would give him the chance to respond with masculine dignity. In shame, Nelson is left with nothing, not even the opportunity to acknowledge the seriousness of what was done to him. In victory, Mike has now certified himself as something more than a badass. He is not only the triumphant and feared avenger, but also the comic genius who—in a single creative act—has now established magnetic leadership and legitimate authority over onlookers. He earns even more respect because his savvy is as impressive as his vengeance.

E. Stickups, Routinized Crime, and the Reframing of Violence

In arguing that violence is strategically avoided, we have suggested that street hustlers are much more defensive and strategic than is usually recognized in the social science literature. In interactions where it appears violence may be necessary for respect on the street, it is usually enough to present yourself as threatening—give a mean glance, tell a violent story, talk some shit, and pull off a good practical joke. These symbolic substitutions depend on third-party onlookers and double as badass status enhancers and as protection against actual physical conflict. In certain interactions, however, violence might appear to be almost impossible to avoid. Such is the case with armed robberies and stickups that are already framed as criminal altercations. Of the five types of potentially violent interactions we are examining, the stickup is the most threatening—the risk of serious physical harm being heightened by three well-known features. Namely, (1) the fact that it is itself a type of criminal interaction that (2) involves the pointing of a gun or other lethal weapon and (3) happens in an instant, with almost no time for the victim to think, much less deliberate. With a pistol pointed close range at the victim's heart, the stickup is indeed the quintessence of what we might call the violent performance.

Empirically, however, stickups and armed robberies rarely lead to serious physical harm. In the eleven years between 1985 and 1995, according to data from the National Incident Based Reporting System, only three out of every one thousand Chicago robberies resulted in a murder or homicide (University of Michigan n.d.). While this still leaves unclear whether less serious physical damage was done, other studies suggest that escalation from robbery to violence is far less than typical. A study by Morrison and O'Donnell (1994) of more than ten thousand armed robberies in London shows that only 7 percent of victims are hurt (usually by something other than a bullet), that a gun was discharged in only 4 percent of the robberies, and that in some cases predators use guns that aren't loaded or even real (Morrison and O'Donnell 1994; Collins 2008). Providing you do not resist but surrender to the predator's demands, you are unlikely to be a target for serious violence (Block 1977).

Stickups involve Hustlas robbing both non-Hustlas and other Hustlas, and in both cases, escalation to physical violence is not common. Our discussions with Hustlas in Woodlawn suggest that—contrary to their exotic presentations—stickups and armed robberies turn out to be relatively banal and prosaic affairs in which it is the predator's weapon that, paradoxically, keeps violence from escalating. According to Hustlas Marcus, Michael, Mike, Leroy, and Jalen, the standard on-the-street stickup entrains predators and victim in well-established interaction chains that are (at least implicitly) governed by the following ritual progression:

1. *Stop what you're doing; this is a stick up.* You are expected to put your hands in the air and to be absolutely silent without looking around, nodding, or even making eye contact. You must keep your eyes focused high and on something abstract in the distance. Eye contact is dangerous, because it suggests recognition, and looking around suggests that you are looking for, as Marcus put it, "a way out of this fucking mess."
2. *Lie down on your stomach, face down.* This tactic, with the gun still pointing at the head, both establishes symbolic dominance and prevents the victim from, as Mike put it, "doing something fucked up, like kicking or something." The victim's face is against the ground to muzzle any potential sound or attempt to call for help.
3. *Gimme respect and you won't get hurt.* Very often this demand is accompanied by a temporary removal of the gun from the victim's field of vision. Much like what we saw in nonviolent "postponements" where Hustlas pass each other on the street, the objective here is for the predator to assert himself as a threatening person—the kind of

person who has and is willing to hurt you but who is, in this instance, willing to show you clemency if you give him respect. In Leroy's terms: "If you get your ass busted or jumped on or someone sticks you up, you gotta just give in, man. If he got the jump on you and is carrying [a gun], you just be like 'Here you go. I'm not looking to get into anything, so here's my money and please let me pass. It's all about showing respect, man. You have to show 'em respect. If you could sum up the street in one word, it's respect. You'll be okay if you have it and if you offer it, end of story."

4. *Let's see what you got motherfucker.* Here, the victim must surrender everything on his person—usually his wallet, money, cell phone, sometimes shoes, and occasionally a symbolic accoutrement (like a hat or article of clothing) to suggest a personal or emotional dimension to the crime.

5. *Keep yo head down, you straight.* The predator establishes situational closure before running off. "You straight" is deployed (or a fist pound or a slight slap on the back) in order to restore unity to the interaction, remind both parties that the robbery was just business, and to reassure the victim that he (the victim) did a good job as victim because it's all over now. Subtly different is the fist pump which implicitly suggests that they *both* did a good job playing their respective roles and that, now that it is over, they can once again greet each other as friends/allies/acquaintances.

Most critical to the nonviolence of stickups and armed robberies is how the predator's weapon frames the situation. While Hustlas point out that the prenominate demands are not always expressed orally, their content is intended to redefine a potentially dangerous situation into one that is, interestingly, both personal and "just business." The personal and emotional weight resides in the predator's "gimme respect"—a demand that is more of a request and which seeks to momentarily drop the logic of the gun, physically remove it from view, and act as if the victim's respect is a freely willed gift. When the gun returns, however, the interaction is restored to a straightforward business transaction in which the robber exchanges mercy for money and consummates it with "you straight." Successfully defined as nonviolent, the interactants can return to life as it was before the stickup. They can now act as if it never happened.

In our discussions, Hustlas help us think about these familiar processes in the context of their own experiences on the Woodlawn streets. For example, consider Jalen's testimony on stickups:

> *Jalen:* They go down like ALL the fucking time. Naw, actually, they used to happen more. But, I been down here and seen armed robberies and holdups and you name it, bro. So here it go: you get caught slippin' and what happens? Some fuckin' punk's all up in you, making jokes and fronting like he's not serious. But, you know you're gonna get ganked, so what you gonna do? So he *[the predator]* waits to make sure no one's around, you know, he's been casing this shit and planning and preparing to get your ass, and you just bought it. So it all goes down, simple as that. It's a fuckin' everyday thing, bro. Most guys don't even use guns—maybe knives—but some do and some just say they got loaded guns, and you know they playing off the fact they ain't got shit. But, either way, you just gotta let it happen. Can't take it personal. I mean you prolly know the punk. All you can do is blame yourself for gettin' caught slipping. Never happened to me bro. My shit's tight. . . . But, that's what I'm saying: watch your back and you straight.
>
> *JK:* Are you less likely to get taken if you show the punk you've got a gun, too?
>
> *Jalen:* Naw, man, just let it happen. Get it over with and then come back at his ass if you have to. It's not about using your gun. You gotta use your eyes, bro.

Although it is likely Jalen would have a different perspective on the armed robbery if it happened to him, it is striking how he rationalizes the crime in the context of the performative rules of the street. In saying "all you can do is blame yourself," Jalen also inverts the traditional moral logic of street crime and suggests the fault lies primarily with the victim—not the predator. While physical violence is preventable if you lower your guard and give in, the armed robbery itself can be avoided if you keep constant vigilance to the maneuvers of the street hustlers who watch your every move. This adds perhaps another layer of definition to the experience of being robbed—its essential avoidability. If you "watch your back" and keep "your shit tight," you are not only likely to escape violence but also to protect yourself from being robbed in the first place.

5. When Violence Does Happen

Momentary postponements, storied accomplishments, shit-talking transformations, transcendent humiliations, nonviolent stickups—all of these are strategic street presentations that preserve the symbolism of violence while obviating its physical expression. Each of these reconfigures threatening interactions into those wherein Hustlas draw on cultural strategies to redefine dangerous situations as peaceable. With that in mind, however, violence does happen in Woodlawn, and it is our task in this section to examine the microinteractional dimensions of how violence breaks out and occasionally escalates to gun fighting and even murder. With that said, violence is generally not intended. When it does happens, it appears to be based on momentary breaks in frame, acts of simple misunderstanding, or—in extreme cases—when strategic logic gets "flooded out" by anger or rage. However, in the language Jalen already used, violence most frequently occurs when you "get caught slipping."

The term "slipping" is itself, perhaps not incidentally, somewhat ambiguous and unclear. *Slipping from what?* or *Slipping into what?* are things we might ask, but to ask the question is of course to miss the point. Slipping is most critically a category of performance that refers to something like letting your guard down and correspondingly applies to a variety of interactional oversights. Jalen already introduced a slip in which he got caught in an armed robbery. More serious examples of slipping can be fateful and sometimes lead to actual violence. Here, we pay attention to three in particular: (1) basic failures to physically recognize an acquaintance passing on the street; (2) a breaking out of frame in already tense situations—like the stickups we have already discussed—that become redefined as violent provocation; and (3) misunderstandings, especially in ambiguous situations like drug deals that arise from missed signals and misinterpretation of cues. In all three of these, the act of slipping itself is essentially accidental, which makes it dangerous precisely because the other Hustla/Hustlas are liable to treat it as an invitation to violence.

A. The Cost of Nonrecognition

The first type, slipping through unawareness of physical copresence, suggests a kind of diss that is made more provocative by its passivity. Earlier, in our discussion of nonviolent passages, we discussed the importance of showing recognition with brief eye contact, a nod of the head, and a casual "What's up, cuz?" To fail to notice you is to suggest that you are not even worth noticing, that I am not here for you because I reside in a world so far above that you're not even visible to me. And, because one cannot know if it was meant as a snub, one can be expected to avoid committing oneself. We rely on Percy for a personal example:

> *Percy:* So this one day I'm walking down the street just minding my business. I walk past these four guys, didn't even think about it, just going to my girl's crib. I'm thinking about her, you know, what I'm gonna do to her. And these four guys like hold me up on the street. Got guns and shanks and shit. These B.D.s roll on me and hit a lick. I mean, it came out of nowhere. Like bam! Like I forgot to bow and shit. Didn't even fuckin' see 'em.

The B.D.s of course interpreted the event quite differently. From Percy's point of view, he was caught slipping, but Black Disciple member Robert (who was present) framed the event quite differently.

> *Robert:* So, yeah, remember that punk Percy? He stepped out, and we was rolling on our own turf, you know—the bitch should know better anyway. And we prepare for, you know, shit to go down, as always, so we just sort of test the waters like we're not even going to actually hit a lick. But when we walk past, Percy just straight rolls past us like we wasn't even there, like this was his fucking block and shit. So who the fuck he think he is, you know, and so we all look at each other like "who's it gonna be," and Samuel just busts on his shit, bro. Shorty got what's coming for him. What a fucking punk, dissing us and shit.
>
> *JK:* But how do you know Percy even saw you? He told us it was an accident.
>
> *R:* Whatever, man. That's what he gets. You gotta stay on point on our block man, and sometimes there isn't time to be like *[in an affectedly "white" tone of voice]* "Excuse me, sir, did you realize that you just walked past us without saying hello?" *[laughing]*

First, note Robert's reliance on the classic "he got what he deserved" trope, which inverts the interaction's moral logic by casting Percy as predator and the Disciples as avengers of wounded pride. Second, there is Robert's critical point about there not being enough time to reconcile things in any way other than violently. On its face, this sounds like a convenient rationalization or way to justify what seems like an impulsive act of aggression toward Percy. But from Robert's point of view, it is the act—not the intention—which compels immediate response. He says, "You gotta stay on point on our block man," suggesting that Percy is at fault even if his failure to recognize was inadvertent because he ought to be more attentive to the fact that he's trespassing on rival gang turf. More subtly, Robert is also alluding to the situational nature of the interaction, which was crucially a four-on-one affair. It is not just that it is easier for a group to assert physical dominance over just one man, but also that the group members are compelled to prove themselves to each other (Collins 2008).

B. Violence in Breaking Frame

The second type of slipping involves frame breaks in situations that are suffused with confrontational tension but are themselves not designed to be violent. Stickups, for example, occasionally become violent when victims don't follow the playbook or act out in ways that are unpredictable. Jalen gives us an example of an episode involving his running buddy Lamar who was shot in the arm and face during a stickup gone wrong.

> *Jalen:* Okay, I can't get into all the details with this, but you know, Lamar was up in his crib, and I was over there with just him fucking around, so we go out to play ball, you know, 63rd over there late-night. So we're playing, and I'm just fucking his shit up with crossovers and whatnot, so at some point L just gives up and throws the ball like a fucking mile down the street. So he's fucking out of his mind angry, and as he's gettin' it, he runs into some big dude, I forget his name, Jimmy's older brother, who just got out. Guy just pulls chrome on L and goes through the motions and shit, like you know, "Gimme that shit" *[wallet, watch, cell phone]* and whatnot. So what does homie do? L reaches for his back pocket and switches up, grabs for his own gun. Crazy motherfucker saw that shit straight up and got no choice but to shoot my boy. Shattered L's cheek or something, all for acting crazy.

In Jalen's story, Lamar walked into the stickup already feeling vengeful and beaten down after the embarrassing loss in basketball, but most crucial here is that both men forward-panicked ("acted crazy"), and Lamar was caught in what might be called a class-two slip. As Jalen points out,

Lamar was partially at fault for breaking the contract implicit in armed robbery, impulsively reaching for his gun and causing Jimmy's brother to do the same.

C. Fateful Misunderstandings

If forward panic is a risk factor associated with relatively well-defined situations like armed robbery, it is also the product of more ambiguous interactions where there is some chance of misunderstanding. We already saw a close-call example of this in Jalen's story about his altercation with K. J., in which Jalen accused K. J. of misinterpreting his offer of protection after the incident with the police. Although the latter abjured the implication, the sheer speed and chaos of get-away situations create an inevitable danger of misunderstandings.

We here rely on Hustlas' discussions of drug deals. Most drug exchanges in Woodlawn are relatively straightforward, involving well-defined rules of territoriality and customs among buyers and sellers that both parties recognize. More dangerous are occasions when Hustlas receive large bids from unknown customers or when they are requested to do the deal in out-of-the-way or unfamiliar settings. These types of encounters are suffused with ambiguity, and there is always a possibility of being caught slipping. Percy reaches into his own experience to provide a (possibly embellished) sense of context:

> Percy: A while, while back, I'm doing my shit, slinging, clocking, you know how the game works. Or maybe you don't *[laughing]*. So me and B. B. get this call on the cell. I mean we don't handle business on cell phone, cops be fucking our shit up otherwise. So it's a call from this guy who wants serious weight, and I won't go into details at risk of incriminating myself in a court of law *[laughing again]*. So he wants to meet us on 79th and Stony, way, way out of the 'hood. I never even been there. But, I'm a shorty, you know, young and dumb, so me and my boy roll out there. . . . We get there, it's already fucking dark as shit, and B. B.'s getting crazy nervous, like "Where are these guys?" and "Are you sure it's not police?" and all that. So sooner or later, this grey Lexus rolls up, tinted windows and shit. So I'm gettin' ready rough for the score. The car stops, and suddenly the guy like rolls his window a little, sticks his eyes

out, glaring at us. Then rolls it up like immediately. I don't know what he's thinking, but B. B.'s suddenly going crazy. He says he knows the motherfucker, that it's a gang thing. Gangster lean and maybe a drive-by, who knows? So B. B. reaches for his gun and fires three shots into the window. We book it, the car's going crazy, guys roll down the window again and are like "Motherfuckers! I thought we were straight!" Nobody was hurt, but window shattered and like. They just wanted to buy some shit man. B. B. straight fucked up. I think there was just something wrong with the window!

Despite our skepticism about some of the details of this story, it is fairly clear that there was a misunderstanding here. Violence was neither intended nor (really) even suggested, but the surrounding events (e.g., the call on the cell, heavy weight, long wait time, and so on) heightened the forward panic that B. B. experienced when he saw the "eyes glaring at us." In such episodes with unusually high levels of situational ambiguity, the precise moment of contact can be a fateful one with brisance realized in the impulsive act of violence.

6. Keeping Violence in Check: A Tentative Note on Guns

Despite "fucking up," B. B. got lucky, and according to Percy, nobody was hurt after the episode in the Lexus. But ambiguity makes violence more threatening, and when violence occurs, there is always a fear that it will become uncontrollable. But as we have argued, the Hustlas organize their interactional world precisely to avoid this kind of violent chaos. This means that when violence does occur, Hustlas often have to take swift action to stem the tide and prevent it from escalating further. Here, we enter into a tentative discussion of how violence, even when it has begun, rarely explodes into forward panic or all-out combat. In particular, we explore how Hustlas—somewhat paradoxically—occasionally use handguns to defuse violent expression and restore the always-precarious sense of cultural order.

To carry a gun—or to be "strapped"—is to signal to others that you are a badass, a player in the high-stakes game of "urban warfare," that you are somebody to be taken quite seriously. Guns evoke "sacred objects," or Durkheimian metaphors, loaded with force imposed on a weaker world that does not ask questions. But among our twenty Hustlas, only two report ever actually firing their gun at another person, and on both accounts, they missed their targets. More surprising is what others told us: that the large majority of gunshots heard in Woodlawn are not signs of violence; they are either errant bullets fired into the air to blow off steam or attempts to alert police to ward off an anticipated threat. The former are the sound and fury of vented anger and the latter a constructive expression of fear for purposes of protection. The Hustla who vents spleen by firing bullets into the air is forcing the world to hear his anger, but it is really more like a desperate wail than a roar. To fire in the air is to literally fire at nobody, but it is also to shoot your gun indiscriminately at the entire world that has wronged you and cannot be pinned down for individual blame. Or, in a different sense, a kind of prayer to the invisible heavens above; words have proved insufficient and must be replaced with a sound that even God cannot fail to hear.

It is the other rationale, firing the gun to elicit police protection, that is suffused with practical significance. In the absence of a reliable law enforcement presence, it is sometimes necessary to alert the police when interactions escalate to the point where violence seems imminent. Hustlas will occasionally fire their guns as a kind of bat signal for the dual protection of summoning the cops and of creating fear of the possibility of summoned cops. The effect is to neutralize a personal threat and to restore a sense of communitywide order. Leroy helps us provide a context for this:

> *Leroy:* But you know, sometimes, I'll tell you what I do: this place is so fucked up that I have to fire my Glock just to get the police's attention. You know when something's about to go down. I see shorties scrapping a couple months ago, man, so I saw this Lexus roll by my block a few times. It stopped and kept going, but kept coming back. So I'm thinking it's about to be some gangster shit—shooting and whatnot. So I like book it to 64th, and first thing I do, I fire my Glock a couple rounds. The police, man, they know that sound; they know it's one of us trying to get 'em out here. I'm Batman; they know that shit. So 5–0 shows up and, guess what—that Lexus just flew up out of here! Those niggas know that sound, too.

Leroy's account is interesting, particularly given that it all happened in what sounds like ambiguous or uncertain circumstances. He didn't know for sure what the guys in the Lexus were planning, whether they were casing the street for a drug deal, a drive-by shooting, or perhaps just to assert symbolic dominance and instill fear. He also did not know whether he himself was in danger, but the fact he had to "book it" suggests he was not ruling out the possibility. What Leroy does, in other words, appears to be the reverse of what his badass image might predict. Rather than evincing invulnerability, the gunshot suggests risk-averse cautiousness in the face of putative danger. Leroy (1) imputes the worst-case scenario involving the Lexus when its behavior may well have been innocuous; (2) flees to an out-of-the-way area to fire his gun; and (3) alerts the police to a scene that might turn out to be a false alarm.

But in comparing himself to Batman, Leroy actually assumes the role of a new kind of badass—in this case a superhero crime fighter who fills a structural hole between the street and the conventional institutions of law and order. And, as other Hustlas suggest, this forging of crime-fighting alliances may not rest exclusively with Leroy:

> *Percy:* Yeah, bro, it's like that. You see some shit about to go down, and you let one go. We all do that shit. I mean how the fuck else do you get 5–0's attention? And they know what's up. We fire one, and they either think a 187's goin' down or it's one of us roundin' their asses out of bed. But, yeah, that's what's up, yo. You gotta take the law into your own hands down here. I got a mother and girl to look out for, yo; I gotta protect. And my bros, you know, we got all that shit worked out. You don't know this shit, but it's like Martin said, in the ghetto we cooperate. Ain't no shame in that. I got you, man. And nobody's fucking with me; I'm a bad motherfucker. Like Shaft.

If Percy's language establishes the conventional young black male distrust with the law enforcement community, it does so in qualified terms. The police may need to have their "asses rounded out of bed," but at least the gunshot gets their attention and successfully elicits their assistance in helping to fight crime. More broadly, what this suggests is that the "bad motherfucker" perhaps cannot afford to be "bad" all the time. Or as Percy intimates, perhaps doing some social good is part of what makes you "bad" in the first place.

7. Conclusion

In the foregoing analysis, we have attempted to challenge much of the received wisdom about how violence works in the inner city. *Pace* the conventional description of urban street life as a Hobbesian world of all-out brutality, we have argued that in many ways in Woodlawn it is just the opposite. Much of what looks like violent inner-city encounters may in fact be intended to reduce the threat of violence via what we have called "symbolic substitutions." More broadly, this suggests that the black urban poor are neither passive victims of unfortunate structural circumstances nor impulsive "super predators" caught in a cultural contagion of low self-control (Hirschi and Gottfredson 1990; Zimring and Hawkins 1997; Wacquant 2008). We have argued for a model in which inner-city residents find themselves interacting in an effort to limit violence and forge a sense of self and social order amidst socioeconomic marginality, the dislodging of the contemporary gang, and the ongoing threat of "Crazy Killers." We say that they "find" themselves, because it is unclear that these strategies are always entirely conscious or premeditated. If as Jack Katz puts it, "only rarely do we actually experience ourselves as subjects directing our conduct," it is in this case because, over time, Hustlas wind up deploying these violence-reduction maneuvers as a matter of course—that is, they become entrained in its rhythms (Katz 1988, 5; see also Katz 1999). For Katz, this nonstrategic strategicness is "magical"; for our Hustlas, it is simply the internalized product of a need to find a modicum of stability and peace amidst the precariousness of inner-city life. That they arise out of need makes our Hustlas rational, but it also makes them less exotic (or more human) than the presentations one usually finds in the mainstream media—or perhaps even in the sociology literature.

But, it is certainly not enough to simply call them "rational," because what also emerges is the extraordinary savvy and sophistication with which Hustlas seem to be able to reflect on their worlds and what it is they are doing. The proverbial "cultural dope" would be unable to articulate Leroy's point that "you gotta learn to use your brain, not animal brawn . . . and I can talk 'em down with this [his head] not with this [his fist]." Nor would he be able to describe the "shit-talking game" with Robert's artfulness—"we are fronting like it don't mean nothing, but your game is on the line, bro." If there is analytical danger in overindulging in folk concepts or in taking these testimonies so seriously, it is a danger that we could not resist, given their explanatory power (Wacquant 2002; Wilson and Chaddha 2009). Such is the potential drawback of stumbling onto such sophisticated informants. But, as it is, we stand firmly behind our arguments—first because we heard such similar testimonies from so many of our Hustlas and, second, because, quite simply, they make sense. Our story is in keeping with Randall Collins's (2008) argument in *Violence: A Microsociological Theory*. It is also in keeping with evidence from the real battlefield—World War II, Korea, and so on—that even frontline soldiers rarely fire their weapons at the enemy and spend most of their time trying to figure out ways to avoid it (Marshall 1947; Grossman 1995; Collins 2008). Finally, it is consistent with the larger arc of western culture—which we must not forget young black men are a part of—documented by scholars from Norbert Elias to Steven Pinker, that the grand march of history has been associated with progressively lower levels of physical conflict (Elias [1939] 2000; Pinker 2011).

But perhaps we ought to be less upbeat—both about history and about the men we studied. As we have already mentioned, perhaps some of the Hustlas' techniques of avoiding physical violence are actually worse than violence. It is not out of the question that being publicly "pantsed" is more wounding than a fist—or even a knife. Nor, as we saw in Robert's "shit-talking game" with Marcus, is it clear that the no-hands rule was particularly beneficial for him. What physical violence has going for it—maybe the only thing—is at least it's honest. That is, at least it comes clean and reveals its seriousness and the passion of its rage—which suggests it may not be enough to call humiliation and shit-talking mere sound and fury, because on the inner-city streets they may signify a good deal more than nothing. Indeed, they may cause internal bleeding.

With that in mind, we make no claims that our findings about peace-keeping in Woodlawn satisfactorily generalize to other inner-city neighborhoods or to other periods in history. What may be true in one Chicago community at one moment in time may be quite different in others, and future research might think about some of these questions in other areas—New York, Los Angeles, Boston, and even other neighborhoods in Chicago. There is also, of course, the matter of time. African American homicide rates have declined more than 50 percent in the last two decades, making it possible that some of the peacekeeping strategies explored here are connected to that nationwide reduction in violent behavior. Points of divergence between this essay and earlier qualitative research—like Anderson (1990, 1999), Bourgois (1995), Venkatesh (2006), and Wacquant (2008)—may reflect different historical frames of reference as much as analytic or substantive disagreement. As such, we intend this essay not just as a challenge but as an invitation to ethnographers to explore spatial differences in inner-city strategies of violence and peace, to historically minded scholars to think about changes in the cultural practices of urban black youth, and finally, to quantitative sociologists to gather data to test the arguments. We hope that this essay will encourage these kinds of future directions, because as much as urban sociology has already said about the proliferation of violence, it has only just begun to think about processes of peace.

Appendix: Profile of Highly Quoted Respondents

Leroy: In his mid-twenties, former mid-/high-level officer in Vice-Lords. Currently works part time as a salaried service professional in an upscale Chicago neighborhood and attends a local two-year college, also part time, pursuing an associate's degree in criminal justice. Leroy has three arrests, including one for drug possession, but he has never been convicted nor has he spent any time in prison. Leroy lives with his daughter and her mother in a one-bedroom apartment.

Mike: Younger brother of Leroy and current drug-dealing member of the Vice-Lords. He is currently on parole for armed robbery. Mike dropped out of high school during his senior year and is presently not employed in the mainstream labor market. He depends on drug-sale commissions to make ends meet and lives with his (and Leroy's) mother—who receives disability payments and is recovering from a crack-cocaine addiction—in a small Woodlawn apartment where he attempts to support his mom and sisters.

Percy: In his early twenties, former "runner," Vice-Lords. He dropped out of high school to pursue "the thug life" then left the Vice-Lords to pursue the GED and prepare for a career in criminal justice. Percy and Leroy are close friends—he calls Leroy his role model—and says that Leroy inspired him to quit the Vice-Lords and "focus on my education," as he put it.

Xman: Mid-twenties, "street soldier," Black Disciples. He dropped out of high school after his junior year to make money working with the Black Disciples and "help my sisters get out of the projects." Xman was incarcerated briefly on a weapons charge in 2009.

Jalen: Early twenties, "street soldier," Black Disciples. Dropped out of high school after his brother was shot and killed during a gang retaliation.

Michael: Mid-twenties, member of Black Stone Rangers. He is a high school graduate and part-time auto mechanic. He is presently applying for technical training and credentialing at a technical institute.

L. L.: Mid-twenties, member of Black Stone Rangers. He is currently charged with manslaughter. He dropped out of high school and has been incarcerated for marijuana distribution and gun possession and was on probation at the time of his most recent arrest.

Robert: Late teens, member of Black Disciples. Recent graduate from high school—the first in his family's history. His older brother and his father are presently incarcerated, and Robert lives with his girlfriend. He has aspirations to be a criminal lawyer and, according to friends, was a very good student who "should be in college like at Harvard."

K. J.: Early twenties, "street soldier," Black Disciples. K. J. dropped out of high school during his senior year. He is currently on probation for involvement in a burglary-turned-robbery.

Nelson: Teenager, member of the Black Disciples. He dropped out of high school at age sixteen.

Marcus: Early twenties, member of the Gangster Disciples. Dropped out of high school during his senior year. He is working on his GED and has ambitions to ultimately become a high school basketball coach.

Lamar: Early twenties, "street soldier," Black Disciples. Dropped out of high school. He has been incarcerated for drug possession and assault.

B. B.: Mid-twenties, member of the Vice-Lords. B. B. dropped out of high school. Has been supporting his mother and three sisters since he was twenty-one with the money he made from the drug trade. B. B. has a number of children and currently lives with his girlfriend and her children in a two-bedroom apartment in Woodlawn.

10

What about the Day After?

Youth Culture in the Era of
"Law and Order"

SUDHIR VENKATESH, *Columbia University*

Introduction

In the last few decades, scholars have grown attentive to the means by which inner city, ethnic minority communities cope with at-risk youth. There are typically two questions that rise to the surface: what propels young people to engage in violent, criminal behavior and how can we help communities improve the lives of troubled youth? I have focused on a related question in my own research: namely, when facing youth involved in delinquent behavior, characterized not only by violence but often by the use of weapons, why do residents of such communities frequently attempt to mediate disputes themselves instead of relying exclusively on calling the police for help?

I stumbled upon this question by observing the daily lives of black Americans who were "stakeholders" in their respective ghetto communities. That is, they had a civic presence or material investment, as well as a title that gave them some measure of status and respect. Teachers, clergy, business owners, social workers, nurses, and the like would respond bravely to incidents of youth violence and criminal offending by attempting to address the conflicts on their own. Rather than relying primarily on the institutions of formal law, they led in creating social order.

One notable case in the community I studied concerned a young man, Carl Rose, who had shot a classmate, John Warren, as a result of a peer-to-peer dispute. Both Rose and Warren claimed to be dating a young woman, also a student in their high school. The three lived in Chicago's Roseland community, a ghetto in Chicago's historic South Side. They came from rival gangs who had been actively fighting for the rights to sell drugs in local parks and public spaces. As the young men's jealousies—and their respective gang's competitive encroachments—spilled over from the schoolyard into the street corner, Carl drew a pistol and injured his counterpart. Warren received treatment at the hospital for various injuries. Members of the community began to mobilize, led by Josiah Pegues, a local minister and social service provider. Josiah quickly spoke to the parents of both men, who agreed that the best of course of action was to persuade their sons to accept Josiah as a mediator. He and a colleague— an assistant high school principal—promised to meet directly with the warring gangs.

When I asked Josiah why he didn't call law enforcement immediately, his curious reply was, "First we need to make things safe around here. Then the police can come and help us." Although many Americans, especially black youth, express distrust of law enforcement, Josiah's perspective is the exception across American society. The expected behavior in such a situation—the cultural norm—would be to allow police to respond to a youth shooting. They are, putatively, the legitimate guarantors of law and order.

But the collective action dynamics in Roseland were different. Residents and local stakeholders were forward looking, acting well before the area was deemed safe by law enforcement. This willingness to initiate an alternate form of mediation is the kind of behavior that leads those in the popular and academic community to wonder whether there exists a moral crisis in American inner cities. Has vigilante justice trumped respect for law and order?

An emphasis on understanding the sociocultural bases of law and order—what I call the "law and order" perspective—is an appealing way to understand the life and times of black youth, particularly for sociologists. With its integration of a scientific sensibility and pragmatic tenets, the combination of which adhere to principles that have animated sociologists for over a century, the "law and order" framework has aided sociologists in examining how ideas foster social action. As an example, one of the inflection points of the "law and order" perspective is the concept of social deviance, which may be understood generally as the failure to comply in attitude and practice to prevailing cultural norms. By orienting analysis around the concept of deviance, the "law and order" framework has spurred vibrant debates about the cultural lives of black youth in particular and the moral outlooks of black Americans in general (see Downey 2008; Young 2006; Duneier 2000).

In the United States, apart from welfare receipt, criminal offending and deviant behavior more generally is by far the most common empirical terrain for understanding matters of ethics, symbolic practices, and lifestyles of disadvantaged young blacks. Deviance specifies an empirical vantage point, namely the study of attitudes, values, and practices that flout conventional codes of conduct, codified law, or both. Second, deviance connotes "deviation," or more specifically, straying from normative modes of social and cultural organization; whether or not the social norm is explicitly defined, it offers a barometer against which to make judgments about the observed behavior.

For the past decade, I have been observing illicit economic exchanges that involve low-income black youth—what is colloquially termed the "underground economy," "informal economy," or "black market" (Venkatesh 2007). The ethnographic vantage point has not included the perspective of self-appointed mediators, like Josiah Pegues, who participate in the regulation of these exchanges. These economies can be highly destabilizing because the involved parties—offenders, victims, mediators—must establish basic ground rules, including shared norms of behavior, for a range of issues such as contract enforcement, pricing, and property rights, and acceptable penalties. It is commonplace to find misunderstandings, disagreement, and, on occasion, the use of physical force to settle disputes. Because the interaction of buyer and trader are not—indeed, *cannot be*—regulated formally by the state, the two parties sometimes require that other agents intervene to help address conflicts. The state may be involved via its law enforcement arm, if a formal legal code is violated, but typically there are civic stakeholders who respond to ensure that social order is maintained. A tour of urban ethnographic studies will reveal fairly quickly a wide range of characters, ranging from sidewalk vendors (Duneier 2000) to pastors (McRoberts 2005) to political officials (Marwell 2007) and even police officers (Moskos 2008), who may intervene informally to help buyer and seller consummate their transaction.

Since these exchanges draw on views of right and wrong and negotiated understandings of permissible and forbidden conduct, they are rooted in values, aspirations, and structures of belief and meaning that circulate among the constituent actors. In other words, they are inherently cultural practices. There may be differences of opinion regarding fair conduct, styles of enforcement, degrees of penalties and punishments, and the like. However, contestation itself is an index of culture via the struggle to determine what is right, just, appropriate, etc.

The daily social regulation of "underground" economies is itself a constituent part of the "law and order" framework. Yet, scholars have neglected the processes of social order maintenance that invariably follow from any incident of deviance. Much of sociology has focused instead on social dynamics of criminal offending—namely, the factors propelling individuals to commit bad acts, rather than the manner by which conflicts are mediated and order restored.[1] It is as if the researcher left the play before the final act.

I argue that this omission has had significant consequences for the capacity to understand the cultural practices of black youth. By failing to examine the full trajectory of offending—which would include the restoration of order—scholars fail to grasp cultural dynamics in their full and complex aspect. In this chapter, I use aspects of crime control and the establishment of social order in the wake of youth deviance to consider how sociologists understand black youth culture, and whether there may be opportunities to improve our analysis without necessarily abandoning the "law and order" perspective altogether. Throughout the pages below, I return to the shooting of John Warren by Carl Rose in order to anchor the discussion.

Racializing Deviance

For many American sociologists, research on deviance is framed by a social problems perspective. Systematic empirical study is married with programmatic responses, though the intended outcome may vary considerably—e.g., deterring individual crime, helping stabilize communities, and building up legitimacy of law enforcement. Though they may differ with respect to their policy recommendations, a common purpose is to inform the design, implementation, and evaluation of remedies for lowering rates of offending and ameliorating the attendant social consequences.[2] Most often, these remedies are rooted in state action, though civil society institutions (e.g., philanthropy, social work, nonprofit organizations) may be incorporated.[3]

With respect to the cultural dimension of deviance, this goal-oriented approach (of the social problems perspective) tends to construe impropriety as culturally exceptional. Sociological studies of deviance emphasize the sociocultural detachment of black youth from a presumed American mainstream. Culture, in this manner, becomes part of the problem that must be rectified so that young people can successfully integrate into the wider society. Culture, viewed as a deficiency, manifests in various forms: perhaps the modal view is rooted in social disorganization theory, whereby deviance is seen as stemming from a lack of shared values that would otherwise enable residents to prevent or deter improper behavior (Kornhauser 1978; Bursik and Grasmick 1993).

In an alternative though less widely accepted formulation, ghetto as problem begets culture as survival. That is, analysts of youth delinquency construct a cultural tug-of-war between "decent" and "street" inhabitants of the inner city (Anderson 2000). A consequence is that culture becomes bifurcated, that is, essentially split between two groups, each of whom are presumed to share distinctive and competing values. One may argue that, in contrast to social disorganization theory, the reader at least can find the existence of a normative component to inner-city culture—for example, Anderson's view that "decent" families attend church and control their use of alcohol and drugs.

Sociological debates on culture and youth must be read against a long history of writing on the influence of norms, behavior, attitudes, and other cultural factors on everyday practice and social organization in black urban communities. Tracing the roots of this intellectual trend would exceed the scope of this chapter. However, it is worth noting that, unlike the British context, in which the sociological construction of culture was built upon a conceit of social actors carrying out aspirational projects—wherein culture was contested albeit shared, rooted in meaning and practice, and formed in direct relation to state ideology and practice—for their U.S. counterparts, culture had another valence in relation to black delinquency: namely, it was theorized as norms and values distinct from the mainstream, capable of generating deviant behavior by itself, and transmitted to succeeding generations either in the home or among networks or neighborhoods of similarly "socially isolated" (Wilson 1987, 189) households.[4]

One finds in social regulation of illicit markets a powerful role for cultural forces. As noted above, underground trading is shaped by views of justice and moral reasoning. The constituent activities transgress normative and legal codes of conduct; nevertheless, actors consider what behavior *ought* to look like, and how the social fabric should be restored when things go awry. The reason is partly that participants never enter into illicit exchange as a one-time commitment: most are embedded in such economies to fulfill various ongoing needs, and so have little choice but to engage in self-governance in order to ensure their ongoing access to illegal gain. They arrive at their exchanges with presumed understandings of appropriate behavior, and they leave knowing the options for redress and resolution of disputes. They are not purely "adaptations" or "survival strategies" for coping with the severe disadvantage, but we would be remiss to theorize them solely as a form of political resistance—indeed, as Kelley points out, these creative expressions are "labors that some African American youth have turned into cold hard cash," and so they are resistant only within limits (Kelley 1997, 44).

So, then, how to develop an alternate framework for understanding culture, if the frameworks discussed previously cannot be imported in whole? A starting point is to consider economic exchanges as involving not only buyers and sellers but also intermediary agents who take responsibility for addressing the conflicts that can ensue. Interpersonal contracts may shape the exchange itself—enabling parties to carry out the transaction according to particular codes of conduct (Venkatesh 2013). But since the procedures and established covenants are likely to be informal misunderstanding, confusion, disagreement, and, at times, discord can easily occur. Inevitably, there must be rapprochement, since, by virtue of necessity alone, the individuals wish to continue operating as underground agents in future transactions. For economies that disproportionately involve youth—who may be gaining familiarity with means of resolving disputes, a third party usually intercedes to ensure that conflicts don't escalate to harmful levels. In inner-city communities, brokers might vary, but they are often familiar faces of civic life—schoolteachers, social workers, store managers, clergy, security guards, and even local beat cops who, like the others listed, have an intimate knowledge of local social dynamics. Such third parties usually intercede proactively in order to provide mediation.

Here, it is worth noting that from the point of view of social order maintenance, incidents of violence or conflict in inner-city communities are best viewed in an historical light: they follow from countless examples in the past where young people have violated either implicit expectations of appropriate conduct or formal law. In this sense, they are certainly violations of cultural norms. But, importantly, we must recognize that such norms are linked up with particular realms of ethical and juridical practice: how one ought to behave, and how one responds to that behavior with sanction, penalty, and punishment, is partly a function of the social context in which violations manifest. In the case of Carl Rose, local police (and some in wider society) may expect him to apologize, leave the gang, forswear violence, and otherwise act according to mainstream norms, backed up by codified law on the books. However, if the past is our guide, Josiah and his fellow stakeholders are more apt to approach Carl with different expectations. They may not ask him to leave the gang forever or seek promises to exit the drug trade; their outcomes may prioritize immediate reductions in shooting, which are not connected to diminished public narcotics sales—in fact, numerous ethnographies suggest that thriving inner-city drug markets are positively correlated with violence-free public space (Bourgois 2002; Venkatesh 2007). Josiah's colleagues may privately desire an end to youth drug trafficking and gang activity, but their efforts may not begin by disclosing these preferences. They may define safety not by the absence of delinquent behavior in toto but instead by the lack of violence and use of weapons during the commission of crimes. As such, their expectations for normative conduct on the part of youth might not necessarily accord perfectly with wider societal standards.

Whether a third party is involved or not, this type of regulation—what Sally Merry and Neal Milner (1995, 20) calls "indigenous justice"—affords scholars an opportunity to examine the cultural forces at play that shape how parties solve problems and reproduce social order. The empirical terrain of social order reproduction is a portal through which to understand the role that culture places in the dynamics of social deviance.

Creating Legitimacy in Roseland

The police arrived immediately after Carl Rose shot John Warren. It would not have been unusual for many residents to call 9–1–1, even if they had little faith that police could mediate the dispute among the youth. Soon after the police arrived on the block where the incident took place, the citywide media arrived—an uptick in city violence in African American communities had recently led to a significant increase in public attention. Several law enforcement officers began making a formal investigation. The process unfolded as expected: officers questioned witnesses, they searched for the gun and traces of the fired bullets, and they convened meetings with the families of the two young men.

As the formal inquiry concluded, a second set of discussions began in earnest. Local stakeholders began debating the most effective means of resolving the conflict between the youth—and their respective gang organizations, if that became necessary. Reverend Josiah Pegues took the lead. He first met with families of the youth to ask their permission to meet with Carl and John. Since he was trusted by the local gang leaders, he knew he could meet with them easily and ascertain their economic interests. And after doing precisely that, he consulted with several people who had established a historical presence in local violence prevention (a hospital clerk, a high school assistant principal, and a former probation caseworker); this group would help Josiah to determine possible courses of action—for example, whether a formal meeting of the gang leaders was necessary and whether they should ask the youth to meet in person to discuss their grievance.

A necessary first step was to ensure that Josiah's work was generally viewed as legitimate. This was not a highly formal process involving presentation of credentials and demonstration of expertise. Instead, Josiah and others in the group simply spoke about their preferred mediation to the young men, the gangs, residents, and other local stakeholders. They made it clear that they would not challenge the gang's drug peddling—it was unrealistic to expect that they could curb their public trade. They would notify local beat cops of their efforts to address the grievances in order that police wouldn't view them as hostile actors. And they would require that Carl relinquish his weapon and turn it into the police—a gesture that would help create legitimacy for their efforts from the local police district commander. Finally, they would require that all parties abide by Josiah's mediation before the process began.

It is worth noting that I met very few residents who wanted to debate the merits of Josiah's "indigenous justice" strategy versus the use of state-sanctioned protocols—that is, the law on the books, the police, the courts, etc. For example, few requested that Josiah include the police in his efforts to mediate the dispute. Nor, for that matter, were they adamant that police take the lead in bringing about peace in the neighborhood. Carl Rose's father offered the most direct explanation for the scant requests to call for greater police involvement in the incident involving his son: "That's just how it's always been. Can't remember a day when it was different."

For nearly two decades, Josiah had demonstrated his ability to resolve conflicts among local youth. The prevailing view was that the police would not be as effective as Josiah in reducing youth violence. Josiah himself was aware of the difference between his own role and that of local police: "The thing to remember is that we don't have much time. These guys will start shooting at each other if you let them think too much about what happened. So, that's why we can't wait for cops, who never come anyway. . . . I can't really say how it got started that we just do for ourselves. My grandfather was a political guy, and his brother owned a restaurant where you would bring in your problems. It could be any kind of problem, and my father and brother would solve it for you. Police never cared about us, so we had to do it for ourselves. And, yes, you paid them to solve it, but I don't take money. Some other people do."

Given that the conflict could escalate—always a possibility when there is gun violence and gangs seeking to protect their economic interests—it is understandable that Josiah and his neighbors were quick to react to this youth conflict by calling on a timeworn method: "do for ourselves." They had great concern not only for the physical health of the two young men but also for any subsequent retaliation, especially that which could lead to injuries to other parties. Some worried that the two young men could recruit others to join their respective gangs, thus escalating the violence and enlarging the scope of those who might be impacted.

The point is not that justice could not be sought—and obtained— through the state apparatus. But the kind of justice residents might win would do little to resolve the conflicts at hand; moreover, the slow pace of bureaucratic procedure would not stem the potential escalation of the conflict between Carl and John.

It is fair to ask how often residents would actively seek out mediators such as Josiah rather than the police, or even tolerate these forms of self-governance. Years ago, in this same neighborhood, I collected incidents of disputes in the underground economy. By no means was I able to identify each and every such economic disagreement or conflict in this community of 45,000—an impossibility given that the underground economy includes innumerable private transactions, from sports bets to sale of sexual services. Over a three-month period, I worked with locals to identify over 2,400 disputes, a little over half of which were characterized by a violation of a legal code (e.g., burglary, robbery, assault) for which the police could claim legal jurisdiction. Yet, for these events, law enforcement responded only 10 percent of the time. Instead, in nearly three-quarters of these events, a third-party intermediary, like Josiah, helped buyer and seller (or creditor and borrower, property owner and renter, etc.) to settle the dispute. Even if we accept these numbers as purely illustrative, they reveal a critical reliance within the community for brokers who can settle matters in a timely manner. (Roughly three-quarters of all underground economic disputes are settled within forty-eight hours.)

Why is third-party mediation so common—for juvenile delinquency and, more generally, underground economic transactions? Perhaps most importantly, working behind the scenes is viewed as meaningful—and the right course of action, from an ethical point of view. It is an actual instance of the kind of "collective efficacy" that otherwise could not be realized by turning matters over to a perceived unreliable police force. Indeed, when couched in the light of state neglect, it is constructed by locals as morally legitimate. As Josiah's friend, the assistant principal who did not live in the area, explained to me, "When you call the cops, you stop and wonder, 'Did I do the right thing? What will others think of me?' See, when you call Josiah, you only think, 'I pray that he will help us, because he's been so good at helping others for a long time.' Until you get to a point where the feeling around here for police is, 'They are on my side,' then Josiah and his friends will always be the one who gets called. And that's not necessarily a good thing, remember. Because a healthy community is one where police help you, not take a backseat to people who take matters into their own hands."

Below, we will have an opportunity to remark on the long-term consequences of failing to utilize police in an effective manner—a point astutely made by the assistant principal. But for now, it is worth pausing to reflect on the developments in this case thus far. One common view held by residents was that putting a few gang members behind bars was futile given that there were many other youths who would take their place. Moreover, although people wanted Carl to be held accountable for his actions, it was no mystery that he was operating at the whim of a more senior, powerful gang leader. The immediate question that hung in the air was whether Josiah could restore the safety of public space for the general population. The clear priority expressed by local residents was to settle any lingering animosities among the disputing parties so that people could move about freely. If Josiah wanted then to bring about a truce among the youth or the gangs, that would be considered an unexpected bonus.

The decision to grant legitimacy to Josiah is not just a consequence of pervasive disdain for police or a widely held belief that police are racist, neglectful, uncaring, and so on (see also Sanchez-Jankowski 1991 for community-policing relations in the context of gang activity). It is quite common in practice to find residents simultaneously supporting the use of intermediaries, complaining about the lack of effective police services, and calling on the state to punish perpetrators and establish safety in a timely manner. One way to understand this apparent contradiction is by noting that there is a temporal aspect to youth delinquency and social order maintenance, which shapes how people act, alone and together, to restore public safety in their communities. Thus far, we have seen that the past plays a critical role in shaping actions in the present. Specifically, there is the general expectation that someone will work outside of the state to address conflicts among youth that threaten public safety. It is common knowledge that the cops will come and leave, but that someone else—a preacher, a schoolteacher, a social worker, a pastor, or other person—will pick up the baton and work more diligently to restore the peace.[5] Josiah's demonstrated expertise at resolving youth conflicts was by no means unique; in fact, though appreciated, it generated little alarm or applause. Residents who had grown up in the area could easily name dozens of people in the past who could play this role.[6]

The case of Carl and John highlights another important temporal aspect to social order maintenance. It showcases two distinct but interrelated sets of practices in youth deviance: the first is the proximate causes that lead to a norm violation or delinquent act, and the second is the consequences of that violation. Too often, social scientists focus on the former. They might only inquire into the social conditions that promote youth aggression—the resources, programs, and policies that might deter crime and violence; the material conditions that send idle youth to the street; and the cultural makeup of young black men that causes them to interact aggressively with one another (cf., Harding 2009; Sullivan 1989).

This is unfortunate, because in impoverished neighborhoods, youth may experience the mediation of local disputes by local stakeholders and community-based organizations as a form of "conventional society." They will likely come into contact with a wide range of individuals who are active in responding to conflicts. It is reasonable to expect that they might be aware of the manner by which community-based entities, from clergy to cops, participate in social order reproduction. The clergy, in particular, play a leading role in creating shared expectations that the church will be a site of informal social control—and, at times, they may work in an informal capacity alongside law enforcement (Winship, Berrien, and McRoberts 2000; Kennedy 2011). Often, however, they are working in a parallel path, providing safe spaces for mediation to occur outside the realm of the law. As McRoberts (2005) writes, "Azusa blurred the line between church and street even further by offering its Ella J. Baker House as a 'gang neutral space' and 'safe space' for young people trying to avoid trouble. Throughout any given day, young people were literally walking in off the street to take advantage of the Uhuru Project's tutoring and job placement services. . . . [I]n the safe space of the Baker House basement, young men held boxing tournaments, which frequently served to settle 'beefs' between individuals and rival crews without resorting to armed struggle" (92).[7]

These local mediation efforts may form part of their *doxa* for determining the meaning of offending and, hence, for a youth's personal decision to offend in the future. As such, these organizational dynamics must be accounted for in understanding at least one significant aspect of youth culture: namely, the perceptions that youth have of their social world. On the one hand, young people will perceive stakeholders, such as Josiah or the Azusa Church, as likely parties to engage at-risk youth, gangs, "crews," etc. in street diplomacy. Conversely, it is critical to note that that the stakeholders themselves may not view the youth in question as simply "criminals," "delinquents," or "norm violators." For example, as Sanchez-Jankowski (1991, 183) writes, "In low-income communities, there can be strong and positive 'social bonds' among residents and delinquent actors. Another reason for bonding from the community's perspective is function: the community needs certain services that the gang provides. Probably the most important service that gangs can provide is protection [which] for low-income communities can take on a number of forms . . . This does not mean that the community is antagonistic toward the police; rather, members of the community realize that the gang has some advantages over the police."

Sociological research often ignores such community-level patterns and fails to see the ways in which these community-level properties set the context for youth attitudes, perceptions, and orientation toward the future. Cobbina and colleagues (2008) study black youth in St. Louis, examining how young people develop fears of crime and victimization. Their objective is to document the role that perceptions play in shaping individual strategies to negotiate neighborhood dangers. Although the researchers acknowledge that "involvement in neighborhood life" could shape perceptions (and, consequently, risk-minimization strategies), neighborhood life was not a fecund space for analytic inquiry. For example, there was relatively little effort made to incorporate the mediation of conflict into the data collection. There did not seem to be much inquiry into the contacts that young people make with those who are active in responding to local violence. These contacts could include not only those working informally to establish order but even agents of law enforcement who, by virtue of the high level of discretion they employ in carrying out arrests, are continually negotiating with youth over the definition and significance of delinquent acts (Moskos 2008, 162). From the discussion of research methods in the Cobbina article, it does not appear that the researchers pushed their respondents to talk about the ways in which criminal and violent incidents were typically addressed in the neighborhood. Thus, it is nearly impossible to discern whether response to crime is one among many factors that shape youth perceptions—and that in turn shape youth behavior.

Without taking into account the scripts for mediation and resolution (see Krupnick and Winship, this volume), we end up failing to take into account the role that cultural factors play in shaping the behavior of black youth in contexts of material disadvantage. We ignore the ways in which various forms of community-level properties can shape the development of social norms—which in turn create the possibilities for young people to make meaningful decisions about their lives. But, to rectify this omission, it is imperative that the sociospatial units of analysis—communities, neighborhoods, public housing projects, etc.—be seen as historically constituted social contexts, in which youth develop perceptions of safety, danger, ally, enemy, resource, and so on, through their relations with other individuals and organizations. However, in practice, these spaces are too often defined as "high-risk ecologies," self-evidently captured with demographic variables like unemployment rate, immigration concentration, and percentage of female-headed households that rarely incorporate the social interventions and mediation strategies. Without this attentiveness to "indigenous justice," we end up with a partial and inadequate understanding of how and why neighborhoods matter in building up norms that make up part of the culture of young people.

Moving Forward

Establishing legitimacy for their efforts was an important task for Josiah and his colleagues, but it did not exhaust their labors. They had other equally critical decisions to make. For example, what was a desirable outcome in this matter? Was it sufficient to create some understanding between the two young men to forgo future violence and use of weapons? Would they seek a similar truce among the gangs? Or were all of these victories pyrrhic as long as local youth participated in the underground economy and settled their disputes with gunfights? Weighing the merits of short-term public safety against long-term stability is an ever-present challenge for those mediating disputes in low-income communities.

Josiah had little time to luxuriate over questions. He obtained the gun from Carl, turned it over to the police, and then brought the youth and their respective gang leaders together. He successfully won thirty days of ceasefire; he then requested that local police increase their own patrols in the area. During this détente, the gangs agreed not to sell drugs publicly within a mile of local schools and only in the parks during the evening, when children were unlikely to play.

Though these small concessions were significant for residents, they were most likely viewed by the outside world as signs of gang cooptation or tolerance of criminality. Always quick-witted and ready with a response for an inquisitive social scientist, he replied matter-of-factly to my query about his level of satisfaction with his "indigenous" diplomacy. "Yeah, I'll agree, it probably doesn't look like much. But these guys need to know I'm going to be here tomorrow. Calling them, chasing them down, making life a little more difficult by showing them someone cares. I can't change yesterday, but tomorrow? Who knows . . ."

Evidently, for Josiah, today's mediation is tomorrow's social context.

For several reasons, researchers studying low-income black communities would do well to recognize events that occur in the aftermath of norm violations—the second set of practices by which locals like Josiah seek to establish order and prevent the escalation of violence. In the short term, any organized mediation or intervention that leads to a cessation of violence or that stops the conflict from escalating can be critical for putting out the fire and restoring order (Winship, Berrien, and McRoberts 2000; Kennedy 2011; Meares and Kahan 1999). But in the longer term, successful interventions can also be viewed as preventative because they shape the potential for subsequent conflict.[8] There is considerable research suggesting that young people are deeply attentive to the local context of mediation and conflict resolution (Bourgois 2002; Sanchez-Jankowski 1991; Pattillo-McCoy 2000). The decision by two youth to draw a knife or wield a gun might be framed by their exposure to successful mediation efforts in their community, by their expectation of a response from law enforcement or a local intermediary, and by any imposed punishments that might be cast upon them by school authorities, parents, and police. The weighting of these practices may not manifest in conscious, utilitarian modes of reasoning, and young people may not be able to provide an explicit assessment in interviews or questionnaires. Nevertheless, these factors may still condition behavior such that dispositions to fight (or not) are adjusted accordingly.[9]

To date, with some notable exceptions (c.f., Phillips and Cooney 2008), social scientists have not actively incorporated these stakeholders into discussions of black youth deviance. Instead, they tend to focus on a very limited part of the timeline, namely "causes" qua factors that occur proximate to the norm violation, such as youth motivations to commit crime. Rarely are the responses incorporated into the analysis either as consequences that highlight community-level properties, such as the degree and effectiveness of forms of collective action, or as themselves contextual properties that shape future violations.

This misrecognition, following Bourdieu's logic, stems in part from a dominant theoretical framing that shapes research. Namely, those who study the dynamics of youth aggression, whether they highlight motivations that are rooted in the psychosocial realm or in the local community, typically see the causal root of the action as beginning with individual thought and action. It matters not whether the youth are considered to be rational, goal-oriented agents with established preferences (Sanchez-Jankowski 1991), peers who are socialized into violence by peer relations (Harding 2009), or conformists to social norms that propel them into violence as a way of achieving a meaningful identity (Anderson 2000). In each, the basic conceptual building block is the willful individual.

But, equal theoretical attention must be paid to the shared meanings and expectations, that is, the community-level dimensions of youth culture that condition behavior. These cultural properties do not form overnight but can ossify over the course of generations. It is by no means a simple matter to document these social dynamics. However, social scientists could plausibly adjust their temporal frames in order to acknowledge such factors. In addition to local conflict mediation, a youth's propensity to commit a violent act may be conditioned by his or her experiences with violence as a child. One could also say that a parent's exposure to violence in his or her own household is a plausible factor that socializes children into perceiving criminal offending as legitimate or desirable. Adequate consideration of proximate causes would require that a researcher widen the timeframe for specification to years, if not decades. The investigator would need to look closely not only at the proximate period—for example, the young person's interaction with peers, their relations to other members of the household—but she would have to search for clues in the distant past and in experiences in childhood (and quite possibly in the upbringing of parents). These analytic gymnastics are not so simple to negotiate in a research study, and so boundaries tend to be drawn that permit ease of data collection—even if there is considerable theoretical justification for seeking information on these more hard-to-reach interpersonal dynamics. In the end, sociologists will impose a priori temporal limit on the range of factors that might plausibly be integrated into the model.

But how boundaries are drawn is nevertheless instructive because it highlights folk (i.e., untested, and often underspecified) assumptions about the social and cultural world of inner-city inhabitants. For example, because pragmatic considerations often reign, sociological research on "causes" of youth criminality can easily lead to the asymmetry discussed above, wherein actions occurring after a criminal incident are presumed to be less critical for determining the etiology of deviant behavior. In particular, the specification of "outcomes" in this approach fails to distinguish between indicator-driven consequences of norm violation and criminality—arrest, jail, school eviction, etc., which are typically accounted for—and community-level attributes, such as mediation patterns and utilization of police, which are absent and which may be relevant to youths' decisions to offend in the future.

To conclude, although sociologists currently look into crime and delinquency in order to make claims about the organization of inner-city black youth culture, they typically begin by presuming a cultural chasm between youth and the wider society. Discussions of crime and offending proceed on the assumption that black youth are being socialized by value systems and norms that are antithetical to mainstream American culture. In this framework, reducing delinquent behavior requires remedying culture.

There are many potential criticisms of this framework—above, we pointed out that the same deviant practices, when viewed as "resistant" or as expressions of discontent, would open up a wider range of possibilities for cultural analysis. We might also revisit the conventional approach that sees deviance as comprised of two distinct spheres of practice. Currently, sociologists tend to arbitrarily separate "causal" forces from those practices that might be conventionally understood as responses to the fallout from events.

By contrast, I would suggest that we see the full range of practices as a continuum. In other words, deviance is a set of performative actions, involving a range of social actors, all of which are situated in structured social contexts. There are certainly different forms of thought and action that occur along this continuum, including the perceptions of those contemplating a deviant act and the subsequent efforts of those who assume responsibility for managing the consequences of deviance. But any particular decision to offend, in which a youth ends up committing a criminal act, is an outcome of a broad field of social practices that involves interactions of that youth with others. In other words, we must find a way to link youth perceptions with activities such as social order reproduction that appear on the surface to occur much later, but that are more accurately understood as forming part of the context through which these perceptions form.

Youth norm violation might be thought of as patterned social actions that create expectations and forms of response by local actors. In the script of youth deviance, there are noteworthy moments at which action congeals. First, communities have particular resources for ensuring that social order is reproduced, including law enforcement personnel, social services, and social workers. Policies and programs can change, but the shifts are typically slow in the making, and so residents and service providers have expectations of each other's conduct (Venkatesh 1997). Second, among the residents themselves, there are patterns of trust and social cohesion that generate expectations of collective action; individuals have routines based on their histories of working together to prevent youth crime and intervene in conflict. So too among youth, one can find associations, peer networks, and formal gangs that behave in predictable ways. Thus, if we are interested in a youth's likelihood to participate in a deviant act, we must take into account the various kinds of expected practices that can affect the young person's decision making. Indeed, young people consider the prospect of offending as a result of observing countless numbers of episodes in which other youth have performed similar actions. This history can shape their understanding of conflict and their decisions to act on feelings of anger or perceptions of injustice.

And since these forms of intervention have an ethical dimension, they must be considered in our general assessments of black youth culture.[10] They are signals to the sociologist of reigning belief systems, dispositions, and structures of meaning. Taking such practices into account can help us avoid a simplistic dichotomy that portrays communities as composites of two divergent value orientations, one criminal and one law abiding. Particularly in social contexts in which there are depleted resources, histories of police neglect and abuse, and identifiable traditions of self-enforcement, we are more likely to see creative interventions that make for strange bedfellows. Individuals may need to put aside animosities to work together to reduce violence and respond to youth in crisis. As they do, they indirectly end up shaping the mores, perspectives, and outlooks of the young people themselves.

11

Culture, Inequality, and Gender Relations among Urban Black Youth

JODY MILLER, *Rutgers University*

In *Getting Played: African American Girls, Urban Inequality, and Gendered Violence* (2008), I examined the seemingly ubiquitous nature of violence against adolescent African American girls living in distressed, racially segregated, urban neighborhoods. Though focused on gendered violence against girls, this work is part of a growing body of research that explores deeper problems concerning how gender inequalities in disadvantaged neighborhoods affect relations between young women and men, and how these inequalities are intertwined with inequalities of race, class, and place (see also Popkin, Leventhal, and Weismann 2008, 2010). To examine such questions fully requires attention to the many intersecting sources of these inequalities, including the relationships between structural and institutional inequalities, the cultural adaptations and situational contexts these help to create and reproduce, and the broader cultural reproductions of gender, race, and class inequalities in which American urban inequalities are embedded.

These intersecting sources of inequality include the important paradox at the core of this volume: despite the deep marginalization of urban African American youth, their place in popular culture—as producers and consumers, and as commodities whose images are sold and highly profitable—is now both omnipresent and highly gendered (Collins 2006). For example, hip-hop and rap music have consistently retained one of the largest market shares in the music industry over the last decade (RIAA 2009). Though this industry is one of the few arenas within popular culture to give a public voice to black youth, it is one of a range of mass media formats that also "constructs and sells a commodified black culture from ideas about class, gender, and age" (Collins 2006, 301), replicating and

369

sometimes exacerbating harmful controlling images of black masculinity and African American young women (Collins 2006; Sharpley-Whiting 2007). Such representations reinforce and crystallize harmful gendered cultural frames among and about urban African American youth.

In this chapter, I examine the relationships between the social conditions of urban African American young men and women and the cultural processes that sustain gender inequalities between them. This chapter is divided into two sections. First, I review previous work by sociologists and urban studies scholars on urban poverty, which has given limited attention to how inequalities of race, class, and place are shaped and reinforced by gender inequality. Second, I examine several key facets of gender inequality particularly harmful to African American women and girls: the sexual objectification and exploitation of young women, including how these are related to each other as well as to prominent features of masculinity among urban young men. Throughout, I note important limitations in our knowledge of the links among inequality, culture, and gender in U.S. urban settings. Finally, I conclude with a discussion of how research on the cultural aspects of poverty can be used to support urban African American young women and young men, as well as to challenge and confront the gendered harms embedded in their daily lives.

Gender Matters

A great deal of scholarly work in the social sciences has given primacy to understanding the experiences of urban African American men and boys, and what some have dubbed the "crisis of young black men" in America (Herbert 2010; Mauer 1999). This crisis is characterized by interrelated features of marginalization of young black men: their increasing economic dislocation and poor educational achievement, particularly in neighborhoods characterized by concentrated urban poverty and racial segregation (Peterson and Krivo 2010; Wilson 2009); their disproportionate experiences of violence as participants and victims (Sampson and Wilson 1995; Stewart and Simons 2006); and their rapidly increased experiences in the criminal justice system resulting from the punitive turn toward mass incarceration that has disproportionately targeted them (Tonry 1996; Western 2007). Much of the recent work on the marginalization of young black men has also begun to reconsider cultural features that are among "the cumulative and often durable effects of residing in poor, segregated neighborhoods" (Wilson 2009, 61; see also Anderson 1999; Harding 2010; Young 2004).

For the most part, though, analyses of the "crises" facing black communities have remained relatively silent on harms to African American women and girls, with limited attention to the impact and functions of gender inequality. Partly this is because one of the most commonly recognized forms of male privilege—an economic dividend in the formal economy—is widely available to white but not black men. As a consequence, many urban scholars focus primarily on "the economic plight of inner-city black males" (Wilson 2009, 62). For example, the sociologist William Julius Wilson (2009) notes that black women have superior educational outcomes than black men, including lower dropout rates and higher college completion rates. Moreover, he suggests that African American women's much greater concentration in service, rather than manufacturing, industries offers them greater protection from the most harmful impacts of economic restructuring.

However, a focus on black men overlooks the substantial gendered harms to black women. Research on the intersecting impacts of race, gender, and class in the labor market, for instance, indicates that the jobs most available to black women in the service economy do not provide strong protections from economic conditions; in fact, black women's wages remain considerably lower than those of black men (Altonji and Blank 1999; Browne and Misra 2003). In addition, urban black women are disproportionately responsible for the economic well-being of their families. This is particularly the case given the growth of single-mother households in poor urban communities, exacerbated by decreases in the "marriageability" of black men in these settings (Wilson 2009, 100–01). Moreover, the increased punitiveness of the welfare state results in even fewer protections for black women (Hays 2004). It makes sense, then, for scholars of urban inequality to be equally concerned with the economic plight of inner-city females.

Ironically, a common cultural frame found in both rap music (Stephens and Few 2007a; Weitzer and Kubrin 2009) and urban young men's characterizations of young women (Harding 2010) is that of the "gold digger"—a woman interested in men primarily for the economic and material resources they can provide. Though a disparaging image, it directs us to not just (more complicated) economic facets of gender relations, but also African American young women's experiences of gendered and raced economic stratification. As sociologist David Harding (2010, 166) points out, African American young men in disadvantaged communities perceive young women as "us[ing] a romantic or sexual relationship as part of th[eir] struggle for material survival," as this is in keeping with larger economic survival strategies in their communities.

Among urban sociologists, however, a more common tendency has been to frame women in disadvantaged black communities primarily in terms of "the fragmentation of the poor black family" (Wilson 2009, ch. 4). Sociologist Elijah Anderson's (1999) *Code of the Street,* for example—one of the most influential contemporary works on inner-city life—discusses young women primarily as girlfriends, sexual partners, and teen mothers. Moreover, as sociologist Loïc Wacquant (2002, 1494–95) has compellingly argued, the *decency* that Anderson often valorizes in his comparative analyses of "street" versus "decent" families is based on a traditional value orientation toward gender relations and women's roles in the family, though this is not explicitly articulated in his analytic framework. Likewise, although analyzing the contradictory cultural frames young men use to understand romantic relationships, sexual behavior, and fatherhood, in *Living the Drama* (2010) Harding does not sufficiently examine how these frames are embedded within cultural ideologies about women and girls that function to reproduce deeply harmful gender inequalities in urban communities, including among youth.

Two additional areas of research have pointed to the disproportionate gendered harms of racial inequality for African American young men: the expansion of the prison-industrial complex and dramatically increased rates of incarceration and criminal justice contact for black men; and their unique risks for violent victimization, including homicide, in the context of the "code of the street." In fact, however, both are implicated in the experiences of African American young women and the cultural reproduction of gender inequalities. As to the former, it is undeniable that, compared to their female counterparts, black men have borne the brunt of mass incarceration as the direct subjects of social control (Western and Wildeman 2009).

Yet, African American young women have not escaped unscathed. They are the fastest-growing segment of the prison population and "constitute a greater proportion of the incarcerated female population than do black males of the incarcerated male population" (Bush-Baskette 1998, 119). In fact, the dramatic and disproportionate increase in incarceration rates for black women on drug charges led criminologist Stephanie Bush-Baskette

(1998, 113) to dub the war on drugs a "war against black women." Moreover, scholars have begun to attend to the "secondary prisonization" experiences of women with incarcerated male loved ones (Comfort 2007; Christian 2005) and the impact on black families of mass incarceration (Western and Wildeman 2009).

An important but less researched topic is "the growing symbiosis between the street and the prison culture due to the astronomical rates of incarceration of young African-Americans from urban centers" (Wacquant 2002, 1492), including what this means for gender relations between young women and men (see Sharpley-Whiting 2007, xvi). Sociologist Ann Nurse (2002), for example, documents a number of ways in which incarceration exacerbates young men's distrust of young women and heightens the circulation of misogynistic discourses. For example, exaggerated displays of masculinity are necessary to avoid victimization in prison; often these are accomplished by denigrating women, with "the intensity of [such] talk and the fact that inmates have little contact with women" heightening the harmful impacts (Nurse 2002, 57). In addition, Nurse found that rumors of infidelity often circulated about young men's romantic partners on the outside, fostering suspicion and damaging relationships. Thus, while mass incarceration is a form of gendered racial oppression, it is not a crisis that uniquely affects young black men and thus its gendered harms to young black women warrant further investigation.

Finally, while many urban scholars examine the connections among racial inequality, concentrated poverty, and violence, this also is too often conceptualized and analyzed as a primarily male problem that requires *young men's* negotiation of the "code" (Anderson 1999) and "structures social relations, reinforces neighborhood identities, organizes local status hierarchies, and influences *boys'* use of space" (Harding 2010, 240; my emphasis). Once again, there is no question that risks associated with gun violence and homicide exact disproportionate harms on young black men. But focusing only or primarily on young men's risks for violence overlooks young, urban African American women's disproportionate and gendered risks for violent victimization as well.

Recent research reveals, for example, that African American girls' risks for nonlethal victimization are dramatically higher than for adolescent girls in other racial groups, and are nearly equal those for African American young men (Lauritsen 2003). In fact, their risk for nonstranger violence, including in their neighborhoods, is higher than that of any other group, *including* their African American male counterparts. These patterns were largely correlated with urban disadvantaged community contexts—a finding confirmed by the recent evaluation of the Moving to Opportunity for Fair Housing Demonstration (MTO). This evaluation revealed that moves to neighborhoods with improved socioeconomic conditions and lower crime were directly beneficial for girls but not boys. Girls who moved as part of the initiative were significantly more likely than those who did not to report "less psychological distress, anxiety, and substance use and they were less likely to be arrested" (Popkin, Leventhal, and Weismann 2008, 2). Neighborhood safety—particularly the decline in sexual harassment and coercion—are primary factors the evaluators point to for explanation (Popkin, Leventhal, and Weismann 2010).

Moreover, sociologist Nikki Jones's work (2010) demonstrates that young women in urban communities also must negotiate street codes and associated risks for violence, and my own work (2008) amply shows that African American girls in urban neighborhoods face heightened risks for gendered violence at the hands of young men. In fact, both of our studies show that the ways in which violence "structures social relations" and "organizes local status hierarchies" (Harding 2010, 240) in urban neighborhoods are built on hierarchical understandings of gender. Moreover, young men's uses of public space—including in their attempts to minimize their own risk—contribute to young women's heightened sense of danger and actual risks for victimization (Cobbina, Miller, and Brunson 2008). For example, for their own safety, young men often travel and spend their time in groups; however, interactional dynamics within male peer groups tend to increase the likelihood that girls will be targeted for sexual harassment or exploitation by these same groups (Miller 2008).

In short, urban scholars' understandings of the challenges facing African American youth in neighborhoods of concentrated segregation and poverty must include attention to the gendered facets of these challenges, including how these conditions build upon and reproduce gender inequalities. A number of feminist scholars have analyzed the intersections of gender, race, class, and sexuality, demonstrating that we can neither examine nor explain adequately the impact of race and class inequalities without serious consideration of their gendered dimensions (Bettie 2003; Collins 1990, 2004; Jones 2010). Bringing this work to the forefront of scholarship on urban African American youth is critical for developing effective strategies to help ameliorate the many challenges they face.

Structure, Culture, and Gender Inequality

We know that "social structure does not exist 'outside' everyday life" (Connell 1993, ix): instead, "broader social forces, properties, and practices . . . [are] constituted in practice" (Fine and Fields 2008, 131). It is these cultural practices we must analyze to understand fully the nature and impact of gender inequality on African American urban youth. Yet, the challenge in studying how culture reproduces gender inequalities is that "explanations focusing on the cultural traits of inner-city residents are likely to draw far more attention from policymakers and the general public than structural explanations will" (Wilson 2009, 43). There is a lengthy history—in public policy and sociology—of asserting a stylized "culture of poverty" thesis that "deliver[s] a vision of the culture of the poor as an all-encompassing, internally consistent, and coherent entity that contributes mightily to their malaise" (Young 2010, 54).

Not only does this focus shift attention away from how youths' cultural frames and interactions are grounded in contexts of structural inequalities such as those built on relations of gender, sexuality, race, class, and age, but it also fails to situate gender inequality and gender relations among African American youth in the larger social order of race and gender: that is, the overarching patterns of social life within society that are arranged on the basis of gender and race (Connell 2002; see also Collins 2004). This means we must situate our analyses of youths' cultural frames, strategies, and performances as emerging from the powerful constraints under which they are produced, and also embed our analyses recognizing the "cultural factors within the broader society" through which urban black youths' gender relations are refracted (Wilson 2009, 75). Our understanding of gender inequality in these settings "should not depend on American exceptionalist notions that the dominant cultural landscape is not wrought with examples of repression against women" (McWilliams 2010, 539; see also Rose 2008; Sharpley-Whiting 2007).

The same holds true for popular culture. As I consider here the overlapping nature of youths' cultural frames about gender, and the images and discourses produced in hip-hop and rap, recognition of the contexts in which this work is produced and consumed is paramount. Sociologists Ron Weitzer and Charis Kubrin (2009, 6–7), for example, note the important pressures placed on rap artists by music industry elites, who "encourage provocative, edgy lyrics . . . to maximize sales," including "misogynistic representations of women." Indeed, a quote by the rapper Too $hort alludes to this process: "wonder why it's like that, well so do I. . . . I get paid real good to talk bad about a bitch." Similarly, the sociologist Patricia Hill Collins emphasizes how "black people's bodies are tied to structures of profitability" (2006, 311): they are "essential to new consumer markets, both as suppliers of commodities that are bought and sold, and as reliable consumer markets . . . [making them] target audiences for their own degradation" (300, 313). Nonetheless, young urban black women and men are a significant portion of the consumers of rap and hip-hop, making their consumption and production of these media an important avenue for research on its impact on gender relations and inequalities.

In addition, though reinforced in popular culture, ideologies about gender and race are profoundly embedded in social life—that is, in "the discursive fields by which [individuals] are constructed or construct themselves" (Daly and Maher 1998, 4). These include deeply engrained notions of fundamental gender difference, which are put to use to create and sustain symbolic boundaries between young women and young men. As the sociologist Mario Small and colleagues (2010, 17) explain, "Symbolic boundaries constitute a system of classification that defines a hierarchy of groups and the similarities and differences between them. They typically imply and justify a hierarchy of moral worth across individuals and groups." These shape the interpretive frameworks that youths bring to their daily lives, and it is through their enactment that some of the most persistent facets of gender inequality are reproduced.

Thus, making sense of the inequalities in gender relations among urban black youth requires examining how broader structural and cultural forces inform and are realized and challenged within the specific organizational contexts of communities of concentrated disadvantage and the microlevel interactions of young men and women within them. As I shift to a detailed discussion of that facet of gender inequality—the sexual objectification of young black women and some of its consequences—I do so with an awareness of these complexities.

The Sexual Objectification of Young Black Women and Its Consequences

Research drawing from nationally representative samples consistently reveals that the highest risks for violence against women are found among those who are younger, never-married, poor, and African American[1] (see

Lauritsen and Schaum 2004). Community context, however, plays a critical role: "Communities in which there are relatively large proportions of households headed by women with children appear to be more dangerous for women" than other settings, and this is "regardless of their own household situation" (Lauritsen and Schaum 2004, 349). Much of my own research thus concerns itself with the peer and social contexts of disadvantaged communities, and how cultural processes in such contexts shape young women's risks for victimization. The sexual objectification of young women plays a critical role and contributes to a continuum of sexual abuse and exploitation, including sexual harassment, sexual coercion and assault, and gang rape.

When my colleagues and I interviewed African American adolescents in impoverished neighborhoods in St. Louis, for example, we found very high rates of sexual victimization among young women: 89 percent (thirty-one of thirty-five) described having been sexually harassed, 54 percent (nineteen of thirty-five) reported experiences with sexual assault or coercion, and nearly one in three (eleven of thirty-five) had experienced multiple incidents of sexual violence.[2] The average age of young women in our sample was just sixteen years old. Though ours was not a representative sample, nonetheless this extent of victimization at such a young age is quite disproportionate to prevalence rates in the general U.S. population (AAUW Educational Foundation 2001; Lauritsen 2003; Lauritsen and Schaum 2004).

Not all of the young men we interviewed engaged in such behaviors, and some were openly critical of them. Nonetheless, the youths we spoke to understood this treatment of girls to be embedded in constructions of masculinity and male entitlement and the sexualization of young women. As seventeen-year-old Ricky explained:

> You got some smooth talkers in our neighborhood. . . . I think it's just to get a image, a name. To make theyselves look big. . . . A lot of guys do it just so other guys can be like, "aw, man, he'll do this" or "he'll do that." . . . Most of 'em just do it for a name, man, just for an image. Try to look like something they not.

The young men that both girls and boys primarily faulted in such sexual mistreatment were those caught up in the street life: specifically, those who are hanging out on the corners with other young men and involved in gangs and drug sales. This is consistent with previous research by sociologists showing that support for the sexual victimization of women tends to be highest in male-dominated settings, where the valorization of narrow conceptualizations of masculinity—including rewarding aggression, competition, and the devaluation of women—is often a prominent cultural feature. Research on offender networks, such as those involved in gangs and drug sales, has consistently found gender stratification, sex typing, and exclusionary practices toward women to be widespread (Maher 1997; Miller 2001; Steffensmeier 1983). Likewise, group loyalty, distrust of outsiders, and limited community scrutiny or intervention create normative conditions that both foster sexually coercive behaviors and reduce the likelihood that such incidents will be penalized (Boswell and Spade 1996; Franklin 2004; Sanday 1981, 1990; Schwartz and DeKeseredy 1997).

Each of these features is prominent in scholars' analyses of street culture in communities characterized by racial segregation and concentrated poverty. Anderson (1999) conceptualizes this as the "code of the street": behavioral expectations for young men that emphasize masculine reputation and respect, achieved through presentations of self that emphasize toughness and independence, a willingness to use violence, and heterosexual prowess demonstrated by means of sexual conquest. Anderson and others trace the dominance of this presentational style to structural dislocation: given "the unique history of racial oppression and persistent denial of access to legitimate avenues of mainstream masculinity construction . . . street reputation, pose, and associated violence become central to [some young] black men's identities" (Mullins 2006, 25). And while "the code" is one of multiple normative frameworks available for young men (Harding 2010), all must be competent in its behavioral rules in order to successfully navigate the social terrains of their neighborhoods (Anderson 1999).

With this comes support for the sexual objectification of young women and attendant consequences such as sexual violence. Such attitudes and resulting activities are an important feature of the "boundary work" (Small, Harding, and Lamont 2010, 18) that young men engage in to construct collective identities based on their differentiation of themselves from young women. This boundary work can be identified across the spectrum of sexually harmful behaviors experienced by young women, starting with those activities often perceived as the most benign, such as school-based sexual harassment. Young men we interviewed, for example, often downplayed the seriousness of sexual harassment by couching it in terms of "play." Explaining why he and his friends routinely "be messing with the girls . . . grab[bing] they bootie," fourteen-year-old Curtis said it was "just to have fun, just playing."

Such play claims, however, were roundly rejected by the young women we spoke to, many of whom recognized boys' behavior as boundary work that came at the expense of the young woman. Sixteen-year-old Anishika explained: "They know right from wrong. But when it's a lot of 'em, they think that stuff is cute, calling girls B's [bitches] and rats and all that stuff. They think that stuff cute . . . but it's not cute." Likewise, fourteen-year-old Nicole lamented, "sometimes boys . . . act like it's funny. But it's not. 'Cause you touchin' a girl and she don't wanna be touched." In fact, despite young men's routine claims that such behavior was "just play," their own accounts belied the notion that their behaviors were simply intended as harmless fun. Several were explicit in describing the derogatory treatment of girls as a way to demarcate their (male) space and make it clear to the girl that she was not welcome.

Moreover, young men sometimes used girls' responses to such behavior as a testing ground, to identify young women who may be vulnerable to more serious forms of sexual abuse. Describing how young men target girls, Ricky continued:

A lot of times they try to find girls that ain't up to the level that they should be. I mean, they might be a little slow on how things go and how the streets work. And then they just prey on innocent people, really, you know what I'm saying. It's usually the ones that they know [are] vulnerable. . . . [The guy'll think], "Well, I'm a smoke this weed with her and I'm a drink this with her, and eventually we gonna do this [have sex]," you know.

The sexual objectification and exploitation of young black women by black men is not only driven by a search for masculine identity. The large presence of young men on the streets is in part a consequence of their exclusion from mainstream institutions such as schools and access to work in the formal economy (Ferguson 2001; Wilson 2009). In addition, as the sociologist Robert Sampson (2009, 272) notes, "crime, disorder, and violence have been overlooked in the feedback processes that help perpetuate" conditions in neighborhoods of concentrated disadvantage. For instance, "there is evidence that fear of violence leads to a 'hunkering down' and shunning of neighborhoods and local institutions that otherwise might support local social control" (ibid.). This contributes to the limited community intervention against young men's involvement in violence, including that directed at young women.

Moreover, young men's solidarity with and commitment to their male peers is guided in part by personal safety concerns (Cobbina, Miller, and Brunson 2008) as well as the important source "of friendship and self-worth" that "allegiance to their male peers" provides "in an environment of low trust" (Fosse 2010, 139). Yet, what this means is that the strategies many young men employ to navigate these structural terrains—hanging out in groups, projecting a "street" persona, sometimes involving themselves with gangs, drug sales, and other crime—are precisely the kinds of cultural adaptations that position girls as "other" and place them at risk for exclusion and victimization (Cobbina, Miller, and Brunson 2008).

Thus, these cultural adaptations are built upon gender inequalities and come at the expense of young women. As thirteen-year-old Antwoin surmised, "The females, all the dudes be wanting to try to freak, you know, have sex with 'em, all that kinda stuff. . . . Boys be wanting to run a train on 'em." In fact, our research shows that the abuse of young women—sexual and otherwise—often takes on a carnivalesque flavor, sometimes involving group-based sexual assault, and is heavily laden with victim-blaming interpretations. In fact, 45 percent of the young men we interviewed (eighteen of forty) described having "run trains" on girls (i.e., group or serial sex, often gang rape), and five of them reported engaging in multiple incidents in the last six months. Importantly, when young men described these incidents, they did not identify them as violence or sexual assault; instead, they constructed them as consensual.

As such, young men's narratives of such incidents warrant scrutiny for interrogating the gendered boundary work utilized to justify (and deny) their sexual abuse of young women, and account for the commonality of such practices. First, accounts of these events were sometimes particularly graphic, focusing specific attention to the details of their sexual performances. For example, thirteen-year-old Frank explained:

There's this one girl, she a real, real freak. . . . She wanted me and my friend to run a train on her. . . . [Beforehand], we was at the park, hopping and talking about it and everything. I was like, "Man, dawg, I ain't hitting her from the back." Like, "she gonna mess up my dick." . . . He like, "Oh, I got her from the back, dude." So we went up there . . . [and] she like, "Which one you all hitting me from the back?" [I'm] like, "There he go, right there. I got the front." She's like, "Okay." And then he took off her clothes, pulled his pants down. I didn't, just unzipped mine 'cause I was getting head. She got to slurping me. I'm like, my partner back there? 'Cause we was in the dark so I ain't see nuttin'. He was back, I just heard her [making noises]. I'm like, "Damn, girl, what's wrong with you?" [More noises] [I'm like], "You hitting her from the back?" He's like, "Yeah, I'm hitting it."

Group processes play a central role in events such as this: its enactment increases solidarity and cohesion among young men, while the female has symbolic status and is treated as an object (Sanday 1990). Numerous studies suggest that gang rape may be particularly common "in the contexts of broader structural violence, including profound marginalization and . . . deprivation" (Wood 2005), as the masculinity constructions that facilitate such behaviors are heightened, due to blocked opportunities for achieving other types of masculine rewards, and because of the dominance of male peer groups in such settings (Franklin 2004). In fact, the African American writer Nathan McCall (1994), in his bestselling autobiography, describes "running trains" as a routine practice among adolescent boys in the neighborhood of his youth:

Although everybody knew it could lead to trouble with the law, I think few guys thought of it as rape. It was viewed as a social thing among hanging partners, like passing a joint. The dude who set up the train got pats on the back. He was considered a real player whose rap game was strong. . . . Even though it involved sex, it didn't seem to be about sex at all. Like almost everything we did, it was a macho thing. Using a member of one of the most vulnerable groups of human beings on the face of the earth—Black females—it was another way for a guy to show the other fellas how cold and hard he was. (44, 50)

The male-dominated contexts found in many disadvantaged urban communities, then, can facilitate not just a gender-blind "street code," but one that includes preoccupations with exaggerated masculinity, a strong sense of male superiority, and sexual entitlement. Attachments to such masculinity constructions increase the likelihood of engaging in sexual aggression (Truman, Tokar, and Fischer 1996; Vass and Gold 1995). In fact, "running trains" appears to function as an interaction ritual, a "means through which cultural meanings about masculinity are transferred and reproduced" (Fine and Fields 2008, 140).

Second, young men's accounts of "running trains" consistently provided interpretations that defined them as consensual. Frank's excerpt above simply implied consent by insisting that the young woman was a "real, real freak." Eighteen-year-old Terence, on the other hand, described an incident that—by putting oneself in the position of the young woman—could easily be identified as coercive and nonconsensual, given the threat inherent in being outnumbered by a group of young men who have congregated for the sole purpose of group "sex." Yet, he maintained that she was a willing participant:

> *Terence:* It was some girl that my friend had knew for a minute, and he, I guess he just came to her and asked her, "Is you gon' do everybody?" or whatever, and she said, "Yeah." So he went first and then, I think my other partna went, then I went, then it was like two other dudes behind me. . . . It was at [my friend's] crib.
>
> *Interviewer:* Were you all like there for a get-together or party or something?
>
> *Terence:* It was specifically for that for real, 'cause he had already let us know that she was gon' do that, so.
>
> *Interviewer:* So it was five boys and just her?
>
> *Terence:* Yeah.
>
> *Interviewer:* And so he asked her first, and then he told you all to come over that day?
>
> *Terence:* We had already came over. 'Cause I guess he knew she was already gon' say yeah or whatever. We was already there when she got there.
>
> *Interviewer:* Did you know the girl?
>
> *Terence:* Naw, I ain't know her, know her like for real know her. But I knew her name or whatever. I had seen her before. That was it though.
>
> *Interviewer:* So when you all got there, she was in the room already?
>
> *Terence:* Naw, when we got there, she hadn't even got there yet. And when she came, she went in the room with my friend, the one she had already knew. And then after they was in there for a minute, he came out and let us know that she was gon', you know, run a train or whatever. So after that, we just went one by one.

By Terence's own account, the girl arrived at a boy's house that she knew and may have been interested in. Waiting for her on arrival were four additional boys whom she did not know or know well. And they had come in advance specifically for the purpose of running a train on her. Terence apparently had not considered the possibility that the young woman may have felt threatened or that she hadn't freely consented. Instead, because his friend said "she was down" for it, Terence took his turn and left.

In fact, adherence to the kinds of masculine ideologies described above is linked to their tendency to discount young women's interpretations of sexual violence. Young men's "certainty" about girls' consent is based on patriarchal definitions of gender and sexuality, built on the belief in male entitlement and constructed in concert with male peers (King 2003; Scully 1990). While such processes are not unique to urban African American communities, they nonetheless represent a significant feature of gender inequality there. Moreover, they appear to be especially salient features of youth culture in urban poor African American communities (Miller 2008). Black feminist scholars, in fact, have traced the sexual objectification of young black women to historical legacies of gendered racial inequality, including, for example, the gross "scientific" objectification of African women in the nineteenth century (Crais and Scully 2008), their use as sexual and reproductive property under slavery (Collins 1990; hooks 1981), and the long history of impunity for men—white and black—who sexually assault them (Davis 1983). Sharpley-Whiting (2007, 64) aptly describes this as "the twin myths of hypersexuality and easy accessibility that emerged in the New World as part and parcel of black women's initiation into what it meant to be chattel."

The Gendered Harms in Holding Young Black Women Responsible

Also critical to the cultural ideologies of sexual objectification and other forms of abuse against young women are the prominent victim-blaming beliefs that buttress them. Feminist scholars conceptualize sexual violence as existing on a continuum: sexual objectification, running "game," and putting pressure on girls for sex are thus linked to more explicitly coercive behaviors, including the threat or use of violence, rape, and gang rape (Kelly 2002). This is a useful conceptualization, because it allows us to examine how normative constructions of gender and sexuality are related to sexual violence (Gavey 1999). Victim-blaming ideologies are present across these forms of sexuality and sexual violence, with young women judged harshly for appearing sexually available, enjoying male sexual attention, having sex outside committed relationships, and having multiple sexual partners. Thus, young women are expected to be the "gatekeepers" of their sexuality, and their failure to do so—even in the case of exploitation or coercion—places primary responsibility in their hands (Squires et al. 2006).

My research links these ideologies to the gender relations that emerge in contexts of intense urban disadvantage and racial inequality and their overlay with "the larger cultural objectification of women and associated norms of hegemonic masculinity" (Weitzer and Kubrin 2009, 26). Other scholars have investigated their relationship to the gendered sexual scripts presented and reinforced through the images and symbolism available to African American youth in popular culture, as "contemporary manifestations of older stereotypes of Black womanhood—the Jezebel, Sapphire, Welfare Mama, and Matriarch" (Stephens and Few 2007a, 51; see also Collins 1990, 2004).

African American young women are a core consumer market of these popular representations, making such imagery and their impact especially significant. As feminist scholar Tracy Denean Sharpley-Whiting (2007, 59) explains: "Even if one dismisses outright causal relationship theories [of rap's relationship to behavior], the urban ghetto (sur)reality [it presents]—pulling trains, forced abortions, and rape—offers a rather forlorn snapshot of young black women's sexual experiences."

In their investigation, psychologists Dionne Stephens and Layli Phillips (2003) identified a diverse array of "bad girl" sexual scripts in hip-hop music videos, positioned against a narrow "good girl" script that included "the normalization of heterosexuality and the celebration of female virginity" (Stephens and Few 2007a, 61). Subsequent investigations examined African American youths' acceptance, usage, and responses to such imagery. Among the authors' findings were that youths saw male sexual desire as "innate and central to their relationships with females," resulting in the acceptance of a sexual double standard in which "the possibility of men engaging in sexual relations with women who followed even the most vilified sexual scripts was not viewed as problematic" (Stephens and Few 2007a, 63; see also Stephens and Few 2007b). As a result, women are positioned as gatekeepers of their sexuality.

There are wide-ranging consequences to the acceptance of and adherence to such beliefs. As Stephens and Few (2007a, 63) note, "These double standard messages regarding male-female 'rules' do not provide women with the skills and attitudes required to negotiate sexual practices effectively." This, they suggest, may be a partial explanation for why, "across preadolescent and adolescent female populations, African Americans experience the highest rates of HIV/AIDS transmission, [other sexually transmitted infections], multiple partners, unplanned pregnancy, nonvoluntary intercourse, sexual abuse, and earliest ages of sexual onset" (ibid., 48).

In addition, in contexts of extreme socioeconomic deprivation, there is compelling evidence that "sex work is permeating the very fabric of African American communities" (Collins 2006, 306), particularly in the form of informal sex-for-money exchanges, wherein young women "engage in casual sex with men" with the "unstated assumptions . . . [that they will] be rewarded with a little financial help" (Collins 2006, 309). As Patricia Hill Collins (2006, 310) explains, "from the outside, these behaviors may seem to be morally lax, yet the impoverished black women engaged in sex-for-money relationships desperately need the money." Moreover, the commodification of their sexuality may be particularly "difficult to disrupt in the context of a powerful mass media that defines and sells images of sexualized black women as one icon of seemingly authentic black culture" (Collins 2006, 310).

There are broader implications as well, negatively affecting multiple domains of the African American community: romantic relationships, relationship conflicts, and intimate partner violence between African American young women and men (Anderson 1999; Burton and Tucker 2009; Fosse 2010; Miller and White 2003); volatility in parents' relationships leading to disruptions in parenting, especially fathering (Augustine, Nelson, and Edin 2009; Edin, Tach, and Mincy 2009); and young women's ability to recognize their bonds with one another to construct a "collective identity" that fosters a "sense of shared belonging" (Small, Harding, and Lamont 2010, 18), and thus build solidarity and alliances, and enhance their collective efficacy as African American young women (Miller 2008; Reid-Brinkley 2008). Though not exclusively to blame for such a range of often deeply challenging outcomes, the cultural constructions of young black women as sexual objects is nonetheless profoundly connected to each of them.

Regarding relationships between young black women and men, for example, research has shown that the twin beliefs in male sexual entitlement and female sexual availability have led to a great deal of suspicion and distrust within relationships (Fosse 2010; Miller and White 2003). My research indicates that while both young women and young men are suspicious of infidelity within their relationships, young men are more likely to report actually being unfaithful in relationships, and they are much more successful in using their own and girls' suspicions to exert control within their relationships. The stigma associated with accusations of infidelity for girls limits its utility as a strategy of empowerment within relationships, while the legitimation of boys as "players" means it is a useful device within boys' gendered "toolkits" for negotiating power within romantic relationships. Moreover, such struggles within relationships lead to high rates of dating violence, often attributed to girls' "out of control" behaviors (see also Miller 2008; Miller and White 2003; Squires et al. 2006).

Such disruptions within relationships, though attributable to multiple additional causes, nonetheless contribute additional harms in the context of parenthood. Sociologist Kathy Edin and colleagues (2009, 152) note that "the role of the father outside the context of a conjugal relationship may be more strongly institutionalized in the black community." Rejecting the "package deal" of fatherhood tied to a romantic relationship with the child's mother can result in instability and fragility in fathers' relationships with their children.

Finally, the pervasiveness of cultural ideologies that blame African American girls is harmful in a myriad of ways for girls themselves. The young women we interviewed, for example, faced not just high rates of victimization, but few avenues—institutional, interpersonal, or cultural—to offer them support in coping with these experiences. Instead, they articulated an understanding, encapsulated in one young woman's adage: "Protect yourself, respect yourself. 'Cause if you won't, guys won't." The latter part of her adage referenced entrenched ideas about male sexual entitlement; the former—"protect yourself"—referenced girls' need, like boys', to develop "street smarts" within urban disadvantaged communities. But the middle facet of her lesson—"respect yourself"—was where perhaps the greatest risk for internalized harm lies for young women, as it is this notion, particularly in a limited resource context, that most leads to the explicit blaming of girls for their sexual mistreatment.

A number of black feminist scholars have analyzed the complicated history and implications of "respectability" among African American women (Collins 2004; Miller-Young 2008). Cultural studies scholar Shanara Reid-Brinkley (2008, 245) explains that while "the strategy of respectability" can destabilize and undermine "racist representations of black women and black people," it comes with particular costs. The "disciplinary character" of such expectations can create harms of their own, impacting both "black women's social allegiances" with one another (238) but also their sexual autonomy and agency: "[T]he 'good' black woman can only be intelligible as a performance if contrasted against the 'bad' black woman. Thus, some women are worthy of protection from misogynistic harassment and violence while other women deserve such treatment because of their performance of femininity" (252; see also Miller-Young 2008). As a consequence, gender inequalities are reinforced and reproduced.

This gendered "politics of respectability and the accompanying culture of silence around sexuality" (Stephens and Phillips 2005, 48) creates additional challenges for young black women living in impoverished urban communities. For example, the need for financial assistance as well as the demographic imbalance of gender ratios resulting from incarceration and violence (Wilson 2009) may lead to particular kinds of strategic choices vis-à-vis romantic and sexual relationships with young men that, combined with such ideologies, may put them at risk. This includes, for example, acquiescing to abusive relationships (Scott, London, and Myers 2002) or "engag[ing] in casual sex with men" with the hope or expectation of being "rewarded with a little financial assistance" (Collins 2006, 309). For this reason, Stephens and Phillips (2005, 48) note, "Collectively, these conflicting messages regarding appropriate behaviors around gender and sexuality indicate that adolescent African American women need distinctly different tools for negotiating their sexuality from women of other cultures."

Conclusion

How, then, might our scholarship be put to use to assist young, urban African American women and men to challenge and confront the gendered harms embedded in their daily lives and relationships, and contribute to reformulations of the cultural scripts behind these? To begin with, it is clear that any hope we have for lasting solutions must address the structural inequalities at the root of urban disadvantage. Such inequalities are not simply based on the race and class inequalities that pattern ecological disadvantage—they are deeply gendered as well. Thus, systematic, ecologically embedded strategies that attend to structural inequalities and build institutional supports for challenging gender inequalities and strengthening young women's efficacy are needed. For example, the MTO evaluation described earlier found that when families moved to neighborhoods with lower poverty, girls' psychological and behavioral outcomes were significantly enhanced. The primary explanations for these changes were decreases in sexual harassment and coercive sexual practices and concomitant feelings of increased safety (Popkin, Leventhal, and Weismann 2008, 2010). Likewise, improved gender responsiveness by the police and school personnel would provide much-needed institutional support for girls, and could help improve relationships within and across gender (Miller 2008).

But what role does culture play in all of this? My analysis here has focused on the most dominant cultural aspects of gender inequality among black youth. These are significant, as culture is meaningfully patterned sociologically across gender, race, and class boundaries. Yet, these cultural features do not constitute an "an all-encompassing, internally consistent, and coherent entity" (Young 2010, 54). In fact, recent research demonstrates that cultural processes, practices, and ideologies among urban black youth are much more heterogeneous than implied by a focus on the hegemonic (Harding 2010). As the sociologist Nathan Fosse (2010, 126) describes, an examination of the cultural logics that black youths articulate reveal "the ways in which culture is contingent, contradictory, indeterminate, and multivocal." Such findings point to sites that are potent for disruption and change. In addition, recognizing that culture does not simply happen to people also opens up new ways of thinking about social change. Engaging youth in critical consciousness-raising efforts, for example, can have meaningful results (Tolman, Hirschman, and Impett 2005; Wyatt 1992).

Moreover, recognizing, as cultural scholars do, "that individuals have access to a toolkit composed of multiple 'cultures' and that subtle priming activates particular cultural frames at particular times" (Fine and Fields 2008, 137) means that we can identify mechanisms for priming African American youth to activate cultural frames that *challenge* rather than reproduce gender inequalities, including the sexualized inequalities I emphasize in my analysis here. Because culture involves human agency, it represents an important site for intervention.

For example, one particularly disheartening finding is the extent to which young women adhere to ideologies blaming other female victims for male violence. Without broader social or institutional supports for addressing violence, they take ultimate responsibility for protecting themselves. The good news is that young women rarely apply such understandings to incidents involving their friends and loved ones. Instead, they describe taking steps to intervene, protect, and support them, and often hold young men—instead of their female loved ones—responsible. An important goal, then, is to find ways to generalize young women's empathetic recognition of their friends' experiences to women in general.

One avenue through which to do so is by assisting young women to "think critically about the messages and images" they receive about gender and sexuality (Tolman, Hirschman, and Impett 2005, 15). With such skills, individually and collectively, young women can develop recognition of their rights and boundaries in relation to young men, and "resist the dominant . . . stories through which their lives have been constructed" (Kenway and Fitzclarence 1997, 129). There are, in fact, promising examples of youth-driven, community-based efforts that assist young black women to collectively challenge gender-based harassment and violence (see Squires et al. 2006, 735–36). Feminist scholars often point to the strengths, resiliency, and independence of African American women (for example, see Collins 1990; hooks 1981). Such qualities have emerged in response to legacies of oppression and can be drawn upon to help young women create positive gender identities and relationships.

We must also identify avenues for disrupting the cultural rewards young black men receive for adhering to the harmful features of hegemonic masculinities in urban communities. Structural dislocations associated with disadvantage play an important role in shaping dominant features of masculinity for young men in poor urban neighborhoods. Thus, a particular challenge lies in providing them with alternative forms of status and prestige. One mechanism for doing so may be to enable their own critical consciousness about the harms adherence to such cultural ideals pose to themselves as well as to their loved ones, both male and female. Research shows that systematic efforts promoting empathy show promise for curtailing violence against women (Winkel and de Kleuver 1997). And, in fact, the young black men discussed in this chapter often demonstrate empathic understanding and are frequently protective of the women in their lives, including their mothers and sisters. Harnessing such empathy and seeking ways to generalize it—to prime compassionate cultural attitudes and beliefs—may offer promise.

Finally, it is critical that efforts do not simply target young women and men separately. Providing youths with opportunities for cross-gender friendships, activities, and discussions has been shown to reduce coercive sexual behaviors among African American young men and foster more egalitarian relationships (Kalof 1995). These offer "positive alternatives to the traditional masculinities that . . . [are] detrimental to the lives and health of both [young] women and men" (Truman, Tokar, and Fischer 1996, 560). Ultimately, our goals must be to harness those cultural features present in black communities to enhance youths' collective action, to facilitate their ability "to interpret their experiences as shared and to rethink their responses as mutual civic imperatives" (Squires et al. 2006, 735).

V

CULTURAL, SOCIAL, *and* MORAL TRIALS

12

Effects of Affluent Suburban Schooling

Learning Skilled Ways of Interacting with Educational Gatekeepers

SIMONE ISPA-LANDA, *Northwestern University*

Introduction

Middle- and upper-middle-class parents' and students' presumed ability to secure educational resources has long attracted public and scholarly attention, connected as it is to a historical legacy of white power and privilege, students' school success, and social reproduction (Lareau 2000; Rosenbaum 1976; Snyder 1973; Willis 1981). It has also been prominent in educational research, with an extensive literature demonstrating how parents' and students' skills in dealing with educational gatekeepers contribute to individual-level academic success and societal-level inequalities (Cucchiara and Horvat 2009; McGrath and Kuriloff 1999; Wells and Serna 1996).

Overall, this literature has stressed the need to consider how social class affects the resources that parents and students bring to their interactions with educational gatekeepers. Thus, qualitative examinations of family practice have dominated the study of upper-middle-class youth advantage (Lareau 2003). Researchers have reported on how middle- and upper-middle-class parents strategically interact with authority figures, especially those within educational institutions. They have also examined how these same parents explicitly coach their children on how to ask for information and attention from education professionals (Devine 2004; Lareau 2003).

In these accounts, schools are often depicted as sites that evaluate, reward, and punish students for cultural skills and dispositions they have acquired at home. Thus, this research misses a major topic of sociological inquiry: how not just families, but also schools, impart youth with

393

important skills, attitudes, and beliefs that, while not part of the official curriculum, powerfully influence students' lifelong achievement. In this chapter, I argue that a renewed focus on how schools act as transformative cultural agents contributes to educational research in two ways. First, it brings the literature on familial culture and educational inequality into greater alignment with research on school contexts and academic attainment.[1] Second, it leads to a more dynamic, accurate depiction of the relationship between privileged schools and their students. Schools, especially affluent suburban ones, provide students with valued cultural resources, including attitudes and beliefs about how to interact effectively with academic gatekeepers such as teachers and counselors.

In this chapter, I extend research on how familial social class position as well as school context contribute to the reproduction of inequality. I do so through an examination of how institutional standards within schools influence students' cultural orientations and skills for dealing with educational gatekeepers. I draw on ethnographic observations and in-depth interviews with two groups of urban black adolescents (in grades eight through ten) with similar familial backgrounds, but starkly different educational environments. Students in one group were enrolled in an urban-to-suburban integration program ($n = 38$) and bussed to schools in affluent suburbs where the majority of students are the children of upper-middle-class, white professionals. In contrast, members of the second group were waitlisted for the suburban integration program and attended low-performing, majority-minority public schools in the central city ($n = 26$).[2] Throughout the chapter, I call these two groups of students "bussed" and "waitlisted" students.

This comparison yielded three key findings. First, bussed students viewed school rules and procedures as malleable and variable. They believed it was possible and advantageous to use specific styles of communication to achieve a desired outcome—whether that be a higher grade, a different track placement, or an apology from a teacher who made a racially insensitive remark. In contrast, their waitlisted counterparts viewed school rules and procedures as fixed entities, with nonnegotiable, unequivocal, and often unpleasant consequences. Second, unlike waitlisted students, bussed students were much more willing to express attitudes and beliefs critical of teacher practices and school rules, frequently through humor, congeniality, or a sense of self-importance. Moreover, teachers and counselors often responded positively to bussed students' attitudes and beliefs, even when they disagreed with their claims. Finally, guidance counselors and other personnel in the suburbs promoted specific skills and beliefs regarding negotiation with authority. For example, coordinators and counselors in some affluent suburban schools (hired by the bussing program to serve the bussed students, but paid by the suburban school districts) explicitly informed bussed students about the strategies that could be used to positively influence other teachers, guidance counselors, and school administrators. Some guidance counselors in affluent suburban schools even attempted to "reform" girls in the bussed group by bringing them into closer compliance with what they believed to be middle-class or non-"ghetto" styles of feminine self-presentation.

This chapter is divided into three sections. First, I review previous research on education, culture, and inequality, focusing on two strands of research. One emphasizes how families and, to a lesser extent, schools impart class-specific cultural knowledge conducive to academic success. The other examines how the socioeconomic and ethnic context of privileged schools affects the academic outcomes of black youth. Second, based on my research, I suggest that, despite similar familial backgrounds, students exposed to upper-middle-class schools are at a distinct cultural advantage for success in professional milieus over those who are not. In the concluding sections of this chapter, I discuss the implications of these findings for current understandings of the consequences of familial background and school contexts. Specifically, I argue for a more dynamic framework for how youth acquire attitudes and beliefs conducive to academic achievement.

Prior Research on Education, Culture, and Inequality

Families, Schools, and Social Class Acculturation

In recent years, much qualitative research on educational inequality has focused on how parents and students interact strategically with important educational gatekeepers, such as teachers or school administrators. These studies have overwhelmingly found that middle- and upper-middle-class families, unlike those from lower classes, obtain desirable educational resources for their children. Researchers believe this is because of parents' assumptions about their personal privilege to such resources, skill in using the language of the experts, social ties with experts, and ability to mobilize collectively on their children's behalf (Brantlinger 2003; Devine 2004; Horvat, Weininger, and Lareau 2003).

While families are key sites of cultural transmission, an almost exclusive focus on that institution has meant that schools have been neglected as important sites of cultural influence (but see Ferguson 2000 and Stevens 2010 for applied exceptions). Two case studies stand out as notable exceptions, albeit in different ways: *Choosing Colleges,* by the education analyst Patricia McDonough (1997), and *Constructing School Success,* by the sociologist Hugh Mehan (1996). Both studies emphasize how students and parents interact strategically with educational gatekeepers. Further, they do so with a focus on the school as an institution where students' skills and orientations about how to interact with educational gatekeepers can be either reinforced or acquired.

In *Choosing Colleges,* McDonough (1997) compares the college guidance environments of high school seniors at four sites: a working-class public school, an upper-middle-class public school, a private preparatory school, and a Catholic school. She finds that each school counseling environment corresponds with the basic social class culture of the families it serves.

Depending on the class-specific cultures of the community, each school "presented different views of the college opportunity structure" that in turn "framed and enabled students' aspirations" (155). Thus, the curricula at the private preparatory school "is designed as college preparatory, assuming that students possess basic familiarity with and have family knowledge of college" (105). In McDonough's study, then, schools reflect and reinforce the class-based attitudes and beliefs that students have already acquired at home.

Similarly, in *Constructing School Success,* Mehan (1996, 212–13) focuses on how the school can be a site of cultural "transformation" and upward social mobility. In his research, Mehan examines how AVID, a tracking program for low-achieving high school students in the San Diego area, can interrupt key reproduction processes. The authors find that AVID coordinators often function in ways similar to the upper-middle-class parents Lareau (2003) studied, imparting valuable cultural skills and beliefs to students through explicit instruction and coaching. For example, Mehan demonstrates that AVID staff often mentor students "on ways to interact with teachers" (88) to obtain desirable academic outcomes. These findings reinforce the notion that education scholars can productively examine the school as a site of dominant cultural transmission.

While both studies examine the school as a site of cultural influence, they reflect two different sets of findings. In McDonough's study, schools primarily reinforced the class-specific attitudes and beliefs of students' families. In contrast, in the research by Mehan, schools offered AVID students a new and unfamiliar set of dispositions and skills, which the AVID students eagerly embraced as critical to educational attainment. However, they also found that when AVID students were viewed as ethnically and economically different and inferior to the rest of the student body, they associated academic success—as well as the styles of interaction with teachers that often lead to academic success—with forced assimilation.

School Contexts and Educational Achievement of Black Youth

Up to this point, I have suggested that schools may be a more powerful influence on students' skills in dealing with educational gatekeepers than indicated by previous research. Next, I turn to a body of research that examines explicitly how the school environment—most notably, its achievement level, proportion of same-race students, and overall socioeconomic composition—affects the educational outcomes of disadvantaged youth (Fuller-Rowell and Doan 2010). This research suggests that two factors in particular impede the academic success of urban black students in majority-white, suburban schools.

First, research on achievement and social acceptance suggests that black students bussed to suburban schools may be socially penalized for requesting access to scarce educational resources (such as placement in AP classes or assistance from a teacher). For instance, the sociologist Karolyn Tyson (2005) found that academically successful ethnic minorities and low-income whites in high-achieving, wealthy schools had trouble finding social acceptance. In these affluent schools, students associated academic success with belonging to the more privileged group. Thus, academically successful students belonging to the less privileged group (either low-income whites or African Americans) reported experiencing animosity and resentment from their equally disadvantaged peers, most of whom were not as successful academically. At the same time, academically successful students from low-income or minority backgrounds felt isolated and demeaned by their wealthier classmates. Their wealthier classmates seemed to question their presence in the high-track courses, perhaps out of feelings of competition.

Second, some research suggests that being in a predominantly white environment can impede black students' bonding with teachers (Alexander, Entwisle, and Thompson 1987; Crosnoe, Johnson, and Elder 2004; Johnson, Crosnoe and Elder 2001). For example, studies have shown a large negative association between the proportion of whites on the teaching staff and measures of African American student–teacher bonding (e.g., Crosnoe et al. 2004). This could be problematic for the academic success of black youth bussed to suburban schools. As the research by Mehan and colleagues demonstrated, teacher–student bonding can be a major conduit to valuable information about the educational system. Moreover, bussed students with poor bonds to teachers may not be open to learning about the opportunity structure from them. Similarly, teachers who are poorly bonded to their students may be less inclined to share informal knowledge about the school, treating them from a more purely formal standpoint. Thus, students with poor bonds to teachers may lack both opportunities and emotional incentives to learn the strategies often used by members of the middle- and upper-middle classes to secure scarce educational resources. Thus, in contrast to the case studies by McDonough as well as Mehan, research on school racial and socioeconomic composition and black students' academic success offers caution when thinking about the opportunities afforded to urban students bussed to upper-middle-class, suburban schools. It suggests a variety of reasons why, despite an apparently advantageous school context, urban black students bussed to upper-middle-class suburban schools may nonetheless be denied opportunities and incentives to learn the interactional styles and strategies that predominate in such contexts.

Research Questions

To examine how affluent suburban schools affect students' attitudes and beliefs about how best to interact with educational gatekeepers, I asked the following questions:

1. How do waitlisted and bussed students understand the opportunities provided by the school?
2. Are waitlisted students less assertive in their interactions with educational gatekeepers than suburban students? If these differences exist, what would explain them?

3. What are the mechanisms through which waitlisted and bussed students learn about the school and the informal ways they can influence their own outcomes (e.g., asking to be placed in a different class)?

In what follows, I first briefly describe the waitlisted students' experiences. Then I focus on the bussed students' school experience, highlighting their beliefs about the variability and malleability of school rules and procedures, their self-expression of critical attitudes and beliefs, and how suburban school staff promoted particular cultural skills and beliefs. Regarding the latter, I show that some counselors and suburban teachers worked with the bussed students to help them achieve an individualized education (i.e., one that takes into account their perceived educational or social needs) by giving them the "inside scoop" on school practices and culture, and training them in strategic self-assertion. These skills and opportunities helped the bussed students cope with racism and discrimination in the highly stratified, majority-white schools. In contrast, waitlisted students in urban charter and public schools perceived few opportunities to use "insider" knowledge to gain access to specialized educational resources, such as assistance on an assignment or alternative coursework.

Waitlisted Students: Lacking Knowledge and Opportunities

Waitlisted students depicted their schools as places in which all students were assigned to the same classes, with little variation in how students were treated. Many waitlisted students had never heard of honors or tracked classes, and said that the teachers "care about all the kids" and try to treat everyone "the same." The sense that the school had few "extra" or "secret" resources that could be devoted to deserving students probably contributed to an atmosphere where assertiveness about asking for special favors was neither necessary nor beneficial. Waitlisted students' comments also suggested that their teachers interpreted self-assertion as "sass" or "attitude."

There are two broad reasons for this difference, and both are important for understanding the mechanisms through which schools can create cultural orientations in students. First, teachers for the waitlisted students perceived challenges to teacher practice or authority as illegitimate, reacting harshly. As the next section shows, this was not true for the bussed students in suburban schools. Second, waitlisted students had fewer opportunities to cultivate skills in self-assertion than bussed students. As a result, their manner of voicing complaints may have been more likely to be interpreted as "attitude."

Indeed, in the schools attended by the waitlisted students, there was nothing analogous to the type of training in self-advocacy that I found in the suburban schools. Perhaps as a result, even when waitlisted students recognized that a bureaucratic mistake had been made, they usually tried to manage their own feelings about it, rather than correcting it, as the bussed students sometimes did. Also, whereas bussed students often consulted with teachers about how to handle difficult situations or choose their courses, the waitlisted students never spoke to their teachers about such issues. The only adults they reported speaking with about school issues were family members—older siblings, cousins, parents, grandparents, and aunts and uncles.

The idea of seeking a teacher's help in solving a problem seemed to be outside the waitlisted students' scope of awareness. More importantly, they seemed much less inclined to label undesirable events as "issues" or "problems" than the bussed students. For example, Reginald, age fifteen, really wanted to be a car mechanic when he grew up. As an eighth grader, he had applied to—and received admission to—The Mechanics School (a pseudonym), a citywide public school.[3] He was excited about the Mechanics School, because it offered hands-on training in fields related to his desired occupation. However, he "ended up" (his words) in a different school, one with a different emphasis (leadership development and service learning). Nonetheless, Reginald never sought to change his school placement, He did not seem to view his placement in the Peace Academy (a pseudonym) as a serious "problem" or "issue."

> INT: Is there anything you don't like about your school?
> Reginald: No, it's okay, I like it.
> INT: Have you ever thought about switching schools?
> Reginald: Yeah, when I first went, because I was supposed to go downstairs to engineers. But I ended up in that school, and they teach the same stuff, and it's fine.

Furthermore, none of the waitlisted students I interviewed mentioned that they had been sent from teacher to teacher in an attempt to make a better and more personally optimal decision about which courses to take. This was an experience that the bussed students often reported.

In addition, as the next section will show, the bussed students reported a variety of situations in which they drew on either humor, congeniality, or a sense of self-importance to express their attitudes and critical beliefs about teacher practices and school rules. Waitlisted students described a very different dynamic with their teachers. There was less of a sense of a "dialogue" or "conversation" about school rules and practices.[4] For example, Brittany, fifteen, a student at a high-poverty pilot middle school, complained that her teachers are always "saying that I should be a better role model, something like that. And then, whatever, whatever *(sighing)* . . ." She remarked that her teachers often rebuked her for what she called her "attitude," or a lack of ritual displays of deference toward authority:

INT: Who would you be a better model for?
Brittany: The sixth graders.
INT: Ooh. What do you think they have in mind? What would they like to see more of?
Brittany: Um, show 'em *[the younger kids at school]* a good example.
INT: Okay. But do you know what they like, what exactly they mean?
Brittany: Like not be loud in hallways, not give attitude, stuff like that.
INT: Okay. Why is it important to not be loud in the hallway, from their view?
Brittany: Because they say it make me look bad.
INT: Do you agree?
Brittany: No.
INT: You don't.
Brittany: No, because I know a lot of people who are loud.
INT: And it doesn't bother you?
Brittany: No! *[emphatically]* No.
INT: So what do they mean when they say don't give attitude? Because I hear teachers say that all the time, and like, I don't know what they mean.
Brittany: Like, they can say something, and you just give attitude to them. For no reason. Yeah.
INT: Do you think you do that, or . . . ?
Brittany: No. I think they give me attitude.

Later in the interview, it became apparent that Brittany lacks the opportunities for challenging authority that the bussed students are acquiring (or are encouraged to acquire). She admitted that she is "loud" and that she acts "rude" sometimes. These may be classic "oppositional" behaviors, and Brittany lacks the skills or opportunities for "refining" them into more socially acceptable protests against school practices and policies. Here, I am not suggesting that all the bussed students have these skills. Rather, I am claiming that all the suburban schools I studied had education professionals *intending* to give those skills to students. Further, bussed students' accounts indicate that, when they challenge school practices using the socially approved techniques, they are neither chastised nor rebuked.

By contrast, the waitlisted students appeared to lack opportunities to learn from adults about how to challenge school rules or authority in ways that would be acceptable to the adults around them. As a result, they may have appeared to be more "belligerent" to their teachers. Janjay, fourteen, a student at an urban charter school who complained she is often in detention, described a typical scenario:

> *INT:* That's annoying. Do you ever get in trouble?
> *Janjay:* No, not really. Just talking back.
> *INT:* Okay. Can you give an example of something you would talk back about?
> *Janjay:* My Spanish teacher tries to tell me I'm talking back in class, which I'm not really doing, so I defend myself, and I get in trouble for it.
> *INT:* Oh really? What happens?
> *Janjay:* Like she tries to tell me I'm talking to other kids in class, and I'm really not. Then I get aggravated with her, so I start saying mad rude stuff to her.

Another waitlisted student who was perpetually in detention, Amira, fourteen, echoed Janjay's story of how irritation and mutual mistrust between a teacher and student escalates into detention for the student. In Amira's account, getting a detention was final and could not be changed through persuasion:

> *INT:* So, like, what gets you in detention?
> *Amira:* For like . . . well sometimes they just give out detention if they are in a bad mood or something, and they, like, tell you to stop, and you're like, "I'm not doing anything," and then they think you're sass talking them, so they give you detention.

Waitlisted students also remarked that their complaints were not taken seriously. Micah, sixteen, told me that her teacher often teases her about how stressed she looks, saying that she "looks constipated" and should "smile" more often. It was evident that Micah communicated clearly to her teachers that she disliked the very strict atmosphere of the school. Nonetheless, Micah intimated that neither her teachers nor her parents took her complaints seriously and did not consider designing a more relaxed environment for her and her classmates:

> *Micah:* My teacher, she tells me I look constipated.
> *INT:* Laughing. Nu-uh!
> *Micah:* Yeah, she'll be telling me that and stuff! And I'm like, "Well, it's cause I'm coming to your class, and you have too many rules [Int note: can't go to the bathroom, can't eat snacks, can't drink water] in your class. It's like I'm in a jail cell or something!
> *INT:* Well it seems like you think there's too many rules. I mean, do you think you could get that changed somehow?
> *Micah:* No way! Are you kidding? Noooo way.

Reginald also described his school as a place where students' assertive questioning of teacher practices or school rules would ruin the fabric of student–teacher relations and lead to negative consequences. He noted a sense that, in his public charter school, students' obedience to school policy—to the rules that, as he says, the teachers "give"—is a necessary precondition for an atmosphere of trust.

> *Reginald:* At our school [a charter school], they teach a lot different I think, than at other high schools. Like they give us certain privileges, so long as we be respectful to the rules that they give . . . 'Cause usually, most schools aren't like that, 'cause they don't trust the kids enough.

Variability and Malleability of School Rules and Procedures

In contrast to the waitlisted students' schooling experiences, teachers and counselors in the suburban schools regularly exposed bussed students to several ideas that conventional wisdom associates with upper-middle-class parenting. First, institutions have particular cultures and differentiated resources, and it is possible and desirable to try to learn more about one's options by talking to people who are "in the know." Second, it is sometimes reasonable to challenge school authority and teacher practices. Finally, there are proper ways for challenging school authority.

Bussed students were keenly aware that, in the suburban schools they attended, there was substantial variation in how students were treated and evaluated (Ispa-Landa 2013). Furthermore, there was a widespread perception that black students, especially those from the city, were automatically sorted into the lowest-achieving tracks.[5] Given these perceptions, the more ambitious bussed students strategized about how best to extract valuable resources from teachers and counselors and sought hints from counselors and other teachers about how best to do so. In fact, a heightened sensitivity to differences in how students were treated resulted in negative feelings about teachers and counselors who "played favorites." For example, Jade, 15, complained:

> *Jade:* I don't like her [a particular counselor]. Like, she tries to hide stuff from kids, like a lot of kids see this about her. Like if there's something going on—like the other day, there was going to be a tour of the [high] school for the kids in middle school . . . and she always makes up excuses to just passively blow you off, like she'll say, "Oh, I have too many people already," or like . . . if there are field trips, she'll be picky-choosy with only the people she wants to go. Like the people who really want to go, she won't have a list. She'll just go and search for the people she wants.

Perhaps the most obvious symbol of a school with differential opportunities is the existence of course tracks (Tyson 2011), and indeed all of the suburban schools had course tracks. Nonetheless, many bussed students told me that they regularly sought guidance and advice from teachers about their course placement. They also reported that their teachers had "sent them" to other teachers to help them make more informed decisions. Take, for example, Dennis's story below about how he decided not to take honors physics. At his suburban school, at least some of his teachers are modeling a worldview in which it is desirable and perhaps even necessary to "get the scoop" about various educational options and resources from other school adults:

> *Dennis:* I talked to some of my teachers about [taking honors physics next year], and it's like, after talking to them about it, I was just like, I don't think I want to do that [take honors] next year.

INT: What did they say?

Dennis: Like, um, my history teacher, he was like, well, you're on the line. Like, you're a really good student, but honors could be kind of tough for you. I was like, "Oh." She was like, you would have to come in for help on your writing, and I was like, well, mmmm, I don't know. And then my physics teacher was like, "Why don't you do honors physics?" cause normally, physics is the hardest subject, but this year, I've been breezing through it . . . and umm, so he had actually, so like he, he had me go talk to this other teacher, who's also like, kind of like my mentor.

Dennis's experiences were typical. Many bussed students reported that teachers modeled a worldview for them in which they had multiple options, and in which they could optimize their chances for a successful outcome through proper information and self-assertion.

Other students told me that they had challenged teacher decisions about which course to take, especially because, in their perception, black students were automatically assigned to the "low" or "stupid" tracks. They expressed their frustration with their course placement to their teachers and guidance counselors, who—at least from the stories they told—appeared responsive to student requests:

Ebo: Well, like when you start out at the high school, they put the black kids in the stupid classes. Like if you're bussed in and going to Hampton High [pseudonym], they put you in the stupidest classes ever. Like Pre-Algebra 1?! Like I can do that stuff; I'm not that stupid!

INT: Oh, is that what they did to you?

Ebo: That's what they did to me, and it's like, I'm not that stupid! So I moved up in math . . . and then like in English, they have like two English classes for freshman year, retarded English, English 2, and mediocre English, which is English 1. And I got out of retarded English, too.

INT: So how did you get out of being in the stupid classes?

Ebo: I just, well, most of the teachers that had me thought I was really smart, by the way I talk, and the grades I get. 'Cause even though I would get like a C for the overall grade, the homeworks were good, and like, I just do bad on the quizzes, but everything else, like my work ethic, it was spectacular to them. And they really liked the way I worked. Even my guidance counselor—she knew I wasn't dumb, like first sight of me. So I asked to get out of the stupid classes.

In short, bussed students not only perceived substantial variability in school rules and procedures, but they also viewed them as malleable through self-assertion.

Self-Expression of Critical Attitudes and Beliefs

Race relations in the affluent suburban schools were problematic and complex (see Ispa-Landa 2013). Nonetheless, bussed students reported a variety of situations in which they drew on either humor, congeniality, or a sense of self-importance to express critical attitudes and beliefs about teacher practices and school rules. Repeatedly, their reports demonstrated that teachers responded positively, either by teasing the student back or through serious attention. These reports suggested a climate where students' self-expression was generally encouraged. Sometimes, this came out in discussions of teachers, when bussed students would describe particular teachers as "funny" or "hilarious." For example, take the following account by Karla, age thirteen:

> INT: So we talked about school, but I'm wondering if you could describe it a little more. Just like in general, how would you describe it?
> Karla: Boring, most of the time, but our teachers are so funny! Like last week, we were in class, and then um Janet, I was sitting next to her and we were talking, and then our teacher, Mr. Hogarty, he was like teaching us with a movie. So were watching this stupid movie, and then I was like, "Mr. Hogarty, why are we watching this movie and you're not teaching us?" And he was like, "Why do you have no friends and you're such a loser?" and like—he's hilarious.

Karla's account of how her teacher responded to her joking critiques of him reveal a very particular school culture. When compared to the waitlisted students' reported experiences, the bussed students' accounts indicate that teachers in affluent suburban schools promoted and cultivated students' sense of agency and control over their education—whether this is expressed in terms of questioning course placement or playfully challenging classroom practice.

When students raised more serious concerns, such as racial dynamics in the classroom, they reported that their teachers sometimes listened, even though teachers' responsiveness did not ameliorate their overall feeling of racial injustice. For example, Apryl, a fifteen-year-old bussed student, told me about a series of tense interactions she has had with her history teacher. Perhaps most remarkably, Apryl reported that she "corrected" the teacher, and that, far from rebuking her for her "attitude," he ended up apologizing to her.

> *Apryl:* So like in my history class, a couple of months ago, a kid, a white student, was talking to the teacher. And I guess he was using slang, and the teacher said, "You're not black." And I was really offended, so I called the teacher out, because he made it sound as if all black people have to say what he [the white kid] said. And he [the teacher] said, "Oh, I made a mistake." And I told him it was a mistake because you didn't correct yourself. I had to correct you; otherwise you would have gone about your business as if you said nothing wrong.
>
> *INT:* So what did he, so what, so what happened?
>
> *Apryl:* After class ended, he like called my name out, but I was really heated, so I stormed out, and the class was over anyway.
>
> *INT:* Wow. You were pissed, huh?
>
> *Apryl:* Right, yeah. The next day, I didn't come to school because I was sick. So the next day after that, he saw me in the hallway, and he said, "Sorry about what I said in class. I have to be more careful about the things I say." And then I was like, "Yeah." I think he was expecting me to say, "Oh, it's alright," but I didn't. So, from then on, well I was always quiet in that class to begin with, but ever since then, I lost a lot of respect for him. And he kind of knows that, so it's . . . whatever.

Apryl also reported that she had told her guidance counselor about the incident, and that they had talked through some of her "options" in how she could deal with it. The teacher's reaction to Apryl could have been the result of being in an environment where student and parent complaints about racially charged comments could lead to teacher dismissal. It is also reasonable to think that Apryl feels she lost the battle—as her "whatever" comment indicates, and her other comment that she is just "quiet" in that class now. Nonetheless, the described sequence of events indicates that she was in an environment where it was not considered belligerent to raise concerns. In Apryl's suburban school, she had the right to verbally challenge her teacher, and he displayed at least a symbolic responsiveness to this challenge; he apologized. The teacher did not reprimand Apryl for expressing her concerns. In fact, none of the adults at her school who were aware of the incident told Apryl that she had "attitude," was showing "sass," or should get detention for "talking back"—common responses to analogous behavior in the waitlisted students' schools.

In sum, bussed students in the suburban schools I studied freely expressed critical attitudes and beliefs regarding teacher practices and school rules, often using congeniality, humor, or a sense of self-importance. Moreover, even when officials disagreed with the students' interpretation of events, as was the case with Apryl, the teachers and guidance counselors did not overtly silence the students. They may not have responded adequately (for instance, by seeking to challenge problematic racial ideologies and practices within the school), but they also did not tell the student that it was inappropriate for him/her to raise concerns.

Training in Self-Advocacy by Education Professionals

Many coordinators working for the bussing program believed that it was part of their job to help the bussed students acquire skills in "self-advocacy." By this, they meant the ability to effectively negotiate with educational gatekeepers whose speech styles and orientations were decidedly middle- or upper-middle class. This training sometimes took place informally, as counselors chatted with bussed students in their offices. It happened formally, too—for example, at a conference for bussed middle school students on how to handle the transition to high school. At this conference, teachers and administrators constantly talked about the importance of "self-advocacy" and "stepping out of your comfort zone" in high school.

The following excerpt from my field notes describes the techniques that Ms. J, an African American drama teacher at one of the suburban high schools, used to impart these self-advocacy skills to bussed eighth-grade students about to enter high school. For her panel, she read vignettes—

problem situations—aloud, and asked the students to come up with what she called "appropriate" responses. Each vignette she read described situations where a student could achieve a better outcome through practices and styles of self-assertion and attention seeking that, according to conventional wisdom, upper-middle-class parents teach their children, both consciously and through everyday modeling. Most of the vignettes were about situations where implicit stereotypes about black people as inferior or delinquent seemed to drive teachers' behavior.

Here are the vignettes that she read aloud to the students:

> *Vignette 1:* You were moved to a higher-level math class because of good grades. The teacher in the new class asks if you are supposed to be there. What should you do?
> *Vignette 2:* The teacher asks a question in class. You are the only one who raises their hand. The teacher doesn't call on you; she waits for others to raise their hands. This happens several times. What should you do?
> *Vignette 3:* Your teacher hands back a language arts essay. You tried really hard. You thought it was really good! It turns out you got a C–. What do you do?
> *Vignette 4:* The assistant principal finds graffiti with the word "URBAN" outside a classroom. She accuses you of doing it, because you're the only student from the city in that classroom.

The students were quite involved in this session, calling out answers and interrupting each other. Through her responses, it was clear that Ms. J was trying to help the students learn strategies and skills for self-assertion that would get positive results in the affluent, majority-white suburban schools, where they might be penalized for calling attention to racial discrimination, but benefit from letting teachers they know they were concerned about their individual success as students.

In Vignette 3 (receiving a C–), Ms. J approved of Renaldo's response—to ask the teacher for a meeting, go over her comments, and "bring the grading rubric with you to the appointment and stuff." Renaldo's response showed his implicit knowledge about teachers' interest in maintaining an appearance of fairness and objectivity by using grading rubrics. It also showed his fluency with a class culture where it is good when students come to meetings prepared to strategize with the teacher, even if it involves a grading dispute. Finally, Renaldo's response indicated his sense of entitlement to teacher attention and respect, another set of dispositions cultivated in suburban schools.

Ms. J also validated students' use of strategic self-assertion when listening to their responses to Vignette 4 about the graffiti incident. When one girl said, "Tell her you didn't do it!" Ms. J asked her to "role-play" the incident with her, asking her, "Do you think she would like it if you were kind of yelling?" Then Ms. J asked Andre what he would do. He said, "I would just say, 'It wasn't me,' and then just walk away." Then another boy said he would "name the people" who did it, because maybe they were trying to get him in trouble. Ms. J asked how much time he would want to put into thinking about that. Finally, another student raised his hand and said, "I would say I didn't do it, and I don't feel right being accused." Ms. J wrapped the session up by saying, "There are a lot of cases where you might have to advocate for yourself in high school; you might have to advocate for yourself right now, for getting recommendations to be in advanced-level courses in high school, and you have to think about how you want to do it."

In my interviews with them, other coordinators working for the bussed students (those not at the self-advocacy conference) confirmed that they believe that lessons in "self-advocacy" within the suburban school context are necessary, especially for students from nondominant groups who may face racial discrimination. I am not suggesting that bussed students lack skills in self-advocacy—they do learn self-advocacy skills at home and from their relatives. However, these self-advocacy skills may not apply in the upper-middle class, predominantly white suburban context, and that is where the coordinators came in. For example, Miss Jackson, a coordinator working for the bussed students at one of the suburban schools, said she makes it her personal mission to let the bussed students know about the manners they will need to ensure that their attempts at "self-advocacy" are well received:

> *Miss Jackson:* This is—is not just about—it's about the academics, yes. But it's about the whole child. So when you leave here, when you leave [school], I want you to be polished and ready to attack the world and say, "Here I am." . . . You know, the majority of us [coordinators] are women, black females, strong. . . . So like, we know, I know how this works, and ain't everybody gonna love you just like

that [like how you are when you're just being how you would be with your friends from home or your family, and not trying to get ahead in the white man's world].

In short, teachers and counselors in the suburban schools regularly exposed bussed students to several ideas that conventional wisdom associates with upper-middle-class parenting. First, institutions have particular cultures and differentiated resources, and it is possible and desirable to try to learn more about one's options by talking to people who are "in the know." Second, it is sometimes reasonable to challenge school authority and teacher practices. Finally, there are proper ways for challenging school authority.

Discussion and Conclusion

Schools as Agents

The findings presented here suggest that in addition to (and perhaps alongside) punishing or rewarding students for the styles of interaction and cultural knowledge they have learned at home or in the neighborhood, schools may also add and layer cultural knowledge and dispositions. Most importantly, I found that in at least some affluent suburban schools, some adults, far from simply rewarding upper-middle-class styles and dispositions, actively taught the students *how* to acquire them. In this way, schools can be culturally transformative agents. To extend the findings of Mehan (1996) and others who have viewed the school as a potentially "transformative" space, I outline here the mechanisms underlying the active inculcation of attitudes and beliefs by teachers and counselors in the suburban schools I studied.

Specifically, in the affluent suburban schools I studied, black guidance counselors and program coordinators, most of whom were female, had a unique "insider/outsider" sensibility. They identified with the bussed students and shared with them an "outside" position of being black in majority-white suburbs. Many (but not all) of the coordinators used this shared outsider position as a platform from which—in their view—they could speak to the bussed students about the ways of middle- and upper-middle-class whites.

Previous research has explored the effects for black students of having black teachers. Findings suggest that having black teachers positively affects the academic achievement of black students (e.g., Crosnoe, Johnson, and Elder 2004). Here, I found that having same-race mentors[6] allows for effective mentoring. Program coordinators' efforts to teach the bussed students skills and strategies were bolstered by their shared background; they knew and had compassion for where their students were "coming from." As a result, they could more effectively tell them where they were going and how to get there.

These experiences contrast greatly with those of the waitlisted students. The sociologist Kathryn Neckerman (2007) has written about the ways in which the decisions of senior educational administrators and superintendents led to inferior and damaging school conditions for generations of black students in Chicago, leading to a legacy of mistrust and resentment. Similarly, the waitlisted students' accounts of their school experiences and run-ins with their teachers evoked a pervasive sense of mistrust. The waitlisted students appeared to be locked in mutually disrespectful standoffs with teachers—recall, for example, Brittany's statement that her teachers give her "attitude," even as they accuse her of doing the same.

What is somewhat counterintuitive, given the model of schooling that has emerged from recent qualitative work on social class and the family, is that bussing coordinators and counselors are able to help adolescents learn new cultural orientations and skills for dealing with educational gatekeepers. In what follows, I discuss how these findings fit into larger debates about what racial integration should and can achieve, suggesting that processes of class socialization can be a critical aspect of the racial integration experience. Further, as I argue, it is this class socialization that may be producing some of the positive outcomes we associate with racial integration.

Racial Integration as a Social-Class Immersion Experience

Another implication of the findings in this chapter is to rethink racial integration as an experience in social class immersion. A large body of research has examined how especially gifted students from disadvantaged backgrounds benefit from attending elite institutions (Cookson and Persell 1991; Kuriloff and Reichert 2003). I extended this research by focusing on a sample of students attending not elite schools, but rather, suburban, majority-white schools more representative of the typical affluent suburban American educational experience.

Minority students selected for admission at top prep schools are probably extraordinarily academically gifted, which differs from the bussed students I studied. Bussed students are more ordinary; many of them would not be eligible for scholarships at top prep schools. As adults, the more average bussed students might rely even more heavily on social skills and the ability to effectively negotiate social situations than extraordinarily bright youth at elite institutions. Academically gifted youth could have the raw talent to make it to the top of certain types of professions, regardless of their cultural skills. However, the bussed youth I discussed in this chapter might be getting a boost for obtaining the types of jobs—increasingly important in a service-dominated American economy—that require excellent communication skills, leadership ability, self-advocacy, and so forth. Thus, the explicit class socialization that I described in this chapter is probably especially important for the types of students that racial integration and bussing programs attract—academically ambitious, but, for the most part, not academically eligible for elite institutions. In developing these findings, I found it useful to view the bussing program as an experience of social-class immersion—a perspective I urge future researchers to consider when thinking about different types of educational opportunity programs.[7]

Accordingly, as this chapter shows, bussed students gained a sense of privilege and entitlement from attending upper-middle-class suburban public schools. Here, a key finding was that counselors and teachers in the suburban schools engaged in explicit class socialization, training their students in how and when to negotiate with authority. This often-ignored advantage has not been previously discussed by scholars within the context of racial integration, nor has it been discussed in debates about how opportunity programs can improve the life chances of urban youth who may not have the test scores to win coveted spots in top private schools.

13

"Try On the Outfit and Just See How It Works"

The Psychocultural Responses of Disconnected Youth to Work

ORLANDO PATTERSON, *Harvard University*
JACQUELINE RIVERS, *Harvard University*

Introduction

One of the defining features of disconnected youth is their chronic unemployment and/or absence from the formal workforce. Many studies have attempted to explain their unemployment in structural terms, or from the perspective of employers' requirements and attitudes (Wilson 1987, 1996; Waldinger 1999; Waldinger and Lichter 2003; Holzer 1996; Wacquant 2008; Pager 2007). Others, a much smaller group, have explored the problem from the perspective of the disconnected, their subjective understanding of why they remain out of work (Anderson 1999, 120–124, 244–5; Young 2003; Venkatesh 2006; Carter 2005). This study works in the phenomenological tradition and attempts to extend what has been found in several ways.

We report findings from a study of chronically unemployed youth who participated in a training program that attempted to prepare them for work in the formal sector by changing their attitudes, values, and norms relating to work and providing them with basic cultural (soft) skills required by employers for entry-level low-skill jobs: presentation of self, dress code, attitudes toward punctuality, interpersonal relations, authority relations, and so on. What this meant was that for several weeks our subjects were trained to think seriously about, and attempt to change, fundamental aspects of their personal beliefs. To the degree that beliefs about

415

work impinge upon most other areas of a person's normative and evaluative belief structure, the exercise had wider significance. It is rare for sociologists to be presented with such subjects, and we attempted to utilize
the opportunity as best we could by studying four research questions.

First, how do the chronically unemployed explain their own failure to
find and keep work?

Second, what norms and values do they espouse, and how do they reconcile these with their work experience? Several previous studies had reported
that, in spite of profound differences from mainstream norms and values
in certain domains and their preference for engagement in the underground economy, disconnected inner-city youth nonetheless espoused
several central mainstream values and normative beliefs such as individualism, materialism, the importance of hard work, and responsibility for
their actions and life outcomes (Wilson 1996, 67–70; Young 2003,
137–45; Cohen 2010, 53). We sought to replicate this seemingly paradoxical finding and further understand it.

Third, to what degree did their street culture configuration conflict with
the attempt to change their work beliefs? In particular, did they view the
program's goals as an assault on their personal, street, or racial identity?

Finally, given their unusual experience in self-examination and normative change, did they develop any broader ethnocognitive and ethnosociological folk theories about their condition?

This last question gets at several central issues raised in ethnomethodology. We follow Garfinkel in assuming that subjects are not "cultural
dopes." Likewise, we agree that one of the puzzles of ordinary life is
people's ability to cognitively retrieve, use, and conceal the complex repertoire of cultural knowledge structures that go into their day-to-day lived
experiences and interactions (Berger and Luckmann 1966; Garfinkel 1967;
Adler and Adler 1987). People hide—often unwittingly, sometimes deliberately—the complexity of their actions, their psychocultural work, so to
speak, both in their interactions and in their reflexive accounts of what
they have accomplished, through the cunning strategy of making the
"familiar, commonplace activities of everyday life recognizable as familiar,
commonplace activities" and thereby not easily discernible (Garfinkel
1967, 9). There are several ways of uncovering these psychocultural strategies. One is the methodological technique of "[making] trouble,"
through breaching experiments that question the coherence and adequacy
of common background knowledge (Garfinkel 1967, ch. 2). Another is to
find naturally occurring, unusual situations that force people into rare

levels of self-revelation, an example being Garfinkel's study of passing by Agnes, a transgendered woman, which revealed the hidden complexities of accomplishing gender in everyday life and its role as a powerful background expectancy in both ordinary and professional relationships (Garfinkel 1967, 118). We consider the experience of our subjects in the ABC program to be of this second type and will report on the ethnosociological reflections of several of the more articulate.

The chapter is organized as follows. Section 2 introduces the ABC training program, summarizing its basic goals and methods. Section 3 reports our respondents' accounts of their work histories, followed, in section 4, by their attitudes toward mainstream work norms and values and their explanations of why they have failed to live up to them. Section 5 reports respondents' reactions to the ABC training program, its effectiveness in changing their work attitudes, and their assessment of the degree to which it conflicts with their ethnic and class identities. Section 6 presents respondents' own ethnosociological theory of their social world, what the ABC training program meant to them, and how they would negotiate the mainstream world of work in light of what they had learned, followed by our outsider sociological view of their ethnotheory and its implications. We end with a brief coda.

ABC and Its Youthful Clients

ABC is a cultural and attitudinal training program designed to prepare the most difficult-to-employ inner-city residents for a successful work experience. The program is a national enterprise with sites in nineteen cities. ABC Boston was the fourth site, established in 1994. The target population is youth who have had very unstable job histories. There is a focus on participants' identifying and taking personal responsibility for decisions they have made that have contributed to their being unemployed. The program develops a work-oriented, "no-excuses" attitude in clients, focusing on the soft skills that poor black youth are often said to lack (Holzer 1996, 54–66, 80–88; Wilson 1996, ch. 5; Newman 1999, 89–97). Graduates are provided with lifelong technical support and some job counseling in their job searches. The goal is to help each graduate get and retain a job, and to ultimately climb the career ladder to "the job"—a stable position with a decent wage and full benefits. The ABC workshop lasts five weeks, including three weeks of training and two weeks dedicated largely to the job search process.

Key to the program is the attitudinal and normative training, which exposes participants to rigorous tests of self-control, coaches them in strategies to manage their emotions in the workplace, and trains them to present an appropriate appearance and demeanor at all times. Activities explicitly aim to increase self-confidence and comfort with public speaking, produce standardized résumés, provide interviewing experience, and develop academic skills. There is concurrently an attempt to create a therapeutic setting intended to foster emotional healing. Consequences for infractions can be severe; violations of the behavior code, such as lack of participation, insubordination, or failure to appear in proper business attire, can result in termination from the program.

Twenty-five youthful inner-city clients participated, sixteen of them males and all but one (a Latino) black. (For a tabular summary of basic demographic data, see the appendix to this chapter.) All but two respondents reported a troubled school history, and several were significantly involved with violence in school. Fourteen had dropped out of high school, and only eleven had at least a high school diploma. Although five had some exposure to college, none had attained a college diploma. Twenty of the twenty-five participants in the sample had a criminal record of some sort, ten of whom described substantial involvement in a criminal life-style. Four had been on probation only as juveniles, five as adults. Two had been detained as juveniles and nine had been incarcerated as adults. Respondents were mainly from poor or working-class families in inner-city neighborhoods. Only three had been raised by both parents, and over half had little or no contact with their fathers by the time they were teenagers. Many mothers were described as either overindulgent or uncaring, though four mothers were strongly praised. Respondents reported very limited and troubled work experiences. Seven of the twenty-five never held a job; only four had experienced any kind of consistent employment, and even these changed jobs frequently. After correcting for incarceration spells (and in one case health issues), the median proportion of time respondents had held a job after leaving high school was 21 percent. Incarceration spells and involvement with crime were important factors contributing to lack of work experience.

One of the researchers visited the ABC Boston site several times per week, an average of four hours each time, for a total of twelve weeks. Three workshop cycles, serving approximately sixty participants, were observed in the spring of 2010. Interviews were also conducted with trainers, the executive director, and the former assistant director of the program. Although ABC has a high attrition rate, all but one of the ABC participants interviewed completed it. The population served by ABC is extremely mobile and unpredictable. Many of the individuals who participated in the orientation for each of the three training cycles observed did not show up for the first day of the training cycle, and many more did not graduate when each cycle ended five weeks later. Interviews were conducted at the program site to enhance access to participants. Once individuals dropped out of the program, it became extremely difficult for the researchers to contact them; as a result, only one individual who did not complete one of the three cycles was successfully recruited for an interview. One respondent had dropped out of the program in an earlier cycle but completed it during the observation period. The one program dropout who was interviewed did not appear to differ in any important way from the others who were interviewed, though she seemed to have had less success dealing with the anger issues that were common in the sample.

Respondents' Accounts of Their Work Records

Respondents emphasized four main sets of factors accounting for their job failures.

Problems with Authority Figures

Most of our interviewees reported that they had difficulty conforming to the normative expectations of those in authority over them. About a quarter of them experienced conflict (with their supervisors or, less frequently, coworkers) severe enough to lead to job termination or voluntarily leaving a position. Frieda, a young drug dealer, explained it this way:

> And the one thing that really, really affected me, even in life, was my attitude. Like, somebody telling me what to do, or basically, somebody telling me something I just don't want to hear.

Henry, though a graduate of a respected suburban school district where he had been a popular and, it appears, adequate student, had dropped out of college and never held a steady job. He lost two jobs that he held very briefly, one due to an altercation with the owner of the store where he worked:

I was doing my job, but I was still kind of training with them, and in other words [the owner] was still hovering over my shoulder, and with me, it was, I felt like he didn't trust me. And he said that to my face, so we had a little, you know, discussion, and he started getting loud to me while I was still trying to maintain a professional, you know, volume, in a relationship with him, but I guess he was getting so mad, and then I started getting aggravated and agitated, and then I felt, you know, he started disrespecting me in the workplace for that, so I was like, you know, I quit, I'm not gonna deal with this. So we got into this little argument, and then I just left.

Unreliability and Instability

Unreliability, an issue frequently cited by employers (Wilson 1996, 113), was another problem that respondents readily admitted to us, as they have done to other researchers (Young 2003, ch. 2). Sarah was typical:

So [my supervisor] just kind of like brushed me off like, "Oh, whatever, like, you are not important." So I said all right, I am not going to do my job. I am going to do what I want to do on my time, and that's what ended up happening. I just came in when I wanted to because everybody else was doing it. . . . One day I looked up the schedule wrong, and I called them, and I am like, "I am on my way"; he's like, "Oh, you are fired." "Why?" He's like, "Oh, you were supposed to be here at eight o'clock this morning."

Closely related to unreliability is instability or an unwillingness to stick to a job, even when it is moderately well paid and there are no problems with employers or coworkers. Ralph, an apparently competent worker, who was frequently called in for extra shifts and made store manager at a large, national shoe retailer, quit several jobs, including his position as a manager, moved out of state, ended up homeless, and became involved with crime:

And I quit after seven months and a half [at a national fast food chain]. . . . The manager just got on my nerves . . . even though he got on my nerves, he was kind of like, a cool boss, because you know, I got more hours, even though on my days off, he was always calling me and ask me if I wanted to work. . . . I wasn't fast like him. He wanted me to have like,] speed. . . . And then we had a district manager that . . . would always come down and say, oh, this is not clean, come and clean this again, and she would just find a lot of stuff. So I went and got a job at [a national shoe retail store].

Being Disrespected and Lacking Respect

Issues centering on respect figured prominently in explanations for their work experience, as one would expect in light of its importance in their street cultural configuration (see Chapter 2 in this volume; cf. Anderson 1999, ch. 2; Young 2003, 92). Often this entailed a sense of grievance about not being respected by employers (and thus is related to problems with authority discussed above), but just as often it related to coworkers. It also involved their own lack of respect for the jobs they held. Elizabeth, who admitted that "my temper doesn't allow me to finish anything," recalled an incident that led to her being fired:

> I did get fired from the job, because the supervisor—I'm the type of person that, it's like, you're sitting here at the register, and there's no reason for me, if I'm coming over to reach over you, to just rudely keep reaching my hand, so I said to the supervisor, "You're being really rude. Every time you want to come over here, you just jump right in front of me." I said it to her nicely the first time, and then, I guess she just—she was just so rude, she didn't care. So she just kept doing it every day, and I was like, "Jasmine, you need to have a little bit more respect." You know, because she was in a manager's position, and she was younger than me, also, but she was in a manager's position so I used to respect her. Like, all right, I'm just going to— because I'm trying to keep my job. But one day, she was trying to do something, and she just like, reached over, but it was like, it was so close to my face, you almost poked me, you know what I mean? And I just blew up on her. I just blew up. And I got fired. We both got fired, actually. But I got fired for that.

It is worth noting that many respondents were able to find jobs when they felt up to it—only seven of them had not worked after leaving high school—rather, they regarded these jobs as not worth keeping. In this regard, they differ from the disconnected youth studied by others (Alford 2004, 92–95, 150–154; Wacquant 2008, 70–74; Wilson 1996, ch. 1). Respondents' reports that job availability was not their main problem is consistent with the recent finding that Boston and San Diego had the lowest percent (13.1 percent and 12.1 percent, respectively) of disconnected youth in all metropolitan areas of the nation (Measure of America 2011). Frequently, they simply quit their jobs or engaged in job-threatening disputes over grievances that seemed trivial or work conditions they considered too onerous (cf. Wilson 1996, 141).

Involvement with Illegal Activities

The strong pull of the *apparent* profitability (Levitt and Venkatesh 2000) and the ready availability of illicit activity greatly influenced the work experience of many of our respondents, not only because of employers' reluctance to hire persons with a prison record but because of the contempt for their jobs engendered by engagement in the illegal economy (see also Anderson 1992; Alford 2004; Venkatesh 2006). As noted earlier, over half of our sample had criminal records. The convenient option of selling drugs undermined the incentive for some respondents to persist in the low-wage jobs they held. Seven of them either quit jobs to engage in crime or led double lives centered on criminal activity, in which a legitimate occupation was a secondary concern. Three of the ten respondents who were habitually involved in crime reported that the entry-level service jobs they held, in most cases briefly, were merely to mask the fact that they were selling drugs or getting money from other criminal activity. Only one man who had been regularly involved in selling drugs took his day job seriously, probably because it paid $500 a week while he was still in high school. Thus, Jim was frequently late for work due to his street life, and after quitting what he himself considered a good job, he didn't look for another, choosing to sell drugs instead:

> I was late quite a few times. That's probably a part to do with my street life that I was living, because I was up all hours of the night, running errands, and I used be late. . . . [After quitting without notice], I continued selling drugs.

Nelson also quit his last, low-paying job because of his conviction that he could earn more in illegal activities: "And I was like, forget this, I'm gonna go sell drugs." John told of getting a job to distract his mother from his illegal activity:

> I'm just goin' be real with you, like, I was never serious about work, to be honest with you, I was like *(laughs)* I was selling drugs, and my

mother got . . . started getting suspicious, and I just pretty much got that job, you know, those jobs, to throw her off track, like, you know . . . but I didn't take neither of them seriously.

In two cases, illegal activities were taken to the workplace. Nelson, a college dropout who had just completed a seven-year term for armed robbery, seemed rueful as he described being fired for stealing on one job and having walked out on another after stealing a small amount of cash. Matt, the other case, presents a more complex figure, refusing or unable to see anything wrong in activities he reported doing that were clearly illegal. He had been on the edge of hustling his whole life. His grandfather had introduced him to the underground economy at an early age, having the boy count cash for him as he sold bootleg alcohol in the park. His uncles were "in the streets," one as an armed robber. Matt saw his father infrequently, but he knew that in addition to having a job, his father was a hustler. Only Matt's grandmother and mother worked. Matt, nonetheless, had a more substantial work history than many of the other ABC youth. A community college dropout, he had experienced brief employment spells and held two full-time jobs with benefits for almost a year each time before quitting. On his last job before "stepping off the porch" and joining his uncles in serious drug dealing, Matt engaged in what he presented as common practice at his job, valet parking customers' cars. He would allow some drivers to park on the street in spots reserved for valet parking but waive the fee in exchange for a tip in cash paid to him. When recounting that he was fired for this behavior, he maintains, first, that it was a common practice, which the new manager decided to change, then that he merely forgot to give the customers their tickets, and, finally, that he was fired for racial reasons. Nonetheless, it is interesting that, for all his unusual socialization into the street life by nearly all his significant male relatives, Matt had enough access to, and knowledge of, mainstream work culture to rack up a better work history than most of the other respondents. It is striking, too, that even with his nonstandard view of acceptable behavior, he was, until the severe downturn in the economy, able to find jobs when he felt like it.

Respondents' Claims of Adherence to Mainstream Norms

Despite the failure of these youth to conform to mainstream work practices, both their attitudes and values toward work and their views of the changes they experienced as a result of ABC training are largely in line with mainstream norms and values pertaining to work. In accounting for their job failures, respondents identified, and denigrated, a specific set of attitudes and personal practices—appearance, laziness, violence, disrespect, insubordination, dropping out of school—as major barriers to achieving their goals. While these may have been activated by their training, the important point is that they expressed full agreement with the program's view that these were very problematic attitudes and ways of self-presentation. Furthermore, our findings nearly exactly replicate those reported by Alford's informants (2004, 137–142, 183–187).

One problem was their appearance, an issue that previous studies have found to be important proxies to employers in evaluating job applicants (Holzer 1996, 57–62). Frieda, an LGBT drug dealer who changed her dress style toward a straight, conventional norm as a result of ABC, put it this way:

> The way they dress, because a lot of people, I see them saying, I don't want to wear that, it looks like something a white girl would wear. But that thing that a white girl would wear would get her a job.

Laziness was another factor cited as a problem by several respondents. Elizabeth was typical:

> Being lazy. Not applying themselves the right way. I only say that from my experience, with myself and my friends, and my lazy brother. He got me into the work that I do now, and now he never wants to work anymore. Oh, give me some work, give me some work, and then the day come, and "Oh, I can't do it. I got to go to this place," and I'm like, you going somewhere to spend money, but you don't want to go make money? Come on, how stupid is that?

Although most respondents were familiar with welfare from childhood experiences and were dependent on others in some way for daily subsistence—the majority were still living with their mothers (parents in one case) or girlfriends or in a program for runaway teens that collaborated with ABC—nearly all were critical of dependency and had reservations about being too long on welfare. Only a few felt that some sort of support was acceptable for more than a short time. Elizabeth, who worked as a casual laborer for many years rejected the notion of depending on government provisions for her living: "I'd rather do [for myself] with a job. I hate not working. I really do." Larry, a nineteen-year-old who had just dropped out of high school had a similar attitude: "I think [welfare's] good for people that don't have jobs, but I think if you're on it you should get a job to get off of it because people become dependent on it." And Sampson, who was subsequently convicted of real estate fraud, espoused a similar position: "I would like (having someone provide for all my needs) but that would make you feel less of a man after a while. So, in other words, I would get an ideal job."

Closely related to respondents' rejection of dependency were their opinions on what the role of government should be in the lives of the poor. Only one respondent thought that the government should be providing more aid for the needy. Several felt that too much government help could breed dependency. The most common response was that the government should provide more jobs, training related to jobs, or help offset the effect of a criminal record in the job market. Anthony, a small-time pimp and aspiring recording artist put it most clearly:

> [The government] don't need to do all that [provide for all my needs]. They could just create more jobs and do what they try to do, improve that. They don't have to do a lot for me—I am going to do that myself—just create more jobs so people can have jobs, help people get jobs.

Several respondents felt that jobs were available and the problem was a lack of application as well as motivation to work. Elizabeth, who described her brother as lazy, saw the same problem in other people, even herself:

> I think [government should do more], in a sense, but I think if people would apply theirselves more, it wouldn't be so hard. Because there's a lot of jobs out here, but a lot of people don't apply for them because they sit around, like I did for a little while, like, I can't get no work. All right, well, if I'm not leaving my house, I'm not going to get a job. . . . I think, I think a lot of people blame stuff on the government, and it's really not so much the government all the time. Regardless of what color you are, you know, anything, a high school diploma. There's a lot of jobs out here that train you, that help you get your diplomas, stuff like that. So it's just a lot of excuses, I think.

The mainstream valorization of work was also frequently espoused. Richard's explanation of why he chose to participate in ABC sounded like a celebration of the work ethic. Observing his girlfriend working hard at ABC inspired him to join:

> That was like a good aura around her, and I wanted it, because I wanted to come home being tired from working all day because that feels good for some unknown reason. Especially when you're not doing nothing, which is like during the day anyway. So I just thought that was progress. She made progress, because we both were in the slump, but she rose above to be progressive and productive, so that's what I wanted to do as well.

Responses to the ABC Program of Cultural and Attitudinal Change

ABC attempted to induce in their clients a greater awareness of the appropriateness of some mainstream behavior in the workplace, an increased ease in accessing several mainstream work norms and attendant cultural knowledge, and a new availability of some behaviors. The organization's key strategies included direct instruction in significant behaviors and attitudes, fostering reflection on personal behavior, providing powerful incentives to modify cultural knowledge and behavior, and facilitating extensive practice of new behaviors. Change among the young clients at ABC occurred in their response to authority, their adoption of a more standard style of dress for work, their conduct in interviews, and their use of appropriate language. For the most part, trainees responded positively to the program's goals and said they saw no personal or identity problems in the psychocultural changes promoted by ABC. Nearly all rejected the notion that the program was trying to impose middle-class or white cultural values and norms on them, although some reservation was expressed about one of the program's cultural goals (which we discuss below). Jane, the one ABC dropout we interviewed, had a particularly troubled history. As a teenager, she had been in a high school for disruptive youth and had been in the custody of child services. Nonetheless, she rejected the idea that the changes were in any way an imposition of an alternate class-based identity or lifestyle, saying, "I don't think it's wrong that they are trying to help you change." Michael used two of ABC's priming concepts—that of the winner (someone who has achieved many of the goals that the ABC participant aspired to) and "the job" (a stable, full-time, well-paid job with benefits)—in his rejection of the idea that the program was indoctrinating them in a white or middle-class culture:

If you want to be a winner, you have to do what the winners do. It doesn't necessarily have to be this group of people or that group of people. It's just, if you want to be a winner, you have to do what the winners do, so I took that in, and I'm working on that. . . . You know, they talk about getting a job, and "the job," and I'm working toward "the job," and that's where the winners are.

Even youth who were fully alert to, and resentful of, the negative, racialized perceptions and stereotypes about inner-city blacks, and especially black men, found no racial undertones in ABC's training. Andre, a teenager with a violent record, described the attitude of society toward black men thus: "We're already stereotyped . . . that we're all upset and ready to fight. Loose cannons, you know. Just ready to do something all the time, violent." Yet he was adamant that the ABC training was in no way racist or a threat to his racial identity. Indeed, Henry, a college dropout who knew all about black identity, found that the changes helped to offset the negative self-image he had as a black man:

I was pretty much myself, the whole time, and to be true with them, and loyal to them, I have to be true and loyal to myself, and that's one reason why I finished the program. . . . I felt good about [the changes]. . . . Oh, I felt bad [about myself as a young black man]. I did. I felt really bad.

Not everyone shared this view. A few respondents perceived the cultural changes to their behavior as racially loaded, but they were resigned to the reality that those were the terms on which they had to negotiate the world, in particular the world of work. Richard, who had lost a number of jobs through his unreliability and behavior on the job, described the need to conform to white standards of behavior:

If we [black people] made the rules, things would be a whole lot different, but I don't want to bring up race too much, but you know it's white people who are making the rules. . . . When you try to go to college, that's who you see behind the desk when you fill out the application and in the interview. And if it's not, he had to work really hard to get there. . . . We're not making the rules, and you can't beat them either. You think you can beat them, but you can't. You don't win in the end. You can try to scam and all you want, but you just can't. And I had to learn it the hard way.

Respondents felt that most of what was transmitted was cultural knowledge and values that they already knew but had disregarded, or had great difficulty doing, which partly explains their lack of resistance. However, in addition to helping participants recognize how important and appropriate some cognitively available but ignored norms and knowledge structures were for the workplace, and in addition to promoting their practice and accessibility, the ABC workshop also introduced some essential new cultural knowledge—concepts and skills—not previously available to participants. These were mainly interviewing skills and the creation of supporting documents for the job search process. They were among the most highly rated aspects of the program. Most participants were familiar with résumés, but some were unfamiliar with cover letters and references, and many were unaware of the practice of thanking a potential employer for an interview. Andre, recently released from incarceration that started while he was still in high school, was very enthusiastic about learning these skills: "I learned how to do a résumé, cover letter. I learned everything to do." These skills had widespread appeal; even Ralph, with one of the most substantial work histories, was grateful for expanding his knowledge of the documents needed to support his job search: ". . . someone will teach you a different way to do a résumé than what somebody else will teach you. Like, what ABC taught me was the original way, the way it's supposed to be done. I never knew about a cover letter, or a reference, or a thank you letter, I never knew none of that. . . ."

Surprisingly, given the importance of fashion among inner-city youth, program participants generally embraced the new norm of business attire when interviewing for a job and even began to adopt such wear in their ordinary lives. Twelve out of twenty-five respondents were surprised and pleased by the response from friends and the public at large when they conformed to ABC's dress code. Kianna had served as a supervisor in a national chain drugstore but found another job with less responsibility because of conflict with her manager and had been out of the workforce for several years due to the birth of her child. She saw in the positive response motivation to keep looking for a job:

I learned, coming to and from ABC, the different type of attention I would attract from certain people. And to me, like, everything they said was right. First impressions are everything. . . . So until I find a job, I feel like I'm going to dress professionally, because I know, I've got résumés on me, I never know when I'm gonna see somebody or go into a place, and I want to be able to speak to them and approach them with what I've got on, and how I look now.

We return here to the important distinction between declarative and procedural knowledge discussed in Chapter 2 (this volume). While the declarative knowledge structures of mainstream culture are partly available to these disconnected youth, the same seems not to be true of its procedural knowledge, precisely because of the social isolation of black youth from mainstream personal interactions where procedural knowledge is mainly acquired. (See also Young 2003, ch. 6). Knowing that you should be on time is not the same as knowing how to be on time. ABC trainers are aware of this distinction and try to train clients in some kinds of procedural knowledge. The process of *practicing* to be on time, for example, makes available previously unknown details and strategies for time management. This constitutes new knowledge, not simply priming the accessibility of already available knowledge structures. Similarly, knowing that work attire is usually worn in a variety of settings is not the same as knowing how important it is in those settings, nor is it the same as knowing how strongly one's choice of dress shapes an employer's impression of a job applicant, although this is one of those tricky areas where the distinction between the declarative and procedural can become blurred. Much the same holds for interpersonal interactions. Referred to as the culture of power by Delpit (1988), these include the direct gaze, the firm dry handshake, and the thank you letter for an interview, among other niceties. Knowing such interactions may seem to be mainly a matter of acquiring declarative knowledge, but doing them properly may be much more difficult, especially since they are best done automatically. The distinction is more critical in the management of stress and interpersonal tensions in the workplace. Norms in this area, and responses to their violation, are difficult to observe, but even when the declarative knowledge of what is expected in interpersonal relations is learned, the procedural knowledge of how to behave, especially if one feels provoked or imagines a slight or disrespectful gesture, is wholly new knowledge for most of these youth, as they themselves readily acknowledged.

We observed one possible deficiency in ABC's training program. In promoting cultural adjustment, reducing negative behaviors that are chronically available from the street culture may be as important as fostering accessibility and availability of positive behaviors. However, ABC had limited success in challenging one highly visible instance of the distinctive street culture: the protective scowl. Attempts to undo the chronic accessibility of the "mean-mug" look and to learn and make more accessible the simple act of smiling more frequently were strongly resisted. While acknowledging the importance of a pleasant demeanor in the workplace, almost all found it difficult to conform to the smiling ideal of the service employee; only six respondents out of the sixteen who reported a need for change in this area seemed to have made substantial progress.

Respondents had two main reasons for their resistance. The first was the need to maintain an appearance that discouraged aggression on the street, and the second was the dissonance between a smiling face and the difficulties men, in particular, encountered in life. Both men and women reported that they maintained an unfriendly expression to reduce the likelihood of being approached by strangers, avoiding either a sexually tinged encounter in the case of women or physical hostility in the case of men. This reaction is common among the urban poor and is well documented in the literature (Anderson 1999, 72–73, 92–93; Carter 2005:, 82–85; see also Krupnick and Winship, Chapter 9 in this volume). Kianna, a young mother with a spotty employment history, explained the necessity for her mean look:

> But when I'm at the train station, I use my look to my advantage, because I don't want to be bothered at all. Because I've been approached negatively by men, so I just put on a mean look, and they don't say anything to me. So I think, yeah, the look is definitely needed.

Both Nelson and John admitted that though they changed dramatically in prison and rejected the violence for which they had once been known, they continued to benefit from the expectation that they would behave as they once had (cf. Young 2003, ch. 2). John deliberately continued to use an aggressive demeanor in order to fend off trouble:

> The kids on the streets and people my age, they know that guy right there is serious. If there's a problem with him, he's not going to argue with you about it, you know what I'm saying? That ain't even me no more, but I still utilize that costume; I still utilize that person, because he's useful, you know, that's what the kids respect. You know, you go ahead and fight him, or just keep your mouth shut. I'm not like that no more; you can talk to me. If you put your hands on me,

I'm going to fight back—you have to defend yourself—but I think that might be the wrong way. People still think that about me, but I'm not like that no more.

Less well documented is the fact that many young black men tend to maintain a front that masks pain, especially emotional suffering. With remarkable candor (which, incidentally, enhanced our confidence in the honesty of their responses), several male respondents, three of them recently out of prison, discussed the fact that their facial expressions reflected a life of pain. This, they explained, began with issues in childhood abuse and punishment (on which, see Nightingale 1993, ch. 3), appeared to intensify during their lengthy incarceration, and persisted subsequently in the disappointment they felt in themselves, and their discouragement at being far behind their peers in achieving the typical benchmarks in life. For these youth, the expectation of a regular smile was onerous. Michael, who recently completed a sentence for shooting another man, said that "coming from the place where I just came from, it's kind of hard to smile every day. Sometimes, you know, I think that it's not warranted, but I try to put it on for the most part, so . . . it's still a work in progress right now."

On a deeper level, these ex-offenders were expressing more strongly what a number of youthful ABC participants revealed: that the requirement to smile, regardless of their sometimes deeply felt emotions, was a violation of themselves. While some respondents' resentment of this mainstream cultural requirement was explicit, for others it was expressed in an uneasy ambivalence. Nelson attributed some of his difficulty with maintaining a smiling attitude to the responsibilities and challenges he faced after being released at the end of a long prison term:

> There is so many things that I have to do to try to catch up to where I need to be. Sometimes I get in arguments with my girlfriend about time; like how I'm supposed to—I'm trying to fit everything in, I'm trying to balance everyone and make everybody happy and it's just hard. I've got so many things to do. I'm trying to make them happy: my mother, my father, my girlfriend, and I still do what I have to do. In terms again of the job, I want to have my own things, so it's like a struggle.

John expressed his feelings more explicitly:

> I had an aggressive demeanor. I always had a mean look, but when people got to know me, they'd be like, you can't judge a book by its

cover, I'm actually pretty cool. Cool, calm, and collected. I'm pretty cool by nature, but like, that's that pain reflected in my features. You have to understand, I've had a very hard life . . . I don't like to be fake, do the fake smile. I've been through a lot, I'm hurting, I'm suffering. That's who I am, accept it, like as long as I do my work, and as long as I'm proficient, and on time, and as long as I do what I'm supposed to do, I don't see why my look, or whatever the case may be, should be of any importance. Like, to a certain extent, as far as being clean, I get, but as far as my facial expression, it's like, are you serious?

Discussion: Two Kinds of Sociological Knowledge

A qualitative sociology of the sort conducted here involves the production of at least two kinds of knowledge: that of the professional sociological observer, and that of the observed. The first part of this section attempts to present, in respondents' own words, the ethnosociological theory of their world as they came to understand it, stimulated by their unusual experience with ABC and us. The second presents our interpretation, as professional observers, studying one domain of the everyday life of a specific group of disadvantaged black youth, including their own ethnosociological interpretations.

"Playing the Game": Insiders' Ethnosociological View

The most remarkable feature of respondents' subjective theoretical reflections was their deep commitment to a dramaturgical interpretation of their life, world, and mode of thinking. As is true of all cultural configurations, some individuals were more adept at expressing the primary frames than others; in our sample this was true of seven especially articulate respondents. What they articulated was Goffmanian theory in the raw, a strong attachment to the metaphor of life as a game and their role as players, a metaphor used originally of pimps and their clients, later extended to men in search of sexual conquest, but now used as a synonym for hustling and making one's way through life generally. (For earlier accounts, see Majors and Billson 1992; Anderson 1999, 150–56, 291; Miller 2008, chs. 3 and 5; Milner and Milner 1973.) They arrived at this, of course, completely independent of Goffman or of any other formal dramaturgical theory. Nonetheless, they did not invent the master metaphor driving their folk sociological theory; rather it is one that has been pervasive in everyday black thought and life from the days of slavery. The trickster of slave lore was the prototypical black player (Levine 1977, 121–33). Wearing the mask was an essential survival strategy under the three and a half centuries of psychological terror that were slavery and Jim Crow, best captured in Dunbar's iconic poem, "We Wear the Mask" (Dunbar 1896), and the notion of playing, and being played, continues to permeate all areas of street culture, from pimping, otherwise known as "playing the game" (Milner and Milner 1973; Ken and Hunter 2007) to troubled gender relations (Miller 2008, ch. 11 in this volume); from selling drugs to selling books and hamburgers (Duneier 2000; Newman 2000; Venkatesh 2006, chs. 1 and 4); or simply being literally good at ballgames. Hannerz found it to be one of the main common features of ghetto-specific culture in the sixties: "Since one's possibilities to protect oneself are limited, a ghetto dweller can only try to keep on his toes to be aware of what is going on. . . . Life is a game, and a lot of people are working their personal games in situations where this is not readily apparent . . ." (Hannerz 1969, 146). The term is now pervasive in hip-hop and street culture; LL Cool J even dedicated a lyric to hip-hop "the game that put me on the map."

This master metaphor may, indeed, be one of the most important features of the distinctive cultural component of inner-city youths, so what is involved here is the use of one important frame to interpret and make sense of what was brought to light by the secondary socialization of the ABC program. To the most criminally involved of the youth we studied, being a player persists as an essential survival strategy—physically, socially, and psychologically. Avery, who had avoided prison or gangs, explained his resistance to smiling by pointing out that the tough, "mean-mug" look was a way of avoiding trouble: "As a guy, I kind of, like, have a mean mug. I don't know, maybe that's how I'm *dodging*." More insightfully, Nelson, recently released from prison, felt he could transition to the mainstream world of work because it simply mirrored the game-playing frame at which he was already adept, only with new players and, presumably, a cultural script that was already available:

I understand that in order for me to get hired I have to look pleasant and I have to talk properly and I have to dress properly. I understand because it's the same way in the street. It mirrors it because when you're in the street you have to look the part, sound the part, and act the part.

This is strikingly reminiscent of what Goffman calls *keying* or "the set of conventions by which a given activity, one already meaningful in terms of some primary framework, is transformed into something patterned on this activity but seen by the participants to be something quite else" (1986, 43–44). Goffman has been criticized for what strikes some as a cynical interpretation of people's impression management, in which role-taking is performed, not to enhance cooperation, but to manipulatively manage others' impressions. The accounts of some of our respondents, however, are fully in line with Goffman. Matt, a drug dealer on probation, explained the skill of impression management learned from his hustling older relatives. He was ready to conform to mainstream standards of dress, he told us, because he had been trained from his youth by his father and grandfather on the importance of avoiding stereotypes of black youth in order to escape detection of criminal activity:

> My grandfather used to tell us all the time, "Take them hats off," when he'd see the kids with the baseball caps. Kids, ones that's out here on the streets, don't know; you've got four people in your car for one, that's no good. You've got four people in your car, four young dudes with baseball caps on in your car, you'll get pulled over [by the police] quick. I'm in the car and not with the sound on, but no hat on. You all four aren't even dirty like I'm dirty [carrying guns or drugs], but I have no hat on, there is no braids. It just looks regular. See that perception though? But I'm doing the worst. They are just going to McDonald's, and they are getting pulled over while I drive right by with probably two guns in the back seat and a whole bunch of drugs on me." It's a perception, it's a stereotype thing, but it's real in this world though. It's really real. . . . Also, my father, when he came around he did his little hustling [as a bookie or running numbers], but when he pulled up he was in shirt and tie.

But it was another respondent, John, who had the most complex understanding of the transformations that he was enacting, one that was as sophisticated, in its own way, as any in the formal dramaturgy of Goffman with its view of self as "not an entity half-concealed behind events, but a changeable formula for managing oneself during them. Just as the current situation prescribes the official guise behind which we will conceal ourselves, so it provides for where and how it will show through" (Goffman 1986, 574). During his seven-year prison term, John had recognized the contempt with which white prison guards regarded the loud, profane style of black inmates, and he had recoiled from being perceived that way himself. He saw his demeanor as a façade that he had constructed to function on the streets, and he still used it to his advantage after his release from prison. But John was working at sorting out what aspects of his behavior reflected the person he saw himself to be, and which were a costume that he could discard. ABC was merely providing another costume for him to try on, he argued, one that he found stuffy and which he would rather not assume on a regular basis but could live with when necessary. We have taken our chapter title from this remarkable expression of ethnosociological theory, which we here cite in full:

And my man was just talking real loud, vulgar, not even conscious of his surrounding, and this cop is just like, "You nigger!" like that. When people around me, I tone that down. Tone it down, for real, because I don't like negative attention, man, and when I started seeing that, I decided to stop . . . for some reason at that moment, I had seen how foolish that individual looked and I was that individual, so I didn't like what I saw, so I basically didn't like some of myself, and I felt like that needed to be changed. There's certain aspects, certain things that I do socially that are not me, and when people point out those things that I do that are not me, then I understand that that's not me. It's just the façade, the illusion I've created. If there's a part of myself that is me, then I'm gonna be like, no, that's me right there, and you have to accept that or keep it moving, you know what I'm saying? To a certain extent, yeah, you're right [that kind of façade is needed on the street]. But people lose sight that it's a façade, but it's like, I know it's a costume. People lose sight of that, and they start believing that the costume is who you really are . . . until people get the time to know me, then they'll see. . . . It's like, you know, it's complicated, because some of my costume is tailored on some of my experiences, some of what I've been through. It's like, the certain pains and certain things. But at the same time, it's, like, my reaction off of what I've been through, the façade, being like, somewhat rude, disrespectful, being abusive, being quick to—that's not who I am, that's not even who I want to be. It's like, because of what I've been through, that's what I've adapted, that's part of that façade, that costume.

[ABC is] trying to groom you to have that like, taste, you know, give you the taste, and somehow make you try on the outfit. You feel me? It's like, go to some of these places and try on the outfit and just see how it works for you. You know what I'm saying? This is a different outfit, though. A different outfit. It's stuffy to me, like, I'm not comfortable.

John was ambivalent about whether the "outfit" that ABC recommended was racist, or whether it was a class-based transformation, but he intended to accept only the aspects that reflected what he saw as his true identity and wear any other aspects only as a costume, if at all.

Like Goffman, too, respondents appear to shift between a view of self as a nonessential, "formula," changing to meet the exigencies of the situation, to a view of a more stable identity that could change its appearance as it played the game required by the situation. Thus, for some, there was the perception that in shaping their behavior and demeanor ABC was not so much altering their identity as providing impression-management tools that could be used as needed in the job market and perhaps dispensed with as easily. In Anthony's words, for example: "It's not changing who I am; it's just making me a better man and making me more powerful. . . . It's teaching you how to play the game the proper way."

Despite the fact that their intensive psychocultural training yielded varying degrees of insight for participants, the process of direct instruction, heightened motivation, personal reflection, and intensive practice used in the ABC program effectively increased the accessibility of targeted, already available, declarative cultural knowledge in addition to providing some new cultural knowledge and the procedural dimension of these declarative knowledge structures. For some of these youth, those who live by their wits, doing ethnographies was an explicit, daily practice; for many of the others, this was an ethnocognitive and ethnosociological discovery—abetted, we suspect, by the observer effect of our own interviews and keenly observed formal sociological work (on which see Duneier 2000, appendix)—an introduction to consciousness of the power of the cultural work occurring endlessly behind the commonplace scenes of their lives.

The Sociological Outsider View

In the introduction, we proposed that subjects' participation in the ABC program constituted a special kind of psychocultural experience, which, by stimulating unusually hard cognitive reflection on their life, world, and themselves, would lift the veil of the camouflaging commonplace and elicit new insights about their world and themselves. This was confirmed. We described participants' ethnosociology as Goffmanian in the centrality of game playing. However, from the perspective of the sociological outsider, it would seem reasonable to inquire into the degree to which the game-playing master metaphor limits their understanding of, and effective functioning in, the mainstream domain of work as well as their own existence in the ghetto and those with whom they associate.

Goffman's conception of framing, in his chapter on "ordinary troubles," points to the kind of trouble that was possible: "Life may be a drama, but to play it properly one must know the script of the role that one is playing for any given activity and the way it is organized," (say, that of being a competent worker). The script, of course, can be interpreted in a variety of ways, allowing for human agency, but in the end the actor's framework must fit the "organizational premises" or frame of the activity.

> It has been argued that these frameworks are not merely a matter of mind but correspond in some sense to the way in which an aspect of the activity itself is organized—especially activity directly involving social agents. Organizational premises are involved, and these are something cognition somehow arrives at, not something cognition creates or generates. Given their understanding of what it is that is going on, individuals fit their actions to this understanding and ordinarily find that the ongoing world supports this fitting. These organizational premises I call the frame of the activity. (Goffman 1986, 247)

When Goffman writes that "the ongoing world supports this fitting" and later that "we are wrong only exceptionally," he is, of course, assuming middle-class Euro-Americans performing in the dominant mainstream world, something he readily admits. But this is precisely the problem for disconnected black youth brought up in the ghetto whose focal cultural configuration is that of the street. "Try on the outfit and see how it fits," may work (to a degree) in the ghetto, but in the mainstream world, one may not have a clue just what the outfit is or how to wear it, and it is precisely in such situations that the "framing of events can lead to ambiguity, error and frame disputes" (Goffman 1986, 343). To be sure, the goal of the ABC program may be defined as providing the declarative and procedural knowledge about the appropriate outfit for the domain of work, and in this regard, a disposition toward playing the role and not worrying about some essential self or identity which may find the role intolerable—assuming that such an essential self exists, which Goffman denies[1]—is an advantage.

There is, however, a further complication. The domains of mainstream America, or any culture for that matter, do not float in isolation. All domains exist in a more complex structure of other domains, either overlapping with them or nested in broader cultural domains. To play the game the right way invariably requires not simply knowing the declarative and procedural knowledge of the domain but the broader normative and value structures that reinforce it. In the view of employers, a "good worker," even for the most low-skilled job, is one who knows the "work ethic" value and the difference between equality norms and authority norms, those of compliance and gratitude, as well as the ways of convincingly enacting them in ongoing interactions. The knowledge and performance of such norms and attendant values, it has been shown, are inversely related to the level of specific skill required of the job: the more deskilled the job the greater the emphasis on them. Thus Holzer (1996) found an emphasis among employers of "relatively high frequency of cognitive and social task performance . . . despite the overrepresentation . . . of high-turnover jobs within firms" (48). Even for these low-skill jobs, employers used elaborate screening procedures that "signal" applicants' suitability. Most black youth with backgrounds such as those of the ABC clients we studied, fail to make it through the first round of screening (because of their criminal background and/or lack of high school diploma or work experience), but even if they pass this first hurdle, they then have to meet the more demanding normative and value-oriented cultural test, what employers call the "attitude" problem of black youth, which leads them to employ immigrants with less education and language skills, but who are perceived as less troublesome and more compliant (Wilson 1996, 111–16, 136; Holzer 1996, 92–93). Ironically, many disconnected youth imagine that it is precisely these social skills that they have, perhaps identifying their skill at hanging out and chillin' with fellow youth, that correlates with similar skill at work (Young 2003, 175–77).

But what of our respondents' espousal of mainstream norms and values? There has to be something to this since nearly all surveys and ethnographic work on low-income black youth report the same. Thus, Young found that "all of the men appeared to subscribe to the traditional American creed—the notion inherent in the 'Protestant ethic'—that hard work begets positive results for getting ahead" (Young 2003, 138–39). Hagedorn (1988, 141) found a similar rejection of racism and an autonomous acknowledgment of their own lack of skills as the reasons given by hardened gang members for their unemployment in Milwaukee during the eighties. Young's (2003) explanation was that the isolation of youth accounts for failure to recognize the role of racism: the more provisionally connected respondents were to mainstream life, the greater the tendency to consider social conditions in explaining their situation, although all were convinced that black men were mainly responsible for their bleak condition (110–12, 132, 144–55). The problem with this explanation is that the more isolated should also have been less committed to the mainstream norm of personal responsibility and the work ethic. Cohen's (2010) explanation is that black youth have internalized these norms and values from their schooling, church, and the media, which they "reiterate when asked to judge behavior," but they "are rarely forced to push . . . beyond that prearranged normative script to think about and make sense of the sexual patterns, the culture, and the family structures that they are producing . . ." (53). Restated in knowledge-activation terms, we may say that there is little opportunity or pressure to make these mainstream norms accessible, and they simply become moribund and inapplicable to their lives, even though they are sufficiently cognitively available to be trotted out when prompted.

An earlier, more forceful version of this explanation, which addresses the issue of game playing, was offered by Rainwater (1970) in his neglected classic:

> If a group becomes totally isolated from the dominant group whose games they cannot play, they will establish normative games of their own, but if they continue to some extent under the influence of the dominant group, their substitute games cannot acquire full normative character. Instead, the games may become pseudo-normative—the players assert to each other that their game has moral justification, but careful observation of actual behavior belies their statement. (394)

The power of the normative game of the dominant group, Rainwater, adds makes it difficult for the competing game to have any cachet. However, in spite of being indoctrinated to recognize the norms of the dominant group, the isolated lower class will, in due course, come to accept their own as the best "substitute games." Another way of interpreting this, drawing on more recent studies in the social psychology of norms (Cialdini and Trost 1998, 155–58), is that the norms of the substitute games of the ghetto are largely observational or descriptive, compared with the persisting but only effortfully accessible injunctive norms of the mainstream. Rainwater drew on Goffman's theory of stigma to argue that the internalization of the dominant norms can lead, "if only for moments," to a sense of shame in agreeing that "he does indeed fall short of what he really ought to be" (Goffman 1963, cited in Rainwater 1970, 394).

It may seem odd that people who subscribe to the street culture with its hypermasculine pride and exaggerated notions of respect would experience any sense of shame, but the ethnographic evidence does indicate that this indeed happens, "if only for moments." It is something, however, that is carefully concealed. Rainwater points out that the more common response is an assertive expression of pride that has at its base "knowing no shame; it is the pride that comes from wholehearted participation in the unconventional opportunities provided by the ghetto world and from learning to be a skilled practitioner of the arts of 'cool' and 'working game'" (1970, 228). More recently, Katherine Newman (2000) found that McJobs and other low-paying jobs overtly carry a great deal of stigma, and such workers must bear the contempt and mockery of uncouth customers as well as prideful, macho street youth. Probing deeper, however, she found that many such workers felt no shame in their game because, however lowly their jobs, they were connected to the formal workforce and knew that in modern America work has become the ultimate value defining personal worth and membership in society. There is a shaft of cultural irony here: the McJob workers' defiant assertion that there is no shame in their game is actually lifted straight from, and thrown right back at, the preexisting street culture of the men who mock them.

Disconnected youth, it turns out, are not immune from the mainstream valorization of work, however cool their usual "working game." They are simply in a state of acute contradiction. As Wilson points out, chronic unemployment leads not only to a lack of income but to the absence of "a coherent organization of the present—that is, a system of concrete expectations and goals," and, to the degree that the experience is shared with others, "to a lack of self-efficacy" (1996, 73–75). Some of the same youth who mocked ghetto workers as they went to work in their uniforms quietly sneaked back to these workers and begged them to recommend them to their employers for one of the McJobs that they publicly ridiculed

(Newman 1999, ch. 4). It is hardly surprising to learn, then, that in moments of self-reflection they do express feelings of shame. Thus Young found that

> sadly, in terms of social status the men most often judged themselves to be losers in the game of life (or at least they were convinced that others saw them in this way). When a man does not work every day, it is easy for him to indict himself, and the people like him who surround him, for their life situation, chastising himself and them for not having worked hard enough, been disciplined, and so on. (2003, 182)

The scowl may indeed be primarily a cultural style, a survival strategy in playing the cool pose game, but it may also be an expression of chronic depression, brought on, in part by the "toxic stress" of growing up in a terribly deprived environment, in part by the deeply hidden sense of shame at being losers in the game of life, of being disconnected from what the dominant culture values most, especially in men: being a working person. Thus, we were struck by several of our male respondents' frequent reference to their experience of constant psychological pain and by the generally negative evaluation of the way they were brought up. As John, one of the most articulate of our respondents, explained, his mean-mug look was really "the pain reflected in my features."

But it does not end here. Playing the game has negative consequences not only for youths attempting to adjust to the outside mainstream world of work and other domains, but for everyone living in the ghetto. "Living the drama" is the way residents of the Boston ghetto described the pervasive violence of their neighborhoods, springing from perpetual gang warfare and feuding over respect, status, and turf (Harding 2010, 18; Anderson 1999, ch. 2). It was much the same for the equally violent gangbangers of Milwaukee, studied by Hagedorn (1988) twenty years earlier: "Corner life can be exciting, the drama of conflict with other gangs and with authorities adds to their appeal to many young people" (101). On reflection, some gang members could see the terrible consequences for themselves and other young men. As a Vice Lords gang member told Hagedorn, "It's just a bad way to go, cause there's always two enemies, really three: the other gang member, the police, and yourself" (140). Had he reflected more, he might have added a fourth, and most victimized, category:

young women caught in what has been called the "playa-pimp-ho-bitch gearshift" of the street and gangsta version of hip-hop culture (Sharpley-Whiting 2007, 13). For too many young men of the street culture, her "body and mind are the object of a sexual game, to be won for his personal aggrandizement" (Anderson 1999, 155–156). The threat and reality of getting played means either cowering like a virtual prisoner in her home or else running the risk of harassment, intimate partner violence, and not infrequently, rapes—all considered "just playing" (Miller 2008, 82).

Coda

In the prolegomena to their sociological masterpiece, Berger and Luckmann (1966, 18) invoked the two basic dictums of the founding fathers of the discipline: Durkheim's rule to "consider social facts as things," and Weber's insistence that for sociology "the object of cognition is the subjective meaning-complex of action." The two imperatives they reconciled in their own pronouncement that "an adequate understanding of the 'reality sui generis' of society requires an inquiry into the manner in which this reality is constructed." In this chapter, we have followed Berger and Luckmann's advice closely. We have attempted to convey, as facts, our respondents' struggle to come to terms with an unusual episode in their lives and have done so by presenting their subjective understanding of what they think was going on and the ways in which it was meaningful to them. Because of the unusual nature of the cultural task they were engaged in, we have been able to go beyond the reporting of their reconstruction and probe into their own theory of their social action and thought—what we have called their ethnosociology and ethnocognition—in a decomposition of the ethnomethodological project.

In doing so, we have pursued, and hopefully realized, an important, if elusive, goal of qualitative sociology, first articulated by the phenomenologists: recognition of the distributed nature of all sociological knowledge—that complementing the systematic reasoning of the sociological observer is the ethnosociological understanding of the observed. This being so, we have tried to respect and give voice to the often implicit theories of social life and thought that inform our subjects' ongoing cultural work. And we close with the words of one of them: "It's like, you know, it's complicated, because some of my costume is tailored on some of my experiences, some of what I've been through. It's like, the certain pains and certain things."

Appendix

Table 13.1 Appendix: Characteristics of the Sample

	Median	Mean
Age in years	22	24
Length of incarceration in yrs. (juvenile or adult)	0.33	2.6
Years employed after high school	.67	1.08
Years of schooling—incl. GED*	12	11.7
Proportion of dropouts	56%	
Proportion with GED	24%	
Proportion with some college	20%	
Proportion less than high school	32%	
Proportion black	96%	
Proportion female	36%	
Proportion immigrant—first or second generation	32%	

*The GED is treated as equivalent to twelve years of schooling, though its impact on work history is not equivalent to that of a high school diploma.

14

Stepping Up or Stepping Back

Highly Disadvantaged Parents' Responses to the Building Strong Families Program

ANDREW CLARKWEST, *Mathematica Policy Research*
ALEXANDRA A. KILLEWALD, *Harvard University*
ROBERT G. WOOD, *Mathematica Policy Research*

The proportion of children raised by a single parent has increased dramatically in recent decades, particularly among low-income families (Ellwood and Jencks 2004). The high rates of single parenthood among low-income families have caused concern because of findings that children growing up in single-parent families are, on average, at greater risk of poor behavioral, health, and academic outcomes, unstable family structure, and poverty than are children raised by their married biological parents (McLanahan and Sandefur 1994; Amato 2005). The Fragile Families and Child Wellbeing Study[1] has provided important new information on unwed couples with children, revealing that the large majority of unwed parents are romantically involved at the time of their child's birth and have high hopes for a stable, enduring marriage (Carlson, McLanahan, and England 2004). Those couples nonetheless face many barriers to achieving these hopes and break up at high rates (Carlson et al. 2005).

Those findings were the impetus for the Building Strong Families (BSF) project, sponsored by the U.S. Department of Health and Human Services' Administration for Children and Families (ACF). The BSF project is an ambitious intervention, offering group-based relationship skills education with trained facilitators to unwed couples who are expecting a child or who have just had a baby. The program's ultimate aim was to promote the well-being of children by improving the quality of unmarried parents' relationships and increasing the likelihood that they remain together. The BSF project was designed to reach new or expecting

444

parents at the "magic moment" around the time of the birth of a child (McLanahan et al. 2003), when unmarried parents are particularly hopeful about the future of their couple relationship and are thought to be most willing to participate in an unfamiliar and relatively time-intensive program aimed at strengthening that relationship.

Mathematica Policy Research[2] conducted an experimental evaluation of the BSF program for ACF in eight evaluation sites. In general, at the time of the fifteen-month follow-up, the BSF intervention did not have statistically or substantively significant effects on couples' relationship status or quality, or on fathers' involvement with their children. Although BSF had little or no effect on couples' relationships overall, impacts varied meaningfully across the eight evaluation sites; for example, the Oklahoma City site's BSF program had a consistent pattern of positive effects at fifteen months. Perhaps most surprisingly, however, at the Baltimore site the BSF intervention had numerous negative effects: at the time of the fifteen-month follow-up survey, Baltimore couples who had been randomly assigned to participate in the BSF program were much *less* likely than control group couples to be romantically involved; fathers assigned to the BSF program were *less* likely to provide substantial financial support for their children or see them regularly; and mothers in the BSF sample were *more* likely to report experiencing a severe physical assault than were mothers in the control group.

The pattern of adverse effects in Baltimore raises important questions about the factors that shape low-income parents' relationships. What was distinctive about the Baltimore program or its participants that may have led to this unexpected and unintuitive pattern of results? More generally, what do the Baltimore results tell us about how cultural contexts, in conjunction with structural conditions, influence efficacy of social policies designed to improve people's well-being? The anomalous results of this type of negative case (Emigh 1997) provide the opportunity for analyses that expand theory about the forces driving family formation among disadvantaged populations and also refine knowledge to improve programs that serve such families.

This chapter is divided into three main parts. First, we describe in more detail the development of the BSF program, its operation, and the main findings of the study.[3] Second, we describe the differences between Baltimore and the other sites. Similar to many other sites, the Baltimore site recruited a sample of predominantly young African American couples.

However, the couples in Baltimore were distinctly more disadvantaged than the couples recruited by other sites, including those sites serving primarily African American couples. Finally, we outline and evaluate several explanations for how high levels of economic and social disadvantage may influence cultural traits—including relationship expectations, the meanings ascribed to being a partner and parent, and levels of trust—that together with limited economic prospects could lead a program like BSF to inadvertently increase relationship instability. We conclude with a discussion on the implications of this study for understanding how ideational and material factors may influence the efficacy of policies designed to improve people's well-being.

Part I: The BSF Program and Findings from the Impact Analyses

The BSF Program

Eight organizations in diverse locations across the United States were selected to implement BSF programs. The objective of the evaluation was to determine whether a well-implemented relationship skills education program could help couples meet their goals for lasting relationships and, in turn, improve the well-being of those couples' children. Project and ACF staff selected the organizations and provided both implementation assistance and monitoring. In most sites (including Baltimore), local organizations built BSF from the infrastructure of existing programs, though the existing organizational structures and services varied across sites.

Couples' participation in the study was strictly voluntary. BSF sites most commonly recruited couples into the study through places that serve expectant or new mothers, such as prenatal clinics, childbirth education classes, hospital maternity wards, and WIC (Women, Infants, and Children) clinics. The sites either used their own staff to approach potential participants directly in those locations or created agreements with the organizations running them to refer potentially eligible participants to BSF (Dion, Avellar, and Clary 2010). Although mothers were often approached first, the consent of both partners was required for BSF eligibility, and most programs strove to meet with the mother and father together to describe the program prior to obtaining consent. Site staff described the program to potential participants as a way to simultaneously improve their relationship as well as do what is best for their child (Dion et al. 2008).

In general, couples were eligible for BSF if they met all of the following five criteria: first, both partners desired to participate; second, the couple was romantically involved; third, the couple was expecting a baby together or had a baby within the last three months; fourth, the parents were not married at the time of conception; finally, both parents were at least eighteen years of age. Potential participating couples were also screened for intimate partner violence prior to determining eligibility. If there was evidence of violence that could be aggravated by BSF participation, the couple was deemed ineligible for BSF and referred to other services.

Although the program did not set any upper age or income restrictions on participation, participants were overwhelmingly young and generally low income. About 42 percent of couples had at least one partner under age twenty-one, and 93 percent had at least one partner age twenty-nine or younger. Couples' average annual earnings were $20,475, well below the median household income in the United States. The program served an ethnoracially diverse sample. About 52 percent of the couples had two African American partners, 20 percent had two Hispanic partners, 12 percent had two white partners, and the other 16 percent were composed of some other combination of partners.

Each BSF program had some flexibility in its structure and curriculum, but all programs shared three components: group sessions on relationship skills, individual support from family coordinators, and assessment and referral to support services. The group sessions on relationship skills typically met weekly, ranging from two to five hours at each meeting, comprising a total of thirty to forty-two hours. Family coordinators were available to assess couples' needs, reinforce relationship skills, provide emotional support, and encourage participation in and completion of the group sessions. Coordinators also provided referrals to auxiliary support services, such as education, employment, and mental health services.

Each site selected one of three research-based curricula adapted specifically for the BSF target population: Loving Couples, Loving Children (LCLC), developed by Drs. John and Julie Gottman; Love's Cradle (LC), developed by Mary Ortwein and Dr. Bernard Guerney; or the Becoming Parents Program for Low-Income, Low-Literacy Couples (BPP), developed by Dr. Pamela Jordan. These types of curricula had shown positive impacts on couples' relationships in samples of mostly married, middle-income, typically white couples (Hawkins et al. 2008). Five of the eight evaluation sites (including Baltimore) chose the LCLC curriculum; two chose the LC curriculum; and one (Oklahoma) chose the BPP curriculum.

The adaptations to the BSF curricula were aimed to better address issues specific to low-income unmarried couples, enhance the cultural sensitivity of the materials, and accommodate a wider range of reading levels. For example, early focus groups revealed that many potential participants had past negative interactions with educational institutions and wished to avoid being lectured about the "right" way to do things. In response to this information, the BSF curriculum was modified to allow couples to share their own experiences and learn from each other, rather than emphasizing a didactic approach. In addition, topics were added to the curriculum that research suggests are particularly important for the target population, including skills for building trust and commitment, managing relationships with children from prior relationships and their parents, and understanding the rewards and challenges of marriage (McConnell et al. 2006).

Findings of the BSF Impact Analyses at Fifteen Months

The eight evaluation sites ultimately enrolled 5,102 couples in the study (see Table 14.1). After agreeing to participate in the study, couples were randomly assigned, with half selected to be offered the chance to participate in the BSF program. The other half was placed in a control group that was offered no services.

The BSF program was expected to increase couples' exposure to relationship skills services. All couples in the BSF group were offered BSF services and actively encouraged to attend the classes, although they were not required to participate. Couples in the control group could seek relationship skills education from sources other than BSF. Among BSF couples, 61 percent reported attending a group session on relationship skills during the fifteen months between random assignment and the follow-up survey. Among control group couples, only 17 percent reported attending a relationship skills group session. When asked about the number of hours they attended the groups, BSF couples reported attending fourteen hours, on average, compared with an average of two hours of group relationship skills education for control group couples.

The BSF fifteen-month impact analysis (Wood et al. 2012) focused on outcomes in the following domains: relationship status, relationship quality, intimate partner violence, coparenting, and father involvement.[4] Across the eight programs as a whole, the program was not found to influence outcomes in any key domain. For example, fifteen months after

Table 14.1 The Eight BSF Programs

Location	Sponsor Organization	Number of Study Couples
Atlanta, Georgia	Georgia State University, Latin American Association	930
Baltimore, Maryland	Center for Urban Families	602
Baton Rouge, Louisiana	Family Road of Greater Baton Rouge	652
Florida: Orange and Broward counties	Healthy Families Florida	695
Houston, Texas	Healthy Family Initiatives	405
Indiana: Allen, Marion, and Lake counties	Healthy Families Indiana	466
Oklahoma City, Oklahoma	Public Strategies, Inc.	1,010
San Angelo, Texas	Healthy Families San Angelo	342
All Programs		5,102

random assignment, 76 percent of BSF couples were still romantically involved, compared with 77 percent of control group couples. Similarly, BSF and control group couples were equally likely to be married to each other at that time (17 and 18 percent respectively) and to be living together, whether married or unmarried (62 percent for both groups). They were also equally happy in their romantic relationships, with average ratings of 8.4 and 8.3 respectively on a relationship happiness scale ranging from 0 to 10.

Despite the overall lack of effects, the evaluation revealed some instances of program success, including a consistent pattern of positive impacts at the Oklahoma City site. However, this program differed from those at other sites in several ways, such as using a curriculum not used by any other site, larger class sizes that included married couples who were not part of the study together with unmarried BSF couples, longer sessions that allowed couples to complete the curricula in fewer weeks, and greater use of financial incentives for participation (Dion et al. 2008; Dion, Avellar, and Clary 2010).

However, the evaluation also uncovered a number of negative program impacts in the Baltimore site (Table 14.2). Notably, at the time of the fifteen-month follow-up survey, only 59 percent of BSF couples in Baltimore were still romantically involved, compared with 70 percent of

Table 14.2 Fifteen-Month Follow-Up Impact Estimates: Baltimore

Outcome	BSF Group	Control Group	Estimated Impact	95% Confidence Interval Lower	Upper
		Relationship Status			
Still romantically involved (%)	59.4	70.3	−10.9***	−19.3	−2.5
Living together, married or unmarried (%)	41.6	45.7	−4.0	−12.7	4.6
Married (%)	7.5	6.8	0.7	−3.8	4.5
		Relationship Quality			
Support and affection[a]	3.01	3.12	-0.11**	-0.22	-0.01
Use of constructive conflict behaviors[b]	3.14	3.18	-0.04	-0.15	0.06
Avoidance of destructive conflict behaviors[c]	2.62	2.62	0.01	-0.11	0.12
Neither reports infidelity (%)	58.3	58.6	-0.3	−8.8	8.2
Mother reports no severe assaults (%)[d]	85.3	90.7	−5.3*	−11.1	0.4
Father reports no severe assaults (%)[d]	79.0	79.4	-0.4	−8.4	7.6
		Parenting and Father Involvement			
Quality of coparenting relationship[e]	4.23	4.32	-0.09*	-0.21	0.0211
Father parenting and involvement					
Lives with child (%)[f]	43.8	51.2	−7.4*	−16.3	1.5
Spends substantial time with child daily (%)[g]	53.1	60.5	−7.3*	−16.2	1.5
Provides substantial financial support (%)[h]	61.2	70.5	−9.3**	−17.9	-0.6
Level of cognitive and social play	4.40	4.64	-0.24*	-0.49	0.01
Absence of parenting stress[i]	3.38	3.37	0.02	-0.10	0.13
Avoidance of frequent spanking (%)[j]	90.5	85.5	4.9	−2.0	11.9
Mother parenting					
Level of cognitive and social play	5.19	5.15	0.05	-0.09	0.19
Absence of parenting stress[j]	3.42	3.41	0.01	-0.09	0.11
Avoidance of frequent spanking (%)[j]	85.3	87.0	−1.7	−8.2	4.8
Sample Size					
All couples	263	262			
Mothers	258	252			
Fathers	202	218			

Source: BSF fifteen-month follow-up survey, conducted by Mathematica Policy Research.

Notes: Impacts are adjusted using a regression controlling for the couple's baseline relationship and demographic characteristics. See Wood, Moore, et al. (2010) for more information.

[a]"Support and affection" is based on six survey items and is measured on a 1-to-4 strongly-disagree-to-strongly-agree scale and is defined for all couples, irrespective of the status of the relationship at fifteen months.

[b]"Use of constructive conflict behaviors" is measured on a 1-to-4 strongly-disagree-to-strongly-agree scale. This measure is defined for all intact couples, as well as for those who are no longer in a romantic relationship but are still in regular contact with each other (talking to each other at least a few times a month).

[c]"Avoidance of destructive conflict behaviors" is measured on a 1-to-4 strongly-agree-to-strongly-disagree scale. This measure is defined for all intact couples, as well as those who are no longer in a romantic relationship but are still in regular contact with each other (talking to each other at least a few times a month). This scale is coded such that positive impacts correspond to the BSF group having less destructive conflict behavior.

[d]Physical assault is measured by the twelve items on the physical assault subscale of the revised Conflict Tactics Scale (CTS2). The measure includes violence from any romantic partner during the past year and is based on the respondent's report of partner's behavior. The severity of violence is based on classifications developed by the creators of the CTS2 (Straus et al. 1996). The developers designated five items as "minor" acts and seven as "severe."

[e]Coparenting is measured on a 1-to-5 strongly-disagree-to-strongly-agree scale and is based on ten items drawn from the Parenting Alliance Inventory.

[f]Fathers are defined as living with the child if both the mother and father report that the father lived with the child at the time of the survey.

[g]Fathers are defined as having spent substantial time with the child if both the mother and father report that during the past month the father spent one hour or more with the child on a daily basis.

[h]Fathers are recorded as having provided substantial financial support if the mother reports that the father covered at least half of the costs of raising the BSF child.

[i]Parenting stress is measured on a 1-to-4 none-of-the-time-to-all-of-the-time scale and is based on own reports to four items from the Aggravation in Parenting Scale.

[j]Frequent spanking is defined as spanking a few times a week or more and is based on self reports.

*/**/*** Statistically significant at the .10/.05/.01 level, two-tailed test.

control group couples. Similarly, the percent of mothers reporting that the father provided financial support was nine points lower in the BSF group (61 percent) than in the control group (70 percent). In addition, women in the BSF program in Baltimore were more likely than women in the control group to report having been severely physically assaulted by a romantic partner in the past year,[5] 15 percent compared with 9 percent. The remainder of this chapter focuses on explanations for the seemingly counterintuitive results at the Baltimore site. Those explanations focus on how material disadvantage influences ideational traits such as family role expectations and partner trust, and how exposure to the BSF intervention could cause partners from highly disadvantaged backgrounds to change the perceptions of their relationships, their partners, or themselves in ways that induced breakups, but that might not be true of individuals from less disadvantaged backgrounds with different family role expectations and patterns of couple trust and commitment.

Part II: Differences between Baltimore and Other BSF Sites

Unlike for Oklahoma City, the differences between BSF's effects in Baltimore and those in other sites cannot be readily explained by differences in delivery of the intervention. The Baltimore program, sponsored by the Center for Urban Families, used a curriculum (LCLC) shared by four other sites and provided it in a fashion similar to those sites. The Center for Urban Families had extensive experience providing employment and fatherhood services to low-income men and had also conducted a parenting program for unmarried couples.

As an organization, the Center for Urban Families differs from other sites in that it is a community-based nonprofit focused on improving the lives of fathers,[6] particularly those living in high-risk areas. The center is located in a high-poverty, predominantly African American neighborhood in West Baltimore. The organization's structure did not appear to greatly affect delivery of BSF services, but it did influence the couples recruited. Although coordinators in Baltimore used some recruiting approaches common to other BSF sites, such as finding couples in prenatal clinics, they emphasized recruiting methods that would allow the program to reach very disadvantaged couples, including those not likely connected to any supportive services. The Center for Urban Families had a history of proactively identifying and recruiting participants for its fatherhood programs using street outreach, approaching men in locations where people gather in the community, such as basketball courts, laundromats, and parks, to speak with them about its programs and services. The program adapted this technique in its BSF recruitment of couples as part of its ongoing commitment to connecting with and serving the population in Baltimore City (Dion et al. 2006; Dion, Avellar, and Clary 2010).

Findings from our implementation analysis (Dion, Avellar, and Clary 2010) suggest that this distinctive recruiting approach allowed the Baltimore site to reach a subset of unmarried couples—and fathers, in particular—that other sites, lacking the same on-the-street neighborhood presence and experience working with fathers in high-poverty areas, were unable to reach. Descriptive information on the couples recruited to the Baltimore site (see Table 14.3) confirms that the site's study sample markedly differs from that of other sites in several aspects.

Table 14.3 Characteristics of Couples Enrolled in Baltimore Compared to Couples Enrolled in Other BSF Sites

Characteristics	Baltimore (Mean)	Other Sites (Mean)	Baltimore Rank (out of eight sites)	Most Similar Site (if Baltimore is at extreme)	Mean of Most Similar Site
Pre-Intervention					
Lives with partner full time (%) (range: 1 to 4)	47	66	8	Baton Rouge	53
Both partners expect to marry (%) (range: 1 to 4)	38	63	8	Atlanta	49
Multiple partner fertility, any (%)	57	46	1	Atlanta	53
Couple earnings	21,762	20,306	2	—	—
Receives TANF or food stamps (%)	58	44	2	—	—
Mother employed (%)	35	32	4	—	—
Father employed (%)	58	76	8	Atlanta	65
Both partners are African American (%)	92	47	1	Atlanta	80
Both partners attend religious services regularly (%)	8	26	8	Florida	19
Fifteen-Month Follow-Up (control group only)					
Romantically involved (%)	69	77	8	Florida	75
Couple lives together full time (%)	45	61	8	Atlanta	53
Father spends time with child daily (%)	59	68	8	Baton Rouge	63
Mother reports that father provides substantial financial support (%)	70	75	8	Oklahoma City	72
Sample Size					
Pre-intervention	602	4,500			
Fifteen-month follow-up (control group only)	262	1,945			

Source: BSF baseline information form, administered by sites, and fifteen-month follow-up survey, conducted by Mathematica Policy Research.

Note: At fifteen months, observations are weighted for survey non-response. See the technical supplement to the BSF fifteen-month impact report (Wood, Moore et al. 2010) for details on data collection and measures.

One characteristic of the Baltimore sample is that it contains the highest proportion of African American couples. Could the negative impacts observed in the Baltimore site be a sign that the BSF programs were ineffective for African American couples in general? Subgroup analysis does not support this interpretation. In the cross-site results, African Americans are the one ethnoracial group in which some positive program impacts are observed (Wood, McConnell, et al. 2010). This suggests that the program did not generally fail in making itself culturally relevant to African Americans and that ethnoracial composition alone cannot account for the Baltimore results.

But the study's Baltimore couples differ from those in other sites in ways that we hypothesize may have influenced BSF's surprising negative effect: more tenuous romantic relationships, greater social isolation, and more severe economic disadvantage among fathers. Baltimore couples' more tenuous relationships are reflected in lower pre-intervention rates of cohabitation, lower expectations of marriage, and higher rates of prior multiple partner fertility. Thus, these couples appear to be embedded in relationships with lower average levels of commitment and higher hurdles to achieving stable, high-quality relationships. Baltimore couples also had much less frequent attendance at religious services, which may simply reflect lower levels of religious interest. However, religious attendance is also an indicator of social integration and support (Ellison and George 1994; Bradley 1995), so the less frequent religious attendance for the Baltimore couples may indicate that they are less embedded in social support networks and more isolated from mainstream service organizations. Lastly, fathers in the Baltimore site were less likely to be employed than in any other site. This may indicate that fathers in the Baltimore site face greater structural barriers to employment, either because the organization succeeded in recruiting a more disadvantaged set of fathers or because of distinctive features of the Baltimore labor market.

Not only is the Baltimore sample at the extreme of the eight sites on all of these measures, on most they are quite a distance from the next closest site. For instance, with respect to marriage expectations, in only 38 percent of Baltimore couples did both partners expect to marry at the time of enrollment, compared to 63 percent across the other seven sites and 49 percent in the next closest site. Only 58 percent of Baltimore fathers were employed at baseline, compared to 76 percent in the remaining sites combined and 65 percent in the next lowest site. And in only 8 percent of Baltimore couples did both partners attend religious services regularly, less than one-third the 26 percent rate overall and less than half the 19 percent rate of the next lowest site.

Apart from these individual-level characteristics, Baltimore couples also were more likely to live in neighborhoods of concentrated poverty. Unlike many other BSF sites, which were located in office parks in largely commercial areas, the Center for Urban Families is located in a high-poverty Baltimore neighborhood. Mathematica's final implementation analysis (Dion, Avellar, and Clary 2010) noted that the organization focused on serving "low-income families, particularly those in high-risk areas" (xv), with the organization's street canvassing occurring in "impoverished West Baltimore" (71). Other sites undoubtedly served some couples living in concentrated disadvantage, but Baltimore was unique in its intentional effort to bring couples from such circumstances into the BSF program.

The Baltimore sample is not an outlier in all areas. For instance, the baseline employment rate for mothers was near the average for the eight BSF sites. This is consistent with the hypothesis that it is the *fathers* reached through the Center for Urban Families' recruitment that are distinctive in their economic disadvantage. The average earnings of Baltimore couples are actually higher than the average in other sites, though this is driven entirely by higher earnings by the mothers. Fathers' earnings are lower in Baltimore than elsewhere.[7]

In sum, the measured characteristics suggest that the unique position of and recruiting by the Center for Urban Families led to a sample of couples whose relationships were less established and whose partners—especially the men—were less connected to major economic and social institutions. These are couples whom we would expect to experience greater relationship instability. The follow-up relationship outcomes for the control group (who were not affected by the intervention) confirm that expectation. As shown in Table 14.3, fifteen months after random assignment, control group couples in Baltimore were much less likely to be living together or romantically involved than control group couples in any other site. And, as might be expected given the higher rates of relationship dissolution, the fathers were much less likely to spend time daily with their children or provide substantial financial support.

Part III: Explaining the Anomalous Findings in Baltimore

Potential Explanations for Negative Program Impacts in Baltimore

Our knowledge of the differences between Baltimore and other BSF sites suggests that the negative impacts in Baltimore are due to differences in the population that the Center for Urban Families was able to reach and recruit rather than differences in delivery of the services. But even if the couples served in Baltimore differed fundamentally from those in other sites, why would the program cause that particular subset of couples to experience more relationship instability than they would have otherwise? The evaluation showed that the program did not reduce couples' employment or earnings, and we have no reason to think that participation in BSF worsened couples' relationship skills. So, in Baltimore, assignment to the treatment group seemingly caused relationships to be more prone to dissolution without worsening couples' circumstances. This implies that the program changed BSF couples' perceptions of their relationships, their partners, or themselves in ways that induced breakups. In this section, we outline some hypotheses for how BSF might have such an impact among couples with particular models of family roles and family formation that are more likely to occur among the most economically disadvantaged and socially isolated couples.[8]

We start from the premise that as family formation has become deinstitutionalized (Cherlin 2004) there is an increasing variety of possibilities for defining romantic and familial relationships and individuals' roles within them. Deinstitutionalization leads to ambiguity in the roles that family members hold, especially for unmarried cohabiting couples (Cherlin 2004; Nock 1995), nonresidential fathers (Hamer 2001; Jarrett, Roy, and Burton 2002), and couples with children from prior relationships (Cherlin 1978; Furstenberg and Cherlin 1994).

In this ambiguous cultural context, individuals have considerable choice in constructing their own definitions of appropriate and healthy relationships. For couples in BSF, we anticipate that their generally disadvantaged material circumstances will shape these interpretations. Poverty affects both the cultural repertoires that individuals have available to them (Swidler 2001) and how they use them to understand their relationships (Fosse 2010). Because poverty limits the material resources that individuals possess, they will tend to adopt expectations for their own roles that fit within their resource limitations. For instance, fathers in poverty often dismiss the provider role as the defining feature of a good father, instead emphasizing the importance of providing an emotional connection with children (Jarrett, Roy, and Burton 2002; Hamer 2001; Waller 2010).

Relationship expectations may also be adapted to fit both individual resources and social norms. The pervasive distrust between partners highlighted in studies of low-income couple relationships (Edin and Kefalas 2005; Waller and McLanahan 2005) can affect individuals' views of the responsibilities that come with their familial roles. For instance, in his interviews with low-income men in Boston, the sociologist Nathan Fosse (2010) finds distrust of women among highly disadvantaged men can become a justification to frame their own role as an intimate partner as one that does not require fidelity.

Although the BSF curricula are focused on developing relationship skills rather than prescribing roles, they nonetheless assume certain types of responsibility and norms of behavior, including sexual fidelity and provision of financial support. Interviews with couples who participated in the BSF curricula revealed that a primary conclusion that couples took from the sessions was the importance of fathers "stepping up" to assume more financial responsibility, provide a better role model for their children, and be more reliable. As one father stated, "I realized that this baby's not gonna raise itself. The baby can't obviously get a job. And I knew, once thinking about it, that she's [his partner] gonna take some time to heal [after surgery] and I had to step up" (Dion, Avellar, and Clary 2010, 27). As such, the curricula may present models of partnerhood and fatherhood that challenge the views held consciously or unconsciously by participants.

From a programmatic perspective, this attempt to challenge and change participants' views may be one of the goals. But as the sociologist Maureen Waller (2010, 120) notes, this sort of challenge could have negative repercussions such that "disadvantaged parents who embrace 'mainstream' ideas about enduring unions may dissolve their relationships." This would occur if the cultural model presented is one that individuals are not (or perceive they are not) able to live up to. The more disadvantaged the population, the more likely the models presented by BSF are to conflict with the ideas that individuals have adopted of what family roles require. As such, the program may challenge individuals' perceptions of themselves as good partners and parents. If individuals see themselves as being able to meet the challenge—such as to provide more economically or be sexually faithful—then it may lead to positive changes for the individual and family. But, if not, it could cause them to distance themselves from their partners and children. For instance, men who see themselves as failing in their role as fathers reduce engagement with their children to protect themselves from that sense of failure or to "shield their children from their own history of personal failings" (Young 2011, 120).

BSF participation and discussions may also lead an individual to realize that the other partner's expectations are different from what the individual had previously understood—or it may simply push those expectations to the fore. For instance, Hamer (2001) recounts the divergence between mothers' expectations of fathers' financial providership in contrast with fathers' own emphasis on providing social and emotional support to their children. Discussions of financial responsibility in the BSF sessions may lead a father to recognize more vividly that his partner has expectations that he is not meeting—an expectation to which the curriculum will lend greater normative heft. If the father is unable or unwilling to fulfill the role, this may introduce conflict and, if the relationship ends, also alter perceptions of fault for the dissolution.

Prior work describes how high economic and relationship prerequisites for marriage deter the decision to marry (Edin and Kefalas 2005; Gibson-Davis, Edin, and McLanahan 2005; Smock, Manning, and Porter 2005). A similar process could deter long-term nonmarital relationships if the accepted expectations rise beyond what partners are able to meet. This process of challenging role definitions and expectations could apply to either fathers or mothers, but we propose that it is more likely to happen to fathers. It has been asserted that there are fewer "good" men who are ready to fill conventional roles as long-term partners or parents (Edin 2000; Wilson and Neckerman 1987). In part, this may be because severe poverty and social isolation impose greater obstacles on the fulfillment of traditional paternal responsibilities—breadwinning—than on traditional maternal responsibilities. While low-income women may find the motherhood role to be a source of satisfaction and domain in which they are able to meet social expectations (Edin and Kefalas 2005), low-income men may find their inability to provide for their families financially a source of shame and frustration (Jarrett, Roy, and Burton 2002; Nelson, Clampet-Lundquist, and Edin 2002). For fathers particularly, then, embracing mainstream beliefs and values of responsible fatherhood or hearing of their partner's desires that they achieve these standards may alter men's own conceptions of their adequacy as fathers and partners. Recall that the fathers in the Baltimore BSF site were much more likely than fathers in other BSF sites to be unemployed at entry into the program. For these fathers, it may be difficult to change their circumstances to "step up" and match mainstream norms of breadwinning fatherhood.

In addition to influencing individuals' views of themselves and their own responsibilities, we hypothesize that BSF could also affect individuals' perceptions of their partners' levels of commitment in ways that may induce relationship instability. This could happen via the decision to participate rather than through the participation itself. In an environment where there are few formal markers of commitment, what seem like advances in the seriousness of a relationship (such as moving in together) frequently occur without explicit discussion or conscious decision making (Manning and Smock 2005). A partner's attitude toward attending sessions could therefore possess substantial signaling value regarding their level of commitment (Hawkins et al. 2012; Stanley, Rhoades, and Whitton 2011).

BSF program operators reported that it was relatively common for one partner (most often the father) to resist attending, while the other was more willing (Dion et al. 2006; Dion, Avellar, and Clary 2010). The partner who is interested in attending may interpret the other partner's resistance to attend as a signal of lack of commitment to the relationship and unwillingness to sacrifice to improve it. In a circumstance where trust is high, the interested partner may not take resistance to attend BSF sessions to reflect a lack of commitment, especially if the other partner has potentially legitimate reasons for not attending—such as time constraints due to job or other commitments. But among the most disadvantaged couples, such reluctance seems more likely to activate suspended distrust. The decision of whether to actively participate in BSF thus could force a decision about the direction of the relationship. In the absence of the program, such a decision point may not have occurred until later, and the relationship may have endured for a longer time, even if it eventually dissolved.

Evidence for the Proposed Explanations

We performed a set of analyses using survey data to test for evidence of the phenomena suggested by the preceding hypotheses. In order to examine whether the increased union dissolution was related to changes in perceived responsibilities of partners, we examined the reasons that Baltimore BSF group members gave for their union dissolutions, comparing those to reasons given by couples from the control group. If the program increased dissolution by altering the meanings that participants attached to relationship roles and the expected behaviors of partners in ways that they may not have been able or willing to meet, then the attributions for dissolution should differ between the groups.

As a test of the hypothesis that the decision to actively participate in the program could induce union dissolution in some cases by raising doubt about a partner's commitment, we examine whether impacts are concentrated among the least committed segment of BSF couples in Baltimore. This should be the group that has established the least amount of trust between partners. In turn, individuals in those relationships would be expected to be the most likely to interpret a partner's reluctance to participate as a lack commitment to the relationship.[9]

In the BSF fifteen-month follow-up survey, individuals whose romantic relationship with their BSF partner had ended were asked to cite reasons for the breakup. Respondents were asked about six potential reasons for dissolution that they could attribute to themselves and/or their partners. The questions were worded as follows: "I am going to read you a list of reasons that people give for why their relationships ended. For each reason, tell me if this is why your relationship with [PARTNER] ended. Was it because you, your partner, or both of you

1. cheated or were unfaithful?
2. went to jail or prison?
3. were abusive or violent?
4. used drugs or alcohol?
5. could not keep a job or contribute enough financially to the family?
6. were not a good parent or role model?"

Respondents could select as many reasons as they felt were relevant. Because of very small counts in some of those responses, we summed across them to create the following measures of

1. whether the respondent faults the father at all;
2. whether the respondent faults only the father;
3. the number of reasons that the respondent faults the father (0 to 6);
4. whether the respondent faults the mother at all;
5. whether the respondent faults only the mother; and
6. the number of reasons that the respondent faults the mother (0 to 6).

Table 14.4 Impact of the Baltimore BSF Program on Reasons Given for Marital Dissolution

Characteristics	All Relationships (experimental)		Dissolved Relationships (not experimental)	
	BSF Group	Control Group	BSF Group	Control Group
Reasons Given by Father				
Faults father at all (%)	14***	6	58***	26
Faults father, not mother (%)	6*	2	23	10
Number of reasons given for faulting father	0.23***	0.07	0.94***	0.26
Faults mother at all (%)	10	8	40	35
Faults mother, not father (%)	2	4	6*	19
Number of reasons given for faulting mother	0.16	0.10	0.69	0.35
Reasons Given by Mother				
Faults father at all (%)	20*	15	63	62
Faults father, not mother (%)	19**	11	59	47
Number of reasons given for faulting father	0.36	0.29	1.11	1.25
Faults mother at all (%)	2	4	6*	17
Faults mother, not father (%)	0	0	1	2
Number of reasons given for faulting mother	0.04	0.05	0.08*	0.25
Sample Size				
Fathers	202	218	53	47
Mothers	258	252	80	62

Source: BSF fifteen-month follow-up survey, conducted by Mathematica Policy Research.
Note: Means are regression adjusted. Observations are weighted for survey non-response. See Wood, Moore, et al. (2010) for details on analysis methods.
***/**/* Difference from control group mean is statistically significant at the .01/.05/.10 level.

The results in Table 14.4 are regression-adjusted group means for each of those measures.[10] The means in the left-hand column are from analyses that include all Baltimore couples, irrespective of whether or not their relationship was intact at fifteen months (420 fathers and 510 mothers). The estimates presented therefore capture how frequently couples' relationships ended with fault attributed to the particular partner. Observations take a value of zero if the relationship was still intact at fifteen months or if it had dissolved but the other partner (the mother or father) was not faulted by the respondent. Consequently, those results are influenced both by the rate of union dissolution and reasons given for dissolution. However, we use this approach because the outcomes we examine are defined for all couples. Therefore, the analysis preserves the benefits of random assignment where research groups can be assumed to be initially equivalent, on average, and any differences between them that emerge and are too large to be due to chance can be attributed to the effect of the program.

The results in the right-hand column are from analyses limited to couples whose romantic relationship had ended by the time of the fifteen-month follow-up (100 fathers and 142 mothers). In contrast to the full-sample results, differences between groups reflect only differences in attributions for breakup rather than both the rate of breakup and attributions. However, because the composition of the samples is determined by relationship dissolution, a post-random assignment factor that could be influenced by the intervention, the analysis is not experimental.

The results show some rather dramatic differences between treatment and control groups in attributing fault for the end of the relationship. Specifically, romantic relationships in the BSF program group are much more likely to end with the father faulting himself than are control group relationships. In the experimental results covering all couples, 14 percent of romantic relationships in the BSF group ended with a dissolution in which the father faulted himself, compared to only 6 percent in the control group. And the average total count of reasons for fault attributed to fathers by fathers was three times greater among those in the BSF group compared to those in the control group. Within dissolved relationships, fathers cite themselves as having at least part of the fault for the breakup in 58 percent of cases in the BSF group, compared to only 26 percent in the control group.

The differences are driven by a few specific areas of fault. The largest is that 19 percent of BSF fathers in dissolved relationships attribute the breakup at least in part to their inability to contribute enough financially to the family, compared to only 4 percent of fathers in dissolved control group relationships. This difference is statistically significant at conventional levels. Other substantively important differences appear in fathers' citing their own incarceration (15 percent in the BSF group versus 9 percent in the control group), substance abuse (9 percent versus 2 percent), and abusive behavior (9 percent versus 4 percent) as at least in part responsible for the end of the couple relationship. Group differences on each of those individual items were not statistically significant, but together they

Table 14.5 Estimated Impacts of Building Strong Families on Fathers' Behaviors and Outcomes Disproportionately Cited as Causes of Union Dissolution in Baltimore

Outcome	BSF Group	Control Group	Estimated Impact	95% Confidence Interval	
				Upper	Lower
Father employed in the past month (%)	66.1	64.9	1.2	−8.2	10.5
Father's earnings in the past year ($)	12,365	12,682	−317	−2,835	2,201
Any binge drinking in the past year (%)	34.4	45.9	−11.5**	−21.6	−1.3
Substance use interfered with work, family, or social life (%)	12.8	13.4	-0.6	−7.7	6.4
Ever arrested since random assignment (%)	48.7	43.3	5.4	−5.5	16.3
Sample Size					
Fathers (all outcomes other than arrests)	202	218			
Fathers (arrests)	263	262			

Source: BSF fifteen-month follow-up survey, conducted by Mathematica Policy Research.

Notes: In order to minimize potential underreporting of interaction with the criminal justice system, the arrests measure is coded with a value of one if either the father or the mother reports that the outcome in question occurred. Multiple imputation is used to fill in the mother's response if the father, but not the mother, responded to the thirty-six-month survey. The sample size is higher for arrests because a value is present if either the father or the mother responded, rather than requiring that the father responded. Further details on the construction of these measures are provided in Wood, Moore, et al. (2010).

***/**/* Impact estimates are statistically significant at the .01/.05/.10 level, two-tailed test.

contribute to the overall differences observed in fathers' attributions in Table 14.4.[11]

These differences are particularly noteworthy because, with the exception of intimate partner violence, BSF did not affect the behaviors and outcomes in question (see Table 14.5). That is, BSF fathers were not any more likely than control group fathers in Baltimore to be unemployed, have been arrested, or have abused drugs or alcohol in the fifteen months after random assignment. Their earnings were, on average, almost identical to the control group, and Baltimore BSF fathers were actually less likely than control group fathers to have engaged in binge drinking in the prior year. Thus the BSF fathers' markedly higher propensity to view their own behavior as having contributed to the end of the relationship appears to be almost wholly due to program impacts on how fathers perceive their own behavior rather than to impacts on the behavior itself.

Regarding the possible exception of intimate partner violence, for which some harmful program impacts were found, it bears noting that BSF mothers in Baltimore were *not* more likely than control group mothers to cite abuse by the partner as a cause of relationship dissolution. Among all couples in both groups, 4 percent of relationships ended with the mother citing the father's abuse as a cause of the dissolution. Among mothers from dissolved relationships, 12 percent of those in the BSF group cited abuse by the partner as a cause, compared to 15 percent in the control group. Prior research has shown that the risk of violence to women increases during a separation (DeKeseredy, Rogness, and Schwartz 2004), and it may well be that the increased rate of intimate partner violence against mothers in the BSF group in Baltimore is a result of the relationship breakup rather than a cause of it.

Mothers in the two study groups did not differ as dramatically as fathers in the reasons they cited for breakups. If anything, mothers in the BSF group appear to have been somewhat less likely than control group mothers to fault themselves. In the analyses that include all couples, regardless of fifteen-month relationship status, BSF group mothers are more likely to fault the father and not themselves. As shown in Table 14.4, among all BSF group couples in Baltimore, 19 percent experienced a relationship dissolution by fifteen months for which the mother faulted the father and not herself, versus 11 percent in the control group. And among mothers whose relationships ended, only 6 percent of those in the BSF group faulted themselves at all, compared to 17 percent in the control group. So, it is possible that participation in BSF also affected mothers' perceptions of appropriate behavior for the fathers. However, this difference is only marginally statistically significant, and there is no statistically significant difference between treatment and control groups in the proportion of all relationships that ended with a dissolution in which the mother cited herself as at fault.

Earlier we also hypothesized that the process of couples deciding whether or not to attend group sessions could provide a signal to each partner of the other's commitment and that this could induce union dissolution if partners disagreed about attending, especially if one partner's reluctance was interpreted as a lack of relationship commitment. Because individuals in less established relationships are likely to have lower levels of trust between partners, we expect that the probability of that process undermining relationship stability would be greatest among the least established couples.

During the process of determining eligibility for the study, couples reported whether they were in a "steady" relationship or one that was only "on-again and off-again." In analyses we performed previously to examine the program's impacts on intimate partner violence, we found the harmful program impacts concentrated among the 20 percent of couples in which at least one partner had reported at baseline that the couple's relationship was only off and on. Among couples in a steady relationship at baseline, 12 percent of BSF group mothers reported some severe physical assault in the fifteen months after random assignment, compared to 9 percent of control group mothers—a difference that is not statistically significant. But among couples in an off-and-on relationship prior to study enrollment, 28 percent of BSF group mothers reported some severe physical assault, compared to 10 percent of control group mothers. The sample size is small, but the group difference is marginally statistically significant at $p < 0.10$.[12]

A similar analysis of relationship stability produces results that are less dramatic but in a similar direction. Among couples who started in a steady relationship, 65 percent of the BSF group were still romantically involved at fifteen months, compared to 74 percent in the control group—a nine percentage point difference that is marginally statistically significant ($p < 0.10$). The magnitude of the difference is larger for on-and-off couples—22 percentage points—with only 36 percent of such couples in the BSF group remaining intact versus 58 percent of corresponding control group couples. The difference in impacts for steady versus on-and-off couples falls short of conventional standards for statistical significance. However, the magnitude of the impacts among on-and-off couples indicates that they disproportionately contribute to the overall negative effects of the BSF program on relationship stability in Baltimore. These results are consistent with the argument that the decision of whether or not to participate could raise concern about lack of commitment to the relationship among couples with the least established relationships in which little trust is likely to have developed.

Conclusion

The BSF demonstration found that the intervention had no effect overall on couple relationships at fifteen months across the eight sites combined. In addition, BSF had little or no effect in most of the evaluation sites individually. However, BSF had a number of negative effects on the young African American couples in Baltimore, increasing relationship dissolution and reducing the level of father involvement with children. Since these effects are the opposite of those intended by the intervention, the Baltimore results are initially a puzzle.

Information about the site obtained from the study's implementation analysis suggest that the pattern of impacts is most likely due to the uniquely disadvantaged set of young African American couples recruited in Baltimore. This chapter has presented some theoretical perspectives on why this may have occurred, focused on how the intervention could undermine the views that participants develop of themselves and their partners using the cultural repertoires available to them within a disadvantaged and isolated economic and social context. We hypothesized that the program curriculum may alter those views in ways that do not fit as well with couples' circumstances as the views with which they had entered the program. In analyses presented here, we find that BSF caused fathers to be more likely to fault themselves for the end of the relationship. Importantly, fathers are more likely to blame themselves for failings like inability to contribute sufficiently financially and for substance abuse, even though the program did not negatively affect fathers' actual employment, earnings, or use of alcohol or illicit drugs.

This finding is consistent with hypotheses that the definitions of partner and father roles encouraged by BSF may differ in important ways from the definitions previously adopted by participating fathers and, in turn, change their views of how well they are fulfilling those roles. If fathers adopt role redefinitions that force them to "step up" in responsibility—or if they perceive that their partners have adopted such expectations—and they feel unwilling or unable to do so, this could precipitate relationship dissolution by causing the father to distance himself from the relationship. We would expect that both the size of the discrepancy between preexisting and newly adopted role expectations and fathers' challenges in meeting those heightened expectations to be more pronounced among Baltimore fathers because of their higher levels of unemployment and social isolation. That is, the role definitions they had created for themselves left them with a larger distance to "step up" to meet the new expectations, while their material circumstances rendered them less able to make that step.

The fact that the program did not cause a similar change among mothers and, if anything, led mothers to be less likely to fault themselves for relationship dissolution, suggests that the gap between how participants had previously framed their relationship roles and the role definitions presented in BSF is much greater for fathers served by the program in Baltimore. Given the dismal economic prospects for the most disadvantaged men in the United States (Sum et al. 2011), like those served by Baltimore's Center for Urban Families, it is to be expected that many fathers would have tended to adopt role definitions that diminished expectations of their contributions in some aspects in order to maintain positive self-evaluations (Hamer 2001; Waller 2010). But the very success of the program in challenging those culturally constructed expectations could inadvertently undermine relationship stability.

The concentration of negative program effects among the least committed couples also suggests that the offer of services resulting from assignment to the treatment group could have forced a decision about the relationship that might not have occurred until later, which is particularly relevant for couples who had not had enough experience together to develop trust in the other and confidence in their commitment to the relationship (Fosse 2010) and for those from highly disadvantaged backgrounds with more fluid family formation patterns where formal, explicit indicators of commitment are less common. It is evident from the program's modest participation rates (Wood, Moore, and Clarkwest 2011) that many individuals were not highly motivated to participate, a fact that could heighten distrust that had been partially suspended by those individuals' more motivated partners.

In addition, the couples' outcomes may have been influenced not just by their own traits but also by those of other participating couples. One factor noted earlier that has been cited as contributing to the positive impacts in Oklahoma is that it was the only site where married and unmarried couples were in the same classes. The more established couples may have served as role models and as sources of hope for couples in earlier relationship stages that they can overcome the challenges they face in meeting high relationship expectations. In Baltimore, not only would

there have been no married couples in the classes, but a larger proportion of unmarried couples would have been less established in their relationships than was the case in other sites. Challenges could well seem
much more daunting among a group of unmarried couples with tenuous
relationships, more obstacles to overcome, and fewer examples among
them of success in doing so.

The results above are framed as being negative because they are contrary to the stated goals of the program, which aims to keep couples
together. However, it is possible that the apparently negative impacts on
relationship dissolution are not all harmful. The relationships of couples
targeted by the program face a high risk of dissolution with or without the
BSF program. As we have seen, this is particularly true of the couples
enrolled in Baltimore. Inducing partners to actively consider the status of
their relationship and reexamine their roles within it may simply speed up
the dissolution of relationships that would have ended before too long in
any event. In some cases, it may be better for that dissolution to occur
sooner rather than later, and it is possible that the reexaminations may
lead to better repartnering outcomes. The negative impacts on father
involvement in Baltimore—in particular the likelihood that fathers regularly spend time with their children and provide them with substantial
financial support—raise concerns. However, it is notable that in spite of
these effects we find no evidence that the Baltimore program adversely
affected the economic well-being of the children of participating couples.
In particular, children of BSF couples in Baltimore were no more likely
than children of control group couples to be living in poverty at the
fifteen-month follow-up or to be living in households that were receiving
public assistance or that had experienced material hardship in the past
year (Wood, Moore, et al. 2010).

Although in some cases an accelerated relationship breakup is the best
outcome for those involved, ideally the intervention would provide tools
allowing most couples to overcome obstacles faced. In addition to the
core relationship skills curriculum, BSF did attempt to provide or arrange
a variety of supportive services—such as employment and mental health
counseling—to help unmarried couples meet the challenges in their relationships. It is possible that, in addition to providing relationship skills
training and other services that directly attack problems, future iterations
of relationship skills interventions could also focus more on ways to
"fram[e] . . . challenges as more tractable, to create a shared identity as a
couple who can 'beat the odds' " (Waller 2010, 120). The Baltimore results

also suggest that future programs may be strengthened by providing supports for couples dealing with relationship breakups and their aftermath, services designed to minimize the risk of intimate partner violence in the context of relationship breakup and to maintain father involvement after relationships end.

The fact that the program's impacts could largely reflect acceleration in the timing of breakups that would eventually have occurred suggests that over time the negative impacts on relationship stability in Baltimore might fade dramatically or reverse.

The results presented here support the call by the sociologists Laura Tach and Kathryn Edin (2011) for greater emphasis in qualitative research on how low-income men "learn to enact the roles of partner and father" (83), how trust and commitment develop in low-income relationships, and how couples' differing perceptions of self and partner affect relationship stability. This is particularly important for researchers evaluating the effects of relationship and marriage education programs serving low-income couples, since these programs have not yet shown the positive impacts that have been observed among more advantaged populations.[13] And as we have seen, the possibility exists of negative impacts among some groups of couples. The success of interventions to improve couples' relationships hinges on their ability to produce a range of changes in thought and behavior—but material disadvantage makes those changes difficult.

Around the time of their child's birth, low-income young fathers express high hopes for their relationships with the child and mother. But they face steep challenges in meeting responsibilities as partners and fathers. In order to be successful, programs that attempt to promote father involvement and positive couple relationships do need to be able to convince young fathers of the importance of stepping up to higher levels of responsibility. But it is important that the steps fathers are encouraged to take are ones that they believe they can achieve and truly have the means to do so. Young fathers have consciously or unconsciously developed mental models of what their roles as parents and partners should entail. Those models are derived from the repertoire of models that they have seen around them and are shaped, in part, to fit what they see as feasible, thus permitting them to maintain an image of themselves as fulfilling their familial responsibilities. Because cultural models have likely been developed to fit circumstances, it is important for family strengthening interventions that involve influencing young fathers' family-related ideas and behaviors to start with an understanding of the models that the men enter with and what difficulties may be introduced for fathers if the program does succeed in changing those mental models. This implies that comprehensive programs that are able to succeed in addressing multiple structural hindrances, along with cultural beliefs, are likely to be required in order to increase relationship stability and father involvement. Without sufficient attention to addressing both what fathers perceive as achievable and what they can realistically achieve, fathers may step back rather than up.

15

Beyond BA Blinders

Cultural Impediments to College Success

JAMES E. ROSENBAUM, *State University of New York, Brooklyn*

JENNIFER STEPHAN, *Northwestern University*

JANET ROSENBAUM, *University of Maryland*

AMY E. FORAN, *Depaul University*

PAM SCHUETZ, *Northwestern University*

Even as some racial barriers in higher education have declined, subtle barriers may remain deeply buried in institutional procedures and cultural assumptions. College access has greatly improved, particularly because of community colleges, but degree completion remains a serious problem. Some researchers and policymakers blame degree completion problems on students' academic deficiencies, but our research indicates that many students do not complete degrees because of nonacademic errors, such as course choices, time allocation, degree plans, and lack of knowledge about the progress toward degree completion. Community colleges can change their procedures to prevent students from making such nonacademic errors—by changing the structure of credentials and increasing clarity in guidance toward degree completion. The current procedures arise from traditional cultural assumptions—what we call "BA blinders"—and we describe nontraditional procedures used in other colleges that reduce these barriers.

Community colleges have reduced the formal barriers of time, distance, and cost. They provide low-cost college access in convenient locations at convenient times. They have also abolished potentially biased admissions requirements. Nonetheless, community college degree completion rates remain low overall (37 percent in eight years) and remain abysmal for African Americans (18 percent; Stephan and Rosenbaum 2009).

The higher education literature often assumes that college dropouts lack the academic ability to handle college. We propose that deficiencies

471

reside partially in the procedures used by community colleges and the demands they make on students. Community colleges have changed dramatically in recent decades, with the addition of a more diverse student body, new programs, and new credentials in response to new labor market demands. Even with these changes that expand access to disadvantaged students seeking labor market-relevant career skills, colleges have maintained requirements that may not be necessary but may increase the barriers to disadvantaged students.

Colleges demand a variety of culturally specific skills, knowledge, resources, and habits, some of which are intrinsic to the purpose of higher education; some, however, may be holdovers from old cultural traditions (Meyer 1977). Demands based in cultural traditions are not a concern if colleges serve only traditional college students who possess these cultural traditions and if the labor market only demands traditional academic skills. Demands based in cultural traditions become problematic when colleges serve new groups of students who do not possess these cultural traditions or when colleges offer programs to prepare for new nontraditional occupations where these cultural traditions may be unnecessary. Given the changes in community colleges that have increased access to disadvantaged students, community college administrators need to evaluate whether community colleges make atavistic demands on students that may not be necessary for addressing current societal needs but do impose larger burdens for disadvantaged students.

Administrators and policymakers often blame college failure on the gap between student achievement and colleges' academic demands, but this gap may not be the only factor. In this chapter, we describe more than six other gaps created by community colleges' procedures that may add burdens to disadvantaged students without providing an academic benefit. These gaps include (1) courses without credits, (2) predictable delays without warning, (3) predictable dropouts without warning, (4) credits without credentials, (5) credits without progress, and (6) credentials without job payoffs.

These gaps are avoidable. As we shall show, community colleges often use traditional college procedures that shape success in many ways. These traditional college procedures define how quickly success can occur, which obstacles must be overcome, how quick successes can be combined with further opportunities, how curriculum pathways can be dependable and fit students' life demands, how effectively mistakes can be prevented or repaired, and how effectively college graduates can turn their degrees into job payoffs. Although most colleges only consider one set of procedures, we describe alternative procedures used by some colleges that radically reduce these gaps and unnecessary barriers to success. Colleges using these new procedures have dramatically better degree completion success rates.

The development of these alternative procedures has implications for theory and practice. For theory, these discoveries indicate that many college failures attributed to students' limited ability may actually arise from mismatches between traditional college procedures and the cultural experiences of nontraditional students. Disadvantaged students experience many kinds of problems in community colleges that arise from the unnecessary demands of traditional college procedures. In contrast, nontraditional procedures avoid making these demands, and they are associated with improved degree completion rates and no decline in labor market payoffs.

For practice, these alternative procedures can be implemented easily and inexpensively. As we shall show, traditional community colleges already have procedures that can be adapted to match the alternative procedures, but these procedures need to be organized, structured, and explained to students. While there is much talk about improving "institutional capability," we believe the capability is already present but college staff must remove their cultural blinders and present alternative procedures.

Three Revolutions

College-for-all has changed the rules. We are living in revolutionary times, where social reality is changing so quickly and so much that our own concepts prevent us from seeing barriers and opportunities. Today, three revolutions are occurring that have transformed community colleges and given them a central role in society.

First, the labor market has undergone a revolution, which affects community colleges. The labor market now includes more mid-skill jobs, including both new jobs and old jobs but with increased skill demands, so more students must attend college to get the skills needed by these jobs—academic, job, social, and professional skills (Grubb 1996; Murnane and Levy 1996).

Second, the number of students attending college has vastly increased. While enrollment in four-year colleges has doubled since the 1960s, enrollment in community colleges has increased fivefold. Community colleges have reduced the barriers to access by having convenient time schedules 24–7 and convenient locations, with 1,100 colleges across the country, including many with satellite campuses near homes and workplaces. Nationwide, more than 80 percent of high school graduates enter higher education in the eight years after high school. Despite big racial gaps in high school and college completion rates, among high school graduates, the racial gap in college enrollment has largely disappeared: 83 percent of whites and 80 percent of blacks and Hispanics enter college (Adelman 2003). Much of the change has occurred in a single kind of institution: community colleges.

Third, the barriers to college entrance have been reduced. Open admissions and low tuition are perhaps the most revolutionary changes. Colleges traditionally were selective and expensive, but today, most community colleges have open admissions and low tuition. As a result, almost anyone can attend, regardless of prior achievement or income.

New kinds of students attend college who traditionally did not (Grubb 1996), which naturally creates new problems. Low tuition has increased access for low-income students, many of whom live in high-risk life circumstances where economic setbacks, illness, and violence can interrupt college at any time. Open admissions policies have increased access for students who have academic skill deficiencies and little confidence. Traditional college procedures were designed to serve traditional college students who do not have these concerns.

Despite their impressive flexibility in reducing entry requirements and adapting to students' time constraints, there has been little thought to which procedures college should use to respond to the new students and new labor market demands. Community colleges mostly have retained traditional college culture and procedures that may not fit the new students or new labor market demands, and perhaps as a result, community colleges have very poor degree-completion rates. As we shall show, some colleges depart from traditional cultural norms, and they devise curricula and procedures that pose more appropriate demands and sacrifices; this likely increases success rates without precluding degree- and job-advancement opportunities. This nation has already made a serious commitment to a "college-for-all" strategy, so it is crucial to understand the massive failures that are now occurring and how colleges can devise alternative procedures that enable students to succeed.

Beyond BA Blinders: Nontraditional Procedures and College Success

Many reformers assume traditional BA degrees are the only goal of college and traditional college procedures are the only conceivable procedures. They devote great energy to trying to transform low-achieving students into traditional students who can meet the traditional demands by imposing massive amounts of remedial courses. That BA-centric approach has been tried many times, and it has failed repeatedly, sometimes with failure rates as high as 83 percent in national studies (see Bailey, Jeong, and Cho 2010). This failure leads some observers to believe these disadvantaged students lack the ability to succeed in college (Murray 2008).

While this approach assumes that nontraditional students lack the ability to handle the academic demands of college, we find that colleges make other nonacademic demands on students. Colleges demand culturally specific information and circumstances that are currently necessary to succeed in college, such as college and labor market knowledge, schedule flexibility, and time and resources to persist without payoffs over long unanticipated durations. In interviews, community college students report a wide variety of mistakes in areas such as course choices, time allocation, and degree plans. Such mistakes threaten students' persistence in college, but they are not related to low academic skills. Many of these mistakes could have been prevented by alternative college procedures. Individuals' "ability" to succeed in college may be changeable—if institutions change their procedures to reduce demands for these cultural attributes.

In the book *Real Education*, Charles Murray (2008) assumes that college dropout indicates low ability of individual students. Murray is partly right: as long as we keep offering the same traditional college procedures, nontraditional students will likely continue to have high failure rates. However, Murray draws the wrong inference: this is not only a statement about individuals' ability; it is also a statement about the demands imposed by traditional procedures on students with nontraditional backgrounds.

Every college graduate knows what "college" is. That is the problem, which we call "BA blinders." Traditional colleges that most of us attended stressed certain traditional cultural norms and procedures. As John Meyer (1971) observed, "college" is defined by the institutional customs and practices that we attribute to colleges, and some of these may be quite irrelevant to producing functional skills. These customs include some obvious elements (athletic teams, mascots, university seals embossed with Latin slogans, dormitories) and many subtle elements, including procedures demanding cultural norms. These customs conjure up images of beautiful college campuses with carefree students studying together, debating metaphysical issues, playing frisbee, and completing a paper assignment during an arduous all-nighter followed by a sunrise euphoria. Nontraditional students may have difficulty with these idyllic images because serious problems are lurking for them that traditional college students are already culturally equipped to navigate.

Our BA blinders include many pervasive but subtle beliefs—that college must encourage all students to pursue a BA degree, to take four years of full-time courses, to expect no interim credentials or payoffs, and to explore many academic fields (labeled "general education"). Traditional college students choose their courses from a wide range of options; they rarely consult counselors, and colleges do not closely monitor their progress. Traditional college students may occasionally take courses that do not count toward their degrees, but traditional colleges may consider such mistakes to be part of the learning process that provide "breadth," and the costs of such deviations are never considered. These traditional norms and procedures, which were designed for traditional college students, pose serious barriers to nontraditional students.

Alternatives are possible, although rarely considered. Colleges can take many forms and use different procedures than the traditional model. We studied another type of college, *occupational colleges*—private accredited colleges that offer career preparation in occupational fields (e.g., technicians, health care, business, etc.). Occupational colleges are accredited to offer college degrees (associate's degrees and sometimes bachelor's degrees) unlike the vast majority of private postsecondary career schools. Occupational colleges are private but not selective, and they enroll large numbers of low-achieving and low-income students, funded by federal and state financial aid, so their students are similarly disadvantaged as those in community colleges.

Surprisingly, despite having five-times-higher tuition than community colleges, private two-year colleges nonetheless have lower-income students than public two-year colleges due to aggressive assistance with loans and state and federal (Pell) grants (which require complicated paperwork). Due to aggressive recruiting and marketing, private two-year colleges also

Table 15.1 Student Composition in For-Profit, Community Colleges, and Four-Year Public Colleges (Percentage of ethnic and income groups in three types of college)

	For-Profit	Community Colleges	Four-Year Public Colleges
African American	.248	.140	.141
Hispanic	.264	.159	.103
Family income if dependent	$36,854	$60,039	$76,509
Family income if independent	$17,292	$31,742	$78,664

Source: Deming, Goldin, and Katz 2012

have higher proportions of African Americans and Hispanics than community colleges.

Analyses of national survey data indicate that community colleges have very low degree-completion rates, while these private occupational colleges have much higher degree-completion rates. Moreover, when we conducted detailed case studies of occupational colleges, we discovered that they use very different college procedures. Having evolved from trade and business schools, occupational colleges have a different cultural tradition than traditional four-year colleges, and, while they now confer accredited college degrees, we found that they use different procedures, which are designed to pose fewer difficulties for nontraditional students and require less cultural know-how and fewer personal resources. Occupational college procedures are based on an entirely different set of cultural norms, and they pose new goals, new strategies, new pathways, new guidance, and new job-placement assistance. These nontraditional procedures are consciously designed to reduce the kinds of difficulties students have in community colleges, and they are likely to explain the better degree-completion rates we found in occupational colleges.

Contrary to Murray's speculation that poor success rates indicate that some students lack the ability for college, the results indicate that colleges can use nontraditional procedures that can reduce mistakes, fix them quickly, and likely improve success rates. These observations suggest that the traditional procedures and norms that we implicitly assume to be necessary parts of colleges (because of our BA blinders) can be altered, and nontraditional norms and procedures can reduce obvious barriers and increase success for nontraditional students.

Instead of offering four-year degrees that take eight years, these procedures offer quick success to build confidence, back-loaded obstacles (which come after initial success), degree ladders with frequent payoffs along the way, clear dependable pathways and time slots (that reduce conflicts with outside obligations), guardrails that keep students on track, and job placement that assures career payoffs.

This chapter describes a range of problems that students experience, not because of a lack of academic ability but because they lack cultural skills, information, and resources. Making students responsible for navigating this cultural gap is an unnecessary requirement. We describe nontraditional procedures, which occupational colleges devise to reduce unnecessary demands that impede students' progress, particularly for disadvantaged students. This study describes many unnoticed procedures that enable student successes that might not otherwise occur.

Findings: Comparing Completion Rates for Comparable Students

While the general features of the three revolutions are well known, recent research using national data has shown some amazing facts—some inspiring, some shocking. Forty years ago, reformers focused on raising students' educational aspirations. Today, lack of high educational aspirations is not the problem: 86 percent of high school graduates plan BA degrees (computed from ELS 2006) and 80 percent of high school graduates enter college in the eight years after high school (Adelman 2003). Even more impressive, there is very little race gap in college entrance: among high school graduates, 83 percent of whites and 80 percent of blacks and Hispanics enter college (ibid.). But this means new kinds of students with new needs and new goals. Colleges must serve these students, who must fit into the new labor market.

While community colleges have provided impressive improvements in access, their completion rates have been poor. Among students who enrolled in community colleges right after high school, only 37 percent get a college degree (associate's degree or higher) in the next eight years. Degree completion varies by students' high school grades. Students in the top third of GPA have a 71 percent graduation rate, while the bottom third has a graduation rate of 25 percent (Stephan 2010). This is good news for high-GPA students. It is also good news for the 25 percent of low-GPA students who succeed: these students get an impressive second chance because of open admissions. But this is not sufficient. Encouraging low-GPA students to attend college, when the vast majority will fail,

Table 15.2 Degree-Completion Rates

	Whites	African Americans	All
Public colleges	47%	19%	37%
Private colleges	59%	64%	57%

Source: Rosenbaum, Deil-Amen, and Person 2006, 13

imposes costs in time and money that many students cannot afford. Moreover, society needs many more students to have skills for the new labor market demands (Carnevale, Rose, and Hanson 2012).

We conducted a comparison across four types of colleges using the National Educational Longitudinal Survey. Following the lead of much prior literature, we compared the outcomes of two-year and four-year public colleges. We concluded that this comparison is largely irrelevant, because these colleges mostly don't have comparable students. Using propensity-matching statistics, we concluded that four-year public colleges have better results for the type of students who typically attend four-year colleges, but they have no better results for typical two-year college students. In other words, for their typical students, community colleges are not failing where four-year colleges are succeeding. Simply getting community college students to attend four-year colleges will not solve the problem of poor completion rates. Similarly, getting community colleges to act more like four-year colleges will not solve the problem either.

However, getting community colleges to use procedures that have been effective in private occupational colleges may be more promising. Private occupational colleges have similar students to public two-year colleges. Indeed, the distribution of student attributes at the two kinds of colleges are nearly identical in terms of prior test scores, grades, and socioeconomic status (SES). We then conduct propensity-matching statistics on degree completion, and we discover that students at private occupational colleges have 20 percentage points better completion rates than students at public two-year colleges for comparable students. Private occupational colleges have a much higher degree-completion rate—57 percent get associate's degree or higher in eight years, compared with 37 percent for community colleges (Stephan, Rosenbaum, and Person 2009). Moreover, the gap is even greater for African Americans.

Of course, one might wonder whether private occupational colleges are merely diluting standards to improve degree-completion rates. Our only

Table 15.3 Earnings outcomes for graduates of two types of college in the National Educational Longitudinal Survey

First College Enter	Number of graduates	Average earnings 1999	95% Confidence Interval
Community College	734	$29,481	$27,324–31,639
Occupational College	61	$28,969	$25,605–32,333

Source: Authors' own calculations from NELS survey

way to examine this question is to see how their graduates do in the labor market. The results indicate that they do about the same. Using the NELS national longitudinal survey, which followed the high school class of 1992 over the eight years following graduation, we compared the earnings of similar students who earned an AA or higher degree. We must caution that very few individuals attended private occupational colleges in the 1990s (and thus few individuals in the NELS sample attended these colleges), yet the results are still remarkable. Among similar students who earned an AA or higher, graduates from the two types of colleges have similar earnings (see Table 15.3).

In sum, private occupational colleges have a much higher degree-completion rate even after propensity matching. Even though private occupational colleges graduate a higher proportion of students, their graduates have similar earnings to community college graduates, which suggests that employers believe they are of comparable value.

This sector has many problems and risks, and our goal is not to recommend that students attend this type of college. Rather, this chapter focuses on discovering what we can learn from their practices for helping students succeed. We find that private occupational colleges use seven distinctive nontraditional procedures that may reduce the kinds of problems that students experience in community colleges.

College Alternatives: Seven Nontraditional Procedures

How do private occupational colleges manage to have much higher degree-completion rates even with comparable students? We conducted detailed analyses of the organizational procedures in seven community colleges and seven occupational colleges in the six-county Chicago metropolitan area. Because our aim is to discover alternative procedures, we purposely chose occupational colleges that we expected to be better than most. We cannot claim that these colleges are typical; our aim, rather, is to discover alternative procedures. Based on close observation and interviews with college staff and students, and over 4,000 surveys with students, we discovered certain characteristic problems that students experienced in community colleges, and we discovered institutional procedures that private occupational colleges used to reduce the chances of these problems. In the following sections, we shall describe these procedures.

1. *Quick successes:* While traditional college procedures assume that the BA is the only goal, nontraditional procedures offer quick credentials on the way to the BA.
2. *Quick payoffs:* While traditional college procedures assume that BAs are required for labor market payoffs, nontraditional procedures offer quick credentials that have labor market payoffs.
3. *Delayed obstacles:* While traditional procedures front-load obstacles (remedial courses, general education), nontraditional procedures delay these obstacles until they are required for higher credentials.
4. *Degree ladders:* While traditional procedures encourage a fail-first sequence, nontraditional degree ladders reverse the sequence and encourage a series of increasingly demanding credentials on the way to a BA.
5. *Structured pathways and time slots:* While traditional procedures offer complex course patterns (which often create credits without credentials), nontraditional procedures offer clear course pathways in predictable time slots.
6. *Guardrails:* While traditional procedures rely on students' choices (which often create mistakes and wasted time), nontraditional procedures use mandatory advising and monitor students' progress to reduce mistakes.
7. *Job placement:* While traditional procedures expect students to search for jobs on their own, nontraditional procedures provide job placement advice and assistance.

1. *Quick successes:* While traditional college procedures assume that the only worthwhile goal is a BA, nontraditional procedures offer quick credentials on the way to the BA.

Traditional college norms work differently in the new reality of community colleges. Wearing BA blinders, community college advisors act as if the BA degree is the only worthwhile goal. In our interviews with community college students, nearly all young students (under age 25) report that college advisors encouraged them to pursue the same four-year BA degrees, and advisors did not tell them how they could get another credential along the way. Of course, advisors do not have to say much to promote BA plans, since students already get this message before they enter college—86 percent of high school graduates plan to get BA degrees (authors' calculations from ELS 2006).

In our interviews, many students refer to a BA degree as a "four-year degree." Unfortunately, our analyses indicate that most community college students do not fare well with their four-year BA plans—few get the degree and almost none get it in four years. Analyzing the NELS national sample of recent high school graduates, we find that among community college students pursuing a BA, only 4 percent get a "four-year BA degree" in four years (Stephan 2010). Another 8 percent take five years, and 16 percent take six to eight years. In other words, only 28 percent get a BA in eight years (and, in the lower third of achievement, only 19 percent of students do so). Therefore, for students who begin in community college, the "four-year BA" is almost a myth, and the BA is rare in even eight years, particularly for those with low achievement. In the next twenty years, another 10 percent of students will eventually complete a degree (Attewell et al. 2008). That is a long time to wait, and it leaves fewer years for earnings payoffs. Community college advisors never refer to it as an "eight-year BA," nor do they warn that it takes many students much longer.

Community colleges also offer other credentials (certificates and associate's degrees), which take less time and have lower academic requirements. We might expect community colleges to inform students about these options, their lower requirements and quicker timetables. They don't. We analyzed community college websites, and we interviewed community college academic advisors. Neither source warns students that the four-year BA usually takes more than four years and is a long shot even in eight years, and neither one encourages students to consider certificates or associate's degrees either as separate goals or along the way to a BA.

Unlike community colleges, private occupational colleges offer students quick credentials along the way. In our study, all seven occupational colleges offered certificates in one year and associate's degrees in two years, and these credentials were conferred automatically along the way to the BA (Rosenbaum, Deil-Amen, and Person 2006). Occupational colleges allow all students to get sub-BA credentials along the way to a BA. Since many students in occupational colleges did poorly in high school, these quick successes in college may improve students' confidence.

2. *Quick payoffs:* While traditional college procedures assume that BAs are required for labor market payoffs, nontraditional procedures offer quick credentials that have labor market payoffs.

Do these sub-BA credentials have labor market payoffs? Aggressive advertising campaigns have made everyone aware of the "$1 million payoff" for a BA, but most of us have no idea what a certificate is worth in the labor market. BA degrees have higher average earnings than lower credentials, but there is substantial variation within each education category and substantial overlap across categories. According to recent research, 43 percent of individuals with certificates have higher earnings than the median person with an associate's degree, and 27 percent have higher earnings than the median earnings for BA degrees. Moreover, 31 percent of those with associate's degrees have higher pay than the average for BA degrees (Carnevale, Rose, and Cheah 2011; cf. Baum and Ma 2010).

While the Carnevale study includes all ages, research also indicates that certificates and associate's degrees have payoffs for young adults. Jacobson and Mokher (2009) show earnings payoffs in Florida for twenty-six-year-olds. Youth with certificates or AAs earn the same as BAs in health-related fields. Only in STEM fields do BAs receive large payoffs (about $15,000 higher earnings per year).

Moreover, although most research focuses on earnings, nonmonetary payoffs are also important. Analyzing a national survey of young adults (ages twenty-six through thirty-one), Janet Rosenbaum (2012; 2013) found that certificates and associate's degrees lead to much better job payoffs on dimensions other than earnings. After controlling for background characteristics (including test scores and parent SES), the analysis showed that certificates and associate's degrees lead to significantly better jobs than high school diplomas on many attributes, categorized by material and psychological rewards:

- *Material rewards:* personal earnings, perceived SES, and health, retirement, and vacation benefits (benefits significant only for associate's degrees, not certificates)
- *Psychological rewards:*

- Job freedom to make important work decisions, career relevant job, job satisfaction, employed in recession
- Job not repetitive, not strenuous, work at desk, and day shift (only associate's degrees)

Indeed, certificates and AA degrees have nearly the same job payoffs as BAs on most of these psychological rewards and benefits. This study indicates that sub-BA credentials confer payoffs on a wide range of job conditions, which may be even more important than earnings on individuals' lives and subsequent careers. In particular, career-relevant, nonrepetitive, and decision-making jobs may lead to higher future career trajectories.

In sum, sub-BA credentials provide substantial payoffs. By age twenty-six to thirty-one, students with certificates or associate's degrees have acquired jobs that are significantly better than those they had previously (as high school graduates), and these jobs provide better financial support in the short term, during college, and afterwards. Moreover, certificates and associate's degrees have better material and psychological rewards than high school diplomas. For students who have limited time, interest, and funds for college and who are at high risk of dropping out on the way to a BA that may take eight years or more, these quick payoffs of certificates and AAs are likely to be valuable, regardless of whether the students continue to higher degrees. Unlike community colleges, occupational colleges make these intervening credentials automatic along the way to a BA and inform students that these quick credentials have labor market payoffs.

3. *Delayed obstacles:* While traditional procedures front-load obstacles (remedial courses, general education), nontraditional procedures delay these obstacles until they are required for higher credentials.

Community colleges have opened their doors to new kinds of students, and even students with low achievement get access. But while students take classes in college buildings, they may not be in "college classes." Two-thirds of students in community colleges are taking at least one remedial course—high school-level courses that don't give college credit (Adelman 2003). The proportion is over 90 percent at some urban community colleges, and many students take several remedial courses (Rosenbaum, Deil-Amen, Person 2006).

Community colleges front-load remedial obstacles. When students first enroll in community college, a placement exam determines whether they take remedial courses and at what level of remediation. Although remedial courses are front-loaded with the hope that they will make later courses easier, that's only true if students survive them. Unfortunately, most students do not. Overall, 46 percent of students referred to reading remediation and 33 percent of those referred to math remediation successfully complete their sequence of developmental education. Many remedial placements have predictable failures: For students referred to the lowest-level remedial courses, completion rates are terrible—29 percent for reading and 17 percent for math (Bailey, Jeong, and Cho 2010). When students are advised to take these courses, they are rarely told that they are being sent on a low-odds path from which only 17 percent successfully emerge. The emphasis on trying to fix academic problems actually makes student success even harder and more remote for the students.

Contrary to the assumption that students need "college-level academic skills" to benefit from college, in fact, eighth-grade academic skills are sufficient for a certificate in many occupational programs, including high-demand fields in computers, health, and business. Indeed, in our interviews with occupational faculty in community colleges, some respondents report that computer networking technicians, medical technicians, and accounting staff only need eighth-grade math skills (or less). "College-level academic skills" may be needed for BAs, but not for certificates, yet advisors' BA blinders prevent them from communicating this information to students.

Community colleges also front-load general education obstacles. Consistent with traditional college procedures, young students are encouraged to take many general education courses. They are told that general education is a good way to explore their interests, but students report that general education does not help them explore their *occupational* interests. They are told that general education courses will give credits for every major, but these courses do not count for many occupational majors. General education may have value on its own, but it is not costless—it demands time and academic competencies that many students lack.

This creates serious gaps—courses without credits and unnecessary risks without warnings. Students think they are in college, but, while they are taking classes in college buildings, they are taking remedial courses without college credits. By being subjected to longer timetables, students face increased risks of their money running out or family crises interrupting college. In addition, remedial and general education courses may not be needed for their first credential. Although these courses may ultimately be useful for a BA degree, low-achieving students may not get that far, and they are not warned that these courses are unnecessary for some college credentials (certificates or applied associate's degrees), they add unnecessary time barriers to a first credential, and they pose high risks of preventing students from completing any credential.

In other words, the college dropout process is more complex than Murray's story about students lacking ability. Largely because of cultural norms associated with BA blinders, students with low academic achievement are advised to pursue a course of action that has low odds of success.

4. *Degree ladders:* While traditional procedures encourage a fail-first sequence, nontraditional degree ladders reverse the sequence and encourage a series of increasingly demanding credentials on the way to a BA.

Because of their cultural preconceptions, advisors encourage young students to pursue all-or-nothing BA degrees, and they rarely tell students about alternative paths that require less remedial coursework and confer quick credentials with labor market value on the way to a BA. Some students discover these alternatives, but they often do so by a costly and risky fail-first process. Analyzing the BPS national survey that followed entering community college students over time, researchers found that 42 percent of students drop out in the first year, 50 percent of them return, and 53 percent of them drop out again (and don't reenter over the next four years; Horn 1999). Despite dropping out, many students try again, but only 14 percent of early dropouts get any credentials. The researchers note that after failing first, some returning students enroll in occupational programs for certificates or applied associate's degrees, which provide quicker credentials.

However, BA blinders prevent students from learning about these alternative options that might have prevented dropout in the first place. The problem is cultural. Community colleges already offer these sub-BA credentials, but advisors discourage them. In interviews we conducted, counselors report that in advising newly entering young students (ages eighteen to twenty-four) they don't mention occupational programs, and some even discourage them if students suggest them. Students are only told about these options if they are returning dropouts or over age twenty-four. We did interview three young students who were in occupational programs, and all three had the backing of relatives who had jobs in skilled trades.

More disturbing, advisors rarely inform students about trade-offs—particularly the predictable long timetables and low odds of getting BA degrees. Students are rarely told about the high dropout rates, the repeated dropouts, the required remedial courses, their noncredit status, their extended timetables, their low odds of completion, or the fact that remedial courses are not required for many sub-BA credentials. Indeed, in the catalog, the euphemism "developmental" is the usual term for remedial courses, and that euphemism is not explained to students. Especially for low-achieving students, this single-minded focus on the BA leads to predictable failures 80 percent of the time, while alternative credentials have much higher odds of success and payoffs.

This withheld information is probably a well-meaning effort to protect all young people from sub-BA programs that advisors consider culturally inferior. Fifty years ago, research reported that community college advisors were "cooling out" students' BA plans with subtle guidance (Clark 1960). Today, instead of cooling out, students drop out, and some dropouts return with "reduced" occupational plans, but advisors are not implicated. Apparently, advisors consider these occupational programs to be lower status, only suitable for students who have become stigmatized by having dropped out. Advisors feel good that they can convey an optimistic message: low-achieving students should aim high and pursue BA plans. Yet in avoiding "cooling out," advisors are withholding crucial information. They aren't warning students of extensive remedial courses that don't give credits, guarantee longer timetables than students expect, and have very low odds of success. The only way students can learn how to avoid remedial courses is to drop out and then return.

This is a costly way to learn. In our interview sample, students take one to four years before returning to college. It is also a risky way to learn. Half of dropouts do not return, so they don't learn about these occupational programs. We might want to reassess the harm of "cooling out" if the alternative is "dropping out" with no return, high costs in time and money, and possibly subsequent failures. Advisors are avoiding cooling out by avoiding candor, and students are being encouraged to make uninformed choices.

In contrast, private occupational colleges put all students on degree ladders that produce quick successes on the way to bachelor's degrees—they create an incremental success ladder where early courses are easy, engaging, and career relevant. As much as possible, they *back-load* remedial courses until after initial successes. Instead of starting college with many noncredit remedial courses that resemble the ones they disliked and did poorly at in high school, students in occupational colleges take courses that are practical and relevant to careers. Within twelve months, students can complete certificates in such fields as computer networking, medical coding, and computer-aided design, which offer good jobs, and many of their credits will count toward associate's and bachelor's degrees. For students who have never done well in school, these successes provide a quick payoff and they give students confidence that they can succeed in college. After such successes, occupational colleges present more demanding courses and remedial content (which is often integrated within occupational courses).

This same option is already possible in community colleges, but it is rarely mentioned. Many community colleges in our sample offer certificates in a number of fields, including computer networking, medical coding, and computer-aided design. Moreover, our analyses indicate that these certificates can lead to degree ladders to associate's degrees and even bachelor's degrees in related fields. Some of the courses count for the higher degrees and some do not, but the intervening credential is a form of insurance that students will get some payoff even if they don't finish the BA. Unfortunately, the emphasis on traditional BA pathways means that community colleges rarely encourage these applied-degree ladders.

5. *Structured pathways and time slots:* While traditional procedures offer complex course patterns (which often create credits without credentials), nontraditional procedures offer clear course pathways in predictable time slots.

While disadvantaged students face highly constrained limits on their time in college, college cultural traditions encourage "exploring" and "electives." Instead of laying out the most efficient set of courses for a degree goal, community colleges let students make their own choices. This may work well for traditional college students whose college-educated parents can offer advice and pay for extra semesters to finish degrees, but it doesn't work well for many students today, including first-generation college students. Because students are encouraged to explore, they waste a lot of time. In the high school class of 1992, 8 percent earned associate's degrees by the year 2000, while another 10 percent had enough credits but no degree (60+ credits; Adelman 2003). Since the labor market only rewards credentials, not isolated credits, credits without credentials give students no payoff in the labor market (Grubb 2002).

Moreover, traditional college norms assume that classes can be offered at any time, and students can fit them into their daily schedules. This assumption works with traditional college students for whom college is their main duty, and work hours and child care are not obligations. Community colleges offer courses that may fill a patchwork of time slots in a week. These courses don't fit together, they may require commuting for nearly every class, and course time schedules change every semester. Unfortunately, many students report that commuting and time conflicts with work or child care sometimes prevent them from taking required courses when they are offered (often they aren't offered when needed).

Instead, private occupational colleges offer structured efficient curricula and dependable time slots, so students choose the right courses and can fit them into the weekly schedule they've already planned. Like a package-deal vacation, these structures let students choose their career goals, and the college packages all the details so students make rapid progress and waste little time. Students don't need to rearrange daycare or work hours every semester, as students report they must do in community colleges. Many students report great satisfaction with this. As one student said, "I am balancing child care, work hours, shopping, cooking, cleaning, and college. I don't want more choices."

In addition, many community college students report that their time in college has been extended because required courses were not available when needed. In contrast, private occupational colleges organize students into cohorts that progress on the same timetable and offer required courses when needed for these cohorts. If community colleges weren't so committed to letting every student choose their own combination of courses, selected programs on a cohort model would let the college promise that required courses were available when needed by cohorts.

These structures are not part of the cultural norms of traditional colleges, but that is actually a relatively recent development. Many of the most selective four-year colleges had many more requirements and even structured curricula over thirty years ago. The sixty-year-old Directed Studies Program at Yale University required students to enroll in most courses together. Even today, a few colleges (e.g., St. John's College) are based on the Great Books curriculum, and they specify a fixed set of courses that all students must take during the first two years. In this case, the BA culture has actually changed away from a structured model that occupational colleges still maintain.

*   *   *

6. Guardrails: While traditional procedures rely on students' choices (despite mistakes and wasted time), nontraditional procedures use mandatory advising and monitor students' progress in order to reduce mistakes.

Community college students make many mistakes, leading to wasted time and dropouts (Rosenbaum, Deil-Amen, and Person 2006). In part, these mistakes arise because first-generation college students can't get advice from their parents who didn't attend college. In part, these mistakes arise because community colleges are complex: they offer many courses, many programs, and complicated rules about requirements. Many of these mistakes lead students to get credits without making progress. Students choose courses that are too easy (and don't aid progress), are too difficult (and risk failure), or don't meet the requirements for their program, degree, transfer, or employment. They miss deadlines, they underestimate degree timetables, and some early credits expire if they don't progress quickly enough. Students don't ask counselors for advice because they don't suspect there is a problem (and because counselors are hard to see). The rules are complex and confusing. In our studies, the researchers (two PhDs who have been studying community colleges for many years) had great difficulties in understanding program requirements from websites and catalogs; some requirements were beyond our comprehension and required further inquiries. At least we knew what questions to ask. The students we interviewed did not know that they needed to ask these questions.

In contrast, occupational colleges offer *guardrails*—frequent mandatory advising (in groups) and monitoring of students' progress and problems), which dramatically reduce mistakes (described in Rosenbaum, Deil-Amen, and Person 2006). They also offer social services to handle life crises (that middle-class students rarely face)—transportation, housing, work, and child care problems. Although community colleges offer advisors, students must initiate the meeting, and many students don't realize they have a problem until it's very serious. Moreover, with over a thousand students for each counselor, meetings are hard to schedule, often requiring appointments to be made months in advance, and meetings are brief and cursory. In contrast, in occupational colleges, students are required to attend advisor meetings several times each term, and since the meetings are in small groups with members of one's same program, students may ask questions that don't occur to others. Occupational colleges also have a student monitoring system, which keeps track of absences, grades, and teacher concerns, and advisors will contact a student who exhibits any warning signs before these problems get more serious (Rosenbaum, Deil-Amen, and Person 2006).

7. Job placement: While traditional procedures expect students to search for jobs on their own, nontraditional procedures provide job placement advice and assistance.

According to cultural tradition in four-year colleges, college students don't have to think about jobs: college degrees guarantee good jobs. That traditional belief may have been true fifty years ago, but it is not true today. Nonetheless, many colleges still operate as if it were true. At the community colleges we studied, career services offices offer optional workshops in interviewing and resume preparation, which are not required or aggressively marketed, perhaps because the office is too small to handle more students (one career office discouraged the student newspaper from mentioning them because the office couldn't handle more students). These offices rarely have connections with employers, and the only specific job information they offer is a bulletin board or website that lists miscellaneous job openings that often are unrelated to program offerings at the college. In effect, these career services are consistent with the traditional assumption that a college degree is a ticket to a good job, and college doesn't have to offer anything beyond that.

In contrast, some occupational programs in community colleges offer mandatory internships (Rosenbaum, Cepa, and Rosenbaum 2013). While internships are not available to students generally in the community college, occupational programs require and help students obtain appropriate internships. Internships contradict two cultural assumptions in traditional colleges. First, they contradict the assumption that learning within the college walls is sufficient. Second, they contradict the assumption that employers will hire based only on a college degree. According to occupational faculty, internships provide vital professional training, and they provide valuable contacts so that employers get a chance to see students in action before making hiring decisions ("try before buying"). In many cases, internships help students get full-time jobs in the same workplace after graduation.

Also in contrast to cultural tradition, some private occupational colleges make job placement help mandatory. Unlike career services offices in community colleges, which are optional and which cover isolated topics,

Table 15.4 Comparison of procedures in two types of colleges

Community College Traditional Procedures	Occupational College Nontraditional Procedures
Deferred payoffs	Quick payoffs
Early obstacles (remedial)	Degree ladders that delay obstacles
Unnecessary complexity	Package deal pathways and preset time slots
Uninformed course choices	Guardrails
Self-directed job search	College-directed job choice and job search
Uninformed job choices	Job placement guidance and assistance

job placement in private occupational colleges is required, structured, and comprehensive across all aspects of the job search process. While career services workshops in community colleges help students make prettier resumes, job placement staff in occupational colleges help students translate course titles into lists of work-relevant skills that employers recognize and value. Instead of assuming that students know how to search for and get a good job, job placement offices assume the opposite, and they provide extensive assistance to teach students about these issues. Students are instructed about getting a telephone answering machine or voicemail, how to leave an appropriate message, and how to locate areas of strong skill-relevant demand (including considering residential moves to improve employment prospects).

Students are also told how to identify a good job. Some of the advice surprised us. Placement staff warn students to be skeptical of the highest paid jobs; they often have bad job conditions. Instead, placement staff urge students to seek skill-relevant jobs and desirable job conditions, which are likely to lead to subsequent advancements. Indeed, job-placement staff spend a lot of time making contacts with local employers who offer good skill-relevant jobs.

Job placement also creates trusted ratings of students. Besides job skills, employers also want soft skills (i.e., persistence, attention to quality, social skills), and this requires subjective ratings. Although employers don't trust ratings from strangers, college placement staff place students every year, so their ratings are trusted. Employers know these placement staff won't mislead them, because that would undermine their effectiveness in future years. Some occupational faculty in community colleges also have such employer links, but they don't have time to use them very often.

Conclusion

Contrary to Murray's one-variable model, which speculates that college dropout is caused by students' limited academic ability, these private occupational colleges make the case that dropout is caused by multiple limiting factors, which nontraditional college procedures can reduce. Even if we used Murray's language about ability, we would have to conclude that traditional college procedures require students to have many other abilities besides academic ability—the ability to persist six to eight years or more (when only four years was expected), the ability to withstand massive remedial obstacles, the ability to persist despite repeated failures, the ability to sort among a multitude of course offerings and figure out complex degree requirements, the ability to know when to seek counseling and find it quickly (when a two-month wait is usual), and the ability to understand and implement a complex job search. Occupational colleges provide alternative procedures that reduce the need for these specific "abilities." With the right procedures, students don't need to endure the extensive and repeated dropout experiences that seem built into community colleges.

Of particular interest, in providing social services, occupational colleges have noticed that students are sometimes overwhelmed by major life crises—transportation, housing, work and child care problems (which are aggravated by low wages and unpredictable crises). Since middle-class students rarely face such life crises, traditional colleges assume that such problems are rare and that they are students' responsibility, so colleges don't provide assistance. In contrast, despite being private and attentive to costs, occupational colleges have figured out that these services are relatively inexpensive and cost effective in helping students persist and complete degrees. They often employ a single staff person to provide quick advice about transportation (low-cost bus passes, carpooling contacts, etc.), housing (apartment listings, homeless shelters), etc. These life crises are sometimes overwhelming to individuals, but they are routine to social services staff who can offer advice and resources for a quick recovery. In effect, these colleges assume that students have more "college ability" when college provides these services. Murray has not considered these other abilities, nor have most reformers.

Nor has Murray (or most college observers) considered that institutions can shape their procedures to reduce the need for these other abilities. If colleges are not restricted by traditional cultural traditions (which make students choose all their courses, solve all their problems, direct their own job searches, etc.), nontraditional procedures in private occupational colleges remove the need for these other abilities. Some abilities which are "necessary" for success in most community colleges are not necessary in colleges using nontraditional procedures. These colleges still require the ability to acquire occupational proficiency, but they manage to get 20 percent more students to attain proficiency and get comparable earnings with a similar pool of students as community colleges. Occupational colleges provide procedures for separating the influence of "academic ability" from other "abilities" like "the ability to persist for many additional unanticipated years" or "the ability to figure out complex degree requirements," by creating procedures that don't require these abilities.

Critics may argue that these other attributes are worthwhile, but we have never seen convincing evidence that the ability to decipher a college catalog predicts success in any occupational field (aside from perhaps college administration). Readers may argue that these attributes are not really abilities. We agree. These many attributes indicate cultural competencies that are strongly influenced by prior experiences, cultural know-how, cultural information, and very specific skills learned in one's cultural upbringing.[1] Occupational colleges force us to examine traditional college procedures and consider alternative procedures that pose fewer and later obstacles and that provide quicker payoffs to encourage success and confidence.

More generally, we propose a "sociology of ability"—that ability is an inference shaped by social context, so ability can be changed by redesigning social context. "Ability" is generally inferred from success in a certain social context. Although the context is not immediately visible on tests, the testing context includes students' understanding of the incentives to do well on the test (Rosenbaum, Schuetz, and Foran 2012). Since ability is regarded as the individual attribute that determines success in college, institutional procedures that affect college success will shape inferences about who has ability. We find that community college procedures shape abilities in a negative fashion by posing unnecessary demands that impose disadvantages on individuals from some cultural backgrounds. When students expect a four-year BA degree, which usually takes six to eight years or more, when they expect college courses and they get high school-level remedial courses, when they need courses that don't fit their time schedules, when scheduling mistakes are frequent and rarely caught in advance, and when they have doubts about job payoffs, students are likely to doubt their ability to succeed, and these doubts may discourage effort and persistence. In contrast, we find that occupational colleges have substantially more students who complete degrees and who get comparable jobs than community colleges do. Occupational colleges manage to increase students' ability to succeed with procedures that encourage quick successes, delay obstacles, specify pathways that fit preset time schedules, prevent or repair course scheduling mistakes, and assure job payoffs. In effect, institutional procedures are shaping students' abilities to succeed.

Occupational colleges act as if Murray's speculative concept of ability is less important than many other abilities (including cultural know-how) which can be rendered unnecessary if colleges use nontraditional procedures. Indeed, unlike Murray, occupational colleges act as if "failures" are not the result of individual students' ability. College can be redesigned to use new procedures. Instead of worrying about some unobservable student attribute (ability), they use procedures that reduce students' failures from college-imposed impediments.

Besides occupational colleges' optimism and greater success, we as social scientists should be impressed by their commitment to principles we believe in—they believe incentives are important and can be improved. They improve incentives through many nontraditional procedures—

by front-loading rewards (identifying desirable credentials and jobs that can be attained quickly),

by presenting quick payoffs,

by back-loading obstacles (delaying remedial and general education until they are needed),

by creating incremental success sequences (degree ladders),

by identifying pathways and time slots (the most efficient sequence of choices to each desirable goal),

by providing guardrails (frequent mandatory advice and monitoring of progress), and

by job placement (extensive information, advice, support, and trusted signals in the job-search process).

These occupational colleges act as if traditional college assumptions are arbitrary and unnecessary to the college mission of preparing youth for productive roles in adult society. They also act as if social and economic contexts matter and are changeable—they actively design procedures to reduce barriers and improve incentives and success. These are assumptions that underlie the theories sociologists use, so it is inspiring and illuminating to see what happens when our assumptions are put into practice in real institutions.[2]

Occupational colleges disagree with our models in one respect—students choose their goals, but not the means (specific courses). While sociologists focus on the way structures limit success, occupational colleges devise structures that increase success. Informed choice is difficult, expensive, and sometimes nearly impossible, and when it fails, students make mistakes that are costly and sometimes irreversible. Instead of bombarding students with mountains of complex, detailed, incomprehensible information, occupational colleges create structured curricula in preset time slots that increase student success by reducing the possibility of mistakes. Occupational colleges target desirable occupations, they create the most efficient path to them, they make it easy for students to follow that path, they offer frequent successes to encourage students who lack confidence, and they provide strong guardrails to monitor progress and provide quick assistance.

To those of us interested in labor markets, job placement staff provide a fascinating model. Dedicating certain staff to do job placement every year creates trusted relationships, because employers know that placement staff will not jeopardize future placements by recommending a substandard graduate. Placement staff know that employers will not misrepresent their jobs because it will make staff reluctant to send high-quality graduates to that employer again. Such trust allows placement staff to provide trusted subjective ratings of hard-to-measure attributes such as soft skills, character, and dependability.

Reformers have become attentive to these issues, and they now demand that colleges receive funding based on their degree completion rates, not just enrollment. That reform is useful, but not sufficient. We also need to identify promising procedures for increasing student success.

Reformers, educators, and researchers all wear BA blinders, which prevent us from seeing alternatives to the traditional college procedures that impede nontraditional students' success. As a result, educators devote vast efforts to encouraging low-achieving students to pursue traditional college procedures but rarely consider alternatives. The usual result is to encourage massive remedial, aimless exploring, and courses that don't count. Colleges don't warn students about predictable delays, early repeated dropouts, and extensive failures. Nontraditional students have terrible outcomes, but they are not solely due to students' academic abilities—their failures are the result of an interaction between their cultural resources and the demands imposed by traditional college norms and procedures. Low-achieving students face long odds with traditional college procedures, and they should be informed of other options for which the odds of success are much greater.

Community colleges are larger and more varied than occupational colleges, so they cannot offer that single model exclusively. But they can offer this model as one option, and they can inform students about their actual odds of success and timetables in the various options. The all-or-nothing BA degree must remain an option, but low-achieving students who have only a 25 percent chance of success should be informed of those odds and of degree-ladder alternatives with better odds and quicker timetables for getting a first credential on the way to pursuing a bachelor's degree. Urging all students to aim high doesn't seem so benevolent when it forces them to repeatedly fail first and still keep returning.

College staff wear the same BA blinders we do, and their cultural biases prevent them from seeing solutions on their own. If reformers are serious about improving outcomes, they need to change not only incentives but also procedures and to provide resources, training, and technical assistance to make these changes happen. This will require that reformers realize the cultural biases that prevent them from considering alternatives, and it will require sociological insight into the kinds of social procedures that can reduce students' mistakes and failures. Research can assist in both of these tasks.

In sum, for many students, community college is a long treacherous stairway. Just like improving a treacherous stairway, colleges can improve their procedures by offering these seven procedures. Community colleges already have elements of these procedures. We just need to remove our BA blinders to see how to use them.

16

Liberalism, Self-Respect, and Troubling Cultural Patterns in Ghettos

TOMMIE SHELBY, *Harvard University*

Scattered across the metropolitan landscape of the United States are many segregated black neighborhoods with high poverty rates (Wilson 1987; Massey and Denton 1993; Jargowsky 1997; Sharkey 2013). Social scientists, ordinary observers, and inhabitants of these spaces often refer to these stigmatized and deeply disadvantaged neighborhoods as "ghettos." Ghetto neighborhoods, in addition to their concentrated poverty, typically have a number of troubling characteristics—alarming rates of violence, street crime, joblessness, teen pregnancy, family instability, school dropouts, welfare receipt, and illicit drug use. Exactly why ghettos persist is, to put it mildly, a complex and controversial question. But many, from all sides of the political spectrum, think that at least part of the explanation has to do with destructive and self-defeating cultural patterns prevalent in ghettos.

In fact, some believe there is a "culture of poverty," or something similar, to be found in America's ghettos.[1] The culture of poverty hypothesis holds that because the segregated black urban poor have lived for so long under such miserable conditions, many (though not all) who live in ghetto neighborhoods have developed attitudes, practices, and self-concepts that inhibit their ability to improve their life prospects. Because of social distance or geographic isolation from mainstream institutions, these cultural traits are transmitted across generations and among peers in ghettos, so that many poor urban black children acquire them, often with catastrophic consequences. Indeed, some of these cultural currents are thought to contribute to perpetuating ghetto conditions and to have become formidable obstacles to ghetto residents taking advantage of the opportunities—say,

498

in education and employment—that are available to them. In particular, some social bases of self-esteem that exist in ghettos would appear to have engendered dysfunctional social identities that, at least in the long run, lead to further impoverishment.

A number of social scientists who study urban poverty (including all contributors to this volume) explicitly reject the culture of poverty hypothesis (e.g., Roach and Gusslin 1967; Valentine 1968; Corcoran et al. 1985; Wilson 1987; Jones and Luo 1999; Lamont and Small 2006). They do not believe there is a culture specific to poverty, for the cultural responses to poverty vary enormously across time and place and between immigrants and natives even in ghetto neighborhoods (see especially, Patterson, Chapter 2, and Tran, Chapter 7, in this volume). Today, many who do scientific cultural analyses of the urban poor (call them the "new cultural analysts") do not accept the idea that there is some totalizing or coherent subculture in poor black communities (Harding, Lamont, and Small 2010). While acknowledging the existence of salient and distinctive cultural patterns in ghetto neighborhoods, they emphasize that there is tremendous cultural heterogeneity even within the same poor black neighborhood. And the cultural traits that are prevalent among the ghetto poor are not generally a straightjacket from which they cannot escape but more often a set of frames or repertoires that the black poor draw on (sometimes implicitly) to navigate their social environment and to make sense of their lives.

Moreover, apart from these empirical and conceptual disagreements, the new cultural analysts reject the label "culture of poverty" because of its misleading associations and political baggage. They are particularly skeptical of those who use the culture of poverty idea to blame the black urban poor for their circumstances and to absolve government of any responsibility for alleviating the plight of the black poor. New cultural analysts often leave open the question of who is ultimately responsible for the disadvantages the ghetto poor face, and even when they do make claims about responsibility, their analyses are generally compatible with government having an obligation to improve the life prospects of the black urban poor. In addition, few believe that the cultural traits of the ghetto poor are the primary causal determinants of the persistence of ghettos or that these traits operate independently of structural factors. Lastly, new cultural analysts rarely invoke the language of "pathology" or "dysfunction" when describing the cultural patterns of the black poor. Indeed, some think that the cultural traits prevalent among the ghetto poor enable them to survive in their social environment.[2]

Still, there are contemporary social scientists and certainly many in the broader public who believe cultural factors help to explain ghetto poverty, even if they insist that structural factors have equal or greater explanatory significance. Among those who think there are cultural aspects to ghetto poverty, some believe there are cultural traits associated with ghettos that hurt poor ghetto residents' chances of improving their lives through mainstream institutions and conventional paths of upward mobility. The issue, then, is not cultural divergence from convention per se. It is that such divergence leads to significantly reduced life prospects given the patterns of social organization typical of contemporary liberal-capitalist societies. What those who take this position today have in common with some older culture of poverty theorists is the following belief: *a significant segment of the ghetto poor diverge culturally from mainstream values and norms, and this divergence generally inhibits their upward mobility or escape from poverty.* I will call this the "suboptimal cultural divergence hypothesis" (or "cultural divergence thesis" for short).

Many social scientists are careful not to make, or even to imply, value judgments about the subjects they study. In their role as empirical researchers, they do not presume to tell the poor (or anyone else) how they ought to live or what they should value. Though perhaps personally motivated by a desire to reduce poverty or even by egalitarian concerns, in their vocation as scientists, many take themselves to be providing empirical analyses of ghetto poverty that show the relationship between cultural processes and structural factors. There are, of course, some social scientists, particularly those who make policy recommendations, who are not reluctant to make value claims or to rely on what they take to be widely held and sound normative judgments. But even here, the normative claims are rarely defended and sometimes are not stated but only implied. Or the inferential links between analytical claims, empirical conclusions, normative assumptions, and policy prescriptions are not explicitly or carefully articulated.

For purposes of this chapter, I will assume the cultural divergence thesis is basically sound. I don't claim to know that the thesis is true and offer no defense of it. But I believe it is a plausible, widely held, and empirically grounded hypothesis worth taking seriously, and I will evaluate some practical prescriptions premised on it. My principal concern will be with what should, and what should not, be done if the thesis is true. Specifically,

I will draw out and reflect on the normative implications of one possible practical response to suboptimal cultural divergence among the ghetto poor. This response, which I will call "cultural reform," is to intervene in the lives of poor ghetto residents to shift their cultural orientation away from these suboptimal traits toward ones that will aid their exit from poverty. To many who care about the plight of the ghetto poor, the need for cultural reform may seem obvious. However, as I will argue, there are cultural reform efforts that cannot be adequately justified to the ghetto poor, particularly those forms that entail government involvement in the reform effort. The focus of this chapter will be on the practical limits, moral permissibility, and overall wisdom of state-sponsored cultural reform. I'm particularly concerned with its compatibility with liberal-egalitarian values. I begin by further clarifying what I take the cultural divergence thesis to entail and then turn to exploring what cultural reform might involve.

1. The Suboptimal Cultural Divergence Hypothesis

While middle- and working-class blacks often live in or adjacent to ghettos and may exhibit suboptimal cultural patterns, I will focus my attention on the black poor who have resided in ghettos for significant periods of time. I'll refer to this group as "the ghetto poor." Nonpoor blacks are often exposed to cultural dynamics in ghettos (Pattillo-McCoy 1999), and some of what I will go on to say will be pertinent to them. But the plight of the ghetto poor is so dire and morally urgent that many believe it is permissible (if not obligatory) to intervene in their lives in ways that would not be justified with respect to the nonpoor.

The category "ghetto poor" is defined in terms of a structural location within U.S. society. Specifically, membership is constituted by a person's racial classification (black), class position (poor), and residential neighborhood (ghetto). The group is *not* defined in terms of shared cultural characteristics. The term "ghetto poor" is not meant as a (more palatable) synonym for "underclass," which is sometimes defined partly in terms of behavioral or cultural traits. And there is no suggestion that the ghetto poor represent a cohesive cultural group or share a unique subculture.

Moreover, the version of the cultural divergence thesis I will consider does not assert that it is a characteristic feature of poor black people in ghettos that they possess a set of debilitating cultural traits. It is now widely acknowledged among cultural analysts that there is considerable cultural diversity among the poor in these neighborhoods. It cannot be said that all or even most of the ghetto poor are in the grip of a self-defeating culture, since many can be characterized as having resisted its pull and many hold to mainstream beliefs and values (Newman 1999; Anderson 1999; Edin and Kefalas 2005; Young 2006; Smith 2007). Even those among the ghetto poor who do diverge from the cultural mainstream are not a culturally homogeneous group, as they often diverge in different ways and to different extents.

However, one can agree that many (perhaps most) poor blacks in ghettos hold mainstream beliefs and values and yet maintain that an alarming number do not and that, moreover, this divergence from the mainstream negatively impacts their life prospects (Vaisey 2010). One might also worry that while some among the ghetto poor have so far evaded the grasp of these suboptimal cultural patterns, they are especially vulnerable to succumbing to their negative influence; and perhaps all black youth residing in or near ghettos, whatever their class background, are vulnerable to being ensnared. Thus although, strictly speaking, not all poor black residents of ghettos are currently in need of cultural reform, they might be viewed as a "high-risk" group that cultural reformers may seek to target.

In the version of the cultural divergence thesis I'll discuss, some of the attitudes and practices among the ghetto poor are viewed as cultural adaptations to severely disadvantaged conditions and mistreatment.[3] They are learned adjustments to socioeconomic hardship and social exclusion. Weak and strong versions of this claim have been defended. According to the weak version, some poor denizens of ghettos have developed ghetto-specific cultural traits but would give them up if they believed they had real opportunities to succeed in mainstream society. For such persons, these cultural traits are (more or less) consciously adopted strategic responses to a perceived lack of opportunity. For instance, William Julius Wilson (1996, 63–64) notes that it might be rational to observe ghetto norms to get by on the mean streets of urban America but that these norms are not conducive to success in the wider society (also see Wilson 2009). He insists that if poor black men and women were provided the job training and employment that would enable upward mobility, most would choose to abandon ghetto-specific cultural traits.

If the weak version of the cultural divergence thesis is correct, cultural reform might nonetheless seem apt. Because of mistaken but widely shared beliefs, some might not realize there are opportunities available that they aren't seizing, or they may not fully appreciate how their cultural characteristics inhibit their success. Some, while willing to abandon ghetto-specific cultural traits if provided adequate opportunities in mainstream society, may find it difficult to fully leave these traits behind without outside intervention. Cultural traits can become preconscious habits or implicit frames ("second nature," as we say), which agents find hard to detect in themselves or to break (e.g., certain speech patterns, worldviews, or modes of bodily comportment). Even if they can shed their suboptimal cultural traits on their own, some may need help acquiring the needed mainstream traits—the relevant cultural competence—that would facilitate their upward mobility. Moreover, presently it may not be feasible to create a fairer opportunity structure or a more equitable distribution of resources. Some might nevertheless be able to escape poverty if they successfully underwent cultural reform, which would enable them to take better advantage of existing opportunities.

According to the strong version, the relevant divergent cultural patterns may have started out as mere strategies for survival under hardship, but some have come to accept these traits as components of their social identity. Individuals have been socialized into these patterns and now maintain them, at least in part, because of their perceived intrinsic value or their association with valued communities. The cultural characteristics in question have become self-perpetuating and, in the absence of outside intervention, will likely remain even if educational and employment opportunities improve, progressive redistributive policies are instituted, and anti-discrimination laws are better enforced.

It is of course possible that, just as there are many among the ghetto poor who do not diverge significantly from the cultural mainstream, there are some from this group to whom the weak divergence thesis applies and some to whom the strong version does. If we treat the strong and weak versions of the cultural divergence thesis as claims about a significant *portion* of the ghetto poor rather than claims about the ghetto poor in general, as I will here, then there is no need to view the two versions of the thesis as incompatible. Moreover, I make no claims about what percentage of the ghetto poor fall into the mainstream, weak divergence, or strong divergence categories, assuming only that a nonnegligible number fall into each.

2. Which Cultural Traits?

There is much disagreement about which cultural patterns prevalent in ghettos are suboptimal from the standpoint of the ghetto poor's socio-economic prospects. However, relying on the work of influential proponents of the cultural divergence thesis (Harrington [1962] 1997; Clark 1965; Moynihan [1965] 1967; Rainwater 1970; Fordham and Ogbu 1986; Sullivan 1989; Majors and Billson 1992; Anderson 1999; Patterson 2000, 2006; McWhorter 2006; Sánchez-Jankowski 2008), it is possible to draw up a list of candidates. Some cultural analyses suggest that some among the ghetto poor have a value-orientation that is in opposition to or incompatible with many conventional measures of success or that disdains what they perceive as "white" paths to success. So, for example, some among the ghetto poor are said to lack conventional occupational ambition or to reject the American work ethic in favor of excessive idleness. Some cultural analysts insist that there are many among the ghetto poor who have hostility or skepticism toward formal education (though perhaps "street wisdom," autodidacticism, or folk knowledge is valued instead). There is said to be pessimism, even fatalism, about the prospects for upward mobility through mainstream channels. Some in ghetto communities are believed to devalue traditional coparenting and to eschew mainstream styles of childrearing. Many of the ghetto poor are thought to distrust established authority, particularly officials of the criminal justice system but also clergy and educators; and this attitude is often accompanied by a belief that such authority is corrupt and thus unworthy of respect. The ghetto poor, particularly poor black youth, are sometimes portrayed as regarding the use of vulgar language (e.g., "nigger" and "bitch") and street vernacular as appropriate in contexts where such modes of expression are widely viewed as uncivil and offensive.

In terms of what is accepted and sometimes valued, many among the ghetto poor are said to have a hedonistic orientation toward intense and immediate pleasure—for example, through frequent casual sex, gambling, drinking, fighting, and recreational drug use—joined with a refusal to delay such gratification and a high tolerance for risk. Many, especially black boys and young men, are thought to regard promiscuity and sexual infidelity as morally acceptable, and they attach little or no stigma to teenage pregnancy, nonmarital childbearing, paternal desertion, or single-mother households. Many are said to be oriented toward crude materialism and leisure and to seek personal prestige through the conspicuous consumption of luxury items and high-status brands. Street crime and interpersonal aggression are tolerated and sometimes embraced, including a readiness to use deception, manipulation, and even violence to achieve one's aims.

Not all of the values allegedly suboptimal for the ghetto poor contrast sharply with the mainstream. The relevant cultural divergence may not be a matter of the values themselves but the way they are held (e.g., tenaciously or weakly); the priority they are given in practice; the way they are interpreted; or the context within which they tend to be expressed and acted on. For example, patriarchal conceptions of masculinity, anti-intellectualism, and materialism are widespread in American society, cutting across lines of race, class, and place. But some among the ghetto poor are believed to enact these values and norms in extreme ways, to give these values and norms much greater precedence in their lives than the average American, to interpret them in nonstandard ways, or to invoke them in inappropriate contexts. In such cases, the divergence from the mainstream is not a matter of the content of the values and norms but the manner in which they are adopted and understood and their role in practical deliberation.

Recall that according to the weak version of the cultural divergence thesis, these cultural traits are components of a repertoire or part of a conceptual frame that agents strategically deploy to advance specific purposes in particular contexts. On the strong version, the traits in question represent more fundamental commitments and may form part of the agent's social identity. Focusing on the latter, we can regard a person's ghetto-oriented and suboptimal beliefs, values, and practices as constituting a *ghetto identity* if (a) they figure prominently in the person's positive self-concept; (b) they are relatively stable across different social contexts (i.e., there is little or no situational code switching); and (c) the agent is resistant to changing them as a matter of principle. Thus, on the strong view, even given a chance to attend (or send their children to) a good school, to obtain a well-paid nonmenial job, or to move to a low-poverty neighborhood, many ghetto residents would still cling to their ghetto identities.

Some cultural practices prominent in American ghettos have symbolic and expressive dimensions—for example, music, visual art, dance, humor, creative linguistic practices, and clothing and hair styles—that cannot be reduced to or explained by ghetto poverty (Lott 1992; Rose 1994, 2008; Kelley 1997; Perry 2004). These expressive and aesthetic traits draw on and extend black cultural traditions that can be traced back for generations prior to the formation of the modern ghetto, and blacks who have never lived in a ghetto or even been poor value and participate in them, along with many who are neither black nor poor. In addition, some dimensions of ghetto cultural life, while perhaps in some sense a collective response to ghetto conditions, have political meaning or intent and so are not simply a matter of coping with, adapting to, or surviving the conditions of poverty. Some rap music, for instance, offers social critiques of ghetto conditions and expresses a spirit of resistance to the structures and dynamics that reproduce these horrendous circumstances (Rose 1994; Shelby, forthcoming). Those who advance the cultural divergence thesis need not deny that the cultural traits of ghetto denizens include such expressive, aesthetic, or political elements, but some may regard them as suboptimal insofar as they inhibit upward mobility among the black poor or spatial mobility out of the ghetto. Consequently, some cultural reformers may seek to limit their influence on the ghetto poor, particularly on black children. Certain strands of hip-hop culture are often targets of cultural reform.

Proponents of the cultural divergence thesis do not generally equate "ghetto identity" with "black identity." To be sure, it is said that poor urban blacks developed and value these cultural traits and that the relevant traits draw on, or have an affinity with, familiar black traditions and folkways. Nevertheless, it is often claimed that those who have a ghetto identity define themselves, not only in opposition to mainstream American culture, but often in opposition to self-concepts associated with blacks who are successful by conventional measures or who attained their success through mainstream avenues. Insofar as a ghetto identity is regarded as "black," it should be thought of as a mode of blackness that many who identify as black reject. Within black vernacular, blacks readily distinguish between "ghetto blacks," "working-class blacks," and "bourgie blacks," and these designations (which are sometimes used as epithets) are meant to track race, class, place, *and* culture (Miller 2008; Farhi 2007). Moreover, many black Americans who think of themselves as having a strong black cultural identity accept the cultural divergence thesis. For instance, in a recent Pew Forum survey (2007), in response to the question "Have the values of middle-class and poor blacks become more similar or more different?" 61 percent of blacks answered "more different." Indeed, many actively participate in cultural reform efforts as part of a program of racial uplift.[4]

3. Cultural Reform

Confronted with compelling evidence in support of the cultural divergence hypothesis, some might acknowledge that cultural change in ghetto neighborhoods is needed but recoil from the idea that government should play an active role in bringing about such changes—that is, apart from making necessary structural changes in the laws and institutions that negatively affect the lives of the urban poor. The approach I want to consider would be less reticent about getting the government involved in effecting cultural changes in the lives of the ghetto poor. Indeed, it might be thought that such state intervention is essential if ghetto poverty and its associated ills are to be adequately addressed.

Cultural reform should be distinguished from mere behavior modification. The state might try to change the behavior of the ghetto poor without attempting to change their cultural traits, regarding any cultural changes that do occur as unintended byproducts or side effects of intended behavioral changes. For instance, the state might use incentives or penalties to induce behavior thought to be more conducive to upward mobility. If refusing to work or using illegal drugs is believed to contribute to poverty, then the government might step in to penalize such behavior with the hope that poor people will choose to work and abstain from illicit drug use. This would be behavior modification, not cultural reform. With behavior modification, there need not be a presumption that the undesirable behavior is part of a learned cultural pattern or cultural identity. The behavior may simply be, for instance, the result of individual (rational or irrational) decision making or habit. If there is a pattern of such behavior in a group, this may simply be a reflection of similar decision making or errors in practical reasoning among those in the group.

By contrast, cultural reform is premised on the assumption that the relevant behavioral changes will only occur, or are more likely to occur, or will be more durable if some cultural traits are modified. Here, there is a presumption that the suboptimal behavior in question is shaped or influenced by a set of cultural patterns. Thus the cultural reformer would harness the power and resources of the state to bring about the desired cultural changes.

There are at least three types of cultural changes that might be sought, and each has different normative implications. The first and least radical would be *cultural augmentation*. Here, the cultural reformer seeks to add to the cultural repertoire of the ghetto poor without attempting to remove or alter any of their existing cultural traits. The idea would be to equip poor blacks with some mainstream cultural tools (sometimes called "cultural capital"), which they could then choose when and whether to use and to what ends. Their prior cultural attachments, whatever they happen to be, would not then be threatened. The second and more radical change is *cultural removal*. This would involve eliminating or neutralizing any existing cultural traits believed to be suboptimal. This type of intervention would not, however, involve instilling new mainstream cultural traits. Cultural removal would work best if, as some cultural analysts insist, most among the ghetto poor already embrace mainstream cultural values and norms. Simply removing or defusing any suboptimal traits might then be sufficient to put them on a path out of poverty. The most radical approach to cultural reform would be *cultural rehabilitation*. It would combine cultural augmentation with cultural removal—getting rid of existing suboptimal traits and replacing them with mainstream cultural traits.

Which types of cultural traits are targets for cultural reform? The particular traits identified for augmentation or removal will affect how controversial and potentially problematic the mode of cultural reform would be. Attempts to change shared *beliefs* among the ghetto poor would be the least controversial, provided the beliefs in question pertain to matters of fact (rather than to what is desirable or valuable) and provided the beliefs are not religious views. For example, if some among the ghetto poor share the belief that formal education will not improve their life prospects or that there are no decent jobs available to them, and if this belief is factually incorrect, then a cultural reformer might try to change this erroneous perception or to prevent its spread.

The cultural reformer might also attempt to change the *skill set* of those targeted for reform. Some cultural analysts maintain that the cultural repertoire of poor blacks includes a set of social skills for operating in ghettos. But these ghetto-specific skills may not be helpful in the wider world and, deployed in the wrong context, may hurt one's chances of success in mainstream society. Effectively navigating the mainstream social world so as to improve one's socioeconomic situation also involves the deft deployment of cultural skills. Insofar as the ghetto poor lack these skills, the cultural reformer might seek to impart them. This type of cultural augmentation is, at least in principle, unobjectionable. Once acquired, the agents can decide whether to make use of this practical know-how and for what purposes, and they can continue to rely on their ghetto-specific know-how if they so choose.

Cultural de-skilling would be another matter. A person can lose an acquired skill if he or she does not use it enough. Either the ability degrades over time or one forgets how to deploy it properly. So de-skilling may be possible if the ghetto poor were deprived of opportunities to use their ghetto-specific skill set or were prevented from drawing on it. Unless the ghetto poor voluntarily went along with this, such a practice, given the constraints it would impose on them, would raise serious questions about the legitimacy of the state's interference with their liberty.

Some customs—shaking hands, saying "thank you," making eye contact, smiling, enunciating words—become *habits*. The cultural reformer may therefore seek to change some cultural habits, either by instilling new habits or breaking old ones. Many customs are preconscious or second nature and performed almost involuntarily. Given how difficult it is to control or break a habit once it has formed, the cultural reform of habits could prove morally problematic.

Even more controversial would be attempts to change the *values* or *cultural identities* of the ghetto poor. Getting into this sensitive terrain might, however, seem unavoidable. Some of the relevant cultural traits that appear to be least optimal (if not destructive)—again, from the standpoint of escaping poverty—do not have to do with factual beliefs, cultural skills, or customary practices. They have to do with ideals and values, with what *ends* are desirable and worthwhile. What constitutes a "good" job? What constitutes "success" in life? What does it mean to be a "responsible" parent or to be in a "healthy" marriage? Is it wrong to smoke marijuana or to use cocaine? Do police officers and laws "deserve" our respect? These and similar questions turn on matters of value. They are normative questions. It is difficult to see how cultural reform could be successful and yet avoid such questions entirely.

Once we know what kind of cultural change is sought and which types of cultural traits are targeted for change, we still need to know which age groups should be targeted. Preadolescent children are the most malleable, so they might seem like the best candidates. Even teenagers in early adolescence (ages ten to fifteen) may seem promising, if more challenging. Provided their parents are adequately informed about and consent to the programs, such initiatives are permissible, even if cultural reform takes the form of cultural rehabilitation. Though parental authority and family autonomy have their limits and can be overridden where there is child abuse, endangerment, or neglect, within these parameters they should be respected. If a parent wants to enroll his or her child into a program or school that engages in cultural reform, this would not be any worse than when parents send their kids to a religious or boarding school.

Things get more complicated with late adolescents (ages sixteen to seventeen) and young adults (ages eighteen to twenty-five). Given their cognitive, emotional, and moral development and the imperative to teach them to run their own lives, late adolescents, though not adults, are properly accorded autonomy over significant domains of their lives (Schapiro 1999). They are also expected to take full responsibility for many of the outcomes of their choices, even when these choices could adversely affect their futures. This is widely acknowledged, even by the U.S. government, as late adolescents are permitted to drop out of school, to accept employment, and to operate motor vehicles, and are sometimes subject to criminal prosecution as adults. Young adults (assuming no serious mental illness or debilitating cognitive disabilities) are rightly treated as fully competent to govern their lives, with all the rights and responsibilities this entails.[5] Thus, cultural reform directed at late adolescents and young adults is potentially more problematic than reform directed at young children. I will leave aside older adults, since they are unlikely to be viewed as good candidates for cultural reform.

Before offering a more in-depth treatment of the practicality and moral permissibility of cultural reform, I need to outline the particular methods the state might use or sponsor to bring about the relevant changes. The cultural augmentation of factual beliefs through the provision of information or rational persuasion is the most benign. Few would object to this, provided it is based on sound scientific research and is devoid of the deception and manipulation characteristic of commercial advertising and political ads. Attempting to eliminate the false factual beliefs of the ghetto poor through information or reasoned argument isn't problematic either.

Things get more complicated with instruction and training programs. Teaching involves the provision of information and dissemination of knowledge but generally goes well beyond this. It can entail skills training, inculcating desirable habits (or breaking undesirable ones), instilling values, and shaping identities. The relevant skills, habits, and values can perhaps sometimes be imparted through lectures, discussion, and the distribution of information. But sometimes a more directive and supervisory approach is the only effective method.

Counseling could also be used as a cultural reform technique. Such counseling might be no more than advice and encouragement, and so almost as benign as the provision of information or the intervention of a friend. But the counseling could take a more explicitly therapeutic form, in which the client is expected to submit to the direction of the counselor. The counseling could also be faith-based, in which nonrational means of persuasion are sometimes used (e.g., the exploitation of guilt or intimations of divine disapproval and sanctions). Would therapeutic or spiritual counseling be problematic as a technique of cultural reform? Much will depend on the power relationship between the counselor and the client and on whether the client has a choice in whether to seek the type of counseling in question. If poor blacks seek counseling because they believe they have suboptimal cultural traits and think counseling would help to change these, then there is little reason to object to the practice.

Of course, if information and reasoned argument, voluntary educational and training programs, and voluntary counseling services were all that were needed to bring about the relevant cultural changes, cultural reform would not raise such difficult moral questions. A more aggressive approach may appear necessary, however. Those selected for cultural reform may not see the need for change even after having been informed of the relevant facts. The cultural traits targeted for change may be recalcitrant, and those individuals singled out for cultural change may not be disposed to participate in the relevant programs. Even those who do choose to participate may not continue with them long enough or may not fully cooperate with those running the programs. This naturally raises the issue of the permissibility of incentives and sanctions.

Incentives, particularly financial ones, may seem benign. However, when they are offered to the poor, especially to those severely disadvantaged, they can be morally troubling. When one is socioeconomically disadvantaged and in need of basic resources, it can be very difficult to turn down a financial offer, especially if one has dependents in need of things you cannot otherwise provide. Thus, many among the ghetto poor might participate in cultural reform programs (say, at the behest of their case workers), not because they see their value and just need a little nudge, but because they desperately need socioeconomic resources. Depending on their alternatives, they may be effectively compelled to submit to cultural reform even if they regard it as demeaning or insulting.

The imposition of sanctions or penalties raises the most serious worries. Not only might the ghetto poor object that they are being forced to submit to a demeaning cultural reform process, but they might also object to any suffering, unpleasantness, indignities, or loss of liberty such penalties would involve. Pointing out that this is for their own good is unlikely to be an adequate response to these complaints.

4. Moral Reform

Relying on distinctions outlined in the previous section, I will largely restrict myself to examining the normative and practical implications of one particular type of cultural reform, which I will designate "moral reform." Moral reform goes beyond correcting mistaken cultural beliefs or expanding the cultural repertoire of the ghetto poor. It is a form of cultural rehabilitation that targets not only beliefs and skills but also habits, values, and identities. The public policy goals of moral reform are to sever or weaken attachment to suboptimal cultural traits and to instill mainstream cultural traits or strengthen attachment to these traits.

The relevant mainstream cultural traits include a value-orientation toward and commitment to hard work, thrift, economic self-sufficiency, delayed gratification, academic achievement, civility, respect for authority, moderation in drink and play, reverence for the institution of marriage, and responsible reproduction and good parenting. Though moral reform is sometimes directed toward young children, I will focus on moral reform directed at late adolescents and young adults (often designated as "youth"), as this raises the most interesting moral issues.

Moral reform might be carried out directly by government agencies or accomplished through publicly funded but privately operated and community-based organizations. The kinds of policies, programs, and techniques I have in mind include the following.[6] Moral reform could involve making work or job training a condition for receiving public aid with a view toward instilling an appropriate work ethic, labor-force attachment, and the value of economic self-sufficiency.[7] Such a program could include empowering social workers with the authority to regulate the lives of those who rely on public assistance. For example, they might threaten to withhold, reduce, or cancel benefits for those who refuse to adhere to work requirements. The government could criminalize "vices" associated with a suboptimal ghetto lifestyle (e.g., drug use, gambling, and prostitution) or make the abandonment of such practices a condition for housing assistance or other aid. There could be programs that exhort and counsel the ghetto poor to make more responsible choices (e.g., about reproduction, marriage, and parenting). Moral reform could involve moving poor people out of ghettos to low-poverty neighborhoods with the expectation that they will come to absorb values and norms of conduct prevalent in these more advantaged communities. The ghetto poor might be given middle-class mentors and role models so that they might come to assimilate mainstream norms and to develop cultural capital. The state might enable greater involvement of faith-based institutions or clergy in the lives of the ghetto poor with the expectation that certain religious beliefs and values might take (stronger) root.[8]

One important thing to keep in mind about such programs and policies is that even when they take the form of incentives and sanctions the point of moral reform is not simply to modify behavior but *to restructure the soul*—to change fundamentally the values, character, and identity of those in the grip of what are regarded as debilitating cultural patterns. To use an expression coined by Kwame Anthony Appiah (2005, ch. 5), moral reform would be a type of "soul making" that a state might engage in to help citizens lead more successful lives. The idea behind moral reform is that once the reform is complete, after the programs are over and the incentives and sanctions are no longer being applied, those who have undergone the reform process will now *govern themselves* in accordance with mainstream norms without further special interventions.

5. "Liberal" Moral Reform?

Social conservatives who advocate moral reform tend to view it (sometimes along with private charity) as the *sole* remedy for ghetto poverty, since they generally regard the basic structure of U.S. society as just and thus not in need of fundamental reform (at least not in an egalitarian direction). Libertarians would presumably not accept moral reform as a legitimate aim of government, at least when dealing with adults. They do not regard the state as having the authority to interfere with the personal choices of adult citizens (though allowances may be made for children). Indeed, they generally believe that it is impermissible for government to take paternalistic actions and that the state's authority is limited to protecting basic rights. On their view, citizens should be free to have a bad character and to embrace self-destructive cultural traits, provided in acting on these dispositions they do not violate the rights of others. Moreover, libertarians generally do not believe the state should institute redistributive schemes to reduce inequality or social welfare measures to alleviate poverty, at least not using tax revenue.

But can liberals, given their basic values, consistently support moral reform? In speaking of "liberals," I don't mean Americans' political self-descriptions or party affiliations. Nor am I referring to advocates of "neo-liberalism"—an ideology that, for example, promotes the use of market rationality and business principles in all social institutions; prefers firms and private organizations (rather than state agencies) to carry out public functions; and views citizens primarily as economic agents (as investors, workers, and consumers).[9] Rather, I have in mind a political morality defined by a distinctive set of value commitments, which might be labeled "liberal egalitarianism," a tradition of thought whose canonical exponents include Immanuel Kant, John Stuart Mill, and John Rawls. In this way, there will be "liberals" (as defined by their self-description, Democratic Party membership, or confidence in markets and privatization) who are not liberals in my sense, because they are not liberal egalitarians.[10] And there will be liberals in my sense who reject the label "liberal" given its current associations (perhaps preferring "progressive").

Thus, a liberal who supported moral reform would presumably view such measures as only *part* of the solution to ghetto poverty. State-sponsored moral reform would have to be joined with policy efforts to make the opportunity structure fairer and the distribution of resources more equitable. Liberals who accept the suboptimal cultural divergence thesis typically regard the relevant cultural traits as a response to unjust structural conditions. These injustices include pervasive racial discrimination (for example, in employment, housing, lending, and law enforcement); diminished life prospects due to unfair economic and educational disadvantages; inadequate social services; and the fact that the social safety net is not large enough and has too many holes to catch all those who fall because of economic restructuring, recessions, and unexpected shifts in the labor market.

I will not directly discuss conservative or libertarian perspectives on moral reform in ghettos, though some of what I will say has implications for these views. While liberals obviously disagree about the extent of its unfairness, they generally agree that the structure of U.S. society is unfair. In fact, a number of prominent liberal thinkers have recently argued that unjust forms of exclusion, unequal opportunities, and economic inequality produced and continue to sustain ghetto poverty (Fiss 2003; Barry 2005; Anderson 2010). Liberals also tend to think that government should do something proactive about poverty, instituting feasible antipoverty measures as necessary. Some might therefore be tempted to accept (or, indeed, may wholeheartedly endorse) moral reform as part of a liberal solution to the problem of ghetto poverty. My aim over the next few sections will be to argue that liberal moral reform is neither wise nor morally coherent. The argument will pivot around the idea of "self-respect."

6. Self-Esteem and Unjust Social Conditions

Self-respect is a value open to a variety of interpretations and definitions. John Rawls (1999, 386–91) emphasizes the importance of ensuring that citizens have an opportunity to develop a sense of self-respect. However, instead of using the term "self-respect" to refer to what Rawls has in mind, I will use "self-esteem" (a term Rawls uses as a synonym). Following others (Darwall 1977; Thomas 1978; Sachs 1981; Boxill 1992, 186–99), I want to distinguish this value from a different though related one that we might also want to call "self-respect," a topic I will turn to in the next section.

Self-esteem has two aspects: (1) a secure conviction that one's fundamental purposes (one's conception of the good) are worthwhile and (2) confidence in one's ability to realize these purposes. So, self-esteem is a kind of self-confidence—confidence in the value of one's basic ambitions and confidence in one's ability to realize these aims. Or, put another way, self-esteem is a combination of self-worth and self-efficacy. We have a healthy sense of self-esteem when we regard our fundamental ends as valuable and consider ourselves competent to secure these ends. We have a diminished or damaged sense of self-esteem when we think our plans in life lack value or we are plagued by self-doubt.

In any pluralist society, where by definition there is deep disagreement about fundamental values, citizens will often adhere to conflicting conceptions of the good life. But a *primary good*, again following Rawls, is something that any rational person can be expected to want regardless of his or her particular conception of the good. Such goods include liberty, leisure, income, and wealth. Self-esteem is a primary good because in its absence none of our practical aims will seem worthwhile or we won't attempt to achieve those things we regard as valuable. Apathy, depression, and despair may take over. Moreover, one generally feels shame when one experiences an injury to one's self-esteem. This shame is a response to one's failure to exhibit the personal qualities and achievements one regards as most worthwhile.

Rawls views self-esteem as a *natural* primary good rather than a social one, because society, and in particular the state, has no mechanism for distributing self-esteem directly.[11] However, there are social bases of self-esteem that a social structure can support or undermine. One's sense of self-worth (the first component of self-esteem) is socially supported when those one admires appreciate and affirm one's values and achievements. One will usually develop and maintain a sense of self-worth provided one belongs to at least one association or community within which one's activities are publicly affirmed. These associative or communal ties also strengthen self-efficacy (the second component of self-esteem), for they reduce the likelihood of failure and provide collective defense against self-doubt when failure does occur.

I agree with Rawls that in a just democratic society, we should expect there to be a diverse array of informal communities and formal associations, within which members will develop ideals that cohere with their aspirations and talents. The question that I want to address, which Rawls does not deal with, is what should we expect in an *unjust* society? In an unjust society, there may also be a variety of communities and associations with their own ideals, and these forms of group affiliation may also develop among those who are severely disadvantaged. Moreover, the cultural traits that characterize some of these communities and associations may have been cultivated in response to, or otherwise shaped by, the unjust institutional arrangements. These affiliations may nevertheless perform essentially the same social function—namely, sustaining and enhancing self-esteem—as their counterparts under just arrangements.

7. Self-Respect and Unjust Social Conditions

Self-respect is to be distinguished from self-esteem. Self-respect can be an element of a person's sense of self-worth. But, unlike self-esteem, the role it plays in constituting self-worth is not contingent on a person's particular ambitions or self-confidence. Self-respect is a matter of recognizing oneself as a rational agent and a moral equal and valuing oneself accordingly (Hill 1991, ch. 1; Boxill 1992, 186–99; Sachs 1981). Self-respect is embodied and expressed in the way one conducts oneself. Those with self-respect live their lives in a way that conveys their conviction that they are proper objects of respect. For example, they resist the efforts of others to mistreat them and openly resent unfair treatment. Moreover, persons with self-respect do not believe that they must earn just treatment—through, say, some display of virtue or personal achievement. They know that their capacity for moral agency alone is sufficient to justify their right to justice.

When a healthy sense of self-respect is widespread in a society, this helps to sustain just practices and to deter injustice. And where there is systemic injustice, the self-respect of society's members often moves them to reform their institutions. Thus, those with a robust sense of justice should be concerned to maintain and foster self-respect in themselves and others.

However, self-respect has value quite apart from its contribution to maintaining or establishing a just society. Its value should not be reduced to how it promotes the general welfare. Moral agents are permitted to preserve, express, and strengthen their self-respect even when doing so would not ameliorate unjust conditions, would not lighten their material burdens, and would be personally costly or risky. Self-respect is thus best understood as a component of a nonconsequentialist moral outlook (Kamm 1992). As the philosophers Thomas Hill (1991, ch. 1) and Bernard Boxill (1992, 186–99) have argued, the person who lacks self-respect fails to have the right attitude about his or her moral status. By putting up with injustice without complaint or protest, one does not give morality the regard it merits. This conception of self-respect focuses on the need to show respect for moral requirements. But those most burdened by injustice have additional reasons to preserve and express their self-respect.

Maintaining one's self-respect in the face of injustice is not simply about respecting the authority of morality. The sense of personal investment in such respect would be inexplicable if self-respect were merely about respecting moral principles. Self-respect has value from a personal point of view and not only from an impartial vantage point (Scheffler 1982). A life lived without a healthy sense of self-respect, particularly for one who is oppressed, is an impoverished life *for the particular person whose life it is.*

Oppression can erode a person's sense of self-respect, causing one to doubt one's claim to equal moral status. We can understand an attack on one's self-respect as an action, policy, or practice that threatens to make one feel or believe that one is morally inferior, that one does not deserve the same treatment as others. As a result of such attacks, one can come to have a damaged sense of self-respect. To maintain a healthy sense of self-respect, the oppressed may therefore fight back against their oppressors, demanding the justice they know they deserve—even when the available evidence suggests that justice is not on the horizon. They thereby affirm their moral worth and equal status.

Agents that take action to affirm their moral standing often take pride in such actions, particularly when these acts entail some personal risks or costs. When one is subject to persistent injustice and yet successfully defends one's self-respect, this is a moral achievement. A robust disposition to resist attacks on one's self-respect can therefore be a source of self-esteem. Such self-valuing is *moral pride*. Conversely, submission to injustice can be a culpable failure that generates *moral shame* in the subject. We surrender or sacrifice our self-respect when we acquiesce to mistreatment or when we suffer such indignities in silence.

Persons with a strong sense of self-respect sometimes refuse to cooperate with the demands of an unjust society. They stand up for themselves, are defiant in the face of illegitimate authority, refuse to comply with unjust social requirements, protest maltreatment and humiliation, and so on, even when they know such actions will not bring about justice or reduce their suffering. Self-respect, then, can be a matter living with a sense of moral pride *despite* unjust conditions.

Though self-respect has intrinsic value and great moral importance, it should not be treated as a trump in moral deliberation. Moral agents need not defend their self-respect at all cost. It is sometimes justifiable or excusable to sacrifice a bit of self-respect to protect others from harm, to avoid grave harm to oneself, or to achieve some worthy goal. Such sacrifices are sometimes necessary, all things considered. However, the agent with a healthy sense of self-respect experiences them *as sacrifices*—as the painful loss of an intrinsically valuable good. When you no longer care that others are wronging you, putting up no resistance, or when you routinely trade fair treatment for mere material gain or social status, you have lost all self-respect.

With these remarks as background, I can briefly state my principal objection to moral reform: even if the suboptimal cultural divergence hypothesis is basically sound, moral reform attacks the ghetto poor's social bases of self-esteem and fails to honor their need to preserve their self-respect. These two consequences create serious practical limitations and moral pitfalls. Moral reform is furthermore incompatible with respect for personal autonomy—that is, with an agent's legitimate claim to govern his or her own life as that agent judges fit. In the remainder of this chapter, I will elaborate on these concerns and then close by sketching an alternative approach that I believe avoids these difficulties, is more in line with core liberal values, and is more likely to be effective in achieving the needed cultural and structural reforms.

8. The Practical Limits of Moral Outreach

As outlined in sections 3 and 4, the methods of moral reform vary greatly. One class of methods, which I'll call "moral outreach," relies on dialogue, lectures, sermons, education, training, and counseling. The idea is to effect a change in cultural patterns through, for example, moral exhortation, role models, counseling services, education programs, or faith-based efforts. Some of these interventions are no more than attempts to convince some among the ghetto poor that their cultural ways are obstacles to their escape from poverty. Other interventions might seek to make some residents of ghettos ashamed of their suboptimal mores, to encourage them to take pride in exemplifying mainstream values and identities, or both. This could be supplemented with attempts to get targets of moral reform to identify less with suboptimal ghetto cultural patterns and more with the successful habits and values of middle-class persons.

The main challenge for moral outreach is getting its targets to listen to these appeals and to take advantage of these programs. Moral outreach would seem to have the best chance of success with those for whom the weak version of the cultural divergence thesis applies—those who strategically employ a ghetto-specific cultural repertoire only because they believe they lack adequate opportunities for socioeconomic advancement. Some willing cooperation with moral reform programs might be forthcoming among those who became convinced that the existing opportunity structure is actually such that they could escape poverty were they to assimilate to more mainstream cultural ways. There might also be some willing cooperation if those targeted for moral outreach were looking for *any* chance at escape from poverty, even if, for example, they knew the opportunity structure is seriously unjust and thus most among the ghetto poor, no matter what reasonable efforts they made, would remain in poverty. They would only have to be convinced that there are more exits from ghetto poverty than there are people actively trying to leave and, with the appropriate cultural changes, they could be among the lucky few.

But what if there are many who have suboptimal ghetto identities (i.e., those for whom the strong version of the cultural divergence thesis applies) *and* the social structure is unfairly stacked against them? Here it seems that moral outreach would have limited success. After all, our conception of the good determines what we feel ashamed of and take pride in; that is, shame and pride are relative to our fundamental goals and to the communities with which we identify. If targets for moral reform reject mainstream values and embrace ghetto identities, as the strong version of the cultural divergence thesis asserts, they will not be readily shamed into conforming to mainstream norms; nor should we expect them to take pride in embodying mainstream virtues. They will have developed alternative sources of self-worth that do not depend on mainstream institutions for validation.

A similar point can be made about self-efficacy. Some among the ghetto poor may be confident that they would succeed, even by mainstream standards, *if the social structure they faced were fairer*. Because they believe their efforts to meet mainstream standards of success are likely to be thwarted by a deeply unjust social structure, these persons may develop alternative ambitions (McGary 1992). Where people blame the unfairness of the social structure for their inability to achieve their aims, they need not experience low self-esteem. And we have even less reason to suspect diminished self-esteem in those cases where, in response to their conviction that their society is unjust, people develop basic aims that they believe to be worthwhile and within reach.[12]

Indeed, the more those perceived as "outsiders," and official agents of the state in particular, attack ghetto identities, the more we should expect those who subscribe to these identities to hold firmly to them. By hypothesis, there are distinctive forms of affiliation in ghetto neighborhoods that are central bases for the positive sense of self-worth of many among the ghetto poor. Those with ghetto identities will therefore demand a compelling reason to change their conception of the good. In the absence of a reasonably just opportunity structure, garnering the esteem of their more advantaged fellows is unlikely to be reason enough.

Recall that the focus of this chapter is on state-operated or state-supported moral reform. In response to the alleged debilitating effects of some ghetto cultural patterns, there are some who propose not government intervention but moral outreach on the part of black elites, a kind of group uplift or self-help (Loury 1995; Cosby and Poussaint 2007). Though such moral appeals may not be inherently objectionable, the strong version of the cultural divergence thesis suggests that this outreach would be rather limited in its effectiveness. Black elites are, in many ways, representatives of the mainstream. They exemplify its values and practices.

Insofar as the ghetto poor are alienated from mainstream values, they are likely to look upon black elites with similar suspicion. This is all the more likely if, as I have argued elsewhere (Shelby 2005, ch. 2), many among the ghetto poor believe that black elites' moral exhortations are motivated less by genuine empathy and group solidarity and more by elites' feeling embarrassed in the eyes of whites by the unruly behavior of poor urban blacks or by their fear that they might be mistaken for one with a ghetto identity.

9. Racism and Cultural Explanations of Black Poverty

There is a second practical limitation to moral outreach. Some of the cultural traits attributed to or associated with the ghetto poor (for example, attitudes toward authority, work, violence, parenting, sex and reproduction, school, and crime) closely resemble well-known racist stereotypes about blacks (their supposed tendencies toward lawlessness, laziness, dishonesty, irresponsibility, gross ignorance, substandard cognitive ability, parasitic reliance on government aid, and sexual promiscuity). Thus, an implication of the cultural divergence thesis is that the conditions of deeply disadvantaged metropolitan neighborhoods have produced a subgroup of blacks who, because of their cultural patterns, exhibit characteristics that racists have long maintained are "natural" to the black race and that these cultural traits are at least part of the explanation for why they are poor. I suspect that this implication is part of the reason many people are suspicious of and sometimes hostile to cultural analyses of black urban poverty—they smell like racist rationalizations for the status quo. To make matters worse, moral reform suggests that the ghetto poor are effectively incapable of altering these suboptimal traits on their own, as it calls for state intervention to change them. Moral reform programs, even voluntary ones, would be implicitly endorsing the idea that poor blacks have personal deficiencies that they alone cannot remedy. In an era when biological racism has been largely discredited and claims that blacks are biologically inferior are not publically acceptable, moral reform will inevitably strike many as the functional equivalent of classic racist doctrines.[13]

Perhaps such a response to moral reform wouldn't be fair. After all, there may be truth in the cultural divergence thesis. The point I want to emphasize, though, is that many among the ghetto poor have reason to believe that some of their fellow citizens are attracted to cultural explanations of black poverty because of racial prejudice and bias. The types of claims made about the black poor, whatever their merit, are often perceived as emanating not from genuine empathy but from racial hostility or indifference to the plight of disadvantaged blacks. In light of this, some poor ghetto denizens may distrust efforts to change the cultural patterns in their neighborhoods. Their suspicion would be well grounded, for some who advocate moral reform no doubt do so because of race-based contempt or a desire to maintain the racial status quo (Bobo, Klugel, and Smith 1997; Holt 2000; Mendelberg 2001; Brown et al. 2003). On grounds of self-respect, then, the oppressed may refuse to avoid "confirming" the stereotypes that are often used to justify their subordination. In the absence of serious structural reform, the suggestion that the ghetto poor do not value hard work and education or that they do not respect the law and are irresponsible parents will strike some among the ghetto poor as yet another racist excuse for not improving social conditions in ghetto neighborhoods.

My point is a practical one: namely, *if* there are some among the ghetto poor who possess ghetto identities, as the strong version of the cultural divergence thesis supposes, then these persons are likely to dismiss outright or strongly resist attempts by representatives of the "mainstream" to undermine or alter those identities. Some moral reform efforts targeted at those with ghetto identities will therefore be self-defeating.

10. Moral Paternalism and Compromises with Injustice

Recognizing the practical limits of moral outreach, moral reformers may give up on this strategy or supplement it with more aggressive measures. Instead of relying on moral outreach alone, they may advocate cultural rehabilitation through a system of rewards and sanctions. This strategy would not depend on the willing or full cooperation of the intended beneficiaries. The moral reformers would attempt to arrange society's incentive structure to produce a deep cultural transformation in their subjects. Their subjects, however, may not (fully) realize what their benefactors are attempting to accomplish, or may not willingly go along, or may not desire the change in themselves the reformers want to effect. In this way, moral reformers work *on*, not *with*, the ghetto poor. Their methods are intended to be effective despite resistance from the black urban poor. Call this mode of moral reform "moral paternalism."

Many liberals find the idea of moral paternalism distasteful. In an ideal world, they would no doubt eschew it. But faced with current social and political realities and in light of their abiding concern to help the poor and disadvantaged, some may be tempted to support some forms of moral paternalism. For example, sympathetic liberals could argue that they do not urge moral reform because they believe the criticisms typically leveled at the ghetto poor are entirely fair or generally spring from nonracist motives. They might simply insist that cultural traits that seem to confirm racist stereotypes make it harder (if not impossible) to generate the good-will among the general public needed to change the structural conditions of ghettos. These liberals may lament the fact that too many Americans regard the ghetto poor as "undeserving" and that, on this ground, these citizens are unwilling to invest the necessary public resources to eliminate urban poverty. However, without the support of at least some of these people, liberal structural reform is not feasible. In response to this political reality, some liberals may be prepared to attach stiff penalties to even minor legal infractions, to impose work requirements on welfare recipients with young children, to aggressively monitor and supervise the behavior of ghetto denizens, and so on, because without cultural and behavioral changes on the part of the black urban poor, structural reform efforts won't be successful.

I have serious doubts about the soundness of the social-theoretic assumptions behind any such strategy, in particular about whether reducing stereotypical behavior and attitudes will garner the desired public goodwill. But even leaving this aside, I would insist that this "liberal pragmatism" threatens the self-respect of the ghetto poor. If, as some cultural analysts maintain, the suboptimal cultural traits of the ghetto poor are a response to societal injustice, then it is not reasonable to expect the urban poor to submit to moral reform to "prove" their worthiness for government interventions to improve structural conditions. Capitulating to the widely held and insulting view that they do not "deserve" better life chances is fundamentally at odds with the ghetto poor maintaining their self-respect. Fair treatment and just social conditions are things they are entitled to in virtue of their status as moral equals and rational agents and cannot be justly withheld on account of their (alleged) unconventional identities or values. The ghetto poor have legitimate justice claims against their government that are not negated by what they do in response to that government's historical and still-persisting failure to honor these claims. As Rawls (1999, 273) rightly points out, as an equal citizen taking part in a system of social cooperation, each acquires legitimate claims on fellow participants as defined by just rules of political association; and we should not regard what a citizen is entitled to by justice as proportional to, nor dependent upon, the quality of his or her moral character.

However, I may seem to have left myself open to the following rejoinder: sometimes advancing the broader cause of justice means compromising with particular injustices. Yes, such sacrifices of self-respect are distasteful and even painful, but they are sometimes necessary in the short term to make progress in the long run. Threatening the self-respect of the current generation of the ghetto poor may simply be the price of the social reform needed to ensure that future generations do not grow up under ghetto conditions.

I do not deny that sacrifices of self-respect can be justified. It may be perfectly reasonable for one to endure some indignities to protect the vulnerable, to preserve one's life, or even to advance the cause of justice. What I reject is the idea that others are permitted to decide for you when you should make such sacrifices. It is one thing to ask or even implore the ghetto poor to sacrifice some self-respect to achieve needed social reforms. It is quite another to demand that they make these sacrifices on pain of penalty or to take measures that effectively force them to accommodate themselves to injustice. Moral paternalism robs the ghetto poor of a choice that should be theirs alone—namely, whether the improved prospects for ending or ameliorating ghetto poverty are worth the loss of moral pride they would incur by conceding the insulting view that they have not shown themselves to be deserving of better treatment. Whether such sacrifices of self-respect are, all things considered, worth it should be left to those who bear the heaviest burdens of the unjust social system liberals seek to reform.

Moreover, using one generation of the ghetto poor as unwilling instruments to bring about justice for the next generation is wrong. We should not treat the ghetto poor as if they did not have purposes, including moral aims, of their own, as if they were mere things that can be turned to purposes, however noble, that we see as fit. As moral agents who should be regarded as equals, they ought to be sought out as willing participants in efforts to bring about just social conditions. In addition, their basic interests in equal liberty and respect should not be treated as tradable for welfare gains for others, not even when the beneficiaries would be their descendants, as this would represent a fundamental compromise in their standing as equal citizens with moral rights.

However, a liberal proponent of moral paternalism might advocate such measures in ghettos, not as a pragmatic political strategy in a conservative era, but based on a sincere belief that certain cultural traits prevalent in ghettos damage the well-being of the ghetto poor, making their already awful situation worse. It might be held, for example, that the ghetto poor do not (fully) appreciate the devastating effect of these cultural traits on their lives. Moral paternalism, then, could be viewed as a compassionate response to suboptimal cultural divergence, even if some among the ghetto poor fail to see how such an intervention is in their best interests.

Nonetheless, the poor in ghettos have reason to find this stance condescending and offensive. Such paternalistic attitudes are fundamentally incompatible with the liberal value of respect for persons. The ghetto poor are free persons and so rightly expect to be accorded the equal respect due all who have this status. Showing that respect means, among other things, regarding persons as capable of revising their conception of the good in response to good reasons and as capable of taking responsibility for their basic ambitions in life (Rawls 1996, 18–20, 72–77). Apart from their interests in meeting their material and physical needs, persons have a fundamental interest in being treated with this kind of respect; and though the liberal desire to meet these other needs is laudable, this goal is not a sufficient reason to override their fellow citizens' claim to be treated as free and equal. In addition, paternalism, as is well known, is hard to justify under just background conditions. Paternalism toward a segment of society acknowledged to be victims of social injustice is all the more suspect.

11. Dignity, Injustice, and the State

There is, however, a third sense of "self-respect" (different from the two discussed in sections 6 and 7) that is relevant to our discussion, and which we might call "dignity." It also has two components: (1) the belief that, no matter one's circumstances, one should do whatever is within one's power to secure one's basic physical, material, and psychological well-being and (2) the will to act on this belief.[14] The dignified person is resilient in the face of adversity and does not allow hardships, even unjust ones, to make him or her feel totally defeated. Constantly wallowing in self-pity and feelings of helplessness, willfully engaging in self-destructive behavior, and no longer caring about whether or how one survives demonstrate that one does not value oneself sufficiently. When people sink to this level of degradation, as some living in ghettos arguably have, it is obvious that they need help whether they recognize this or not. Thus one might argue that moral paternalism, while *pro tanto* unjustified, is permissible in such extreme cases.

So let us suppose that some among the ghetto poor, unbeknownst to them, do need help freeing themselves from a culture of defeatism and debasement, and information, persuasion, and voluntary programs would be insufficient to the task. Still, I think it would be morally problematic for a person or organization, *qua representative of the state*, to presume to be the appropriate agent to provide this unrequested help, at least when this assistance takes the form of moral paternalism. The freedom of the ghetto poor is already constrained by unjust conditions, which the state has failed to remedy. It would add insult to injury for the state to further constrain their freedom with a view to preventing them from making themselves worse off. In short, the problem is this: given its failure to secure just social conditions, the state lacks the moral standing to act as an agent of moral reform. The state could perhaps earn this standing, but only after it had made real and sustained efforts to establish a just social structure, thus establishing its legitimacy and goodwill in the eyes of those it seeks to help.[15]

Moreover, what might appear to be a tragic loss of dignity might, in fact, be an affirmation of self-respect. Though their actions may seem to signify diminished dignity, those with suboptimal cultural characteristics might not have given up on life and might not be suffering from weakness of will. Rather, they have reasons to view their outlook as a realistic stance in light of their government's wrongful actions (from malign neglect to vicious assaults) and their fellow citizens' self-serving contempt. They can permissibly choose to accept the risks and bear the consequences of their cultural attitudes and practices rather than attempt to live in accordance with mainstream values while lacking the necessary resources and opportunities. And they can do so with a sense of moral pride. Perhaps what they most need and desire, then, is not unsolicited state-sponsored help but basic social justice. One way to respect this reasonable stance would be to recognize their prerogative to decide when their defiant behavior and suboptimal cultural traits are worth the personal costs and risks.

12. Moral Reform and Duties to Others

The form of liberal egalitarianism I am advancing does not rely on the dubious idea that the oppressed can never be morally criticized for how they respond to injustice. Not all criticisms of the unjustly disadvantaged are problematic victim-blaming. Moral criticism of the ghetto poor is sometimes warranted despite the unjust conditions that circumscribe their lives (Boxill 1994; Shelby 2007). Those mired in ghetto poverty, just like many among the nonpoor, do sometimes have ambitions that are not in fact worthwhile but morally base and wrong. They sometimes choose immoral means to achieve their legitimate goals. And they sometimes give undue weight in deliberation to some of their group affiliations. So, for example, it is morally objectionable that some use deadly violence to secure luxury goods and social status, that some degrade and sexually assault others, and that some allow gang loyalty to trump what should be overriding moral considerations like respecting the rights of others and assisting the weak and vulnerable. These bases of self-esteem are not worthy of our respect and are appropriately condemned.

Moreover, the ghetto poor, like the rest of us, have moral duties to others that are not voided because of unjust social conditions. So, for instance, we should all refrain from violent aggression against others and should not abuse, endanger, abandon, or neglect the children in our care. There are, and should be, legal proscriptions against these wrongful actions, even when they are perpetrated by the unjustly disadvantaged. Accordingly, it will sometimes be permissible and even morally required for the state to use coercive means to ensure that these duties are fulfilled and their corresponding rights protected. Thus, one legitimate rationale for intervening in the lives of the ghetto poor is to protect innocent persons, including children, from legally proscribed harmful immoral conduct. It is a requirement of social justice that the state play this role in the lives of those within its territorial jurisdiction. A state that fails to do so in a conscientious, impartial, and consistent way treats those under its rule unjustly, just as it does when it fails to secure a fair distribution of the benefits and burdens of socioeconomic cooperation. When this protective function goes unfulfilled under unjust social conditions, like those that exist in ghetto neighborhoods, the state compounds the burdens on the oppressed and undermines its own legitimacy in their eyes.

However, this raises the difficult question of whether moral reform of criminal offenders can be justified on the grounds that it is needed to protect third parties from harmful wrongdoing. So, for example, the cultural rehabilitation of criminals might be regarded as a crime-prevention measure, as an effort to reduce recidivism. Or, more controversially, moral reform could be directed at parents who have abused or neglected their children. This abuse and neglect might be attributed to suboptimal parenting styles acquired through intergenerational or peer influence. Perhaps moral reform would be justified in these cases. This isn't obvious, though. When the criminal justice system or children's protective services do intervene to protect the rights of persons against the wrongful actions of others, moral reform may not be needed, advisable, or even permissible. Behavior modification without cultural rehabilitation—for example, punitive measures—may be all that is called for and justifiable. But I will not pursue this complex issue here, as it is not my principal focus.

My concern in this chapter is with how cultural patterns in ghettos may hold back the socioeconomic advance of some in their grip and whether moral reform is a legitimate antipoverty strategy. I am not addressing whether moral reform is an appropriate response to criminal deviance or parental maltreatment of children. State interventions aimed at ensuring that people fulfill their moral responsibilities to others have a different normative status from interventions aimed at ensuring that people do not harm their own interests. It is the latter rationale for moral reform that is the subject here. My objection is to moral reform whose objective is helping the black urban poor escape poverty.

13. Two Responses from the Political Left

Many on the political left are adamantly against state-sponsored moral reform, especially in the context of societal injustice. They believe that government should not be in the business of structuring the intimate lives or moral consciousness of embattled citizens but should rather focus its efforts on protecting basic liberties, ensuring a fair distribution of resources, and maintaining a just opportunity structure. There are two important leftwing responses to the cultural divergence thesis, both of which deny the validity of the thesis itself. The first insists that the cultural lives of the ghetto poor do not actually diverge from the mainstream (Reed 1999, ch. 6). These leftists point out that the attitudes and practices associated with the ghetto poor—laziness, hedonism, devaluation of academic achievement, materialism, promiscuity, rudeness, substance abuse, lack of respect for authority, nonmarital reproduction, irresponsible parenting, and violence—are also pervasive among the affluent and the vaunted middle class. The cultural patterns found in the ghetto are not specific to it but are part of a much broader cultural current within the United States. The difference, they maintain, is that the poor have far fewer resources than their more advantaged fellow citizens. This means that they are much less able to bear the costs of this lifestyle. Thus some of the burdens of the ghetto poor's choices (e.g., higher taxes, urban blight, school disruption, and street crime) are shifted onto those with greater means. Many among the affluent resent this fact and therefore adopt a punitive, authoritarian, or paternalistic response to the disadvantaged living in the deteriorated urban core. But this resentment is unjustified, for the distribution of benefits and burdens of social life in the United States is profoundly unfair, and thus the responsibility for these "negative externalities" cannot be (solely) placed on the ghetto poor. Moreover, targeting the ghetto poor for moral reform is hypocritical, as many so-called mainstream Americans possess the same cultural traits they decry.

A second response from the left is to accept that cultural patterns in ghettos diverge from the mainstream but to insist that this divergence is not suboptimal (Stack 1974; Steinberg 2011). According to this view, group cultures are adaptive collective responses to the structural environment. The ghetto poor are simply responding rationally to the constraints of high ghetto walls—though perhaps they do not conceive of their values and practices in such terms—with the result being, not a suboptimal culture, but a culture that fits the external environment. This culture would change, perhaps swiftly, with improved material circumstances and greater protection of civil rights, as the formerly poor would rationally adapt to their better conditions. Thus, if we tear down these walls, that is, make the social structure more just, we would thereby effect a positive change in the culture of ghettos without having to resort to moral reform.

These two positions are important rivals to liberal moral reform. Though I will not assess them here, I mention them because they are alternatives worthy of serious consideration and because I want to distinguish them from the one I have been defending. I close, then, by briefly sketching a different kind of response to the cultural aspects of ghetto poverty, a liberal-egalitarian response that does not depend on rejecting the suboptimal cultural divergence hypothesis.

14. Self-Esteem, Self-Respect, and Collective Resistance to Injustice

I begin with the following normative premise. To be reasonably just, a liberal-democratic, market-based society must (a) ensure that discrimination does not diminish persons' life chances, (b) maintain the conditions for fair equality of opportunity (i.e., eliminating, as far as possible, the effects of class origins on individuals' relative life chances and labor-market competitiveness), and (c) provide a guaranteed social minimum and adequate social services so that no one is forced to live in degrading forms of poverty. I realize many reject this liberal-egalitarian stance, even some who regard themselves as "liberals." My goal here is to defend an approach to ghetto poverty from a liberal-egalitarian perspective, not to defend liberal-egalitarian values. Moreover, I would also insist that, as a factual matter, these principles of justice are not currently realized in the United States (Shelby 2007, 2012). If the normative premise and the factual claim are correct, it will almost certainly take a progressive social movement to realize liberal-egalitarian ideals, for there is currently strong resistance to such structural reform. And if we want to build and sustain such a movement, it is not enough to act on behalf of the disadvantaged. We should also enlist their active involvement, including the participation of the ghetto poor.

The effort to garner their cooperation faces a number of challenges, however. One challenge is brought into focus by the cultural divergence thesis. The thesis holds, on at least some variants, that the stigma, blight, segregation, crime, lack of opportunity, and material deprivation of ghetto neighborhoods have shaped the ambitions, values, practices, and identities of many of their inhabitants. In particular, a salient cultural attitude in ghettos (though not exclusive to them) is widespread political cynicism or apathy, a general belief that the social system is irredeemably corrupt and that meaningful structural change cannot be achieved. This is hardly surprising, since a familiar response to long-term, second-class citizenship is an absence of civic engagement and an acceptance of unjust conditions as inevitable. If, as the cultural divergence thesis maintains, such attitudes encourage the development of corresponding social identities and forms of group-based self-esteem, then if an inclusive progressive movement is to emerge, it may be necessary for some of the cultural attitudes and practices of the ghetto poor to change after all. Without this change, the politically alienated among the ghetto poor cannot be regarded as suitable allies in a collective fight for just social conditions.

The difficulty is how to effect this cultural change without undermining the self-esteem, attacking the self-respect, or calling into question the dignity of those who have been most burdened by social injustices. Are there considerations in favor of a change in their cultural ways that it would be reasonable for the ghetto poor to accept? Considerations that threaten their self-respect, convey paternalistic sentiments, or question their dignity are not reasonably acceptable, for reasons I have explained. Moreover, as a practical matter, it might help the cause of social justice if alternative social bases of self-esteem were developed or made available without being coupled with a moralizing attack on ghetto cultural patterns. Even if their resistance to changing their cultural attachments is not entirely reasonable, many among the segregated black urban poor will naturally reject any suggestion that their cultural ways are having a corrosive effect on their life chances, for some have found meaning, solace, and self-worth in these cultural traits. In addition, as I have argued, the state lacks the moral standing to demand that the ghetto poor change their cultural perspective or practices, at least until it establishes a more just social scheme. So it falls to concerned private citizens and associations to convince the politically alienated among the ghetto poor that active political resistance to the current social arrangement is not futile, that organizing, mobilizing, and putting political pressure on government officials can yield positive results.

My suggestion, then, is to make an appeal (perhaps indirectly) to the self-respect of the ghetto poor. Since political resistance to injustice expresses and boosts self-respect, the black urban poor have reasons of self-respect to participate in a movement for social change. These are reasons the ghetto poor can reasonably accept, and many of course are already moved by them. Because the injustices characteristic of ghettos are threats to the self-respect of the black poor—that is, these injustices can potentially weaken their confidence in their equal moral worth—engaging in a collective struggle for social justice with others similarly committed can restore or fortify the self-respect of the ghetto poor.

In addition, maintaining a robust sense of self-respect in the face of injustice can enhance self-esteem. Persons can increase their moral pride by successfully protecting themselves against threats to their self-respect. They can do this, not only through defying conventional authority or transgressing mainstream norms, but by protesting wrongs perpetrated against them, preventing others from violating their rights, or criticizing the beliefs and values that are used to justify their suffering and disadvantage.

Efforts to change the basic structure of U.S. society should include the ghetto poor, not just as potential beneficiaries of such efforts, but as potential allies. There are already grassroots organizations and activists working to empower the ghetto poor and to increase their political participation. These efforts should be supported, joined, extended, and emulated. Not only could this dramatically increase the numbers of those pushing for social reform, but it might also help to sustain or create alternative sources of self-esteem for those attracted to suboptimal cultural values and practices. Many could find self-worth, in the form of moral pride, in working together with others to bring about just social conditions. But for this to occur on a large scale, forms of political solidarity that foster a commitment to the values of justice and mutual respect would need to be strengthened. Consequently, each member of these political associations could have their activities affirmed by the other members, thereby buttressing individual and collective self-efficacy. Provided these alliances produced some concrete political victories and realistic hope for further gains, the result might well be the creation of more constructive social bases of self-esteem than those the ghetto poor sometimes embrace today. Those who want to act in solidarity with the ghetto poor can therefore legitimately encourage them to find self-esteem in the joint pursuit of justice.[16]

Conclusion

What Have We Learned?

ORLANDO PATTERSON, *Harvard University*
ETHAN FOSSE, *Harvard University*

What We Have Learned about Culture

There is no such thing as *the* culture of poverty. In fact, the originator of the phrase, Oscar Lewis, can hardly be said to have endorsed what has now become the standard stereotypical argument on how culture is related to poverty. In this caricatured portrayal, culture has a deterministic, negative influence on the lives of the poor, leading to a downward spiral of pathology. Understandably, scholars and policy analysts alike have rejected such a portrayal of the lives of the poor. Recent attempts at rehabilitating the culture concept have tentatively gone only halfway toward its retrieval as a critical factor in any understanding of the plight of the poor, especially the black poor, still intimidated by this caricature and the facile mantra that all mention of the concept entails a blaming of the victim.

If there is no such thing as the culture of poverty, the fact remains that for disadvantaged black youth, like all people, culture is the fundamental component of social life—that which separates the behavior of *Homo sapiens* from other species. The question, then, is not whether culture matters but how. The contributors to this volume have boldly addressed this problem and have offered many well-documented examples of how culture works—as enabling agent, constraining force, and provider of goals, meanings, and ways of knowing as well as the metaphors and other shared schemas with which to think, feel, and express ourselves.

Running through all the chapters of this volume is a balanced view of cultural processes that are seen as the product, on the one hand, of relatively stable, shared schemas of ideas, narratives, metaphors, and beliefs, formal and informal rules or norms, and specific as well as ultimate values

533

and, on the other hand, their more flexible pragmatic application in social interactions, which allow for agency, individualism, and creativity, though within limits set by practical rules of engagement that take account of status, power, and context.

The chapters further demonstrate that disadvantaged black neighborhoods, like other urban neighborhoods of America, are socially and culturally variegated, consisting of at least three main groups (the inner-city middle- and lower-middle class, the working class [including the working poor], and the disconnected), the members of which observe one or more of four cultural configurations (adapted mainstream, black proletarian, street, and the hip-hop). Contrary to what has been claimed, we found that this cultural and social heterogeneity is not in itself problematic but, instead, a source of support and creativity. What is problematic for all who live in these neighborhoods is the street configuration of the disconnected minority, which is embraced by no more than a quarter of their populations, and often substantially less. The sociocultural complexity of inner-city black youths' neighborhoods is especially well documented in the chapters by Sampson on variation in moral and normative responses, Tran on ethnic differences between native blacks and youth of West Indian descent, Venkatesh on varying community resources for dealing with violence, Fosse the differing cultural dimensions of structurally disconnected youth, and Miller on gender differences, as well as Patterson's delineation of the major groups and cultural configurations.

Another important general conclusion that has emerged from these studies is that culture works interactively with structural forces—that is, socioeconomic, institutional, network, and environmental processes. Having rejected the vulgar Marxist view that culture is merely epiphenomenal, to be treated, at best, as a dependent variable; the more orthodox view of contemporary cultural sociology that it is a mere bundle of toolkit resources to be used at will by free-floating agents in endless meaning making and boundary work, constrained only by situation and context; and the more humanistic, Geertzian dogma of the "cultural-studies" congregation that it is a text, a web of significations, to be hermeneutically interpreted; these studies have not gone to the opposite "strong program" extreme advocated by Jeff Alexander (2003), which claims that culture can be autonomous in its impact on social structures and people's social life. Rather, the studies underscore that *both culture and structure matter in describing and understanding the lives of poor black youth,* or any other group, for that matter. To be sure, the relative weight of cultural versus structural forces in interactively explaining outcomes will vary. Thus, for example, Clarkwest and his coauthors show how the interaction of extreme poverty and differences in the role expectations and valuation of marriage between program officers trying to encourage stable marriage and their clients resulted in the counterintuitive hastening of the collapse of the clients' relationships. Dehejia and his colleagues show that the buffering effects of church attendance when growing up remains strong, even after controlling for a range of structural variables. On the other hand, Patterson's analysis of youth violence indicates that environmental and health factors such as chemical toxicity, parental poverty, overcrowding, and weak or nonexistent institutional presence largely account for the high levels of violence in the inner cities and that cultural processes mainly mediate these epidemiologically early environmental impacts.

What We Have Learned about Black Youths' Views on Culture and Society as well as Their Own Condition

One of our most striking findings is that black youth have a sophisticated understanding of cultures: not only are they not "cultural dopes," but they do not view the world this way either. To put it another way, crude theories of culture and poverty are more the exclusive province of academics than the poor themselves. For example, Patterson and Rivers discovered that black youth have a highly sophisticated, dramaturgical view of the world, an ethnosociology, so to speak, that rivals Goffman's in its thoroughgoing use of the metaphor of the social world as a stage or a game on which the self is enacted in response to other players and the appropriate script. This view of the interaction between structure and culture is reflected in the opinions of black youth themselves on the problems facing black men and the possible reasons underlying some of the major predicaments they face, such as the fact that they are more likely than black women to be incarcerated and involved in criminal activity, in part because of their greater disposition to play risky life games.

Another important point emphasized is the seeming paradox that, although among the most socially isolated groups in America, black youth are nonetheless fully exposed to the declarative aspects of America's mainstream popular culture and have influenced its musical, broader entertainment, and athletic domains more than any other minority group and in some domains more than the Euro-American majority. Indeed, as Marshall reminds us, a turning point in the history of American mainstream popular culture was achieved during one week in October 2003 when all of the top ten positions on Billboard's pop chart were filled by black artists, nine of them in the inner-city created rap genre. It is hardly surprising that the typical Euro-American imagines the African American population to be somewhere between 23 and 30 percent of the U.S. population, or over twice its actual size (Patterson 1997, 56). This, we have learned, has both its positive and negative aspects. Black youth's complete immersion in mainstream popular culture, documented in Chapter 2 by Patterson, has not only allowed them to powerfully engage with, and transform, important segments of it but also explains their deep commitment to some of the most fundamental values of the mainstream—its individualism, materialism, admiration for the military, and insistence on taking near-complete responsibility for their own failures and successes—but it has also meant exposure to, and assimilation of, the mainstream's own most undesirable values: the celebration of violence, sexism, anti-intellectualism, primal honor, and extreme consumerism.

Following on what was mentioned above, black youth are surprisingly critical of themselves and take responsibility for their predicament. When President Obama (2014a), in his recent speech announcing his new Brother's Keeper policy initiative aimed at improving the lives of black youth, stated that "It may be hard, but you have to reject the cynicism that says the circumstances of your birth and the lingering injustices of society define you and your future," he was saying something with which the great majority of black youth are in complete agreement; it is mainly older middle-class black Americans and their social science allies who would find it "hard" to agree with him. When asked to evaluate the problems facing black men, 92 percent of black youth, aged eighteen to twenty-four, say that "young black men not taking their education seriously enough" is a "big problem," while 88 percent say likewise for "not being responsible fathers."[1] Notwithstanding, black youth also cited structural issues, with large majorities saying poverty (66 percent), lack of good jobs (85 percent), and racial discrimination (60 percent) are also big problems facing young black men.[2] Moreover, if anything, young black men are just as critical of themselves as black women. Somewhat surprisingly, black youth are more likely than white youth to say that black men are to blame for their own problems.[3] Asked whether or not they think the problems facing black men are more a result of what "white people have done to blacks" or more a result of what "black men have failed to do for themselves," 16 percent of black youth cite the former, while 67 percent choose the latter (with 18 percent saying both factors are equal). In comparison, white youth are more likely to say the problems facing black men are due to what "white people have done to blacks" (31 percent), while 41 percent blame young black men, and 28 percent say both are equally important reasons.

The findings highlighted earlier notwithstanding, 54 percent of black youth in 2011 still say that racism is a big problem. Interestingly, this varies by gender, with 59 percent of black women saying this is a big problem, compared to 42 percent of black men. The evidence suggests that this is in part due to the greater structural connection of young black women than men: they are more likely to experience problems of racism in the workplace and educational system precisely because they are not removed from them. As expected, we found that larger proportions of black men are likely to say that police discrimination is a major problem in their neighborhoods and communities.[4]

We also learned that black men are likely to say they are at least partly responsible for problems related to violence between men and women. When asked about whether or not black men show the "proper respect" toward black women, the findings are striking: 74 percent of young black women and 61 percent of young black men say that black men do not show "proper respect" toward black women. Furthermore, of those who agree, large majorities of young black men and women say this is a "very serious problem" (63.4 percent males versus 60 percent women). Although large majorities say black men do not show the proper respect toward black women, this is not wholly reflected in black youth's perception of the level of sexism. Thus we find that 39 percent of black youth say sexism is a big problem, while 46 percent say it is a somewhat big problem.[5] As expected, there is a gender difference, with approximately 40.5 percent of young black women saying sexism is a big problem as compared to 34 percent of young black men. There is a curious disconnect here: acknowledging disrespect does not proportionately translate into recognition of a serious problem of sexism.

The emphasis on both structural and cultural factors is not limited to a global assessment of the problems facing young black Americans: when asked about particular issues facing black Americans, black youth are again likely to say both structural and cultural causes are important. This is apparent in what we found regarding three major issues: the high rate of out-of-wedlock births, the education and employment gap between black men and women, and the higher level of incarceration among black men than women.

Large majorities say structural factors are a big reason for out-of-wedlock birth: 54 percent give as a big reason the fact that that many black men "don't feel they can support a family financially," and 69 percent report likewise for the statement that "too many young black men are in prison or have been killed." Black youth also believe cultural factors are a "big reason," but neither is a majority viewpoint: 45 percent give as a big reason the view that "black men are less likely [than black women] to value marriage," while 38 percent say that "black women are reluctant to marry men who have less education and lower incomes." Interestingly, these findings did not vary by gender, suggesting a general consensus on the underlying causes, except that young black men were more likely to say black women are reluctant to marry men with lower levels of education and less incomes (43 percent versus 34 percent), although this did not reach conventional levels of statistical significance. In short, black youth view both structural and cultural causes as big reasons for the high rate of out-of-wedlock births among black Americans, with a higher percentage citing structural causes.

Another major issue focuses on the fact that the average black woman is more highly educated (two thirds of all bachelor's degrees and 60 percent of all doctorates among African Americans are held by women) and more employed, especially in management, professional and related occupations, where she earns more because of her greater presence although, in all occupations taken together, black women still earn 85% of black men in average weekly earnings (BLS 2014a, 2014b). When asked about the causes of this disparity, 38 percent of black youth say that a big reason is that whites are more comfortable with black women than black men, 48 percent cite greater discrimination against black men, and 40 percent report the greater likelihood of a criminal record among black men. However, 49 percent of black youth also say that a big reason is that black women "work harder" than black men, suggesting that black youth also believe cultural factors are important in explaining the gender achievement gap. Notwithstanding, there are some basic gender differences, suggesting that these explanations lack some consensus: young black men are much more likely than young black women to say that the higher percentage of criminal records among black men (52 percent versus 28 percent for women) and the claim that whites feel more comfortable around black women than black men (45.6 percent versus 31 percent) are big factors. In summary, black youth report both structural and cultural reasons for the achievement gap between men and women, although men are more likely to emphasize structural factors.

The third issue we highlight is the high rate of incarceration of young black men compared to other young people. When asked about the reasons for this, black youth view structural forces as major causes, such as the fact that more black men grow up in poverty (64 percent), police are more likely to target black men than their white counterparts (60 percent), courts are more likely to convict black men than white men (50 percent), black men have fewer job opportunities (47 percent), and schools are failing black men (42 percent). However, black youth also think that incarceration is, at least in part, due to the fact that black men are less likely to think committing crimes is wrong (43.4 percent) and that "many black parents aren't teaching their children right from wrong" (57.4 percent). Although not reaching conventional levels of statistical significance, we find further evidence that young black women are more likely to view cultural reasons as important, while young black men are more likely to cite structural conditions.[6]

What We Have Learned about the Cultural Aspects of Poverty

The studies in this volume emphasize a number of important themes on the cultural aspects of poverty, especially as it relates to black youth. First, cultural continuity is vital to examining how culture is related to poverty. To put it another way, there is a deep cultural continuity over time. For example, Robert Sampson shows in his chapter that neighborhoods inherit near-identical structural and cultural conditions decades later. Patterson also argues that there is a deep undercurrent of vernacular African American culture, especially among the working class, that informs their resilient outward changes and adaptations to the slings and arrows of outrageous racial environments. We see it, too, in the anti-heroic street character of the player whose cultural ancestry reach back deep into the slave past, or several of the characteristic gestures of hip-hop, which Lhamon (2000) traces all the back to the eel dancers at Catherine's Market in the early decades of nineteenth-century New York.

Second, culture is not always a constraint or an overtly negative influence on the lives of the poor. While it is true that culture can be expressed

as anger, discontentment, depression, violence, and other patently negative outcomes, as we have documented, the chapters in this volume also
show how culture can have a positive impact on black youth. We have
already noted how religious membership can buffer against the negative
effects of growing up in conditions of severe structural disadvantage,
helping youth become resilient despite exposure to a multitude of risks.
Similarly, Van Tran documents the ways in which the adapted, neo-
immigrant cultural configuration of second-generation West Indians partially shields their youth from the onslaughts of the street culture.[7] Most
remarkably, Wayne Marshall shows that hip-hop music is vital for the self-
expression of black youth—in a few cases propelling them to enormous
economic and occupational success. From his chapter, we learn further,
that the hypersegregation and poverty of black youth has meant that they
had limited, if any, access to the instruments and procedural training in
music or the funds to visit concerts and museums. This led them to rein-
terpret the declarative musical knowledge to which they were fully exposed
via the mass media and to repurpose available technologies for new musical
ends, with explosive creative consequences. Thus the turntable, an instrument for reproducing music, became an instrument for producing music
in the invented art of turntabling; popular hits became samples in rap
renditions; the walls of ghetto shops, unsecured by the uncaring police,
became the canvas for graffiti art, and so on. There are few greater testimonies to the innate cultural capacity and adaptability of human beings,
especially what Tomasello (2001) calls the cultural "rachet effect"—our
capacity to create new artifacts and symbolic representations from what
we already have, however meager—than the construction and rise to
national and global prominence of hip-hop from the formal institutional
desert and material desolation of America's inner cities.

Third, culture consists of nested contexts, from micro to macro, which
can frame actions, but this usually involves meaning maintenance rather
than meaning making. One implication is that a shared understanding and valued interactional schema can have different consequences,
depending on the context as well as the status and relative power of the
parties involved. For instance, the sociologist Simone Ispa-Landa found
that evaluations of assertiveness among female students differed greatly in
urban compared to suburban schools. What to black, working-class girls
from the inner city are cherished representations of self and ethnic identity—joyous laughter and squeals of good humor, verbal contestations
in ghetto girl-talk, expressions of female pride and assertiveness, and

protective "don't mess with me" glances—are viewed by upper-middle-class suburban white girls as crass, loud, and un-gentrified cultural practices. This is not a case of meaning making or even of meanings changing in different contexts, as orthodox cultural sociologists would have it, but examples of what affect-control theorists call meaning maintaining. Usually, when there are differences, people head off potential conflict by adjusting their behaviors and expressions to signal their shared schematic understandings or meanings. However, in the absence of such shared understandings, as was the case between the white and black girls studied by Ispa-Landa, both parties stick to their familiar schemas, rigidly maintaining their meanings, resulting in resentment, unresolved conflict, or sullen avoidance. Similarly, the contrasting integration of the black inner-city boys into the school and suburban setting is a reflection, not of meaning making, or even reinterpretation, but also of meaning maintaining, though with a different outcome. Upper-middle-class white boys and girls viewed the cultural schemas and performances of black boys—their seeming toughness, their sartorial style, their walk, talk, and athleticism—as highly desirable expressions of cool, hip-hop masculinity, maintaining their suburban stereotypes and valorization of such cultural practices. In this case, the black boys, far from resenting this interpretation of their cultural practices, adjusted by reinforcing these shared understandings of inner-city youth masculinity, in many cases changing their behavior to conform to the shared schematic meanings, even when it was not true of them, as were the cases of the far-from-cool black boys coming from respectable inner-city homes, who talked the talk, walked the walk, and jumped the jump, to the delight of the white boys who eagerly invited them to their homes for weekends and the pretty blond girls who competed for dates with them. Again, there was no meaning making here and not a trace of boundary work, but instead a bourgeois meaning maintenance about black masculinity carried through with the full collaboration of the black boys (not to mention, the utter disgust of the black girls).

The context of actions, then, is essential to understanding how cultural schemas influence patterns of behavior, and the point is made by almost all the other authors in this volume. To take other examples, although violent activity is often measured and analyzed legally as isolated instances of deviance, the sociologist Sudhir Venkatesh contends that this is largely misguided. Understanding the causes and consequences of violence entails understanding relations and contexts, such as relationships among other people on the street, involvement with large-scale institutions of the state, and community-level cultural contexts. Only by addressing the myriad forms of how culture is related to the social context of violence can it be more clearly understood and effectively prevented. It was noted, further, that a cultural schema can extend well beyond particular configurations or geographies. For example, as shown by Jody Miller in her chapter on sexual violence, the cultural aspects of violence are grounded in the everyday interactions among some inner-city youth, but they also extend far beyond, mirrored and reinforced in other realms such as popular culture, the prison system, and cultural ideologies of masculinity.

Fourth, a numerical minority can have a disproportionate impact on cultures and neighborhoods. Although many black youth grow up in poor neighborhoods with high levels of violence, this generalization ignores the role of a numerical minority in affecting the cultural context of a neighborhood or community. For example, in the chapter by Kathy Edin and colleagues, all youth in a poor neighborhood must alter their behaviors to deal with the problematic behaviors of a minority who commit the most violent crimes. Similarly, in their chapter on cultural aspects of violence, Krupnick and Winship illustrate the micro-rituals most youth enact to avoid triggering violence, most of which is committed by a relatively small percentage in the neighborhood they examine. Patterson's study marshals the evidence for a similar reign of terror on whole neighborhoods emanating from the minority of no more than 25 percent living by the street culture. A related point on the rule of the numerical minority is that even one or two role models may be enormously beneficial in buffering against the negative effects of growing up in a disadvantaged context. For example, the work by Jody Miller suggests that men, in particular, would benefit from role models. As well, Edin and colleagues document convincingly the importance of positive extra-familial role models in helping youth deal with living in a neighborhood of poverty and high rates of crime. What our studies make clear is that it is extremely inaccurate and egregiously unfair to smear entire neighborhoods of black youth with the violence and thug-life of the minority who terrorize them.

Fifthly, *one of the most important things we have learned from this study is that segregation matters*; it has colossal negative consequences, especially for poor black youth, but also for others living in these segregated neighborhoods, including middle-class youth, a point already well made by Mary Pattillo (1999) and more recently compellingly established by Sharkey (2013). Our studies pinpoint the mechanisms by which ghettoization inflicts its damage. One such mechanism is the fact that ghettos are environmentally toxic, including massive exposure to chemical contamination from both past accumulations and current exposure. A second mechanism is overcrowding, which interacts with cultural practices such as child-rearing patterns, sexual and gender values and notions of territoriality to create high levels of child abuse, exposure to violence, adult sexuality, and gang membership. The final mechanism is what Wacquant (2008) has called institutional desertification, a claim fully supported by the studies in this volume. To be more specific, what's lacking is formal institutional support since, left to themselves, residents have developed their own supportive networks and sometimes makeshift, sometimes, highly structured institutional resources (on which, see Small 2009). Households in severely disadvantaged neighborhoods lack protection from the police, who are often preoccupied with the losing war on drugs that has fueled the nation's historically unprecedented rates of incarceration, making criminals of nonviolent youth whose only crime often was to have been in the wrong place at the wrong time or to have used the wrong version of drugs. Other critical institutions such as schools, which serve vital institutional services besides formal learning, are often removed in the name of policy efficiency, with no clear impact on the educational opportunities of the affected students. Moreover, as shown in the chapters by Patterson, Edin and colleagues, Tran, and Sampson, many black youth are not only removed from the institutions of school but also those of meaningful, well-paying work.

Perhaps the most significant effect of ghettoization is one strongly emphasized by Patterson in Chapter 2: exclusion from the procedural knowledge or tacit cultural capital of the mainstream that comes only from growing up and networking with other mainstream children and youth (Massey and Denton 1993; Massey 2004; also Charles, Dinwiddie, and Massey 2004). Patterson's meta-study makes clear that such procedural knowledge is acquired early in upbringing and is cumulative. Closely related, too, is the twin evil of isolation from the social networks, or social capital, that comes through growing up with peer groups destined for success in middle-class, mainstream society. One consequence of this is that the few black youth who make it are forced to navigate multiple cultural worlds, across contexts, as shown in the chapters by Ispa-Landa, as well as Rosenbaum and colleagues. Segregation, there can now be no doubt, especially the hypersegregated condition of concentrated poverty under which most black youth live, and nearly all the disconnected, is a root cause of their plight—the major, though by no means the only, source and structural multiplier of their cultural schemas and practices. There will be no appreciable change in their condition until what Martin Luther King called the "beloved community" of a truly integrated America comes about.

Culture and Policy

In this section, we will first underscore a number of general themes related to culture and social policy, then, in light of what we have learned, turn to a brief consideration of some of the better-known programs aimed at alleviating the condition of black youth.

First, culture is not immutable, as is commonly believed, especially by structuralist social scientists and most policymakers. Policies explicitly incorporating cultural change can be efficacious. Indeed, the history of change in America indicates that deep-seated cultural values, beliefs, and ideas may be easier to change than established structural ones. Compare, for example, the centuries-old cultural system known as Southern Jim Crow or the broader national culture of racism that informed almost all Euro-American values and beliefs about African Americans up to the 1960s with the system of structural inequality that social scientists and policymakers have spent countless decades of research studying in the belief that it is more mutable and amenable to social policy. What does the history of America over the past half-century show? On the one hand, the complete dismantling of the Jim Crow system and a radical transformation in Euro-American values on race, to the degree that young Euro-Americans are, arguably, the least racially prejudiced group of whites in the world; and, on the one hand, the extreme growth of inequality in America. Consider, too, the dramatic changes in Americans' attitudes toward gays and single-sex marriage, women's attitude to work, or attitudes toward blacks in the culture of sports and entertainment, and compare these cultural changes to the structural rigidity of the ghettos and of sex-segregation in the workplace. What, we are justified in asking, is the truly immutable force?

Secondly, we have learned that rarely are individuals uniformly for, or against, a particular set of values and beliefs, and often people can hold seemingly contradictory viewpoints. As was pointed out in the first chapter by Patterson, people are quite adept at code switching as they move from one cultural configuration to another. For example, the chapter by Patterson and Rivers shows that a program overtly promoting cultural change with regard to work did not offend disconnected youth. A primary reason for this is that many of the youth felt that they could freely reject those aspects of the program they did not like, or switch to norms and declarative cultural knowledge that were available, though not normally accessible (corroborated by Fosse's chapter on the values of disconnected youth), so the program did not appear paternalistic or domineering to them. Their real problem is that they were nearly completely lacking in the procedural knowledge, as well as a good portion of the declarative cultural literacy beyond the popular culture, necessary for their enactment.

Third, although past research has focused on how the poor are different culturally from other populations, several chapters underscore that the culture of elites and policymakers is just as important in understanding the reproduction of poverty as the cultures of the poor themselves. This is particularly relevant regarding the implicit norms and values undergirding policymaking. For example, James Rosenbaum and colleagues compellingly show how the cultural views of elites, which privilege a four-year college degree with certain requirements as normative, can have severely negative consequences for the upward mobility of the poor. Furthermore, an excessive elite emphasis on test scores can lead to a neglect of emotional, psychosomatic, and other health problems that are as needful of attention in their own right, and may also be the very source of educational failure.

Fourth, the chapters in this volume emphasize that some policy interventions are likely to take a long time, even one or more generations, to have any impact, and hasty assessments will likely lead to misleading and unnecessarily pessimistic conclusions. A major case in point was the quasi-experimental Movement to Opportunity study by a large group of economists, which basically concluded that movement out of the ghetto to non-ghetto housing had almost no effect except on young women's mental health (Sanbonmatsu et al. 2011). Massey and Clampet-Lundquist (2008) have offered one important criticism of this work: its design was flawed since the areas to which the treated individuals moved were nearly all racially segregated. However, of equal importance is the deprivation pointed out above: that black youth in disadvantaged areas—and this includes the disadvantaged middle class—are nearly completely excluded from the acquisition of procedural cultural knowledge vital for success in nearly all domains of mainstream life. Furthermore, as Patterson reported in Chapter 2, many of the cognitive and behavioral problems that beset disadvantaged black youth begin very early in life and are later reinforced by toxicity in the environment, and such cognitive impairments are life-long, often getting worse as individuals age. Moreover, as suggested in the chapter by Fosse, even if youth are not geographically segregated, they may nonetheless be structurally disconnected from the institutions of work and school. Thus, to have assumed that movement from a severely deprived neighborhood to a somewhat better-off segregated environment would have had any significant impact in a relatively short timeframe, as the directors of the MTO study did, was highly questionable, ignoring, as Robert Sampson (2008) pointed out, a century of sociological research on neighborhood effects.

In light of the above, let us briefly consider some of the better known of these youth-targeted programs, several of which are considered best practices. There are a considerable number of them, offered at all levels of government, and in the private sector (Koball et al. 2011). Some are aimed at job training, mainly through existing educational institutions and workforce investment programs (Eyster et al. 2012), while others attempt to prevent high-risk behaviors or offer support for those in crisis such as runaways or youth aging out of foster care, addicted to drugs, or suffering psychological trauma. Other programs attempt to reduce aggression and antisocial behavior, such as the family-based Multisystemic Therapy, and the school based Too Good for Violence. Programs such as Family Matters target parents of children ages twelve to fourteen, and those such as Guiding Good Choices, and the ABC program we studied attempt to improve interpersonal and other "soft" skills. There are also numer-ous out-of-school-time programs and precollege outreach ones such as Upward Bound.

Among the largest and best known of the federal programs are the Job Corps, begun in 1964 under Johnson's War on Poverty, aimed at youth fourteen to twenty-four, which now has 124 training centers across the country, serving 60,000 at risk youth annually; the National Guard's Youth ChalleNGe program, sponsored by the Department of Defense, aimed at improving education and life skills; and YouthBuild, adminis-tered by the Department of Labor's Employment and Training Admin-istration, which teaches skills through employment in building and rehabbing homes for poor families in the participants' own communities. Of special note are also many community-focused programs funded both locally and by the federal government, such as the Youth Opportunity (YO) programs that build life skills and offer places for recreation, short-term employment, and community service, as well as academic remediation. Finally, there is the Building Strong Families Program (BSF) evaluated in Chapter 14 of this volume, which was initiated and funded to the tune of $300 million by the Bush administration.

In addition to these mainly government-funded programs, there are a large number administered by NGOs funded in part by government, but also by private foundations, small individual donors, and philanthropists. Among those that have received the greatest national attention are the Harlem Children's Zone, which takes a holistic approach to intervention, offering support to young parents and families, as well as special learning environments in its charter schools; Turnaround for Children, which works with schools to address the psychological well-being of poor children; and Nurse-Family Partnership, which employs specially trained nurses to provide prenatal and home infancy care, as well as advice on partner relationship, economic self-sufficiency, and spending habits through age twelve of the parents' firstborn.

How effective are these programs, and how do our studies help us understand why some fail and others succeed? Most, unfortunately, have not been rigorously evaluated, especially the NGOs, but the conclusions from those that have been are mixed, ranging from moderate successes to nearly complete failures, such as the Building Strong Families program (Koball et al. 2011; Dworsky 2011; Eyster et al. 2012; Clarkwest, Killewald, and Wood, this volume). A four-year randomized evaluation of the Job Corps found that it moderately increased literacy and the earning of GEDs and vocational certificates and reduced criminal behavior; there were also short-term gains in earnings, but these do not last over time. However, the program is not cost effective: per person gains ($4,000) do not outweigh the per person cost ($16,000) (Schochet, Burghardt, and McConnell 2008). More impressive outcomes have been achieved by the National Guard's Youth ChalleNGe. Graduates of the program attain higher educational levels and earn 20 percent more than a control group of nonparticipants (Millenky et al. 2011), and a recent RAND evaluation estimates "$2.66 in social benefits for every dollar expended, for a return on investment of 166 percent," these benefits accruing "mostly in the form of higher lifetime earnings attributable to higher levels of educational attainment induced by the program" (Perez-Arce, Loughran, and Karoly 2012). Interestingly, evaluations of YO programs, similar to the kind of interventions led by President Obama before he took up public office, show marked improvements among youth in years of schooling, employment, and job participation rates, and a significant decline in the proportion of disconnected youth in the targeted communities, compared with similar communities without the programs (DIR Inc. 2007). Oddly, while the effects of this program were generally positive for blacks, it did reduce the full-time employment rate for white youth and increased the unemployment rate of Hispanics (DIR INC 2007, 63–71), suggesting that what works in some domains for one ethnic group may not for another. Youth participants also perceived these programs in very positive terms, claiming that they provided "safe spaces, quality youth and adult relationships, enhanced training and education services, and opportunities to be productive" (DIR Inc. 2007, 97).

The evaluations of NGOs produce equally mixed results. This is true of one of the most celebrated programs, the Harlem Children's Zone (HCZ) and Promise Neighborhood system, which has become the model for a nationwide "cradle to career" government intervention instituted by the Obama administration in 2010, with over $160 million allocated so far (U.S. Department of Education 2013). The strategy of this program is to incorporate the entire community in the effort to improve the educational performance of African American disadvantaged children and youth, including a Baby College, aimed at enhancing the childrearing practices of young mothers. A widely cited evaluation by Dobbie and Fryer (2009) found extraordinary improvements in the educational performance of HCZ students, especially in math, but could find no support for the program's claim that the broader sociocultural intervention contributed to their educational improvement. A later evaluation by the Brookings Institute (Croft and Whitehurst 2010) was more critical, concluding that, although the students performed above average for the New York public schools, their test scores were substantially below those of the best-performing charter schools such as the KIPP (Knowledge is Power Program) schools and that the broader social intervention had no detectable effect on the educational outcome of the students (Croft and Whitehurst 2010). While the Brookings evaluation of HCZ is unassailable with respect to the program's exaggerated educational claims, its own evaluation is itself flawed in the narrow, educational vision it holds of the well-being and general condition of children and youth in the inner cities. If the studies of this volume have demonstrated anything, it is the fact that the condition of black children and youth are burdened by a tragic catalog of disorders originating in their mothers' wombs. To assess programs aimed at improving their well-being solely in terms of their performance on school test scores strikes us as an unusual example of policy-oriented tunnel vision.

Indeed, the Brookings study, in this same vein, goes on to question the effectiveness of one of the best NGOs working on behalf of the holistic well-being of poor black children and youth—the extremely well regarded Nurse-Family Partnership, mentioned earlier—inaccurately reporting the result of a very rigorous, and positive, evaluation of the program (Olds et al. 2010; Kitzman et al. 2010). This evaluation found that by the age of twelve of the firstborn child, mothers visited by the program's nurses had significantly less impairment due to alcohol and other drug use; had longer relationships with their partners; had a greater sense of mastery of their world; and, as an added boon, the program paid for itself when the substantially reduced reliance on food stamps, Medicaid and AFDC, and Temporary Assistance to Needy Families over the first twelve years of the first child's life were taken into account. Further, the children of mothers visited by the nurses used less cigarettes, alcohol, and marijuana and were less psychologically disturbed. In addition, children of mothers with low psychological resources and whose children were most at risk scored significantly higher in math and reading when compared to the control group. In light of the prenatal beginnings of the problems of disadvantaged youth, it seems reasonable to expect that intervention focused on this period would be the most effective, and the Nurse-Family Partnership program confirms as much. Recall also the finding of Patterson and Rivers (Chapter 13, this volume) that black male youth and young adults, including even the most outwardly hardened with prison records reported, constant feelings of psychological pain, a deep-seated anguish that no doubt originates in infancy and childhood. Hence, any program that substantially lessens the likelihood of twelve-year-old children "having internalizing disorders that [meet] the borderline or clinical threshold" must be considered extraordinarily successful, measured not in narrow test scores, but in pain tests.

It is useful to compare this program with another, Turnaround for Children,[8] which attempts to address the psychosocial problems of poor children in mainly K–8 schools through mental health professionals working with school teachers and officials to improve the "socio-behavioral functioning" of students (Cantor 2011; turnaroundusa.org; Ark 2013). *Turnaround for Children* is one example of a broader policy being adopted by several educational districts around the nation that seeks to implement a more supportive school climate for students, complementing the focus on reading, math, and science with the "social, emotional, ethical, and civic dimensions of student learning" (Cohen 2010). While we applaud the objectives of these programs, the case of Turnaround for Children is not encouraging. With implementations in several states, mainly New York where it began, and an intervention cost of a quarter of a million dollars per school, Turnaround for Children has been widely hyped, several times in the usually reliable *New York Times* (Phillips 2011; Nocera 2012), but we could find no independent evaluation presenting evidence that the program works. Indeed, the schools in which it intervened all did considerably worse than average in New York's recently revised testing system, even after taking into account the location and socioeconomic background of the schools' students (Phillips 2011).[9]

In February 2014, President Obama (2014b) announced the most ambitious program of his presidency aimed directly at improving the condition of African American male youth (along with Hispanic Americans and Native Americans): "My Brother's Keeper," the primary goal of which is a public-private "blueprint for action by government, business, non-profit, philanthropic, faith and community partners," to "develop sustained and direct mentoring relationships that will play vital roles in the lives of young people" (White House, 2014a). In conjunction with mentoring, the program aims to support locally initiated, comprehensive efforts that address the "educational, physical, social and emotional needs of young people—and that span multiple life stages from cradle-to-college" (White House, 2014a). Foundations have already committed more than $200 million over the next five years. Many of the program's objectives address issues raised in several of the chapters of this volume: eliminating suspensions and expulsions in early learning settings; closing the word gap between low income African American and middle class children; implement early health and developmental screening, which hopefully, will give early notice of the effects of environmental toxicity and emotional trauma; promote alternative disciplining methods in schools and focus on those schools and districts responsible for the majority of African American dropouts; promote post-secondary education;[10]

increase labor force participation and employment through summer employ-ment and pre-apprenticeships and enhance employment opportunities through greater infrastructure investment, job training, and raising of the minimum wage; and reduce violence and incarceration through the scaling-up of successful anti-violence and gang prevention programs, greater partnership between neighborhoods and law enforcement offi-cials, greater use of alternatives to incarceration, and the reduction of ethnic bias in the juvenile and criminal justice systems as well as removal of the obstacles to reentry into the workforce for ex-prisoners (White House, 2014b). This is an enormously important policy initiative, and if only half of its objectives are achieved it is likely to have significant impact on the lives of young African Americans. According to Jennifer Epstein, reporting in politico.com on 2/27/2014, it has been reported that the President is strongly committed to its successful execution and, indeed, that he plans to make its implementation his main activity after his presidency.

All of these programs amount to attempts, in one way or another, at cultural change. As pointed out by Tommie Shelby, in the most prosaic form, cultural change is simply an alteration of people's values, norms, and beliefs about the world, a practice now so widespread in the American system of education that it is rarely admitted as a massive project of cul-tural change. President Obama clearly shares this view in his repeated "tough love" injunctions to black leaders, a position that has not always endeared him to them. In general terms, cultural changes come about in two ways. First, change can be brought about through structural, tech-nical, and environmental changes, as well as through new laws that pro-vide incentives for people to change or oblige them to adapt their beliefs and cultural expectations. Thus, increased labor market participation and growing income led to marked changes in women's attitudes toward divorce and the institution of marriage, as well as out-of-wedlock birth; and, as noted earlier, the Civil Rights Act of 1964 as well as the Supreme Court desegregation of schools, combined with the increased integration of blacks in the workplace, led to the radical cultural shifts on race men-tioned earlier.

Secondly, change may be promoted through direct interventions, using various techniques of persuasion, which is what the programs discussed above attempt to do. Persuading people to change is easier if the ideas or practices being introduced can be seen to be consistent with previ-ously held beliefs, or at least not inconsistent with them—a psychological principle long established in social judgment theory (Sherif and Sherif 1976). Trying to persuade young, cohabiting, unemployed African Americans to marry is inconsistent with both male and female shared understanding that a husband should be a provider; and with male preference for extramarital relations as well as females' rejection of, and pessimism about, marital infidelity. Similarly, our study of ABC's effort to change black youths' work attitudes and habits in the Boston area found that while they were prepared to learn nearly all of the declarative knowledge and most of the norms and values of the formal workplace, there was real difficulty in presenting a smiling, conciliatory face (an important requirement in many working-class jobs, such as sales), since this conflicted with the ingrained view that a "mean mug" was essential for survival in the inner city. Work norms were also inconsistent with the high valuation of being shown personal respect, closely related to which was the reluctance to accept authority figures, especially on the part of males who grew up in fatherless households and with single mothers unable, or too tired, to exercise discipline after mid-adolescence. Additionally, while some may consider it a cliché, a fundamental prerequisite for successfully persuading people to change are change agents who are either role models or are persons with skills that are both admired and considered achievable.

The impressive effects of the Nurse-Family Partnership program is understandable in these terms. Young mothers are obviously motivated to change in ways that improve their health and enhance the life chances of their children and themselves. The choice of nurses as change agents and models is clearly a critical element in the success of the program. Nursing is a very prestigious occupation, especially among young African American women, a large proportion of whom work in the health industry as hospital and nurse's aides and aspire to become fully qualified nurses themselves. What nurses do and seek to communicate are also easily understandable and meaningful; additional nonhealth messages about economic self-sufficiency and relationship with partners are therefore more easily embedded and communicable, and more receptive to clients. Communication also takes place in the familiar environment of the client's home. Partly for similar reasons, the success of the National Guard's Youth ChalleNGe program is also understandable: as noted in Chapter 2, the military is greatly admired by African American children and youth who spend a considerable amount of time playing military-themed video games, watching war movies, and, more importantly, observing many cases of the lives of troubled friends and older youth turned around by their stint in the army, not to mention successful adult role models, both local and national, such as former Chairman of the Joint Chiefs of Staff, General Colin Powell, and Vice Chief of Staff of the Air Force, General Larry Spencer. The situation is quite different in the school environment where Turnaround for Children attempts to treat and change psychologically troubled and traumatized children, usually with agents who are not familiar, attempting to treat problems that may not be recognized or that may be considered signs of weakness, especially among boys with emerging street versions of masculinity. Smaller schools with better-qualified and better-paid teachers and counselors, supplemented by extended and properly staffed after-school programs and learning communities, have been proven to work much better (for evaluations of which, see Bloom and Unterman 2012; Black et al. 2009; Kemple 2008).

Conclusion

In the final analysis, if the sociocultural problems that beset the lives of disadvantaged black American youth are to change, they will only come about through a combination of external and internal changes. By external changes we refer to interventions such as movement from the toxic environment of the inner cities (observable positive effects of which will require at least a generation, possibly longer) and/or their detoxification and reconstruction; the ending of unjust and counterproductive mass incarceration and the demonstrably failed War on Drugs; the provision of working-class jobs paying a livable wage; the continued expansion of good charter schools along the lines of the KIPP academies, as well as smaller public schools with after-school programs that will keep kids out of trouble until their overworked single parents return home; and the greatly expanded provision of prenatal, postnatal, and preschool care. Complementing such changes should be expanded support for direct-intervention and remedial programs that have been proven to work such as Job Corps (its limitations notwithstanding), Youth ChalleNGe, YouthBuild, and the Youth Opportunity community programs. We applaud the Obama administration's scaling up of the Promise Neighborhood program and the more recent and far-reaching Brother's Keeper policy initiative, especially the requirement of rigorous evaluations of each implementation, which hopefully will avoid the hype and unsustainable cost of the Harlem Children's Zone program.

However, we should make it absolutely clear that, even with the successful implementation of all the above-mentioned programs, there will be no substantial change among the millions of disadvantaged youth and their families in the inner cities until black Americans assume full responsibility for the internal social and cultural changes that are essential for success in the broader mainstream capitalist society. We pointed out earlier that black youth are likely to agree with President Obama's recent injunction to reject the view that circumstances beyond their control define them and their future. However, their likely reaction to the second of his injunctions, is a different matter: that it was up to "all the young men who are out there to seize the responsibility for their own lives." One of the many complexities in the values of black American youth is that their mainstream acceptance of responsibility for their own condition is not matched by that other mainstream value: a willingness to do what it takes to change the socioeconomic aspects of their lives within the limits allowed by their circumstances, limits that, while severe (as we have certainly delineated in this volume) are nonetheless not totalizing, denying all agency.

We are not suggesting total personal transformation here, for as our studies have made clear, black Americans are in many respects among the most American of Americans, a major force in the nation's popular cultural and political life. We have seen that black youth are capable of quite radical change in the aesthetic domain and other areas of popular culture. Learning to read at grade level should be no more demanding cognitively, emotionally, and physically, than learning to play a skillful game of basketball. We have seen, too, that black youth share several of the most important mainstream values that have propelled their country to greatness. These values, however, have got to be actualized through the pursuit of increased cultural literacy in the nonpopular domains of the mainstream culture, a rejection of the group's (all-too-American) anti-intellectualism, along with much deeper commitment to a love of learning for its own sake that will match their educational aspirations and solve the chronic aspiration-achievement paradox among them. Required, too, are a greater genuine respect for women, in music and practice, and the valuing of stable gender relations.

Above all, African Americans must find a way of providing a viable household environment with authoritative caregivers and positive role models for their children. The present, terribly broken arrangement in which over 70 percent of all African American children (Ventura 2009) and over 80 percent of poor ones are being born to households bereft of a second adult, headed by overstressed, overworked, and underpaid single mothers who lose nearly all control of their male children by mid-adolescence when they are most in need of guidance and support, is not just unsustainable; it is an ethnic and national tragedy. It is also a wholly unnatural situation in comparative sociological and American terms; for while the ethnographic data indicate a wide range of household arrangements throughout the world for bringing up children, one constant underlying this variation, especially in advanced societies, is that some provision is made for the reliable emotional and material support and consistent socialization of children, usually by two adults, of whatever gender and in whatsoever kind of relationship they choose (Leeder 2004, 22–47). This is still the case for the great majority of Americans, although the issue is often clouded by citation of the misleading and largely irrelevant statistic that the majority of American households are no longer of the conjugal type.[11] The truth is that over 70 percent of Euro-American children are born to married women, and 68 percent of the remainder are born to cohabiting couples (straight or gay), most of whom eventually get married. In other words, the overwhelming majority of white (and Asian) children, and almost all middle- and upper-class ones, are born and raised in supportive households with two caregivers, whatever the marital patterns of their parents. The problem, really, is not one so much of out-of-wedlock birth as of out-of-care childrearing; two-thirds of children are born out of wedlock in Iceland and over half in Sweden and Norway, but there is hardly a problem for children, who grow up in secure two-adult households strongly supported by their welfare states (Ventura 2009).

We do not propose to tell African Americans what kind of household arrangements or union patterns they should choose for the safe and nourishing environment of their children—that is a decision best left to the wisdom of the African American crowd. What we do say is that a better arrangement must be found if the mass of African Americans, especially their youth, are ever to participate fully in the complex, post-industrial society in which they live, and that this might require a social movement akin to the civil rights revolution, though one now directed at internal social and cultural transformation, facilitated, to be sure, by strong and sympathetic government and private sector support. If it could be done with such overwhelming success for the external, public sphere, it can certainly be done for the internal, private sociocultural and personal sphere. For a group that has contributed so much to the industry, civic life and culture of their great nation, African Americans and their youth deserve much better, from their government and economy and from themselves.

Notes

Introduction

1. Wacquant was later to emerge as coauthor and leading interpreter of Pierre Bourdieu, the world's most renowned student of culture and, in his own right, one of the most original theorists and investigators of the interaction of cultural and structural forces in the rise of hyperghettoization and mass incarceration in America.
2. For a critical assessment of contemporary cultural sociology, see Orlando Patterson, "Making Sense of Culture," *Annual Review of Sociology*, Vol. 40 (2014):1–30.

1. The Nature and Dynamics of Cultural Processes

1. For a more detailed elaboration and analysis, see my paper, "Making Sense of Culture," in *Annual Review of Sociology*, Vol. 40 (2014):1–30.

2. The Social and Cultural Matrix of Black Youth

1. A recent study of middle-class delinquency by Hassett-Walker (2010) finds more delinquency (measured by number of arrests in 1996) among middle-class than poor black youths: 8.2 percent versus 7.9 percent. However, her definition of middle class, based solely on a mean parental income of $22,259 ($32,159 in 2012 dollars) is badly flawed. At best, she is really comparing working-class with working-poor and poverty-level black Americans. Her dependent variable also underestimates both the levels of delinquency and the differences between the SES classes.
2. This is a sociology honors thesis from post–2000, done partly under my supervision and for which I was the first reader. The author has declined to have the thesis, or parts thereof, published, my repeated entreaties notwithstanding. I am respecting the author's privacy by not listing his/her name. Apart from its superb academic quality, the thesis is unusual in the

559

extraordinary degree of access the author had to the students and teachers studied. The author was, in fact, only three years removed from being a student him-/herself at the same high school when the study was conducted. I know of no other sociological study of black youth in which the author was this close in age, ethnicity, class, and cultural familiarity to the subjects studied.

3. I sympathize with Prudence Carter's view that knowledge of the African American vernacular culture should be considered another form of cultural capital that educators ought to take account of. I am pessimistic about this happening in view of the experiences of Jamaica and Haiti, both black-ruled societies with educational systems completely under the control of bourgeois blacks, but which have steadfastly resisted attempts to incorporate the islands' highly developed and thoroughly studied creoles (see Carter 2005, 137–74).

4. The sense of gratitude to God is also found among men, even among otherwise unbelieving, disconnected youth (Young 2004, 80). What is distinctive among black working-class women is the functioning of this value as part of a triadic spiritual configuration.

5. Originating with Donohue and Levitt (2001), the paper argues that crime began to fall eighteen years after abortion legalization due to the reduction of the number of unwanted children, who are those most likely to commit crimes. Legalization accounts for up to 50 percent of the later drop in crime. For a summary of critiques and counterarguments, see the Wikipedia article "The Impact of Legalized Abortion on Crime." Reyes's paper, the latest in the controversy, is one of the most thorough and largely supports the original thesis, in addition to taking account of the role of lead.

6. Whether this is an inherent feature of post-industrial economies, or a peculiarity of America's, is open to question. Some have argued that there is no good reason why low-skilled jobs should pay nonlivable wages. See Steven C. Pitts, *Job Quality and Black Workers* (Berkeley, CA: Center for Labor Research Education, 2008), especially Chapters 4–5.

3. The Values and Beliefs of Disconnected Black Youth

1. Youth who are married to a connected spouse and are parenting are also sometimes excluded from the definition used by researchers and policymakers, presumably because they are working in the home and can rely on the income of their spouses. In the data here, I cannot make this distinction without sacrificing comparability of estimates across data sources.

2. Note that the definition used by other researchers, principally demographers and economists, is narrower than that used here because they tend to use questions that capture youth who are unemployed and not in school for a longer period of time than at a particular cross section.

3. Besharov and Gardiner (1998) further define disconnectedness by those who are not married. I exclude this variable from measuring disconnection since many youth cohabit or maintain stable relationships in absence of a formal marital contract.

4. Note that the level of structural disconnection among youth had been increasing before the 2008 financial crisis. For example, Wight et al. (2010) calculate that the level of disconnected youth in the American population increased from 10 percent in 2010 to 14.8 percent by 2010 based on the Current Population Survey.

5. However, as expected, disconnected black youth are less likely to say that they loaned or gave money to family or friends to help with expenses (64.9 percent versus 57.2 percent).

6. Specifically, the summary overview is the average for each domain after adjusting for year of the survey and sample size. These were obtained fitting a multilevel model in which the first level consists of the questions, and the second level consists of the survey with a second-level predictor for survey year and sample size.

7. The findings in this section are based on predicted probabilities from the stereotype logistic models, described in the methods section. Note that predicted probabilities may be interpreted as a " percent chance," such that, for example, a predicted probability of 0.45 can be equivalently interpreted as a 45 percent chance of the outcome. For all results, the predicted probabilities are expressed in reference to the topmost category of the outcome variable mentioned.

8. Some surveys show an even starker difference. For example, data from 2006 shows that only 9.6 percent of disconnected black youth are very satisfied with their life as a whole, compared to 44.6 percent of connected black youth.

9. These questions are from a 2011 survey; nearly identical questions from 2006 show a similar set of findings.

10. However, we find no evidence that structurally disconnected black youth are less likely to date someone of a different race. The data show that 67.3 percent of disconnected black youth have dated someone of a different race, in contrast to 65.7 percent of connected black youth. We also find only slight evidence of a gender effect, with young black men more likely than black women to report that they've dated someone of a different race (71.3 percent versus 62.8 percent).

11. These findings are similar across two sets of surveys, one from 2006 and another from 2011. The findings here are from the 2011 survey. One exception to the pattern of perceived mistreatment is that *connected* black youth are more likely to report that they receive poorer treatment at restaurants or stores (63 percent versus 53 percent). One possible explanation is that

connected black youth have more diverse social networks and are thus more likely to encounter interactions with others of higher social classes and different races.

12. These findings are somewhat divergent from a recent report on disconnected youth, which has argued that disconnected youth are relatively optimistic (Bridgeland and Milano 2012). For example, the authors report that nearly three in four are very confident or hopeful that they will be able to achieve their goals in life, including continuing their education and getting a good job (ibid., 8). The findings here suggest that these estimates mask differences within age, gender, and racial groups; moreover, the authors of this report do not compare the responses of those who are structurally connected from those who are disconnected.

13. This is consistent with previous research on disconnected youth, which has shown that many view their lack of education and work experience as a major challenge to becoming structurally connected (Bridgeland and Milano 2012).

14. Since some of these outcomes measure the values and beliefs of black men and women, I re-ran the analyses with an additional term, allowing for a four-way interaction that now includes whether or not the respondent is female. In a large number of cases, the predicted probabilities from the interaction were statistically significant. However, I found statistically significant results showing that black women do not view life as getting worse for black women, they are much less likely to blame themselves for the declining black marriage rate, and they are decidedly more optimistic than black men about their overall life conditions.

15. I also find that black youth, regardless of gender or disconnection status, overwhelmingly say that being close to their family is very important (92.3 percent compared to 89.7 percent).

16. Note that these estimates are derived from regression models that adjust for marital status and region of birth, among other variables.

17. There is a similar but steeper intergenerational pattern among white Americans, with the percentages at 53.7 percent, 69.1 percent, and 73.5 percent, respectively.

18. However, when asked about rich people in particular (rather than "getting ahead" more generally), a larger percentage of both disconnected and connected black youth say that knowing the right people and being born to inheritance are more important reasons (44.1 percent versus 40.9 percent).

19. In fact, out of the 220 variables analyzed, 182 were statistically significant at the $\propto = 0.10$ level between disconnected black youth and connected black youth.

20. For example, as is well documented, jazz and blues arose from the crucible of slavery, immigration, and poverty in Congo Square in New Orleans.

21. Among the clearest structural disruption is geography, which has led to cultural differences in how agriculture is produced to the spread of religious thought (e.g., Christianity spreading through Europe but not as easily due to the expanse of Asia, including the Ural Mountains, the deserts of the Middle East, and the Atlantic Ocean).

22. For instance, rather than asking a respondent, "Have you experienced discrimination?" I would include a question such as "How severe is discrimination in today's society?" The distinction is that I am attempting to measure cultural outcomes rather than self-reported behaviors. I, however, make an exception when examining the sociocultural networks of the respondents, since the questions tap into the respondents' beliefs about their networks and not their own actions as such.

23. Additional variables include views on whether or not the economic system is "stacked against" black men, concerns about racial discrimination and treatment by the police, evaluations on the perceived closeness to other racial groups, and views on whether or not black and white Americans have the same goals and values. Variables related to views on why respondents think black women are not marrying black men (and vice versa), perceived causes of the higher level of educational attainment of black women compared to black men, and whether or not the quality of life of black women has been improving. Similarly, variables related to views of black men include the perceived obstacles men face in the workforce, the degree of the problems facing black men (e.g., racial discrimination, joblessness, exposure to violent crimes), and the possible role of black men in the declining black marriage rate. Due to the limited space in this chapter, however, these analyses are not included in the findings section.

24. I exclude here questions on religion and politics due to space constraints. Regarding questions on religion, these include measures of values and beliefs about belief in a god, the importance of having a religious life overall, whether or not one's religious culture is "worth keeping," and the importance of shared moral values to one's life.

25. This model is similar to the multinomial logistic and ordered (i.e., ordinal) logistic model in that it is appropriate for categorical outcomes. Note that in a multinomial logistic model, the categories are unranked, while the ordered logistic regression model follows a ranking.

26. An alternative approach would be to use a continuous variable for age, and then calculate the predicted probabilities for all analyses set at values of age ranging from eighteen to twenty-four inclusively. The results do not substantially change with this approach. Moreover, with this approach there is the disadvantage of some ambiguity about what age to set the predicted probabilities as well as the appropriate functional form for the age variable in the model.

4. Hip-Hop's Irrepressible Refashionability

1. Pioneered by French composers such as Pierre Schaeffer in the 1940s and 1950s, *musique concrète* is an approach that employs sound recordings as the central building blocks for composition, rather than, say, scores to be realized by performers. Originally involving the work-intensive splicing of tape recordings of trains and other "nonmusical" sounds gathered in the field, *musique concrète* as a conceptual practice became far more commonplace as an approach in the era of digital samplers, especially in the wake of sample-based hip-hop innovators such as Marley Marl, Dr. Dre, the Bomb Squad, and Prince Paul.

2. See, for example, Eshun 1998 and Reynolds 1998.

3. For a glimpse at Tupac's global resonance, especially in Africa, see, for example, Sommers 2003 and Jacobs 2011.

4. FruityLoops, now known as FL Studio, is but one example—if perhaps the most commonplace—of today's popular music production software programs. In addition to allowing countless kids (or adults) to compose music in their homes, it has also been used to create genuine chart-topping hits, the most famous of which is no doubt Soulja Boy Tellem's "Crank That" (2007).

5. For additional statistics giving a sense of YouTube's scale, see, for example, YouTube Team 2011 and Schonfeld 2008.

6. See Kevin Driscoll's (2009) master's thesis for a detailed genealogy of the mixtape, especially with regard to the digital turn, in the context of a broader discussion on technical innovations among black youth in hip-hop.

7. The Pew Research Center has published a number of studies of technology use by black youth (as well as other demographic groups). See Smith 2010 for a summary of recent findings.

5. Continuity and Change in Neighborhood Culture

1. These leading arguments have been challenged and sometimes pitted against each other. But Quillian's (1999, 2012) important analyses show that they are not necessarily in conflict and can be synthesized: racial segregation and middle-class outmigration are interdependent mechanisms that are simultaneously in operation. "Neighborhood effects" research in general has also been challenged, especially by economists and largely on technical grounds (e.g., see Dietz 2002; Kling et al. 2007). I take up a discussion of neighborhood effects and their critics in more detail elsewhere (e.g., see Sampson, 2008; 2012, Chapters 2, 3, and 15).

2. See also the work of Cialdini and colleagues (1990), especially the distinction between injunctive and descriptive or heuristic norms. Although I cannot distinguish empirically between these two types, I expect that public other-regarding behaviors are more linked to descriptive norms that are visual in nature and observable (e.g., people picking up discarded material; interactions and personal interventions; posted signs of collective meetings).

3. There are a number of assessments elsewhere (Harding 2010; Lamont 2000; Patterson 2004, 2009; Small et al. 2010). See also Wilson (2009) on the integration of structural and cultural forces within the context of explaining inner-city life, and Small's (2004) integration of Goffman's (1974) frame analysis with neighborhood narratives on organizational participation. My focus here is aimed at neighborhood-level processes and the explanation of continuity.

4. This section is taken with permission from Sampson (2012, Chapter 9).

5. The merger of empirical and normative principles is explored in what Thacher (2006) calls the "normative case study." Using Jane Jacobs's (1961) classic work as the main example, Thacher argues that bringing philosophical and normative considerations of desired behavior into the picture improves our empirical explanation of neighborhood-level processes. For example, Thacher (2006, 1641) argues that the descriptions of city life by Jacobs "helped to clarify the things that are intrinsically good or bad for humans—features of city neighborhoods that are attractive not just because of the consequences they have for values we already understand clearly (as in the case of street eyes) but also because they reflect values we previously perceived only dimly if at all (as in the case of the vitality of cities and opportunities for contact they offer)" (1641). See Sampson (2012, Chapter 9) for further reflection on what philosophical and normative considerations offer for our understanding of the "good community."

6. To Rawls's list we can add safety and security. There is a long literature that comes to the same conclusion: across groups there is a great deal of consensus on rankings of seriousness of crimes and the desire for security (Kornhauser 1978). Richard Sennett (2012) has written more recently on the desired role and positive consequences of cooperation in everyday life.

7. A common experimental game gives players A and B a set amount of money. A can offer any amount to B, and, if accepted, both get to keep the money. If B rejects the offer, no one gets a penny. Rational choice theory predicts that because any amount of money is a gain for both, no offer should be rejected, and A should make a low initial offer. But B will reject A's offer if it is perceived as unfair, and the opening offers of A are typically much higher than selfish models predict. There is also comparative evidence that a city's rate of helping strangers is a cross-culturally meaningful characteristic of a place (Levine et al. 2001).

8. The main statement on procedural justice is Tyler (1990). The link between Rawls's and Tyler's legitimacy principles deserves further scrutiny. For innovative work on bringing "social identity" into mainstream economic theory, see Akerlof and Kranton (2010).

9. As distinct from personal ties that aid survival in poor communities. Dense webs of family and kinship ties in disadvantaged environments have long been argued (Stack 1974).

10. Donations to United Way have been proposed (Chamlin and Cochran 1997), but there are sharp disagreements in society over the role of charity versus the State, and United Way in particular has suffered withering criticism. The financial ability to give is also confounded.

11. I only sketch the basic design and variable construction here for both the lost letter and cardiopulmonary resuscitation studies. For details see Sampson (2012, 217–220).

12. This chapter is not the place for detail on research design, variable construction, and analytic techniques. For details see Sampson (2012, 77–92). My goal is to sketch the outlines of a theory of neighborhood continuity and its consistency with basic empirical tests.

13. The original label proposed by Sampson and Bartusch (1998) for this scale was simply "legal cynicism." Because the questions ask about broad conceptions of ethical behavior (e.g., "no right and wrong ways"; "okay to do anything you want") and not just about "the law," however, "moral cynicism" is perhaps the more accurate description. For a stricter focus on legal cynicism that includes indicators of police satisfaction as well, see Kirk and Papachristos (2011).

14. These data are based on records originally collected by the National Center for Charitable Statistics (Sampson 2012, 196).

15. Concentrated disadvantage includes percent poverty, public assistance, female-headed families, unemployment, and racial isolation in the form of percent black. African Americans are disproportionately exposed to all the constituent indicators of resource disadvantage (Sampson 2012, Chapter 5). Residential stability is measured by a standardized scale combining the average length of home residence and the rate of home-ownership. Diversity is measured by a Herfindahl index that taps race, ethnicity, language, and immigrant status, where a higher score reflects more heterogeneity. Population density is persons per square mile.

16. Although it might be the case that poor areas have fewer mailboxes, letters were randomly distributed throughout the neighborhoods such that the majority of drops were not in close proximity to a mailbox—typically one had to pick up the letter and mail it somewhere else. I would further argue that the controls for land use and housing type adjust for "mailbox proximity" across community areas. Size and density, stand-ins for foot traffic, were also adjusted.

17. At the community-area level, the t-ratio reflecting the association of non-profit density with letter-return rates was 2.97 (p < .01), after adjusting for other community factors.

18. When I controlled for community-level perceived disorder, the association of racialized disadvantage with high cynicism/low altruism was cut roughly in half. Observed disorder was not significant. This result suggests that perceived rather than actual disorder is a mechanism of cultural continuity (see also Sampson 2012, Chapter 6).

19. The journalist Ta-Nehisi Coates has recently provided a provocative and well-documented historical account of the legacies of slavery and racial dominance that continue to divide American cities. A key institutional mechanism he highlights is housing policy, such as the red-lining of black neighborhoods in the twentieth century by the federal government and the deliberate targeting of urban black neighborhoods by banks for sub-prime loans in the early twenty-first century, further intensifying the link between racial segregation and concentrated poverty (Coates 2014).

6. "I Do Me"

1. The phrase "caught up in the streets," as used by the young men in our sample, could mean selling drugs or being in a gang, but more commonly it meant being regularly involved with neighborhood "drama" such as street violence, often as a member of a neighborhood clique or gang. At times, these fights involved weapons.

2. It should also be noted that the characteristics of the adults who raised them were very disadvantaged as well. Almost all were single parents for whom employment rates were very low, welfare histories ubiquitous, drug addiction and incarceration high, and stress-related physical problems and mental health challenges common.

3. We also include one respondent whom we interviewed as part of the preliminary field testing of our interview guide.

4. Respondents and their friends and family are referred to by pseudonyms. The names of a particular respondent's housing project, his neighborhood, and schools attended have been changed throughout the paper.

5. This is similar to Anderson's "going for bad" (1999, 100).

6. The importance of family as a designation that signifies loyalty can also be seen through the way that some youth used terms like *brother* or *cousin* to refer to select friends who were not actually blood related but who were loyal and whom they felt could be trusted.

7. A number of youth in our sample had older siblings who were involved in criminal activity. While these siblings occasionally provided social connections

to drug dealers or advice for how to get away with criminal activity in the neighborhood, it was also common for them to caution the younger children in the family not to take the same route.

8. Carter (2007) introduces the notion of cultural straddling among black students in racially mixed schools.

9. Hacks are a common form of transportation throughout Baltimore.

10. Franklintown is a black working-class neighborhood that is in decline.

11. The tuition of this community college is lower than the national average, but we could not verify whether or not it is the least expensive in the United States.

12. Source: American Community Survey 2005–2009 five-year estimates.

7. More Than Just Black

1. I am grateful to Andrew Deener, Ethan Fosse, Philip Kasinitz, Jennifer Lee, Orlando Patterson, Wendy Roth, and Rob Smith for their comments on previous drafts of this paper. I am also grateful to Philip Kasinitz, John Mollenkopf and Mary Waters for providing me with access to the geo-coded IMSGNY data.

2. See also Kasinitz et al. (2008).

3. For further and technical details of the ISGMNY study, see the Methodological Appendix in Kasinitz et al. (2008).

4. I use "native blacks" to denote respondents who were born in the United States to native-born African American parents, "native whites" to denote respondents who were born in the United States to native-born European American parents, and "West Indians" to denote respondents who were born in the United States to parents who were born in the West Indies.

5. See Model (2008) for a recent summary of this literature.

6. The NEET rate accounts for those who are "not engaged in education, employment, training, or caregiving."

7. Since these two analyses are based on "male respondents only," the sample size is rather small.

8. For more details, please see Tran (2011).

9. Figures reported are predicted probabilities for the three ethnic groups. These probabilities were calculated from logistic regression models with "native white" as the reference category, holding all other covariates at their mean values. "College graduate" indicates having a bachelor's degree by age 25 whereas "Professional" indicates being in a professional occupation by age 25. These logistic models adjust for respondent's age, gender, parental education, number of adult earners in household while growing up, family structure, number of children in household while growing up, and number of moves between the ages of 6 and 18. The models for "College graduate" and "Professional" only include respondents above the age of 25. The models for

"Arrested" and "Incarcerated" only include male respondents. The model for "Teen parent" only includes female respondents. Full logistic regression results available upon request from the author.

10. Neighborhood concentrated disadvantage is an index measure based on the four items at the tract level: percent poverty, percent unemployed, percent on public assistance, and percent female-headed households with children.

11. Neighborhood concentrated affluence is an index measure based on three items at the tract level: percent with a bachelor's degree or more, percent in managerial and professional occupation, and percent household with income greater than $70,000.

12. For the purpose of this analysis, neighborhoods were defined using census tracts at three time points: where the respondent was born (i.e. birth neighborhood), lived the longest between the ages of 6 and 18 (i.e. childhood neighborhood), and lived at the time of the survey (i.e. adult neighborhood). The figures are unadjusted mean values for each ethno-racial group.

13. The bars are the coefficients for the West Indian dummies in the multivariate analyses where the reference group is "native black". Analyses limited to respondents who are not currently living with parents. "Unadjusted" models controlled for ethnic origin, age and gender. "Adjusted" models included the full set of controls: ethnic origin, age, gender, parental education, parental employment status, family structure, number of siblings respondent grew up with, respondent's education and income, times moved between the ages of 6 and 18, years in current neighborhood, public housing project living while growing up, neighborhood disorder and cohesion index.

14. West Indians attended high schools that are further away from their neighborhoods and often of better quality compared to native blacks. For further details, please see Tran (2011, ch. 7).

8. The Role of Religious and Social Organizations in the Lives of Disadvantaged Youth

1. This research was funded by the Annie E. Casey Foundation. We thank them for their support but acknowledge that the findings and conclusions presented in this paper are those of the authors alone and do not necessarily reflect the opinions of the Foundation. Luttmer also gratefully acknowledges funding from the National Institute on Aging through Grant Number T32-AG00186 to the National Bureau of Economic Research. We thank Jon Gruber, Dan Hungerman, Chris Ellison, and conference participants for useful suggestions and helpful discussions. All errors are our own.

2. While we do not consider being nonwhite to be a disadvantage per se, it may be associated with disadvantages (such as experiencing racism or discrimination) that we are unable to capture in our other measures.

3. None of the 168 estimates of buffering effects is even marginally significantly negative, so we cannot reject the hypothesis of a positive buffering effect for any disadvantage-outcome combination at the 10 percent level.

4. If religious parents have a lower threshold for saying that the child is in trouble (e.g., skipping church qualifies as trouble), then "troubled" children of religious parents have on average less severe trouble than "troubled" children of nonreligious parents. As a result, we would expect troubled children of religious parents to have better outcomes later in life even if religion does not directly help youth overcome the negative consequences of being in trouble.

5. We use the religious attendance of the parent who was selected as the "main respondent" by the NSFH.

6. Body mass index (BMI) is defined as weight in kilograms divided by height in meters squared. We followed the National Heart, Lung and Blood Institute (part of the National Institutes of Health) in defining a healthy body weight as $18.5 \leq BMI < 25.0$.

7. An instrumental variable for religion has been suggested by Gruber (2005), namely the percent of individuals in the same locality who, based on their ethnic background, are predicted to share the respondent's religious denomination. For our relatively small sample, however, this instrument yielded estimates that were so imprecise that they did not provide evidence either way on whether our main results can be interpreted causally.

8. The magnitude of the buffering effects is generally reasonable (between zero and one) for the significant buffering effects. However, estimates of buffering effects sometimes become unreasonably large when the direct effect of disadvantage on the outcome measure is small because this direct effect enters in the denominator of the formula for buffering effects. However, the resulting unreasonably large buffering effects are never statistically significant.

9. Under the null hypothesis of no effect, the observed t-statistics are a draw from a distribution with zero mean and unknown covariance structure. By bootstrapping our sample 10,000 times and recalculating the t-statistics of our 168 disadvantage-outcome combinations, we obtain the correlation matrix of our t-statistics. We then draw 100,000 vectors of 168 t-statistics from a distribution with mean zero and this correlation matrix. This creates a probability distribution for each percentile of the distribution of t-statistics, which we summarize by the mean and 0.5 and 99.5 percentiles.

9. Keeping Up the Front

1. Some statistical elaboration is needed to document this claim. According to the Chicago Police Department, there are seventy-three active gangs and

between 68,000 and 150,000 gang members in the Chicago metropolitan area. In the three-year period between 2009 and 2011, there were 786 "gang-related" murders. In 2011 (to November 30), the figure was 264. If we use the 68,000 gang-member baseline, this means that *at most* 1 in 90 gang members was murdered over the three-year period ending in 2011, and *at most* 1 in 260 gang members was murdered in the first eleven months of 2011. The rates would of course be much lower if we used the 150,000 gang-member baseline and if we were able to precisely account for the fact that many "gang-related" victims are not gang members. Either way, these statistics support the point that even among gangs, specifically in the context of the tens of thousands of interactions in which they are involved, murder is quite unusual. See the Chicago Crime Commission's (2012) *The Gang Book* pp. 13, 307–10.

2. We wish to thank the following for their thoughtful comments on this chapter in its various incarnations: Randall Collins, Elijah Anderson, Jack Katz, Orlando Patterson, Ethan Fosse, Chris Muller, Saurabh Bhargava, Joseph Podwol, Elizabeth Graff, Jean K. Carney, and Constantin Fasolt. We extend our deepest gratitude to the young men in Woodlawn, our twenty respondents who call themselves "Hustlas," whose unflagging trust, patience, and support made this project possible from conception to completion.

3. Readers familiar with the microinteractionist tradition in sociology will immediately note the influence of Erving Goffman's seminal (1974) *Frame Analysis* on the present typology of performative categories. "Keying," "Fabrication," and "Reframing," in particular, are monikers we borrow directly from Goffman. See Erving Goffman (1974) *Frame Analysis: An Essay on the Organization of Experience.* Boston, MA: Northeastern University Press. See pp. 40–82 for "Keys and Keyings"; pp. 83–122 for "Designs and Fabrications"; and pp. 21–39, 201–46, and 496–559 for a discussion of frames. See also Goffman 1959, 1961, 1963, 1967, 1969.

4. As an interaction ritual, street shit-talking bears some resemblance to other historically black improvisational art, such as jazz music and the more recent phenomenon of hip-hop freestyle battles—the latter analyzed in Jooyoung Lee's incisive 2009 paper "Battlin' on the Corner: Techniques for Sustaining Play." Like jazz and freestyle hip-hop, much of the artistry to shit-talking involves the "smoothness" of the interaction rhythm and on the appearance of effortless improvisation that conceals the sweat and stress involved in the process. Shit-talking's connection to hip-hop is particularly striking in another, more structural sense inasmuch as both seem to be linguistic adaptations to racism and oppression. Viz, Orlando Patterson's (1994) point that rap music developed as a "cultural response to historic oppression and racism, a system for communication among black communities throughout the United States." Also note that shit-talking is very similar to what others have

called "Joaning" (Rainwater 1970) or "Playing the Dozens" (Abrahams 1962). For a further discussion of the role of verbal battles in street life, see Dollard 1939; Haley and Malcolm X 1964; Lauria 1965; Hannerz 1969; Kochman 1970, 1981; Guffy 1971; Labov 1972; Brenneis and Padarath 1975; Majors and Billson 1992; Smitherman 1997; Morgan 2002; Alim 2004, 2006; Lee 2009).

5. This idea of using retaliatory language—rather than actual violence—to "keep everyone scared of you" has affinities with Gerald Suttles's account of street-gang disputes in his 1968 *The Social Order of the Slum* (see pp. 200–02). While Suttles is primarily describing *between*-group altercations, notably Italians versus African Americans, he finds similarly that rumors and linguistic promises of violent revenge almost never materialize into actual physical conflict. Suttles calls these faux phenomena "predicted" gang fights.

6. The practical joke is a situation where Erving Goffman may have uncharacteristically gotten it wrong. In *Frame Analysis,* Goffman repeatedly categorizes practical jokes as "benign" fabrications, which in this case is to overlook its resolutely malignant intention. Henri Bergson ([1900] 2000) makes a similar mistake in his treatment of laughter when he suggests a fundamental similarity between a practical joke and a runner who slips. While they both share what Bergson calls "mechanical inelasticity," the presence of the mischievous jokester in the former makes all the difference. What Goffman and Bergson seem to forget—and is applicable in Nelson's experience—is that in the practical joke the onlookers are not merely laughing at the victim, they are also laughing *with* the perpetrator. This can only compound the victim's embarrassment because it splits him off (or alienates him) from the social community. See Bergson's *Laughter: An Essay on the Meaning of the Comic.*

10. What about the Day After?

1. Elijah Anderson's many illuminating studies of the publicly situated coping strategies of inner-city inhabitants may seem a notable exception. However, his focus tends to be on the ways individuals anticipate danger and seek to avoid threatening situations with "streetwise" behavior. There is relatively little attention to the ways in which social actors actually address conflicts, broker disputes, and restore order. The essays in this volume, by Edin and by Krupnick and Winship, do address such issues.

2. In the sphere of juvenile delinquency, a contrastive example of the analytic deployment of culture as potentially ameliorative is Cross (2003). Cross suggests that systemic forces do not reinforce dysfunctional or impotent cultural traits, such as values or attitudes, but instead "neutralize" their potency for helping black youth to overcome the temptations to commit crime.

3. This use of knowledge is not entirely alarming, but it is one of only several analytic paths one might choose. Many of the essays in this volume provide a contrastive case, thereby helping us to broaden the theoretical frameworks that might be harnessed to understand various youth behavior. Some readers might also be familiar with the tradition of "cultural studies" that emerged in the United Kingdom via the writings of Stuart Hall, Paul Gilroy, Dick Hebdige, and others at the so-called Birmingham School (During 2003). Cultural studies practitioners viewed deviance not just as an act that violates social norms but also as one that is an intentional practice, imbued with meaning, and always positioned in relation to wider social institutions. The general preference was to speak of youth resistance as opposed to criminality, political motives as opposed to deviant values, and symbolic expression instead of norm violation.

4. It might be objected that the view of Anderson, Stack, and others who emphasized the adaptive competence of black culture remain as exceptions, but I would disagree.

5. For an assessment of Chicago police officers' relations with community members, see Tracey Meares. 2002. "Praying for Policing." *California Law Review* 90: 1593.

6. Historical studies of Chicago are filled with such cases of local stakeholders settling disputes when the state abdicates its responsibility to protect person and property. See Kevin J. Mumford's *Interzones: Black and White Sex Districts in Chicago and New York in the Early Twentieth Century;* and Nathan Thompson's *Kings: The True Story of Chicago's Policy Kings and Numbers Racketeers.*

7. See also Mary Pattilo-McCoy. 1998. "Church Culture as a Strategy of Action in the Black Community." *American Sociological Review* 63 (6): 767–84.

8. It is worth pointing out that the distinction is not purely a semantic one, but substantively significant. The Federal Bureau of Investigation, to offer one example, uses this logic to record its overall performance. The FBI's category of record, "deferments," is meant to capture the work of the authorities that prevent future crimes.

9. We might also add that formal organizational initiatives aimed at violence reduction and crime prevention will incorporate the individuals and organizations that settle conflicts and mediate disputes. These initiatives sometimes take the form of law-enforcement sponsored programs aimed at reducing recidivism; some of the most innovative are community courts and alternative-sentencing programs that incorporate individuals with a proven expertise in conflict resolution with local offenders. They can be joint productions, as in the example of community policing, whereby state and civic actors share responsibility for preventing socially destructive behavior (Skogan and Hartnett 1997). Alternatively, as in the case of Chicago's CeaseFire program,

community-based organizations can "interrupt" violence through creative diplomacy and intervention that works entirely outside the auspices of the state. These organizational initiatives share a common thread, namely the inclusion of experts, with the ability to mediate disputes, in prevention-based efforts that seek to deter youth offending.

10. A historical survey reveals that examples of self-enforcement are by no means specific to black urban communities. They predate the monopolization of force by the modern democratic state. But, even in liberal democracies it is possible to find examples of social groups that orient action toward a body of law—customary or formal—based on particularistic principles, with only minimal regard for the wider authorities and passersby who respond unfavorably. At times, these adherents may broadcast the capacity for self-enforcement as a sign of collective strength and moral integrity. For example, in numerous urban neighborhoods the Jewish "Shomrim," a volunteer force in Hasidic communities routinely and unapologetically adjudicates social violations according to religious edicts as opposed to secular law. From domestic abuse to burglary, its proponents advertise that criminal incidents will be addressed by the Shomrim, with little formal involvement by police or other government representatives. Similarly, the Word of Wisdom enabled tens of thousands of polygamists to live in direct opposition to state laws that forbid such marriage contracts; leaders in the Mormon communities not only operate in full view of state legislators, who seem incapable of eliminating these transgressions, but they use this stalemate as a sign of their own presumed cultural superiority. Self-enforcement need not be held by up by its proponents in such defiant terms. Korean, Arab, and Mexican communities in the United States routinely draw on credit associations, the proceeds of which are not reported as income and the violations of which are not policed by the state. Systems of enforcement that accompany these financial transactions are rarely spoken about publically or championed. In all the aforementioned cases, there is some type of criminal act: a financial transaction is not reported to the government, a physical assault has ensued, someone has consciously decided to obstruct the work of law enforcement, and so on. However, there are few sociological interpretations that frame the behavior of these groups as culturally deficient or marginal: there is little social scientific or popular interest in these examples qua signs of criminality. Thus, the entire culture of Jews, Mormons, Koreans, and so forth is generally perceived to be intact and in no need of fundamental alteration. Indeed, for the most part, scholars and the wider public are quick to celebrate these examples of locally bounded regulation as signs of cultural strength, not moral failure.

11. Culture, Inequality, and Gender Relations among Urban Black Youth

1. Though beyond the scope of my discussion here, American Indian women also parallel African American women in risks for violent victimization (Lauritsen and Schaum 2004).

2. Our project involved surveys and in-depth qualitative interviews with seventy-five black adolescents in St. Louis, including thirty-five young women and forty young men. Youths were drawn from a local community agency and several schools and included those who had been deemed "at risk" by virtue of exposure to detrimental social conditions (see Gibbs 1990, 40) or reported participation in moderate or serious delinquency. For an overview of the study methodology, see Miller 2008.

12. Effects of Affluent Suburban Schooling

1. In particular, I have in mind the well-developed literature on school socio-economic and ethnic composition and teacher–student relationships (Crosnoe 2009; Crosnoe, Johnson, and Elder 2004; Fuller-Rowell and Doan 2010).

2. For additional data, I interviewed coordinators and teachers in the suburban schools ($n = 9$).

3. The Mechanics School (a pseudonym) is closing (2010–2011 is the last year it is in operation) under the "Redesign and Reinvest" initiative.

4. I am not discussing the waitlisted students who are in boarding schools or elite exam schools here, because, for a number of reasons, they are outliers and are not directly comparable to either the bussed or the waitlisted students.

5. This perception was confirmed by a district-level report from one of the public school districts I studied. This report showed that a disproportionate number of black students in that district were placed in remedial courses or labeled as having special needs.

6. Bussing program coordinators are hired by the suburban school districts to serve the bussed students.

7. I do not believe we should reduce the meaning of racial integration programs to class immersion opportunities. Rather, in my own research, I sometimes found that conceptualizing the bussing program as a class immersion experience helped me generate new and important questions about what it was achieving, and why.

13. "Try On the Outfit and Just See How It Works"

1. Like our respondents, somewhat inconsistently. Thus, in his discussion of framing, Goffman dismisses as a "lamentable bias" the view that there can be a "deeper, more genuine" self of the individual beyond the role he plays (1986, 270), but sixteen pages later, he assures us that individuals do have a biography—"a single, continuing personal identity, beyond that performance" (1986, 286).

14. Stepping Up or Stepping Back

1. Fragile Families is the first large nationwide study focusing on children born to unmarried parents. More information on the study, which is conducted jointly by Princeton University and Columbia University, can be found at http://www.fragilefamilies.princeton.edu/.
2. Mathematica is an employee-owned research organization that provides objective analysis across several areas of social policy, including health, education, family support, employment, disability, and international development. See http://mathematica-mpr.com for additional information.
3. For a more detailed discussion of the BSF intervention and its evaluation see Wood, McConnell, et al. (2010) and Wood, Moore, et al. (2010).
4. The primary outcomes examined in the study, by domain, were: *Relationship status:* couple is still romantically involved, couple lives together (married or unmarried), couple is married; *Relationship quality:* relationship happiness, support and affection, use of constructive conflict behaviors, avoidance of destructive conflict behaviors, and sexual fidelity; *Intimate partner violence:* mother reports no severe physical assaults, father reports no severe physical assaults; *Co-parenting:* quality of co-parenting relationship; *Father involvement:* father lives with child, father spends substantial time with child daily, and father provides substantial financial support. See Wood, Moore, et al. (2010) for details on measures.
5. This could include violence experienced in subsequent relationships after dissolution of the relationship with the BSF partner.
6. At the time BSF began, the organization was called the Center for Fathers, Families, and Workforce Development (CFWD).
7. Mean earnings provide a misleading comparison of economic well-being across sites given the higher cost of living in Baltimore, the only East Coast site in the study. Other BSF locations, such as Indiana, Oklahoma, and Texas, tend to have much lower costs of living. And despite the relatively high wages, Baltimore couples' rate of TANF and food stamps usage was 58 percent—14 percentage points higher than the mean in other sites.

8. One potential argument against the assertion that the negative Baltimore results were driven by the particular level of economic disadvantage, social isolation, and underlying propensity for relationship instability is that the cross-site analysis did not tend to find negative impacts for couples with those types of characteristics. One exception is that the program's impact on couples with multiple-partner fertility was negative relative to the impact on couples in which neither partner had a child from a prior relationship. We observed a negative impact among couples in which at least one partner had a child from another relationship, but no such impact among couples without multiple-partner fertility. And, as noted earlier, the uniqueness of the Baltimore couples may not be fully captured by measured traits. The Center's unique location, mission, and street-level recruiting approach targeting men and focusing on disadvantaged neighborhoods seem likely to have attracted a set of participants—and fathers in particular—that differ qualitatively from participants in other sites.

9. This test was suggested by Scott Stanley in a personal communication with the authors.

10. Although the random assignment design should produce fully equivalent samples (at least for the sample that includes all Baltimore couples), the regressions include a broad range of characteristics of partners and couples both to increase statistical precision and to adjust for any small differences that might emerge by chance or as a result of survey non-response. See Wood, Moore, et al. (2010) for a full description of the analysis approach and covariates included in impact analyses.

11. There were no substantively important differences between study groups in fathers' propensity to cite their own infidelity or parenting as a cause for relationship dissolution.

12. In response to these findings, program eligibility rules were modified in Baltimore so that only when both partners described themselves as in a "steady romantic relationship" were they eligible for enrollment.

13. Mathematica recently began an ACF-sponsored study of Healthy Marriage and Responsible Fatherhood Grantees, which includes an intensive qualitative study of couples to help shed important light on those types of questions.

15. Beyond BA Blinders

1. Moreover, the same might be true for the "academic abilities" that Murray posits. Four-year-old children who are exposed to word games and complex verbal interaction with adults are acquiring cultural know-how which enables them to learn more from the same experiences (such as *Sesame Street*; Cook

1975) and perform better on academic tests that purport to measure "academic ability."

2. We are not saying that all private occupational colleges operate this way or that they are necessarily models, but they clearly indicate alternatives that are rarely considered in community colleges, and they contradict the cultural assumptions we usually make if we wear BA blinders. Moreover, although we studied some of the best private occupational colleges, they devised procedures that likely could be implemented in most community colleges. Given that research has found that community college students have great difficulties persisting over many years (particularly when those years are extended without warning), that they often choose courses that don't count for their degrees, and that they have grave doubts that they are making progress toward degrees and job payoffs, the nontraditional procedures created in occupational colleges seem well designed to address these problems. This comparison indicates that a single kind of organization can shape its procedures in ways that improve success, and incidentally, reduce the kinds of "abilities" needed to succeed in the organization.

The ingredients are already present in many community colleges. In recent research, we have discovered that many community colleges already offer pieces of this structured program as a choice option, but only to "adults," not to young students, and it is not systematic. When students get their remedial placement test scores, they should be informed about these options and probabilities, some of which require fewer remedial courses. For low-achieving students, a structured "package-deal" program would improve their chances of quick success, give them intervening milestones on a degree ladder to a BA, and provide a backup option if they have difficulty (and many will). We should also monitor their progress to catch problems quickly. This will reduce the repeated dropout sequence, which is demoralizing, wastes time and money, and loses many students.

16. Liberalism, Self-Respect, and Troubling Cultural Patterns in Ghettos

1. The idea that there exists a culture of poverty is old. One can even find a version of it articulated in W. E. B. Du Bois's *The Philadelphia Negro* (1899), with its emphasis on the cultural deficits of newly urbanized blacks, especially the so-called submerged tenth. The phrase "culture of poverty" came into popular use because of the influence of Oscar Lewis's *Five Families* (1959), which focused on Mexican urban communities. The theory is developed in relation to the black urban poor in such well-known texts as Michael Harrington's *The Other America,* Kenneth Clark's *Dark Ghetto* (1965), and

Daniel Patrick Moynihan's "The Negro Family: The Case for National Action" (1965).

2. The substantive differences between the new cultural analysts and Oscar Lewis (the originator of the concept "culture of poverty") may not be so stark. For a defense of the view that the classic culture of poverty theory, as articulated by Lewis, has been subject to gross distortion and misrepresentation, by those on the left and the right, see Harvey and Reed (1996).

3. It is worth noting that there are advocates of the suboptimal cultural divergence thesis who do not believe that this set of cultural characteristics is, or ever was, an adaptation to poverty, slavery, Jim Crow, or any other unjust social conditions. For example, Thomas Sowell (2005) has argued that black ghetto culture is actually the remnants of Southern white "redneck" culture, which has its origins in those regions of the British Isles from which white American Southerners came. The cultural traits that Sowell attributes to blacks in the ghetto (and to poor rural whites) are much the same as those cultural of poverty theorists attribute to poor blacks. Charles Murray (1984), by contrast, has argued that a culture of poverty, both in black ghettos and white slums, arose as a response to liberal welfare policies that encouraged the poor to depend on federal aid rather than strive to be economically self-sufficient. These antipoverty policies, he claims, created perverse incentives that led to a dramatic rise in nonmarital births, family breakdown, crime, and other social ills. I will not discuss these variants of the cultural divergence thesis.

4. For discussions and critiques of black elite advocacy of cultural reform, see Dyson 2005; Pattillo 2007, ch. 2; Cohen 2010, chs. 2–3.

5. Despite having the right to vote and enlist in the military, eighteen- to twenty-year-olds do not have the right to buy alcoholic beverages in the United States. I leave this controversial exception aside.

6. For defenses of such measures, see the essays in Mead 1997. Also see Kaus 1992.

7. Some of these measures have been instituted through the Personal Responsibility and Work Opportunity Reconciliation Act (1996). However, moral reform is not the only type of justification or rationale offered in their defense. The same could be said about the Moving To Opportunity experiment sponsored by the U.S. Department of Housing and Urban Development.

8. For a careful analysis of church-state collaborations in poor black neighborhoods, see Owens 2007.

9. For critiques of the neoliberal dimensions of moral reform, see Wacquant 2009; and Soss, Fording, and Schram 2011.

10. For a brief but particularly helpful discussion of the place of liberal political morality in American and British political history, see Dworkin 1985, 181–204.

11. Some people have lower self-esteem than they otherwise would because of clinical depression, which can sometimes be effectively treated. Government could enable those who need it to get access to such treatment. But this is not the same as distributing self-esteem; it is a way of repairing damaged self-esteem.

12. The argument of this paragraph and the previous one are offered on the assumption that not all ghetto identities are the product of false consciousness, rationalization, or bad faith. That is, I am assuming that these identities have not all been formed as an unconscious psychological defense mechanism against a debilitating sense of personal failure and individual incompetence. I take it that some ghetto identities are consciously adopted in light of the sincere and justified judgment that U.S. society is unjust and that the ghetto poor in particular do not have a fair shot in life as a result. For a classic defense of the view that some ghetto identities are rationalizations that stave off a sense of failure and incompetence, see Liebow 1967.

13. It might be thought that a race-neutral moral reform policy that targets *all* poor people would not run into this problem. But this is not so clear. There is a long history of "race-neutral" policies with racist intent—from policies that concern voting rights to the criminal justice system to welfare—and most blacks would seem to be aware of this history.

14. Michele M. Moody-Adams (1997) suggests something like this conception of self-respect.

15. There are other circumstances under which it may be permissible for a public official (e.g., a social worker or police officer) to intervene paternalistically to help those who, because of unjust treatment by the state, have become incapable of helping themselves. For instance, this may be acceptable when the would-be benefactor is acting as a private citizen rather than in his or her official capacity as a representative of the state.

16. For helpful comments on previous drafts of this chapter, I thank Eric Beerbohm, Lawrence Blum, Moshe Cohen-Eliya, Nir Eyal, Ethan Fosse, Marilyn Friedman, Christopher Jencks, Lawrence Lessig, Christopher Lewis, Jonathan Marks, Orlando Patterson, Brandon Terry, Andrew Valls, Daniel Viehoff, Erik Olin Wright, and an anonymous referee. Material from this chapter was presented at Emory University, Harvard University, Miami University, Michigan State University, University of Illinois Urbana-Champagne, University of Michigan, University of North Carolina Chapel Hill, University of the Witwatersrand, Washington University, and Yale University. I thank these audiences for their comments and criticisms. Research for this project was generously supported by the Edmond J. Safra Center for Ethics at Harvard University.

Conclusion

1. Analyses are based on data from the 2006 African American survey.
2. In contrast, when asked to evaluate what issues constitute a "big problem" facing black men, 62.1 percent of white youth cite becoming involved in crime, 54.9 percent say drug and alcohol abuse, 54 percent say "not taking their education seriously enough," 53.7 percent say poverty, 40.1 percent say "not having good jobs," 33.9 percent say "not being responsible fathers," 37.7 percent say racial discrimination.
3. Note that this difference could be due to desirability bias, with white youth giving the answers they believe are appropriate. One way to check this is to determine whether the race of the interviewer is related to the responses of white youth. Ordinal logistic regression analyses indicated no statistically significant relationships (at $\propto=0.10$) between the race of the interviewer and the responses by white youth to the questions discussed here.
4. Analysis is based on data from the Pew Survey of 2008 and the Black Youth Project Survey.
5. Analysis based on data from the 2011 Kaiser Black Women Survey. One resolution of this apparent discrepancy is that black youth may believe that black men do not show the proper respect for women for reasons other than overt sexism.
6. For example, 45.5 percent of young black women (compared to 41.7 percent of young black men) say that black men being less likely to think committing crimes is wrong is a big reason and 60.6 percent (compared to 54.3 percent of young black men) say likewise for parents not teaching their children right from wrong.
7. The question of immigrant selectivity in regard to their first-generation parents is irrelevant to the point being made here, and in Tran's chapter: that culture matters, *not* whether a West-Indian-American cultural configuration is superior to African American, an utterly spurious issue as far as we are concerned.
8. Not to be confused with the Obama Administration's national school turnaround program of the Department of Education, announced in 2009 (see Kutash et al. 2010).
9. An independent evaluation cited by the program and its admirers, presumably done by the American Institutes of Research, could not be located or provided by them after repeated requests; and an in-house evaluation of school staff response to the program's effort to establish clear and consistent protocols found a "decrease of school staff satisfaction when viewing the clarity of protocols taught to them at the beginning of the year" (Foster 2013).

10. On post secondary educational improvements, the recommendations of the *Presidential Task Force 90-Day Report* are somewhat conventional, such as expanding access to AP classes and dual enrollment options in high school. The task force would do well to consider the recommendations of Rosenbaum et al., presented in Chapter 15 of this volume.

11. Discussions of family or household types should not be confused with discussion of the distribution of children in different household arrangements, as so often happens, especially among apologists who wish to underplay differences between blacks and other Americans.

References

Introduction

Anderson, Elijah. 1979. *A Place on the Corner*. Chicago: University of Chicago Press.

———. 1992. *Streetwise: Race, Class and Change in an Urban Community*. Chicago: University of Chicago Press.

———. 1999. *Code of the Street: Decency, Violence, and the Moral Life of the Inner City*. New York: Norton.

———. 2008. *Against the Wall: Poor, Young, Black and Male*. Philadelphia: University of Pennsylvania Press.

Barth, Fredrik. 1969. *Ethnic Groups and Boundaries: The Social Organization of Culture Difference*. New York: Little Brown.

Berezin, Mabel. 1994. "Fissured Terrain: Methodological Approaches and Research Styles in Culture and Politics." In *The Sociology of Culture*, edited by Diana Crane, 91–116. Cambridge, MA: Blackwell.

Billingsley, Andrew. 1968. *Black Families in White America*. Englewood Cliffs, NJ: Touchstone Books.

Bonnell, Victoria E., Lynn Hunt, and Hayden White, eds. 1999. *Beyond the Cultural Turn: New Directions in the Study of Society and Culture*. Berkeley: University of California Press.

Carter, Prudence. 2005. *Keepin' It Real: School Success Beyond Black and White*. New York: Oxford University Press.

Clark, Kenneth. 1965. *Dark Ghetto*. New York: Harper and Row.

Drake, St. Clair, and Horace R. Cayton. 1945. *Black Metropolis: A Study of Negro Life in a Northern City*. New York: Harcourt, Brace and Co.

Draper, Theodore. 1971. *The Rediscovery of Black Nationalism*. New York: Viking.

Du Bois, W. E. B. 1899. *The Philadelphia Negro: A Social Study*. Philadelphia: University of Philadelphia Press.

Frazier, E. Franklin. 1940. *Negro Youth at the Crossways*. Washington, D.C: American Council of Education.

———. 1948. *The Negro Family in the United States*. Chicago: University of Chicago Press.

Gibbs, Jewellle ed. 1988. *Young, Black, and Male in America*. Dover, MA: Auburn House Publishing Co.

Gouldner, Alvin. 1970. *The Coming Crisis of Western Sociology*. New York: Basic Books.

Habermas, Jürgen. 1981. "Talcott Parsons: Problems of Theory Construction." *Sociological Inquiry*. Vol.51, Issues 3–4: 173–196.

Hannerz, Ulf. 1969. *Soulside: Inquiries into Ghetto Culture and Community*. New York: Columbia University Press.

Harding, David J. 2010. *Living the Drama: Community Conflict and Culture among Inner-City Boys*. Chicago: University of Chicago Press.

Ladner, Joyce. 1972. *Tomorrow's Tomorrow: The Black Woman*. New York: Doubleday.

———, ed. 1973. *The Death of White Sociology*. New York: Vintage.

Lamont, Michele, and Mario Small. 2010. "How Culture Matters for the Understanding of Poverty: Enriching Our Understanding." In *The Colors of Poverty: Why Racial and Ethnic Disparities* Persist, edited by Ann Lin and David Harris, 76–102. New York: Russell Sage.

Lamont, Michele, Mario Luis Small, and David J Harding. 2010. "Introduction: Reconsidering Culture and Poverty." *The ANNALS of the American Academy of Political and Social Science* 629 (1): 6–27.

Lareau, Annette 2003. *Unequal Childhood*. Berkeley: University of California Press.

Lewis, Oscar. 1961. *Children of Sanchez*. New York: Random House.

———. 1966. *La Vida: A Puerto Rican Family in the Culture of Poverty*. New York: Random House.

Massey, Douglas, and Mary Denton. 1993. *American Apartheid*. Cambridge, MA: Harvard University Press.

Moynihan, Daniel Patrick. 1965. *The Negro Family: The Case for National Action*. Washington, D.C: Office of Planning and Policy Research, Dept. of Labor.

Murray, Charles. 1984. *Losing Ground: American Social Policy, 1950–1980*. New York: Basic Books.

Obama, Barack. 2014. "President Obama's Full 'My Brother's Keeper' Speech. 02/27/2014." Politico Video. Retrieved 02/28/2014 at politico.com

Patterson, Orlando. 1977. *Ethnic Chauvinism: The Reactionary Impulse*. New York: Stein & Day.

———. 1997. *The Ordeal of Integration*. Washington, D.C: Civitas/Counterpoint.

Patterson, Orlando. 2001. "Taking Culture Seriously: A Framework and an Afro-American Illustration." In *Culture Matters: How Values Shape Human Progress,* edited by Lawrence E. Harrison and Samuel P. Huntington, 202–18. New York: Basic Books

———. 2004. "Culture and Continuity: Causal Structures in Socio-cultural Persistence." In *Matters of Culture: Cultural Sociology in Practice,* edited by Roger Friedland and John Mohr. New York: Cambridge University Press.

———. 2006. "A Poverty of Mind," *The New York Times* (Op-Ed, March 26, 2006)

———. 2014. "Making Sense of Culture," *The Annual Review of Sociology* 40: 1–30.

Powdermaker, Hortense. 1939. *After Freedom: A Cultural Study of the Deep South.* New York: Viking.

Rainwater, Lee. 1970. *Behind Ghetto Walls.* Chicago: Aldine.

Rainwater, Lee, and William Yancey. 1967. *The Moynihan Report and the Politics of Controversy.* Cambridge, MA: MIT Press.

Sanchez-Jankowski, Martin. 2008. *Cracks in the Pavement: Social Change and Resilience in Poor Neighborhoods.* Berkeley: University of California Press

Scanzoni, John H. 1971. *The Black Family in Modern Society: Patterns of Stability and Security.* Boston: Allyn and Bacon.

Small, Mario L. 2004. *Villa Victoria: The Transformation of Social Capital in a Boston Barrio.* Chicago: University of Chicago Press.

Smith, Sandra. 2006. *Lone Pursuit: Distrust and Defensive Individualism among Black Poor People.* New York: Russell Sage.

Stack, Carol. 1974. *All Our Kin.* New York: Basic Books.

Valentine, Charles, ed. 1968. *Culture and Poverty: Critique and Counterproposals.* Chicago: University of Chicago Press.

Venkatesh, Sudhir. 2002. *American Project: The Rise and Fall of a Modern Ghetto.* Cambridge, MA: Harvard University Press.

———. 2009. *Off the Books: The Underground Economy of the Urban Poor.* Cambridge, MA: Harvard University Press.

Wacquant, Loïc, and Wilson, William Julius. 1989. "The Cost of Racial and Class Exclusion in the Inner City." *Annals of the American Academy of Political and Social Sciences.* 501, 1: 8–25.

Williams, J. Allen, and Robert Stockton. 1973. "Black Family Structures and Functions: An Empirical Examination of Some Suggestions Made by Billingsley." *Journal of Marriage and the Family* 35 (1): 39–49.

Wilson, William Julius. 1978. *The Declining Significance of Race.* Chicago: University of Chicago Press.

Wilson, William Julius. 1987. *The Truly Disadvantaged.* Chicago: University of Chicago Press.

———. 1989. Introduction to *Dark Ghetto,* by Kenneth Clark, ix-xxii. 2nd ed. Hanover, NH: Weslyan University Press.

———. 2009. *More Than Just Race: Being Black and Poor in the Inner City.* New York: Norton

Young, Jr., Alford A. 2004. *The Minds of Marginalized Black Men.* Chicago: University of Chicago Press.

1. The Nature and Dynamics of Cultural Processes

Akerlof, George. 1982. "Labor Contracts as Partial Gift Exchange." *Quarterly Journal of Economics* XCVII, No. 4: 543–69.

Alim, H. Samy. 2008. "Straight Outta Compton, Straight *aus Munchen*: Global Linguistic Flows, Identities, and the Politics of Language in a Global Hip Hop Nation." In *Global Linguistic Flows: Hip Hop Cultures, Youth Identities, and the Politics of Language,* edited by H. Samy Alim, A. Ibrahim, and A. Pennycook, 1–24. New York: Routledge.

Anderson, Elijah. 1999. *Code of the Street: Decency, Violence & the Moral Life of the Inner City.* New York: W. W. Norton & Co.

Anderson, Susan, G. B. Moskowitz, I. V. Blair, and B. A. Nosek. 2007. "Automatic Thought." In *Social Psychology: Handbook of Basic Principles,* 2nd ed., edited by Arie W. Kruglanski and E. Tory Higgins, 138–75. New York: Guilford Press.

Argyris, C. L., and D. A. Schon. 1978. *Organizational Learning.* Reading, MA: Addison-Wesley.

Atran, Scott. 2006. "Sacred Values and the Limits of Rational Choice: Conflicting Cultural Frameworks in the Struggle Against Terrorism." In *In the Same Light as Slavery,* edited by Joseph McMillan, 151–177. Washington, D.C.: NDU Press.

Balestrino, Alessandro, and C. Ciardi. 2008. "Social Norms, Cognitive Dissonance and the Timing of Marriage." *Journal of Socio-Economics* 37 (6): 2399–410.

Bardi, Anat, and Shalom Schwartz. 2003. "Values and Behavior: Strength and Structure of Relations." *Personality and Social Psychology Bulletin,* 29 (10): 1207–20.

Barth, Fredrik. 1993. "Are Values Real? The Enigma of Naturalism in the Anthropological Interpretation of Values." In *The Origin of Values,* edited by Michal Hechter et al., 31–46. New York: Aldine De Gruyter Inc.

Benet-Martinez, V., J. Leu, F. Lee, and M. Morris. 2002. "Negotiating Biculturalism: Cultural Frame Switching in Biculturals with Oppositional versus Compatible Cultural Identities." *Journal of Cross-cultural Psychology* 33: 492–516.

Biernacki, Richard. 2000. "Language and the Shift from Signs to Practices in Cultural Inquiry." *History and Theory* 39 (3): 289–310.

Bloom, F. E., and A. Lazerson. 1988. *Brain, Mind, and Behavior.* New York: Freeman.

Bourdieu, Pierre. 1977. *Outline of a Theory of Practice*. Translated by Richard Nice. New York: Cambridge University Press.

———. 1979. *Algeria 1960: The Disenchantment of the World, the Sense of Honour, the Kabyle House or the World Reversed*. Translated by Richard Nice. Cambridge: Cambridge University Press.

———. 1986. "The Forms of Capital." In *Handbook for Theory and Research in the Sociology of Education,* edited by J. Richardson, 241–58. New York: Greenwood.

———. 1990. *The Logic of Practice*. Cambridge, MA: Polity Press.

Bourgois, Philippe. 1996. *In Search of Respect: Selling Crack in El Barrio*. New York: Cambridge University Press.

Brewer, W. F. 1987. "Schemas versus Mental Models in Human Memory." In *Modelling Cognition,* edited by P. Morris, 187–97. Chichester: Wiley.

Brewer, W. F., and G. V. Nakamura. 1984. "The Nature and Functions of Schemas." In *Handbook of Social Cognition,* Vol. 1, edited by R. S. Wyer & T. K. Srull, 119–60. Hillsdale, NJ: Erlbaum.

Burke, P. J., and J. E. Stets. 2009. *Identity Theory*. New York: Oxford University Press.

Cerulo, Karen, ed. 2010. "Brain, Mind and Cultural Sociology." *Poetics* (Special Issue), 30 (2).

Chen, Xiang. 2004. "Scripts and Conceptual Change." In *Science, Cognitive, and Consciousness,* edited by P. Li, X. Chen, and H. X. Zhang, 96–117. Nanchang: Jiangxi People's Press.

Chwe, Michael. 1999. "Structure and Strategy in Collective Action." *American Journal of Sociology* 105: 128–56.

Cialdini, Robert, and Melanie Trost. 1998. "Social Influence: Social Norms, Conformity, and Compliance." In *The Handbook of Social Psychology,* edited by Daniel Gilberte, Susan Fiske and Gardner Lindzey, Vol. 2: 151–92. New York: Oxford University Press.

Cohen, Kathy J. 2012. *Democracy Remixed: Black Youth and the Future of American Politics*. New York: Oxford University Press.

Coleman, James S. 1990. *Foundations of Social Theory*. Cambridge, MA: The Belknap Press.

Cook, Karen S., and Russell Hardin. 2001. "Norms of Cooperativeness and Networks of Trust." In *Social Norms,* edited by Michael Hechter and Karl-Dieter Opp, 327–47. New York: Russell Sage.

D'Andrade, Roy G., and Claudia Strauss. 1992. *Human Motives and Cultural Models*. New York: Cambridge University Press.

Denzau, Arthur T., and Douglass C. North. 1994. "Shared Mental Models: Ideologies and Institutions." *Kylos* 47 (1): 3–31.

DiMaggio, Paul. 1997. "Culture and Cognition." *Annual Review of Sociology* 23: 263–87.

DiMaggio, Paul, and W. Powell. 1983. "The Iron Cage Revisited: Institutional Isomorphism and Collective Rationality in Organizational Fields." *American Sociological Review* 48: 147–60.

Douglas, Mary. 1986. *How Institutions Think.* Syracuse, NY: Syracuse University Press.

Drissel, David. 2009. "Hip-Hop Hybridity for a Glocalized World: African and Muslim Diasporic Discourses in French Rap Music." *The Global Studies Journal* 2 (3):121–42.

Dubreuil, Benoit. (2010) *Human Evolution and the Origins of Hierarchies: The State of Nature.* New York: Cambridge University Press.

Epstein, S. 1989. "Values from the Perspective of Cognitive-Experiential Self-Theory." In *Social and Moral Values,* edited by N. Eisenberg, J. Reykowski, and E. Staub, 3–22. Hillsdale, NJ: Lawrence Erlbaum Associates.

Feather, N. T. 1995. "Values, Valences, and Choice: The Influence of Values on the Perceived Attractiveness and Choice of Alternatives." *Journal of Personality and Social Psychology* 68: 1135–51.

Fine, Gary. 1979. "Small Groups and Culture Creation: The Ideoculture of Little League Baseball Teams." *American Sociological Review* 44: 733–45.

———. 2001. "Enacting Norms: Mushrooming and the Culture of Expectations and Explanations." In Hechter and Opp 2001, 139–64.

Fine, Gary Alan, and Corey D. Fields. 2008. "Culture & Microsociology: The Anthill & the Veldt." *Annals of the American Academy of Political and Social Sciences* 619: 130–48.

Fischer, Claude. 1975. "Toward a Subcultural Theory of Urbanism." *American Journal of Sociology* 80 (6): 1319–41.

Fiske, A. P., and P. Tetlock. 1997. "Taboo Trade-offs: Reactions to Transactions That Transgress the Domain of Relationships." *Political Psychology* 18: 255–97.

Forster, Jens, and Nira Liberman. 2007. "Knowledge Activation." In *Social Psychology: Handbook of Basic Principles,* 2nd ed., edited by Arie W. Kruglanski and E. Tory Higgins, 201–231. New York: Guilford Press.

Freilich, Morris, and Frank A. Schubert. 1989. "Proper Rules, Smart Rules, and Police Discretion," In *The Relevance of Culture,* edited by Morris Freilich, 218–244. New York: Bergin & Garvey.

Gates, Henry Louis, Jr. 1988. *The Signifying Monkey: A Theory of African-American Literary Criticism.* New York: Oxford University Press.

Hagedorn, John. 1998. *People and Folks: Gangs, Crime and the Underclass in a Rustbelt City.* Chicago: Lake View Press.

Haidt, Jonathan. 2012. *The Righteous Mind: Why Good People are Divided by Politics and Religion.* New York: Penguin.

Hechter, Michael, Lynn Nadel, and Richard Michod, eds. 1993. *The Origin of Values.* New York: Aldine De Gruyter Inc.

Hechter, Michael, and K. D. Opp, eds. 2001. *Social Norms*. New York: Russell Sage Foundation.

Heise, David R. 2002. "Understanding Social Interaction with Affect Control Theory." In *New Directions in Sociological Theory*, edited by Joseph Berger and Morris Zelditch, 17–40. Boulder, CO: Rowman & Littlefield.

Higgins, E. T. 1996. "Knowledge Activation: Accessibility, Applicability and Salience." In *Social Psychology: Handbook of Basic Principles*, edited by E. T. Higgins and A. W. Kruglanski, 133–68. New York: Guilford.

Hitlin, Steven, and Jane A. Piliavin. 2004. "Values: Reviving a Dormant Concept." *Annual Review of Sociology*, 30: 359–93.

Hong, Ying-Yi, and LeeAnn Mallorie. 2004. "A Dynamic Constructivist Approach to Culture: Lessons Learned from Personality Psychology." *Journal of Research in Personality* 38: 59–67.

Horne, Christine. 2001. "Sociological Perspectives on the Emergence of Norms." In Hechter and Opp 2001, 3–34.

Hutchins, Edwin. 1995. *Cognition in the Wild*. Cambridge, MA: M.I.T. Press.

Ignatow, Gabriel. 2007. "Theories of Embodied Knowledge: New Directions for Cultural and Cognitive Sociology?" *Journal for the Theory of Social Behavior* 37 (2): 115–35.

Inglehart, Ronald. 1990. *Culture Shift in Advanced Industrial Society*. Princeton, NJ: Princeton University Press.

Inglehart, Ronald, and Wayne Baker. 2000. "Modernization, Cultural Change and the Persistence of Traditional Values." *American Sociological Review* 65: 19–51.

Inglehart, Ronald, and Christian Welzel. 2005. *Modernization, Cultural Change, and Democracy*. New York: Cambridge University Press.

Lakoff, George. 2009. *The Political Mind*. New York: Penguin.

Lakoff, George, and Mark Johnson. 2003. *Metaphors We Live By*. Chicago: University of Chicago Press.

Lamont, Michele. 2009. *How Professors Think: Inside the Curious World of Academic Judgment*. Cambridge, MA: Harvard University Press.

Lamont, Michele, and Marcel Fournier, eds. 1993. *Cultivating Differences: Symbolic Boundaries and the Making of Inequality*. Chicago: University of Chicago Press.

Larson, Deborah Welch. 1994. "The Role of Belief Systems and Schemas in Foreign Policy Decision-Making." *Political Psychology* 5 (1): 17–33.

Lefkowitz, Joel. 2003. *Ethics and Values in Industrial-Organizational Psychology*. Mahwah, NJ: Lawrence Erlbaum Associates.

McBride, Allan, and Robert Toburen. 1996. "Deep Structures: Polpop Culture on Television." *The Journal of Popular Culture* 29 (4): 181–200.

McGraw, Peter A., and Philip E. Tetlock. 2005. "Taboo Trade-Offs, Relational Framing, and the Acceptability of Exchanges." *Journal of Consumer Psychology* 15 (1): 2–15.

Merleau-Ponty, Maurice. 1945. 1962. *Phenomenology of Perception.* London: Routledge.

Moskos, Peter. 2009. *Cop in the Hood.* Princeton: Princeton University Press.

Myers, Fred. 1998. "Reflections on a Meeting: Structure, Language, and the Polity in a Small-Scale Society." In *The Matrix of Language,* edited by D. Brenneis and R. Macaulay, 234–57. Boulder, CO: Westview

North, Douglass. 1991. "Institutions." *The Journal of Economic Perspectives* 5 (1): 97–112.

O'Gorman, Rick, David S. Wilson, and Ralph R. Miller. 2008. "An Evolved Cognitive Bias for Social Norms." *Evolution and Human Behavior* 29: 71–78.

Owens, Timothy, Dawn Robinson, and Lynn Smith-Lovin. 2010. "The Three Faces of Identity." *Annual Review of Sociology* 36: 477–99.

Padgett, John F., and Walter W. Powell. 2012. *The Emergence of Organizations and Markets.* Princeton, NJ: Princeton University Press.

Patterson, Orlando. 2001. "Taking Culture Seriously: A Framework and an Afro-American Illustration." In *Culture Matters: How Values Shape Human Progress,* edited by Lawrence E. Harrison and Samuel P. Huntington, 202–18. New York: Basic Books.

———. 2004. "Culture and Continuity: Causal Structures in Socio-Cultural Persistence." In *Matters of Culture: Cultural Sociology in Practice,* edited by Roger Friedland and John Mohr, 71–109. New York: Cambridge University Press.

———. 2010. "The Mechanisms of Cultural Reproduction: Explaining the Puzzle of Persistence." In *Handbook of Cultural Sociology,* edited by John Hall, Laura Grindstaff, and Ming-Cheng Lo, 140–152. London: Routledge.

Pinker, Steven. 2007. *The Stuff of Thought: Language as a Window into Human Nature.* New York: Viking.

Pollard, Velma. 2000. *Dread Talk: The Language of Rastafari.* Montreal: McGill-Queens University Press.

Rokeach, M. 1973. *The Nature of Human Values.* New York: Free Press.

Rosch, Eleanor. 1978. "Principles of Categorization." In *Cognition and Categorization,* edited by E. Rosch and Barbara Lloyd, 27–48. Hillsdale, NJ: Lawrence Erlbaum Associates.

Russell, Robert. 1992. "An Examination of the Effects of Organizational Norms, Organizational Structure, and Environmental Uncertainty on Entrepreneurial Strategy." *Journal of Management* 18 (4): 639–58.

Sahlins, Marshall. 2000. *Culture in Practice.* New York: Zone Books.

Saussure, Ferdinand de. 1977. *Course in General Linguistics.* Glasgow: Fontana/Collins.

Schank, R. C., and Abelson, R. 1977. *Scripts, Plans, Goals, and Understanding.* Hillsdale, NJ: Erlbaum Assoc.

Schwartz, S. H. 1977. "Normative Influence on Altruism." In *Advances in Experimental Social Psychology,* edited by L. Berkowitz, Vol. 10: 221–79.

Scott, W. Richard. 2005. "Institutional Theory: Contributing to a Theoretical Research Program." In *Great Minds in Management: The Process of Theory Development,* edited by Ken G. Smith and Michael A. Hitt, ch. 22. New York: Oxford University Press.

Shore, Brad. 1998. *Culture in Mind.* New York: Oxford University Press.

Smith, Eliot R. 1994. "Procedural Knowledge and Processing Strategies in Social Cognition." In *Handbook of Social Cognition, Vol. 1: Basic Processes,* edited by Robert S. Wyer, Jr. and Thomas K. Srull, 99–102. Hillsdale, NJ: Lawrence Erlbaum Associates.

Sperber, Dan. 1996. *Explaining Culture: A Naturalistic Approach.* Malden, MA: Blackwell Publishers.

Stryker, Sheldon, and Peter J. Burke. 2000. "The Past, Present, and Future of an Identity Theory." *Social Psychology Quarterly* 63 (4):284–97.

Swidler, Ann. 1986. "Culture in Action." *American Sociological Revie,* 51 (2): 273–86.

Ten Berge, Timon, and Rene van Hezewijk. 1999. "Procedural and Declarative Knowledge: An Evolutionary Perspective." *Theory & Psychology* 9 (5): 605–24.

Therborn, Goran. 2004. "Back to Norms and Normative Action." *Current Sociology* 50 (6): 863–80.

Van Leeuwen, Theo. 2005. *Introducing Social Semiotics.* New York: Routledge.

Wacquant, Loïc. 2004. "Habitus." *International Encyclopedia of Economic Sociology,* 31, edited by Jens Beckert and Milan Zafirovski, 315–319. New York: Routledge.

Weber, Max. 1949. " 'Objectivity' in Social Science and Social Policy." *Max Weber on the Methodology of the Social Sciences.* Translated and edited by Edward Shils and Henry Finch, 49–112. Glencoe, IL: Free Press.

Vaisey, Stephen. (2008). "Socrates, Skinner and Aristotle: three ways of thinking about culture in action," *Sociological Forum* 23, 3: 603–613.

Vaisey, Stephen. (2009) "Motivation and Justification: A Dual-Process Model of Culture in Action," *American Journal of Sociology,* 114: 1675–715.

Venkatesh, Sudhir. 2006. *Off the Books: The Underground Economy of the Urban Poor.* Cambridge, MA: Harvard University Press.

2. The Social and Cultural Matrix of Black Youth

Acs, Gregory. 2011. *Downward Mobility from the Middle Class: Waking from the American Dream.* Washington, DC: Pew Charitable Trust: Economic Mobility Project.

Ahmed, Insanul. 2012. "Who Is Danny Brown?: Growing Up in Detroit" *Complex Music,* accessed 6/13.2013, http://www.complex.com/music/2012/01/who-is-danny-

Akerlof, George. 1998. "Men Without Children." *The Economic Journal* 108 (447): 287–309.

Akerlof, George, Janet L. Yellen, and Michael L. Katz. 1996. "An Analysis of Out-of-Wedlock Childbearing in the United States." *The Quarterly Journal of Economics* 111 (2): 277–317.

Alba, Richard D., and Victor Nee. 2005. *Remaking the American Mainstream: Assimilation and Contemporary Immigration.* Cambridge, MA: Harvard University Press.

Alexander, Michelle. (2010). *The New Jim Crow: Mass Incarceration in the Age of Colorblindness.* New York: The New Press.

Alim, H. Samy. 2006. *Roc the Mic Right: The Language of Hip Hop Culture.* (New York: Routledge)

Alleyne-Green, B., V. Coleman-Bower, and D. Henry. 2012. "Dating Violence Perpetration and/or Victimization and Associated Sexual Risk Behaviors among a Sample of Inner-City African American and Hispanic Adolescent Females." *Journal of Interpersonal Violence* 27 (8): 1457–73.

Alvarez, Luis. 2008. *The Power of the Zoot: Youth Culture and Resistance During World War II.* Berkeley: University of California Press.

Anderson, Craig, Leonard Berkowitz, Edward Donnerstein, L. Rowell Huesmann, James D. Johnson, Daniele Linz, Neil M. Malamut, and Ellen Wartella. 2003. "The Influence of Media Violence on Youth." *Psychological Science in the Public Interest* 4: 81–110.

Anderson, Elijah. 1992. *Streetwise: Race, Class and Change in an Urban Community.* Chicago: University of Chicago Press.

———. 1999. *Code of the Street.* New York: Norton.

———. 2008. Ed. *Against the Wall: Poor, Young, Black and Male.* Philadelphia: University of Pennsylvania Press.

Arnold, Paul. 2008. "DX-clusive: Plies Lied about Criminal Past," HIPHOP DX, http://www.hiphopdx.com/index/news/id.7397/title.dx-clusive-plies-lied-about-criminal-past.

Ballard, M. E., A. R. Dodson, and D. G. Bazzini. 1999. "Genre of Music and Lyrical Content: Expectation Effects." *Journal of Genetic Psychology* 160 (4): 476–87.

Banks, E. C., L. E. Ferretti, and D. W. Shucar. 1997. "Effects of Low Level Lead Exposure on Cognitive Function in Children: A Review of Behavioral, Neuropsychological, and Biological Evidence." *Neurotoxicology* 18 (1): 237–81.

Baumrind, Diana. 1991. "The Influence of Parenting Style on Adolescent Competence and Substance Abuse." *Journal of Early Adolescence* 11: 56–95.

Bell, Daniel. 1976. *The Cultural Contradictions of Capitalism*. New York: Basic Books.

Bell, E. E. and S. M. Nkomo (1998) "Armoring: Learning to Withstand Racial Oppression," *Journal of Comparative Family Studies* 29 (2): 285–296.

Bodvarsson, Orn, and Hendrik Van den Berg. 2009. *The Economics of Immigration*. New York: Springer.

Boyd, Todd, ed. 2008a. *African Americans and Popular Culture*. New York: Praeger.

Boyd, Todd. 2008b. *Young, Black, Rich, and Famous: The Rise of the NBA, the Hip Hop Invasion, and the Transformation of American Culture*. New York: Doubleday.

Bradley, Robert H., R. F. Corwyn, H. P. McAdoo, C. Garcia Coll. 2001a. "The Home Environment of Children in the United States, Part I: Variations by Age, Ethnicity and Poverty Status." *Child Development* 72 (6): 1844–67.

———. 2001b. "The Home Environment of Children in the United States, Part II: Relations with Behavioral Development through Age Thirteen." *Child Development* 72 (6): 1868–86.

Brooks-Gunn, J., Pamela Klebanov, and Fong-Rue Liaw. 1995. "The Learning, Physical, and Emotional Environment of the Home in the Context of Poverty: The Infant Health and Development Program." *Children and Youth Services Review* 17 (1–2): 251–76.

Brown, Cecil. 2003. *Stagolee Shot Billy*. Cambridge, MA: Harvard University Press.

Brown, Ray B., and Pat Brown, eds. 2001. *The Guide to United States Popular Culture*. Madison: The University of Wisconsin Press.

Brungage, W. Fitzhugh, ed. 2011. *Beyond Blackface: African Americans and the Creation of American Popular Culture, 1890–1930*. Chapel Hill, NC: University of North Carolina Press.

Bureau of Justice Statistics. 2011. *Homicide Trends in the United States, 1980–2008*. Washington, DC: U.S. Department of Justice, Office of Justice Programs, NCJ 236018.

———. 2012a. *Violent Crime Against Youth, 1994–2010*. Washington, DC: U.S. Department of Justice, Office of Justice Programs, NCJ 240106.

———. 2012b. *Correctional Populations in the United States, 2011*. Washington, DC: U.S. Department of Justice, Office of Justice Programs, NCJ 239972.

Bureau of Labor Statistics. 2012a. *College Enrollment and Work Activity of High School Graduates*. Washington, DC: Bureau of Labor Statistics. Release date April 2012: http://www.bls.gov/news.release/hsgec.htm.

———. 2012b. *A Profile of the Working Poor, 2010*. Washington, DC: U.S. Department of Labor, Report 1035.

———. 2013. *Employment Status of the Civilian Population by Race, Sex and Age*. Washington, DC: U.S. Department of Labor, Report 1035. Release date May 5, 2013: http://www.bls.gov/news.release/empsit.t02.htm.

Carter, Prudence. 2001. "Between a 'Soft' and a 'Hard' Place: Issues of Gender Identity in the Schooling and Job Behaviors of Low-Income Minority Youth." *Sociological Studies of Children and Youth* 8: 211–33.

———. 2005. *Keepin' It Real: School Success Beyond Black and White*. New York: Oxford University Press.

Center on the Developing Child at Harvard University. 2010. Cambridge, MA: Harvard University.

Chang, Jeff, ed. 2006. *Total Chaos: The Art and Aesthetics of Hip-Hop*. New York: Basic-Civitas.

Cheng, Chi-Ying, Fiona Lee, and V. Benet-Martinez. 2006. "Assimilation and Contrast Effects in Cultural Frame Switching: Cultural Integration and Valence of Cultural Cues." *Journal of Cross-Cultural Psychology* 37: 742–60.

Child Trends Data Bank. 2013. "Child Maltreatment: Indicators on Children and Youth," accessed, http://www.childrensdatabank.org.

Chiu, Chi-Yue, and Ying-Yi Hong. 2007. "Cultural Processes: Basic Principles." Edited by Kruglanski and Higgins, 785–804.

Chung, J. C., P. J. Callahan P. J., C. W. Lyu et al. 1999. "Polycyclic Aromatic Hydrocarbon Exposures of Children in Low-Income Families." *J Expos Anal Environ Epidemiol* 1:193–225.

Clarkwest, George Andrew. 2005. "African American Marital Disruption: What's History Got to Do With It?" PhD diss., Harvard University.

Cohen, Cathy. 2010. *Democracy Re-Mixed*. New York: Oxford University Press.

Cramer, Maria, M. E. Irons, A. Johnson, J. Russell, and A. Ryan. "68 Blocks: Life, Death, Hope." *Boston Globe,* December 7, 2012.

Dahl, Gordon, and Stefano Della Vigna. 2009. "Does Movie Violence Increase Violent Crime?" *The Quarterly Journal of Economics* 124 (2): 677–734.

Del Caro, Adrian. 1989. "Dionysian Classicism, or Nietzsche's Appropriation of an Aesthetic Norm." *Journal of the History of Ideas* 50 (4): 589–605.

DeNavas-Walt, C., B. Proctor, and J. Smith. 2012. *Income Poverty and Health Insurance Coverage in the United States: 2011*. U.S. Census, Current Population Reports.

Denno, D. W. 1990. *Biology and Violence: From Birth to Adulthood*. New York: Cambridge University Press.

Dienstbier, Richard A. 1989. "Arousal and Physiological Toughness: Implications for Mental and Physical Health." Paper 216, May 21, 2013, http://digitalcommons.unl.edu/psychfacpub/216.

Dietrich, K. N., et al. 1991. "Lead Exposure and the Cognitive Development of Urban Preschool Children: The Cincinnati Lead Study Cohort at Age 4 Years." *Neurotoxicology and Teratology,* 13 (12): 203–11.

Dietrich, K. N., M. D. Ris, P. A. Succop, O. G. Berger, and R. L. Bornschein. 2001. "Early Exposure to Lead and Juvenile Delinquency." *Neurotoxicology and Teratology* 23 (6): 511–18.

Dietz, W. H., and S. L. Gortmaker. 1985. "Do We Fatten Our Children at the Television Set: Obesity and Television Viewing in Children and Adolescents." *Pediatrics* 75: 807–12.

Dill, Bonnie Thornton. 1980. " 'The Means to Put My Children Through': Childrearing Goals and Strategies among Black Female Domestic Servants." In *The Black Woman,* edited by LaFrances Rodgers-Rose. Beverly Hills, CA: Sage.

Dixon, Travis, Y. Zhang, and K. Conrad. 2009. *Group Processes and Intergroup Relations* 12 (2):345–60.

Donohue, John, III, and Steven D. Levitt. 2001. "The Impact of Legalized Abortion on Crime." *Quarterly Journal of Economics* 116 (2): 379–420.

Drake, St. Clair, and Horace R. Cayton. 1945. *Black Metropolis: A Study of Negro Life in a Northern City.* New York: Harcourt, Brace.

Drucker, Ernest. 2013. "Drug Law, Mass Incarceration and Public Health." *Oregon Law Review* 91: 1097–1128.

Drum, Kevin. 2013. "America's Real Criminal Element: Lead." *Mother Jones* Jan-Feb.

Du Bois, W. E. B. 1899. *The Philadelphia Negro: A Social Study.* Philadelphia: University of Philadelphia Press.

Duneier, Mitchell. 1992. *Slim's Table: Race, Respectability, & Masculinity.* Chicago: University of Chicago Press.

———. 1999. *Sidewalk.* New York: Farrar, Straus and Giroux.

Dyson, Michael. 2004. "The Culture of Hip-Hop." In *That's the Joint: The Hip-Hop Studies Reader,* edited by Forman and Neal, 61–68.

East Harlem Juvenile Gang Task Force. 2011. *2011 Strategic Plan.* New York: Harlem Community Justice Center.

Edelman, Peter, Harry Holzer, and Paul Offner. 2006. *Reconnecting Disadvantaged Young Men.* Washington, DC: Urban Institute Press.

Edin, Kathryn, and Maria Kefalas. 2005. *Promises I Can Keep: Why Poor Women Put Motherhood Before Marriage.* Berkeley: University of California Press.

Ellison, Ralph. 1967. "A Very Stern Discipline: An Interview with Ralph Ellison." *Harper's Magazine* March.

Engerman, Stanley, Richard Sutch, and Gavin Wright. 2004. "Slavery." In *Historical Statistics of the United States,* Millennial Edition, edited by Susan B. Carter, Scott Gartner, Michael Haines, et al. New York: Cambridge University Press.

Ferguson, Ann Arnett. 2000. *Bad Boys: Public Schools in the Making of Black Masculinity.* Ann Arbor: University of Michigan Press.

Fischer, Claude S. 2008. "Paradoxes of American Individualism." *Sociological Forum* 23 (2): 363–372.

Floyd, Samuel A., Jr. 1995. *The Power of Black Music: Interpreting Its History from Africa to the United States.* New York: Oxford University Press.

Ford, Kahlil R. 2009. "Making Meaning of the Messages: Transmission and Reception of Racial Socialization among African American Dyads." PhD diss., University of Michigan.

Forman, Murray. 2003. *The 'Hood Comes First: Race, Space, and Place in Rap and Hip-Hop.* Middletown, CT: Wesleyan University Press.

Forman, Murray, and Mark Anthony Neal. 2004. *That's the Joint: The Hip-Hop Studies Reader.* New York: Routledge.

Frank, Robert H., and Philip J. Cook. 1995. *The Winner-Take-All Society.* New York: Free Press.

Frazier, E. Franklin. 1940. *Negro Youth at the Crossways.* Washington, DC: American Council of Education.

———. 1948. *The Negro Family in the United States.* Chicago: University of Chicago Press.

Freccero, Carla. 1999. *Popular Culture: An Introduction.* New York: New York University Press.

Frederick, Marla. 2003. *Between Sundays: Black women and everyday struggles of faith.* Berkeley: University of California Press.

Furstenberg, Frank, Jr. 1993. "How Families Manage Risk and Opportunity in Dangerous Neighborhoods." In *Sociology and the Public Agenda,* edited by William Julius Wilson, 231–58. New York: Sage.

———. 2000. "The Sociology of Adolescence and Youth in the 1990s: A Critical Commentary." *Journal of Marriage and the Family* 62: 896–910.

Furstenberg, Frank, Jr., Thomas Cook, Jacquelynne Eccles, Glen Elder Jr., and Arnold Sameroff. 1999. *Managing to Make It: Urban Families and Adolescent Success.* Chicago: University of Chicago Press.

Gan, Su-lin, D. Zillman, and M. Mitrook. 1997. "Stereotyping Effect of Black Women's Sexual Rap on White Audiences." *Basic and Applied Social Psychology* 19 (3): 381–99.

Gans, Herbert. 1988. *Middle American Individualism.* New York: Oxford University Press.

Garfinkel, Harold. 1967. *Studies in Ethnomethodology.* New York: Prentice Hall.

Gennetian, Lisa, L. Sanbonmatsu, L. Katz, J. Kling, M. Sciandra, J. Ludwig, G. Duncan, and R. Kessler. 2012. "The Long-Term Effects of Moving to Opportunity on Youth Outcomes." *Cityscape* 14 (2): 137–67.

George, Nelson. 1998. *Hip Hop America.* New York: Viking Penguin.

George, Nelson. 2004. "Hip-Hop's Founding Fathers Speak the Truth" In *That's the Joint: The Hip-Hop Studies Reader,* edited by Murray Forman and Mark Anthony Neal, 45–60. New York: Routledge.

Gephart, Martha A. 1997. "Neighborhood and Communities as Contexts for Development." In *Neighborhood Poverty: Vol. 1,* edited by Jeanne Brooks-Gunn, Greg Duncan, J. Lawrence Aber. New York: Russell Sage.

Giroux, Henry A. 1998. "Teenage Sexuality, Body Politics, and the Pedagogy of Display." In *Youth Culture: Identity in a Post-Modern World,* edited by Jonathon S. Epstein, 24–55. Malden, MA: Blackwell Publishing.

Goffman, Erving. 1972. *Relations in Public.* New York: Harper and Row.

Green, Gary P., Leann M. Tiggs, and Daniel Diaz. 1999. "Racial and Ethnic Differences in Job-Search Strategies in Atlanta, Boston, and Los Angeles." *Social Science Quarterly* 89 (2): 263–78.

Guillermo-Gil, Rebollo, and Amanda Moras. 2012. "Black Women and Black Men in Hip-Hop Music: Misogyny, Violence and the Negotiation of (White-Owned) Space." *Journal of Popular Culture* 45 (1): 118–132.

Gunn, Raymond. 2008. "David's Story: From Promise to Despair." In *Against the Wall,* edited by Elijah Anderson, 28–37.

Hagan, John, and Holly Foster. 2001. "Youth Violence and the End of Adolescence." *American Sociological Review* 66: 874–99.

Hannerz, Ulf. 1969. *Soulside: Inquiries into Ghetto Culture and Community.* New York: Columbia University Press.

Hansen, C. H. 1995. "Predicting Cognitive and Behavioral Effects of Gangsta Rap." *Basic and Applied Social Psychology* 16 (1–2): 43–52.

Harding, David J. 2010. *Living the Drama: Community Conflict and Culture among Inner-City Boys.* Chicago: University of Chicago Press.

Harris, Angel L. 2011. *Kids Don't Want to Fail: Oppositional Culture and the Black-White Achievement Gap.* Cambridge, MA: Harvard University Press.

Harvard School of Pubic Health. 2013. "Television Watching and 'Sit Time' Online." Accessed April 22, 2013.

Hassett-Walker, Connie. 2010. "Delinquency and the Black Middle Class: An Exploratory Study." *Journal of Ethnicity in Criminal Justice* 8 (4): 266–89.

Hebdige, Dick. 1990. *Cut 'n' Mix: Culture, Identity and Caribbean Music.* New York: Routledge.

Hirsch, E. D., Jr. 1987. *Cultural Literacy: What Every American Needs to Know.* Boston: Houghton Mifflin.

———. 2006. *The Knowledge Deficit.* Boston: Houghton Mifflin.

Hoberman, John. 1997. *Darwin's Athletes: How Sport Has Damaged Black America and Preserved the Myth of Race.* Boston: Houghton Mifflin Co.

Hofstadter, Richard. 1966. *Anti-Intellectualism in American Life.* New York: Vintage.

Holloway, Susan D., B. Fuller, M. F. Rambaud, and C. Eggers-Pierola. 1997. *Through My Own Eyes: Single Mothers and the Cultures of Poverty.* Cambridge, MA: Harvard University Press.

Holzer, Harry. 1996. *What Employers Want: Job Prospects for Less-Educated Workers.* New York: Russell Sage Foundation.

Huesmann, L. R., J. Moise-Titus, C. Podolski, and L. D. Eron. 2003. "Early Exposure to TV Violence Predicts Aggression in Adulthood." *Developmental Psychology* 39: 201–22.

Iton, Richard. 2008. *In Search of the Black Fantastic: Politics and Popular Culture in the Post-Civil Rights Era*. New York: Oxford University Press.

Jacobs, Bruce, and Richard Wright. 2006. *Street Justice: Retaliation in the Criminal Underground*. New York: Cambridge University Press.

Jaynes, Gerald. 2008. "The Effects of Immigration on the Economic Position of Young Black Males." In *Against the Wall: Poor, Young, Black and Male*, edited by Elijah Anderson, 87–101.

Jeynes, William H. 2005. "The Effects of Parental Involvement in the Academic Achievement of African American Youth." *Journal of Negro Education* 74 (3): 260–74.

Johnson, Jeffrey, Patricia Cohen, Elizabeth M. Smailes, Stephanie Kase, and Judith Brook. 2002. "Television Viewing and Aggressive Behavior during Adolescence and Adulthood." *Science* 295: 2468–71.

Johnson, J. D., L. A. Jackson, and L. Gatto. 1995. "Violent Attitudes and Deferred Academic Aspirations: Deleterious Effects of Exposure to Rap Music." *Basic and Applied Social Psychology* 16(1–2): 27–41.

Kasinitz, Philip, J. H. Mollenkopf, M. C. Waters, and J. Holdaway. 2008. *Inheriting the City: The Children of Immigrants Come of Age*. Cambridge, MA: Harvard University Press.

Kaufman, Peter. 2005. "Middle-Class Social Reproduction: The Activation and Negotiation of Structural Advantages." *Sociological Forum* 20 (2): 245–72.

Kearney, Melissa S., and Phillip B. Levine. 2014. "Media Influences on Social Outcomes: The Impact of MTV's *16 and Pregnant* on Teen Childbearing." Working Paper 19795, 1–43. Cambridge, MA: National Bureau of Economic Research.

Kelley, Robin D. G. 1994. *Race Rebels: Culture, Politics, and the Black Working Class*. New York: Free Press.

Kitwana, Bakari. 2002. *The Hip-Hop Generation*. New York: Basic/Civitas.

———. (2005). *Why White Kids Love Hip-Hop: Wankstas, Wiggers, Wannabes, and the New Reality of Race in America*. New York: Basic Civitas.

Kmec, Julie, and Frank Furstenberg, Jr. 2002. "Racial and Gender Differences in the Transition to Adulthood: A Longitudinal Study of Philadelphia Youth." In *New Frontiers in Socialization*, vol. 7, edited by Richard A. Settersten, Jr. and Timothy J. Owens, 435–70. Amsterdam: JAI.

Kornblum, William, and Terry Williams., 1998. *Growing Up Poor*. Lexington, MA: Lexington Books.

Kotlowitz, Alex. 1992. *There Are No Children Here*. New York: Anchor.

Kubrin, Charles E. 2005. "Gangstas, Thugs and Hustlas: Identity and the Code of the Street in Rap Music." *Social Problems* 52 (3): 360–78.

LaFree, Gary, Eric Bauner, and Robert O'Brien. 2010. "Still Separate and Unequal? A City-Level Analysis of the Black-White Gap in Homicide Arrest Since 1960." *American Sociological Review* 75 (1):75–100.

Lacey, Karyn. 2007. *Blue-Chip Black: Race, Class, and Status in the New Black Middle Class.* Berkeley: University of California Press.

Lane, Roger. 1986. *Roots of Violence in Back Philadelphia, 1860–1900.* Cambridge, MA: Harvard University Press.

Lareau, Annette. 2003. *Unequal Childhood.* Berkeley: University of California Press.

Lena, Jennifer C. 2006. "Social Context and Musical Content of Rap Music, 1979–1995." *Social Forces* 85 (1): 479–95.

Levine, Lawrence. 1977. *Black Culture and Black Consciousness.* New York: Oxford University Press.

Lhamon, W. T., Jr. 1988. *Raising Cain: Blackface Performance from Jim Crow to Hip-Hop.* Cambridge: Harvard University Press.

Logan, John R. 2011. "Separate and Unequal: The Neighborhood Gap for Blacks, Hispanics and Asians in Metropolitan America." Accessed, 6/10/2013 http://www.s4.brown.edu/us2010/Data/Report/report0727.pdf.

Lopez, Mark and D'Vera Cohn. 2011. *Hispanic Poverty Rate Highest in New Supplemental Census Measure.* Washington, DC: Pew Research Hispanic Trends Project Hispanic Poverty.

Lott, Bernice. 2002. "Cognitive and Behavioral Distancing from the Poor." *American Psychologist* 57 (2): 100–10.

Lott, Eric. 1993. *Love and Theft: Blackface Minstrelsy and the American Working Class.* New York: Oxford University Press.

Lyman, Stanford, and Marvin Scott. 1967. "Territoriality: A Neglected Sociological Dimension." *Social Problems* 15 (2): 236–49.

Lynch, Michael. 2012. "Revisiting the Cultural Dope." *Human Studies* 35: 223–33.

MacLeod, Jay. 1995. *Ain't No Makin' It: Aspirations and Attainment in a Low-Income Neighborhood.* Boulder: Westview Press.

Majors, Richard and Janet M. Billson. 1992. *Cool Pose: The Dilemmas of Black Manhood in America.* New York: Lexington Books.

Marcus, D. K., Fulton, J. J., and Clarke, E. J. 2010. "Lead and Conduct Problems: A Meta-Analysis." *Journal of Clinical Child and Adolescent Psychology,* 39: 234–241.

Marshall, Wayne G. 2007. *Routes, Rap, Reggae: Hearing the Histories of Hip-Hop and Reggae Together.* PhD diss., Dept. of Music/Ethnomethodology, University of Wisconsin–Madison.

Martinez, Theresa. 1997. "Popular Culture as Oppositional Culture: Rap as Resistance." *Sociological Perspectives* 40: 265–86.

Mauer, Marc. 2013. "The Changing Racial Dynamics of Women's Incarceration." Washington, DC: The Sentencing Project. Accessed http://sentencingproject.org/doc/publications/rd_Changing%20Racial%20Dynamics%202013.pdf.

May, Reuben A. 2008. *Living Through the Hoop: High School Basketball, Race, and the American Dream*. New York: New York University Press.

Mayer, Susan E., and Christopher Jencks. 1989. "Growing Up in Poor Neighborhoods: How Much Does it Matter?" *Science* 243 (4897): 1441–1445

Mayer, Susan E. 1997. *What Money Can't Buy: Family Income and Children's Life Chances*. Cambridge, MA: Harvard University Press.

MC Hammer. (1990) "Here Comes the Hammer" (Music Video) Uploaded on youtube, Nov. 8, 2013.

McCall, Nathan. 1994. *Makes Me Wanna Holler*. New York: Random House.

McCord, William, J. Howard, B. Friedberg, and E. Harwood. 1969. *Life Styles in the Black Ghetto*. New York: Norton.

McLanahan, Sara. 1997. *Growing Up with a Single Parent: What Hurts, What Helps*. Cambridge, MA: Harvard University Press.

McRoberts, Omar. 2005. *Streets of Glory: Church and Community in a Black Urban Neighborhood*. Chicago: University of Chicago Press.

Measure of America. 2011. *One in Seven: Ranking Youth Disconnection in the 25 Largest Metro Areas*. New York: Social Science Research Council.

Mickelson, Roslyn. 1990. "The Attitude-Achievement Paradox among Black Adolescents." *Sociology of Education* 63 (1): 44–61.

Mielke, Howard W., and Sammy Zahran (2012). "The urban rise and fall of air lead(Pb) and the latent surge and retreat of societal violence," *Environmental Inernational* 43: 48–55.

Miller, Jody. 2008. *Getting Played: African American Girls, Urban Inequality, and Gendered Violence*. New York: New York University Press.

Moskos, Peter. 2008. *Cop In the Hood*. Princeton, NJ: Princeton University Press.

National College Athletic Association. 2012. "Estimated Probability of Competing in Athletics beyond the High School Interscholastic Level." Modified September, 17, 2012, accessed April 22, 2013, http://www.ncaa.org/sites/default/files/Probability-of-going-pro-methodology_Update20123_0.pdf.

National Scientific Council on the Developing Child. 2004a. *Young Children Develop in an Environment of Relationships*: Working Paper No.1. Retrieved from www.developingchild.harvard.edu

———. 2004b. *Children's Emotional Development is Built into the Architecture of Their Brains*: Working Paper No.2. Retrieved from www.developingchild.harvard.edu

———. (2006). Early Exposure to Toxic Substances Damages Brain Architecture: Working Paper No.4. Retrieved from www.developingchild.harvard.edu

———. (2008/2012). Establishing a Level Foundation for Life: Mental Health Begins in Early Childhood: Working Paper No. 6. Updated Edition. http://www.developingchild.harvard.edu

———. (2010a). Persistent Fear and Anxiety Can Affect Young Children's Learning and Development: Working Paper No.9. Retrieved from www .developingchild.harvard.edu

———. (2010b). Early Experiences Can Affect Gene Expression and Affect Long-Term Development: Working Paper No.10. Retrieved from www .developingchild.harvard.edu

Neal, Mark Anthony. 1999. *What the Music Said*. New York: Routledge.

Needleman, H., A. Schell, D. Bellinger, A. Leviton, and E. Allred. 1990. "The Long-Term Effects of Exposure to Low Doses of Lead in Childhood: An 11-Year Follow-up Report." *New England Journal of Medicine* 322 (2): 83–88.

Nevin, R. 2000. "How Lead Exposure Relates to Temporal Changes in IQ, Violent Crime, and Unwed Pregnancy." *Environmental Research* 83 (1): 1–22.

Newman, Katherine. 2000. *No Shame in My Game: The Working Poor in the Inner City*. New York: Vintage.

Nielsen. 2011. "State of the Media: U.S. TV Trends by Ethnicity." Accessed 2/3/2013, http://nielsen.com/us/en/insights/reports/2011/tv-trends-by-ethnicity.html.

Nielsen. 2012. "African American Consumers: Still Vital, Still Growing 2012 Report." Accessed 2/3/2013, http://nielsen.com/us/en/insights/reports/ 2012/african-american-consumers-still-vital-growing–2012-report.html

Nietzsche, Friedrich. 1954. *The Portable Nietzsche*. Translated and introduced by Walter Kaufmann. New York: Penguin Books.

———. 2008. *The Birth of Tragedy*. Translated by Douglas Smith. New York: Oxford University Press.

Nightingale, Carl. H. 1993. *On the Edge: A History of Poor Black Children and Their American Dreams*. New York: Basic Books.

O'Conner, Carla. 1997. "Disposition toward (Collective) Struggle and Educational Resilience in the Inner City: A Case Analysis of Six African American High School Students." *American Educational Research Journal* 34 (Winter): 593–629.

Ogbar, Jeffrey O. G. 2007. *Hip-Hop Revolution: The Culture and Politics of Rap*. Lawrence: The University of Kansas Press.

Ogbu, J. U. 1993. "Differences in Cultural Frame of Reference: International Roots of Minority Child Development" [Special issue]. *International Journal of Behavioral Development* 16: 483–506.

Oyserman, Daphna, M. Kemmelmeir, S. Frybero, H. Brosh, and T. Hart-Johnson. 2003. "Racial-Ethnic Self Schemas." *Social Psychology Quarterly* 66 (4): 333–48.

Pager, Devah. 2008. "Blacklisted: Hiring Discrimination in an Era of Mass Incarceration." In *Against the Wall*, edited by Elijah Anderson, 71–86.

Parker, Holt N. 2011. "Toward a Definition of Popular Culture." *History and Theory* 50: 147–70.

Patterson, Orlando. 1972. "Toward a Future That Has No Past: On the Fate of Blacks in the Americas." *The Public Interest* (Spring) 27: 25–62.

———. 1991. *Freedom in the Making of Western Culture*. New York: Basic Books.

Patterson, Orlando. 1997. *The Ordeal of Integration*. New York: Basic Civitas.

———. 1998a "Broken Bloodlines: Gender Relations and the Crisis of Marriages and Families Among Afro-Americans." In Orlando Patterson, *Rituals of Blood*, 1–168. New York: Basic/Civitas.

———. 1998b "American Dionysus: Images of Afro-American Men at the Dawn of the Twenty-First Century," in *Rituals of Blood*, 233–289. New York: Basic/Civitas.

———. 2008. "Black Americans." In *Understanding America*, edited by Peter Schuck and J. Q. Wilson. New York: Public Affairs.

Pattillo-McCoy, Mary. 1999. *Black Picket Fences: Privilege and Peril among the Black Middle Class*. Chicago: University of Chicago Press, 2000.

Pattillo-McCoy, Mary. 1998. "Church Culture as a Strategy of Action in the Black Community." *American Sociological Review* 63 (6): 767–84.

Patton, Erin O. 2009. *Under the Influence: Tracing the Hip-Hop Generation's Impact on Brands, Sports, and Pop Culture*. Ithaca, NY: Paramount Marketing Publishing, Inc.

Pendal, Rolf, E. Davies, L. Freiman, and R. Pitingolo. 2011. *Neighborhood Poverty and the Urban Crisis of the 2000s*. Washington, DC: Joint Center for Political and Economic Studies.

F. Perera, V. A. Rauh, W. Y. Tsai, P. Kinney, D. Camann, D. Barr, T. Bernert, R. Garfinkel, Y. H. Tu, D. Diaz, J. Dietrich, and R. M. Whyatt. 2003. "Effects of Transplacental Exposure to Environmental Pollutants on Birth Outcomes in a Multiethnic Population." *Environmental Health Perspectives* 111 (2): 201–05.

Perkins, William E. 1996. *Droppin' Science: Critical Essays on Rap Music and Hip Hop Culture*. Philadelphia: Temple University Press.

Perry, Imani. 2004. *Prophets of the Hood: Politics and Poetics in Hip-Hop*. Durham, NC: Duke University Press.

Peterson, Richard A., and Roger M. Kern. 1996. "Changing Highbrow Taste: From Snob to Omnivore." *American Sociological Review* 61 (5): 900–07.

Pew Forum on Religion and Public Life. 2010a. *A Religious Portrait of African Americans*. Washington, DC.: Pew Research Center.

———. 2010b. *Religion among the Millennials*. Washington, DC.: Pew Research Center.

Phillips, M., J. Brooks-Gunn, G. J. Duncan, P. Klebanov, and J. Crane. 1998. "Family Background, Parenting Practices, and the Black-White Test Score

Gap." In *The Black-WhiteTest Score Gap,* edited by Christopher Jencks and M. Phillips, 102–45. Washington, DC.: Brookings Institution Press.

Pinker, Steven. 2007. *The Stuff of Thought: Language as a Window into Human Nature.* New York: Viking.

Polanyi, Michael. 1958. *Personal Knowledge: Towards a Post-Critical Philosophy.* Chicago: University of Chicago Press.

Pryde, Kitty. 2013. "My Thoughts on This Whole Danny Brown Oral Sex Thing." *Noisey/Vice* (blog). http://noisey.vice.com/blog/my-thoughts-on-this-whole -danny-brown-oral-sex-thing.

Quyen, Q. Tiet, David Huizinga, and Hilary Byrnes. 2010. "Predictors of Resilience among Inner City Youths." *Journal of Child and Family Studies,* 19: 316–78.

Rainwater, Lee. 1970. *Behind Ghetto Walls.* Chicago: Aldine.

Raley, R. Kelly, and Larry Bumpass. 2003. "The Topography of the Divorce Plateau: Levels and Trends in Union Stability in the United States after 1980." *Demographic Research,* 8: 245–60.

Rankin, Bruce H., and James M. Quane. 2002. "Social Context and Urban Adolescent Outcomes: The Interrelated Effects of Neighborhoods, Families, and Peers on African-American Youth." *Social Problems* 49 (1): 79–100.

Reyes, Jessica (2007). "Environmental Policy as Social Policy? The Impact of Childhood Lead Exposure on Crime." Cambridge, MA: NBER Working Paper No.13097.

Rich, Motoko, and John Hurdle. "Rational Decisions and Heartbreak on School Closings." *New York Times,* March 08, 2013, Education Section. www.nytimes.com/3013/03/09/rational-decisions-and-heartbreak-on -school-closings.html

Riley, Alexander. 2005. "The Rebirth of Tragedy out of the Spirit of Hip Hop: A Cultural Sociology of Gangsta Rap Music." *Journal of Youth Studies* 8 (3): 297–311.

Risley, Todd R., and Betty Hart. 1995. *Meaningful Differences in the Everyday Experience of Young American Children.* Baltimore, MD: Paul H. Brookes Publishing.

Rebollo-Gil Guillermo, and Amanda Moras. 2012. "Black Women and Black Men in Hip Hop Music: Misogyny, Violence and the Negotiation of (White-Owned) Space." *Journal of Popular Culture.* 45.1: 118–132.

Rodman, Hyman. 1963. "The Lower-Class Value Stretch." *Social Forces* 42: 205–15.

Rokeach, M. 1973. *The Nature of Human Values.* New York: Free Press.

Rose, Tricia. 1994. *Black Noise: Rap Music and Black Culture in Contemporary America.* Hanover: Wesleyan University Press.

———. 2008. *The Hip-Hop Wars: What We Talk About When We Talk About Hip-Hop—And Why It Matters.* New York: Basic Books.

Ruggles, Steven, and Catherine Fitch. n.d. "Trends in African-American Marriage Patterns." Minnesota Population Center, http://www.hist.umn.edu/~ruggles/black_marriage.ppt.

Rule, S. "Generation Rap." *The New York Times,* April 3, 1994, section 6, 41–45.

Salganik, M. J., and Watts, D. J. 2009. "Social Influence: The Puzzling Nature of Success in Cultural Markets." In *The Oxford Handbook of Analytical Sociology,* edited by Peter Hedstrom and Peter Bearman, 315–341. Oxford: Oxford University Press.

Sampson, Robert. 2013. *Great American City: Chicago and the Enduring Neighborhood Effect.* Chicago: University of Chicago Press.

Sampson, Robert, Jeffrey Morenoff, and Felton Earls. 1999. "Beyond Social Capital: Spatial Dynamics of Collective Efficacy for Children." *American Sociological Review* 64: 633–60.

Sampson, Robert, Jeffrey Morenoff, Stephen Raudenbush. 2005. "Social Anatomy of Racial and Ethnic Differences in Violence." *American Journal of Public Health* 95: 224–32.

Sampson, Robert, Stephen Raudenbush, and Felton Earls. 1997. "Neighborhoods and Violent Crime: A Multilevel Study of Collective Efficacy." *Science* 277: 918–24.

Sampson, Robert, Patrick Sharkey, and Stephen Raudenbush. 2008. "Durable Effects of Concentrated Disadvantage on Verbal Ability among African-American Children." *Proceedings of the American National Academy of Sciences* 105: 845–52.

Samuels, David. 2004. "The Rap on Rap: The 'Black Music' That Isn't Either." In Forman and Neal 2004, 147–53.

Sanchez-Jankowski, Martin. 2008. *Cracks in the Pavement: Social Change and Resilience in Poor Neighborhoods.* Berkeley: University of California Press.

Schwartz, Gretchen. 1987. "A Good Idea Gone Wrong." *Educational Leadership* 45 (4): 77.

Sharkey, Patrick. 2012. *Neighborhoods and the Black White Mobility Gap.* Washington, DC: Pew Foundation.

———. 2013. *Stuck in Place: Urban Neighborhoods and the End of Progress Toward Racial Equality.* Chicago: University of Chicago Press.

Sharpley-Whiting, and T. Denean. 2007. *Pimps Up, Ho's Down.* New York: New York University Press.

Simons, Ronald, Leslie Simons, Man K. Lei, and Antoinette M. Landor. 2013. "Relational Schemas, Hostile Romantic Relationships, and Beliefs about Marriage among Young African American Adults." *Journal of Social and Personal Relationships* 29 (1): 77–101.

Smith, R. Drew. 2001. "Churches and the Urban Poor: Interaction and Social Distance." *Sociology of Religion* 62 (3): 301–13.

Smith, Saundra S. 2005. "'Don't Put My Name on It': Social Capital Activation and Job-Finding Assistance among Black Urban Poor." *American Journal of Sociology* 111 (1): 1–57.

Squire, James R. 1987. "Basic Skills Are Not Enough." *Educational Leadership* 45: 76–77.

Staples, Robert. 1982. *Black Masculinity: The Black Male's Role in American Society.* San Francisco, Black Scholar Press.

Steinberg, Laurence, Susie Lamborn, Sanford Dornbusch, and Nancy Darling. 1992. "Impact of Parenting Practices on Adolescent Achievement: Authoritative Parenting, School Involvement, and Encouragement to Succeed." *Child Development* 63: 1266–81.

Storey, John. 2006. *Cultural Theory and Popular Culture.* Athens: University of Georgia Press.

A Study of Gender Differences, Culture, and Academic Performance among Black Youth in an Integrated, Middle Class, Suburban High School Located in the Northeastern U.S. Cambridge, MA: Department of Sociology, Harvard University.

Thompson, Franklin, and W. P. Austin. 2003. "Television Viewing and Academic Achievement Revisited." *Education* 24 (1): 194–202.

Toll, Robert C. 1974. *Blacking Up: The Minstrel Show in Nineteenth Century America.* New York: Oxford University Press.

Townsend, Tiffany G. 2008. "Protecting Our Daughters: Intersection of Race, Class, and Gender in African American Mothers' Socialization of Their Daughters' Heterosexuality." *Sex Roles* 59: 429–42.

Turnage, B. F. (2004) "African American Mother-Daughter Relationships Mediating Daughter's Self-Esteem. *Child and Adolescent Social Work Journal* 22 (2): 155–173.

Turney, Kristin, Rebecca Kissane, and Kathryn Edin. 2012. "After Moving to Opportunity: How Moving to a Low-Poverty Neighborhood Improves Mental Health among African American Women." *Society and Mental Health* 3 (1): 1–21.

Tyson, Karolyn. 2011. *Integration Interrupted: Tracking, Black Students and Acting White after Brown.* New York: Oxford University Press.

U.S. Census Bureau. 2011. "Age and Sex Composition in the United States, 2011: Blacks Alone." Accessed 03/05/2012., http://www.census.gov/population/age/data/2011comp.html.

Useem, Bert, and Anne M. Piehl. 2008. *Prison State: The Challenge of Mass Incarceration.* New York: Cambridge University Press.

Venkatesh, Sudhir. 2000. *American Project: The Rise and Fall of a Modern Ghetto.* Cambridge, MA: Harvard University Press.

———. 2006. *Off the Books: The Underground Economy of the Urban Poor.* Cambridge, MA: Harvard University Press.

Verba, Sidney, and Gary Orren. 1985. *Equality in America: A View from the Top.* Cambridge, MA: Harvard University Press.

Wacquant, Loïc. 2001. "Deadly Symbiosis: When Ghetto and Prison Mesh." *Punishment and Society* 3 (1): 95–133.

———. 2004. *Body & Soul: Notebooks of an Apprentice Boxer.* New York: Oxford University Press.

———. 2008. *Urban Outcasts: A Comparative Sociology of Advanced Marginality.* Cambridge, MA: Polity.

Waldinger, Roger. 1996. *Still the Promised City? African-Americans and New Immigrants in Post-Industrial New York.* Cambridge, MA: Harvard University Press.

Washington, Julie A. 2001. "Early Literacy Skills in African-American Children: Research Considerations." *Learning Disabilities Research and Practice* 16 (4), 213–21.

Watkins, S. Craig. 2005. *Hip-Hop Matters: Politics, Pop Culture, and the Struggle for the Soul of a Movement.* Boston: Beacon Press.

Wernette, D. R., and L. A. Nieves. 1992. "Breathing Polluted Air: Minorities Are Disproportionately Exposed." *EPA Journal* 18: 16–17.

West, Cornel. 1982. *Prophesy Deliverance! An Afro-American Revolutionary Christianity.* Philadelphia: Westminster.

Western, Bruce, and Christopher Muller. 2013. "Mass Incarceration, Macrosociology, and the Poor." *The Annals of the American Academy of Political and Social Sciences* 647: 166–89.

Western, Bruce, and Becky Pettit. 2010. *Collateral Costs: Incarceration's Effects on Economic Mobility.* Washington, DC: Pew Charitable Trust.

White, Harrison. 1992. *Identity and Control.* Princeton, NJ: Princeton University Press.

Wilkinson, Deanna L. 2003. *Guns, Violence and Identity among African American and Latino Youth.* New York: LFB Scholarly Publishing.

Willis, Paul. 1977. *Learning to Labor: How Working Class Kids Get Working Class Jobs.* New York: Columbia University Press.

Willis, Paul. 1990. *Common Culture.* Milton Keynes, U.K.: Open University Press.

Wilson, William Julius. 1987. *The Truly Disadvantaged.* Chicago: University of Chicago Press.

———. 1997. *When Work Disappears: The World of the New Urban Poor.* New York: Knopf.

———. 2009. *More Than Just Race: Being Black and Poor in the Inner City.* New York: Norton.

Wingood, Gina, R. DiClemente, J. Bernhardt, K. Harrington, S. Davies, A. Robillard, and E. Hook III. 2003. "A Prospective Study of Exposure to Rap Music Videos and African American Female Adolescents' Health." *American Journal of Public Health* 93 (3): 437–39.

Wright, John Paul, Danielle Boisvert, and Jamie Vaske. 2009. "Blood Lead Levels in Early Childhood Predict Adulthood Psychopathy," *Youth Violence and Juvenile Justice* 7: 2008–222.

XXL Staff. 2010. "Is Jail Ever a Good Thing? Street Cred or Incredibly Wrong." Accessed 06/21/2012, http://www.xxlmag.com/news/bloggers/2010/10/is-jail-ever-a-good-thing-street-cred-or-incredibly-wrong.

Young, Alford A., Jr. 2004. *The Minds of Marginalized Black Men.* Chicago: University of Chicago Press.

Zillmann, D., C. F. Aust, Kathleen D. Hoffman, Curtis Love, V. L. Ordman, J. T. Pope, P. D. Seigler, & R. J. Gibson. 1995. "Radical Rap: Does It Further Ethnic Division?" *Basic and Applied Social Psychology* 16: 1–25.

3. The Values and Beliefs of Disconnected Black Youth

Ajzen, I. 2001. "Nature and Operation of Attitudes." *Annual Review of Psychology* 52 (1): 27–58.

Anderson, John A. 1984. "Regression and Ordered Categorical Variables." *Journal of the Royal Statistical Society. Series B (Methodological)*: 1–30.

Belfield, Clive, and H. Levin. 2007. *The Price We Pay: Economic and Social Consequences of Inadequate Education.* Washington, DC: Brookings Institution Press.

Belfield, Clive R., Henry M. Levin, and Rachel Rosen. 2012. *The Economic Value of Opportunity Youth.* Washington, DC: Corporation for National and Community Service.

Bell, Daniel. 1965. "The Disjunction of Culture and Social Structure: Some Notes on the Meaning of Social Reality." *Daedalus* 94 (1): 208–22.

Besharov, Douglas J. 1999. *America's Disconnected Youth: Toward a Preventive Strategy.* ERIC. Retrieved December 21, 2013, http://www.eric.ed.gov.ezp-prod1.hul.harvard.edu/ERICWebPortal/recordDetail?accno=ED443988.

Besharov, Douglas J., Child Welfare League of America, and American Enterprise Institute for Public Policy Research. 1999. *America's Disconnected Youth: Toward a Preventive Strategy.* Washington, DC: CWLA Press: American Enterprise Institute for Public Policy Research.

Besharov, Douglas J., and Karen N. Gardiner. 1998. "Preventing Youthful Disconnectedness." *Children and Youth Services Review* 20 (9): 797–818.

Borofsky, Robert, Fredrik Barth, Richard A. Shweder, Lars Rodseth, and Nomi Maya Stolzenberg. 2001. "When: A Conversation about Culture." *American Anthropologist* 103 (2): 432–46.

Bridgeland, John, and Tess Mason-Elder. 2012. "National Roadmap for Opportunity Youth." Retrieved January 7, 2014, http://www.civicenterprises.net/MediaLibrary/Docs/Opportunity%20Youth%20National%20Roadmap%20Final%202012.pdf.

Bridgeland, John M., and Jessica A. Milano. 2012. "Opportunity Road: The Promise and Challenge of America's Forgotten Youth." Retrieved January 8, 2014, http://www.vamentoring.org/images/uploads/resources/Opportunity_Road_2012.pdf.

Burd-Sharps, Sarah, and Kristen Lewis. "One in Seven: Ranking Youth Disconnection in the 25 Largest Metro Areas," 2013. http://www.voced.edu.au/content/ngv62538.

Carr, Patrick J. 2001. "The Dignity of Working Men: Morality and the Boundaries of Race, Class and Immigration by Michele Lamont." *American Journal of Sociology* 107 (2): 503–5.

Carter, Prudence L. 2003. "Black Cultural Capital, Status Positioning, and Schooling Conflicts for Low-Income African American Youth." *Social Problems* 50 (1): 136–55.

Cherry, R. 1995. "The Culture-of-Poverty Thesis and African Americans: The Work of Gunnar Myrdal and Other Institutionalists." *Journal of Economic Issues* 29 (4): 1119–32.

Coward, Barbara E., Joe R. Feagin, and J. Allen Williams. 1974. "The Culture of Poverty Debate: Some Additional Data." *Social Problems* 21 (5): 621–34.

D'Andrade, R. G. 1981. "The Cultural Part of Cognition." *Cognitive Science* 5 (3): 179–95.

Eckholm, Erik. 2006. "Plight Deepens for Black Men, Studies Warn." *The New York Times,* March 20. Retrieved September 2, 2011, http://www.nytimes.com/2006/03/20/national/20blackmen.html.

Edelman, Peter B., Harry J. Holzer, and Paul Offner. 2006. *Reconnecting Disadvantaged Young Men*. The Urban Insitute. Retrieved December 21, 2013, http://books.google.com.ezp-prod1.hul.harvard.edu/books?hl=en&lr=&id=cs6vtSJSfzUC&oi=fnd&pg=PR9&ots=i4CmFRmbEf&sig=n90PmU9PLm0KgqH3R1qxlfHDp4E.

Eisenstadt, S. N. 1986. "Culture and Social Structure Revisited." *International Sociology* 1 (3): 297–320.

Elliott, Delbert S., David Huizinga, and Scott Menard. 1989. "Multiple Problem Youth: Delinquency, Substance Use, and Mental Health Problems." Paper presented at a research conference held in conjunction with the Alcohol, Drug Abuse, Mental Health Administration and the Office of Juvenile Justice and Delinquency Prevention in April 1984. Retrieved December 21, 2013, http://doi.apa.org.ezp-prod1.hul.harvard.edu/psycinfo/1989-98128-000.

Hagan, J., C. Shedd, and M. R. Payne. 2005. "Race, Ethnicity, and Youth Perceptions of Criminal Injustice." *American Sociological Review* 70 (3): 381–407.

Jordan, Will J., and Robert Cooper. 2003. "High School Reform and Black Male Students Limits and Possibilities of Policy and Practice." *Urban Education* 38 (2): 196–216.

Kaufman, J., and O. Patterson. 2005. "Cross-National Cultural Diffusion: The Global Spread of Cricket." *American Sociological Review* 70 (1): 82–110.

Lomax, Michael E. 2000. "Athletics vs. Education: Dilemmas of Black Youth." *Society* 37 (3): 21–23.

Lundy, Garvey F. 2003. "The Myths of Oppositional Culture." *Journal of Black Studies* 33 (4): 450–67.

MacDonald, Robert. 1997. *Dangerous Youth and the Dangerous Class*. Florence, KY: Routledge. Retrieved December 21, 2013, http://books.google.com. ezp-prod1.hul.harvard.edu/books?hl=en&lr=&id=4mW9bwR5onMC&oi=fnd&pg=PA1&dq=youth+black++structurally+disconnected&ots=jbZ2HHps6I&sig=sgvR0_C5svKKVX_jUlBCxmk4Yuc.

———. 2008. "Disconnected Youth? Social Exclusion, the 'Underclass' and Economic Marginality." *Social Work & Society* 6 (2): 236–48.

MacDonald, Robert, and Jane Marsh. 2001. "Disconnected Youth?" *Journal of Youth Studies* 4 (4): 373–91.

MaCurdy, Thomas, Bryan Keating, and Sriniketh Suryasesha Nagavarapu. 2006. "Profiling the Plight of Disconnected Youth in America." *William and Flora Hewlett Foundation*. Retrieved December 21, 2013, http://www.econ.brown.edu/fac/Sriniketh_Nagavarapu/Disconnected%20Youth-v34-with%20tables.pdf.

Mincy, R. B. 2006. *Black Males Left Behind*. Washington, DC: Urban Institute Press.

O'Donnell, L., A. Myint-U, C. R. O'Donnell, and A. Stueve. 2003. "Long-Term Influence of Sexual Norms and Attitudes on Timing of Sexual Initiation among Urban Minority Youth." *Journal of School Health* 73 (2): 68–75.

Patterson, Orlando. 2004. "Culture and Continuity: Causal Structures in Socio-Cultural Persistence." *Matters of Culture: Cultural Sociology in Practice* 71–109.

Pfeiffer, Friedhelm, and Ruben R. Seiberlich. A Socio-Economic Analysis of Youth Disconnectedness. SSRN Scholarly Paper. Rochester, NY: Social Science Research Network, April 1, 2010. http://papers.ssrn.com.ezp-prod1.hul.harvard.edu/abstract=1597117.

Schudson, Michael. 1989. "How Culture Works." *Theory and Society* 18 (2): 153–80.

Smeeding, T., I. Garfinkel, and R. B. Mincy. 2009. "Young Disadvantaged Men: Fathers, Families, Poverty, and Policy: An Introduction to the Issues." Paper presented at the Institute for Research on Poverty Working Conference on Young Disadvantaged Men: Fathers, Families, Poverty and Policy, 14–15 September, University of Wisconsin–Madison.

Strayhorn, Terrell L. 2009. "Different Folks, Different Hopes: The Educational Aspirations of Black Males in Urban, Suburban, and Rural High Schools." *Urban Education* 44 (6): 710–31.

Sullivan, R. E. 2003. "Rap and Race." *Journal of Black Studies* 33 (5): 605–22.

Turner, Alezandria K., Carl Latkin, Freya Sonenstein, and S. Darius Tandon. 2011. "Psychiatric Disorder Symptoms, Substance Use, and Sexual Risk Behavior among African-American out of School Youth." *Drug and Alcohol Dependence* 115 (1): 67–73.

Twenge, Jean M., and Jennifer Crocker. 2002. "Meta-analyses comparing Whites, Blacks, Hispanics, Asians, and American Indians and Comment on Gray-Little and Hafdahl (2000)." *Psychological Bulletin 128*(3): 371–408.

Wight, Vanessa, Michelle M. Chau, Yumiko Aratani, Susan Wile Schwarz, and Kalyani Thampi. 2010. "A Profile of Disconnected Young Adults in 2010." Retrieved January 7, 2014, http://academiccommons.columbia.edu.ezp-prod1.hul.harvard.edu/catalog/ac:135726.

Wilson, William Julius. 1987. *The Truly Disadvantaged: The Inner City, the Underclass, and Public Policy.* Chicago: University of Chicago Press.

———. 2009. *More Than Just Race: Being Black and Poor in the Inner City.* New York: Norton.

———. 2010. "Why Both Social Structure and Culture Matter in a Holistic Analysis of Inner-City Poverty." *The ANNALS of the American Academy of Political and Social Science* 629 (1): 200–19.

Woods, L. K., and R. J. Jagers. 2003. "Are Cultural Values Predictors of Moral Reasoning in African American Adolescents?" *Journal of Black Psychology* 29 (1):102.

4. Hip-Hop's Irrepressible Refashionability

Arnold, Eric. 2010. "Why We Need (Real) Gangsta Rap Right Now." *Colorlines* September 13, 2010, accessed March 13, 2012, http://colorlines.com/archives/2010/09/why_we_need_real_gangsta_rap_right_now.html.

Caramanica, Jon. 2010. "Tossing Out Rhymes and Dollar Bills." *New York Times,* December 3, 2010, accessed March 13, 2012, https://www.nytimes.com/2010/12/04/arts/music/04soulja.html.

Chang, Jeff. 2005. *Can't Stop Won't Stop: A History of the Hip-Hop Generation.* New York: St. Martin's Press.

Charnas, Dan. 2010. *The Big Payback: The History of the Business of Hip-Hop.* New York: Penguin Books.

Driscoll, Kevin. 2009. "Stepping Your Game Up: Technical Innovation among Young People of Color in Hip-Hop." Master's thesis, MIT, Cambridge, MA, accessed March 13, 2012, http://cms.mit.edu/research/theses/KevinDriscoll2009.pdf.

Eshun, Kodwo. 1998. *More Brilliant Than the Sun: Adventures in Sonic Fiction.* London: Quartet Books.

Gunst, Laurie. 1995. *Born Fi' Dead: A Journey Through the Yardie Underworld*. Edinburgh: Payback Press/Canongate Books.

Jacobs, Sean. 2011. "Tupac in Africa," *Africa Is a Country* (blog), September 15, 2011.Accessed March 13, 2012, http://africasacountry.com/2011/09/15/tupac-in-africa/.

Jay-Z. 2010. *Decoded*. New York: Spiegel & Grau.

Lange, Patricia G., and Mizuko Ito, eds. 2009. *Hanging Out, Messing Around, Geeking Out: Living and Learning with New Media*. Cambridge, MA: MIT Press.

Lewis, Randy. 2003. "All-Black Top 10 Is a Billboard Hot 100 First." *Los Angeles Times*. October 9, 2003. Accessed March 13, 2012, http://articles.latimes.com/2003/oct/09/news/wk-quick9.

Marshall, Wayne. 2005. "Hearing Hip-Hop's Jamaican Accent." *Institute for Studies in American Music Newsletter* 34 (2): 8–9, 14–15.

———. 2006. "Giving Up Hip-Hop's Firstborn: A Quest for the Real after the Death of Sampling." *Callaloo* 29 (3): 868–92.

———. 2007. "Kool Herc." In *Icons of Hip Hop: An Encyclopedia of the Movement, Music, and Culture*, edited by Mickey Hess, 1–26. Westport, CT: Greenwood Press.

McWhorter, John. 2008. *All about the Beat: Why Hip-Hop Can't Save Black America*. New York: Gotham Books.

Neal, Mark Anthony. 2004. "Up From Hustling: Power, Plantations and the Hip-Hop Mogul." *Socialism and Democracy* 18 (2): 157–82. Accessed March 13, 2012, http://sdonline.org/36/up-from-hustling-power-plantations-and-the-hip-hop-mogul/.

Noz, Andrew. 2010. "The Decade in Rap Mixtapes." *NPR Music*. January 14, 2010. Accessed March 13, 2012, https://www.npr.org/templates/story/story.php?storyId=122319397.

———. 2011. "Lil B: Understanding Rap's New Rebel." *NPR Music*. January 27, 2011. Accessed March 13, 2012, https://www.npr.org/blogs/therecord/2011/01/27/133245953/lil-b-understanding-raps-new-rebel.

Reynolds, Simon. 1998. *Generation Ecstasy: Into the World of Techno and Rave Culture*. Boston: Little, Brown and Co.

Rose, Tricia. 1994. *Black Noise: Rap Music and Black Culture in Contemporary America*. Hanover & London: University Press of New England.

———. 2008. *The Hip Hop Wars*. New York: Basic Books/Perseus.

Schloss, Joseph. 2004. *Making Beats: The Art of Sample-Based Hip-Hop*. Middletown, CT: Wesleyan University Press.

Schonfeld, Eric. 2008. "ComScore: YouTube Now 25 Percent of All Google Searches." *TechCrunch*. December 18, 2008. Accessed March 13, 2012, http://techcrunch.com/2008/12/18/comscore-youtube-now–25-percent-of-all-google-searches.

Simmons, Russell. 2002. *Life and Def: Sex, Drugs, Money, & God*. New York: Three Rivers Press.

Smith, Aaron. 2010. "Technology Trends Among People of Color." *Pew Internet & American Life Project*. September 17, 2010. Accessed March 13, 2012, http://pewinternet.org/Commentary/2010/September/Technology -Trends-Among-People-of-Color.aspx.

Sommers, Marc. 2003. "Youth, War, and Urban Africa: Challenges, Misunderstandings, and Opportunities." In *Youth Explosion in Developing World Cities: Approaches to Reducing Poverty and Conflict in an Urban Age,* edited by Blair A. Ruble, et al., 25–46. Washington DC: Woodrow Wilson International Center for Scholars.

Sublette, Ned. 2008. *The World That Made New Orleans*. Chicago: Lawrence Hill Books.

Watkins, Craig. 2009. *The Young and the Digital: What the Migration to Social Network Sites, Games, and Anytime, Anywhere Media Means for Our Future*. Boston: Beacon Press.

West, Cornel. 2009. *Brother West: Living and Loving Out Loud: A Memoir*. New York: Hay House, Inc.

Williams, Thomas Chatterton. 2010. "President Obama's 'Rap Palate.'" *Wall Street Journal*. October 6, 2010. Accessed March 13, 2012, http://online.wsj .com/article/SB10001424052748703859204575526401852413266 .html?mod=%20WSJASIA_newsreel_opinion.

YouTube Team. 2011. "Thanks, YouTube Community, for Two BIG Gifts on Our Sixth Birthday!" *Broadcasting Ourselves: The Official YouTube Blog* (blog). May 25, 2011. Accessed March 13, 2012, http://youtube-global.blogspot.com /2011/05/thanks-youtube-community-for-two-big.html.

5. Continuity and Change in Neighborhood Culture

Akerlof, George A., and Rachel E. Kranton. 2010. *Identity Economics: How Our Identities Shape Our Work, Wages, and Well-Being*. Princeton, NJ: Princeton University Press.

Anderson, Elijah. 1999. *Code of the Street: Decency, Violence and the Moral Life of the Inner City*. New York: W. W. Norton & Company, Inc.

Bachrach, Christine. 2014. "Culture and Demography: From Reluctant Bedfellows to Committed Partners." *Demography* 51: 3–25.

Beckett, Katherine, and Steve Herbert. 2010. *Banished: The New Social Control in Urban America*. New York: Oxford University Press.

Bobo, Lawrence. 2001. "Racial Attitudes and Relations at the Close of the Twentieth Century." In *America Becoming: Racial Trends and Their*

Consequences, edited by N. J. Smelser, W. J. Wilson, and F. Mitchell, 264–301. Washington, DC: National Academy Press.

Briggs, Xavier de Souza, Susan J. Popkin, and John Goering. 2010. *Moving to Opportunity: The Story of an American Experiment to Fight Ghetto Poverty*. New York: Oxford University Press.

Chamlin, Mitchell B., and John K. Cochran. 1997. "Social Altruism and Crime." *Criminology* 35: 203–27.

Cialdini, Robert B., Raymond R. Reno, and Carl A. Kallgren. 1990. "A Focus Theory of Normative Conduct: Recycling the Concept of Norms to Reduce Littering in Public Places." *Journal of Personality and Social Psychology* 58: 1015–1026.

Coates, Ta-Nehisi. 2014. "The Case for Reparations." *The Atlantic* June: 54–71.

Darity, William Jr. 2011. "The New (Incorrect) Harvard/Washington Consensus on Racial Inequality." *Du Bois Review* 8: 467–95.

Dietz, Robert D. 2002. "The Estimation of Neighborhood Effects in the Social Sciences: An Interdisciplinary Approach." *Social Science Research* 31: 539–75.

Drake, St. Clair, and Horace R. Cayton. 1993 [1945]. *Black Metropolis: A Study of Negro Life in a Northern City*. Chicago: University of Chicago Press.

Duncan, Cynthia. 2009. *Worlds Apart: Why Poverty Persists in Rural America*. New Haven, CT: Yale University Press.

Ehrenhalt, Alan. 2012. *The Great Inversion and the Future of the American City*. New York: Alfred A. Knopf.

Ellickson, Robert C. 1991. *Order without Law: How Neighbors Settle Disputes*. Cambridge, MA: Harvard University Press.

Friedman, Thomas L. 2005. *The World Is Flat: A Brief History of the Twenty-First Century*. New York: Farrar, Straus and Giroux.

Gans, Herbert. 2011. "The Moynihan Report and Its Aftermaths: A Critical Analysis." *Du Bois Review* 8: 315–27.

Giddens, Anthony. 1991. *Modernity and Self-Identity: Self and Society in the Late Modern Age*. Cambridge: Polity.

Goffman, Erving. 1971. *Relations in Public*. New York: Basic.

———. 1974. *Frame Analysis: An Essay on the Organization of Experience*. Cambridge, MA: Harvard University Press.

Hannerz, Ulf. 1969. *Soulside: Inquiries into Ghetto Culture and Community*. Chicago: University of Chicago.

Harding, David J. 2010. *Living the Drama: Community, Conflict, and Culture among Inner-City Boys*. Chicago: University of Chicago Press.

Horne, Christine. 2001. "Sociological Perspectives on the Emergence of Norms." In *Social Norms*, edited by M. Hechter and K.-D. Opp, 3–34. New York: Russell Sage Foundation.

Hwang, Jackelyn, and Robert J. Sampson. 2014. "Divergent Pathways of Gentrification: Racial Inequality and the Social Order of Renewal in Chicago Neighborhoods." *American Sociological Review* 79: 726–751.

Iwashyna, Theodore J., Nicholas A. Christakis, and Lance B. Becker. 1999. "Neighborhoods Matter: A Population-Based Study of Provision of Cardiopulmonary Resuscitation." *Annals of Emergency Medicine* 34: 459–68.

Jacobs, Jane. 1961. *The Death and Life of Great American Cities*. New York: Random House.

Kirk, David S., and Andrew V. Papachristos. 2011. "Cultural Mechanisms and the Persistence of Neighborhood Violence." *American Journal of Sociology* 116: 1190–1233.

Kling, Jeffrey, Jeffrey Liebman, and Lawrence Katz. 2007. "Experimental Analysis of Neighborhood Effects." *Econometrica* 75: 83–119.

Kornhauser, Ruth Rosner. 1978. *Social Sources of Delinquency: An Appraisal of Analytic Models*. Chicago: University of Chicago Press.

Lamont, Michèle. 2000. *The Dignity of Working Men: Morality and the Boundaries of Race, Class, and Immigration*. Cambridge, MA and New York: Harvard University Press and Russell Sage Foundation.

Levine, Robert V., Ara Norenzayan, and Karen Philbrick. 2001. "Cross-Cultural Differences in Helping Strangers." *Journal of Cross-Cultural Psychology* 32: 543–60.

Lewis, Oscar. 1969. "Culture of Poverty." In *On Understanding Poverty: Perspectives from the Social Sciences,* edited by D. P. Moynihan, 187–220. New York: Basic Books.

Liebow, Elliott. 1967. *Tally's Corner: A Study of Negro Streetcorner Men*. Boston: Little, Brown.

Marshall, Wayne G. 2014. "Hip-Hop's Irrepressible Refashionability." In *The Cultural Matrix,* edited by Orlando Patterson and Ethan Fosse, 167–197. Cambridge, MA: Harvard University Press.

Massey, Douglas S., and Nancy Denton. 1993. *American Apartheid: Segregation and the Making of the Underclass*. Cambridge, MA: Harvard University Press.

Massey, Douglas S., and Robert J. Sampson. 2009. "Moynihan Redux: Legacies and Lessons." *Annals of the American Academy of Political and Social Science* 621: 6–27.

Milgram, Stanley, L. Mann, and S. Hartner. 1965. "The Lost Letter Technique: A Tool of Social Research." *Public Opinion Quarterly* 29: 437–38.

Morgan, Marcyliena. 2009. *The Real Hiphop: Battling for Knowledge, Power and Respect in the LA Underground*. Durham, NC and London: Duke University Press.

Moynihan, Daniel P. 1965. "The Negro Family: The Case for National Action." Washington, DC: Office of Policy Planning and Research, U.S. Department of Labor.

Nunn, Nathan, and Leonard Wantchekon. 2011. "The Slave Trade and the Origins of Mistrust in Africa." *American Economic Review* 101: 3221–52.

Patten, Alan. 2011. "Rethinking Culture: The Social Lineage Account." *American Political Science Review* 105: 735–49.

Patterson, Orlando. 2000. "Taking Culture Seriously: A Framework and Afro-American Illustration." In *Culture Matters: How Values Shape Human Progress,* edited by L. E. Harrison and S. P. Huntington, 202–18. New York: Basic Books.

———. 2004. "Culture and Continuity: Causal Structures in Socio-Cultural Persistence." In *Matters of Culture: Cultural Sociology in Practice,* edited by J. Mohr and R. Friedland, 71–109. New York: Cambridge University Press.

———. 2009. *The Mechanisms of Cultural Reproduction: Explaining the Puzzle of Persistence.* Cambridge, MA: Harvard University.

Quillian, Lincoln. 1999. "Migration Patterns and the Growth of High-Poverty Neighborhoods, 1970–1990." *American Journal of Sociology* 105: 1–37.

———. 2012. "Segregation and Poverty Concentration: The Role of Three Segregations." *American Sociological Review* 77: 354–79.

Rawls, John. 1971 [1999]. *A Theory of Justice.* Cambridge, MA: Harvard University Press.

———. 1993. *Political Liberalism.* New York: Columbia University Press.

Sampson, Robert J. 2008. "Moving to Inequality: Neighborhood Effects and Experiments Meet Social Structure." *American Journal of Sociology* 114: 189–231.

———. 2012. *Great American City: Chicago and the Enduring Neighborhood Effect.* Chicago: University of Chicago Press.

Sampson, Robert J., and Dawn Jeglum Bartusch. 1998. "Legal Cynicism and (Subcultural?) Tolerance of Deviance: The Neighborhood Context of Racial Differences." *Law and Society Review* 32: 777–804.

Sampson, Robert J., Patrick Sharkey, and Stephen W. Raudenbush. 2008. "Durable Effects of Concentrated Disadvantage on Verbal Ability among African-American Children." *Proceedings of the National Academy of Sciences* 105: 845–52.

Sennett, Richard. 2012. *Together: The Rituals, Pleasures and Politics of Cooperation.* New Haven, CT: Yale University Press.

Small, Mario. 2002. "Culture, Cohorts, and Social Organization Theory: Understanding Local Participation in a Latino Housing Project." *American Journal of Sociology* 108: 1–54.

———. 2004. *Villa Victoria: The Transformation of Social Capital in a Boston Barrio.* Chicago: University of Chicago Press.

Small, Mario Luis, David J. Harding, and Michèle Lamont. 2010. "Reconsidering Culture and Poverty." *Annals of the American Academy of Political and Social Science* 629: 6–27.

Stack, Carol. 1974. *All Our Kin: Strategies for Survival in a Black Community.* New York: Harper and Row.

Stout, Lynn. 2006. "Social Norms and Other-Regarding Preferences." In *Social Norms and the Law,* edited by J. N. Drobak, 13–34. New York: Cambridge University Press.

Suttles, Gerald D. 1984. "The Cumulative Texture of Local Urban Culture." *American Journal of Sociology* 90: 283–304.

Swidler, Ann. 1986. "Culture in Action." *American Sociological Review* 51: 273–86.

Thacher, David. 2006. "The Normative Case Study." *American Journal of Sociology* 111: 1631–76.

Tyler, Tom R. 1990. *Why People Obey the Law.* New Haven, CT: Yale University Press.

Wacquant, Loïc. 2010. "Urban Desolation and Symbolic Deinigration in the Hyperghetto." *Social Psychology Quarterly* 73: 215–19.

———. 2014. "Marginality, Ethnicity and Penality in the Neoliberal City: An Analytic Cartography." *Racial and Ethnic Studies Review* 37: 1687–1711.

Wilson, William Julius. [1987] 2012. *The Truly Disadvantaged: The Inner City, the Underclass, and Public Policy.* Chicago: University of Chicago Press.

———. 2009. *More Than Just Race: Being Black and Poor in the Inner City.* New York: Norton.

6. "I Do Me"

Anderson, E. 1999. *Code of the Street: The Moral Life of the Inner City.* New York: W. W. Norton.

Carter, P. 2007. *Keepin' It Real: School Success Beyond Black and White.* New York: Oxford University Press.

Clampet-Lundquist, S., K. Edin, J. R. Kling, and G. Duncan. 2011. "Moving Teenagers Out of High Risk Neighborhoods: How Girls Fare Better than Boys." *American Journal of Sociology* 116 (4): 1154–89.

Duneier, M. 1992. *Slim's Table: Race, Respectability, and Masculinity.* Chicago: University of Chicago Press.

Durham, R. E., and E. Westlund. 2011. *A Descriptive Look at College Enrollment and Degree Completion of Baltimore City Graduates.* Baltimore: Baltimore Education Research Consortium.

Ellen, I. G., and M. A. Turner. 1997. "Does Neighborhood Matter? Assessing Recent Evidence." *Housing Policy Debate* 8 (4): 833–64.

Furstenberg, F., T. D. Cook, J. Eccles, and G. H. Elder. 1999. *Managing to Make It: Urban Families and Adolescent Success.* Chicago: University of Chicago Press.

Hannerz, U. (1969) 2004. *Soulside.* Chicago: University of Chicago Press.

Harding, D. J. 2009. "Violence, Older Peers, and the Socialization of Adolescent Boys in Disadvantaged Neighborhoods." *American Sociological Review* 74 (3): 445–64.

———. 2011. "Rethinking the Cultural Context of Schooling Decisions in Disadvantaged Neighborhoods: From Deviant Subculture to Cultural Heterogeneity." *Sociology of Education* 84 (4): 322–39.

Laub, J. H., and R. Sampson. 2003. *Shared Beginnings, Divergent Lives: Delinquent Boys to Age 70*. Cambridge, MA: Harvard University Press.

Leventhal, T., and J. Brooks-Gunn. 2000. "The Neighborhoods They Live In: The Effects of Neighborhood Residence on Child and Adolescent Outcomes." *Psychological Bulletin* 126 (2): 309–37.

MacLeod, J. 1995. *Ain't No Makin' It: Aspirations and Attainment in a Low-Income Neighborhood*. Boulder, CO: Westview Press.

Massey, D. S., and N. A. Denton. 1993. *American Apartheid: Segregation and the Making of the Underclass*. Cambridge, MA: Harvard University Press.

Newman, K. S. 1999. *No Shame in My Game: The Working Poor in the Inner City*. New York: Vintage and Russell Sage.

Sampson, R., J. Morenoff, and T. Gannon-Rowley. 2002. "Assessing 'Neighborhood Effects': Social Processes and New Directions in Research." *Annual Review of Sociology* 28: 443–78.

Wilson, W. J. 1987. *The Truly Disadvantaged: The Inner City, the Underclass, and Public Policy*. Chicago: The University of Chicago Press.

7. More Than Just Black

Agius-Vallejo, Jody. 2012. *Barrios to Burbs: The Making of the Mexican-American Middle Class*. Stanford, CA: Stanford University Press

Anderson, Elijah. 1990. *Streetwise: Race, Class, and Change in an Urban Community*. Chicago: University of Chicago Press.

———. 1999. *Code of the Street: Decency, Violence, and the Moral Life of the Inner City*. New York: W. W. Norton.

———. 2008. *Against the Wall: Poor, Young, Black, and Male*. Philadelphia: University of Pennsylvania Press.

Bashi, Vilna Francine. 2007. *Survival of the Knitted: Immigrant Social Networks in a Stratified World*. Stanford, CA: Stanford University Press.

Brown, Susan K. 2007. "Delayed Spatial Assimilation: Multi-Generational Incorporation of the Mexican-Origin Population in Los Angeles." *City & Community* 6: 193–209.

Crowder, Kyle D. 1999. "Residential Segregation of West Indians in the New York/New Jersey Metropolitan Area: The Roles of Race and Ethnicity." *International Migration Review* 33: 79–113.

Crowder, Kyle D., and Lucky M. Tedrow. 2001. "West Indians and the Residential Landscape of New York." In *Islands in the City: West Indian Migration to New York,* edited by Nancy Foner, 81–114. Berkeley: University of California Press.

Edin, Kathryn, and Maria Kefalas. 2005. *Promises I Can Keep: Why Poor Women Put Motherhood before Marriage.* Berkeley: University of California Press.

Foner, Nancy. 2001. *Islands in the City: West Indian Migration to New York.* Berkeley: University of California Press.

Harding, David J. 2010. *Living the Drama: Community, Conflict, and Culture among Inner-City Boys.* Chicago: University of Chicago Press.

Iceland, John. 2009. *Where We Live Now: Immigration and Race in the United States.* Berkeley: University of California Press.

Kasinitz, Philip. 1992. *Caribbean New York: Black Immigrants and the Politics of Race.* Ithaca, NY: Cornell University Press.

———. 2001. "Invisible No More? West Indian Americans in the Social Scientific Imagination." In *Islands in the City: West Indian Migration to New York,* edited by Nancy Foner, 257–76. Berkeley: University of California Press.

Kasinitz, Philip, John H. Mollenkopf, Mary C. Waters, and Jennifer Holdaway. 2008. *Inheriting the City: The Children of Immigrants Come of Age.* New York; Cambridge, MA: Russell Sage Foundation; Harvard University Press.

Lacy, Karyn R. 2007. *Blue-Chip Black: Race, Class, and Status in the New Black Middle Class.* Berkeley: University of California Press.

Lamont, Michèle, and Mario Small. 2008. "How Culture Matters for the Understanding of Poverty: Enriching our Understanding." In *The Colors of Poverty: Why Racial and Ethnic Disparities Persist,* edited by Ann Lin and David Harris, pp. 76–102. New York: Russell Sage Foundation.

Lee, Jennifer, and Min Zhou. 2014. "The Success Frame and Achievement Paradox: The Costs and Consequences for Asian Americans." *Race and Social Problems* 6 (1): 38–55.

Model, Suzanne. 2008b. *West Indian Immigrants: A Black Success Story?* New York: Russell Sage Foundation.

Mollenkopf, John H., Philip Kasinitz, and Mary C. Waters. 1999. "Immigrant Second Generation in Metropolitan New York" (ISGMNY). Ann Arbor, Mich.: Inter-University Consortium for Political and Social Research. Available at: http://www.icpsr.umich.edu/icpsrweb/ICPSR/studies/30302 (accessed June 15, 2014).

Neckerman, Kathryn M., Prudence Carter, and Jennifer Lee. 1999. "Segmented Assimilation and Minority Cultures of Mobility." *Ethnic and Racial Studies* 22 (6): 945–965.

Patterson, Orlando. 1995. "The Culture of Caution: The Roots of [Colin] Powell's Decision [not to Run for the Presidency of the U.S]." *The New Republic,* November 27, 1995.

————. 2000. "Taking Culture Seriously: A Framework and an Afro-American Illustration." In *Culture Matters: How Values Shape Human Progress,* edited by Lawrence E. Harrison and Samuel P. Huntington, 202–18. New York: Basic Books.

————. 2004. "Culture and Continuity: Causal Structures in Socio-Cultural Persistence." In *Matters of Culture: Cultural Sociology in Practice,* edited by Roger Friedland and John W. Mohr, 71–109. New York: Cambridge University Press.

Pattillo, Mary. 2013. *Black Picket Fences: Privilege and Peril among the Black Middle Class,* 2nd edition. Chicago: University of Chicago Press.

Portes, Alejandro, and Ruben G. Rumbaut. 2001. *Legacies: The Story of the Immigrant Second Generation.* Berkeley, CA: University of California Press.

Portes, Alejandro, and Min Zhou. 1993. "The New Second Generation: Segmented Assimilation and Its Variants." *The Annals of the American Academy of Political and Social Science* 530: 74–96.

Reid, Ira D. A. 1939. *The Negro Immigrant: His Background, Characteristics, and Social Adjustment, 1899–1937.* New York: Columbia University Press.

Sampson, Robert J. 2012. *Great American City: Chicago and Enduring Neighborhood Effects.* Chicago: University of Chicago Press.

Smith, Robert C. 2014. "Black Mexicans, Conjunctural Ethnicity, and Operating Identities: Long-Term Ethnographic Analysis." *American Sociological Review* 79 (3): 517–548.

Smith, Robert C. 2006. *Mexican New York: Transnational Lives of New Immigrants.* Berkeley: University of California Press.

Sowell, Thomas. 1978. "Three Black Histories." In *Essays and Data on American Ethnic Groups.* Edited by Thomas Sowell, 7–64. Washington, DC: The Urban Institute.

Tran, Van C. 2011. "How Neighborhood Matters, and for Whom? Disadvantaged Context, Ethnic Cultural Repertoires and Second-Generation Social Mobility in Young Adulthood." PhD diss., Harvard University, Cambridge, MA.

Venkatesh, Sudhir Alladi. 2000. *American Project: The Rise and Fall of a Modern Ghetto.* Cambridge, MA: Harvard University Press.

————. 2006. *Off the Books: The Underground Economy of the Urban Poor.* Cambridge, MA: Harvard University Press.

Vickerman, Milton. 1999. *Crosscurrents: West Indian Immigrants and Race.* New York: Oxford University Press.

Waldinger, Roger D. 1996. *Still the Promised City?: African-Americans and New Immigrants in Postindustrial New York.* Cambridge, MA: Harvard University Press.

Waters, Mary C. 1999. *Black Identities: West Indian Immigrant Dreams and American Realities.* New York; Cambridge, MA: Russell Sage Foundation; Harvard University Press.

Waters, Mary C., and Philip Kasinitz. 2010. "Discrimination, Race Relations, and the Second Generation." *Social Research* 77 (1): 101–32.

Waters, Mary C., and Jennifer Sykes. 2009. "Spare the Rod, Spoil the Child? First and Second Generation West Indian Child Rearing Practices." In *Across Generations: Immigrant Families in America,* edited by Nancy Foner, 72–97. New York: New York University Press.

Wilson, William J. 1987. *The Truly Disadvantaged: The Inner City, the Underclass, and Public Policy.* Chicago: University of Chicago Press.

———. 2009. *More Than Just Race: Being Black and Poor in the Inner City.* New York & London: W. W. Norton & Company.

8. The Role of Religious and Social Organizations in the Lives of Disadvantaged Youth

Aaronson, Daniel. 1997. "Sibling Estimates of Neighborhood Effects." In *Neighborhood Poverty, Vol. II,* edited by J. Brooks-Gunn, G. Duncan, and L. Aber, 80–93. New York: Russell Sage Foundation.

Altonji, Joseph, Todd Elder, and Christopher Taber. 2005. "Selection on Observed and Unobserved Variables: Assessing the Effectiveness of Catholic Schools." *Journal of Political Economy* 113 (1): 151–84.

Anderson, Patricia M., Kristin F. Butcher, and Phillip B. Levine. 2003. "Maternal Employment and Overweight Children." *Journal of Health Economics* 22 (3): 477–504.

Anderson, Patricia M., Kristin F. Butcher, and Diane Whitmore Schanzenbach. 2007. "Childhood Disadvantage and Obesity: Is Nurture Trumping Nature?" Manuscript, Dartmouth College.

Antel, John J. 1992. "The Intergenerational Transfer of Welfare Dependency: Some Statistical Evidence." *The Review of Economics and Statistics* 74 (3): 467–77.

Bitler, Marianne P., and Janet Currie. 2004. "Does WIC Work? The Effect of WIC on Pregnancy and Birth Outcomes." *Journal of Policy Analysis and Management* 24 (1): 73–91.

Black, Sandra, Paul J. Devereux, and Kjell G. Salvanes. 2005. "Why the Apple Doesn't Fall Far: Understanding Intergenerational Transmission of Human Capital." *American Economic Review* 95 (1): 437–49.

Brooks-Gunn, Jeanne, and Greg Duncan. 1997. "The Effects of Poverty on Children." *The Future of Children* 7 (2): 55–71.

Case, Anne, and Lawrence F. Katz. 1991. "The Company You Keep: The Effects of Family and Neighborhood Effects on Disadvantaged Youths." NBER Working Paper 3705.

Case, Anne, and Lawrence F. Katz. 1991. "The Company You Keep: The Effects of Family and Neighborhood Effects on Disadvantaged Youths." NBER Working Paper 3705.

Clark, Andrew, and Orsolya Lelkes. 2005. "Deliver us from Evil: Religion as Insurance." Manuscript, PSE, Paris.

Currie, Janet. 1997. "Choosing among Alternative Programs for Poor Children." *The Future of Children* 7 (2): 113–131.

Currie, Janet, and Rosemary Hyson. 1999. "Is the Impact of Health Shocks Cushioned by Socioeconomic Status?: The Case of Birth Weight." *American Economic Review* 89 (2): 245–50.

Currie, Janet, and Enrico Moretti. 2003. "Mother's Education and the Intergenerational Transmission of Human Capital: Evidence from College Openings." *Quarterly Journal of Economics* 118 (4): 1495–1532.

Dahl, Gordon B., and Lance Lochner. 2005. "The Impact of Family Income on Child Achievement." *American Economic Review* 102 (5): 1927–1956.

Dehejia, Rajeev, Thomas DeLeire, and Erzo F. P. Luttmer. 2007. "Insuring Consumption and Happiness through Religious Organizations." *Journal of Public Economics* 91 (1–2): 259–79.

Dehejia, Rajeev, Thomas DeLeire, Erzo F. P. Luttmer, and Josh Mitchell. 2009. "The Role of Religious and Social Organizations in the Lives of Disadvantaged Youth." In *The Problems of Disadvantaged Youth: An Economic Perspective*, edited by Jonathan Gruber, 237–74. Chicago: University of Chicago Press for the National Bureau of Economic Research.

DeLeire, Thomas, and Ariel Kalil. 2002. "Good Things Come in Threes: Single-Parent Multigenerational Family Structure and Adolescent Adjustment." *Demography* 39 (2): 393–412.

Diener, Ed, Daniel Kahneman, and Norbert Schwarz, eds. 1999. *Well-Being: The Foundations of Hedonic Psychology.* New York: Russell Sage Foundation.

Duncan, Greg J., and Jeanne Brooks-Gunn. 1997. *Consequences of Growing Up Poor.* New York: Russell Sage Foundation.

Duncan Greg J., W. Jean Yeung, Jeanne Brooks-Gunn, and Judith R. Smith. 1998. "How Much Does Childhood Poverty Affect the Life Chances of Children?" *American Sociological Review* 63 (3): 406–23.

Ellison, Christopher G. 1991. "Religious Involvement and Subjective Well-Being." *Journal of Health and Social Behavior* 32 (1): 80–99.

Evans, William N., Wallace E. Oates, and Robert M. Schwab. 1992. "Measuring Peer Group Effects: A Study of Teenage Behavior." *Journal of Political Economy* 100 (5): 966–91.

Freeman, Richard B. 1986. "Who Escapes? The Relation of Churchgoing and Other Background Factors to the Socioeconomic Performance of Black Male Youths from Inner-City Tracts." In *The Black Youth Employment Crisis*, edited by Richard B. Freeman and Harry J. Holzer, 353–76. Chicago: University of Chicago Press.

Gruber, Jonathan, and Daniel Hungerman. 2006. "The Church vs. The Mall: What Happens When Religion Faces Increased Secular Competition?" *Quarterly Journal of Economics* 123 (2): 831–862.

Guralnick, Michael J. 2004. "Family Investments in Response to the Developmental Challenges of Young Children with Disabilities." In *Family Investments in Children's Potential: Resources and Parenting Behaviors That Promote Success,* edited by Ariel Kalil and Thomas DeLeire, 119–39. Mahwah, NJ: Lawrence Erlbaum.

Hanson, Thomas L., Sara McLanahan, and Elizabeth Thomson. 1997. "Economic Resources, Parental Practices, and Children's Well-Being." In *Consequences of Growing Up Poor,* edited by Greg J. Duncan and Jeanne Brooks-Gunn, 190–238. New York: Russell Sage Foundation.

Iannaccone, Laurence R. 1998. "Introduction to the Economics of Religion." *Journal of Economic Literature* 36 (3): 1465–95.

Korenman, Sanders, and Jane E. Miller. 1997. "Effects of Long-Term Poverty on Physical Health of Children in the National Longitudinal Survey of Youth." In *Consequences of Growing Up Poor,* edited by Greg J. Duncan and Jeanne Brooks-Gunn, 70–99. New York: Russell Sage Foundation.

Lillard, Dean R., and Joseph Price. 2007. "The Impact of Religion on Youth in Disadvantaged Families." Manuscript, Cornell University.

Mayer, Susan E. 1997. *What Money Can't Buy: Family Income and Children's Life Chances.* Cambridge, MA: Harvard University Press.

McCullough, Michael E., William T. Hoyt, David B. Larson, Harold G. Koenig, and Carl Thoresen. 2000. "Religious Involvement and Mortality: A Meta-Analytic Review." *Health Psychology* 19 (3): 211–22.

McLanahan, Sara, and Gary Sandefur. 1994. *Growing Up with a Single Parent.* Cambridge, MA: Harvard University Press.

McLanahan, Sara, and Gary Sandefur. 2006. "The Intergenerational Effects of Compulsory Schooling." *Journal of Labor Economics* 24 (4): 729–60.

Oreopoulos, Philip, Marianne E. Page, and Ann Huff Stevens (2008). "The Intergenerational Effects of Worker Displacement." *Journal of Labor Economics* 26 (3): 455–500.

Page, Marianne E. 2004. "New Evidence on Intergenerational Correlations in Welfare Participation." In *Generational Income Mobility in North America and Europe,* edited by Miles Corak, 226–244. Cambridge: Cambridge University Press.

Page, Marianne, Ann Huff Stevens, and Jason Lindo. 2007. "Parental Income Shocks and Outcomes of Disadvantaged Youth in the United States." In *An Economics Perspective on the Problems of Disadvantaged Youth,* edited by Jonathan Gruber, 213–235. Chicago: University of Chicago Press for the National Bureau of Economic Research.

Pargament, Kenneth I. 2002. "The Bitter and the Sweet: An Evaluation of the Costs and Benefits of Religiousness." *Psychological Inquiry* 13 (3): 168–81.

Shea, John. 2000. "Does Parents' Money Matter?" *Journal of Public Economics* 77 (2): 155–84.

Smith, Judith R., Jeanne Brooks-Gunn, and Pamela K. Klebanov. 1997. "Consequences of Living in Poverty for Young Children's Cognitive and Verbal Ability and Early School Achievement." In *Consequences of Growing Up Poor*, edited by Greg J. Duncan and Jeanne Brooks-Gunn, 132–89. New York: Russell Sage Foundation.

Smith, Timothy B., Michael E. McCullough, and Justin Poll. 2003. "Religiousness and Depression: Evidence for a Main Effect and the Moderating Influence of Stressful Life Events." *Psychological Bulletin* 129 (4): 614–36.

Strawbridge, William J., Sarah J. Shema, Richard D. Cohen, Robert E. Roberts, and George E. Kaplan. 1998. "Religiosity Buffers Effects of Some Stressors on Depression but Exacerbates Others." *Journal of Gerontology Series B: Psychological Sciences and Social Sciences* 53 (3): 118–26.

Sweet, James A., and Larry L. Bumpass. 1996. "The National Survey of Families and Households—Waves 1 and 2: Data Description and Documentation." Center for Demography and Ecology, University of Wisconsin–Madison (http://www.ssc.wisc.edu/nsfh/home.htm).

———. (2002). "The National Survey of Families and Households—Waves 1, 2, and 3: Data Description and Documentation." Center for Demography and Ecology, University of Wisconsin–Madison (http://www.ssc.wisc.edu/nsfh/home.htm).

Sweet, James A., Larry L. Bumpass, and Vaughn Call. 1988. "The Design and Content of the National Survey of Families and Households." Center for Demography and Ecology, University of Wisconsin–Madison, NSFH Working Paper No. 1.

9. Keeping Up the Front

Abraham, Roger. 1962. "Playing the Dozens." *Journal of American Folklore*. 75: 209–10.

Alim, Samy H. 2004. *You Know My Steez: An Ethnographic and Sociolinguistic Study of Styleshifting in a Black American Speech Community*. Durham, NC: Duke University Press.

———. 2006. *Roc the Mic Right: The Language of Hip Hop Culture*. New York: Routledge.

Anderson, Elijah. 1978. *A Place on the Corner*. Chicago: University of Chicago Press.

Anderson, Elijah. 1990. *Streetwise*. Chicago: University of Chicago Press.

———. 1999. *Code of the Street: Decency, Violence, and the Moral Life of the Inner City*. New York: Norton.

Bateson, Gregory. 1971. "The Message 'This is Play.'" In *Child's Play*, edited by R. E. Herron and B. Sutton-Smith, 261–66. New York: Wiley.

Becker, Howard. (1963) 1997. *Outsiders: Studies in the Sociology of Deviance.* New York: Free Press.

Bergson, Henri. (1900) 2000. *Laughter: An Essay on the Meaning of the Comic.* New York: Dover Publications.

Block, R. 1977. *Violent Crime.* Lexington, MA: Lexington.

Bourgois, Philippe. 1995. *In Search of Respect: Selling Crack in El Barrio.* Cambridge: Cambridge University Press.

Brazier, Arthur. 1960. *Black Self-Determination: The Story of The Woodlawn Organization.* New York: Eerdmans.

Brenneis, Don, and Ram Padarath. 1975. "About Those Scoundrels I'll Let Everyone Know: Challenge Singing in a Fiji Indian Community." *The Journal of American Folklore* 88 (349): 283–91.

Collins, Randall. 2004. *Interaction Ritual Chains.* Princeton, NJ: Princeton University Press.

———. 2008. *Violence: A Microsociological Theory.* Princeton, NJ: Princeton University Press.

Dollard, John. 1939. "The Dozens: Dialectic of Insult." *American Imago* 1: 3–25.

Drake, St. Clair, and Horace Cayton. (1945) 1993. *Black Metropolis: A Study of Negro Life in a Northern City.* Chicago: University of Chicago Press.

Durkheim, Emile. (1912) 1964. *The Elementary Forms of Religious Life.* New York: Free Press.

Elias, Norbert. (1939) 2000. *The Civilizing Process: Sociogenetic and Psychogenetic Investigations.* Oxford: Blackwell Publishing.

Garfinkel, Harold. 1967. *Studies in Ethnomethodology.* Englewood Cliffs, NJ: Prentice-Hall.

Goffman, Erving. 1959. *The Presentation of the Self in Everyday Life.* New York: Doubleday.

———. 1961. *Encounters: Two Studies in the Sociology of Interaction—Fun in Games & Role Distance* . . . Indianapolis, IN: Bobbs-Merrill.

———. 1963. *Behavior in Public Places: Notes on the Social Organization of Gatherings.* New York: Free Press.

———. 1967. *Interaction Ritual: Essays on Face-to-Face Behavior.* New York: Doubleday.

———. 1969. *Strategic Interaction.* Philadelphia: University of Pennsylvania Press.

———. 1974. *Frame Analysis: An Essay on the Organization of Experience.* Boston: Northeastern University Press.

Grossman, Dave. 1995. *On Killing: The Psychological Cost of Learning to Kill in War and Society.* Boston: Little, Brown.

Guffy, Ossie. 1971. *Ossie: The Autobiography of a Black Woman*. New York: Norton Press.

Hagedorn, John M. 1998. "Gang Violence in the Postindustrial Era." In *Youth Violence*, edited by Michael Tonry and Mark H. Moore, 365–419. *Crime and Justice Series*, no. 24. Chicago: University of Chicago Press.

Hagedorn, John M. 2009. *A World of Gangs: Armed Young Men and Gangsta Culture*. Minneapolis: University of Minnesota Press.

Haley, Alex, and Malcolm X. 1964. *The Autobiography of Malcolm X*. New York: Grove Press.

Hannerz, Ulf. 1969. *Soulside: Inquiries into Ghetto Culture and Community*. New York: Columbia University Press.

Hansberry, Lorraine. *A Raisin in the Sun*. (1959) 2004. New York: Vintage.

Harcourt, Bernard. 2006. *Language of the Gun: Youth, Crime, and Public Policy*. Chicago, IL: University of Chicago Press.

Hirschi, Travis, and Michael Gottfredson. 1990. *A General Theory of Crime*. Stanford, CA: Stanford University Press.

Holmes, Richard. 1985. *Acts of War: The Behavior of Men in Battle*. New York: Free Press.

Jackall, Robert. 2005. *Street Stories: The World of Police Detectives*. Cambridge, MA: Harvard University Press.

Kahneman, Daniel. 2003. "Maps of Bounded Rationality: Psychology for Behavioral Economics." *The American Economic Review* 93(5): 1449–1475.

Kahneman, Daniel. 2011. *Thinking, Fast and Slow*. New York: Farrar, Strauss and Giroux.

Katz, Jack. 1988. *Seductions of Crime: On the Moral and Sensual Attractions of Doing Evil*. New York: Basic Books.

———. 1999. *How Emotions Work*. Chicago: University of Chicago Press.

Keegan, John. 1976. *The Face of Battle: A Study of Agincourt, Waterloo, and the Somme*. New York: Random House.

———. 1993. *A History of Warfare*. London: Hutchinson.

Klein, Malcolm, and Cheryl Maxson. 2010. *Street Gang Patterns and Policies*. Oxford: Oxford University Press.

Kochman, Thomas. 1970. "Rapping in the Ghetto." In *Soul*, edited by Lee Rainwater. Chicago: Aldine.

———. 1981. *Black and White Styles in Conflict*. Chicago: University of Chicago Press.

Labov, William. 1972. *Language in the Inner City: Studies in the Black English Vernacular*. Philadelphia: University of Pennsylvania Press.

Lauria, Anthony Jr. 1965. "'Respeto,' 'Relajo,' and Inter-Personal Relations in Puerto Rico." *Anthropological Quarterly* 37 (2): 53–67.

Lee, Jooyoung. 2009. "Battlin' on the Corner: Techniques for Sustaining Play." *Social Problems* 56 (3): 578–98.

Majors, Richard, and Janet Mancini Billson. 1993. *Cool Pose: The Dilemmas of Black Manhood in America*. New York: Simon & Schuster.

Marshall, S. L. A. 1947. *Men against Fire: The Problem of Battle Control*. Norman, OK: University of Oklahoma Press. Originally published by William Morrow, New York.

McRoberts, Omar. 2003. *Streets of Glory: Church and Community in a Black Urban Neighborhood*. Chicago: University of Chicago Press.

Morgan, Marcyliena. 2002. *Language, Discourse, and Power in African American Culture*. Cambridge, UK: Cambridge University Press.

Morrison, Shona, and Ian O'Donnell. 1994. *Armed Robbery: A Study in London*. Oxford: Oxford University Press.

Park, Robert E., and Ernest W. Burgess. 1925. *The City: Suggestions for the Study of Human Nature in the Urban Environment*. Chicago: University of Chicago Press.

Patterson, Orlando. 1994. "Ecumenical America: Global Culture and the American Cosmos," *World Policy Journal* 11 (2): 103–17.

———. 2000. "Taking Culture Seriously: A Framework and an Afro-American Illustration." In *Culture Matters*, edited by Lawrence Harrison and Samuel Huntington, 202–18. New York: Basic Books.

Pinker, Steven. 2011. *The Better Angels of Our Nature: Why Violence Has Declined*. New York: Viking.

Radcliffe-Brown, Alfred. (1952) 1965. *Structure and Function in Primitive Society*. New York: Free Press.

Rainwater, Lee. 1970. *Behind Ghetto Walls: Black Families in a Federal Slum*. New York: Transaction Books.

Sampson, Robert J., and William Julius Wilson. "Toward a Theory of Race, Crime, and Urban Inequality." In *Crime and Inequality*, edited by John Hagan and Ruth D. Peterson, 37–56. Stanford, CA: Stanford University Press, 1995.

Sanchez-Jankowski, Martin. 1991. *Islands in the Street: Gangs and American Urban Society*. Berkeley, CA: University of California Press.

Skogan, Wesley. 1990. *Disorder and Decline: Crime and the Spiral of Decay in American Neighborhoods*. New York: Free Press.

Smitherman, Geneva. 1997. "'The Chain Remain the Same': Communicative Practices in the Hip-Hop Nation." *Journal of Black Studies* 28 (1): 3–25.

Suttles, Gerald D. 1968. *The Social Order of the Slum: Ethnicity and Territory in the Inner City*. Chicago: University of Chicago Press.

Thornberry, Terence P., Marvin D. Krohn, Alan J. Lizotte, Carolyn A. Smith, and Kimberly Tobin. 2003. *Gangs and Delinquency in Developmental Perspective*. New York: Cambridge University Press.

Thrasher, Frederic. 1927. *The Gang: A Study of 1313 Gangs in Chicago*. Chicago: University of Chicago Press.

University of Michigan. N.D. *National Archive of Criminal Justice Data.* < http://www.icpsr.umich.edu/icpsrweb/NACJD/NIBRS/>.

Venkatesh, Sudhir. 1997. The Social Organization of Street Gang Activity in an Urban Ghetto." *American Journal of Sociology.* 103 (1): 82–111.

Venkatesh, Sudhir. 2000. The *American Project: The Rise and Fall of a Modern Ghetto.* Cambridge, MA: Harvard University Press.

———. 2006. *Off the Books: The Underground Economy of the Urban Poor.* Cambridge, MA: Harvard University Press.

Wacquant, Loïc. 2002. "Review Symposium Scrutinizing the Street: Poverty, Morality, and the Pitfalls of Urban Ethnography." *American Journal of Sociology* 107 (6): 1468–1532.

———. 2003. *Body and Soul: Notebooks of an Apprentice Boxer.* Oxford: Oxford University Press.

———. 2008. *Urban Outcasts: A Comparative Sociology of Advanced Marginality.* New York: Polity Press.

Wilson, William Julius. 1996. *When Work Disappears: The World of the New Urban Poor.* New York: Knopf.

Wilson, William Julius, and Anmol Chaddha. 2009. "The Role of Theory in Ethnography." *Ethnography* 10 (4): 549–64.

Woodlawn Preservation and Investment Corporation. 2005. *Woodlawn: Rebuilding a Village: Quality of Life Plan.* <http://www.newcommunities.org/cmadocs/woodlawnqofl2005.pdf>.

Zimring, Franklin, and Gordon Hawkins. 1997 *Crime is Not the Problem: Lethal Violence in America.* Oxford University Press.

10. What about the Day After?

Anderson, Elijah. 2000. *Code of the Street: Decency, Violence, and the Moral Life of the Inner City.* New York: W. W. Norton.

Bourgois, Phillipe L. 2002. *In Search of Respect: Selling Crack in El Barrio.* Cambridge: Cambridge University Press.

Bursik, Robert J., Jr., and Harold G. Grasmick. 1993. *Neighborhoods and Crime: The Dimensions of Effective Community Control.* New York: Lexington.

Cobbina, Jennifer E., Jody Miller, and Rod K. Brunson. 2008. "Gender, Neighborhood Danger, and Risk-Avoidance Strategies Among Urban African-American Youths." *Criminology* 46 (3): 673–709.

Cross, William E., Jr. 2003. "Tracing the Historical Origins of Youth Delinquency and Violence: Myths and Realities." *Journal of Social Issues* 59 (1): 67–82.

Downey, Douglas B. 2008. "Black/White Differences in School Performance: The Oppositional Culture Explanation." *Annual Review of Sociology* 34: 107–26.

Duneier, Mitchell. 2000. *Sidewalk.* New York: Farrar, Strauss and Giroux.

During, Simon. 2003. *The Cultural Studies Reader.* 2nd ed. London; New York: Routledge.

Gans, Herbert J. 2011. "The Moynihan report and its aftermaths." *Du Bois Review: Social Science Research on Race* 8 (2): 315–327.

Harding, David J. 2009. "Violence, older peers, and the socialization of adolescent boys in disadvantaged neighborhoods." *American sociological review* 74 (3): 445–464.

Kelley, Robin D. G. 1997. *Yo'mama's disfunktional!: Fighting the culture wars in urban America.* Beacon Press.

Kennedy, David. 2011. *Don't Shoot: One Man, A Street Fellowship, and the End of Violence in Inner-City America.* New York: Bloomsbury.

Kornhauser, Ruth R. 1978. *Social Source of Delinquency.* Chicago: University of Chicago Press.

Marwell, Nicole. 2007. *Bargaining for Brooklyn: Community Organizations in the Entrepreneurial City.* Chicago: University of Chicago Press.

Massey, Douglas S., and Nancy Denton. *American Apartheid: Segregation and the Making of the Underclass.* Harvard University Press, 1993.

Meares, Tracey, and Dan M. Kahan. 1999. *Urgent Times: Policing and Rights in Inner City Communities.* New York: Beacon.

McRoberts, Omar M. *Streets of Glory: Church and Community in a Black Urban Neighborhood.* University of Chicago Press, 2005.

Merry, Sally Engle, and Neal A. Milner. 1995. *The Possibility of Popular Justice.* Ann Arbor: University of Michigan.

Moskos, Peter. 2008. *Cop in the Hood: My Year Policing in Baltimore's Eastern District.* Princeton, NJ: Princeton University Press.

Pattillo-McCoy, Mary. 2000. *Black Picket Fences.* Chicago: University of Chicago Press.

Phillips, Scott, and Mark Cooney. 2008. "Aiding Peace, Abetting Violence: Third Parties and the Management of Conflict." *American Sociological Review* 70 (2): 334–354.

Popkin, Susan. 2000. *The Hidden War.* New Brunswick: Rutgers.

Rose, Tricia. 1994. *Black Noise: Rap Music and Black Culture in Contemporary America.* Hanover, NH: University Press of New England.

Sampson, Robert J. 2009. "Racial Stratification and the Durable Tangle of Neighborhood Inequality." *Annals of the American Academy of Political and Social Science* 621 (1): 260–280.

Sampson, Robert J., and W. Byron Groves. 1989. "Community structure and crime: Testing social-disorganization theory." *American Journal of Sociology* 94 (4): 774–802.

Sanchez-Jankowski, Martin. 1991. *Islands in the Street: Gangs and American Urban Society.* Berkeley: University of California Press.

Carol B. Stack. 1975. *All Our Kin: Strategies for Survival in a Black Community*. New York: Basic Books.

Skogan, Wesley G., and Susan M. Hartnett. 1997. *Community Policing, Chicago Style*. New York: Oxford University Press.

Sullivan, Mercer. 1989. *Getting Paid: Youth Crime and Work in the Inner City*. Ithaca, NY: Cornell University Press.

Sun, Ivan Y., Ruth Triplett, and Randy R. Gainey. 2004. "Neighborhood Characteristics and Crime: A Test of the Model of Social Disorganization." *Western Criminology Review* 5 (1): 1–16.

Venkatesh, Sudhir. 2013. "Underground Markets as Fields in Transition: Sex Work in New York City." In *Sociological Forum* 28 (4): 682–699.

Venkatesh, Sudhir. 1997. "The Three-Tier Model: How Helping Occurs in Poor Communities." *Social Service Review* 71 (4): 574–606.

———. 2007. *Off the Books: The Underground Economy of the Urban Poor*. Cambridge, MA: Harvard University Press.

Wilson, William Julius. 2012. *The Truly Disadvantaged: The Inner City, the Underclass, and Public Policy*. Chicago: University of Chicago Press.

Winship, Christopher, Jenny Berrien, and Omar McRoberts. 2000. "Religion and the Boston Miracle: The Effect of Black Ministry on Youth Violence." In *Who Will Provide? The Changing Role of Religion in American Social Welfare*, edited by M. J. Bane, B. Coffin, and R. Thiemann. Boulder, CO: Westview Press.

Young, Alford Jr. 2006. *The Minds of Marginalized Black Men: Making Sense of Mobility, Opportunity, and Future Life Chances*. Princeton: Princeton University.

11. Culture, Inequality, and Gender Relations among Urban Black Youth

AAUW Educational Foundation. 2001. *Hostile Hallways: Bullying, Teasing and Sexual Harassment in School*. New York: AAUW Educational Foundation.

Altonji, Joseph G., and Rebecca M. Blank. 1999. "Race and Gender in the Labor Market." In *Handbook of Labor Economics, Volume 3, Part C*, edited by Orley C. Ashenfelter and David Card, 3144–258. Amsterdam: Elsevier.

Anderson, Elijah. 1999. *Code of the Street: Decency, Violence, and the Moral Life of the Inner City*. New York: W. W. Norton & Company.

Augustine, Jennifer March, Timothy Nelson, and Kathryn Edin. 2009. "Why Do Poor Men Have Children? Fertility Intentions among Low-Income Unmarried U.S. Fathers." *The ANNALS of the American Academy of Political and Social Science* 624: 99–117.

Bettie, Julie. 2003. *Women Without Class: Girls, Race, and Identity*. Berkeley: University of California Press.

Boswell, A. Ayres, and Joan Z. Spade. 1996. "Fraternities and Collegiate Rape Culture: Why Are Some Fraternities More Dangerous Places for Women?" *Gender & Society* 10: 133–47.

Brown, Irene, and Joya Misra. 2003. "The Intersection of Gender and Race in the Labor Market." *Annual Review of Sociology*. 29: 487–515.

Burton, Linda M., and M. Belinda Tucker. 2009. "Romantic Unions in an Era of Uncertainty: A Post-Moynihan Perspective on African American Women and Marriage." *The ANNALS of the American Academy of Political and Social Science* 621: 132–48.

Bush-Baskette, Stephanie R. 1998. "The War on Drugs as a War Against Black Women." In *Crime Control and Women: Feminist Implications of Criminal Justice Policy*, edited by Susan Miller, 113–29. Thousand Oaks, CA: Sage.

Christian, Johnna. 2005. "Riding the Bus: Barriers to Prison Visitation and Family Management Strategies." *Journal of Contemporary Criminal Justice* 21: 31–48.

Cobbina, Jennifer, Jody Miller, and Rod K. Brunson. 2008. "Gender, Neighborhood Risk, and Risk Avoidance Strategies among Urban African American Youth." *Criminology* 46: 501–37.

Collins, Patricia Hill. 1990. *Black Feminist Thought: Knowledge, Consciousness, and the Politics of Empowerment*. New York: Routledge.

———. 2004. *Black Sexual Politics: African Americans, Gender, and the New Racism*. New York: Routledge.

———. 2006. "New Commodities, New Consumers: Selling Blackness in a Global Marketplace." *Ethnicities* 6: 297–317.

Comfort, Megan. 2007. *Doing Time Together: Love and Family in the Shadow of the Prison*. Chicago: University of Chicago Press.

Connell, R. W. 1993. "Foreword." In *Masculinities and Crime*, edited by James W. Messerschmidt, vii–xvi. Lanham, MD: Rowman & Littlefield.

———. 2002. *Gender*. Cambridge: Polity Press.

Crais, Clifton, and Pamela Scully. 2008. *Sara Baartman and the Hottentot Venus: A Ghost Story and a Biography*. Princeton, NJ: Princeton University Press.

Daly, Kathleen, and Lisa Maher. 1998. "Crossroads and Intersections: Building from Feminist Critique." In *Criminology at the Crossroads: Feminist Readings in Crime and Justice*, edited by Kathleen Daly and Lisa Maher, 1–17. Oxford: Oxford University Press.

Davis, Angela Y. 1983. *Women, Race and Class*. New York: Vintage Books.

Edin, Kathryn, Laura Tach, and Ronald Mincy. 2009. "Claiming Fatherhood: Race and Dynamics of Paternal Involvement among Unmarried Men." *The ANNALS of the American Academy of Political and Social Science* 621: 149–77.

Ferguson, Ann Arnett. 2001. *Bad Boys: Public Schools in the Making of Black Masculinity*. Ann Arbor: The University of Michigan Press.

Fine, Gary Alan, and Corey D. Fields. 2008. "Culture and Microsociology: The Anthill and the Veldt." *The ANNALS of the American Academy of Political and Social Science* 619: 130–48.

Fosse, Nathan Edward. 2010. "The Repertoire of Infidelity among Low-Income Men: Doubt, Duty, and Destiny." *The ANNALS of the American Academy of Political and Social Science* 629: 125–43.

Franklin, Karen. 2004. "Enacting Masculinity: Antigay Violence and Group Rape as Participatory Theater." *Sexuality Research & Social Policy* 1: 25–40.

Gavey, Nicola. 1999. "'I Wasn't Raped, But . . . ': Revisiting Definitional Problems in Sexual Victimization." In *New Versions of Victims*, edited by Sharon Lamb, 57–81. New York: New York University Press.

Gibbs, Jewelle Taylor. 1990. "Mental Health Issues of Black Adolescents: Implications for Policy and Practice." In *Ethnic Issues in Adolescent Mental Health*, edited by Arlene Rubin Stiffman and Larry E. Davis, 21–52. Newbury Park, CA: Sage Publications.

Harding, David J. 2010. *Living the Drama: Community, Conflict, and Culture among Inner-City Boys*. Chicago: University of Chicago Press.

Hays, Sharon. 2004. *Flat Broke with Children: Women in the Age of Welfare Reform*. New York: Oxford University Press.

Herbert, Bob. "Too Long Ignored." *New York Times*. August 20, 2010.

hooks, bell. 1981. *Ain't I a Woman*. Boston: South End Press.

Jones, Nikki. 2010. *Between Good and Ghetto: African American Girls and Inner City Violence*. New Brunswick, NJ: Rutgers University Press.

Kalof, Linda. 1995. "Sex, Power and Dependency: The Politics of Adolescent Sexuality." *Journal of Youth and Adolescence* 24: 229–49.

Kelly, Liz. 2002. "The Continuum of Sexual Violence." In *Sexualities*, edited by Ken Plummer, 127–39. London: Routledge.

Kenway, Jane, and Lindsay Fitzclarence. 1997. "Masculinity, Violence and Schooling: Challenging 'Poisonous Pedagogies.' " *Gender and Education* 9: 117–33.

King, Neal. 2003. "Knowing Women: Straight Men and Sexual Certainty." *Gender & Society* 17: 861–77.

Lauritsen, Janet L. 2003. "How Families and Communities Influence Youth Victimization." *OJJDP Juvenile Justice Bulletin*. Washington, DC: U.S. Department of Justice.

Lauritsen, Janet L., and Robin J. Schaum. 2004. "The Social Ecology of Violence against Women." *Criminology* 42: 323–57.

Maher, Lisa. 1997. *Sexed Work: Gender, Race and Resistance in a Brooklyn Drug Market*. Oxford: Clarendon Press.

Mauer, Marc. 1999. *The Crisis of the Young African American Male and the Criminal Justice System*. Washington, DC: U.S. Commission on Civil Rights.

McCall, Nathan. 1994. *Makes Me Wanna Holler: A Young Black Man in America.* New York: Vintage Books.

McWilliams, Marco A. 2010. "Review of Tricia Rose, *The Hip Hop Wars.*" *Educational Studies.* 46: 537–39.

Miller, Jody. 2001. *One of the Guys: Girls, Gangs, and Gender.* New York: Oxford University Press.

———. 2008. *Getting Played: African American Girls, Urban Inequality, and Gendered Violence.* New York: New York University Press.

Miller, Jody, and Norman A. White. 2003. "Gender and Adolescent Relationship Violence: A Contextual Examination." *Criminology* 41 (4): 1501–41.

Miller-Young, Mireille. 2008. "Hip-Hop Honeys and Da Hustlaz: Black Sexualities in the New Hip-Hop Pornography." *Meridians: Feminism, Race, Transnationalism* 8: 261–92.

Mullins, Christopher W. 2006. *Holding Your Square: Masculinities, Streetlife, and Violence.* London, UK: Willan Press.

Nurse, Ann M. 2002. *Fatherhood Arrested: Parenting from within the Juvenile Justice System.* Nashville, TN: Vanderbilt University Press.

Peterson, Ruth D., and Lauren J. Krivo. 2010. *Divergent Social Worlds: Neighborhood Crime and the Racial-Spatial Divide.* New York: Russell Sage.

Popkin, Susan J., Tama Leventhal, and Gretchen Weismann. 2008. *Girls in the 'Hood: The Importance of Feeling Safe.* Metropolitan Housing and Communities Center, Brief No. 1. New York: The Urban Institute.

———. 2010. "Girls in the 'Hood: How Safety Affects the Life Chances of Low-Income Girls." *Urban Affairs Review* 45: 715–44.

Recording Industry Association of America (RIAA). 2009. "2008 Consumer Profile." www.riaa.org.

Reid-Brinkley, Shanara R. 2008. "The *Essence* of Res(ex)pectability: Black Women's Negotiation of Black Femininity in Rap Music and Music Video." *Meridians: Feminism, Race, Transnationalism* 8: 236–60.

Rose, Tricia. 2008. *The Hip Hop Wars: What We Talk About When We Talk About Hip Hop—and Why It Matters.* New York: Basic Civitas Books.

Sampson, Robert J. 2009. "Racial Stratification and the Durable Tangle of Neighborhood Inequality." *The ANNALS of the American Academy of Political and Social Science* 621: 260–80.

Sampson, Robert J., and William Julius Wilson. 1995. "Toward a Theory of Race, Crime and Urban Inequality." In *Crime and Inequality,* edited by John Hagan and Ruth D. Peterson, 37–54. Stanford, CA: Stanford University Press.

Sanday, Peggy Reeves. 1981. "The Socio-Cultural Context of Rape: A Cross-Cultural Study." *Journal of Social Issues* 37: 5–27.

———. 1990. *Fraternity Gang Rape: Sex, Brotherhood, and Privilege on Campus.* New York: New York University Press.

Schwartz, Martin D., and Walter S. DeKeseredy. 1997. *Sexual Assault on the College Campus: The Role of Male Peer Support*. Thousand Oaks, CA: Sage.

Scott, Ellen K., Andrew S. London, and Nancy A. Myers. 2002. "Dangerous Dependencies: The Intersection of Welfare Reform and Domestic Violence." *Gender & Society* 16: 878–97.

Scully, Diana. 1990. *Understanding Sexual Violence*. Boston: Unwin Hyman.

Sharpley-Whiting, T. Denean. 2007. *Pimps Up, Ho's Down: Hip Hop's Hold on Young Black Women*. New York: New York University Press.

Small, Mario Luis, David J. Harding, and Michèle Lamont. 2010. "Reconsidering Culture and Poverty." *The ANNALS of the American Academy of Political and Social Science* 629: 6–27.

Squires, Catherine R., Laura P. Kohn-Wood, Tabbye Chavous, and Prudence L. Carter. 2006. "Evaluating Agency and Responsibility in Gendered Violence: African American Youth Talk about Violence and Hip Hop." *Sex Roles* 55: 725–37.

Steffensmeier, Darrell. 1983. "Organizational Properties and Sex-Segregation in the Underworld: Building a Sociological Theory of Sex Differences in Crime." *Social Forces* 61: 1010–32.

Stephens, Dionne P., and April L. Few. 2007a. "Hip Hop Honey or Video Ho: African American Preadolescents' Understanding of Female Sexual Scripts in Hip Hop Culture." *Sexuality & Culture* 11: 48–69.

———. 2007b. "The Effects of Images of African American Women in Hip Hop on Early Adolescents' Attitudes toward Physical Attractiveness and Interpersonal Relationships." *Sex Roles* 56: 251–64.

Stephens, Dionne P., and Layli D. Phillips. 2003. "Freaks, Gold Diggers, Divas and Dykes: The Socio-Historical Development of African American Female Adolescent Scripts." *Sexuality & Culture* 7: 3–47.

———. 2005. "Integrating Black Feminist Thought into Conceptual Frameworks of African American Adolescent Women's Sexual Scripting Processes." *Sexualities, Evolution and Gender* 7: 37–55.

Stewart, Eric A., and Ronald L. Simons. 2006. "Structure and Culture in African-American Adolescent Violence: A Partial Test of the Code of the Street Thesis." *Justice Quarterly* 23: 1–33.

Tolman, Deborah L., Celeste Hirschman, and Emily A. Impett. 2005. "There is More to the Story: The Place of Qualitative Research on Female Adolescent Sexuality in Policy Making." *Sexuality Research and Social Policy* 2: 4–17.

Tonry, Michael. 1996. *Malign Neglect: Race, Crime, and Punishment in America*. New York: Oxford University Press.

Truman, Dana M., David M. Tokar, and Ann R. Fischer. 1996. "Dimensions of Masculinity: Relations to Date Rape Supportive Attitudes and Sexual Aggression in Dating Situations." *Journal of Counseling and Development* 74: 555–62.

Vass, Jason S., and Steven R. Gold. 1995. "Effects of Feedback on Emotion in Hypermasculine Males." *Violence and Victims* 10: 217–28.

Wacquant, Loïc. 2002. "Scrutinizing the Street: Poverty, Morality, and the Pitfalls of Urban Ethnography." *American Journal of Sociology* 107: 1468–1532.

Weitzer, Ronald, and Charis E. Kubrin. 2009. "Misogyny in Rap Music: A Content Analysis of Prevalence and Meanings." *Men and Masculinities* 12: 3–29.

Western, Bruce. 2007. *Punishment and Inequality in America*. New York: Russell Sage Foundation.

Western, Bruce, and Christopher Wildeman. 2009. "The Black Family and Mass Incarceration." *The ANNALS of the American Academy of Political and Social Science* 621: 221–42.

Wilson, William Julius. 2009. *More Than Just Race: Being Black and Poor in the Inner City*. New York: W. W. Norton & Company.

Winkel, Frans Willem, and Esther de Kleuver. 1997. "Communication Aimed at Changing Cognitions about Sexual Intimidation: Comparing the Impact of a Perpetrator-Focused versus a Victim-Focused Persuasive Strategy." *Journal of Interpersonal Violence* 12: 513–29.

Wood, Kate. 2005. "Contextualizing Group Rape in Post-Apartheid South Africa." *Culture, Health and Sexuality* 7: 303–17.

Wyatt, Gail E. 1992. "The Sociocultural Context of African American and White American Women's Rape." *Journal of Social Issues* 48: 77–91.

Young, Alford A. Jr. 2004. *The Minds of Marginalized Black Men: Making Sense of Mobility, Opportunity, and Future Life Chances*. Princeton, NJ: Princeton University Press.

———. 2010. "New Life for an Old Concept: Frame Analysis and the Reinvigoration of Studies in Culture and Poverty." *The ANNALS of the American Academy of Political and Social Science* 629: 53–74.

12. Effects of Affluent Suburban Schooling

Alexander, Karl L., Doris R. Entwisle, and Maxine S. Thompson. 1987. "School Performance, Status Relations, and the Structure of Sentiment: Bringing the Teacher Back In." *American Sociological Review* 52 (5): 665–82.

Bettie, Julie. 2003. *Women Without Class: Girls, Race, and Identity*. Berkeley: University of California Press.

Brantlinger, Ellen A. 2003. *Dividing Classes: How the Middle Class Negotiates and Rationalizes School Advantage*. New York: Routledge.

Carter, Prudence L. 2005. *Keepin' It Real: School Success beyond Black and White*. Oxford; New York: Oxford University Press.

Cookson, Peter, and Caroline Persell. 1991. "Race and Class in America's Elite Preparatory Boarding Schools: African Americans as the Outsiders Within." *The Journal of Negro Education* 60(2): 219–228.

Crosnoe, R. 2009. "Low-Income Students and the Socioeconomic Composition of Public High Schools." *American Sociological Review* 74 (5): 709–30.

Crosnoe, Robert, Monica Kirkpatrick Johnson, and Glen H. Elder, Jr. 2004. "Intergenerational Bonding in School: The Behavioral and Contextual Correlates of Student-Teacher Relationships." *Sociology of Education* 77 (1): 60.

Cucchiara, M. B., and E. M. N. Horvat. 2009. "Perils and Promises: Middle-Class Parental Involvement in Urban Schools." *American Educational Research Journal* 46 (4): 974.

Devine, Fiona. 2004. *Class Practices: How Parents Help Their Children Get Good Jobs.* Cambridge; New York: Cambridge University Press.

Ferguson, Ann Arnett. 2000. *Bad Boys: Public Schools in the Making of Black Masculinity.* Ann Arbor: University of Michigan Press.

Fordham, Signithia. 1993. "'Those Loud Black Girls': (Black) Women, Silence, and Gender 'Passing' in the Academy." *Anthropology & Education Quarterly* 24 (1): 3–32.

———. 1996. *Blacked Out: Dilemmas of Race, Identity, and Success at Capital High.* Chicago: University of Chicago Press.

Fuller-Rowell, Thomas E., and Stacey N. Doan. 2010. "The Social Costs of Academic Success across Ethnic Groups." *Child Development* 81 (6): 1696–713.

Gibson, Margaret A. 1988. *Accommodation without Assimilation: Sikh Immigrants in an American High School.* Ithaca, NY: Cornell University Press.

Grant, Linda. 1984. "Black Females' 'Place' in Desegregated Classrooms." *Sociology of Education* 57 (2): 98–111.

Horvat, Erin McNamara, Elliot B. Weininger, and Annette Lareau. 2003. "From Social Ties to Social Capital: Class Differences in the Relations Between Schools and Parent Networks." *American Educational Research Journal* 40 (2): 319–51.

Ispa-Landa, Simone. 2013. "Gender, Race, and Justifications for Group Exclusion: Urban Black Students Bussed to Affluent Suburban Schools." *Sociology of Education* 86 (3): 218–233.

Johnson, Monica Kirkpatrick, Robert Crosnoe, and Glen H. Elder, Jr. 2001. "Students' Attachment and Academic Engagement: The Role of Race and Ethnicity." *Sociology of Education* 74 (4): 318.

Kuriloff, Peter, and Michael Reichert. 2003. "Boys of Class, Boys of Color: Negotiating the Academic and Social Geography of an Elite Independent School." *Journal of Social Issues* 59(4): 751–769.

Lareau, Annette. 2000. *Home Advantage: Social Class and Parental Intervention in Elementary Education.* Lanham, MD: Rowman & Littlefield Publishers.

———. 2003. *Unequal Childhoods: Class, Race, and Family Life.* Berkeley: University of California Press.

McDonough, Patricia M. 1997. *Choosing Colleges: How Social Class and Schools Structure Opportunity.* Albany, NY: Suny Press.

McGrath, Daniel J., and Peter J. Kuriloff. 1999. "'They're Going to Tear the Doors off This Place': Upper-Middle-Class Parent School Involvement and the Educational Opportunities of Other People's Children." *Educational Policy* 13 (5): 603–29.

Mehan, Hugh. 1996. *Constructing School Success: The Consequences of Untracking Low Achieving Students.* Cambridge [England]; New York: Cambridge University Press.

Mehan, Hugh, Lea Hubbard, and Irene Villanueva. 1994. "Forming Academic Identities: Accommodation without Assimilation among Involuntary Minorities." *Anthropology & Education Quarterly* 25 (2): 91–117.

Neckerman, Kathryn M. 2007. *Schools Betrayed: Roots of Failure in Inner-City Education.* Chicago: University of Chicago Press.

Rosenbaum, James E. 1976. *Making Inequality: The Hidden Curriculum of High School Tracking.* New York: Wiley.

Schippers, Mimi. 2007. "Recovering the Feminine Other: Masculinity, Femininity, and Gender Hegemony." *Theory and Society* 36 (1): 85–102.

Snyder, Benson R. 1973. *The Hidden Curriculum.* Cambridge, MA: MIT Press.

———. 2010, April 12. "How Not to Do Education Research." In *Culture and Social Analysis Workshop at the Sociology Department of Harvard University.* Cambridge, MA.

Stevens, Mitchell. 2010. "How Not to do Education Research." Presented at the Culture and Social Analysis Workshop at Harvard University, April 12, Cambridge, MA.

Tyson, Karolyn. 2003. "Notes from the Back of the Room: Problems and Paradoxes in the Schooling of Young Black Students." *Sociology of Education* 76 (4): 326.

Tyson, Karolyn, William Darity Jr., and Domini Castellino. 2005. "It's Not 'a Black Thing': Understanding the Burden of Acting White and Other Dilemmas of High Achievement." *American Sociological Review* 70(4): 582–605.

Tyson, Karolyn. 2011. *Integration Interrupted: Tracking, Black Students, and Acting White after Brown.* New York: Oxford University Press.

Wells, A. S., and I. Serna. 1996. "The Politics of Culture: Understanding Local Political Resistance to Detracking in Racially Mixed Schools." *Harvard Educational Review* 66 (1): 93–119.

Willis, Paul E. 1981. *Learning to Labor: How Working Class Kids Get Working Class Jobs.* New York: Columbia University Press.

13. "Try On the Outfit and Just See How It Works"

Adler, Patricia, and Adler, Peter. 1987. "Everyday Life Sociology." *Annual Review of Sociology* 13: 217–35.

Anderson, Elijah. 1992. *Streetwise: Race, Class and Change in an Urban Community.* Chicago: University of Chicago Press.

———. 1999. *Code of the Street: Decency, Violence, and the Moral Life of the Inner City.* New York: W. W. Norton.

Berger, Peter, and Thomas Luckmann. 1966. *The Social Construction of Reality.* New York: Doubleday.

Carter, Prudence. 2005. *Keepin' It Real : School Success Beyond Black and White.* New York: Oxford University Press.

Cialdini, Robert B., and Melanie R. Trost. 1998. "Social Influence: Social Norms, Conformity, and Compliance." In *The Handbook of Social Psychology,* Vol. 2, edited by D. Gilbert, S. Fiske, and G. Lindzey, 151–92. New York: Oxford University Press.

Cohen, Cathy J. (2010). *Democracy Remixed: Black Youth and the Future of American Politics.* New York: Oxford University Press.

Delpit, Lisa. 1988. "The Silenced Dialogue: Power and Pedagogy in Educating Other People's Children." *Harvard Educational Review* 48: 280–98.

Dunbar, Paul L. 1896. *Lyrics of Lowly Life.* New York: Dodd, Mead & Co.

Duneier, Mitchell. 2000. *Sidewalk.* New York: Farrar, Straus and Giroux.

Garfinkel, Harold. 1967. *Studies in Ethnomethodology.* Englewood Cliffs: Prentice Hall.

———. 1986. *Frame Analysis: An Essay on the Organization of Experience.* Lebanon, NH: Northeastern University Press.

Goldthorpe, John, D. Lockwood, F. Bechhofer, and J. Platt. 1969. *The Affluent Worker in the Class Structure.* Cambridge: Cambridge University Press.

Hagedorn, John M. 1988. *People and Folks: Gangs, Crime and the Underclass in a Rustbelt City.* Chicago: Lake View Press.

Hannerz, Ulf. 1969. *Soulside: Inquiries into Ghetto Culture and Community.* New York: Columbia University Press.

Harding, David. J. 2010. *Living the Drama: Community, Conflict, and Culture among Inner-City Boys.* Chicago. University of Chicago Press.

Holzer, Harry J. 1996. *What Employers Want: Job Prospects for Less-Educated Workers.* New York: Russell Sage.

Ken, Pimpin', and Karen Hunter. 2007. *Pimpology: The 48 Laws of the Game.* New York: Simon Spotlight, Simon and Schuster.

Levine, Lawrence. 1977. *Black Culture and Black Consciousness: Afro-American Folk Thought from Slavery to Freedom.* New York: Oxford University Press.

Levitt, Steven, and Sudhir Venkatesh. 2000. "An Economic Analysis of a Drug-Selling Gang's Finances." *Quarterly Journal of Economics* 13: 755–89.

Majors, Richard, and Janet Billson. 1992. *Cool Pose: The Dilemmas of Black Manhood in America*. Lexington, MA: D. C. Heath and Co.

Measure of America. 2011. *One in Seven: Ranking Youth Disconnection in the 25 Largest Metro Areas*. New York: Social Science Research Council.

Miller, Jody. 2008. *Getting Played: African American Girls, Urban Inequality, and Gendered Violence*. New York: NYU Press.

Milner, Christina, and Milner Richard. 1973. *Players: The Secret World of Black Pimps*. Boston: Little, Brown.

Newman, Katherine. 1999. *No Shame in My Game: The Working Poor in the Inner City*. New York: Vintage.

Nightingale, Carl H. 1993. *On the Edge: A History of Poor Black Children and Their American Dreams*. New York: Basic Books.

Pager, Devah. 2007. *Marked: Race, Crime, and Finding Work in an Era of Mass Incarceration*. Chicago: University of Chicago Press.

Rainwater, Lee. 1970. *Behind Ghetto Walls: Black Families in a Federal Slum*. Chicago. Aldine.

Sharpley-Whiting, T. Denean. 2007. *Pimps Up, Ho's Down: Hip Hop's Hold on Young Black Women*. New York: New York University Press.

Venkatesh, Sudhir. 2006. *Off the Books: The Underground Economy of the Urban Poor*. Cambridge, MA: Harvard University Press.

Wacquant, Loïc. (2008). *Urban Outcasts: A Comparative Sociology of Advanced Marginality*. Malden, MA: Polity Press.

Waldinger, Roger. 1999. *Still the Promised City?: African-Americans and New Immigrants in Postindustrial New York*. Cambridge, MA: Harvard University Press

Waldinger, Roger, and Michael Lichter. 2003. *How the Other Half Works: Immigration and the Social Organization of Labor*. Berkley and Los Angeles, CA: University of California Press.

Wilson, William Julius. 1987. *The Truly Disadvantaged: The Inner City, the Underclass, and Public Policy*. Chicago, IL: University of Chicago Press.

———. 1996. *When Work Disappears: The World of the New Urban Poor*. New York: Knopf.

Young, Alford A. 2003. *The Minds of Marginalized Black Men: Making Sense of Mobility, Opportunity, and Future Life Chances*. Princeton, NJ: Princeton University Press.

14. Stepping Up or Stepping Back

Amato, Paul R. 2005. "The Impact of Family Formation Change on the Cognitive, Social, and Emotional Well-Being of the Next Generation." *Future of Children* 15: 75–96.

Bradley, Don E. 1995. "Religious Involvement and Social Resources: Evidence from the Data Set 'Americans' Changing Lives.'" *Journal for the Scientific Study of Religion* 34: 259–67.

Carlson, Marcia, Sara McLanahan, and Paula England. 2004. "Union Formation in Fragile Families." *Demography* 41: 237–261.

Carlson, Marcia, Sara McLanahan, Paula England, and Barbara Devaney. 2005. *What We Know About Unmarried Parents: Implications for Building Strong Families Programs*. Princeton, NJ: Mathematica Policy Research.

Cherlin, Andrew. 1978. "Remarriage as an Incomplete Institution." *American Journal of Sociology* 84: 634–650.

Cherlin, Andrew J. 2004. "The Deinstitutionalization of American Marriage." *Journal of Marriage and Family* 66: 848–61.

DeKeseredy, Walter S., McKenzie Rogness, and Martin D. Schwartz. 2004. Separation/Divorce Sexual Assault: The Current State of Social Scientific Knowledge. *Aggression and Violent Behavior* 9: 675–91.

Dion, M. Robin, Sarah A. Avellar, and Elizabeth Clary. 2010. *The Building Strong Families Project: Implementation of Eight Programs to Strengthen Unmarried Parent Families*. Washington, DC: Mathematica Policy Research.

Dion, M. Robin, Sarah A. Avellar, Heather H. Zaveri, and Alan M. Hershey. 2006. *Implementing Healthy Marriage Programs for Unmarried Couples with Children: Early Lessons from the Building Strong Families Project*. Washington DC: Mathematica Policy Research.

Dion, M. Robin, Alan M. Hershey, Heather H. Zaveri, Sarah A. Avellar, Debra A. Strong, Timothy Silman, and Ravaris Moore. 2008. *Implementation of the Building Strong Families Program*. Washington DC: Mathematica Policy Research.

Edin, Kathryn. 2000. "Few Good Men: Why Poor Mothers Don't Marry or Remarry." *American Prospect* 11: 26–31.

Edin, Kathryn, and Maria Kefalas. 2005. *Promises I Can Keep: Why Low-Income Women Put Motherhood before Marriage*. Berkeley: University of California Press.

Ellison, Christopher G., and Linda K. George. 1994. "Religious Involvement, Social Ties, and Social Support in a Southeastern Community." *Journal for the Scientific Study of Religion* 33: 46–61.

Ellwood, David, and Christopher Jencks. 2004. "The Spread of Single-Parent Families in the United States since 1960." In *The Future of the Family*, edited by D. P. Moynihan, T. Smeeding, and L. Rainwater, 25–65. New York: Russell Sage Foundation.

Emigh, Rebecca Jean. 1997. "The Power of Negative Thinking: The Use of Negative Case Methodology in the Development of Sociological Theory." *Theory and Society* 26: 649–84.

Fosse, Nathan Edward. 2010. "The Repertoire of Infidelity among Low-Income Men: Doubt, Duty, and Destiny." *The ANNALS of the American Academy of Political and Social Science* 629: 125–43.

Furstenberg, Frank F., and Andrew J. Cherlin. 1994. *Divided Families: What Happens to Children When Parents Part.* Cambridge, MA: Harvard University Press.

Gibson-Davis, Christina M., Kathryn Edin, and Sara McLanahan. 2005. "High Hopes but Even Higher Expectations: The Retreat from Marriage among Low-Income Couples." *Journal of Marriage and Family* 67: 1301–12.

Hamer, Jennifer. 2001. *What It Means to Be Daddy: Fatherhood for Black Men Living Away from Their Children.* New York: Columbia University Press.

Hawkins, Alan J., Victoria L. Blanchard, Scott A. Baldwin, and Elizabeth B. Fawcett. 2008. "Does Marriage and Relationship Education Work? A Meta-Analytic Study." *Journal of Consulting and Clinical Psychology* 76: 723–34.

Hawkins, Alan J., Scott M. Stanley, Victoria L. Blanchard, and Michael Albright. 2012. "Exploring Programmatic Moderators of the Effectiveness of Marriage and Relationship Education Programs: A Meta-Analytic Study." *Behavior Therapy* 43: 77–87.

Jarrett, Robin L., Kevin M. Roy, and Linda M. Burton. 2002. "Fathers in the 'Hood: Insight from Qualitative Research on Low-Income African-American Men." In *Handbook of Father Involvement: Multidisciplinary Perspectives*, edited by Catherine S. Tamis-LeMonda and Natasha Cabrera, 211–48. Mahwah, NJ: Lawrence Erlbaum Associates.

Manning, Wendy D., and Pamela J. Smock. 2005. "Measuring and Modeling Cohabitation: New Perspectives from Qualitative Data." *Journal of Marriage and Family* 67: 989–1002.

McConnell, Sheena, Robert Wood, Barbara Devaney, Sarah Avellar, M. Robin Dion, and Heather H. Zaveri. 2006. *Building Strong Families: The Evaluation Design.* Princeton, NJ: Mathematica Policy Research.

McLanahan, Sara, Irwin Garfinkel, Nancy Reichman, Julien Teitler, Marcia Carlson, and Christina Norland Audigier. 2003. *The Fragile Families and Child Wellbeing Study: Baseline National Report.* Princeton, NJ: Bendheim-Thoman Center for Research on Child Wellbeing.

McLanahan, Sara, and Gary Sandefur. 1994. *Growing Up with a Single Parent: What Hurts, What Helps.* Cambridge, MA: Harvard University Press.

Nelson, Timothy J., Susan Clampet-Lundquist, and Kathryn Edin. 2002. Sustaining Fragile Fatherhood: Father Involvement among Low-Income, Noncustodial African-American Fathers in Philadelphia. In *Handbook of Father Involvement: Multidisciplinary Perspectives*, edited by Catherine S. Tamis-LeMonda and Natasha Cabrera, 525–53. Mahwah, NJ: Lawrence Erlbaum Associates.

Nock, Steven L. 1995. "A Comparison of Marriages and Cohabiting Relationships." *Journal of Family Issues* 16: 53–76.

Smock, Pamela J., Wendy D. Manning, and Meredith Porter. 2005. "'Everything's There Except Money': How Money Shapes Decisions to Marry among Cohabitors." *Journal of Marriage and Family* 67: 680–96.

Stanley, Scott M., Galena K. Rhoades, and Sarah W. Whitton. 2010. "Commitment: Functions, Formation and the Securing of Romantic Attachment." *Journal of Family Theory & Review* 2: 243–47.

Straus, Murray A., Sherry L. Hamby, Sue Boney-McCoy, and David B. Sugarman. 1996. "The Revised Conflict Tactics Scales (CTS2): Development and Preliminary Psychometric Data." *Journal of Family Issues* 17: 283–316.

Sum, Andrew, Ishwar Khatiwada, Joseph McLaughlin, and Sheila Palma. 2011. "No Country for Young Men: Deteriorating Labor Market Prospects for Low-Skilled Men in the United States." *The ANNALS of the American Academy of Political and Social Science* 635: 24–55.

Swidler, Ann. 2001. *Talk of Love: How Americans Use Their Culture*. Chicago: University of Chicago Press.

Tach, Laura, and Kathryn Edin. 2011. "The Relationship Contexts of Young Disadvantaged Men." *The ANNALS of the American Academy of Political and Social Science* 635: 76–94.

Waller, Maureen R. 2010. "Viewing Low-Income Fathers' Ties to Families through a Cultural Lens: Insights for Research and Policy." *The ANNALS of the American Academy of Political and Social Science* 629: 102–24.

Waller, Maureen R., and Sara S. McLanahan. 2005. "'His' and 'Her' Marriage Expectations: Determinants and Consequences." *Journal of Marriage and Family* 67: 53–67.

Wilson, William Julius, and Kathryn M. Neckerman. 1987. "Poverty and Family Structure: The Widening Gap between Evidence and Public Policy Issues." In *The Truly Disadvantaged*, edited by W. J. Wilson, 232–59. Chicago: University of Chicago Press.

Wood, Robert G., Sheena McConnell, Quinn Moore, Andrew Clarkwest, and JoAnn Hsueh. 2010. *Strengthening Unmarried Parents' Relationships: The Early Impacts of Building Strong Families*. Princeton, NJ: Mathematica Policy Research.

———. 2012. "The Effects of Building Strong Families: A Healthy Marriage and Relationship Skills Education Program for Unmarried Parents." *Journal of Policy Analysis and Management* 31: 228–235.

Wood, Robert G., Quinn Moore, and Andrew Clarkwest. 2011. *BSF's Effects on Couples Who Attended Group Relationship Skills Sessions: A Special Analysis of 15-Month Data*. Princeton, NJ: Mathematica Policy Research.

Wood, Robert G., Quinn Moore, Andrew Clarkwest, JoAnn Hsueh, and Sheena McConnell. 2010. *Strengthening Unmarried Parents' Relationships: The Early Impacts of Building Strong Families. Technical Supplement*. Princeton, NJ: Mathematica Policy Research.

Young, Alford A. Jr. 2011. "Comment: Reactions from the Perspective of Culture and Low-Income Fatherhood." *The ANNALS of the American Academy of Political and Social Science* 635: 117–22.

15. Beyond BA Blinders

Adelman, Clifford. 2003. *Principal Indicators of Student Academic Histories in Post Secondary Education, 1970–2000.* Washington DC: U.S. Department of Education, Institute of Education Sciences.

Attewell, Paul, David E. Lavin, Thurston Domina, and Tania Levey. 2008. "Passing the Torch: Does Higher Education for the Disadvantaged Pay Off across the Generations?" *Journal of Economic Literature* 46 (2): 431–33.

Bailey, Thomas, Dong Wook Jeong, and Sung-Woo Cho. 2010. "Referral, Enrollment, and Completion in Developmental Education Sequences in Community Colleges." *Economics of Education Review* 29: 255–270.

Baum, Sandy, and Jennifer Ma. 2010. *Education Pays.* Princeton, NJ: College Board.

Carnevale, Anthony. 2009. "Postsecondary Education Goes to Work." Center on Education and the Workforce, Georgetown University. Working Paper. May 15, 2009.

Carnevale, Anthony P., Stephen J. Rose, and Ban Cheah. 2011. "The College Payoff: Education, Occupations, Lifetime Earnings." Georgetown University Center on Education and the workforce. August 5. http://www9.georgetown.edu/grad/gppi/hpi/cew/pdfs/collegepayoff-summary.pdf

Carnevale, Anthony P., Stephen J. Rose, and Andrew Hanson. 2012. "Certificates: Gateway to Gainful Employment and College Degrees." Georgetown University Center on Education and the Workforce. June.

Clark, Burton R. 1960. "The 'Cooling-Out' Function in Higher Education." *American Journal of Sociology* 65 (6): 569–76.

Cook, T. D. (1975). *"Sesame Street" Revisited.* New York: Russell Sage Foundation.

Deming, David J., Claudia Goldin, and Lawrence F. Katz. 2012. "The For-Profit Postsecondary School Sector: Nimble Critters or Agile Predators?" *Journal of Economic Perspectives* 26 (1): 139–64.

ELS. 2006. Educational Longitudinal Survey. National Center for Educational Statistics. Washington, DC: U.S. Dept of Education.

Grubb, W. Norton. 1996. *Working in the Middle.* San Francisco: Jossey-Bass.

———. 2002. "Learning and Earning in the Middle, Part I: National Studies of Pre-Baccalaureate Education." *Economics of Education Review* 21: 299–321.

Horn, Laura. 1999. "Stopouts or Stayouts? Undergraduates Who Leave College in Their First Year." U.S. Department of Education, NCES 1999–087.

Jacobson, L., and Mokher, C. G. (2008). *Pathways to Boosting the Earnings of Low-Income Students by Increasing Their Educational Attainment.* Report prepared for the Bill & Melinda Gates Foundation by Hudson Institute and CNA. http://www.hudson.org/files/publications/Pathways%20to%20Boosting.pdf

Marcotte, Dave E., Thomas Baily, Carey Borkoski, and Greg S. Kienzl. 2005. "The Returns of a Community College Education: Evidence from the

National Education Longitudinal Survey." *Education Evaluation and Policy Analysis* 27 (2): 157–75.

Meyer, John. 1977. "The Effects of Education as an Institution." *American Journal of Sociology* 83: 55–77.

Murnane, Richard J., and Levy, Frank. 1996. *Teaching the New Basic Skills: Principles for Educating Children to Thrive in a Changing Economy.* New York: The Free Press.

Murray, Charles. 2008. *Real Education.* New York: Crown Press.

Rosenbaum, James, Kennan Cepa, and Janet Rosenbaum. 2013. "Beyond the One-Size-Fits-All College Degree." *Contexts* 12 (1): 49–52.

Rosenbaum, James, Regina Deil-Amen, and Ann Person. 2006. *After Admission: From College Access to College Success.* New York: Russell Sage Foundation Press.

Rosenbaum, James, Pam Schuetz, and Amy Foran. 2012. "The Least Understood Tests in America: Remedial Placement Tests and How Community Colleges Could Better Convey Incentives for School Effort." Presented at the Conference for Building Better Students: Preparation for Life After High School. Washington, DC.

Rosenbaum, Janet. 2012 "Degrees of Health Disparities: Health Status Disparities between Young Adults with High School Diplomas, Sub-Baccalaureate Degrees, and Baccalaureate Degrees." *Health Services and Outcomes Research Methodology.* doi: 10.1007/s10742–012–0094-x.

———. 2013. "Money Isn't Everything: Do Sub-BA Credentials Lead to Non-Monetary Job Rewards?" Unpublished manuscript. State University of New York, Brooklyn, NY.

Stephan, Jennifer. 2010. "Is an Associates Degree a Dead End?" Unpublished analyses. National Educational Longitudinal Survey, Northwestern University, Institute for Policy Research.

Stephan, Jennifer L., and James E. Rosenbaum. 2009. "Permeability and Transparency in the High School-College Transition." In *AERA Handbook on Education Policy Research,* edited by D. Plank, G. Sykes, and B. Schneider, 928–41. Washington, DC: American Educational Research Association.

Stephan, Jennifer L., James E. Rosenbaum, and Ann E. Person. 2009. "Stratification in College Entry and Completion." *Social Science Research* 38 (3): 572–93.

16. Liberalism, Self-Respect, and Troubling Cultural Patterns in Ghettos

Anderson, Elijah. 1999. *Code of the Street: Decency, Violence, and the Moral Life of the Inner City.* New York: Norton.

Anderson, Elizabeth. 2010. *The Imperative of Integration.* Princeton, NJ: Princeton University Press.

Appiah, Kwame Anthony. 2005. *The Ethics of Identity*. Princeton, NJ: Princeton University Press.

Barry, Brian. 2005. *Why Social Justice Matters*. Cambridge, MA: Polity.

Bobo, Lawrence, James R. Klugel, and Ryan A. Smith. 1997. "Laissez-Faire Racism: The Crystallization of a Kinder, Gentler, Antiblack Ideology." In *Racial Attitudes in the 1990s*, edited by Steven A. Tuch and Jack K. Martin, 15–41. Westport, CT: Praeger.

Boxill, Bernard R. 1992. *Blacks and Social Justice*. Rev. ed. Lanham, MD: Rowman & Littlefield.

———. 1994. "The Culture of Poverty." *Social Philosophy and Policy* 11: 249–80.

Brown, Michael K., Martin Carnoy, Elliot Currie, Troy Duster, David B. Oppenheimer, Marjorie M. Shultz, and David Wellman. 2003. *Whitewashing Race: The Myth of a Color-Blind Society*. Berkeley: University of California Press.

Clark, Kenneth. 1965. *Dark Ghetto: Dilemmas of Social Power*. New York: Harper & Row.

Cohen, Cathy. 2010. *Democracy Remixed: Black Youth and the Future of American Politics*. New York: Oxford University Press.

Corcoran, Mary, Greg J. Duncan, Gerald Gurin, and Patricia Burin. 1985. "Myth and Reality: The Causes and Persistence of Poverty." *Journal of Policy Analysis and Management* 4: 515–36.

Cosby, Bill, and Alvin F. Poussaint. 2007. *Come On, People: On the Path from Victims to Victors*. Nashville: Thomas Nelson.

Darwall, Stephen L. 1977. "Two Kinds of Respect." *Ethics* 88: 36–49.

Du Bois, W. E. B. 1899. *The Philadelphia Negro*. Philadelphia: University of Pennsylvania.

Dworkin, Ronald. 1985. *A Matter of Principle*. Oxford: Oxford University Press.

Dyson, Michael Eric. 2005. *Is Bill Cosby Right? Or Has the Black Middle Class Lost Its Mind?* New York: Basic Books.

Edin, Kathryn, and Maria Kefalas. 2005. *Promises I Can Keep: Why Poor Women Put Motherhood before Marriage*. Berkeley: University of California Press.

Farhi, Paul. 2007. "'Hot Ghetto' Leaves Some Blacks Cold." *Washington Post*, July 22, 2007. http://www.washingtonpost.com/wpdyn/content/article/2007/07/20/AR2007072000481.html.

Fiss, Owen. 2003. *A Way Out: America's Ghettos and the Legacy of Racism*. Princeton, NJ: Princeton University Press.

Fordham, Signithia, and John Ogbu. 1986. "Black Students' School Success: Coping with the Burden of 'Acting White.'" *Urban Review* 18: 176–206.

Harding, David, Michèle Lamont, and Mario Luis Small, eds. 2010. "Reconsidering Culture and Poverty." *The Annals of the American Academy of Political and Social Science* 629: 6–29.

Harrington, Michael. (1962) 1997. *The Other America: Poverty in the United States*. New York: Touchstone.

Harvey, David L., and Michael H. Reed. 1996. "The Culture of Poverty: An Ideological Analysis." *Sociological Perspectives* 38: 465–95.

Hill, Thomas, Jr. 1991. *Autonomy and Self-Respect.* Cambridge, UK: Cambridge University Press.

Holt, Thomas C. 2000. *The Problem of Race in the Twenty-First Century.* Cambridge, MA: Harvard University Press.

Jargowsky, Paul A. 1997. *Poverty and Place: Ghettos, Barrios, and the American City.* New York: Russell Sage Foundation.

Jones, Rachel K., and Ye Luo. 1999. "The Culture of Poverty and African-American Culture." *Sociological Perspectives* 42: 439–58.

Kamm, F. M. 1992. "Non-Consequentialism, the Person as an End-in-Itself, and the Significance of Status." *Philosophy & Public Affairs* 21: 354–89.

Kaus, Mickey. 1992. *The End of Equality.* New York: Basic Books.

Kelley, Robin D. G. 1997. *Yo' Mama's Disfunktional! Fighting the Culture Wars in Urban America.* Boston: Beacon Press.

Lamont, Michèle, and Mario Luis Small. 2006. "How Culture Matters for the Understanding of Poverty: Enriching Our Understanding." In *The Color of Poverty: Why Racial and Ethnic Disparities Exist,* edited by David Harris and Ann Lin, 76–102. New York: Sage Foundation.

Lewis, Oscar. 1959. *Five Families: Mexican Case Studies in the Culture of Poverty.* New York: Basic Books.

Liebow, Elliot. 1967. *Tally's Corner: A Study of Negro Street Corner Men.* New York: Little and Brown.

Lott, Tommy L. 1992. "Marooned in America: Black Urban Youth Culture and Social Pathology." In *The Underclass Question,* edited by Bill E. Lawson, 71–89. Philadelphia: Temple University Press.

Loury, Glenn C. 1995. *One by One from the Inside Out: Essays and Reviews on Race and Responsibility in America.* New York: Free Press.

Majors, Richard, and Janet Billson. 1992. *Cool Pose.* Lexington, MA: Heath.

Massey, Douglas S., and Nancy A. Denton. 1993. *American Apartheid: Segregation and the Making of the Underclass.* Cambridge: Harvard University Press.

McGary, Howard. 1992. "The Black Underclass and the Question of Values." In *The Underclass Question,* edited by Bill E. Lawson, 57–70. Philadelphia: Temple University Press.

McWhorter, John. 2006. *Winning the Race: Beyond the Crisis in Black America.* New York: Gotham Books.

Mead, Lawrence M., ed. 1997. *The New Paternalism: Supervisory Approaches to Poverty.* Washington, DC: Brookings Institution.

Mendelberg, Tali. 2001. *The Race Card: Campaign Strategy, Implicit Messages, and the Norm of Equality.* Princeton, NJ: Princeton University Press.

Miller, Veronica. 2008. "Bourgie R Us." *The Root,* August 4. http://www.theroot.com/views/bourgie-r-us, accessed June 19, 2012.

Moody-Adams, Michele M. 1997. "Race, Class, and the Social Construction of Self-Respect." In *African-American Perspectives and Philosophical Traditions*, edited by John P. Pittman, 251–66. New York: Routledge.

Moynihan, Daniel Patrick. (1965) 1967. "The Negro Family: The Case for National Action." In *The Moynihan Report and the Politics of Controversy*, edited by Lee Rainwater and William L. Yancey, 41–124. Cambridge, MA: MIT Press.

Murray, Charles. 1984. *Losing Ground: American Social Policy 1950–1980*. New York: Basic Books.

Newman, Katherine S. 1999. *No Shame in My Game: The Working Poor in the Inner City*. New York: Russell Sage.

Owens, Michael Leo. 2007. *God and Government in the Ghetto: The Politics of Church–State Collaboration in Black America*. Chicago: University of Chicago Press.

Patterson, Orlando. 2000. "Taking Culture Seriously: A Framework and an Afro-American Illustration." In *Culture Matters: How Values Shape Human Progress*, edited by Lawrence E. Harrison and Samuel P. Huntington, 202–18. New York: Basic Books.

———. 2006. "A Poverty of Mind." *New York Times*, March 26.

Pattillo, Mary. 2007. *Black on the Block: The Politics of Race and Class in the City*. Chicago: University of Chicago Press.

Pattillo-McCoy, Mary. 1999. *Black Picket Fences: Privilege and Peril among the Black Middle Class*. Chicago: University of Chicago Press.

Perry, Imani. 2004. *Prophets of the Hood: Politics and Poetics in Hip Hop*. Durham, NH: Duke University Press.

Pew Forum. 2007. *Blacks See Growing Values Gap between Poor and Middle Class*. Washington, DC: Pew Research Center.

Rainwater, Lee. 1970. "The Problem of Lower-Class Culture." *Journal of Social Issues* 26: 133–48.

Rawls, John. 1996. *Political Liberalism*. New York: Columbia University Press.

———. 1999. *A Theory of Justice*. Rev. ed. Cambridge: Harvard University Press.

Reed, Adolph, Jr. 1999. *Stirrings in the Jug: Black Politics in the Post-Segregation Era*. Minneapolis: University of Minnesota Press.

Roach, Jack L., and Orville R. Gursslin. 1967. "An Evaluation of the Concept 'Culture of Poverty.'" *Social Forces* 45: 383–92.

Rose, Tricia. 1994. *Black Noise: Rap Music and Black Culture in Contemporary America*. Hanover, NH: Wesleyan University Press.

———. 2008. *The Hip Hop Wars*. New York: Basic Books.

Sachs, David. 1981. "How to Distinguish Self-Respect from Self-Esteem." *Philosophy and Public Affairs* 10: 346–60.

Sánchez-Jankowski, Martín. 2008. *Cracks in the Pavement: Social Change and Resilience in Poor Neighborhoods.* Berkeley: University of California Press.

Schapiro, Tamar. 1999. "What Is a Child?" *Ethics* 109: 715–38.

Scheffler, Samuel. 1982. *The Rejection of Consequentialism.* Oxford: Oxford University Press.

Sharkey, Patrick. 2013. *Stuck in Place: Urban Neighborhoods and the End of Progress Toward Racial Equality.* Chicago: University of Chicago Press.

Shelby, Tommie. 2005. *We Who Are Dark: The Philosophical Foundations of Black Solidarity.* Cambridge, MA: Harvard University Press.

———. 2007. "Justice, Deviance, and the Dark Ghetto." *Philosophy & Public Affairs* 35: 126–60.

———. 2012. "Justice, Work, and the Ghetto Poor." *Law & Ethics of Human Rights* 6: 70–96.

———. Forthcoming. "Impure Dissent: Hip Hop and the Political Ethics of Marginalized Black Urban Youth." In *From Voice to Influence: Understanding Citizenship in a Digital Age,* edited by Danielle Allen and Jennifer Light. Chicago: University of Chicago Press.

Smith, Sandra Susan. 2007. *Lone Pursuit: Distrust and Defensive Individualism among the Black Poor.* New York: Russell Sage.

Soss, Joe, Richard C. Fording, and Sanford F. Schram. 2011. *Disciplining the Poor: Neoliberal Paternalism and the Persistent Power of Race.* Chicago: University of Chicago Press.

Sowell, Thomas. 2005. *Black Rednecks and White Liberals.* San Francisco: Encounter Books.

Stack, Carol B. 1974. *All Our Kin: Strategies for Survival in a Black Community.* New York: Harper and Row.

Steinberg, Stephen. 2011. "Poor Reason: Culture Still Doesn't Explain Poverty." *Boston Review,* January 13. http://www.bostonreview.net/BR36.1/steinberg.php.

Sullivan, Mercer L. 1989. *"Getting Paid": Youth Crime and Work in the Inner City.* Ithaca, NY: Cornell University Press.

Thomas, Laurence. 1978. "Rawlsian Self-Respect and the Black Consciousness Movement." *Philosophical Forum* 9: 303–14.

Vaisey, Stephen. 2010. "What People Want: Rethinking Poverty, Culture, and Educational Attainment." *Annals of the American Academy of Political and Social Science* 629: 75–101.

Valentine, Charles. 1968. *Culture and Poverty: Critique and Counter-Proposals.* Chicago: University of Chicago Press.

Wacquant, Loïc. 2009. *Punishing the Poor: The Neoliberal Government of Social Insecurity.* Durham: Duke University Press.

Wilson, William Julius. 1987. *The Truly Disadvantaged: The Inner City, the Underclass, and Public Policy*. Chicago: University of Chicago Press.

———. 1996. *When Work Disappears: The World of the New Urban Poor*. New York: Knopf.

———. 2009. *More Than Just Race: Being Black and Poor in the Inner City*. New York: Norton.

Young, Alford A. 2006. *The Minds of Marginalized Black Men: Making Sense of Mobility, Opportunity, and Future Life Chances*. Princeton, NJ: Princeton University Press.

Conclusion

Alexander, Jeffrey. 2003. *The Meanings of Social Life: A Cultural Sociology*. New York: Oxford University Press.

Ark, Vander. 2013. "Fortified Environments Can Turnaround the Adverse Impacts of Poverty." *Education Week*, August 12, 2013, http://blogs.edweek.org.

Black, Alison, Marie-Andree Somers, Fred Doolittle, Rebecca Unterman, and Jean Grossman. 2009. *The Final Report from the Evaluation of Enhanced Academic Instruction in After-School Programs*. New York: MDRC.

Bloom, Howard S., and Rebecca Unterman. 2012. *Sustained Positive Effects on Graduation Rates Produced by New York City's Small Public High Schools of Choice*. New York: MDRC.

BLS (Bureau of Labor Statistics). 2014a. Characteristics of the Employed: Table 10: Employed persons by occupation, race, Hispanic or Latino ethnicity, and sex. Retrieved on 7/9/2014 from www.bls.gov/CPS

———. 2014b. Economic News Release: Table 2: Median usual weekly earnings of full-time wage and salary workers by selected characteristics, quarterly averages, not seasonally adjusted.Retrieved on 7/9/2014 from www.bls.gov/CPS

Cantor, Pamela. 2011. "How we help failing schools." (New York) *Daily News*, Accessed December 19, 2011. Online.

Charles, Camille Z., Gniesha Dinwiddie, and Douglas S. Massey. 2004. "The Continuing Consequences of Segregation: Family Stress and College Academic Performance." *Social Science Quarterly* 85 (5): 1353–73.

Cohen, Jonathan. 2010. "The New Standards For (New School Climate Standards from the National School Climate Council)." *Principal Leadership* September 2010: 28–32 Retrieved 9/15/2013 from: schoolclimate.org.

Croft, Michelle, and Grover Whitehurst. 2010. *The Harlem Children's Zone, Promise Neighborhoods, the Broader, Bolder Approach to Education*. Washington, DC: Brookings.

Dobbie, Will, and Roland G. Fryer. 2009. "Are High Quality Schools Enough to Close the Achievement Gap? Evidence from a Social Experiment in Harlem." NBER Working Paper 15473. Cambridge, MA.

Dworsky, Amy. 2011. "Federally Funded Education and Job Training Programs for Low-Income Youth." *The Prevention Researcher* 18 (4): 16–20.

Eyster, Lauren, T. Derrick-Mills, J. Trutko, J. Compton, A. Stanczyk, and D. S. Nightingale. 2012. *Implementation Evaluation of the Community-Based Job Training Grant Program*. Washington, DC: The Urban Institute.

Foster, Megan K. 2013. "A Program Evaluation of the Effectiveness of Turnaround's Model of Implementing and Operating Clear and Consistent Protocols within Schools." http://megankfoster.wordpress.com/2013 /09/19/a-program-evaluation-of-the-effectiveness-of-turnarounds-model -at-implementing-and-operating-clear-and-consistent-protocols-within -schools.

DIR (Decision Information Resources) Inc. 2007. *Youth Opportunity Grant Initiative: Impact and Synthesis Report*. Retrieved on 6/20/2013 from wdr .doleta.gov

Kemple, James. 2008. *Career academies: Long-Term Impacts on Labor Market Outcomes, Educational Attainment, and Transitions to Adulthood*. New York: Manpower Development Research Corporation.

Kitzman, Harriet, David Olds, Robert Cole, Carole Hanks, Elizabeth Anson, Kimberly Arcoleo, Dennis Luckey, Michael Knudson, Charles Henderson, and John Holmberg. 2010. "Enduring Effects of Prenatal and Infancy Home Visiting by Nurses on Children." *JAMA Pediatrics* 164 (5): 412–18.

Koball, Heather, Robin Dion, Andrew Gothro, and Maura Bardos. 2011. *Synthesis of Research and Resources to Support At-Risk Youth*, OPRE Report 2011–22. Washington, DC: Office of Planning, Research and Evaluation, Administration for Children and Families, U.S. Department of Health and Human Services.

Kutash, Jeff, E. Nico, E. Gorin, K. Tallant, and S. Rahmatyullah. 2010. *School Turnaround: A Brief Overview of the Landscape and Key Issues*. Boston: FSG Social Impact Advisors.

Leeder, Elaine. 2004. *The Family in Global Perspective: A Gendered Journey*. Thousand Oaks, CA: Sage Publications.

Lhamon, W. T., Jr. 2000. *Raising Cain: Blackface Performance from Jim Crow to Hip Hop*. Cambridge, MA: Harvard University Press.

Massey, Douglas. 2004. "Segregation and Stratification: A Biosocial Perspective." *Du Bois Review* 1 (1): 7–25.

Massey, Douglas, and Nancy A. Denton. 1993. *American Apartheid: Segregation and the Making of the Underclass*. Cambridge, MA: Harvard University Press.

Massey, Douglas, and Susan Clampet-Lundquist. 2008. "Neighborhood Effects on Economic Self-Sufficiency: A Reconsideration of the Moving to Opportunity Experiment." *American Journal of Sociology* 114: 107–43.

Millenky, Megan, Dan Bloom, Sara Muller-Ravett, and Joseph Broadus. 2011. *Staying the Course: Three-Year Results of the National Guard Youth ChalleNGe Evaluation.* New York: MDRC.

Nocera, Joe. 2012. "Addressing Poverty in Schools." *The New York Times,* July 27, 2012.

Obama, Barack. 2014a. "President Obama's full, 'My Brother's Keeper' Speech. 02/27/2014." Politico Video. Retrieved 02/28/2014 at politico.com.

Obama, Barack. 2014b. Presidential Memorandum—Creating and Expanding Ladders of Opportunity for Boys and Young Men of Color, White House Briefing Room. Retrived March 1, 2014 from whitehouse.gov.

Olds, David, Harriet Kitzman, Robert Cole, Carole Hanks, Kimberly Arcolo, Elizabeth Anson, Dennis Luckey, Michael Knudson, Charles Henderson, Jessica Bondy, and Amanda Stevenson. 2010. "Enduring Effects of Prenatal and Infancy Home Visiting by Nurses on Maternal Life Course and Government Spending Follow-Up of a Randomized Trial Among Children at Age 12 Years." *JAMA Pediatrics* 164 (5): 419–24.

Patterson, Orlando. 1997. *The Ordeal of Integration.* Washington, DC: Civitas.

Pattillo, Mary. 1999. *Black Picket Fences.* Chicago: University of Chicago Press.

Perez-Arce, Louay Constant, David Loughran, and Lynn Karoly. 2012. *A Cost-Benefit Analysis of the National Guard Youth ChalleNGe Program.* Santa Monica, CA: RAND.

Phillips, Anna M. 2011. "Calming Schools by Focusing on Well-Being of Troubled Students." *New York Times,* November 14, 2011.

Sampson, Robert J. 2008. "Moving to Inequality: Neighborhood Effects and Experiments Meet Social Structure." *American Journal of Sociology* 114 (1): 189–231.

Sanbonmatsu, Lisa, Jens Ludwig, Lawrence F. Katz, Lisa Gennetian, Greg Duncan, R. C. Kessler, E. Adam, T. McDade, and S. Tessler Lindau. 2011. *Moving to Opportunity for Fair Housing Demonstration Program: Final Impacts Evaluation.* Washington, DC: U.S. Department of Housing and Urban Development, Office of Policy Development and Research.

Schochet, P., J. Burghardt, and S. McConnell. 2008. "Does Job Corps Work? Impact Findings from the National Job Corps Study." *American Economic Review* 98 (5): 1864–86.

Sharkey, Patrick. 2013. *Stuck in Place: Urban Neighborhoods and the End of Progress Toward Racial Equality.* Chicago: University of Chicago Press.

Sherif, Carolyn W., and Muzafer Sherif. 1976. "Attitude as the Individual's Own Categories: The Social Judgment-Involvement Approach to Attitude and

Attitude Change." In *Attitude, Ego-Involvement, and Change,* edited by C. W. Sherif and M. Sherif, 105–139. Westport, CT: Greenwood Press.

Small, Mario. 2009. *Unanticipated Gains: Origins of Network Inequality in Everyday Life.* New York: Oxford University Press.

Tomasello, Michael. 2001. *The Cultural Origins of Human Cognition.* Cambridge, MA: Harvard University Press.

U.S. Department of Education. 2013. "Promise Neighborhoods: Program Description." https://www2.ed.gov/programs/promiseneighborhoods/index.html?exp=0#description.

Ventura, Stephanie. 2009. *Changing Patterns of Nonmarital Childbearing in the United States.* NCHS Data Brief, No. 18. Washington, DC: Centers for Disease Control and Prevention.

Wacquant, Loïc. 2008. *Urban Outcasts: A Comparative Sociology of Advanced Marginality.* Cambridge, MA: Polity.

White House. 2014a. *Fact Sheet & Report: Opportunity for All: My Brother's Keeper Blueprint for Action,* Retrieved June 14, 2014 from whitehouse.gov.

White House. 2014b. *My Brother's Keeper Task Force Report to the President, May 2014.* Retrieved June 14, 2014 from whitehouse.gov.

Contributors

Andrew Clarkwest
Senior Researcher
Mathematica Policy Research

Rajeev Dehejia
Associate Professor of Public Policy
Robert F. Wagner Graduate School of
   Public Service
New York University

Thomas DeLeire
Professor of Public Policy
McCourt School of Public Policy
Georgetown University

Kathryn Edin
Professor of Sociology
Johns Hopkins University

Amy E. Foran
Human Development and Social
   Policy
Northwestern University

Ethan Fosse
Doctoral Student in Sociology
Harvard University

Simone Ispa-Landa
Assistant Professor of Human
   Development and Social Policy
Northwestern University

Alexandra A. Killewald
Assistant Professor of Sociology
Harvard University

Joseph Cushing Krupnick
Doctoral Student in Sociology
Harvard University

Erzo F. P. Luttmer
Associate Professor of Economics
Dartmouth College

Wayne Marshall
Lecturer on Music
Harvard University

Jody Miller
Professor of Criminal Justice
Rutgers University

Josh Mitchell
Research Associate
Income and Benefits Policy Center
Urban Institute

Orlando Patterson
John Cowles Professor of Sociology
Harvard University

Jackie Rivers
Doctoral Student in Sociology
Harvard University

653

James E. Rosenbaum
Professor, Human Development and
  Social Policy
Professor, Sociology, Weinberg
  College of Arts and Sciences
Sociology Faculty Fellow
Institute for Policy Research
Northwestern University

Janet Rosenbaum
Assistant Professor
School of Public Health
University of Maryland

Peter Rosenblatt
Assistant Professor of Sociology
Loyola University Chicago

Robert J. Sampson
Henry Ford II Professor of the Social
  Sciences
Director of the Boston Area Research
  Initiative at the
Radcliffe Institute for Advanced Study
Harvard University

Pam Schuetz
Instructor
Higher Education Administration and
  Policy
Faculty in Residence
Northwestern University

Tommie Shelby
Professor of African and African
  American Studies and of Philosophy
Harvard University

Jennifer Stephan
Post-Doctoral Fellow
Institute for Policy Research
Northwestern University

Van C. Tran
Assistant Professor of Sociology
Columbia University

Sudhir Venkatesh
Professor of Sociology
Columbia University

Christopher Winship
Diker-Tishman Professor of Sociology
Harvard University

Robert G. Wood
Senior Fellow
Mathematica Policy Research

Queenie Zhu
Doctoral Student in Sociology and
  Social Policy
Harvard University

Index